Committed to the Church and the Country

JDV Philosophy Series - 9

Committed to the Church and the Country

Exploring the Theological Contribution of
Prof Dr Kurien Kunnumpuram SJ on Caring and Sharing

Editors:
Kuruvilla Pandikattu SJ
PT Mathew SJ

Jnana-Deepa Vidyapeeth

&

Christian World Imprints

First Published in 2019 by

Jnana-Deepa Vidyapeeth
Ramwadi, Nagar Road, **Pune-411014**
jdvoffice@jdv.edu.in
www.jdv.edu.in
Phone: +91 20 41036111

&

Christian World Imprints
Christian Publishing & Books from India
C-3, Shop No. 14, Ground Floor
Wazirpur Industrial Area, **Delhi-110052**
cwidelhi2017@gmail.com
www.ChristianWorldImprints.com
Phone: +91 11 41526079

ISBN: 978-93-5148-397-7 (HB)
ISBN: 978-93-5148-398-4 (PB)

"Published with the help of the Institute of Missiology – Germany"

Printed in India.

CONTENTS

JDV PHILOSOPHY SERIES - 9

Since 1893 Jnana-Deepa Vidyapeeth has been pioneering philosophy discussion and debate inspired by prominent personalities like Richard De Smet, Jean de Marneffe, Salvino Azzopardi, Cyril Desbruslais, Noel Sheth, John Vattanky, etc. It has been in the forefront of promoting Indian philosophy and making philosophical thinking relevant for contemporary times. In its effort to reach out to like-minded scholars, JDV Philosophy Series has been visualized as a catalyst for interdisciplinary thinking and contemporary exploration on social issues fostering holistic liberation, integral development and creative engagement.

JDV Philosophy Series

1. Salvino Azzopardi: ***Epistemology and Phenomenology of Religions*** (2018)
2. Kuruvilla Pandikattu & Thomas Karimundackal (eds): ***Melodies from the Flute***: For Prof Noel Sheth SJ (2018)
3. Kurien Kunnumpuram: ***Freedom and Joy*** (2018)
4. Cyril Desbruslais SJ: ***Postmodernity: An Indian Christian Philosophical Appraisal*** (2019)
5. Cyril Desbruslais SJ: ***Metaphysics Philosophy of Be-ing for Today*** (2019)
6. John Peter Vallabadoss: ***Indian Thinkers: Modern and Contemporary Period*** (2019)
7. Thomas Karimundackal & Kuruvilla Pandikattu (eds): ***Logic and Love***: For Prof John Vattanky SJ (2019)
8. Fabian Jose UMI: ***Relevance of Thomas Merton's Spirituality for the Consecrated Life in India*** (2019)
9. Kuruvilla Pandikattu & PT Mathew (eds): ***Committed to the Church and the Country***: For Prof Kurien Kunnumpuam SJ (2019)
10. Cyril Desbruslais SJ: ***The Philosophy of God*** (2019)

EDITORIAL

This volume of theological reflections is to honour Prof Dr Kurien Kunnumpuram SJ, Professor (Emeritus), Systematic Theology, Jnana-Deepa Vidyapeeth, Pune. After having specialised in Vatican II, he has been teaching various subjects like Theological Anthropology, Ecclesiology and Priesthood for more than thirty years. After his retirement, he has been editing two journals, *Jnanadeepa: Pune Journal of Religious Studies* and *Asian Journal of Religious Studies*.

Dr Kunnumpuram is a versatile personality: a committed professor of theology, creative thinker, prolific writer, gentle mentor and compassionate guide to many people. As a professor of theology, he has been the pioneer to introduce and enable the vision of Vatican II to the Indian Church. As a thinker, he has contributed significantly to an Indian theology that is both contextual and relevant. As a writer, he has founded *Jnanadeepa: Pune Journal of Religious Studies* and edited *Asian Journal for Religious Studies*, besides his own numerous books. As a mentor, he has been inspiring a countless number of students in their academic and affective progress. As a guide, he has been accompanying numerous persons in their intellectual and spiritual journey. In short, he has been a critical, creative and gentle personality who has touched the lives of many people respectfully and reverentially! He cherished freedom, affirmed the human dignity and accepted others as they are and rejoiced in the happiness of others!

Coming to the academic part: as a theologian and teacher, he has been pleading for a Church that is more human and promoting human persons who are more liberated and liberating. He has been consistently pleading for a spirituality that is rooted in a personal encounter with God and in the deepest human values! One of his last contributions to theology has been single-handedly editing the collected works of Samuel Rayan, a six-volume work. A remarkable contribution to the Indian Church!

Considering his invaluable contribution to Indian Christian Theology, we are bringing out a compilation of articles in his honour. The articles are related to the themes that have been dear to Kurien: Church, human beings and spirituality. Some articles are based on his chosen writings and are meant to continue the path of theological reflection on the Indian soil.

After elaborate planning and exchange of views, a seminar was organised at Kozhikode (Calicut), Kerala, on October 17-18, 2018, with the wholehearted support of the Jesuit Province of Kerala. Eighteen theological papers were presented during these two days. Kurien had a stroke on 17 Nov 2017, and he was bedridden, and so he could not take part in this Seminar which he was eagerly preparing for. Unfortunately, just five days after the seminar, on Sunday, October 23, 2018, Kurien passed away peacefully and joyfully!

After the seminar, some more papers were added to explore Kurien's contribution to Indian Christian theology from various angles. Thus, this volume has thirty-four articles – all being expressions of love and gratitude to Kurien for what he has been personally and professionally. The introductory article by MK George SJ, then Provincial, Kerala Province of the Society of Jesus, is adapted from his inaugural address at the seminar. It gives an overview of Kurien as a person and a theologian who has contributed significantly to the Indian Church. The other articles are organized into five broad sections. The first section is on Caring for the Indian Church. Francis X D'Sa SJ, a colleague and friend of Kurien, explores the need to return to the original charism of the Church based on the cosmotheandric vision of Raimon Panikkar. The next article by Isaac Padinjarekuttu dwells on the spirit of Vatican II as the impetus for Church renewal, a theme close to the heart of Kurien. This is followed by a critical study of Onesimus in Philemon by Arul Samy ALCP/OSS, a renowned scripture scholar. Sr Shalini Mulackal PBVM challenges the Church to reclaim its prophetic mission for the poor. Paul Thelakat, reflects on the repeatable tragedy that Church at all times is confronted with. Thomas Karimundackal studies a new way of being a prophetic priest in India based on the Prophet Amos. This is followed by an article by Evelyn Montero, who pleads for a renewed participation of the poor and underprivileged in the life and spirituality of the Indian Church. This is followed by a fervent plea for radical change in the Church, by Kochurani Abraham, a feminist theologian. Denis Rodrigues, a lay thinker and close associate of Kurien, concludes this section by pleading for a mystical Church, inspired by Karl Rahner.

The second section deals with the Church's basic openness to the world. Two American biologists discuss the future of evolution and evolutionary biology, leading us to encounter the possible collective destiny of the human family. Christian Bauer from the University of Innsbruck and a close admirer of Kurien, focuses on Church's interaction with the social media through "*Inter mirifica* heute: Eine Relecture im digitalen Zeitalter." The issue of dialoguing with other religions is further reflected on by Andreas Vonach, Old Testament scholar, University of Innsbruck, when he reflects on the relevance of *Nostra Aetate* with special reference to Hinduism and Buddhism. The next two articles pay attention to the theme of ecology. The first one by Isaac Parackal relates ecology to the Eucharist, and the other by A.L. Christopher Roach, a systematic theologian, dwells on the anthropology and ecology in *Laudato Si'*, topics close to the heart of Kurien. The final article in this section is by Job Kozhamthadam; he deals with the Church's openness to the world in general and science in particular.

Dialoguing with other religions is the theme of the next section. The article by Joseph Mattam SJ explores the general principles in dialoguing with other religions. Anoopa Anto MSMI, inspired by Kurien, studies the salvific significance of other faiths in the teachings of post-conciliar documents. Mathew Chandrankunnel CMI tries to draw the wisdom from Christian, Buddhist and Hindu religious practices. James Ponniah dwells on shared religious spaces in different religions that can promote mutually beneficial encounter among religions. Sebastian Painadath SJ, a close colleague of Kurien, compares the spiritual experiences of the Upanishads (*advaita*) and the early Christian fathers (*theosis*). The final article by VM Jose investigates the liberative and societal dimension of authentic religious experiences.

The fundamental human search for truth and quest for dignity is the theme of the next section. As a basic condition for this search, Johnson J. Puthenpurackal OFM Cap raises some fundamental questions on theological truths. The article by Nishant A. Irudayadason explores the relationship between theory and praxis with special reference to theology. M.D. Joseph reflects on our collective search for truth, based on the philosopher-saint, Edith Stein. The last two articles of this section deal with human dignity, a major theme in Kurien's thought. Bishop (Emeritus) Thomas Menamparampil, reflects on the meaning of human rights in a globalised world, while J. Charles Davis discusses the two faces of dignity in terms of "Secured Worth" and "Required Recognition."

The last section of the book deals with spirituality that humanises, a theme to which Kurien devoted his entire life. Stephen Chundanthadam SJ tries to understand Kurien's own spirituality in terms of "fullness of life." Dr Victor Ferrao dwells on carnal hermeneutics and the dynamics of divine-human love. This is followed by an article by P.T. Mathew SJ, co-organiser of the Seminar and co-editor of the book, on "formation of the heart" that is badly missing in the training of priestly candidates today. The article of Surekha Lobo focuses specifically on spirituality that humanises, drawing inspiration from Kurien himself. Paulraj Mariapusham dwells on the love commandments in St. Paul's letters, a theme personally encouraged by Kurien.

The concluding article is by Kuruvilla Pandikattu, co-editor of the book. It draws on hope, joy and freedom, which remain the core values Kurien nourished, both as a Christian and as an author, as elaborated in his last book. It visualises a Christian living that is rooted in Christ joyfully and lovingly and at the same time affirms the freedom, dignity and worth of fellow human beings!

As for the title of this edited work: *Committed to the Church and the Country: Exploring the Theological Contribution of Prof Dr Kurien Kunnumpuram SJ on Caring and Sharing.* As we know, Kunnumpuram has been a person passionately devoted to the Church and the Nation. He was rooted in the rich heritage of India and that of the Church. He embraced the values, vision and ethos of India and the Church. He felt entirely at home in the Indian culture and Christian fellowship. His was truly a life of devotion to the country and commitment to the Church. He cared deeply for the Church and the country. He shared freely his deep faith and hope both with the Church and the nation! Further, he himself was a man of personal care, concern for others and share. We hope that the readers of this book will be good citizens and committed Christians!

We, as editors, acknowledge our indebtedness to members of the Kerala Province of the Society of Jesus for initiating this venture. It was Fr MK George SJ, then Provincial who mooted the idea of the Seminar, out which came out this Memorial Volume. We are also grateful to the new Provincial Fr EP Mathew SJ, who has been very much a source of constant support. Fr Kurien belonged to the Kerala Province and kept close contact with its members, even when he was working in Pune, India.

We would like to thank the three communities; Prof Kurien has been closely associated with: Papal Seminary community along with Fr Bhausaheb Sansare SJ, Rector and Fr Vincent Crasta SJ, Administrator, where Prof Kurien spent more than forty years. Jnana-Deepa Vidyapeeth, along with Fr Selva Rathinam SJ, President and Fr Jose Thayil SJ, Registrar, where Prof Kurien has been academically involved; and De Nobili College Community, along with Fr Edward Mudavassery SJ, Rector and Fr Jacob Kulangara SJ, Administrator. It is these communities that gave Prof Kurien a proper ambience to live and flourish!

May this volume be a modest contribution, inspired by the life of Prof Kurien Kunnupuram, SJ, to foster a shared and collective life of love, joy, peace and freedom for every individual in our vast human family! May this book further the vision of Kurien Kunnumpuram, SJ who accepts, affirms and respects every individual!

Kuruvilla Pandikattu SJ
PT Mathew SJ
(Editors)

Pune
July 8, 2019 (Birthday of Kurien Kunnumpuram)

Contributions of Fr Kurien Kunnupuram SJ to Indian Christian Living: Introductory Remarks

MK George SJ

General Counsellor and Regional Assistant for South Asian Jesuits, Rome

Let me welcome you all warmly to the Christ Hall campus. There are rich history and the confluence of different missions in this soil: Vice-Province of Malabar, Goa, Madurai, and claims for itself roots back to the pre-suppression days of the Society of Jesus. Just, for instance, the oldest School in Kerala, 225 years, is now a Jesuit school and in the city, which I am glad you would be visiting.

As you follow the trail in the campus, listen to the stories, beginning with the last resting place to the once pond now a small well, round the small grotto to the cowshed and around the school …am sure you will talk to the trees, some of the old ones….coconuts…they too have their story…

Calicut city, now Kozhikode, has a rich heritage. The era of enlightened Zamorins of Calicut fascinates historians even today. The landing of Vasca da Gama is a historical fact. Going back in history, writing about the voyage of Mahuan, the chronicler of the first Chinese imperial expedition under Cheng Ho,1 405 A D onwards, it is reported: "Calicut, after all, was the objective of the Admiral's great voyages; this was Mahuan's 'great country of Western Ocean'. The principal city of the magical Malabar coast, it was a necessary port of call for traders and adventurers alike. Marco Polo visited Calicut on his way back home from Kublai Khan's China. The Chinese didn't just stop here; they built homes and warehouses….But modern Calicut seems to have no history at all"(MGS Narayanan 2018: 16). But if you walk around and observe closely just around where our school is, you will find locations where various visitors and business men had their warehouses and business centres.

When you go to the beach, you would really be walking along the historical path of Mahatma Gandhi who addressed a gathering on 14 January 1934. Several national leaders like Khan Abdul Gaffar Khan, Jawaharlal Nehru, Krishna Menon and Indira Gandhi spoke on this historic beach, a beach which had once welcomed numerous Arab and European merchant adventurers who came by sea.

Listen to this blurb from MGS' book: "No colossal pyramids, enduring palaces, or meditating mausoleums to witness its history. Breeze is still blown as somebody whistles from the silent bed of the Arabian Sea. In the remote days of history, it fanned the coconut palms that invited pirates, traders, horses and flags of creeds through Hippalus, the windway. Hustles of land breeze returned news about calico, the fragrance of spices, and delicacies of Malabar sweet meat…"

To continue: "Factories were established, and the kingdom of Kozhikode signalled colonialism in India…Battles alias wars were fought…but peace returned soon to ports and the markets. Forts were not rebuilt, or palaces were not reinforced…Whisper of gossips continued, and when the kingdom became history, there were no monuments to attests its past glory…However, Calicut testifies a great heritage and culture in witness to its history".

We are gathered here today to share about the contributions of Fr. Kurien Kunnupuram. By its very nature, particularly given the condition in which he remains today, I cannot but be personal. Let me begin with a regret I carry around. On 17th September, I was getting ready for a long trip and Fr. Kurien asked me, "George take me out for dinner". I apologized, explaining to him how I had to get ready for the travel but promised him that I would take him out when I returned. Now, I do not know whether I will ever be able to do that for him. A regret for life.

Fr. Kurien was extremely caring towards me. He would enquire after my health, work and plans. He would always have a suggestion or two. He would edit whatever I wrote, even till a month ago. I would read to him, and he would correct me. He had reached a stage where he could not read anymore but could listen and respond.

Most importantly, I remember him as a man who challenged me to grow. Even as late as a day before my travel, he asked me: "When are you going to put together the articles you wrote? I will edit them for you. You could get the help of the secretary!' He wanted me to publish, reflect and live the *magis* that we profess.

So it is with a lot of emotional content too that I speak at this inaugural function. I thank Fr. Kurien for his caring and challenging ways.

There is always an anxiety that remains in me when I talk to groups like this: Do I have anything to tell you which you do not know already? I have it now too.

What should a seminar of this type really do?

There is, of course, a ritual or obligatory dimension to it. We feel obliged to acknowledge someone who has done such a yeomen service to thousands of students, readers and believers. Just think of his one contribution alone, collecting and publishing Samuel Rayan's contributions, it speaks of why we are gathered here. It is a spontaneous, thanksgiving exercise. Unfortunately, he is not listening face to face.

But in this exercise, we celebrate and thank for Fr. Kurien's rich theological and human contributions to humanity and to us personally.

There is also the challenge of carrying on a tradition: a tradition of intellectual, educational depth and of publishing academically. It is only when we intensify our effort in one of these areas that this seminar finds its fruition.

There is also, I imagine, the challenge of completing the work he has left undone. I am reminded of what Bernard Shaw said, "Life is no brief candle to me. It is a sort of splendid torch which I have got a hold of for the moment, and I want to make it burn as brightly as possible before handing it on to future generations." Fr. Kurien is passing on a burning torch, we need to carry it on and pass on to new generations.

In his book *Called to Serve* (2012), Kurien asks himself: "How do I make sense of my priesthood? What makes my priesthood meaningful to me is the honest effort to walk in the footsteps of Jesus who said, 'I came that they may have life, and have it abundantly.' It has been my earnest endeavour to be a life-giving and growth-promoting person. Whether and to what extent I have been successful in my endeavour only God knows". Maybe some of us here will bear witness to it too. He says specifically in his chapter on 'My priestly life and ministry', written on the occasion of the Golden Jubilee of his Ordination that he has all his life been a professor of theology, who enjoyed the occasional sacramental calls, preaching of the Word, retreat ministry, counselling ministry and spiritual direction. This is what he said "This is the way I look at my priesthood. At the time of my priestly ordination, God made a promise to be with me, to empower me and guide me. It is God's grace that has touched and transformed me. If my priestly ministry has been in any way effective, it is because of God's constant assistance". (p.70).

What I would like to recall to myself from reading Kurien is the way he searched for the Divine and the human in his life and the way he tried to integrate both the divine and human. In a chapter on the Spirituality of the Priest, he talks of the four ways in which the religious traditions of humankind have encountered the divine: First, the experience of God in nature, as the power behind the natural phenomenon. He points out that such an experience usually leads to belief in nature gods. He cites the example of Hinduism. He refers to Rom 1,18-20 and Wisdom 13 to demonstrate this path. Secondly, there is the experience of God in the depths of one's being. "God-ward movement often takes an inward direction. This leads to the cultivation of interiority." He cites Upanishads as a witness to this kind of experience of God. So too, St. Augustine who said, God, is more intimate to me than I am to myself. Christian mystics found the same path too. Third, there is the experience of God mediated through the rites and doctrines of religions. 'This is probably the most valued form of God-experience in popular Catholicism, in which the frequent reception of the sacraments is highly esteemed. This approach, of course, is found in other religions too. Fourthly, there is 'the experience of God in inter-human relationships and socio-political involvements. This form of God-experience is, I believe, typical of the biblical tradition. The foundational God-experience of Israel was the Exodus- the experience of God in the liberation of slaves. Israel also experienced God as the one who was active on its behalf in the decisive moment s of its history. And the early Christians experience God in the life, death and resurrection of Jesus, who was done to death as a political criminal. For us Christians, the human person is the privileged locus of God experience – We encounter God, first of all, in Jesus of Nazareth, and then in every man, woman and child.'

He goes on to quote Charles Davis to say, "the Christian religion has always been thoroughly political, with social and political action the major vehicle of the distinctively Christian religious experience. Briefly, Christians find God in their neighbour rather than in their inner consciousness or the cosmos" (pp 104-105).

Fr. Kurien's call to priests to practice a spirituality of active involvement in the lives of people and to practice an integrated spirituality – integrating life, prayer and work, instead of 'scattering their energies in many directions' (Vat II) finds an echo in the challenges of Catholic Church all over the world and particularly so in India and Kerala. Fr. Kurien believes that to follow Christ is to become increasingly human.

He quotes the challenges that a Priest faces today: It is to move from a model of the priest as Sacerdos – a sacred person with sacred power to fulfil sacred functions, celebrating sacraments – to being a builder and leader of the Christian community as envisaged by the Vat II. "Gathering the faithful and building a true Christian Community by the proclamation of the word, the celebration of the Eucharist and pastoral care. Ultimately, a priest moves into being a Prophet of God." As a prophet of God's Kingdom, a priest is the builder of the alternative community; an alternate perception of reality and letting people see their own history in the light of God's freedom and his will for justice. It is a non-institutional involvement with our people and their struggle for a new society as well as in our recapturing the spirit of the prophets.

Fr. Kurien enumerates some of the challenges faced by a priest today:

- Like the prophets of the Kingdom, particularly addressing the challenges of Globalization and Atheism
- Challenge of Freedom
- Challenge of Communion; building a culture of solidarity
- Challenge of Justice
- Challenge of Peace, particularly addressing violence against Dalits and religious minorities
- Challenge of Joy
- Challenge of innovation
- Challenge of Leadership

Fr. Kurien also talks of the friendship of priests with women and the need to respect women. He says, "I suggest that priests look upon these women as collaborators in the ministry and involve them in the formulation and implementation of pastoral policies. Priests have to respect women's right to articulate their needs and interests as well as their vision of the Church and society. Women must have a say in the making of decisions which affect their life and work" (p.93).

I would like to argue that these articulations of Fr. Kurien help us understand the crisis that priests face today in Kerala and the world over in terms of their relationship with women, and women religious. His views provide us with a framework within which we can both understand the present crisis and propose solutions for the same.

I did not see him using the word clericalism that has become much more widespread and is critically analyzed. Clericalism is definitely behind the crisis that has gripped the Church today. "The price paid by the clergy was pride and arrogance and a presumption of entitlement, which made them a cast which dominated rather than served – that enforced rather than led. It created two ranks of Christians" (Eric Hodgens 2018).

A solution to the crisis definitely has to come from the conversion of heart in the clergy from power to service. Changing the lifestyle and curriculum of seminaries so that they cease to be academies of clericalism.'

This then is the biggest contribution Fr. Kurien has made to theological pursuits. His writings and his inputs provide for us a framework within which we can analyze the present context and plan for a new and transformed future.

The times we live in are difficult. Social, Political and cultural forces far beyond our control shape our lives even in the nitty-gritty of how we wake up, how we clean ourselves, eat, pray, love or live. Therefore, as Fr. Kurien repeated reminded us to be an effective priest and religious we constantly need to study scientifically our society, respect the cultural diversity and celebrate the pluralistic nature. In a situation where identity politics rules the roost and everyone is vying with each other to prove themselves, what does the Christian message of self-emptying mean?

One thing is obvious. We cannot go about doing business as usual. Our way of thinking has to be different, narratives re-written and styles of living very diverse. The difficulty is that nobody knows for sure how to go about.

But there is one clarity, I am sure. It is about the call for credibility in life. That we walk our talk, that people feel and experience that we are what we preach. It is here that I have a prayer: that this seminar becomes a moment to re-look at life and make decisions and follow up with changes in life, which will make us men and women of integrity.

Seeking God's blessings and with your permission, I inaugurate this Seminar on the Theological contributions of Fr. Kurien Kunnupuram. God bless! Jai Hind!

Bibliography

Hodgens, Eric. *Byways: Memories from a Catholic Seminary*. Churchill, VIC: Alella Books, 2018.MGS Narayanan. Calicut*: T*he City of Truth Revisited. Calicut: University of Calicut Publication Division, 2018.

Kunnumpuram, Kurien. *Called to Serve*. Mumbai: Mumbai: St. Paul's. 2012.

(This is the revised inaugural address by Rev Fr MK George SJ, then Provincial, Kerala Province of the Society of Jesus, delivered at the Seminar in honour of Prof Kurien Kunnumpuram SJ, conducted on October 17-18, 2018, at Kozhikode, Kerala.)

PART ONE

CARING FOR THE CHURCH

1

To Call to Return to the Original Church

Francis X. D'Sa SJ
Professor (Emeritus), Jnana-Deepa Vidyapeeth, Pune

Abstract: *Pope Francis's pontificate has signalled openness to different cultural approaches. This is being exploited differently by different cultures and power groups. The theologians in India inspired by R. Panikkar's Christophany have opened up to the Revelations in the Indic Religions. Regarding the Church, Panikkar has shown that the Church was understood in the New Testament and the Church Tradition till the Reformation as always existing and came to be on earth along with Creation. Today however the Church as an institution has replaced the original intuition so completely that the original now sounds strange.*

Keywords: *Pope Francis, Raimundo Panikkar, Christophany, Church.*

He [the Christ] is the image of the Invisible God, the first-born of all creation,
for in him all things were created, in heaven and on earth, visible and invisible,
whether thrones or dominations or principalities or authorities
all things were created through him and for him.
He is before all things, and in him, all things hold together.
He is the head of the body, the church;
he is the beginning, the first-born from the dead,
that in everything he might be pre-eminent.
For in him, all the fullness of God was pleased to dwell
whether on earth or in heaven,
making peace by the blood of the cross. Col 1:15-20 (RSV)[1]

1 See the same in contemporary [American] language, Eugene H. Peterson, *The Message* (Colorado Springs/Colorado: Navpress Publishing, 1993, footnote 42.

Introducing the Theme

After the time of the Vatican II Council some of the discussions among Indians theologians centred mainly on degrees of 'belonging' [to the Church]. Behind this loomed the picture of concentric circles. The circles nearer the centre signified a deeper degree of belonging while the peripheral circles indicated a weaker link.[2]

Undergirding this was the concern for our sisters and brothers from other [faith] traditions. It was a time when the question of identity (person, nature, culture, religion) was becoming gradually thematic. 'Third-world' nations had already become or were soon to become politically free from colonial rule.

Today, there is a much greater political self-consciousness among India's theologians and also a certain inner theological freedom (thanks to Pope Francis), compared to the times when Cardinals Joseph Ratzinger and later his student Gerhard Mueller headed the Office of the Congregation for the Doctrine of Faith (CDF). We have come so far that even Cardinals do not hesitate to criticize the Pope in public, as do Cardinals Mueller, Burke and Sarah, what in their own time as centres of power was unheard of!

Mueller claims, he can be of service to Pope Francis in warding off potential schisms in the Church, schisms he sees looming on the horizon thanks to Pope Francis' ambiguous formulations because of his lack of theological background.[3] Burke gives the impression that as a canon-lawyer he can clearly discern exactly where Pope Francis is going off the beaten doctrinal path and Sarah is sure neither liturgy nor Vatican II are Pope Francis' cup of tea. There is lot of good will in all three of them and they have gone on record that they are willing to help the Pope to overcome the chinks in the different aspects of his theological armour. With friends like these Francis will be well protected against doctrinal, moral, liturgical and other shortcomings. All this shows how the times they are a-changin![4]

However, there are other Cardinals like Walter Kasper who support the Pope. Kasper is impatient with people who have been accusing the Pope of heresy.[5] He insists that there is no sign of any heresy here. Kasper was

---

2 See Kurien Kunnumpuram, *Ways of Salvation* (Jnana-Deepa Vidyapeeth Publications, Pune, 1971).

3 Recently the Emeritus Pope has sharply criticized those who believe Pope Francis has no theology.

4 Critics of Pope Francis forget the resonance he is producing in secular circles. See James Carroll, "The Transformative Promise of Pope Francis, Five Years On." How the Leader of the Catholic Church became a hero of the secular world. *The New Yorker*. The Daily. March 13, 2018.

5 See *La Croix International* March 7, 2018: Stop accusations of heresy, says Cardinal Kasper. Pope Francis' views on allowing the Sacraments for those who remarry not heretical — criticism of 'Amoris laetitia' misplaced.

a longtime Professor of Theology at the University of Tubingen, Germany. Later on, as a Bishop (and then as Cardinal) he was President of the Pontifical Council for Promoting Christian Unity. Pope Francis considers him "a good theologian", his kind of theologian; the Pope is impressed by his insistence on mercy in the guidance of divorced couples.

Some of the clergy and laity (in reality a small but vociferous group) opposing the alleged new doctrine of the Pope on divorce in *amoris laetitia*, seem to lack awareness of the nature of theology. Even some who are teaching (moral) theology take their subject as a collection of (juridical) propositions that over the years the Church has formulated "once and for all time". They forget that the Church's teaching is a living guidance to concrete people of a particular time and culture who understand things in a definite manner, and differently from the way their ancestors did.[6]

Take, for instance, the phenomenon of divorce and the simple, yes, almost simplistic, way our ancestors understood it and the complex system that *we* are entangled in! There is a chasm of a difference between their pre-understanding and ours. We cannot overlook historical differences such as these, especially when discussing familiar matters. Faggioli is absolutely right when he insists, "Catholic teaching is not a mineral. It is an animal". Everything is under the sway of the historical process, even the mineral (*pace* Faggioli). The pragmatic popular eye may be blind where the historical process is concerned but not necessarily the trained discerning eye of the seasoned historian. Everything is registered in a person's DNA. However, it requires a researching historian to bring out the processes hidden therein.

In addition to the overwhelming group that supports Pope Francis that Cardinal Kasper stands for there is a third group, the group (of Bishops) from Africa that has severe cultural reservations regarding gays, lesbians and transgender people.[7] This African group, if it is to be taken seriously, needs to work out how this is connected with African culture specifically, and show how much of it is culture and how much cultural prejudice, and how much

---

6 As Villanova University`s theologian Massimo Faggioli puts it, "Francis is not interested in reformulating church doctrine… Catholic teaching is not a mineral. It is an animal. It moves and adapts, it grows". See Peter Feuerherd's report on the dialogue between Ross Douthat ("the skeptical conservative columnist for the New York Times") and Massimo Faggioli ("an unabashed Francis booster and Villanova University theologian") at Fordham's Lincoln Center. See Peter Feuerherd's report on the dialogue on Jan. 31, 2018 between Ross Douthat and Massimo Faggioli in *National Catholic Reporter*, Feb 2, 2018.

7 I have no numerical evidence to support this, except to report what we read in the media. The head of the Catholic Bishops' Conference of Asia, Cardinal Oswald Gracias, a canon lawyer and member of the Pope's G-8, when asked in an interview on a national television programme about his position regarding catholic gays and lesbians replied that, like Pope Francis, he too held that they were legitimate members of the Catholic Church.

of it is doctrinally derived, etc.[8] We from the outside have to wait, listen and observe – not only what African bishops and theologians say and assert, but also what their creative thinkers, writers and poets say in their traditions and in the literature they produce.

Having said this, we now proceed to the main theme of this contribution. There are two important reasons why the discussion on "belonging" has not reached even today the shores of relevance. The first is because the Christ of these discussions was 'limited' to the Christ of the Christians[9] in spite of the fact that the Christ of the New Testament is a comprehensive and holistic Christ through whom this world and all that is, came into being and remains in being. This is the Christ that Raimon Panikkar highlights in his *Christophany*[10], the Christ who is open to and builds bridges with the cultures and Revelations of other religions as also with those who believe that they are outside the world of Revelation.

Secondly, the Church that was at the centre of the controversial reflections on the Church arising from the time of the Reformation were probably not derived from the world of such a Christophany but were, to a great extent, a product of doctrinal developments.

1. The mystery, hidden from the Beginning …

Panikkar spells out in nine Sūtras the specificity of Christophany, i.e., the Christic Experience![11] As is usual with Panikkar, he rarely goes into details, leaving it to us to work them out with the help of his other writings.

(1) "Christ is the Christian Symbol for the Whole of Reality."[12]

---

8 Like e.g. cultural prejudice against blacks and coloured people in some first-world countries.

9 See Keshub Chunder Sen, "That Marvellous Mystery– The Trinity," in: *Keshub Chunder Sen's Lectures in India* (London/Paris/New York/Melbourne: Cassel & Company, 1904), 32: In the midst of this large assembly I deny and repudiate the little Christ of popular theology, and stand up for a greater Christ, a fuller Christ, a more eternal Christ, a more universal Christ. I plead, for the eternal Logos of the Fathers, and I challenge the world's assent. This is the Christ who was in Greece and Rome, in Egypt and India. In the bards and the poets of the Rig Veda was he. He dwelt in Confucius and in Sakya Muni. This is the true Christ whom I can see everywhere, in all lands and in all times, in Europe, in Asia, in Africa, in America, in ancient and modern times. He is not the monopoly of any nation or creed. All literature, all science, all philosophy, every doctrine that is true, every form of righteousness, every virtue that belongs to the Son, is the true subjective, Christ whom all ages glorify.

10 Raimon Panikkar, *Christophany: The Fullness of Man* (Maryknoll/New York: Orbs Books, 2004).

11 *Christophany*, 141.

12 *Christophany*, 144ff.

The first and most important statement of Panikkar's comment on Christophany can be treated as: (a) Christ as Symbol; (b) Christ as Christian Symbol and (c) for the Whole of Reality. From these themes a larger Christian understanding of the Christ should emerge, on the one hand; on the other, such a Christic understanding should make it unmistakably clear that it is only a Christian understanding that we are talking about and that the approach does not subsume all the other traditions regarding the Absolute Mystery!

In this context, it is necessary to clarify Panikkar's approach to symbol. For him a symbol *makes present* that reality of which it is a symbol. Straightforward as the statement appears to be, it means more than meets the eye. Here a symbol unlike a sign works on the ontological, not on the epistemological level because "symbolizes" says, "makes really present", not represents, what it symbolizes. A face, e.g., really makes present a person. When one sees a face one sees the person whose face it is. Where the face is, there is also the being whose face it is. A symbol makes present the being it symbolizes.[13] "Makes present" is indeed very different from "stands for" or "represents". Makes present is ontological, stands for is epistemological.

Thus, for instance, when we state that Christ symbolizes the whole of Reality it refers to makes present as a certain face makes a certain body present to one who knows a certain person. Our Sūtra insists that Christ is the face, the symbol, of all Reality. But the face is not the whole of Reality; it is the symbol for the whole of Reality. In Panikkar's words, it is *pars pro toto*[14], the part standing for the whole. Besides, it is only the Christian symbol, not the universal symbol for all believers. Other traditions have their own approaches to, other symbols for this Mystery. In our times, Christians need to affirm this belief because its nexus with Reality was not and is not always proclaimed thus. Sacred secularity is very relevant for our age. It is the functional equivalent of finding God in all things.

(2) "The Christian Recognizes Christ *In* and *Through* Jesus."[15]

The First Sūtra *might* put off believers from other traditions. The purpose of the Second Sūtra clarifies the place of Jesus with regard to the Christ for Christians. Their door to the Christ is different, not separate, from

---

13 See Panikkar, *Myth, Faith and Hermeneutics. Cross-Cultural Studies* (New York: Paulist Press, 1979), *passim*, esp. 4-6.

14 Panikkar, A Self-Critical Dialogue, in: Joseph Prabhu (Ed.), *The Intercultural Challenge of Raimon Panikkar* ((Maryknoll/Ney York: 1996), 244-245.

15 *Christophany*, 149ff.

that of other traditions. The Christian door, so to say, is Jesus. There is no doubt about the historical nature of Jesus. But this historical character as such has been important for some cultures where history has played a dominant role. But the colonial powers that brought Christianity to the "colonized" countries used it as an argument against countries where history is not an important category and hence was not considered a positive factor in their respective cosmovisions. This turned out to be a real hindrance in the work of mission and evangelization. It hindered the growth of a positive attitude towards Christianity among the native religions because the Christianity they came in touch with was a colonial Christianity that pretended to speak for all Christians. Moreover, they [over-]stressed the historical character of Jesus of Nazareth which the others found hard to accept. And this overstress has come in the way of its interaction with Asian cultures. Speaking generally, Asian cultures have a different stance towards time and history.[16] It is understandable that western Christian missionaries couldn't appreciate the specific contribution of Asian cultures with regard to time and vice versa.[17] The transhistorical consciousness of their cultures has evoked a negative reaction from Christian missionaries, and the historical consciousness of the Christian traditions have hampered a free and open dialogue right up to our times. Actually, this Sūtra is a stepping-stone towards dialogue by stating where Jesus stands. Historical consciousness and transhistorical consciousness are two different kinds of time-experience.[18]

(3) "The Identity of Christ Is Not the Same as His Identification."[19]

The Third Sūtra introduces a clarification that is as profound as it is philosophical. Identity is has to do with the "who", whereas identification focuses on the "what". Identity is neither logically deducible nor is it externally perceptible to the senses. Identification refers to the articulation of the experience of a certain individual but that is not to be confused with

---

16 See my Time, History and Christophany, in: Peter Phan/Young-chan Ro (Eds.), *RAIMON PANIKKAR. A Companion to His Life and Thought* (Cambridge: James Clarke & Co., U.K., 2018), 171-193.

17 For a brief general discussion on this see R. Panikkar, "Time and Sacrifice: The Sacrifice of Time and the Ritual of Modernity," in *The Study of Time III: Proceedings of the Third Conference of the International Society for the Study of Time, Alpbach, Austria* (New York: Springer, 1979),

18 Panikkar *The Cosmotheandric Experience. Emerging Religious Consciousness.* Ed. by Scott Eastham (Maryknoll/New York: Orbis Book, 1993). Also, Panikkar, "Concepts of Time: Ancient and Modern - Kalasakti: The Power of Time," in: Kapila Vatsyayana/Côme Carpentier de Gourdon (Eds.), *Raimundo Panikkar: A Pilgrim Across Worlds* (New Delhi: Niyogi Books, 2016), 222-247.

19 *Christophany*, 153.

the identity of the person. We know so many individuals in the course of our lives (work, profession, etc.) that there will not be much difficulty in locating the differences between their identifications. However, in a deep relationship of friendship we might get some "intimation" of identity. Coming to know the identification of Jesus as done by different Christian, Hindu, Muslim and other historical groups is a different kind of task. These descriptions are more of an external kind. However, coming to know the identity of a person like Jesus of Nazareth is possible, if at all, through meditative and ascetical practices and this is a never-ending, life-long process.[20] What the present Sūtra is drawing attention to is the fact that even for Christians it is far from being a cakewalk to the identity of the Christ!

(4) "Christians Do Not Have a Monopoly on the Knowledge of Christ."[21]

This is one of the more fundamental Sūtras of Christophany. The Name Christ may lead Christians to imagine that Christ is exclusively theirs. Christophany makes it clear that this is not so. Christ is the Christian Name for, the Christian door to, the Absolute Mystery. One of the major tasks of Christophany from the Christian perspective, is to confirm that Christ symbolizes that Mystery to whom all belong and in whom all exist. Furthermore, each Tradition has its own Name for this Mystery! To confirm this, the Sūtra explicitly asserts that Christians do not have a Monopoly on the Knowledge of Christ. Even to Christians Christ remains a Mystery! It is to the Christians that he proclaims, I am the way, the truth and the life. He is not asking the followers of other religions to give up their religion and its teaching. But if anyone follows him (in both the senses of the word), then for that person too he is the way, the truth and the life.

(5) "Christophany Transcends Tribal and Historical Christology."[22]

Sūtra Five is aware of its roots in "Yahweh, the God of the Hebrews, a tribal God, one among many others, often more powerful or in any event equally cruel."[23] It was the merit of the prophets of Israel to convert the Hebrews' tribal God into the God for all and of all.[24] With prophetic insight Panikkar adds here: "The task of Christians – perhaps our *kairos* – may be *the conversion – yes, conversion – of a tribal christology into a*

20 *Christophany*, 39-140.

21 *Christophany*, 156.

22 *Christophany*, 161ff.

23 *Christophany*, 162.

24 Ibid.

christophany less bound to a single cultural current."[25] The Christology that India has inherited mostly from the West is 'historical' Christology. It has not only overstressed the historical aspect and is therefore somewhat of a misfit in the Indic context where the sense of history is not better but very different indeed. "Christophany does not contest the historicity of Jesus. It merely affirms that history is not the only dimension of the real and that *Christ's reality is thus not exhausted with Jesus's historicity*."[26] Panikkar asserts that the historical overstress is clear even in Vatican II. "The cosmovision of the council thereby effectively forgot the angelic and cosmic dimension of reality and ignored the perspectives of other cultures."[27] The concern here is about connectivity with other cultures – to be enriched by their insights and their critique. Very few scholars refer to Panikkar's diatopical hermeneutics[28] – the effort to relate *topoi* of different cosmovisions!

(6) "The Protological, Historical, and Eschatological Christ Is a Unique and Selfsame Reality, Distended in Time, Extended in Space, and Intentional in Us."[29] We can paraphrase this thus: The Christ that always existed, the one who lived in history and the one whom we shall encounter at the end of time is the selfsame reality. This Sūtra is best understood on the backdrop of the cosmotheandric experience.[30] Time is a constituent of Man who experiences continuity of time in the events of life (*distended in space*), not discrete moments. Man, also experiences things as *extended in space*; here there is continuity of space. However, Man does not stop with what he experiences in time and space but longs to follow this up. Man yearns for "more", wants the narrative to go on beyond (*intentional*).

(7) "The Incarnation as Historical Event Is Also Inculturation."[31]

Admittedly the language of the Sūtra vis à vis Panikkar's comment might be somewhat confusing: "As a historical act in time and space, the incarnation is also a cultural event, intelligible only within a particular religiocultural context, that of a specific history. The divine incarnation

25 Ibid. My italics.

26 Ibid. My italics.

27 *Christophany*, 163.

28 See my Raimon Panikkar's Diatopical Hermeneutics: Meister Eckhart's World of holistic Thinking and the Bhagavadgītā's Experience of the World of Wholeness, in: *Jnanadeepa. Pune Journal of Religious Studies*. Befriending the Other. Vol. 20/1-2. Jan-Dec 2016, 107-128.

29 *Christophany*, 165ff.

30 Panikkar, *The Cosmotheandric Experience: Emerging Religious Consciousness* (Maryknoll/New York: Orbis Books, 1993).

31 *Christophany*, 170ff.

as such is, however, not a historical event but a divine trinitarian act."[32] I make sense of all this thus: The incarnation as a divine trinitarian act is *in* history but it is not *of* history. Our acceptance of this happening as a divine trinitarian act is an act of faith. The act of faith is not the product of a logical or rational process but as something that makes sense. We do this in so many cases without finding this to be irrational.[33] Furthermore, the incarnation is intelligible, if at all, in the particular context of the prophets who opened up the people to God's larger world of mercy and salvation. The uncritical acceptance of the world of history Panikkar calls 'historiolatry' [34]. His contention is that with the acceptance of the heliocentric system "not only was the earth no longer considered the center of the universe, but the angels, demons, and spirits, which constituted parts of that cosmovision began to vanish and Christ began to lose his cosmic function - which had been obvious in the canonical scriptures as centre of the entire universe (Ephesians 1:21; Colossians 2:10)."[35] After that, the Church's [implicit] surrender was to colonial thinking –"one single culture is sufficient to embrace and understand the whole spectrum of human experience"[36]. Basically, Sūtra Seven intends to integrate traditional Christology ("in history") with Christophany ("not of history") - "the quintessence of Christ's mystery – *totus Deus et totus homo* ('the whole God and the whole man')".[37] To understand the Sūtra we have to recall Panikkar's distinction between *mythos* and *logos*. Their exigencies on the trinitarian level are different and we must be aware of them especially when Panikkar speaks of non-duality. As a further help he suggests: "We should distinguish *experiential Christianness* from *cultural Christianity* and *doctrinal Christendom*."[38] These distinctions are essential today for theologizing cross-culturally. What should be common to all Christians is *experiential Christianness*. This unites Christians and at the same time, this will help keep them faithful to their cultural specificity and open to doctrinal diversity. The other really important point in the commentary on this Sūtra is about

32 *Christophany*, 170.

33 We smile back when a child smiles at us, we laugh when we hear a joke, we cry when we share in the sorrow or pain of a friend, we rejoice when our team wins a game, etc., etc. The Rational is only one level of our being! There are many other levels of our being where things make sense without the Rational.

34 *Christophany*, 170, Panikkar writes: "…I have often criticized the implicit 'historiolatry' of a certain kind of theology".

35 *Christophany*, 170.

36 *Christophany*, 171.

37 *Christophany*, 172.

38 *Christophany*, 175.

inculturation. One aspect of inculturation is the attempt to enter into a world of meaning that is not one's own, it is the endeavour to understand the world that one is trying to enter. Though the incarnation is a unique phenomenon, Panikkar considers the Judaic background a suitable site for the incarnation (obviously *a posteriori*) because the coming of the Divine into the Judaic world of meaning had been well prepared by their prophets for quite some time in its history - despite the unrelenting resistance of the Jewish leaders to Jesus in the Gospels; *and* despite the brave struggles of the early Councils to work out trinitarian and christological formulations to unite the Greek and the Latin faithful. As a historical note one may add that none of the trinitarian formulations has really found resonance among the faithful, resonance that is born of theological understanding.

(8) "The Church Is Considered a Site of the Incarnation."[39]

Pace the modern mentality which considers the Church primarily as an *institution*, this Sūtra reminds us that from early tradition (*ecclesia ab Abel*) its prime understanding and role is that of an *organism* that expresses the Mystery of the Reality of the Cosmic, the Human and the Divine. In Panikkar's words:

In the first fifteen centuries, in contrast [to the 'image of the church as something similar to a civil institution' created by the Reformation clash], Christians were virtually unanimous in believing in what today is called 'the cosmic church' (*mystērion kosmikon tēs ekklēsias*)-although immersed in secular affairs that it considered sacred.[40]

He holds that Vatican II returned to the ampler understanding of the church as *mystērion tou kosmou* or the *sacramentum mundi* - that is, the mystery of the universe, not the mystery of the church! What was lost in translation from *mystērion* to *sacramentum* was "the global nature of the church's sacraments". That is why the ancients spoke of the church as existing from the time of Abel (*ecclesia ab Abel*). "The idea that God created the world out of love for the church was considered virtually synonymous with the idea of the mystical body. This meant that God created the world for the purpose of divinizing his creation by making it become his own body, with Jesus as head and we the members."[41]

Here Panikkar quotes a number of church fathers: Clement of Alexandria spoke of the church of the first-born – *ekklēsia prōtotokōn*. Panikkar goes on to quote Tertullian: "wherever the three are, that is to say the Father,

39 *Christophany*, 176ff.

40 *Christophany*, 177.

41 *Christophany*, 177.

the Son and the Holy Spirit, there is the church which is the body of the three". *Extra ecclesiam nulla salus* was formulated by Origen and Cyprian and accepted by all. There *ecclesia* meant the "place of salvation". St. Ignatius of Antioch said similarly: "Where Jesus Christ is, there is the catholic church." Panikkar reminds us that the primary meaning of the Greek word *katholikē* is cosmic and soteriological. Already Pope Pius XII had warned against identifying this church directly with an institution.[42]

With a fresh critical consciousness, Christophany returns to these fundamental truths: the place of the incarnation is Man, indeed 'the flesh'. The place of man is the earth, indeed the church in its journey. The goal of this pilgrimage is plenitude, not nothingness (not to be confused with emptiness). It is this, which constitutes Christian hope. The human adventure is ecclesial, cosmic, and divine.[43]

Apart from Panikkar's theology of hope that is clearly at work here, implied in the larger perichoretic process are *creatio continua* and *incarnatio continua*. The former refers to the creative cosmotheandric dance of the Cosmic, the Divine and the Human, and the latter to the constant divinizing of all that is known as Man. It is good to remember that when we speak for heuristic purposes like this, we are converting theological poetry into prose and with that, we are changing the focus from the moon to the finger that points to the moon.

(9) "Christophany Is the Symbol of the Mysterium Coniunctionis of Divine, Human, and Cosmic Reality."[44]

The ninth and last Sūtra is about the Sacrament of Networking of the whole of the cosmotheandric process. Panikkar, who was fairly familiar with the Texts of the Greek and the Latin Fathers of the Church employed polysemic words. The church was the *mystērion tou kosmou*, in Latin *sacramentum mundi*. Thus, *sacramentum mundi* was not so much or primarily the Sacrament of the World but the mystery of the universe. We too are part of this Mystery, this Sacrament, this holistic vision called Christophany.[45] Man as a poet is primarily tasked with making [sense] (=*poēsis*) of the universe around us through networking. This networking has to do with appropriating or, more precisely, realizing our ontic relatedness. True, for the Western Church, Christianity is a historical religion, but its historicity is neither primary nor originary. It has exposed multiple negative historical developments, e.g. its rigorous

42 *Christophany*, 177.

43 *Christophany*, 178-179.

44 *Christophany*, 180ff.

45 *Christophany*, 176.

defense of monotheism at the price of its trinitarian uniqueness; its claim of one centre of intelligibility at the service of colonialism where other independent centres have been made subservient; its acceptance of the historical monopoly of truth as if presence were necessarily and always of a historical nature, etc.[46] Whatever its merits, one needs to be made aware of the pernicious and perilous effects of historicity on transhistorical consciousness. Temporality, not historicity, is a basic characteristic of reality.[47] Temporality shares in Christophany, but it does not exhaust Christophany's essential transhistorical reality.[48] What the last Sūtra sums up is this: Christophany *brings into being*, that is, *brings together* what it brings into being and *holds together* what it brings into being. Far from being a collection of dead objects, Man realizes, the universe is an organic living being. Treating this universe as a collection of dead objects will gradually spell the beginning of *our* end.

2. The Church of Reality

The First Sūtra spoke of Christ as the Christian symbol for the whole of reality. That means that *outside of* and *apart from* [the cosmotheandric] Christ there is nothing. That is the reason that Panikkar asserts "that the Christian tradition does not separate the understanding of Christ from that of creation"[49]. This is obvious from Panikkar's foundational thesis of the cosmotheandric constitution of all reality. Every single being is real because of its cosmotheandric constitution. From here, Panikkar argues:

> Precisely because religion, in the best sense of the word, is the most profound human dimension that 'binds' (*religa*) us to the rest of reality through its most intimate constitutive bonds, it is not reducible to an exclusive belonging to any particular human group. On the contrary, It is precisely the conscious belonging to the reality that makes us Christians and happens precisely through a very concrete bond by means of which we are not only fully human

46 In such a cosmovision only the historical is taken to be real, to be true!

47 *Christophany*, 167: "Our experience of the world shows that everything of which we are conscious is temporal, etc." See footnote 43.

48 Panikkar, *The Cosmotheandric Experience*, *Part Two: The End of History*. The Threefold Structure of Human Time-Consciousness, 79-137. Most thinking on history, whether Indian or Western has been partial and one-sided. Panikkar, "Time and Sacrifice: The Sacrifice of Time and the Ritual of Modernity," in *The Study of Time III: Proceedings of the Third Conference of the International Society for the Study of Time, Alpbach, Austria* (New York: Springer, 1979). Also, his "Concepts of Time: Ancient and Modern - Kalasakti: The Power of Time," in: Kapila Vatsyayana/Côme Carpentier de Gourdon (Eds.), *Raimundo Panikkar: A Pilgrim Across Worlds* (New Delhi: Niyogi Books, 2016), 222-247.

49 *Christophany*, 165.

> but also fully real, although in a contingent and limited way. It is within and through this concreteness that we are able to realize, to the extent of our limitations, the fullness of our being-as microcosm and *mikrotheo*s.[50]

It is of paramount importance to understand the significance of these reflections and realize their consequences.

The threefold bond of the Cosmic, the Human and the Divine binds every single being, without exception - all of which constitutes the Real. Accordingly, the Reality of the Church includes every single being, though obviously not in a univocal manner. This requires a twofold comment: The poetic task and the practical task of the Human. The first has to do with the task of meaning in life that all religions and philosophies have constantly and continuously struggle to provide; included in which are the pastoral and pedagogical concerns. The second focuses on the life-styles that societies develop, their efforts to respond to the patterns of meaning in life put forward, the question of whether Governments and institutions provide enough opportunities to implement them and the doubts and discussions of the public regarding all this.

Thus, the idea of Church far from being churchy harks back to the Mystery of the Christ who is the head of the body, the church. Here is a *paraphrase* of the Letter to the Colossians quoted at the beginning of this article (Col 1:15-20).

> We look at the Son and see the God who cannot be seen. We look at this Son and see God's original purpose in everything created. For everything, absolutely everything, above and below, visible and invisible, rank after rank after rank of angels – everything got started in him and finds its purpose in him. He was there before any of it came into existence and holds it all together right up to this moment. And when it comes to the church, he organizes and holds it together, like a head does a body.
>
> He was supreme in the beginning and – and leading the resurrection parade – he supreme in the end. From beginning to end he is there, towering far above everything, everyone: So spacious is he, so roomy, that everything of God finds his proper place in him without crowding. Not only that, but all the broken and dislocated pieces of the universe – people and things, animals and atoms – get properly fixed and fit together in vibrant harmonies, all because of his death, his blood poured down from the Cross.[51]

---

50 *Christophany*, 169.

51 Eugene H. Peterson, *The Message* (Colorado Springs/Colorado: Navpress Publishing, 1993). See paraphrase of Col 1:15-20. See the RSV translation of the same text at the head of this article.

3. The Reality of the Church

Whatever one's stand *vis à vis* this argument may be, it should give us pause to think. The juridical-and-institutional approach that has prevailed in the Church in the last centuries of its history is neither the favourite nor the favoured way of the ancient traditions of the Church. More importantly, it is abundantly clear that in some, if not in most cases, the mystical dimension, the main constituent that authenticates the Church, have been minimized if not lost. It has to be urgently retrieved if it is to be the Church of Jesus the Christ.

More: If the Church is to become the *agora* of and for all peoples, then it has to be founded on Reality, which is the common foundation stone of all cultures and religions. No being, no group, no tradition can afford to neglect a foundation other than the cosmotheandric foundation. That is the commonality that every single being shares with every other being. That is the logic that has to be followed in the revision of our rights and duties. The perspective cannot anymore be anthropocentric or anthropic. Indeed, this was the root cause of the ecological crisis, making Man the centre of our concern. This mistake cannot be repeated. Henceforth all creative efforts, no matter in which field, have to be cosmotheandric. This is the path to wholeness and recovery.

Cosmotheandrism is not *a* school of thought or a direction of work or an area of spirituality. It is to be the background of all thinking, work and spirituality. Or to be more precise, cosmotheandrism is the structure of Reality. We do not construct it, it is always and already there as our basic structure. One has gradually to become aware of it and make it thematic.

Awareness is a short form for self-awareness; one cannot produce it on one's own. It is a gift of the Holy Spirit. Anyone practising the Buddhist vipassana exercise knows how long it takes just to 'get into it'! Battling distractions, one does not know whether one will ever reach a point, that will be distraction-free!

Be that as it may, even self-awareness like every reality is cosmotheandric. This may seem far-fetched, but it is not so. The *expressing* of this issue is the cosmic dimension as this makes us aware of what we are talking about. Our *awareness* itself is the human dimension. And what it embodies and points to is the *depth-dimension*, the inexpressible.

Awareness, the Christian word for it is discernment, is the secret of life. It heals all separations not by artificially juxtaposing things but by turning polarizations into polarity. "Love your enemies and pray for your persecutors; only so can you be children of your heavenly Father, who makes his sun rise on good and bad alike, and sends the rain on the honest and the dishonest." Even the sun and the rain follow this love-commandment as it belongs to his Father's order of the day, Jesus says, on the cosmic level! And in Jesus' final commission, we are instructed: "Go forth to every part of the world and proclaim the Good News to the whole creation." The mission-command appears to embody the *process* of the beautiful metaphor of the *anakephalaiōsis* of Ephesians 1:10.

2

Life in the Spirit of Vatican II

Isaac Padinjarekuttu
Professor of Church History and Dean at Oriens Theological College, Shillong, Meghalaya

Abstract: *In the person of Kurien Kunnumpuram, we see someone celebrated for his theological contributions, spiritual insights and commitment to Christian humanism. And the thread that runs through his entire life as a theologian, spiritual guide, scholar and teacher is his unwavering commitment to a Church that embodies the spirit of Vatican II. And for Kurien, what symbolized the Vatican II Spirit is freedom because it belongs to the very nature of the human person as we see in the deceptively simple sentence, all but lost in the documents of Vatican II: "Authentic freedom is an exceptional sign of the divine image within the human person." It is this commitment to freedom that has made his reflections on the Church and life in the Church refreshingly new, relevant and appealing to all. Kurien's motto has been, "Reach out to life with both hands" as seen on a picture hanging on the wall in front of him. And there can be no genuine life without genuine freedom. Kurien always fought against an un-free Church and theology, an un-free religion and spirituality, and, therefore, this short paper is a plea to revive the spirit of the Second Vatican Council in the Church in general and theology in particular.*

Vatican II was a revolution and revolutions can be stalled for a time, but cannot be stopped. Therefore, it may be wiser to conclude that the vast movement of transformation begun by Vatican II will not be easily ended either externally or internally. Hopefully, the Church will genuinely accept the spirit and implications of Vatican II in realizing a "people of God" ecclesiology, in a stress upon both a working collegiality and the genuine centrality of the Eucharist within the Church, especially the local Church in the warm recognition of the values of pluralism and freedom within and between particular Churches as within human society generally and in a commitment to work and find Christina holiness within the struggle for justice and peace in solidarity with the poor. But for that to happen, the Church has to become humble.

Keywords: *Vatican II, freedom, Christian humanism, Church open to the world.*

On the Sunday after the Encyclical *Humanae Vitae* (1968) of Pope Paul VI was published, the American Jesuit, Horace Mckenna, preaching to an impoverished congregation at St. Aloysius parish in Washington D.C. apparently left the impression that despite the encyclical there was still room for the exercise of individual conscience. After the Mass, a lawyer came up to him and asked: "Do you think you can reconcile what you said with loyalty to the Holy Father?" "Yes, I think, I can," replied the priest. The lawyer retorted: "I don't see how you can say that. Let me make up an example. If you were working for the President of the United States, and he gave you a bag of rose seeds, and told you to plant them in the Rose Garden of the White House, and you didn't do it, would you say you were being loyal?" "I think so," said the Jesuit, "if the Rose Garden was already full."[1]

In the person of Kurien Kunnumpuram, a Jesuit of a similar mould is being honoured and celebrated for his theological contributions, spiritual insights and commitment to Christian humanism. And the thread that runs through his entire life as a theologian, spiritual guide, scholar and teacher is his unwavering commitment to a Church that embodies the spirit of Vatican II. And for Kurien, what symbolized the Vatican II Spirit is freedom because it belongs to the very nature of the human person as we see in the deceptively simple sentence, all but lost in the documents of Vatican II: "Authentic freedom is an exceptional sign of the divine image within the human person."[2] It is this commitment to freedom that has made his reflections on the Church and life in the Church refreshingly new, relevant and appealing to all. Kurien's motto has been, "Reach out to life with both hands" as seen on a picture hanging on the wall in front of him. And there can be no genuine life without genuine freedom. Kurien always fought against an un-free Church and theology, an un-free religion and spirituality, and, therefore, this short paper is a plea to revive

1 Walter J. Burghardt, S.J., *Long Have I Loved You. A Theologian Reflects on His Church* (Maryknoll, New York: Orbis Books) 2000, 413.

2 *Gaudium et Spes*, 17.

the spirit of the Second Vatican Council in the Church in general and theology in particular.

The Story of Catholic Theology

Before the twelfth century, theology was an exposition of Scripture by appeal to the established tradition of ecclesiastical authorities. So Augustine said to the Manichaeans: "I would not believe in the gospel if the authority of the Catholic Church did not lead me to do so."[3] A theologian had authority not on the ground of his own interpretations but only if his insights were consistent with those of his predecessors and the received doctrinal tradition. Even the best theological synthesis of the Middle Ages was basically reconciling it with the past voices. By the modern period, this authority was to be found in the Roman Pontiff, who is considered the most authentic interpreter of Revelation in Scripture and Tradition. The Reformers also basically shared the idea that truth was not to be found in the individual or collective acts of theologising but in the fidelity to divine Revelation. The only difference was that for them it was only Scripture, but for the Catholics, it also included Tradition. But they the Reformers also introduced another element into theology, the freedom of the theologian to study, to criticise and thus the responsibility of the theologian to delve into the truth through his creativity.[4] It is the Enlightenment that took this idea of freedom and autonomy further and effected a paradigm shift and even rejected the truth claims of both Scripture and Tradition, placing them in opposition to human reason. The Christian Churches had to defend the integrity of their theological vision against this subjective approach.

What came to the rescue of theology was Romanticism. Truth, the Romantics claimed, was discoverable not in some objective metaphysical referent but only in its historical development. Divine Revelation is not static but rather can be conceived as a process and hence, experience plays an important role and so the "role of individual creativity in theological reflection was remarkably enhanced. The theologian was no longer seen as mimetically representing an objective revelation but as imaginatively constructing the immediate, though historical, the experience of salvation."[5] Here begins the tension between the Magisterium and the theologian in the nineteenth and twentieth century. This paradigm found itself in conflict with the classical paradigm "as defined at Trent, affirmed at Vatican I, and promulgated throughout the Modernist controversy and its aftermath until Vatican II."[6] The

---

3 Johannes Quasten, *Patrology*, vol. IV (Allen, Texas: Christian Classics) 426.

4 John E. Thiel, "Theological Responsibility: Beyond the Classical Paradigm", *Theological Studies* 47(1986) 578.

5 *Ibid.*, 578-79.

6 *Ibid.*, 586.

most forceful repudiation of it came in the wake of the Modernist controversy by Pope Pius X in his *Pascendi dominici gregis* of 1907. The Pope assailed the Modernist pride which "leads them to hold themselves up as the rule for all." No doubt, a number of positions of Modernism were a threat to Catholic Christianity. On the other hand, the condemnation showed no appreciation of the positive values the movement represented: faith as personal encounter, relation between psychology and religion, sense of mystery, pastoral function of theology, less mechanical role for authority, new insights into development of dogma, fresh stress on the organic nature of the Church and the importance of the laity, greater respect for scriptural scholarship and natural science, a newer framework for church-state relationships, a call to abandon a Catholic cultural ghetto, etc.[7] More harmful was the aftermath of the condemnation which created an intellectually oppressive situation in the Church which lasted practically till the eve of Vatican II.

The Challenge of Vatican II

Vatican II had to recognize a new man, a new woman and a new world that had emerged after the post-World War II period. A new epoch had come to birth. A new epoch is born when there is a consensus about ideals and standards, consensus about what is meaningful at all, about what is obvious and simply beyond argument, a consensus about what counts as relevant, worthwhile and significant, or pointless or ridiculous.[8] The period surrounding Vatican II was a new epoch although the Church seemed unaware of its existence. This was as an epoch in which traditional religion and theology were becoming rather irrelevant. The God they presented could not be experienced by anyone. In an age increasingly concerned with man's temporal destiny and temporal development, an age that has discovered the person and is passionately concerned with emphatically personal realms of responsibility, identity and liberty, traditional methods of philosophy and theology with their concern for objectivity, known and judged according to universal norms supplied by the Church was not acceptable. Contemporary man and woman searching desperately for meaning were not attracted to such a philosophy and theology. The world had shifted from the classical mentality where truth floats serenely in a pace unaffected by persons and events, to historical consciousness where truth is ever writhing in the "joys and the hopes, the griefs and the anxieties of the men of this age."[9] Search for certainty is less significant than the quest for intelligibility. There is also a profound affirmation of freedom. A human being cannot be understood apart from his freedom. The Second Vatican Council

7 Walter J. Burghardt, *Long Have I Loved You…*, 26.

8 See Fergus Kerr, "*Theology in the Godforsaken Epoch*", *New Blackfriars*, 46 (1965) 665-72.

9 *Gaudium et Spes*, 1.

understood some of these modern aspirations, and we see traces of them, for example, in the affirmation of religious freedom as a human right, based on the very dignity of the human person. Philosophy would characterize this radical shift as one from essence to the existence, which for the Church would mean that living in the doctrine of Christianity is more important than speculating on it. There is a dynamic interrelation of the self and the world, the awareness that experience of the world of things was not as important as the experience of the world of persons, that experience is never a closed circle but always open to further development.

Within Catholicism and outside, the traditional search for certainty has been replaced by the quest for understanding. Understanding how God speaks to men and women today, disclosing himself to men and women today, in persons and events and situations rather than through propositions and abstract truths. And one is not sure just where the secular experience ends, and religious experience begins. There is "less attachment to the incontrovertible proposition, more profound attachment to the God to whom all propositions point; less clarity in the meaning of experience, the greater conviction that religious experience cannot be "cribbed, and confined" by law or system.[10]

It is good to point out that many of these ideas were already present in the "words of the holy fathers"[11] spoken centuries ago. In that sense, the Council was basically going back to the "sources" in trying to answer the new questions of the modern world. One of the important facets of patristic thought was that there was no gap between theology and spirituality. "If you are a theologian, you will pray truly. And if you pray truly, you are a theologian," said, Evagrius Ponticus.[12] The gap was created later when it was made into a system, a set of ideas. For the Fathers, theology was a search, not only for the truth of God but for God's very self.

Moreover, the search was carried on not by reason alone, but the whole person because it is the whole person that must respond to the revealing God. So patristic theology is a spirituality. It was produced not in theological laboratories but grew out of live problems in the Church and society, pain, persecutions and sufferings; it was not timeless, extra-temporal and static. A second important facet of patristic theology was the Fathers' experience of Scripture. True, they did not have the tools that we have, and they were accused of too much subjectivism and allegory, but they did not commit the sin of "straining out the gnats and swallowing the camel"[13] through lifeless exegesis. They were able to see God and his works in Scripture. "It is this feeling of faith

10 Walter Burghardt, *Long Have I Loved You...,* 38.

11 *Dei Verbum*, 8.

12 *De Oratione*, 61.

13 Mt 23:24.

that we must recapture if we too want to understand what the Bible is trying to tell us. Then it will be that many of the false problems will vanish. We shall find in the Bible the truth in its totality because we shall be searching for it there alone where God put it."[14] Theology for the Fathers was their experience of Scripture within the Church. We need to recapture their familiarity with Scripture, their love for Scripture, their search for Christ in Scripture, which prompted Jerome to say that ignorance of Scripture is ignorance of Christ. The third facet of patristic theology was its understanding of the Church. For the Fathers, the Church is primarily a communion, not a pyramid but a body. This one communion shares jointly in Christ's light and life. This one communion jointly communicates Christ's truth and grace to men and women. This experience of the Church as communion was not so much a thought-out theory as a lived-out reality. It was expressed warmly in the patristic imagery of the Church as "mother" with all the faithful responsible for the common life of the community.[15] There were heresies, sects, schisms, etc. but the Christian Church during the patristic era could suffer these without devastating rupture to its oneness. There were different theological currents, schools and tendencies, but all coexisted within the one Church. There were geographical and cultural mentalities but not to the destruction of the one body. Despite divergences in race and culture, in language and mentality, in exegesis and theology, Basil of Caesarea could write: "The faith we profess is not one thing in Seleucia, another in Constantinople, another in Zela, another in Lampsacus, and still another at Rome. The faith that circulates today is no different from the faith of yesterday; it is always one and the same."[16] This oneness was not an abstract unity parroted by bishops in council, it was a life, and its foci were the local church and the Eucharist. This communion was imperilled in an established Church torn internally where Christian emperors like Constantine could control ecclesiastical policy and bishops like Cyril of Alexandria could call a fellow-bishop "the new Judas" and Rome and Constantinople could challenge each other with unchristian coldness. But still, in the patristic age, the magic word was not authority but community. And the Eucharist was still capable of linking hostile hands in love, still the most powerful force for building up the Body of Christ. That is the reason why Henri de Lubac clearly perceived that there could not be any renewal of the Church without the study of the Fathers.

Thus, at Vatican II, the council Fathers came back to the thesis that theology has to be authentically biblical and historical because it has to wrestle

---

14 Pierre Benoit in A. Robert and A. Tricot, eds., *Initiation biblique* (3rd ed.), (Tournai: Desclee, 1954) 43.

15 C. Plumpe, *Mater ecclesia: An Inquiry into the Concept of the Church as Mother in Early Christianity* (Washington DC: Catholic University of America, 1943).

16 Letter, 251 4, *Patrologia graeca* 32, 937.

with the biblical event and the progressive efforts of the Christian ages to grasp it and express it and live it. Theology has to be anthropological in that it has to search out human beings as they are; it has to be pastoral in that its burning questions will rise in significant measure from the anguish of contemporary man and woman. It will be ecumenical in that other Christians will not be primarily adversaries but co-operators in common concern, the effort of faith not simply to understand but to unite in love. It will be eschatological in its awareness of a pilgrim people in the movement now and tomorrow and every day, thorough the demonic and salvific, to the consummation of their corporate oneness in Christ.[17] Vatican II's contribution to theology was not primarily in its formal acceptance of a particular approach, for example, to ecclesiology or revelation; although its documents on these matters are immensely significant, the Council's importance for theology lies rather in the new location it proposed for theological reflection. It proposed that the Church ought to be characterized by a profound engagement with the reality of the world's experience: no longer a Church set apart from the world within an institutional Christendom, but a Church that enters into profound solidarity with the experience of human society, and takes humanity seriously in the unfolding of its history. This new location of the Church's identity prescribes a new location for the theological activity. Human history becomes the *locus theologicus* for the post-conciliar theologian.[18] The new stage on which post-conciliar theology is to speak is set unambiguously in the middle of human history and experience. Christian theology in every age must address the question of how Jesus is significant for a culture.

The Situation after Vatican II

Avery Dulles clearly perceived that in consequence Catholic theology moved "into a period radically unlike the past few centuries, necessitating an abrupt shift of theological style comparable in magnitude to the shift that occurred with the dissemination of printed literature in the sixteenth century."[19] The process was not without problems because uncritical reception of modern trends in natural science, philosophy, sociology etc. by theology can mask the fact that "Catholic theology is always a reflection on the faith of the Church, practised within the community of faith, with a view to serving

17 Walter J. Burghardt, S.J., "Vatican II and Catholic Theology in America", in *Vatican II: An Interfaith Appraisal*, ed. John H. Miller, C.S.C. (Notre Dame: University of Notre Dame, 1966) 626-41.

18 John McDade, SJ, "Catholic Theology in the Post-conciliar Period", in Adrian Hastings, ed., *Modern Catholicism* (London SPCK. 1991) 422-23.

19 Avery Dulles, S.J., *The Craft of Theology: From Symbol to System* (New York: Crossroad, 1992) 3.

and enhancing the spiritual life of that community."[20] But still, within this framework, the post-conciliar Church has thrown out remarkably powerful movements within theology which have proved the words of Karl Rahner right, that Vatican II signalled the emergence of a "world Church" from an initially Judaeo-Christian, and subsequently European, cultural matrix. Latin American Liberation Theology, which had tremendous impact on Asia as well, Asian Theologies in dialogue with the religions of Asia, Feminist Theology, Dalit Theology from India, Tribal Theologies from various parts of the world, African Theology, etc. are examples of the post-conciliar insight into the priority of the landscape of lived experience in the articulation of theological doctrine. The priority has been in establishing local theologies appropriate to the lived experience of the community. Theology since the Council has been rooted in the Church's experience of asking difficult questions about what it means to be the Church of Christ in the contemporary world; It has to find ways of understanding itself as a living, varied, changing community whose identity is established, not prior to, but as a function of, its relationship to the world in which God's Kingdom grows. This has led to preference, on the part of theology, for inductive approaches, in which the context in which theology is conducted becomes a constitutive feature of theological reflection. If at the heart of human history is the mystery of Christ, and if at the heart of contemporary history is poverty, violence, oppression and injustice on a massive scale, then theology is led to see the contemporary form of its task as a reversal of the *maxi ubi ecclesia, ibi, Christus* (Where the Church is, there is Christ). It becomes instead, *ubi Christus, ibi ecclesia* (Where Christ is, there is the Church), and is expanded to mean "Where the poor are suffering, there must the Church (and its theology) be."[21] Thus the centre of interest has shifted to creating local theologies appropriate to the lived experience of the community. There are difficulties inherent in this approach as the Church wrestles with the place of pluralism in the Church. Repeated stress upon the benefits brought by diversity and pluralism is a recurrent theme of the Council documents. This returns again and again in a variety of contexts, and the Council has called for ecclesial, liturgical and theological pluralism. It calls for a genuine diversity "even in the theological elaborations of revealed truth"[22] and speaks of "lawful freedom of theological enquiry to which laity and clergy alike have a right."[23]

---

20 Avery Dulles, S.J., "The Future of Seminary Theology," *Catholic International* 8, no. 1 (January 1997) 39.

21 John McDade, 442.

22 *Unitatis Redintegraio*, 22.

23 *Gaudium et Spes*, 62.

Differing theological formulations, we are assured are "often to be considered as complementary rather than conflicting."[24]

But it has not been easy to practice this value, especially in the decades following the Council. The Vatican had taken action against several theologians, requiring clarification on disputed points, silencing some of them for a period, and prohibiting publication or teaching, declaring that a theologian is not suitable to teach Catholic theology or withdrawing the right to be called a Catholic theologian etc. It signalled a determination, on the part of the Roman authorities to constrain theological development within narrow limits than were generally envisaged in the Council halls. Such actions have the potential of making Vatican II and its aftermath just another brief aberration within Catholic history comparable to the conciliar movement of the fifteenth century. For the supporters of this view, the reforms of Vatican II could at best be considered administrative rather than theological. For them, in many aspects the Council has already gone too far and reining in the rebellious horses is absolutely necessary for its very survival.

On the other hand, there are others who believe that the pluralist forces within the Church cannot be and should not be tamed by anyone and the reforms envisaged by Vatican II should be taken to their logical conclusion. The pendulum should swing back with a new phase of more radical reforms and only a pluralistic Catholic Christianity will be able to respond without losing its core identity to the needs of a truly world Church and of the ongoing transformation of human consciousness and intellectual understanding. But there is the real danger of a third possibility. As both these groups are trying to vie with each other, the Church will decline. The pull factors of conservatism will sap the vitality of area after area of ecclesial strength, thus preventing the liberals from going any further. Clericalism in the Church, still widespread in most parts of the world, will make impossible the development of alternative models of ministry. The intellectual strength of Catholicism will fade under pressure of a rather fundamentalist theology taught in seminaries. The Church will irreversibly decline as in some parts of the world it is already doing. Manifestly, so vast a body does not collapse overnight, and much of the decline can be masked for decades. It will retain its strength more in some places than in others. It will continue to win some local battles but its overall role as a credible world community of faith and love, a body that can be ignored by no one, a living tradition that combines humanity and the most sophisticated rational understanding with divinity and mystical insight, will simply dwindle away leaving the Church as a narrowing fellowship upon the margins of history.

24 *Orientalium Ecclesiarum*, 17.

Conclusion

It is, of course, impossible for the historian to foresee the future. It is undeniable that the Church was by and large quite slow in assimilating the spirit of Vatican II and implementing its decisions. But Vatican II was a revolution and revolutions can be stalled for a time, but cannot be stopped.[25] Therefore, it may be wiser to conclude that the vast movement of transformation begun by Vatican II will not be easily ended either externally or internally. The Church will hopefully genuinely accept the spirit and implications of Vatican II in realizing a "people of God" ecclesiology, in a stress upon both a working collegiality and the genuine centrality of the Eucharist within the Church, especially the local Church in the warm recognition of the values of pluralism and freedom within and between particular Churches as within human society generally and in a commitment to work and find Christina holiness within the struggle for justice and peace in solidarity with the poor. But for that to happen, the Church has to become humble. Revelation makes no sense without the human being's answer in faith. This response that takes place in history as a definite experience, in a concrete language, also belongs to the content of revelation. We are not adding anything to revelation here but are interpreting revelation. Neither part is independently the whole of revelation. So a completely objective content of revelation outside of history is a questionable concept. The whole of revelation and faith exist in history. No zone is immune from the storms of man's history, no zone of pure theology. But the Spirit who is constantly active in the Church, and whose 'strength is revealed in weakness', preserves the identity of the Christian faith intact, and helps it to 'remain in the truth' through the vicissitudes of history. Creative faithfulness to the Gospel is possible only in a changing and developing history. Therefore, to suppress the freedom of theology in the name of truth is no service to the truth.

It is a known fact all over the world truth claims are associated with violence, arrogance, intolerance and indoctrination. But there is truth and it has to be found, and dialogue is the only possible way for it. But this dialogue is only reasoning together and learning together. Claiming that you have got the truth wrapped up breeds violence and intolerance. Believing that together, we may arrive at the truth can heal differences. We are all pilgrims. We do not know all the answers in advance. The Church must be seen as a community of those who teach, but also those who learn. The Church must have the courage to proclaim its convictions but the humility to learn from others. St. Augustine

---

25 John J. Markey, "George Washington, Napoleon, John Paul II and the Future of Vatican II Revolution," in *Seattle Theology and Ministry Review* 3 (2003) 14-25 quoted by Kurien Kunnumpuram, SJ, "Towards a New Church: An Investigation of the Theological Orientations of Vatican II," in Isaac Padinjarekuttu and Teiborlang Lyngdoh, *Catholic Church in Transition* (Shillong: Oriens Publications, 2106) 46.

said: "Whoever thinks that in this mortal life one may so disperse with the mists of the imagination as to possess the unclouded light of unchangeable truth understands neither what he seeks nor who he is that seeks it."[26] The Church has to protect itself from runaway secularism masqueraded as *aggiornamento,* but the Church leaders have also a special responsibility to balance their legitimate concern for vigilance about Catholic identity against the urgency of fostering creative Catholic thinking and activism. Clarity does not have to mean paralysis, and discernment does not have to mean turning a deaf ear to new perspectives because of anxiety about their provenance or possible implications. In other words, even if personalities or movements in the Church sometimes give bishops and other authorities heartburn, that doesn't mean they have nothing to contribute on any possible subject.

---

26 In Timothy Radcliffe, "Europe's Challenge," *The Tablet, 7 May, 2005, 10.*

3

More than a Slave: Characterization of Onesimus in Philemon - A Contextual Reading

K. Arul Samy ALCP/OSS

Apostolic Life Community of Priests in the Opus Spiritus Sancti (ALCP/OSS)

Abstract: *In the present article, the author attempts to explore the manner in which Paul characterizes Onesimus, a slave from Colossae (Col 4:9), who ran away from his master for the guilt of possible theft (Phlm. 18). Onesimus was converted to Christ by Paul. Paul's intention after conversion was to rehabilitate Onesimus. Thus, Paul sent him back to Philemon, his master with the letter a poignant plea that he be received no longer as a slave but as a brother in Christ and a beloved in the Lord. Paul's argumentative language is displayed at its best in the most intimate and personal letter that Paul wrote. In it, he deals with an accepted institution in the Ancient Near East, namely human slavery. It is highly unlikely that Paul attacked slavery directly nor was it strategically desirable for him to do so for the sake of the proclamation of the Gospel. However, Paul calls upon the spirit of Christ and of equality to break down the social barriers that were so dehumanizing.*

Keywords: *Slave, Master, Characterization, Philemon, Onesimus, Child, Brother, and Beloved*

Introduction

Metaphors and Images play prominent roles in both oral and written communication; the New Testament is no exception. Its writings, particularly those of Paul, abound with anthropological (Church[1], Synagogue[2], Community and Communion[3], Body of Christ[4], Bride of Christ and of the Lamb[5], Saints[6], Children of Abraham[7]), agricultural (Field, Vineyard, Olive Tree[8]), and at times, architectural (Temple or Sanctuary[9], House[10], the Way[11]) images and analogies to explain what is meant by the term 'church' and how its members ought to relate with one another.

Prof. Dr. Kurien Kunnumpuram, SJ, in whose honor this article is written, was truly passionate about the church, especially the church in India.[12] He was a dreamer of a church which would truly be Indian and authentically Christian;

---

1 The term 'church' (Gk: *ekklesia*) is used 114 times in NT. Interestingly, it is found just three times in the Gospels (Mt 16:18 and twice in Mt 18:17). Paul uses it 62 times mostly to refer to the local Christian community or a group of communities. Only occasionally, Paul refers to the whole church (Gal 1:13; 1 Cor. 12:28) in a universal sense (Col 1:24; Eph. 5:29).

2 The term 'synagogue' is used 56 times in the entire NT. It is often found in the Gospels and Acts of the Apostles. It is also found in James 2:24 and Rev 2:9; 3:9. Scholars wrangle over whether synagogue in the NT era still refers mainly to the assembly of people on the Sabbath, or also to the place where they gathered. However, the term 'synagogue' consistently refers to a Jewish assembly, whereas a Christian community of believers is designated to as an *ekklesia*.

3 The terms 'community' and 'communion' (Gk: *koinonia*) refer to a relationship of fellowship or friendship among believers based on participation in Christ (Phil 3:10; 1 Pet 4:13) and sharing common life in the Spirit (2 Cor. 13:13; Phil 2:1) by way of baptism (1 Cor. 12:13) and the Eucharist (1 Cor. 10:16-17). This communion is also manifested by sharing goods in common use (Acts 2:44; 4:32; Gal 6:6). Paul's mission to support the poor financially in the Jerusalem church is a concrete sign of this communion among believers (Rom 12:13; 15:25).

4 The 'Body of Christ' is a noteworthy Pauline metaphor for the church (1 Cor. 12:12-31), as a community of different members with different gifts and ministries (Rom 12:4-8; 1 Cor. 12:4-7) banded together in the same Spirit by baptism (1 Cor. 12:13) and the Eucharist (10:17). Colossians (1:18--2:19) and Ephesians (1:22-23) employ the same image, but insist that Christ is the head of the body (Col 2:19; Eph. 4:15-16).

5 Eph. 5:22-33; Rev 19:7; 21:2, 9; 22:7.

6 Acts 9:13, 32; Rom 1:7; 12:13; Phil 4:22; 1 Cor. 1:2; 2 Cor. 1:1; Rev 17:6.

7 Gal 3:29; Rev 3:12; 21:2. Along with it the phrases like 'New Israel and New Jerusalem' also appear.

8 God's field (1 Cor. 3:6-9), or vine (Jn. 15:1-11) or olive tree (Rom 11:17-24).

9 1 Cor. 3:16-17; 2 Cor. 6:16.

10 God's family or houschold in Gal 6:10; Eph. 2:19 or house in 1 Cor. 3:10-17; Eph. 2:20; 1 Tim 3:15; Heb. 10:21; 1 Pet 2:5; 4:17.

11 In the Gospel of Mark, some individuals follow Jesus 'on the way' (10:52). Jesus calls himself 'the Way' in the gospel of John (14:4-6) and later, 'the Way' is used as a group designation for the early Christians in Acts (9:2; 18:25-26; 19:9, 23; 24:14, 22).

12 I was fortunate to listen to his dreams and visions during my study years at JDV from 1995-1998.

a church that becomes more human, and a church that houses human beings who are both liberated and liberating. In other words, he dreamt of a church which is truly a community of friends; which is evident from his writings.[13]

The present article attempts to study the manner in which Paul characterizes Onesimus, a slave from Colossae (Col 4:9), who ran away from his master for the guilt of possible theft (Phlm. 18). Onesimus was converted to Christ by Paul. Then Paul sent him back to his master with the letter a touching appeal that he be received no longer as a slave but as a brother in Christ. Paul's persuasive and strong argumentative language is displayed at its best in the most intimate and personal letter that Paul wrote. In it, he deals with an accepted institution in the Ancient Near East, namely human slavery. It is highly unlikely that Paul attacked slavery directly, nor was it strategically desirable for him to do so for the sake of the proclamation of the Gospel. However, Paul calls upon the spirit of Christ and of equality to break down the social barriers that were so dehumanizing. He goes on to convince Philemon that Onesimus is, in fact, a brother and a beloved in the Lord.

1. Characterization as a Mode of Communication

When we study the letters of St. Paul, we think not only of Paul, the writer, but we think of the many addressee, the various Christian communities, for whom he has written those letters. Paul, without fail, mentions some of the prominent individuals in these communities for a win-win situation. Paul becomes famous for his rich use of images and metaphors for individuals and communities alike. In short, he is fully engaged in characterization with the sole aim of building the Christian communities in the Ancient Greco-Roman world without compromising the basic traits of Christianity. Characterization or character drawing is as old as humanity itself. Therefore, characterization is not a strange phenomenon in both the sacred and profane literature of the Ancient Near East, particularly in the Old Testament and the New Testament.

It is good to state what certain terminologies mean right at the beginning. For example, what is a character? A character as a count noun may refer to a character or many characters who might appear in a literary work as humans and individuals. Character as a mass noun refers to moral, mental, and social traits about the individuals[14]. Characterization is the way in which attributes and dispositions of any kind are assigned by a narrator to a character. It also refers to the process by which those traits are interpreted by narratees as about that character. Broadly, there are two types of characterization: direct and indirect. For D.L. Stamps, "Character and characterization refer to the way

13 For select Bibliography see: https://en.wikipedia.org/wiki/Kurien_Kunnumpuram.

14 KOEN DE TEMMERMAN & EVERT VAN EMDE BOAS (Eds.), Characterization in Ancient Greek Literature (SAGN 4), Leiden – Boston 2018, XII.

persons are presented in the story. The presentation includes what a person says and the way a person acts. Characterization is also developed by what others say about them, how they function in the plot, and what the narrator says about them"[15]. They are further divided and subdivided into many groups. For our purpose, it is good to know that metaphorical characterization primarily relies on the alignment or opposition of a character with someone or something else, with respect to certain points of similarity or difference[16]. Metaphorical characterization can again be explicit or implicit, intertextual or intra-textual, which can either function based on comparison or of contrast[17].

Scholars and students alike have been using metaphorical analysis as a scientific tool for the study of biblical texts. No more is the use of metaphors is considered as beautification of a text with some sort of style, delight, or pleasure to the senses and to the minds. Metaphors have the power to bring forth new meanings[18]. In other words, the use of metaphor can open up a new sphere of the word that is deeply hidden. It can serve as a pointer to the reality, which is called the heuristic valence[19], which is nothing but seeing "something as something else"[20].

Additionally, metaphors have the ability to provoke the audience[21]. As such, the metaphorical predicates of a text have the paraenetic valence[22], which is to bring about a desirable result effectively among the readers or listeners. In other words, metaphorical characterization of someone has the ability to move and make an impact on the readers. It aims at feeling, impressions, and the thought pattern of the readers and helps them in arriving at an intended practical solution. It is broadly seen as a strategy adopted by the writer/speaker to get what he wanted from his readers/listeners.

---

15 D. L. STAMPS, Rhetorical and Narratological Criticism, in: S. E. Porter (Ed.), Handbook to Exegesis of the New Testament (NTTS 25), Leiden – Stuttgart – Köln 1997, 231.

16 KOEN DE TEMMERMAN & EVERT VAN EMDE BOAS (Eds.), Characterization XIV.

17 KOEN DE TEMMERMAN & EVERT VAN EMDE BOAS (Eds.), Characterization XIV.

18 P. RICOEUR, Die lebendige Metapher, mit einem Vorwort zur dt. Ausgabe, übers. von R. Rochlitz (Übergänge. Texte und Studien zu Handlung, Sprachen und Lebenswelt; Bd. 12), München 1986, 28.

19 CH. G. MÜELLER, Gottes Pflanzung – Gottes Bau – Gottes Tempel. Die metaphorische Dimension paulinischer Gemeindetheologie in 1 Kor 3,5-17 (FuSt 5), Frankfurt/Main 1995, 59-61.

20 M.J. BORG, Reading the Bible again for the first time. Taking the Bible seriously but Not literally, New York – Harper San Francisco 1989, 41.

21 R. ZYMNER, Uneigentlichkeit. Studien zur Semantik und Geschichte der Parabel, Paderborn – München – Wien – Zürich 1991, 220.

22 H. WEDER (ed.), Die Sprache der Bilder. Gleichnis und Metapher in Literatur und Theologie (Zeitzeichen. Bd. 4), Gutersloh 1989, 111.

In recent years, the number of publications that have applied metaphor theory for the exegesis of biblical texts keeps on growing along with several studies on specific Pauline metaphors that have emerged. It is not our concern to state them all here. Our main concern is to apply metaphorical characterization to Paul's letter to Philemon.

2. Characterization of Onesimus by Paul

Paul's authorship of the letter to Philemon is accepted even by those who reject his authorship of Colossians. He writes as a prisoner[23]. As the shortest letter, it is very close in format to the model of Hellenistic letters that are intercessory in nature[24]. The addressees are Philemon, Apphia[25], Archippus and the church that is in the house of Philemon. The church seems to be very small in size. Philemon, the main addressee, is characterized as a dear friend and co-worker. He could have served either as the head of a Christian house-church or as the host of a Christian house-church, or both. Apphia, characterized as 'our sister', is the only lady to be mentioned by Paul in the list of the recipients in all his letters. Is she the wife or the sister of Philemon? Scholars are divided[26]. Certainly, she must have not only enjoyed a highly respectable position within the church but also for Paul. She has a special role to play about his appeal to take Onesimus back into their household. Paul, after usual address and greetings (1-3), extends his thanksgiving, which actually serves as an exordium to win over the heart of Philemon (4-7). The body of the letter is filled with the main appeal, re-appeal, and expansion of the appeal (8-22). The letter ends with final greetings and blessings (23-25).

a. Child

Paul calls Onesimus 'my child' in verse 10, whose 'father' he has become in his imprisonment. Interestingly, even in this shortest letter, there are many instances where child-father and childhood-fatherhood related terms and expressions or language of begetting occur. Paul by calling Onesimus 'my child' recognizes certain developments that have taken place in his imprisonment, namely Onesimus has learned to do certain duties of a child

23 The place and the date are very much disputed: from Ephesus (ca. 55), Caesarea (58-60) and Rome (61-63).

24 Letter to Philemon is comparable to the shorter letter of Pliny the Younger appealing to Sabinianus for a young freedman who sought refuge in Pliny's house. Cf. R. E. BROWN, An Introduction to the New Testament New York – London – Toronto – Sydney – Auckland 1997, 503.

25 H.-J. VENETZ, Frauen von Rang und Namen. Ein anderer Blick in paulinische Gemeinden, in: BiKi 57 (2002) 133.

26 CH. G. MÜELLER, Frühchristliche Ehepaare und paulinische Mission (SBS 215), Stuttgart 2008, 43-46.

in prison such as honouring, obeying, caring, and supporting Paul in his old age. On the other hand, as a 'father', Paul has most likely extended his authority, given instructions and education about important affairs such as rhetoric, travel, general education, physical training and control of tongues in speech and religion particularly about Christianity. Additionally, Paul showed affection and love to Onesimus, who was a runaway slave. This reciprocal giving and taking resulted in a new relationship between Paul and Onesimus.

In a world where the hierarchy[27] was so crucial, Paul maintained it and at the same time transcended it by donating a new identity to Onesimus: namely that of a child to Paul within the new family, i.e. the church, which is not something unusual for Paul[28]. Ronald F. Hock has rightly pointed out that Paul has used a strategy called *ethopoiia* (character drawing), which begins with the present, then moves on to the past and finally looks to the future. Accordingly, Paul starts with an appeal about Onesimus to Philemon. Then he goes on to recall the past from verses 10-15, wherein he remembers about the uselessness of Onesimus in the past. He also expresses his desire to keep him but not without Philemon's consent, and then finally remembers why the slave ran away from his master at all. Looking into the future with hope, Paul expects that Philemon will accept Onesimus back into his household, no longer as a slave but as a beloved brother. If he owes anything to Philemon, Paul himself will repay (16-19)[29].

b. Brother

In the plea of Paul Onesimus is characterized as a brother. By means of this epithet Onesimus is identified as a fellow Christian like anyone else, including Paul and Philemon. Additionally, and more significantly, it has to be noted that Paul has introduced kinship language or the language of belonging. It is not something strange for Paul[30]. Paul has already called Onesimus a child. It is rightly noted that Paul's use of kinship language was primarily to insist without any compromise the bonds that bind Christians to one another as members of the same family. The context that drives Paul to use the language of belonging is primarily one of division or scandal, which could serve as internal and external obstacles to unity within the community as it is the case

27 J. JEREMIAS, Jerusalem in the Time of Jesus: An Investigation into Economic and Social Conditions during New Testament Period, Philadelphia 1988, 317-345.

28 KAR YONG LIM, Metaphors and Social Identity Formation in Paul's Letters to the Corinthians, Eugene OR 2017, 98-112.

29 RONALD F. HOCK, Paul and Greco-Roman Education, in: J. PAUL SAMPLEY (ed.), Paul in the Greco-Roman World: A Handbook, Harrisburg – London – New York 2003, 210.

30 RAYMOND F. COLLINS, First Corinthians (Sacred Pagina Series 7) Collegeville, Minnesota 1999, 45.

in 1 Corinthians (1 Cor. 1:10-11; and chapters 6-11)[31]. Philemon could very well take Onesimus to the secular judiciary for the liabilities that Onesimus caused to him. In other words, legally, Philemon could punish his slave very severely. What Paul promises to repay can be actually claimed through the intervention of the secular courts. However, Paul reminds Philemon through the use of the language of kinship that the case of Onesimus now has to be settled within the community of Christians, particularly by the benevolent intervention of Philemon himself, who enjoys certain administrative powers over the church there.

In this plea, Paul does not argue the case simply in terms of the standard set by the secular world. The secular world had different and strict standards of behaviour between masters and slaves or even ex-slaves. Instead, Paul pleads the case on the grounds of mercy. Paul begins the whole persuasion with a new set of relationships: those between Christians. Unfortunately, Paul does not tell us about what Onesimus thinks about having run away from Philemon: does he repent like the prodigal son or is he stubborn like the elder son in the gospel of Luke? We have no idea at all. Paul is very silent on this matter. However, it is good to remind ourselves that Paul has already exercised his authority over Onesimus during the period of imprisonment, and has given enough instructions about various affairs, including Christianity, which made him embrace Christianity as his religion. That is the reason why Paul now calls Onesimus a beloved brother in Christ.

As a beloved brother in Christ, Onesimus could very well now represent Paul in his work and mission. Now he is entrusted with a mission of carrying the very letter that Paul writes to Philemon. Paul is hopeful that Onesimus will be treated in the same manner as Paul himself. Paul's hope for a relationship of fellowship between Philemon and himself is now almost dependent on how Onesimus is received and treated. Paul requests that Philemon prepare a guest room for him, which indicates that the entire case could have been settled as Paul has persuaded. The consequence of settling the case as Paul persuaded is that Philemon not only accepted Onesimus as a fellow Christian but also, he cancelled out all the outstanding debts and other legal punishments that he might have otherwise claimed against Onesimus in the secular courts.

Paul's plea begins in verse 7, where he recalls his own experience. The experience is worthy of recall since it brought both joy and encouragement. What is that experience? It is the love of Philemon in taking care of the holy ones, which is narrated as the hearts of the holy ones have been refreshed. This act of Philemon serves as the starting point for Paul to present his case to him. It is interesting to note that in verses 5-7, one can notice that the theme of love and faith are repeated, particularly the love and faith of Philemon. In verse 7,

31 RAYMOND F. COLLINS, First Corinthians 45.

Onesimus is characterized as the heart that belongs to Paul. However, Paul does not want to keep him without the consent of Philemon. Now Paul expects that Philemon himself would refresh the heart of Paul just as he refreshed the hearts of the holy ones. Some see here a hint that Paul expects Philemon to free Onesimus from the slavery.[32]

In all, Paul does not in any way, limit the freedom of Philemon. He has freedom; not only as to how he can receive but also if he needs to free Onesimus from all the legal punishments and debts. Paul only pleads that the debt could be levied on Paul himself. Paul persuades Philemon to forgive Onesimus and keep him with him or to return him back to Paul to aid him in his missionary work.[33]

3. Message for us Today

The Catholic churches in India are as complex and varied as India itself. They consist of three churches (Latin, Syro-Malabar and Syro-Malankara) with almost 174 dioceses. It is natural to have differences between people, cultures, languages and races. There cannot be mathematical unity. However, not-withstanding the many positives and blessings in the churches in India, there are certainly many unhealthy differences, rivalries and tensions among Christians and Christian churches in India. When one hears about the conflict between Dalit Christians and high caste Christians, women and men, rich and poor, urban and rural, hierarchy and laity, one really wonders and asks; is the church truly living according to the foundational values of Christ? In areas like social justice, equity, human dignity, and social peace, the churches in India have to grow. It is not enough to just be friendly with people of lower castes or status, the poor, children, or women or laity. An atmosphere of mature love has to be created in our homes, churches and institutions so that Christians who are our own brothers and sisters feel at home. These places are to become places of love, care, acceptance, healing, joy and integration.

Jesus, our Master and Lord, was not just a friend. Jesus calls his disciples as his closest and intimate friends. He transcended the master-servant relationship and alignment. Jesus in the Gospels helps us to see God, others and oneself in a unique way. That unique way is beautifully summarized by Pope Francis in his recent Apostolic Exhortation as follows: "Jesus clears a way of seeing two faces, that of the Father and that of our brother. He does not give us two more formulas or two more commands. He gives us two faces, or better yet, one alone: the face of God reflected in so many other faces. For in every one of our brothers and sisters, especially the least, the most vulnerable,

32 PHEME PERKINS, Reading the New Testament, Mahwah, New Jersey, 1988, 149.

33 PHEME PERKINS, Reading the New Testament, 150.

the defenceless, and those in need, God's very image is found."[34] Jesus wanted the church and its members to be at the service of the dignity and destiny of the entire cosmos, including that of humanity.[35]

Paul, through his letter to Philemon, does exactly what was expected of an Apostle of Christ: he brings the healing power of God's grace in the life of Onesimus. Onesimus was a prisoner who needed transformative and intimate love, and Paul gave him exactly that. As a result, Onesimus, the prisoner who had lived under the hardest conditions, now becomes a Christian. Paul becomes a father to him in faith, and Onesimus becomes a child. They are no longer strangers. Paul has gone out of his way to practice the Spirit of Christ.

Paul also presents us with a picture of equality in an early Christian community without challenging the much-practised elements of authority, slavery and hierarchy. Paul refers to the new converts like Onesimus as his children. As such, he brought gladness and joy to these new converts. As a responsible father, Paul guards and corrects, and more importantly helps them to integrate into the Church, which is their new family. In this new family, the categories of the secular world do not play prominent roles. All are called to recognize their only Master, and that is Jesus, the Lord. Also, he challenges them and makes use of them in building up this church.

Conclusion

In conclusion, I have a couple of practical suggestions to improve our way of living as members of the Church in India. First of all, Deacons, Priests, Bishops and all those engaged in pastoral works are to imbibe the spirit of Paul in going out of themselves and strive to become mediators between God and men and women; particularly the marginalized in our society, failing which, we will end up being just managers of our own institutions. God has anointed the leaders of the Christian communities to be there for others, especially the poor, prisoners, the sick and those who suffer from isolation. Paul and Onesimus were both in prison. However, Paul was certainly treated differently than Onesimus due to his Roman citizenship. There was a huge divide between them, even in prison. However, Paul did not wait for Onesimus to come to him: he went after him to encounter, encourage and transform him. Therefore, in the pastoral duties, the pastors are to go out to meet their sheep in their own circumstances and situations.

Secondly, the Church could mean many things to many people. However, for us Catholics, she is our mother since she is the bride who brings forth the children of light, who in turn become pillars of holiness, sources of inspiration, and challengers of the truth. Onesimus and Philemon become true children of

34 POPE FRANCIS, *Gaudete Et Exsultate* (19 March 2018), 61.

35 Pastoral Constitution on the Church in the Modern World: *Gaudium et Spes* 29.

the church by being obedient listeners to what Paul had to say to them. They listened to Paul's desire to have communal unity in the church at the house of Philemon. A dispute has been amicably resolved. More importantly, they have transformed their lives according to the expectations of Paul. The Churches in India need what I call, the grace of engaging with all the members of the church so that no one will be left alone to suffer from rejection and isolation, but all will be embraced to take shelter in our earthly home, the Church.

4

Ways of Salvation and the Way of Salvation

Jacob Parappally MSFS
Dean of Theology, Tejas Vidya Peetha, Bengaluru-560074

Abstract: *Every religion offers salvation or liberation. Since the time of Cyprian of Carthage, the Catholic Church held the exclusive Christian claim that there is no salvation outside the Church (Extra Ecclesiam nulla salus). However, at the Vatican II there was a re-visioning and a renewed understanding of salvation that that went beyond absolute exclusivism to a recognition of the role of other religions in the economy of salvation. Based on the teachings of Vatican II, the author shows that in Jesus Christ, the incarnation of God's Communion within the Trinity as well as God's communion with humans and their world all authentic ways of salvation find their uniqueness and legitimate space distinct but not separate from Christ, the Way! Extra communionis nulla salus (Outside Communion no salvation)!*

Keywords: *Salvation, Church, Communion, Religions.*

Every religion claims to offer the certainty of salvation or liberation to its adherents if they follow the way shown by it faithfully, consistently and perseveringly till the end of one's life. Some religions claim that the way shown by them is the only way to be followed to attain salvation or liberation. There are others who would do not deny the possibility of salvation in and through the following beliefs and practices of religions other than their own but would claim at least a certain kind of superiority over other religions. Since the time of Cyprian of Carthage the Catholic Church held the exclusive

Christian claim that there is no salvation outside the Church (*Extra Ecclesiam nulla salus*). However, at the Vatican II there was a re-visioning and a renewed understanding of salvation that that went beyond absolute exclusivism to a recognition of the role of other religions in the economy of salvation.

Immediately after the Vat II Council it was Kurien Kunnumpuram entered into an engaging dialogue with the teachings of Vatican II on the salvation of those who are not the members of the Church. It was his concern that the multi-religious context of India with many religions which claim to be ways of salvation challenges Christian faith about the claim of salvation exclusively through Christ and his Church. It is the concern of every Christian believer in India to understand the meaning of his or her salvation through Christ and his Church in the face of Hinduism and other religions of India which claim to be ways of salvation. In the foreword to his book *Ways of Salvation*[1], which was a revised version of his doctoral dissertation submitted to the University of Innsbruck in 1967, he articulated the problem of religious pluralism that confronts every Christian believer in India. He observes that for a long time the Catholic Church showed little interest in entering into dialogue with other religions "leaving the Indian Christian a frustrated and marginal figure, ill-equipped for his mission in this pluralistic society". The Second Vatican Council opened the Church to the outside world and encouraged dialogue with other religions. Kunnumpuram contributed to the understanding of the theological significance of other religions in God's plan of salvation according to the teachings and insights of the Vatican II and highlighted the importance of entering into dialogue with other religions as an imperative to the self-understanding of Church which is essentially missionary by its nature. At the end of his research on the approach of Vatican II to world religions Kunnumpuram affirmed that the approach of the Church was positive as the Council recognized the place and function of world religions in the divine economy of salvation. Itdiscovered and acknowledged the presence of the seeds of the Word and the fruits of the Spirit in them. Therefore, the need for a theology of Non-Christian religions and developing a theology of Christian Missions were seen that time, immediately after the Council, as the task ahead for the Church, especially, the Indian Church.

The recognition of the place and function of non-Christian religions in the divine economy of salvation and the presence and action of the Holy Spirit in the hearts of the people of other religions call for a deeper reflection on the nature of the Church itself and its place in the world. Kunnumpuram says, "We need a clearer grasp of its [Church's] place in God's plan for the world. We must learn to regard the Church as the home of all peoples and religions. Thus we realize that is our Christian duty to recognize and appreciate the positive

1 Kurien Kunnumpuram, *Ways of Salvation,* Pune: Pontifical Athanaeum, 1970

values in all religions, in a spirit of faith in God who has scattered his graces and insight among the nations of the earth. Genuine faith is always ready to acknowledge him wherever it encounters him."[2] During the fifty years after Kunnumpuram had made his study on the teachings of Vatican II on Church's understanding of the place and role of other religions in the divine plan of salvation there have been important papal encyclicals[3] and other magisterial teachings, hundreds of theological books and articles on dialogue with other religions and on the need and the relevance of Christian missions. However, it is difficult to find in them a definitive statement about recognizing other religions as ways of salvation that give other religions their legitimate place in the divine plan without a paternalistic or condescending attitude of the Church.

A theology of religion that sees other religions only as preparation for the gospel or ways that are to be fulfilled in Christ and in His Church may satisfy a Christian believer who experiences Jesus Christ as the fullness of revelation. Such an understanding of other religions satisfies one who is confronted by the nagging question about the salvation of millions of people who are not the members of the Church or not even heard of Jesus Christ or even they have heard of the gospel and Christ yet do not accept it as a better way of salvation than what they believe in. Why and how should, then, the Church fulfil its missionary mandate to proclaim Christ and make disciples of all nations, baptizing them in the name of the Father and of the Son and the Holy Spirit (cf. Mt 28:18) if all religions are ways of salvation? Would not the understanding that all religions as ways of salvation sap the energy and enthusiasm of thousands of missionaries all over the world who toil day and night risking even their own lives for proclaiming Christ and work for the implanting of the Church? The legendary missionary zeal was for the salvation of the souls living outside the bark of Peter?

By going beyond the clear statement expressing the traditional belief of the Church that *extra ecclesiam nulla salus* or outside the Church there is no salvation in the Second Vatican Council, the Church made itself very vulnerable. It is certain that a negative approach to other religions and the exclusive claim of salvation in and through the Church engender missionary zeal and enthusiasm as it was seen in the Church before Vatican II. In spite of the positive approach to other religions and acknowledging their place in the economy of salvation some missionaries continue to hold the pre-Vatican II negative attitude towards other religions in their missionary approach to other religions. In this context, how do we reconcile the self-understanding of the

---

2 *Ways of Salvation,* p. 95

3 Eg. *Evangelii Nuntiandi, Christifideles Laici, Redemptoris Missio, Dialogue and Proclamation: Reflection and Orientations on Interreligious Dialogue and The Proclamation of The Gospel of Jesus Christ, etc.*

Church and its commitment to follow the missionary mandate entrusted to it and still adhere to the positive approach to other religions and their offer of ways of salvation to humans? How can Church remain a home for all peoples and religions in the light of the teachings of Vatican II as envisioned by Kunnumpuram? In this paper an attempt is made to reconcile the apparent contradiction between the Ways of Salvation and the Way of Salvation. Do the Ways of Salvation reduce the importance and uniqueness of the Way of Salvation? How are the Ways of Salvation related to the Way of Salvation? Is the proclamation of Christ and his Kingdom to those who follow other Ways of Salvation still relevant?

I. Vatican II on the Salvific Meaning of Other Religions

No other ecumenical council in the history of the Church took seriously the plurality religions and their salvific meaning as the Second Vatican Council. It attempted to discover its own identity in relation to other religions and its mission to the people of other religions from its new insight into the meaning of revelation. The *Dogmatic Constitution Divine Revelation* viewed revelation in relation to the events of salvation history. The salvific interventions of God in history culminated in Christ and he is the perfection of revelation. From this new understanding of revelation which is summed up and climaxed in Christ was a departure from the "neo-scholastic intellectualism for which revelation chiefly meant a store of mysterious supernatural teachings"[4]. It opened the possibility of discovering the presence and action of God in all that is good in other religions. The teaching of Vatican II on other religions evolves from this new understanding of revelation.

The important teachings of Vatican II on non-Christian religions are found scattered in various documents of the Council. The Declaration on Church's Relation to Non-Christian Religions (*Nostra Aetate)* affirms that "other religions found everywhere try to counter the restlessness of the human heart, each in its own manner, by proposing "ways," comprising teachings, rules of life, and sacred rites. The Catholic Church rejects nothing that is true and holy in these religions. She regards with sincere reverence those ways of conduct and of life, those precepts and teachings which, though differing in many aspects from the ones she holds and sets forth, nonetheless often reflect a ray of that Truth which enlightens all people. Indeed, she proclaims, and ever must proclaim Christ 'the way, the truth, and the life' (John 14:6), in whom men may find the fullness of religious life, in whom God has reconciled all things to Himself"[5]. The Catholic Church does not reject anything true and

4 Kurien Kunnumpuram, *Ways of Salvation,* Pune: Pontifical Athanaeum, 1970, p. 80; J.Ratzinger, "Revelation Itself", in *Commentary on the Documents of Vatican II,* ed., Vorgrimler, London, 1969, p. 172.

5 *Nostra Aetate* No. 2

holy in other religions as well as affirms that they reflect a ray of the Truth that enlightens all people. Indeed, according to the Christian faith Christ is this Truth and the Way! It can be legitimately concluded that the Council recognizes everything holy and true in other religions flow from that Truth whose ray is found in these religions.

How are the religions related to Christ the Truth and his Church so that it possible for those who follow these religions to find salvation? *Lumen Gentium* clearly states, "Nor is God far distant from those who in shadows and images seek the unknown God, for it is He who gives to all people life and breath and all things, and as Saviour wills that all humans be saved. Those also can attain to salvation who through no fault of their own do not know the Gospel of Christ or His Church, yet sincerely seek God and moved by grace strive by their deeds to do His will as it is known to them through the dictates of conscience"[6]. If salvation is only through the Way and Truth that Christ is, then the salvation is both offered and received only through him whose Spirit is mysteriously at work in everything good, holy and acceptable to God in all these religions. It is through this mysterious action of God they are saved if they remain open to that Truth that enlightens every human. The document on the Missionary Activity of the Church, *Ad Gentes*states, "God in ways known to himself can lead those inculpably ignorant of the Gospel to that faith without which it is impossible to please him".[7]

According to Kunnumpuram, "The Second Vatican Council recognizes that non-Christian religions possess many positive values such as truth and goodness, grace and holiness. It regards these values as a sort of secret presence of God, as the seeds of the Word and the fruits of the Spirit. The Council realizes that these religions cannot be considered merely as natural religions, since they contain supernatural elements, even saving faith. Despite error, sin and human depravity, non-Christian religions are a preparation for the Gospel, as they have an intimate tendency, an inner dynamism towards Christ and his Church. For those who have not yet been existentially confronted with Christianity, non-Christian religions can serve as ways of salvation, in the sense that God saves these human beings in and through the doctrines and practices of these religions".[8] Going further from these conclusions the question can be raised about the theological reasons for recognizing the non-Christian religions as Ways of Salvation because they have 'an intimate tendency, an inner dynamism towards Christ and Church'. What is the source of this inner dynamism towards Christ and Church?

---

6 *Lumen Gentium* , No.16

7 *Ad Gentes* No.2

8 *Ways of Salvation,* p. 91

II. Recent Teaching of the Church on Salvation

All the previous magisterial teachings before Vatican II affirmed the necessity of being a member of the Church for salvation and at the same time categorically stated who cannot obtain salvation. We have seen that with Vatican II there is broadening of the understanding of the possibility of salvation for others who do not belong to the Catholic Church through mysterious ways known to God alone.[9]

The Letter *Placuit Deo* published on 22 February, 2018, by the Congregation for the Doctrine of Faith headed by Cardinal Ladaria addressing all the bishops of the Catholic Church on certain aspects of salvation is the first document in the history of the Church which explains at least certain aspects of salvation. Though it is not a comprehensive document on salvation it liberates the notion of salvation from its traditional individualistic, spiritualistic and other-worldly understanding.

The salvation that God offers us is not achieved with our own individual efforts alone, as neo-Pelagianism would contend. Rather, salvation is found in the relationships that are born from the incarnate Son of God and that form the communion of the Church. Because the grace that Christ gives us is not a merely interior salvation, as the neo-Gnostic vision claims, and introduces us into concrete relationships that He himself has lived, the Church is a visible community. In her we touch the flesh of Jesus, especially in our poorest and most suffering brothers and sisters. Hence, the salvific mediation of the Church, "the universal sacrament of salvation",assures us that salvation does not consist in the self-realization of the isolated individual, nor in an interior fusion of the individual with the divine. Rather, salvation consists in being incorporated into a communion of persons that participates in the communion of the Trinity. Both the individualistic and the merely interior visions of salvation contradict the sacramental economy through which God willed to save the human person.[10]

In the context of Pope Francis' attack on neo-Pelagian individualism and the neo-Gnostic disregard for the body, the document affirms, "In the face of these two trends, the present Letter wants to reaffirm that salvation consists in our union with Christ, who, by his Incarnation, death and Resurrection has brought about a new order of relationships with the Father and among human persons, and has introduced us into this order, thanks to the gift of his Spirit, so that we are able to unite ourselves to the Father as sons in the Son, and become one body in the "firstborn among many brothers" (Rom 8:29)."[11] The document further says, "At no moment in history did God stop offering his

9 *Lumen Gentium* , No.16

10 *Placuit Deo* No.12-13

11 *Ibid.*, 4

salvation to the sons and daughters of Adam (cf. Gen 3:15), establishing his covenant with all of humanity in Noah (cf. Gen 9:9) and, later, with Abraham and his descendants (cf. Gen 15:18). Therefore, divine salvation takes on the creaturely order shared by all humanity and accompanies their concrete journey in history".[12]

The mission of the Church is to communicate the experience which begins in the historical existence and is fulfilled in the eschatological communion with the Trinity so that those who are objectively saved through their ontological union with Christ may experience wholeness here and now. The document says: "The awareness of the fullness of life into which Christ the Saviour introduces us propels Christians onward in the mission of announcing to all the joy and light of the Gospel. In this work, Christians must also be prepared to establish a sincere and constructive dialogue with believers of other religions, confident that God can lead "all people of good will in whose hearts grace works in an unseen way" towards salvation in Christ."[13]

Some have tweeted that '*Placuit Deo* reads like a summary of *Dominus Iesus.*' However, those who have really analysed the document *Placuit Deo* would not miss the opening of a new theological vision of salvation, though it may be sketchy, presented in this document compared to the narrow and exclusive understanding of the Church and salvation through Jesus Christ in *Dominus Iesus.* Austen Ivereigh, Pope Francis' biographer and supporter in tweet implied that *Placuit Deo* advances the formula *Extra Ecclesiam nulla salus.* It must be stated that this document is not a repetition of the traditional axiom that there is no salvation outside the Church. It opens up new avenues for theological reflection on Christian understanding of salvation that salvation or wholeness essentially consists in *Communion.*

III. Communitarian Dimension of Salvation

Both the Second Vatican Council and the recent document on certain aspects of salvation *Placuit Deo*a ffirm the communitarian dimension of salvation. Whether within the Church or beyond the Church in other non-Christian religions salvation is through communion and salvation is ultimately communion. Even in the *Relatio* referring to non-Christian religions in the 1964 schema on Church says, " "All grace takes on a communitarian character and tends to the Church"[14] The Constitution on Church, *Lumen Gentium* affirms this when it says, "At all times and in every race God has given welcome to whosoever fears Him and does what is right. God, however, does not make men holy and

---

12 *Ibid., 8*

13 *PlacuitDeo,* No.15.

14 *Relatio Super Schema Const.Dogma. De Eccclesia,* 1964.p. 53: " *Omnis autem gratia quondam indolem communitariam induit et ad Ecclesiam respicit".*

save them merely as individuals, without bond or link between one another. Rather has it pleased Him to bring men together as one people, a people which acknowledges Him in truth and serves Him in holiness. He therefore chose the race of Israel as a people unto Himself."[15] Divine purpose is human well-being or wholeness is through communion with God and communion with others.

The source of communion among humans is the Trinitarian communion of the Father, Son and the Spirit. The Decree on the Missionary Activity of the Church says: "This decree, however, flows from the "fount - like love" or charity of God the Father who, being the "principle without principle" from whom the Son is begotten and Holy Spirit proceeds through the Son, freely creating us on account of His surpassing and merciful kindness and graciously calling us moreover to share with Him His life and His glory, has generously poured out, and does not cease to pour out still, His divine goodness. Thus He who created all things may at last be "all in all" (1 Cor. 15:28), bringing about at one and the same time His own glory and our happiness. But it pleased God to call men to share His life, not just singly, apart from any mutual bond, but rather to mold them into a people in which His sons, once scattered abroad might be gathered together (cf. John 11:52)."[16] The divine plan for humans is that they live, move and have their being in communion which begins in their historical existence and fulfilled in the eschatological communion with God, the Absolute Communion.

The essential communitarian dimension of any religion and the social nature of humans have their source in the Trinitarian communion and in the reality of Christ. In the Declaration on Religious Freedom (*Dignitatis Humanae*) - Church acknowledges the communitarian dimension of religions and the social nature of humans." The social nature of man, however, itself requires that he should give external expression to his internal acts of religion: that he should share with others in matters religious; that he should profess his religion in community."[17]

The Christian faith-experience affirms that every human being is created in the image and likeness of God, the Trinity and therefore every human being is Trinitarian or communitarian by nature. It is by their essential communitarian nature humans are persons. The social nature of humans is rooted in as well as the expression of the essential Trinitarian nature of human being. The capacity of humans for transcendence can be considered as their Father-dimension, their transparency or openness as the Son-dimension and their immanence or interiority as the Spirit-dimension. Thus communion is the beginning and end or the source and destiny of humans, indeed, it is their communion with the

15 *Lumen Gentium* , No.9

16 *Ad Gentes*2

17 *Dignitatis Humanae* 3

Absolute Communion or the Trinitarian life that brings final fulfillment of humans as humans.

Every type of human community has its source and model in the Trinitarian communion. Trinity is the source of human community because every human is the image of the Trinity and therefore communitarian and this essential nature is lived existentially in communities. Trinity is the model for communitarian life because in the Trinity there is absolute self-giving among the Persons of the Trinity and therefore, the Trinity is absolute unity or love. The revelation of God as Trinity is also the revelation of the meaning of plurality of everything that exists in the world and all forms of plurality. In the Trinity the Persons are distinct but not separate. The distinction or difference among the Persons of the Trinity is for communion and therefore it justifies all distinctions or differences that lead to communion. The ways of authentic communion among humans too are different and distinct but not separate from the Trinitarian communion historically manifested in Jesus Christ the Way. It is the Christian faith-experience that Jesus Christ, the incarnation of Absolute Communion is indeed the Way of salvation.The Church is the sacrament of Christ, the incarnate communion of God.

In Jesus Christ everything is united as he is the Alpha and the Omega of the entire creation. Everything is created in him and for him. "He is the image of the invisible God, the first-born of all creation; for in him all things were created, in heaven and on earth, visible and invisible, whether thrones or dominions or principalities or authorities -- all things were created through him and for him. He is before all things, and in him all things hold together"(Colossians 1:15-17). By assuming humanity, Jesus Christ, the Word, includes everyone before him, after him and contemporaneous with him. "He is the head of the body, the church; he is the beginning, the first-born from the dead, that in everything he might be pre-eminent"(Colossians 1:18). In his body, the Church, all are included though their relation to the body may differ. The ontological union of every human being with Christ and the interrelatedness of the entire humanity in Christ through incarnation make objective salvation of humans possible. All those ways of salvation, however, they are perceived, understood and their demands are lived with a sincere heart by those who follow those ways cannot be separated from the Way of Salvation, Jesus Christ and his body the Church! The ways of salvation offered by non-Christian religions are distinct from the explicit way of salvation in Jesus Christ and his body the Church but cannot be separated from Christ or his Church. If so, can we not say that those who are walking on those ways are, in fact, walking with Christ and united with Christ, the Way, thoughit may not be known to them?

The mission or the proclamation of the good news continues to be an imperative placed on every disciple. It means that Jesus Christ, the incarnation of Absolute Communion, and his Church the Sacrament of Christ need to be offered to all humans to experience wholeness or salvation through communion in a new way hitherto unknown to them. Its newness consists in revealing to humans that the heart of salvific communion is self-emptying love revealed in Jesus Christ and actualized through the Spirit of God .It is also a part of the mission to recognize and affirm that all other ways of authentic communion as the expression of God, the Absolute Communion because outside communion there is no salvation – *extra communionis nulla salus*!

Conclusion

The Second Vatican Council's recognition of the presence of seeds of Word and the rays of Truth in non-Christian religions was a great relief for Christians who were encountering daily the reality of a plurality of religions and each of them claiming to be the way of salvation for its adherents. Immediately after the Council it was Kurien Kunnumpuram who recognized that the teachings of Vatican II on non-Christian religions scattered in various documents offered the Church in India the possibility to enter legitimate dialogue with other religions especially Hinduism. In the context of India he envisioned a new self-understanding of the Church that it becomes a home for all religions and all peoples. The task ahead for the Church, according to him, was to develop a new theology of religions and a relevant Missiology that takes into account the new approach of the Church towards other religions which claim to be ways of salvation. The challenge of Kurien Kunnumpuramto develop a relevant ecclesiology and a Missiology can be responded to adequately if the self-understanding of Church as the Sacrament of Christ the incarnation of Absolute Communion lives and relates with all humans as a home of communion and proclaims that outside communion there is no salvation. It can be theologically shown that in Jesus Christ, the incarnation of God's Communion within the Trinity as well as God's communion with humans and their world all authentic ways of salvation find their uniqueness and legitimate space distinct but not separate from Christ, the Way! *Extra communionis nulla salus – Outside Communion no salvation!*

5

A Challenge to Become the Church of the Poor

Shalini Mulackal PBVM
Professor of Systematic Theology,
Vidyajyoti School of Theology, New Delhi

Abstract: *As an adult member and as a Consecrated person in the church, the author looks at the Indian situation and the role the Church is called to play in this context. She is convinced that there is a close link between the radical following of Jesus and reaching out to those on the margins. There are millions in our country who go to bed hungry every day. Poverty and absolute poverty is a reality in our country in spite of the economic growth the country claims to make. Wealth is concentrated into fewer and fewer hands, and the gap between the rich and poor are widening day by day. In this context, the Church's commitment to the poor is not an option but an integral part of our call as Christians and as followers of Jesus. We cannot practice our faith by bracketing off this commitment. The church in India needs to make a preferential option for the subaltern groups and work for their well-being.*

Keywords*: Church of the poor, Two feet theory, Preferential option for the poor, Subalterns, Tribals.*

Introduction

When I reflect on my vocation to religious life, I realize that the feeling of compassion I had towards the poor and the suffering was at the root of my saying 'yes' to religious life.[1] Even as a young girl I desired to do something to alleviate pain and misery of those made poor. During my initial formation, I came to know that Nano Nagle, the Foundress of Presentation Sisters, spent her whole life for the education of the poor children in Ireland. Her heart was moved with compassion when she saw the situation of the poor during the Penal Laws in the 18th Century Ireland. Being from a wealthy and influential family, she was smuggled to France and there she was educated. It was on her return that she realized the plight of the poor in Ireland. The history of many religious orders has similar stories of their Founders responding to the needs of the poor at a particular time in a particular place.

Where did I pick up this spirit of compassion? Of course, it is from the Church, from the Bible and from my Christian upbringing. Today as an adult member and as a Consecrated person in the Church I would like to critically look at the Indian situation and the role the Indian Church is called to play in this context. I am convinced that there is a close link between the radical following of Jesus and reaching out to those on the periphery. This short paper is an attempt to reflect on this link in the present day context of India.

1. Poverty and People Made Poor

For decades, India had been trying to combat poverty through several policies and programmes. "Growth mediated Approach," "Capability Approach," "Safety-net Approach," and alternatively the "Area Specific Approach" have been adopted for the eradication of poverty. Despite all these, more than 400 million persons in India continue to live in conditions of extreme poverty earning income less than US $ 1 a day. However, poverty ratio is not uniform throughout India. It is as high as 46. 4 per cent in Orissa, 41.4 per cent in Bihar, 40.3 per cent in Jharkhand, 39.6 per cent in Uttar Pradesh to merely 5.4 per cent in Jammu & Kashmir. Orissa remains the worst-hit State, with a rural poverty of 60.8 per cent followed by Bihar with urban poverty at 43.7 per cent.[2]

Poverty can be defined from various perspectives, namely, Income perspective, Basic needs perspective or Capability perspective.[3] But today the understanding of poverty world-wide includes Income or consumption poverty, Human poverty in terms of Human (under) development, Social exclusion, Ill beings, (lack of) Capability and functioning, Vulnerability, Inequality of income and consumption, Livelihood Unsustainability, Lack of basic human

1 This is a slighly modified from a paper presented at a panel during the General Body meeting of CBCI on 3rd March 2016 at St. John's Medical College, Bangalore.

2 See Manish Dev, *GDP Growth and Poverty: An Analytical Study of Poverty Reduction Strategies and Achievements during Plans in Indian States* (New Delhi: Deep & Deep Publications, 2011), 5.

3 See Manish Dev, *GDP Growth and Poverty*, 31-32.

needs, Violation of basic human rights, Relative deprivation, and Lack of dignity, self-respect, security and justice.[4] Poverty can be conceptualized both as income poverty and human poverty. Human Poverty is defined by impoverishment in multiple dimensions-deprivations in a long and healthy life, in knowledge, in decent standard of living, in participation, etc.[5]

A number of studies in India have established that people belonging to scheduled castes, scheduled tribes and other backward castes have the largest share of the poor. Women of these vulnerable classes are the worst affected segment of society. This makes one believe that poverty has a gender dimension. According to the former UN Secretary-General Kofi Annan, "Gender equality is more than a goal in itself. It is a precondition for meeting the challenge of reducing poverty, promoting sustainable development and building good governance." Majority of women in India are still a deprived lot. Consequently, we have exceptionally high rates of malnutrition, especially among women and girl children. Tradition requires that women eat last and the least throughout their lives, even when pregnant or lactating.

Despite several constitutional safeguards, millions of Dalits are still facing discrimination. They are deprived and discriminated lot- economically and socially. The shocking incident of suicide committed by Rohit Vemula is a case in point. Rohit killed himself on 17th January 2016 leaving a powerful letter behind in which he mentions, "The value of man was reduced to his immediate identity and nearest possibility. To a number. To a vote. To a thing... My birth is my fatal accident."Scheduled castes or Dalits as they call themselves constitute 16.23 per cent of India's population. They have been socially ostracized, economically exploited and politically disempowered. As a result, they are denied their God-given human dignity and self-worth. The incidence of poverty among Dalits is higher as compared to the general population. More than 52 per cent of them are landless agricultural workers, and only 19.9 per cent are cultivators. Due to lack of access to fixed sources of income, a high rate of underemployment and low wages, Dalit households are often faced with low income and high incidence of poverty.

Tribals/Adivasis are marginalized in every walk of life despite several constitutional safeguards. They are the victims of major economic reforms in terms of mega projects which displaced many tribal people. The mining projects in Orissa, Jharkhand, West Bengal, Chhattisgarh, Madhya Pradesh and Andhra Pradesh ruined the lives of thousands of tribal people. A large number of them who are living below the poverty line are landless, with no

---

4 See Manish Dev, *GDP Growth and Poverty*, 12.

5 See Manish Dev, *GDP Growth and Poverty*, 23.

productive assets and with no access to sustainable employment and minimum wages.[6]

2. Biblical and Theological Reflection

Why should the Church be committed to the poor? Why should the Church have a preferential option for the poor? Why should the Church work for alleviating poverty in the world? Biblical revelation is loud and clear about God's actions in history. The foundational experience of the Hebrew people is of liberation from the oppressive situation of Egypt. It was a situation of ill-being and not well-being. They were oppressed under their task masters. God tells Moses, "I have observed the misery of my people who are in Egypt: I have heard their cry on account of their taskmasters. Indeed, I know their sufferings, and I have come down to deliver them..." (Ex 3:7-8).

God's special concern for the poor, the orphans and the widows is seen all through the Bible. "You shall not abuse any widow or orphan. If you abuse them, when they cry out to me, I will surely heed their cry..." (Ex 22: 22-24). The prophets spoke vehemently when there was injustice done to the poor. God is not pleased with sacrifices and offerings where the poor are oppressed. Prophet Isaiah says, "Wash yourselves; make yourselves clean; remove the evil of your doings from before my eyes; cease to do evil, learn to do good; seek justice, rescue the oppressed, defend the orphan, plead for the widow" (Is 1:16-17). Again through prophet Amos, God strongly condemns all those who oppress the poor and treat them unjustly (Amos 4:1; 5:11-12; 8:4-6).

According to the Gospel of Luke, Jesus begins his public ministry with the Nazareth manifesto (Lk 4: 18- 19). Jesus understands his mission as bringing good news to the poor, proclaiming liberty to captives, giving sight to the blind and letting the oppressed go free. He not only preached but put it into action the same manifesto. He touched the wounded, and the broken, the sick and the possessed and healed them, he fed the hungry, he was a friend to the outcasts and shared meals with them (Lk 8: 40-56; 9: 10-17, 37-43; 13: 10-17; 15: 1-2). No one can be a follower of Jesus without having his attitude and actions towards those who are on the margins of society. The parable of the Good Samaritan (Lk 10: 25-37), the story of the rich man and Lazarus (Lk 16: 19-31), the conversion of Zacchaeus (Lk 19: 1-10), the criteria for entering the Kingdom (Mt 25: 31-46), all these illustrates Jesus' concern towards those on the periphery and those in need. One cannot be a follower of Jesus without putting on this attitude and action of Jesus.

Moreover, there is a beautiful description of the Church at its very origins. "There was not a needy person among them, for as many as owned lands or houses sold them and brought the proceeds of what was sold. They

6 See Manish Dev, *GDP Growth and Poverty*, 251-255.

laid it at the apostles' feet, and it was distributed to each as any had need" (Acts 4: 34-35). St. James is forthright when it comes to our attitude towards the poor. He warns the Christians of his time against partiality shown to the rich and ignoring the poor (James 2:1-7). Concern for the needy and the neglected cannot be separated from being a Christian. The Church, through its many social encyclicals, has been teaching time and again the impossibility of practising and preaching Christian faith without the concern and care for the less privileged. The document *Gaudium et Spes* of Vatican II speaks clearly about Church's ongoing concern for working towards creating a just world for all.

Talking about the option for the poor, Pope Francis says that "For the Church, the option for the poor is primarily a theological category rather than a cultural, sociological, political or philosophical one. God shows the poor "his first mercy." This divine preference has consequences for the faith life of all Christians since we are called to have "this mind… which was in Jesus Christ" (Phil 2:5). This is why I want a Church which is poor and for the poor" (EG, 198). He further says that the worst discrimination which the poor suffer is the lack of spiritual care. The great majority of the poor have a special openness to the faith; they need God, and we must not fail to offer them his friendship, his blessing, his word, the celebration of the sacraments and a journey of growth and maturity in the faith. Our preferential option for the poor must mainly translate into a privileged and preferential religious care (EG, 200).

3. The Response of the Church

Recently I happened to visit some mission stations in the diocese of Ujjain. I was very much impressed and happy to see the work done by the Church in those remote villages where there are no schools or dispensaries. The Church is really empowering the poor through education. In many dioceses, the religious and the clergy are engaged in serving the poor, especially the Dalits and the Tribals in remote villages. *Caritas India* is rendering great service to the poor throughout our country. The Church also runs orphanages, institutions for the care of the elderly, the disabled, the abandoned, terminally ill, persons, suffering from HIV and AIDs, leprosy, etc. All these are commendable acts of charity, indeed. Can the Church in India be complacent to think that it is doing its part?

In the present day situation when millions of people are below the poverty line, the Church needs to recommit itself for the poor. The Church needs to take another step forward. According to me, the following areas seem to be important to ponder upon.

The Predominant Image of the Church

In spite of the Church's engagement with the poor, the predominant image of the Indian Church seems to be 'Church of institutions' and not 'Church of the poor.' We are around 2.3 per cent, and we run more than 20 per cent of the educational institutions. It is not wrong to run institutions, but it has its own adverse impacts. Not only we create an image of affluence, but some of us working in such institutions imbibe a spirit of elitism. This is very much seen in the lifestyle of some Church personnel working in elitist institutions. How do we run these institutions while holding on to our preferential option for those made poor? How do we ensure that priests/religious sisters/ brothers/lay faithful who work in our institutions have a heart for the poor? We also need to increase our presence among the urban poor and balance our Institutional presence with that of our incarnational presence among those on the periphery.

Anti-Poor Attitudes and Actions

Recently one woman told me that she stopped working in one of our Christian schools as a supportive staff because she felt that she was not treated with respect. One of the basic Christian affirmations is the recognition of the dignity of all human persons. We need to introspect about how we uphold the dignity of the poor who are our employees. Often we, as administers and employers, are not sensitive to those most vulnerable. Influenced by the market economy and neo liberal policies, many of our institutions today follow the dictum of "hire and fire." The practice of having contract workers in our institutions is a gross injustice done to the employees who are often struggling to survive.

Too Feet Theory

The charitable institutions of the Church are doing wonderful service in taking care of the many destitute poor and disabled persons. In the given context of millions struggling under income poverty and human poverty, we need to use both our feet. The first foot is the church's engagement in charity work. The second foot should involve the Church in securing justice for the poor. This would include advocacy and lobbying for policies that would aim at poverty alleviation, implementation of pro-poor policies, analysing new policies of the govt. in terms of its impact on the poor, etc. This would require us to be familiar with our Constitution, knowledge of the various amendments which are specifically aimed at empowering the powerless and also the study of various policies of both Central and State governments with regard to the poor, Dalits, Tribals, women, etc. This would mean that we make all efforts to secure the rights of the poor and the marginalized. We need to participate much more as church run NGOs at *Jantar Mantar* with other NGOs demanding for the rights of the poor or saying 'No' to Govt Policies that are anti-poor.

The church's commitment to the poor means that we raise our voices together with secular-minded people when the rights of the poor are violated or when atrocities are committed against them. It is important to create infrastructure at CBCI level for this purpose. An expert committee could be entrusted with the task of studying what is going on in the country and make immediate and appropriate responses in the form of a statement or any other form when issues emerge. For instance, when the whole country was under the grip of Rohit's suicide, the Church's voice and its stand were missing in the public space.

Preferential Option for the Subaltern Groups

Among the poor, the situation of women, especially women from Dalit and Tribal backgrounds, need special attention. In light of the plight of Dalits and Adivasis, the Church needs to make a preferential option for them. The Dalits are not only economically poor, but they are at a disadvantaged position even when they come to institutions of higher learning. I think the church needs to espouse the cause of Dalits, especially. We cannot allow many more Rohit's to take their life away because of the oppressive structures of society. Church's commitment to the poor means the Church's commitment to the Dalits of this country.

Simple Lifestyle

The Church needs to be a model in sustainable living and life style if the church is serious about her commitment to the poor. We must put into practice what we preach i. e, *reduce*, *reuse* and *recycle*. Consumerism results in environmental destruction and the worst victims of such environmental degradation are the poor. As part of our commitment to the poor, we need to consciously consume less, be it food or clothing or any other consumer goods. Simple lifestyle should be visible in the way we build our churches, other buildings, dwelling places, etc. It should reflect in the type of transport we use, the kind of food we consume, and the type of hospitals we visit. When millions of children die every year due to lack of primary health care, can we think of wasting money on ourselves for our comfort and conveniences? Are we morally justified?

Concluding Remarks

There are millions in our country who go to bed hungry every day. Poverty and absolute poverty is a reality in our country in spite of the economic growth the country claims to make. Wealth is concentrated into fewer and fewer hands, and the gap between the rich and the poor are widening day by day. In this context, the Church's commitment to the poor is not an option, but it is an integral part of our call as Christians and as followers of Jesus. We cannot practice our faith by bracketing off this commitment. The church in India needs to make a preferential option for the subaltern groups and work for their well-being.

The Church is challenged to become a church of the poor and not to take pride in its present image as the 'Church of institutions.' To correct its present image, the church needs to increase its incarnational presence much more among the urban poor while continuing the great work it is doing with the rural poor. Moving a step further, the church should not limit its social activities only to charitable works but need to work also for justice for the poor and the oppressed.

6

Repeatable Tragedy of Don Quixote

Paul Thelakat
Editor, Light of Truth, Ernakulam

Abstract: *The tragedy of the church today is that there are many who are called to the mad ways of life – the prophetic, poetic and mystic call to be in the world but not of the world. But some return from possession to the sanity of life. They still put on the Persona or the mask - the attire and the habit, but are no more influenced or have the identity of the optics or vision. They have become sane with worldly ways and outlooks, and the habits born indicate the contradistinction within. They slowly succumb to the what T.S. Eliot called the last Temptation: "To do right things for the wrong reasons." As Cervantes wrote, "But in this degenerate age, fraud and a legion of ills infecting the world, no virtue can be safe, no honour be secure; while wanton desires diffused into the hearts of man, corrupt, the strictest watches and the closes retreats which though as intricate and unknown as the labyrinth of Crete, are no security for chastity." But Eliot made his point of the Last Temptation thus: "Now is my way clear, now is the meaning plain: Temptation shall not come in this kind again. The last temptation is the greatest treason: To do the right deed for the wrong reason."*

Keywords: *TS Eliot, Don Quixote, Last temptation, Treason.*

1. The Possession

The Ingenious Nobleman of named Alonso Quixano who reads so many chivalric romances loses his sanity and decides to become a knight-errant, reviving chivalry and serving his country, under the name Don Quixote de la Mancha. A simple farmer, Sancho Panza follows his squire, who often employs a unique, earthy wit in dealing with Don Quixote's rhetorical orations on antiquated knighthood. Don Quixote does not see the world for what it is and prefers to see it as it should be, or we may say he imagines that he is living out a knightly story. He sells his property to buy books, and his brain is eaten by those readings. Every book is a version of the world. So he may be said to have been possessed of the epic midlevel phenomenon called the knight. So there are three charterers in the classic novel of epic nature, Alonso, who is struck by the ideal world of the knight, vests himself as a knight. It is literally a story of possession. He is not himself; he is other. The two have become one, the double acts as one. A person who is moon-struck or struck by another world. He is really confused as Baudelino of Umberto Eco: "I confuse between what I see with what I wish to see" The Man of La Mancha: "the greatest madness of all is to see life as it is and not as it should be." He paints it all in his mind exactly as he wants it to be. Bishop Berkeley's philosophical observation is especially apt in this context, "Esse est percipi": to be is to be perceived. Berkeley's argument is that man cannot know an object as it is, but only as he perceives it. Therefore, all that an individual knows about is his world, his reality, is their unique perception of it. In Don Quixote, the illusion is necessary because it undermines conventional perception and provides another way to view reality. The third charterer is, as Kafka rightly wrote, "A free man, Sancho Panza philosophically followed Don Quixote on his crusades, perhaps out of a sense of responsibility, and had of them a great and edifying entertainment to the end of his days."

2. The Hard Times

Don Quixote, a Spanish novel by Miguel de Cervantes published in two parts in 1605 and 1615, is the most influential work of literature from the Spanish Golden Age and the entire Spanish literary canon. A founding work of modern literature, it is the work of a writer who lived at the time of William Shakespeare and died in the same year of (1616) as Shakespeare. Perhaps the most significant work of fiction ever published is also the best literary work ever written. Cervantes writes it at the time of the Spanish Inquisition. The Spanish Inquisition was started in 1462 to deal with problems of potential heresy or continued Judaizing among the converted, many of whom had only recently converted to Christianity. Later, the emphasis of the organisation expanded to include prosecution of Protestants who opposed the particular interpretation of Christianity of the Catholic Church, which was deemed "dangerous" for their role in the dissemination of heretical ideas. The result was near-hysteria among the authorities that led to a well-orchestrated surge of widespread hatred of heretics. The public furore further empowered Inquisitors. Following the exposure of these Protestant groups, both the offices of Spanish regent Philip II and Pope Sixtus V acquired new levels of support. There followed dramatic public spectacles organised to demonstrate the power of the Inquisition and to instil in the masses a dread of heresy. No fewer than 100 men and women were condemned to be burnt alive at such public spectacles. Writing at such time was very dangerous, and so the story is written in codes and mysterious designs of concealing the content, and its form is shaped by a literary man who also worked as a spy. Leo Strauss exposes the truth about its style: "Persecution, then, gives rise to a peculiar technique of writing, and in addition to that to a peculiar type of literature, in which the truth about all crucial things is presented exclusively between the line… It has all the advantages of public communication without having its greatest disadvantage—capital punishment for the author."

3. Evangelical Writing

The most important question: who is Quixote? Miguel de Unamuno calls Cervantes "Don Quixote's evangelist" who most profoundly understood his spirit. Although Don Quixote is mocked for his idealism by both the ignorant and the educated, he functions as a misunderstood saviour, as Christ does in the Christian Bible. Unamuno speculates that if Christ were to return, the critics of quixotism "would take him for a madman or a dangerous agitator and would seek to give him an equally ignominious death." Don Quixote hurtled into action and exposed himself to the mockery of mankind; he was thus one of the purest examples of true humility. We will never recover our ancient spirit until we turn mockery into truth and until we play Quixote in dead earnest, not in a routine and unbelieving way, wrote Unamuno. Cervantes by his ingenuity, identifies the Roman period of persecution with the Spanish Inquisition. 'Ichthus' is used as a substitute for Jesus Christ the Saviour, because the corresponding Greek 'Ichthus' is a pregnant anagram, containing the initials of the words: 'Jesus Christ, Son of God, Saviour.'" Cervantes says, "Some educated men believe that these were the fish that Saint Peter, by order our God and Lord, pulled out of the sea." Don Quixote, the novel, contains graphic and linguistic distortions aimed at extending meanings and revealing hidden messages.

The intellectual freedom and the ethical treatment of human beings that Unamuno finds always meet with opposition and oppression. He quixotically defended personal freedom and quality of life. Thus quixotism, instead of defending the faith as a general concept from the repressive bureaucracy of the church, as well has promoting individual religious freedom in ecclesiastical structures and rules as its theme. The quixotic believer cannot merely believe in the existence of love and compassion, but also has to act to alleviate suffering and promote dignity. Thus, in quixotism, religious principles are not merely pieces of knowledge, but guidelines to be put into practice in life. Quixote says, "I know that the path of virtue is very narrow, and the road of vice broad and spacious; I know that their ends and goals are different, because the broad and easy road of vice ends in death, and the narrow and toilsome one of virtue ends in life." It is practically the same as in Sermon on the Mount of Mathew Ch.5.

4. The Abductors of Our Lady

In Part one chpter 52 we find Quixote marching against a church procession of penitents or flagellants who are hooded and are wiping themselves carrying the statue of Our Lady in procession. He did not stop for the shouts of Sancho calling after him, "Where are you going, Senor Don Quixote? What devils have possessed you to set you on against our Catholic faith? Plague take me! Mind, that is a procession of penitents, and the lady they are carrying on that stand there is the blessed image of the immaculate Virgin. Take care what you are doing, senor, for this time it may be safely said you don't know what you are about." He stops the procession and demands, "I will say it in one," replied Don Quixote, "and it is this; that at once, this very instant, ye release that fair lady whose tears and sad aspect show plainly that ye are carrying her off against her will, and that ye have committed some scandalous outrage against her; and I, who was born into the world to redress all such like wrongs, will not permit you to advance another step until you have restored to her the liberty she pines for and deserves." The accusation that they have kidnapped the lady meets with derision, and he is beaten down. He does not bother, he says, "There is undoubtedly still some educated clown that will come and tell me I confuse logical truth with moral truth, as well as a mistake with a lie, and that there can be someone who is led to do something by an obvious illusion and succeeds, no matter what their purpose is. To which I would say that then the illusion is the most truthful truth and that there is nothing more logical than morality. And I will be true to everything I have said. And that's enough." Don Quixote entered the road and stood there. He launched his challenge, and that was when a herd of bulls and steers came and knocked him down, and trampled on him. That's what happens when you challenge people in order to defend a truth; bulls and steers, and even oxen come and trample you. Many critics came to view the work as a tragedy for Don Quixote's idealism, and nobility are viewed by the post-chivalric world as insane and are defeated and rendered useless by common reality.

5. The Return to Sanity

The story ends with his return home, a *ghar vapsi* from the exodus of life and he told his most trusted follower, "Forgive me, my friend, for the opportunity I gave you to seem as mad as I, making you fall into the error into which I fell, thinking that there were and are knights-errant in the world." "Oh!" responded Sancho, weeping. "Don't die, Senor; your grace should take my advice and live for many years because the greatest madness a man can commit in this life is to let himself die, just like that, without anybody killing him or any other hands ending his life except those of melancholy. Look, don't be lazy, but get up from that bed and let's go to the countryside dressed as shepherds, just like we arranged: maybe behind some bush we'll find Senora Dona Dulcinea disenchanted, as pretty as you please. If you're dying of sorrow over being defeated." "Senores," said Don Quixote, "let us go slowly, for there are no birds today in yesterday's nests. I was mad, and now I am sane; I was Don Quixote of La Mancha, and now I am, as I have said, Alonso Quixano the Good." Finally, we read his tombstone: "Here lies the mighty Gentleman who rose to such heights of valour that death itself did not triumph over his life with his death. He did not esteem the world; he was the frightening threat to the world, in this respect, for it was his great good fortune to live a madman, and die sane."

Indeed it a tragedy; "the tragic sense of life" of the Spanish Christ. But it could be read as the tragedy of any call to the Christian way of life of a priest, religious or a bishop. It is indeed the story of one called and possessed by the Other, the Kingdom of God. In the *Spectres of Marx* of Derrida, we read the on-going influence of Marx. It is the story of contagion or influence of Christ. The resurrected Christ possesses us, and we are in His shoes. Mary Magdalene said to the gardener "Sir, if you have carried him away, tell me where you have laid him, and I will take him away" (Mt.20:15). Any priest acts in the person of Christ, carries him, takes up his garments and acts on His behalf. The ordained minister can be an instrument in the production of grace because he is the instrument of Christ, the minister of Christ, and another Christ. According to St Augustine, a priest acts in the name and in the person of Christ, and Christ baptizes. The call of Christ to live and act as he did in this time and space, every Christian is called to be editions of Christ in the context to which one is called.

A Christian lives not by light but by faith, which is a perspective or an optics of seeing the world and its realities. The optics become ethics of life, which is so different from the world and its sanity. Plato in Phaedrus claimed that he preferred God-sent madness to man-made sanity. He spoke of madness because of "the divine disturbance in human conduct." These he called to four categories: poets, prophets, mystics and lovers. Evangelist John wrote that Jesus was accused of being possessed and mad. "He hath a devil and is mad" (Jn 10:20). The mad man is the minority of one.

The Concluding Remarks

The tragedy of the church today is that there are many who are called to the mad ways of life – the prophetic, poetic and mystic call to be in the world but not of the world. But some become sane and return from the evil possession to the sanity of life. They still put on the Persona or the mask - the attire and the habit, but are no more influenced or have the identity of the optics or vision. They have become sane with worldly ways and outlooks, and the habits born indicate the contradiction within. They slowly succumb to the what T.S. Eliot called the last Temptation: "To do right things for the wrong reasons." The Chorus of the *Murder* in the Cathedral speaks while the Knights kill the archbishop, and Eliot implies by this stage direction that the words are the chief point of interest, not the deed: "In life, there is no time to grieve long. But this, this is out of life, this is out of time, An instant eternity of evil and wrong." The Archbishop was between the thrones of King and God. It would be the highest perversity and mockery to do the habit of Christ and seek to secure power or acquire political might. The temptations are strong and varied. Cervantes, who died as a penniless poor Franciscan Third Order, made a point of temptation: "O happy age, which our first parents called the age of gold! Not because gold, so much adored in this iron age was then easily purchased, but because those two fatal words mine and thine were distinctions unknown to people of those fortunate times; for all things were in common in that blessed age… But in this degenerate age, fraud and a legion of ills infecting the world, no virtue can be safe, no honour be secure; while wanton desires diffused into the hearts of man, corrupt, the strictest watches and the closes retreats which though as intricate and unknown as the labyrinth of Crete, are no security for chastity." But Eliot made his point of the Last Temptation thus: "Now is my way clear, now is the meaning plain: Temptation shall not come in this kind again. The last temptation is the greatest treason: To do the right deed for the wrong reason."

7

A Call to Prophetic Priesthood: A Hermeneutical Reading of Amos 7:10-17

Thomas Karimundackal SJ
Jnana-Deepa Vidyapeeth, Pune 411014

Abstract: *Priesthood degenerates when priests become the custodian of the establishment rather than servants of God. Situated in a historical context, Amos 7:10-17 presents a confrontation between Amaziah, the priest of Bethel and Amos, the prophet of Yhwh. While Amaziah remains as a sad reminder for the priests, Amos sets a prophetical model for the priests. Amos 7:10-17 is a reminder of what would happen if the priests disregard their call and go after their natural inclinations to cling on to power and prestige. It makes a strong appeal to those who are called to be the priests of God to listen to God's words and thus lead the people to the liberation which God provides. Amos 7:10-17 is relevant for the Church where the priesthood is becoming more and more of an institutionalized one. Thus, Amos 7:10-17 stands as a challenge and warning to the priesthood of our times. At the outset, this paper makes an overview of the priesthood in Israel, its ministries and obligations. Then it analyses Amos 7:10-17 exegetically and structurally. Finally, it gives a theological and hermeneutical reading of Amos 7:10-17 eliciting its contemporary relevance.*

Keywords: *Amos, Amaziah, priesthood, prophetical priesthood, Church.*

Today a priest is understood as a prophet due to the similar elements that they share in common. This enables us to realise that today, we do not merely need priests, but priests with a prophetic nature. As Pope Francis reminds us it is a call to move from clericalism to a pastor whose call is to be with the people to share their joys and sorrows, dreams and aspirations, comforts and sufferings in all walks of life. It is a call to deny the honour and glory, power and prestige to be identified with the people, especially with the marginalized by 'smelling the sheep' as a shepherd of the faithful community. Fr. Kurien has written extensively on the priesthood, its theology and praxis and called for the priesthood to shape tomorrow's Church. It is my great pleasure to reflect on a theme very dear to Fr. Kurien and to actualize it, I read Amos 7:10-17 exegetically and hermeneutically.

Situated in a historical context, Amos 7:10-17 presents a confrontation between Amaziah, the priest of Bethel and Amos, the prophet of Yhwh. Amaziah fails to do his Yhwh-given responsibilities towards Yhwh and his people by ignoring the word of Yhwh that came to him through the prophet Amos and thus invites Yhwh's judgment on himself and the nation. When Amaziah commands Amos not to prophesy at Bethel, Amaziah aligns himself with the king rather than with God. Accordingly, Amaziah has to face its consequence, namely Yhwh's judgment on himself and the nation.

Amaziah's narrative in Amos 7:10-17 stands as a challenge and warning to the priesthood of our times. This narrative is relevant for the church where priesthood is becoming more and more of an institutionalized one. Today, the Church and priesthood degenerate due to their undue concern for institutionalization. Amaziah's failure as a priest has severe consequences on himself and over the nation. Likewise, the failure of the priests is reflected in the spiritual life of people in the Church today. Amos 7:10-17 shows what would happen to those who reject the word of God and those who disregard their calling. In this pericope, Amaziah stands as a temptation to be omitted in the priesthood and Amos as a model to be imitated.

A perusal of the priestly ministry and obligations in the Old Testament would help us understand Amos 7:10-17 in a better way as it basically calls for a prophetic priesthood.

1. Priesthood in Israel: Ministries and Obligations

In the Old Testament priests are given a number of duties like offering sacrifices on behalf of the people (Exod 29:38-46; Lev 1-7), guarding the tent of meeting (Num 18:3), blessing the people (Num 6:22), attending the vessels of the holy place like lamp stand, altar of incense and bread of the presence (Exod 27:20-21; 30:7-8; Lev 24:5-9), distinguishing clean and unclean, sacred and profane (Lev 10:10), declaring them clean when warranted (Lev 13:14), teaching the law (Deut 33:10; Mal 2:7), administering justice under the law (Deut 17:8), encouraging people before the starting of battle (Deut 20:2) etc. All the above said duties of the priests can be classified into two categories:

duties with regard to the house or temple of the Lord and duties in relation to the people of Israel.

1.1. Duties in Relation to the House or Temple of the Lord

Mainly two kinds of duties come under this section: duties of guarding or attending the temple and that of the offering of the sacrifice on the altar.

- The primary duty of a priest is to guard the temple of God and its treasures (Num 3:8, 38). They are called to serve at the sanctuary of the Lord, doing service at the tabernacle; they shall be in charge of all the furnishings of the tent of meeting (Num 3:7-8). They shall be ministers in the sanctuary, having oversight at the gates of the temple, and serving in the temple, to keep the charge of the temple, to come near to Yhwh to offer Him the fat and the blood (Ezek 44:11,15). At the heart of the priest's character was holiness (Exod. 39:30; Ezek. 44:11). He was called to wholeness, symbolized by his exclusion from the altar if he had any physical impairments (Lev 21:17).
- The cultic personnel in the desert were entrusted with the duty of guarding the tabernacle and the Ark (Num 1:53: 3:23, 28-29, 32, 35, 38), carrying the tabernacle or Ark when needed (Num 4:58: Josh 3:3-4; 4: 10). When the Ark is recovered from the Philistines and established in Kiriath-Jearim, the house of Abinadab became its Sanctuary, and Abinadab's son consecrated as its guardian (1 Sam 7:1). The lips of a priest should guard knowledge, people should seek instruction from his mouth, for he is the messenger of the Lord of hosts (Mal 2:7). They are asked to assess impurity of the people (Lev 13-15) for the sake of removing pollution and defilement of the sanctuary (Lev 13:31) and the land (Lev 18:25).

Thus in the Old Testament, the very essence of priesthood lies in the fact that they were guardians of Yahweh's temple.

Another function with regard to the temple of God is to offer sacrifices on behalf of the people.

- In 1 Sam 2:28, we read that the priests have been chosen to go up to the altar, to incense, to smoke, and to carry the ephod. They alone had access to the sanctuaries of Israel.
- Offering incense and trimming the wicks of the lamps on the lampstand both in the morning and evening was the duty of the high priest (Exod 30:7-8; Lev 24:1-4).

- The high priest has to offer sacrifice in the holy of holies on the Day of Atonement for the forgiveness of the sins of the people (Lev 16:2.12-13).
- The book of Leviticus chapters 1-6 describes various offerings which a priest has to offer for the people: Voluntary sacrifices (Lev 1-3) and mandatory Sacrifices (Lev 4:1-6:7). Thus, we see that offering sacrifices was essential to the priesthood in Israel.

1.2. Duties in Relation to the People of Israel

As a shepherd, a priest has to lead his community by way of blessing and interceding, instructing and monitoring.

1.2.1. Priests as Intercessors

One of the primary duties of the priest in the Israelite society is to bless the people (Num 6:22-27). Intercession has been another essential responsibility of priests in the Old Testament. We can look at the moving example of Abraham, interceding for the city of Sodom (Gen 18:16-32), interceding for his son Ishmael (cf. Gen 17:18), interceding for Abimelech's family (cf. Gen 20:17). Moses, because of his priestly leadership, offers an example of priestly intercession: He intercedes for the removal of plagues (cf. Exod 15:25 ff.); for water at Rephidim (cf. Exod 17:4); for victory over Amalek (cf. Exod 17:8-16); intercedes for the people after their worship of the golden calf (cf. Exod 32:11-14,21-34; 33:12ff; Deut 9:18 ff); after the renewal of the tables of stone (cf. Exod 34:9); at the setting forth and stopping of the Ark (Num 10:35ff.); after the burning at Taberah (cf. Num 11:2); for the healing of Miriam's leprosy (cf. Num 12:13); after the return of the spies (cf. Num 14:13-19); through Aaron for the end of the plague (cf. Num 17:9-15); after the bit of poisonous serpents (cf. Num 21:7); for direction in the case of the daughters of Zelophehad (cf. Num 27:5); for a successor (cf. Num 27:15); for the people for their entrance into Canaan (cf. Deut 3:23ff.); for the rebellious people (cf. Deut 9:25-29); to offer prayer for the nation (cf. Deut 26:15); Another image that shows the intermediary role of the priests is the twelve stones on the breast piece and the names of the twelve tribes engraved on the shoulder stones (Exod 28:15-29). The very garments of the high priest symbolize that he represents the people of God before the Lord.

1.2.2. Priests as Instructors of the Torah

Priests as the bearers of Urim and Thummim deliver Yhwh'smessage to the people (Deut 33:10). They are called to teach the people (Lev 10:8-11). They are to inform people of the ceremonial regulations, distinguishing between clean and unclean, sacred and profane (Lev 10:8-11). They are often recognized as the ones to give rulings about the Torah and its meaning as well as all cultic matters (Mic 3:11; Zeph 3:4: Ezek 44:24: Hag 2:11-13).

Moreover, they are entrusted with the duty of blessing the people and declaring the blessings of the Lord for the people (Deut 6:22f). Thus, as a teacher of the law his responsibility towards the people lies more in teaching them what is good and bad (Deut 30:1-10), in giving them instructions regarding the cultic matters etc. Thus primarily for the people, he is a teacher.

1.2.3. Priests as Monitors of the Society

Priests also served as the conscience of the society by functioning as judges (Deut 17:9). As judges, they are called to resolve controversy (Deut 21:5). Pronouncing ritual and civil judgments were part of their duty. They were the symbol of social cohesion initiating grounds for reconciliation amidst conflicts in the society. In 2Chr 19:8, we see that the king Jehoshaphat established tribunals in Jerusalem comprising priests and elders for the cases of Yahweh and for civil disputes. Amariah, the chief priest, was the authority in the cases governed by religious law and Zebadiah, the governor of the house of Judah, for those governed by the civil law (2Chr 19: 11). Priests are to maintain peace and harmony among the people by settling down the conflicts among the people.

1.2.4. Priests as Leaders of the Community

Priests have taken leadership roles in the governance of society. In 2 Kgs 11-12, we see Jehoiada, the priest, giving instructions to the people. In the book of Haggai, we see that Joshua is not only the just head of the priests but also acts as the provincial governor of Zerubbabel (Hag 1:1,14; 2:2). Joshua's duties here seem to involve mainly those relating to the temple and cult, but since these were central to the province of Judah, the duties of the high priest were already starting to overlap with those of civil leader. Thus, we see that apart from the religious life of the people, priests also served as leaders of the community.

2. The Text and Translation of Amos 7:1017

וישׁלח אמציה כהן בית־אל אל־ירבעם מלך־ישׂ רא לאמר קשׁר עליך עמוס בקרב בית ישׂראל לא־תוכל הארץ להכיל את־כל־דבריו:	7:10	And then Amaziah the priest of Bethel sent to Jeroboam king of Israel, saying, Amos has conspired against you in the midst of the house of Israel: the land is not able to bear all his words.

כי־כה אמר עמוס בחרב ימות ירבעם וישׂראל גלה יגלה מעל אדמתו :	7:11	For thus Amos has said, Jeroboam shall die by the sword, and Israel must go into exile away from his land.
ויאמר אמציה אל־עמוס חזה לך ברח־לך אל־ארץ יהודה ואכל־שם לחם ושם תנבא:	7:12	And then Amaziah said to Amos, seer, go, flee away to the land of Judah, and there eat bread, and prophesy there:
ו בית־אל לא־תוסיף עוד להנבא כי מקדשׁ־מלך הוא ובית מ מלכה ה וא:	7:13	But prophesy not again any more at Bethel, for it is the sanctuary of the king and it is the house of the king
ויען עמוס ויאמר אל־אמציה לא־נביא אנכי ולא נביא אנכי כי־בוקר אנכי ובולס שׁקמים:	7:14	And then answered Amos, and said to Amaziah, I am not a prophet, and I am not a prophet's son; but I am a herdsman, and a dresser of sycomore trees:
ויקחני יהוה מאחרי הצאן ויאמר אלי יהוה לך הנבא אל־עמי ישׂראל:	7:15	And the Lord took me from following the flock, and the Lord said to me, Go, prophesy to my people Israel.
ועתה שמע דבר־יהוה אתה אמר לא תנבא על־ישׂראל ולא תטיף על־בית ישׂחק:	7:16	And now hear the word of the Lord: you say, prophesy not against Israel, and drop not your word against the house of Isaac.
לכן כה־אמר יהוה אשתך בעיר תזנה ובניך ובנתיך ב חרב יפלו ואדמתך בחבל תחלק ואתה על־אדמה טמאה תמות וישׂראל גלה יגלה מעל אדמתו	7:17	Therefore thus says the Lord; your wife shall be a harlot in the city, and your sons and your daughters shall fall by the sword, and your land shall be divided by line, and you shall die in an unclean land: and Israel shall surely go into exile away from its land.

3. A Structural Reading of Amos 7:10-17

Amos 7:10-17 can be divided into two parts (vv.10-11 and vv.12-17), each reporting a different event. The narrative begins with Amaziah's message to the king (vv.10-11), And then Amaziah confronts the prophet (vv.12-17). As it stands, the first scene serves primarily to set the stage for the second. In the first part, what we have is Amaziah's accusation against Amos. Amaziah sent a message to the king, which consisted of an accusation of the unlawful activity of Amos (v10). Then, he provides the supporting evidence in the form of a citation of the prophet's words (v11).

In the second scene (vv.12-17), there is a confrontation between two parties, i.e., Amos and Amaziah. The second scene can be further divided into two: Arnaziahs dispute with Amos (vv.12-13) and Amos' response (vv.14-17). As the scene begins, Amaziah challenges Amos and commands him not to prophesy in Israel and asks him to leave the country (vv.12-13). In reporting to Jeroboam, Amaziah has accused Amos of unlawful activities (vv10-11), but when he addresses Amos, he speaks in terms of jurisdiction: "do not prophesy here because it is king's sanctuary" (v.13). Thus, we see that Amaziah's attack is not really against Amos but against the Lord, who sent Amos. However, Amos responded to him directly by declaring the authenticity of his words. In his response to Amaziah, Amos takes the issue to be one of authority (v.15). Amos tries to answer both the questions of legality and jurisdiction by telling that it is Yhwh who sent him (v.15). Then Amos speaks the word of the Lord to Amaziah (vv.16-l7) using what Amaziah has just said to show his guilt, i.e., the failure to listen to the word of God(v.13). There is an elaborate description of the punishment that is to come upon Amaziah for his denial of the word of God (v.17). Both the nation and his family will be punished due to the sin of Amaziah. Nation will go to exile, and the family will fall by the sword, and his death will be in an unclean land.

1. First Scene: Amaziah's Charge against Amos to Jeroboam (vv.10-11)
   a. The accusation against Amos (v. 10)
   b. The Proof for the Accusation (v .11)
2. Second Scene: Amaziah's Confrontation with Amos (vv.12-17)
   a. Amaziah's Dispute Speech (vv.12-13)
   b. Amos' Response (vv.14-17)

4. A Close Reading of Amos 7:10-17

Amos 7:10-17 is all about the confrontation between Amos and Amaziah. Amos' preaching against the political and religious establishment in 7:9 leads Amaziah into conflict with Amos (7:10-17).The story narrates beautifully how Amaziah the priest of Bethel is judged by Yhwh for his denial of the word of Yhwh that came to him through the prophet Amos.

The first scene (vv.10-11) is about Amaziah's accusation against Amos. Amaziah tries to present Amos as a political conspirator (v.10) as he is misquoting and misinterpreting Amos' words in order to provoke the king to act against Amos (v.11). He deliberately leaves out those things that are directly related to religion and sanctuaries. He articulates only those things that affect the king. His concern is all about the security of the king and his kingdom. Accordingly, he wants to protect his position in the state and religion. To safeguard his position, he tries to remove all the obstacles that come on his way even if it is the prophet. In doing so, he proves himself as the guardian of the establishment and the representative of the State. Thus, as a priest, he becomes the custodian of the State and its affairs, instead of becoming the custodian of the house of God. Thus in vv.l 0-11, Amaziah becomes the spokesperson of the king and the state.

In the second scene (vv.12-17), Amaziah turns against the prophet in his own standards, considering him as one who prophesies for his material benefits (v.12a). Priesthood for Amaziah is a matter of position and money. By calling Amos as a *hozeh* (חֹזֶה), Amaziah considers him as a professional prophet who lives by his tongue. Amaziah does not consider the words of Amos as the words of God; rather he treats them as purely human words. Amaziah asks him to leave Israel (v.12a) and thus prohibits the word of God to be heard in Israel (v.13), which in God's sight becomes the greatest sin he has ever done. By commanding Amos not to prophesy in Israel he misrepresents the message of God to the people (cf. 2:12). The judgment upon Amaziah and nation in v.17 is mainly because of his rejection and prohibition of the word of God.

In response to Amaziah's accusation in vv10-11 Amos tries to justify his actions in vv.14-15. In order to counteract Amaziah's accusation that Amos is a professional prophet who lives by his tongue, Amos recalls his own professions to live with, i.e., sheep tender and a dresser of sycamore trees (v.14). Therefore, Amos does not need to come to Bethel and prophesy there for his bread. His present activity at Bethel now is due to the direct divine intervention in his life (v.15). The Lord took him from following the sheep and asked him to go and prophesy to his people in Israel. Thus, Amos stands in sharp contrast with Amaziah who for the sake of position and material security in life forgets his God-given duty as a priest. For Amos, what is important, the word of God and the liberation of the people and not his personal security.

In vv.16-17 Amos now turns to Amaziah by pronouncing judgment against him. The basis for Amos' Judgment against Amaziah is in tune with 2:12 where the Lord pronounces judgment against Israel saying: "but you made the Nazirites drink wine, and commanded the prophets, saying, 'You shall not prophesy'." In v.10 Amaziah accuses Amos of standing against the king. On the contrary, here, Amos accuses Amaziah of standing against God and his words. Therefore, judgment is inevitable.

Judgment has both personal and national significance, i.e., judgment upon Amaziah and his family and judgment upon the nation (v.17). There is a gradation in the punishments listed starting from his wife becoming a harlot in the city (v.17a). Then his sons and daughters shall fall by the sword (v.17b), which probably indicates the end of his family line. The loss of his inheritance of the land (v.17c) is even more belittling because the inheritance of the Promised Land is one of the promises Yhwh has given to the people of Israel. The judgment comes to its climax when he is left to die in an unclean land (v.17d). His death in an unclean land is not only the physical death of the person but also the total alienation of the priestly office from Amaziah. His sons will not be able to succeed him as priests, for they would fall by the sword (v.17b). There is also no hope that his daughters will marry some priests and bear him grandchildren in the office of the priesthood, for they also will be killed. Finally, the possibilities that new children be born to Amaziah before being deported who may later become a priest is also deemed by referring to the shameful fate of his wife. Because his wife would become a public prostitute, the child born from her would be considered a child of adultery and unworthy of becoming a priest. Thus, Yhwh's judgment affects Amaziah in all its severity; it marks the end of his family and his priesthood.

The final judgment is that Israel shall go into exile (v.17e). This is the sum and substance of his prophecy in the book. The prophet has constantly been pointing out the people's failures and asking them to mend their ways. However, they do not heed their ears to his word. Both priests and people indulge in complacency and sinfulness. Priest neither observes his duty faithfully (7:10-13) nor are the people ready to be corrected (4:6-13). Therefore, the nation, together with its leaders, is going to be judged for their denial of the word of the Lord (v.16). Amaziah has the responsibility to teach the law of Yhwh. He has to realize the word of the Lord, and he has to make sure that the word of God is preached to the people.

Nevertheless, his concern is to maintain the stability of the establishment (v. 10). He is concerned about the cause of the king rather than that of Yhwh and his people. He is more like a guardian of the State and the king. Thus, his failures in fulfilling the priestly duties lead to the condemnation and destruction of the people.

Thus, the narrative in vv.10-17 shows what would happen to those who forsake the God-given duties and embraces the values of the State and establishment. The ultimate message of Amos 7:10-17 is that the final word is with Yhwh. Though Amaziah and his state-sponsored religion try to stop Yhwh and his Prophet, Yhwh takes the ultimate decision. At the beginning of the pericope, Amaziah commands Amos to flee to Judah (v.12), but towards the end, Amaziah himself is going to be out of his country (v.17). Amaziah is guilty of rejecting the word of God and of prohibiting it from being proclaimed. It is not the priest but God who has the last word.

5. Theological Implications of Amos 7:10-17

Priesthood degenerates when priests become the custodian of the establishment more than spokespersons of Yhwh and His words. The great temptation in history for priesthood had been this: to support the power centres and to enjoy the privileges that it offers. Those who had been exceptions to this rule had to pay a high price for their convictions. Like Amos, they have to face rejection from the people as well as from the authorities. As chosen ones, those who fail to do their God-given responsibilities, be it as individuals or as a nation will have to bear the consequences. This is the sum and substance of this pericope (Amos 7:10-17). God gave Amaziah a unique calling. But he did not live up to his expectations. By his consecration, he has been set apart for God and his people. However, Amaziah forgot his call to be the guardian and the servant of the temple of God and became a mere servant at the king's house. He had to ensure that God was represented properly and he had to seek God's will. His role had to be the religious role but he played the role of a political employee.

On the other hand, Amos' prophetic ministry invites us to bring in a prophetic dimension to the exercise of priestly ministry. He remains as a threat to the status-quo and as a scandal to the citizens who performed all the prescribed rituals faithfully but whose heart was far from God. Following themes can be highlighted from this pericope:

5.1. Failure to Acknowledge God

Amaziah considers the king as the supreme authority over the people. Primarily he seeks king's will and not of God's will. As a royal employee, his loyalty is more to the king than to God, and consequently, he becomes the spokesperson and the royal servant of the State. He is conscious of the rights of the king but not that of God. While prohibiting Amos to speak at Bethel (v.13), he seems to consider religion as subordinate to the State. According to him, the sanctuary belongs to the king (v.13). For Amaziah, it is not God, but the king and his temple are at the centre of religion and cult. His failure to acknowledge God and to do the God-given responsibilities invites punishment upon him and his family and upon the nation.

5.2. Guarding the True Religion or Establishment?

Amaziah is very much concerned to safeguard the establishment and the religion supported by the establishment. This is clear from the accusation that he makes against prophet Amos. He accuses Amos as a political conspirator (v.10). He considers Amos as a danger to the state and state-sponsored religion (v.11). In accusing Amos, Amaziah misinterprets and misquotes Amos's words so that he can provoke the king to act against Amos. He omits those things that are about religious matters and presents only those that would directly affect the king and his people. Thus, Amaziah wants to present himself as a loyal and responsible servant of the king and the State while presenting Amos as a political conspirator.

5.3. Rejection of the Word of God

Amaziah rejects both the word of God and the prophet. He considers the prophet and prophecy in his own standard. Priesthood for Amaziah is a matter of prestige, authority and the means for his livelihood. Therefore, he considers Amos as one who is prophesying for his material benefit (v.12). Here he thinks that Amos also is like him. He rejects Amos' preaching and his God-given mission. The phrase "thus Amos has said' in v.11 shows that he is trying deliberately to hide the truths of Amos' words. He wants to present them as the words of Amos. As a priest, he should have realized the ways of the Lord more than others.

5.4. Challenging the Authority of God

Amaziah challenges the authority of God by prohibiting Amos to prophesy in Israel (v.13). Amaziah does not want God's truth and righteousness to be proclaimed in Israel because it might undermine his comfortable position. In v.15 God asks Amos to "go and prophesy in Israel" but in v.13 Amaziah says "do not prophesy in Israel."Amaziah takes the opposite direction and wants Amos to go back to Judah (v.12). The reason for prohibiting Amos from speaking at Bethel is that Amaziah thinks that Amos is stirring things up and spoiling the smooth flow of affairs. Here, Amaziah is continuing the sin of Israel as the Israelites silence the voice of God (2:6-16). In short, Amaziah is complacent, comfortable and challenges the authority of God.

5.5. Being Called by Yahweh

Amos acknowledges the divine commission that he had and the divine mandate for his preaching (v.15). He is not boasting about his present activity. He is convinced that God has chosen and commissioned him which is the basis of his prophesying. God's will is of supreme interest and the exclusive rule for Amos. He is doing the mission of God. He treats the prophetic office as an entirely unmerited dignity. His exercise of it is without ulterior motives. He is not prophesying at Bethel in order to satisfy his material needs. He can find his means of livelihood from his twofold occupations. When Amaziah sarcastically addresses him as hozeh (חֹזֶה), he says that he is neither a prophet nor son of a prophet (v.13a). Thus, he stands in sharp contrast with Amaziah, who is delighted in being the high priest of Bethel, and enjoying all the privileges that it provides.

5.6. Commitment to the Mission Entrusted

Amos is not discouraged at the face of opposition from the part of Amaziah; rather he remained faithful to proclaim the word of the Lord (vv.16-17). Fully aware of what he is doing, he prophesies judgment upon Amaziah and his family and his tragic death in a foreign land (v.17). He does not consider his personal safety important, rather he makes the conversion of Israel a personal concern and his life-effort. Amaziah's prohibition does not make any effect on Amos rather he takes it as a challenge. It only leads him to repeat and emphasize the judgment against Amaziah.

6. Hermeneutical Relevance of Amos 7:10-17

Having seen the theological implications of Amos 7:10-17, the question is how can we live out the prophetic dimension of the priesthood here and now?

- In Amos 7:10-17 Amaziah reminds us to resist the natural inclination to cling on to the establishment. If the primary concern of a priest is to safeguard the establishment, then he cannot live his priestly life in a meaningful way. Whenever priesthood becomes a means for one's livelihood and means for power, money, prestige, etc., it degenerates, and it becomes a burden for the people. It becomes a cause for the scandal for the people. When priesthood becomes an overly cultic and institutional one, it cannot fulfil the prophetic mission but would rather end up in conflict with the charisma.
- Amaziah also reminds us that we should not neglect the word of God. As the people 'set apart' the priests are called to realize the voice of God and to respond to it prophetically. The primary concern in the priestly life is to communicate God's message to the people. The failures in the priestly obligations have led Amaziah into conflict with the prophet Amos. Amaziah failed to uphold the teachings of the Torah by rejecting the word of God. Priests are called to be faithful to their call, teachings of the Church and the priestly obligations.
- Amos stands as a powerful image of prophetic priesthood. Amos is convinced of his call and does his God-given responsibility faithfully even at the face of opposition. The prophetic image of Amos invites us to be convinced of our call. One is called to priesthood not because he is better than others but simply because God chose him.
- Amos was in deep union with the Lord, and consequently, he could decipher and proclaim the word of the Lord to the people fearlessly. The priests of today are called to cherish an intimate personal union with the Lord. Only, if a priest is in love with God, will he be able to move people's hearts and open them to the Lord's merciful love.

- God's choice involves a mission, i.e., to speak in God's name and with his authority. Amos is called to commit himself to a God-given mission. Amos is neither discouraged with the poor response of the people to the word of God nor frightened by the threat of the authorities. His commitment is only to God and to his word. With the humble acceptance of what he is and the conviction of being called by God and the persistence in the mission entrusted even in difficult situations, Amos stands as a model for the contemporary priesthood.
- Amos also challenges us to be faithful to God even at the face of opposition. Just as Amos, the priest of today has to go to the people fearlessly to announce God's word. He should be a defender of the poor, the exploited and the abandoned, and should work as a promoter of peace, justice and reconciliation. As Amos is, the basic identity of a priest should be that of a collaborator and trusted co-worker of the Lord.
- Amos 7:10-17 also invites us to rediscover the greatness of priesthood. Amaziah has lost the sense of the greatness of his priesthood by becoming the spokesperson of the state and state-sponsored religion. The vocation of a priest today is to be a man of joy and hope, teaching people that life is worth living in its fullness.

In short, in Amos 7:10-17while Amaziah remains as a sad reminder for the priests, Amos sets a prophetical model for the priests. It is a reminder of what would happen if the priests disregard their call and go after their natural inclinations to cling on to power and prestige. Amos 7:10-17 makes a strong appeal to those who are called to be the priests of God to listen to God's words and thus lead the people to the liberation which God provides.

Bibliography

Andersen, Francis I, and David Noel Freedman, *Amos: A New Translation with Introduction and Commentary, The Anchor Yale Bible, London: Yale University Press, 2008.*

Badia, Leonard F. Amos: Model for Pastoral Ministry, *The Bible Today* 20/3 (1982), 161-165.

Campos, Martha E. Structure and Meaning in the Third Vision of Amos (7:7-17), *The Journal of Hebrew Scriptures* 11/3 (2011), 51-78.

Cody, Aelred, *A History of Old Testament Priesthood*, Rome: Pontifical Biblical Institute, 1969.

Coote, Robert B., *Amos among the Prophets: Composition and Theology,* Philadelphia: Fortress Press, 1981.

Craigie, P. C., *Twelve Prophets: Hosea, Joel, Amos. Obadiah and Jonah*, The Daily Study Bible Series. Philadelphia: John Knox Press, 1984.

Garland, David D., *Amos: A Study Guide Commentary*, Grand Rapids: Zondervan, 1966.

Grabbe, Lester L., and Alice Ogden Bellis (eds). *The Priests in the Prophets: The Portrayal of Priests, Prophets and Other Religious Specialists in the Latter Prophets,* New York: T & T Clark, 2004.

Guenther, A. R., Hosea, Amos, *Believers Church Bible Commentary,* Scottsdale: Herald Press. 1998.

Harper, W. R., *A Critical and Exegetical Commentary on Amos and Hosea,* New York: C. Scribner's Sons, 1905.

Hayes, John H. *Amos: His Times & His Preaching, The Eighth Century Prophet*, Nashville: Abingdon Press, 1988.

Holmgren, F, *Priests and Prophets: Spirituality and Social Conscience,* Worship 79/4 (2005): 304-316.

Irudaya, Raj. Prophetic Priesthood Today, *Jnanadeepa* 11/2 (2010), 36-49.

Jeremias, Jorg. *The Book of Amos: A Commentary*. The Old Testament Library, Louisville: John Knox Press, 1995.

Kunnumpuram, Kurien, *Shaping Tomorrow Church: Formation of Priests and Religious for India,* Mumbai: St. Pauls' Publication, 2006.

Leithart, Peter J. Attendants of Yahwehs House: Priesthood in the Old Testament, *Journal for the Study of the Old Testament*, 85 (1999), 3-24.

Noble, Paul R. Amos and Amaziah in Context: Synchronic and Diachronic Approaches to Amos 7-8, *Catholic Biblical Quarterly,* 60 (1998), 423-439.

Raja, Maria A., Priests amidst Conflicts, *Jnanadeepa* 11/2 (2010), 50-74.

Raja, R.J. Priests and Priesthood in the Bible, *Ignis* 1 (2010), 13-23.

Rausch, Thomas P., *Priesthood Today: An Appraisal,* New York: Paulist Press, 1992.

Stephen J., Rosetti, *The Joy of Priesthood,* New York: Ave Maria Press, 2000.

8

The 'New' People of God in India

Evelyn Monteiro SCC
Professor (Emeritus), Systematic Theology, JDV, Pune

Abstract: *Post-Vatican II, in the pursuit of an updated public image and role, the Church revisited its centuries-old grandiose governing structure and attributed a certain primacy to the relationship of the Church with cultures, religions and the world. This resulted in crucial shifts in ecclesiological models with consequential pastoral and mission implications for India. To counter the excesses of the institutionalized-patriarchal ecclesial model, the values of the historical-anthropological stance were emphasized, and plurality and inclusiveness were welcomed. In this context, the author pleads for a Church of the People of God that goes forth to the excluded in the existential and geographical peripheries of India. She goes forth as a loving mother who tends the wounded of broken marriages and families, accompanies the disturbed children and enterprising youth, and nurtures the lonely and abandoned. As a merciful father, the Church searches for excluded laywomen and men and integrates them in her life and mission. The Church of the People of God is not pigeoned-holed into any abstract standard. Her missionary outreach strategies evolve from the struggles of people and from grassroots realities of life. Becoming a Christ-centred Church is an on-going commitment to be for and with the 'new' people of God in the changing contexts of the times, the author affirms.*

Keywords: *People of God, Peripheries, Ecclesiology, Pope Francis.*

Prof Kurien Kunnumpuram's article "Towards a New Ecclesiology in the Light of Vatican II"[1] had aroused my interest when I first read it as a student of theology. Later I used some of the paradigm shifts he speaks about in my teaching to introduce the main ecclesiological thrust of Vatican II. This brief essay discusses an emerging paradigm of the Church as a community of diverse faces, which is gaining immense ground in the contemporary world.

Post-Vatican II, in the pursuit of an updated public image and role, the Church revisited its centuries-old grandiose governing structure and attributed a certain primacy to the relationship of the Church with cultures, religions and the world. This resulted in crucial shifts in ecclesiological models with consequential pastoral and mission implications for India. To counter the excesses of the institutionalized-patriarchal ecclesial model, the values of the historical-anthropological stance were emphasized, and plurality and inclusiveness were welcomed (*Evangelii Nuntiandi* cf. GS 29, Gal 3:28). "By divine institution the Holy Church is ordered and governed with a wonderful diversity" (Rom 12:4-5) and with the 21st century bringing in a new era of pluralism, the Church is urged to forge a new and creative mode of being Church to fashion a new humanity with that "wonderful diversity."

I do not intend to present a new ecclesial paradigm but rather build on one given to us at Vatican II and founded on Scripture, namely, Church as People of God, also dear to Pope Francis. This conciliar portrait that bore promising signals towards birthing an ecclesial model of inclusiveness was couched within the hierarchical framework of the 'Church of officialdom'. The latter prevented the Church from becoming a congregation of the faithful from every race (LG 13) and a "fellowship of life, charity and truth" (LG 9) where "all share a true equality with regard to the dignity and the activity common to all the faithful for the building up of the Body of Christ" (LG 32).

Who are the 'New' People of God within the Church in India?

The evolved perception of the Church today is that Christians, Muslims, Hindus and all peoples (LG 9-17) constitute the People of God. However, in this essay, I am restricting my reflections to only one section of the People of God, namely the laywomen and men to underline the Church's urgent response to contemporary pastoral concerns and issues.

Globalization promotes multi-cultural and religious communities the world over and Indian Catholic communities are also drawn into that phenomenon. There is a growing migrant Catholic community in the country bearing multicultural/ethnic, caste, religious and ritual identities. The Catholic communities are also facing the challenges of the 'generational-gap' with a

1 Kurien Kunnumpuram, SJ, "Towards a New Ecclesiology in the Light of Vatican II," in *The Indian Church of the Future, Mumbai,* St Paul's, 2007, pp. 81-112. Fr Kurien K, SJ was my professor of theology and mentor.

rapidly growing millennial generation with their quasi-invisible presence in the Church and an equally increasing number of senior members who faithfully fill the pews of the Church. Such transformation prompts myriad searching questions on how to be Church in a relevant way in today's changing contexts.

Jesus did not commission the apostles to form an exclusive group of disciples. Rather he said, "Go and make disciples of all nations" (Mt 28:19) for God's salvation is for everyone (cf. GS 22). "To those who feel far from God and the Church, to all those who are fearful or indifferent," Pope Francis says, "The Lord, with great respect and love, is also calling you to be a part of his people" (EG 113). In this regard, he urges, "The Church must be a place of mercy freely given where everyone can feel welcomed, loved, forgiven and encouraged to live the good life of the Gospel" (EG 114). Who are the 'new' people of God today that the Church must welcome, be merciful to and encourage to live the good life of the Gospel?

The Marginalized Lay Women and Men

Clericalism and patriarchy, the cancerous disorders that still afflict the Church in India, continue to marginalize laywomen and men, restrict their prophetic role and impede their creative initiatives and missionary zeal. The laity, whose identity and role are defined in contrast to the ordained clergy, are usually assigned symbolic involvement in the life and mission of the Church. *Evangelii Gaudium* 102 sets right this distorted understanding, "Lay people are, put simply, the vast majority of the people of God. The minority – ordained ministers – are at their service." Unfortunately, the silent and passive presence of this vast majority of people of God is seen only in the pews of the Church. A few among them are engaged in Parish Councils, Pastoral and Financial Committees and various other Diocesan and National Commissions.

Laymen and women are not aware of their baptismal responsibility because they "have not been given the formation needed to take on important responsibilities" (EG 102). Sadly, their involvement in lay ministries remain confined to limited Church tasks and "is not reflected in a greater penetration of Christian values in the social, political and economic sectors" (EG 102).

There is an urgency to evoke the baptismal agency of the laity and engage them in the mission of transforming the world. What is conspicuously wanting is the theological formation for the empowerment of the laity that will enable them to exercise responsibly their triple functions of common priesthood (cf. LG 10-12). "We need lay people who take risks, who get their hands dirty, who are not afraid of making mistakes, who go forward … who dare to dream,' emphasized Pope Francis for "The Church should always value the transformative power of faith-filled laity who are willing to serve the Gospel."[2]

2 The Plenary Assembly of the Pontifical Council for the Laity in 2016.

A true missionary disciple is one who reflects Christ in his life. Paul, Phoebe, Junia, Andronicus and many other lay men and women in the early Church who full of the Holy Spirit and of faith not only proclaimed the Good News but became the good news through their witnessing lives. (Acts 11:21f). Likewise, we have many faith-filled laymen and women who live the beatitudes by their witnessing life and are willing to serve the Gospel today. Why do we not value the transformative power of faith-filled laity and invite them to use their proficiency, expertise and talents in the life and mission of the Church? A true Church of the People of God contests any form of clericalism. The clergy must learn to walk with the laity, listen and learn from realities of their life and engage them actively to bring newness in the life and mission of the Church. The laity's involvement and collaboration will go a long way to eradicate the many social evils like intolerance, social discriminations, corruption, etc. plaguing the Indian society.

Family: The Domestic Church and Pillar of Society: Need for On-going Formation

A new global media and technological culture is invading the contemporary society and affecting every sphere of life. Families today encounter many socio-economic, religious and cultural challenges. The stability of family and transmission of faith and values are at stake. Family structure is changing, and the nuclear family unit is promoted.

The family that used to be the first school of the society and nation and custodian of values no longer enjoys that status. The sacred value of married and family life upheld in Indian culture is changing. Single-parent families, unwed mothers, divorced couples and live-in relationships are on the rise. Instead of side-lining and ostracizing those singles parents or couples who live in 'irregular' situations, the Church has the responsibility to reach out to them, understand and integrate them in the community (cf. *Amoris Laetitia*, 49).[3]

Every layperson is an integral member of the ecclesial community. The laity can render service to bring about reconciliation in broken families and among separated couples and help disturbed children, victims of this new situation afflicting family life today. Pastoral family cells to reach out to such families can be formed in parishes and dioceses. The family of Nazareth is a model for every Christian family to live the sacramental communion for the good of humanity. Mary and Joseph are a constant inspiration of fidelity to fulfill God's plan amid many trials and struggles, and Jesus, their only Son who under their guidance, allowed himself to grow in wisdom and knowledge

---

3 Evelyn Monteiro, "Une Eglise pour et avec les pauvres en Inde: Un engagement ecclesial, " *Spiritus, Revue d'experiences et de recherché missionnaires,* Les Pauvres: au Coeur de l'Eglise? No 232, September 2018, pp. 323-336, p. 335.

(Lk 2:52). The Church must integrate lay men and women in the mission of restoring the sacredness of married and family life and of enabling families to build homes of love and harmony and become active agents of development of the society and nation (CCC no. 898).

On-going Christian and family formation of married couples and families is the dire need of the times. Given the stress and varied demands and challenges of life today, problems between spouses, among children and with extended family members are escalating. Job opportunities and demands and the culture of 'wanting more' often force couples to live separately. Infidelity and addiction to alcohol or drugs and to pornography affect the well being of the family. Infants and children are kept in the crèche or nursery or in the care of domestics. Elderly family members are often abandoned and left to live on their own. Formation in continual marital fidelity, in responsible parenthood, acceptance and caring of physically or mentally challenged children and the elderly is of primary importance. Laymen and women with their varied professional competences and rich experiences can reach out to families in their struggles.

Another area of pastoral care, particularly in the urban context is to welcome and integrate couples of mixed marriages– inter-religious, inter-cultural/ethnic, inter-caste, inter-ritual into the ecclesial community. Mixed marriages are a welcoming sign of openness, breaking away from traditional taboos and dividing socio-cultural boundaries. The clergy in collaboration with lay men and women can help families to be open to such contemporary changes and build communities of fellowship and solidarity among the faithful, making the Church a 'home' for all.

There is a dearth in engaging lay men and women in leadership roles, as consulters, resource persons, as family and youth Counsellors even though many of them have a fund of knowledge, experience and wisdom. With adequate training in family counseling, committed lay couples would be good resource persons to restore the sacredness of marriage and life-long marital commitment in unstable married life and broken families.

Connecting with the Youth

India counted 411 million people between the age of 18 and 35, making it a leading country of millennials by 2020 according to the UN's Population Database in 2016. The country's more than 400 million millennials or those born after 1982, account for a third of India's population and 46% of its workforce. The youth of this generation are better educated, better connected to information, and better linked to the world than those of earlier generations. They are creative, ingenious and enterprising. They are also part of a rising middle class.[4] However, unsupervised family life, consumerism and cyber addiction are also birthing a 'poor' generation of false hopes and virtual dreams.[5] The millennials aspire for a better future but their question is how to keep this dream and their faith together.[6]

At Philadelphia (US) in 2014, Pope Francis raised the following pertinent questions: "How many young people in our parishes and schools have the same high ideals, generosity of spirit, and love for Christ and the Church! Do we challenge them? Do we make space for them and help them to do their part? To find ways of sharing their enthusiasm and talents with our communities, above all in works of mercy and concern for others?"[7] With most clergy and parishes more concerned with safeguarding tradition and institutionalized power, the youth in India have doubts regarding the Church's ability to guide and accompany them and respond to their searching questions on faith, God, morals, ethics, etc. on their life's journey.

The Church does not appear to be an attractive and friendly community for them to be part of. What we need is a Church capable of meeting the young on their life's journey and of entering into their conversation, speaking and understanding their language, and investing 'youth power' for the betterment of the society. The preferential option for the peripheries needs to be translated into preferential understanding and care of children, youth and young adults in the Church (cf. EG 200).[8]

The Urban People of God of Many Faces

The People of God is incarnate in the peoples of the earth, each with its own culture (EG 115). The history of the Church shows that Christianity does not have simply one cultural expression but rather also reflects "the different faces of the cultures and peoples in which it is received and takes root."[9]

The urban People of God reflects this diversity in a new way today. Apart from the long-time diminishing settlers, one notices a mosaic of new and different faces occupying the pews of the urban parishes. Urban parishes

---

4 Morgan Stanley report, based on its AlphaWise survey. https://www.forbes.com/sites/.../indias-millennials-to-drive-growth-in-four-key-sectors.

5 Evelyn Monteiro, "Une Eglise pour et avec les pauvres en Inde.." *Op. cit.* p. 335.

6 Evelyn Monteiro, SCC, "Women Religious: Reviewing and Reinventing Mission Pathways," in *Prospects and Pathways in India, Missio Ad-Inter Gentes*, Edited by Lazar T. Stanislaus, SVD, Mumbai, St Paul's, pp. 97-132, p114.

7 Tom McGrath, "In Homily, Pope Francis Calls for Greater Role for Laity .... And Women?",http://www.phillymag.com/news/2015/09/26/pope-francis-philadelphia-homily/#qRcdocpWMcwK7ySE.99.

8 *Evelyn Monteiro, SCC, "Women Religious: Reviewing and Reinventing Mission Pathways, " Op.* cit. p. 116.

9 John Paul II, Apostolic letter, *Novo Millennio Ineunte*, 6 Jan 2001, 40.

are more heterogeneous than before with a blend of parishioners of varied languages, cultures and rites. Mass migration of displaced rural and indigenous people dispossessed of their land and identity like Joseph and Mary in Egypt, inter-religious/caste/cultural marriages and families, 'floating' parishioners like IT employees who are 'in and out' of the parish communities, young career and job seekers who are engaged in professional studies and training, lonely elderly and infirmed abandoned or left in the care of domestics among the middle and upper class and many others are crafting an urban landscape of multi-cultural parishes as well as breaking down traditional walls of linguistic, class, caste divisions.

In this mosaic of nameless People of God frequenting our Churches, how essential it is to identify and know the numerous anonymous people in our parishes and welcome and integrate them in the community for the Church is 'a people for everyone' (EG 112). In this diversity of peoples who experience love and fellowship, the Church witnesses to that 'wonderful diversity'; to her genuine catholicity through the "beauty of her varied face"[10]

The urban landscape is also a locus for new evangelization. No uniform and rigid mission-plan can be designed. Instead each context teaches us something new. Our pastoral ministry will have to include meaningful ways to communicate the Good News, especially to the young sheep. We also have a special mission of assisting the masses of displaced and indigenous migrants to be integrated into the parishes and the civil society.[11] The Indian Bishops Labour Office that has set up an online service to register migrant workers, promote safe migration and provide pastoral care, counseling and welfare assistance must be implemented in every diocese.

Place of the Poor in God's People

Consumerism and technology have brought about a feverish pursuit of frivolous pleasures that breed individualism and indifference. A financial system that rules rather than serves rejects ethics as well as God. It blunts one's conscience and sedates our feelings of compassion at the outcry of the poor and excluded, and deadens our social responsibility towards them (EG 52, 54).

We need agents of ethics to create a counter-cultural resistance to the self-centred hedonism of capitalism and corruption and to bring about a more humane social order. God's heart has a special place for the poor so much so that He himself "became poor" (2 Cor 8:9) and Jesus' mission-manifesto was primarily geared towards proclaiming "the good news to the poor" (Lk4:16-18). We are called to find Christ in the poor, to lend our voice to their causes, to

10 Ibid.

11 Evelyn Monteiro, SCC, "Women Religious: Reviewing and Reinventing Mission Pathways," *Op. cit*. p. 119.

be their friends, to listen to them, to speak for them and embrace the mysterious wisdom which God wishes to share with us through them" (EG 198).

Conclusion

A Church of the People of God goes forth to the excluded in the existential and geographical peripheries of India. She goes forth as a loving mother who tends the wounded of broken marriages and families, accompanies the disturbed children and enterprising youth, and nurtures the lonely and abandoned. As a merciful father, the Church searches for excluded laywomen and men and integrates them in her life and mission. The Church of the People of God is not pigeoned-holed into an abstract standard. Her missionary outreach strategies evolve from the struggles of people and from grassroots realities of life. Becoming a Christ-centred Church is an on-going commitment to be for and with the 'new' people of God in the changing contexts of the times.

9

Crisis Crying Out for Change: Ecclesiastical Signposts

Kochurani Abraham
Indian Christian Women's Movement

Abstract: *Today the Catholic Church is going through a very critical phase in its history as the crisis is provoked not by an 'outside' enemy but from within. The Church stands exposed before the world in being confronted by a very grave crisis of credibility and integrity. The author hopes that it will be a wake-up call for the Church to face the issues in a non-defensive manner with a deep openness to the Spirit of God, that the very crisis becomes a turning point for growth and revitalization. For the Church, it is an opportunity to return to its founding vision, to enflesh the Gospel vision and to engage consciously in the politics of the reign of God. This will enable the Church to grow beyond a male-centred, ritualistic, cultic and charitable organization and become a potent leaven that acts as a catalyst of change, a sign and sacrament of salvation in the world today.*

Keywords: *Church in crisis, Need for change, Ecclesiology, Ecclesiogenesis.*

It is generally observed that in the present times, the Catholic Church is facing its most serious crisis since the Reformation[1], a crisis of a different nature from what has been its lot in the recent past. In the latter part of the 20th century, with the secularisation of Europe and the consequent dwindling of ecclesiastical

1 Church historian Massimo Faggioli makes this assertion. See his article "The Catholic Church's Biggest Crisis Since the Reformation", *Foreign Affairs, 11 October 2018.*

membership and participation, it was a crisis of diminishing numbers in the West. Whereas in the East, particularly in countries where Christianity is a minority religion as in the Asian continent, the crisis confronting the Church was due to attacks on its presence and mission from fundamentalistic religious and political forces. While these challenges could be disconcerting to the established ecclesiastical identity in the diverse global situations, it could still be handled with greater composure as the 'enemy' was from outside, and the Church could bank on its moral and spiritual resources to confront it. However moving into the 21st century, the Catholic Church in going through a very critical phase in its history as the crisis is provoked not by an 'outside' enemy but from within. The Church stands exposed before the world is being confronted by a very grave crisis of credibility and integrity.

The extensive reporting of clergy sexual abuse from different parts of the world has signaled to a global epidemic affecting the Church, something that cannot be contained as a virus afflicting mainly the North and the Western parts of the world. The severity of the problem got intensified not just for its persistence but for the fact that it implicated high level Church officials in the abuse and its cover-up.[2] Even the Pope was accused of covering up and not acting on reports of abuse by top church officials as brought out in the 'Vigano letter'.[3] Analysts of the Vigano letter point out that a new wave of sexual abuse revelations seems to have deepened preexisting divisions in the Church that is bitterly divided between progressive and conservative wings. While the progressive groups have defended the Pope, for the conservatives, the letter seemed to vindicate such distrust by accusing the current papacy and its supporters in the church of complacency towards what Viganò called a "pro-gay ideology" and "homosexual networks" among the clergy. In Viganò's opinion, this was the cause of the abuse crisis.[4]

Besides the issue of clergy sexual abuse, strong critique is voiced against churches that function as commercial enterprises generating huge revenue through its ministries and these Churches are seen as encapsulating the very essence of materialism. In such situations of corruption, it is noted that though a 'Church' seems to be doing quite well, it is actually creating a major crisis in that it destroys the credibility of the Gospel and the Church.[5]

---

2 *Ibid.*

3 The Vigano letter refers to an open letter by Archbishop Carlo Maria Viganò, a former papal diplomat, published in August 2018, in which he accuses Pope Francis of knowing about American Cardinal McCarrick's sexual abuses for years and helping to cover them up. Viganò concluded by calling on the pope to resign.

4 Faggioli, The Catholic Church's Biggest Crisis Since the Reformation", *Op cit.*

5 Rah, S.-C., 2009, *The Next Evangelicalism. Freeing the Church from Western Cultural captivity*, InterVarsity Press, Downers Grove.

Reading into the crisis afflicting the Church, diverse interpretations are given by prominent theologians and public intellectuals. While this situation is seen as indicative of the 'approaching end of the church'[6] it is also argued that the real crisis of the Church is primarily a question of the Church not being able to 'be Church'.[7] It is widely acknowledged that the Church is in bad shape and if it is not able or willing to undergo a process of radical transformation, the Church – as an institution – will disappear.[8] These predictions find an echo in the opinions expressed by the younger generation who admit to 'wrestling with the "God question" as well as 'the meaning of the Church.'[9] As expressed by a university student, "The institutional model has in recent centuries served to give Roman Catholics a strong sense of corporate identity. I feel that in contemporary times, especially regarding the sex abuse crisis, this statement does not hold. Catholic institutions and individuals have abandoned their strong sense of corporate identity in an attempt to separate themselves from the system that perpetuated this abuse."[10]

Crisis in the Indian Church

Until recent times, the Indian church seems to have enjoyed rather a 'crisis-free' existence before the global eye as it was not tainted by major sex scandals or corruption issues that had surfaced into the public view. Besides, it has always basked in glory for its apostolic contributions particularly in the field of education and for its numerical strength of professionally religious personnel in spite of being a small minority in the religiously plural context of India. The Indian church has withstood the challenges posed by politicized religious fundamentalism and the outbreak of nationalistic assertions of the Hindutva forces in this land. However, this aura of ecclesiastical vitality is being challenged by the eruption of major sex scandals and scams in the present times.

Certainly we do not take the Indian Church here as a monolithic entity forgetting its diversity for reasons of ritual differences, multiple ethnic identities, divisions in the name of gender, class, caste and other factors. All the same, before the people of other faiths of the Indian society as well as when seen from a global point of view, scandal in any ecclesial community of

---

6 Hauerwas, S., 2013, *Approaching the end. Eschatological reflections on Church, politics and life*, Grand Rapids: William B. Eerdmans Publishing Company, ix–xi.

7 Dreyer,W., 'The real crisis of the church', *HTS Teologiese Studies/Theological Studies* 71(3), 2015.1. 10.4102/hts.v71i3.2822.

8 Heitink, G., 2007, *Eenkerk met karakter: Tijdvoorheroriëntatie*, UitgeverijKok, Kampen as cited by Wim A. Dreyer in "The real crisis of the Church."

9 Massimo Faggioli , 'The Church of the abuse scandal is the only Church we know', La Croix 21 May 2019.

10 *Ibid.*

India would bear the 'Indian church' tag. In this context, the eruption scandals relating to land dealings and sexual abuse in some of the most tradition-bound and conservative communities of the Church in India has triggered a crisis, shaking the very foundations on which the 'ecclesiastical empire' had been established.

As we know various scams may be present in the Church itself, resulting in deep-seated divisions within the highly clericalized hierarchical structures. The laity is also divided between those who seek transparency in Church dealings and those who want to keep the untarnished the public image of the Church intact, no matter how mucky its internal affairs are. The lack of discernment in ecclesiastical decision making and the lack of moral responsibility towards the material resources entrusted to the leaders for the fulfilment of the Church's mission, all seem to point a critical finger at the very ecclesiastical institution. According to a Circular issued by a diocese, "What happened to the Archdiocese is not only a financial crisis but also a moral lapse. Facts that there was no transparency and ignorance of Canon law also raise serious moral concerns. Though the Archdiocese can recover from the financial crisis to a great extent, issues related to morality will prevail."[11] In and through the land scam crisis, what is made starkly evident is the Gospel principle that one cannot serve God and Mammon at the same time.

Over the past few years in India, the reporting of clergy sex abuse has been on the increase, particularly in South India with many cases of molestation and rape and even alleged murder of the victims coming to light.[12] Among the many cases of clerical sexual abuse in India, one that has caught global attention is the recent case of the alleged rape of a nun by a bishop, who is meant to be the patron of her Institute. While this case has triggered very many protests and debates across India, and the investigation is still going on, what has provoked a deep ecclesiastical crisis is the fact that the official Church leadership took a silent distance from the case and the victim/survivor. This scandalous case also brought to surface the deep divide in the Indian Church between those who support the accused bishop and those who stand with the nun; the way gender concerns are addressed by the Church hierarchy with public expressions of support extended to the accused but having failed to set up even a fact-finding commission to assess the truth of the allegations. The irony of the case is that while there is a defensive silence on the part of

11 Excerpts from a Circular issued by Ernakulam-AngamaliSyro-Malabar Church on 27 December 2018. For more details on the land scam that has brought the Church into a crisis, see "Land deal has led to financial crisis, says Archdiocese" in *The Indian Express*, 29 December, 2018

12 See M.G. Radhakrishnan, "Rising cases of sexual abuse within the church in Kerala force clergy to rethink on homosexuality", *India Today*, 17 September, 2011; See also Priestly Predators, *The Outlook*, 20 January, 2017.

Church leaders before the accusations meted out against the alleged offender, the victim/survivor and her companion nuns who dared to take the issue to public attention -on failing to receive justice from the hierarchy-stand accused of crossing the limits of ecclesiastical conduct.[13]

The Challenges Posed by the Crisis

In the context of clergy sex abuse reaching shocking heights globally, critical concerns about the very future of the Church are raised from different fronts. Some well meaning people ask with certain angst to the clergy involved in the scandals: "Why are you trying to destroy the Catholic Church?"[14] Ironically, the same question is raised by many in the Church when the media and people seeking reform in the Church address the deeper concerns underlying the scandals. Apparently Church life seems easier if the issues are put under the carpet instead of dealing them. Or it could be that the sex abuse crisis abides because the complex hierarchical culture refuses to die and refuses to investigate itself in order to identify the flagrantly immoral elements within it.[15]

All too often, persons abused by clergy report that their complaints to bishops and other diocesan officials were met with varying degrees of denial, arrogance and incompetence.[16] Though the reasons behind the inability of the Church to effectively address clergy sexual abuse are many, clericalism is seen as a major enabler of this problematic. As observed by Thomas Doyle,a noted Canon lawyer, clericalism is grounded in the erroneous belief that clerics form a special elite and, because of their powers as sacramental ministers, they are superior to the laity. Although the clergy constitute a minuscule fraction of the world's Catholic population, they wield all of the power in the Church. The Church's governmental structure, therefore, is both hierarchical and monarchical by definition and, according to official Catholic teaching, intended so by divine will. Doyle argues that far from being merely a tragic moment in the Church's history, sexual abuse and related cover-ups are the fruits of a systemic disorder in the church, the toxic clericalism.[17] In his opinion, the

---

13 The case, its allegations and counter allegations has been brought out by the visual and print media over the last one year. The Kerala Conference of Catholic Bishops (KCBC) issued a Statement on 12 September2018 saying that the protest against the accused bishop has crossed the limits and the stir is unacceptable. See *The Hindu*, 13 September, 2018.

14 Eugene Cullen Kennedy,The hierarchical spirit that will not die, National Catholic Reporter, Jun 4, 2019.

15 *Ibid.*

16 U.S. Bishops' Dallas Meeting, Charter for the Protection of Children and Young People, cited by John J. Coughlin, Boston College Law Review Volume 44 Issue 4,pp. 977-997.

17 Thomas Doyle, Clericalism: Enabler of Clergy Sexual Abuse,Mary Gail Frawley-O'Dea and Virginia Goldner (eds), *Predatory Priests, Silenced Victims, The Sexual Abuse Crisis*

situation is more critical as Canon law gives the ordained rights and privileges that are not available even to rulers in any democratic country. Accused clerics are not brought before civil courts, but tried by a canonical forum and Canon law is totally impotent in bringing about a just Church and society.[18]

In light of the failure on the part of Church leadership to handle this crisis, serious questions are raised about hierarchical authority and the centralised way of exercising power in the Church. The use of religious power when coupled with money power creates a situation where the corruption of power is made easy. And absolute power corrupts absolutely if hierarchical leaders are bent on protecting the hierarchical complex, its assets, its property, and its leadership. The interplay of sex, power and money then becomes the major cause behind the scandals afflicting the Church.

The global outbreak of this crisis apparently declares aloud the scriptural dictum that 'the time has come for judgement to begin with the house of God' (1 Pet. 4: 17). This entails a serious reconsideration on what it means to be Church, how it needs to be structured, the place and role of the laity, particularly women and the like. The challenge facing the Church is to 'be Church' and to 'stay Church'. The discrepancy between the true nature and empirical manifestation of the Church leads to crisis, loss of integrity and regression.[19] Or as Dreyer observes, the real crisis of the Church is its inability to 'be Church' – sometimes not even conscious of what the Church is or should be and sometimes deliberately ignoring it for personal gain. When the 'Church' dilutes into mere human activity, it is not Church anymore. No human effort will avert the deepening crisis if the Church itself does not understand the real nature of the crisis and continually reform to be what it is.[20]

Crisis Calling for a New *Ecclesiogenesis*?

It is widely acknowledged that embedded in any crisis is an invitation for growth. People who have grown through crises in their lives testify that they have been birthed anew, though going through the birth pangs can be very difficult and demanding. The same is true of the Church as a body, which though marked deeply by human imperfections, has the potential to emerge

and The Catholic Church, The Analytic Press Mahwah, New Jersey London, 2007, pp. 147-162

18 Doyle, The Sexual Abuse Crisis is Not a Crisis, https://consciencemag.org/2019/04/03/the-sexual-abuse-crisis-is-not-a-crisis/ fbclid=IwAR0t3u2woDiyfCLtWRWftWoZobymJF

19 Busch, E., 2004, *The great passion: An introduction to Karl Barth's theology*, transl. G.W. Bromley & D.L. Guder (eds.), Grand Rapids:William B. Eerdmans Publishing Company, pp. 246–247.

20 Wim A. Dreyer, "The Real Crisis of the Church" *HTSTeologiese Studies / Theological Studies* | Vol 71, No 3 | a2822 | DOI: https://doi.org/10.4102/hts.v71i3.2822

anew when open to the renewing touch of the Spirit. Then, even the worst crisis can become a turning point for the Church.

Growth implies renewal from within, and we can see that in the unfolding history of the Catholic Church, this call has resounded at different crisis moments. It is a call for a new way of being, letting go of the old. This entails letting the new emerge from the crisis as in the call to be 'born again', which is a Gospel imperative for entry into the Reign of God. This call that is generally applied to the conversion stories of individuals applies also to the life story of the Church. It is a call to born anew from within , echoing St. Bede's classic statement that "every day the Church gives birth to the Church"[21] In this call we hear the patristic idea of rejuvenation of the Church, which found a resonance in the affirmation by the Second Vatican Council that "the Spirit by the power of the Gospel rejuvenates the Church" (LG 4). This process of rejuvenation can be an *ecclesiogenesis,*[22] where 'a new way of being Church' evolves from the messy crisis when we allow the Spirit to hover over the chaos. *Ecclesiogenesis* happens when "a new church is taking shape in the womb of the old" and this is seen as "the most promising development within Roman Catholicism today."[23]

For e*cclesiogenesis* to happen, the faithful Christians need to engage in a serious rethinking on what it means to be Church. It demands open and sincere conversations on the crisis from within and this entails an intense discernment with deep openness to the Spirit in freedom on what it means to be Church. This implies rethinking ecclesiology anew, so that the Church can be born again to what it is meant to be. However, as Watkins argues ecclesiology will only be 'authentic' when it can 'speak truthfully about concrete realities' and actual practices need to be given their rightful place in the theological talk about the Church. Practices are indeed bearers of theology and potentially a theological voice spoken from the heart of the Church, which has authority.[24]

---

21 St Bede the Venerable, *Explanatio Apocalypse* bk 2: *Nam et Ecclesia, quotidiegignit Ecclesiam* (PL 93 166 d) cited by Henri de Lubac in *The Splendour of the Church* (Michael Mason trans, New york, Sheed and Ward 1956), p.109.

22 This expression I borrow from the liberation theologian Leonardo Boff who introduced the term *ecclesiogensis* to show how the base communities in the Latin American context reinvent the Church. See Boff*Ecclesiogenesis*: *The Base Communities Reinvent the Church,* Maryknoll NY: Orbis Books, 1986.

23 C. Rene Padilla, A New Ecclesiology in Latin America, International Bulletin of Missionary Research, Volume: 11 issue: 4 (1987), pp. 156-164.

24 Clare Watkins, Practical Ecclesiology: What Counts as Theology in Studying the Church? In Peter Ward (ed) Perspectives on Ecclesiology and Ethnography, Grand Rapids, MI, Eerdmans, 2012, ch. 9 cited by Paul Avis in Paul Avis ed, Oxford Handbook of Ecclesiology, Oxford University Press, 2018, p.18.

For this *ecclesiogensis*, it is imperative that the Christian faithful exercise theological and spiritual agency. Social theorists speak of agency as 'the capacity to make a difference.'[25] Generally, among the Catholic faithful, theological agency is considered the prerogative of the clergy. Very few among the faithful avail theological training as in a country like India and the rest consider themselves 'lay' in the literal sense of the word, limiting their ecclesiastical engagements to mere cultic and ritualistic practices.. Unless Christian faithful emerge from their ecclesiastical infantilism and come of age as a Church community, ecclesiastical crisis may lead to destructive effects than paving the way for *ecclesiogenesis*. A deep sense of crisis when combined by an intense desire for healing, growth and change can lead to 'ecclesiological renaissance', borrowing an expression of the noted ecclesiologist Veli-Matti Kärkkäinen who uses this expression to indicate the 'revived interest in the Church'.[26] There needs to be a revived interest in being Church on the part of the faithful, not just to safeguard its long established identity for the establishment's sake but to revive its true spirit as a Christian community at the service of the Reign of God. According to Hans Küng, the Church will only survive if it could move past the Enlightenment, Reformation and the Middle Ages to the origins of the Church in the early Jesus movement. This does not imply a simplistic idealisation or reduplication of the Jesus movement, rather an identification with the kingdom of God which became manifest with the incarnation of Christ.[27]

For the Christian faithful[28] to come of age in the Church, the feudalistic hierarchical settings though long established as divinely ordained arrangements need to give way to more democratic structures where women, men and people of other gender/sexual orientations who are imbued by the Spirit take leadership positions and play an active role in the Church's decision/policy-making bodies. Then, the power structures of the Church will give way to Gospel potency of the Spirit, and the Church will engage in an ongoing discernment on its mission in service of the Reign of God.

The cry for change in the face of the present crisis in the Church is raised from many fronts. People are asking for mechanisms in the Church where the faithful have a potent say and have it heard. They claim that 'parishioners must have a direct say in the merit appointments of priests and bishops. Directors of

---

25 See Giddens A. *The Constitution of Society*, Cambridge: Polity Press, 1984, p.14

26 See Veli-Matti Kärkkäinen, *An Introduction to Ecclesiology: Ecumenical, Historical and Global Perspectives*, Downers Grove: InterVarsity Press, 2002, 7.

27 Küng, H., 2003, *The Catholic Church: A short history,* transl. J. Bowden, The Modern Library, New York.

28 I am purposely avoiding the use of laity or lay people for its meaning of being distinct from the clergy or for the connotations of being the ordinary people as different from the professionals of religion.

diocesan boards and trustees of Church assets must include equal numbers of laity and clergy.'[29] Others demand the rights and responsibilities of the baptised faithful to have an effective voice in the decision-making of our Church.[30] The Leadership Conference of Women Religious speaks of refashioning the leadership structures of the church in order to address the issue of clericalism and ensure that power and authority are shared with members of the Christian faithful. In their opinion, the revelations of the extent of abuse indicate clearly that the current structures must change if the church is to regain its moral credibility and have a viable future.[31]When concerned Christian faithful in the Catholic Church are seeking change, the time has come for a true *ecclesiogenesis* where the Church evolves in a new way without the clergy-laity divide.

Conclusion

The cry arising from the crisis is not for a mere perfection of the members of the ecclesiastical establishment. The Church will always remain holy and sinful at the same time, as Luther taught in his famous *simul iustus, simul peccator*. Crisis here is meant to be a wake-up call for the Church to face the issues in a non-defensive manner with a deep openness to the Spirit of God, that the very crisis becomes a turning point for growth and revitalization. For the Church it is an opportunity to return to its founding vision, to enflesh the Gospel vision and to engage consciously in the politics of the reign of God. This will enable the Church to grow beyond a male-centred, ritualistic, cultic and charitable organization and become a potent leaven that acts as a catalyst of change, a sign and sacrament of salvation in the world today. And, this would be the way of being Church that Kurien Kunnumpuram would have dreamt of.

29 See Francis Sullivan,The Catholic Church must make these seven changes now,https://cathnews.co.nz/2019/03/25/seven-changes/

30 https://www.catholicchurchreform.org/216/index.php/get-involved/letters-to-the-pope/25-for-a-voice-in-the-decision-making-of-our-church./

31 See LCWR Statement on the Sexual Abuse of Sisters by Clergyhttps://lcwr.org/media/news/lcwr-statement-sexual-abuse-sisters-clergy

10

The Future of Christianity: Rahner's World Church

Denis Rodrigues
Consultant, Pune

Abstract: *The Second Vatican Council was meant to be the Catholic Church's response to the evolutionary imperative: Adapt to changing environments or go extinct! But if the events of the past decades are any indication, then the adaptation has not been enough – or it is not in the right direction. What the Church needs now is not just a re-engineering but a radical reconstruction. That is something Karl Rahner had foreseen some forty years ago in a talk given in 1979, well before the worst of the crisis facing the Church today had begun to make itself seen and felt. Rahner saw in the Second Vatican Council "the Church's first official self-actualization as a world Church" albeit "in a rudimentary form still groping for identity". This required a process of transition through a "de-Europeanizing of the Church" so that it could properly inculturate itself into the contemporary cultures of Asia and Africa. This was the task undertaken by Kurien Kunnumpuram, the pioneer of Vatican II in India and other contemporary theologians.*

This demands also an experience of the source of Christian kerygma. The "final and fundamental substance" of the kerygma can be found only in participating in the very experience of Jesus. How this will happen and what results it will have we do not know, any more than the first Christians in Jerusalem could have envisaged the Christian Churches as they exist today.

Of this however we can be sure. If there is to be a world Church in the future it will definitely be very different from the ones we have today.

Keywords: *Catholic Church, Indian Church, World Church, Vatian II, kerygma.*

Vatican II was meant to be the Catholic Church's response to the evolutionary imperative: Adapt to changing environments or go extinct! But if the events of the past decades are any indication, then the adaptation has not been enough – or it is not in the right direction. What the Church needs now is not just a re-engineering but a radical reconstruction. That is something Karl Rahner had foreseen some forty years ago in a talk given in 1979, well before the worst of the crisis facing the Church today had begun to make itself seen and felt. Rahner saw in the Second Vatican Council "the Church's first official self-actualization as a world Church"[1] albeit "in a rudimentary form still groping for identity." This required a process of transition through a "de-Europeanizing of the Church" so that it could properly inculturate itself into the contemporary cultures of Asia and Africa.[2]

The Final and Fundamental Substance of the Church

For Rahner, such a transition to a fundamentally new world Church was not unthinkable because there had already been an earlier transition equal in scope to what was now required. According to him there have been three great epochs in the Church's history:

"First, the short period of Jewish Christianity. Second, the period of the Church in a distinct cultural region, namely, that of Hellenism and of European culture and civilization. Third, the period in which the sphere of the Church's life is, in fact, the entire world. These three periods signify three essential and different basic situations for Christianity and its preaching."[3]

The first transition from a Jewish to a Gentile Christianity "introduced a radically new period in Church history, a Christianity that was not the export of Jewish Christianity to the Diaspora but instead a Christianity which, for all its relationship to the historical Jesus, still grew on the soil of paganism."[4]

This transition involved changes, which according to Rahner "Jesus certainly did not anticipate and which can scarcely be cogently derived from Jesus' own explicit preaching or from the preaching about the salvific meaning of his death and resurrection" in Jewish Christianity.

---

1 Rahner, Karl. "Towards a Fundamental Theological Interpretation of Vatican II," *Theological Studies* Volume: 40 issue: 4, p. 717.

2 Ibid, see p. 723.

3 Ibid, p. 721.

4 Ibid.

That first transition would seem to Rahner to be sufficient precedent to provide theological justification for a contemporary transition from" a Christianity of Europe (with its American annexes) to a fully world religion. "Though there are major differences in the two situations, according to Rahner the difference between the historical situation of Jewish Christianity and the situation into which Paul transplanted Christianity as a radically new creation is not greater than the difference between Western culture and the contemporary cultures of all Asia and Africa into which Christianity must inculturate itself' today. And hence "the second break, towards a world Church, naturally has or must acquire a completely different content than the first break, towards the Gentile Church of antiquity and the Middle Ages."[5]

For Rahner, a confirmation for the need of a new beginning lies in the fact that "modern missionary history shows that Christianity as a Western export actually succeeded neither with the high cultures of the East nor in the world of Islam, precisely because it was Western Christianity and sought in that way to establish itself in the rest of the world, without risking a really new beginning or breaking with many continuities that seem self-evident to us." For the past several centuries (if not a millennium) Christianity has encountered world cultures as a western export. As long as the exporters were seen as culturally superior or economically or politically more powerful, this approach met with such success. But the success was merely skin deep and was easily sloughed of when the circumstances changed.

What makes this quest even more urgent is the fact that even in its own milieu of the West, Christianity is losing its impetus. It is clearly no longer the salt of the West let alone of the earth. It is no longer leavening the bread of the Western cultural sphere.

Rahner is quite clear that what is required today is a "return to the final and fundamental substance of the Christian message, to formulate from it anew the whole of ecclesial faith with the natural creativity that corresponds to the actual historical situation. For Rahner, this "final and fundamental substance" of the kerygma, has what he calls a 'natural creativity' that makes a new creation of a genuine world possible.

We are faced here with two questions. First, what exactly is this 'final and fundamental substance' that Rahner is talking about. And second, if it does exist, is it possible for us to access it in the here and now. Rahner himself is quite clear that this reduction or return to the final and fundamental substance as the first step towards a new expression of the whole content of faith is not easy."[6]

5 Ibid p. 724.

6 Ibid, p. 725.

An Analogy From Biology

The issue here boils down to a question of transfer of information of a very special and critical kind. Perhaps modern biology can help here, not so much with providing answers as with pointing out to the mechanism required. In all organisms, we have what are called stem cells and somatic cells. All cells can divide and form new cells. But while somatic cells can only form cells exactly like themselves, stem cells have a higher potency, which makes it possible for them to develop into a variety of different somatic cells. We can apply this analogy to the Church today. What Rahner calls the Western Church is like a somatic church cell which can only generate new Church cells which are basically the same as what it is. It lacks the potency to create "a new expression of the whole content of faith". For this, we need to access the kerygmatic stem cells which are produced by an organism in its embryonic stages. These stem cells are of different potencies

- Totipotent cells can form all the cell types in a body plus the extraembryonic or placental cells. Embryonic cells within the first couple of cell divisions after fertilization are the only cells that are totipotent.
- Pluripotent/Multipotent cells can give rise to all of the cell types that make up the body.
- Somatic cells can only develop cells of the same type.[7]

We can now try to apply this scheme by analogy to the successive levels of the transmission of the kerygma, from Jesus to the disciples/ Jewish Church and then through the mediation of the New Testament to different churches of Western Christianity and finally to those in Asia and Africa.

The transfer from Jesus to his disciples was on the level of the totipotent cell. They received the kerygma in its full potency. This transference was not so much conceptual as existential and happened through constant interaction over the years at the human level so that they slowly developed that 'mind which was in Christ Jesus', as they became 'other Christs". This is why when the disciples were looking for a replacement for Judas, the major consideration for the apostles was that it had to be 'someone who was with us from the beginning".

The transfer of the kerygma from the immediate disciples of Jesus to the Gentile Church, on the other hand, would have been on the level of the Pluripotent/Multipotent cell. This level of transmission was capable of generating a 'new creation' and the Gentile Church was genuinely a new beginning, growing as Rahner puts it "on the soil of paganism." The means of transmission was initially through the direct testimony of the first disciples and

7 Ref Kelly, Evelyn.B., *Stem Cells*, Greenwood Press, Westport , p. 7.

then, indirectly, through the written witness of the New Testament. However, these Christian Scriptures have an in-built limitation in that they are 'the word of God in the words of men". In terms of the stem cell analogy, these were only pluripotent/multipotent cells and could not transmit their own potency. The 'product' (the Gentile Church) of this transmission was therefore on the level of a somatic kerygma, and this could only produce products like itself. As this Church spread and evolved, with the New Testament as its medium, through the Middle-Ages and the feudal and national states in Europe and later America, it basically remained at the same somatic stage, and it was this Western church that was 'exported' to Asia and Africa. All subsequent proclamation was on the somatic level, which did not integrate into what can be termed the 'cultural DNA' of those cultures.

How to Access the Embryonic "Final and Fundamental Substance"

It should be clear that if we continue doing the kerygma in the way it has been done in the past two millennia, then we shall continue to get the type of results that we have been getting. We need a paradigm shift in the way we proclaim the gospel of Jesus. Rahner himself, in this work, doesn't seem to provide a way out of this impasse. He is aware that we cannot say exactly with "what conceptuality " or through what "basic formulas of faith" (ibid) we must make the future proclamation. However, in an earlier work, he does seem to indicate an entirely new approach.

In 1974 he wrote that "the Christian of the future will either be a mystic or will not be a Christian at all."[8] Expanding that, would he also have said that the Church of the future will either have its foundations in mystical experience or it will not stand at all. And this mystical experience can only be the experience of Jesus: not of Jesus as an object of experience, but of Jesus as being the subject of the experience. The totipotency of the proclamation is in the person of Jesus and only in the person. The "final and fundamental substance" of the kerygma is the person of Jesus. And the person of Jesus can only be encountered in the Gospels. But this encounter will not arise from the exegetical effort, but rather in the direct and immediate experience of the man Jesus: in a mystical experience of Jesus s a person.

Experiencing Jesus: Concluding Remarks

Tony de Mello used to say that we never experience the power of the gospel because we have been 'inoculated' against catching a full dose of it. We read about Jesus but never really know him. de Mello used to tell the story of a man named Anthony Bloom and of how he came to know Jesus. This is how Bloom described the incident:

8 *Theological Investigations* XX, 149

> I was an atheist in the truer sense of the word – there was no God in my experience, no God in my life. And therefore, there was no ultimate meaning in my life; all the meaning of life could be summed up in the necessity of survival.
>
> And then one day I happened to read the Gospel. It happened by the act of God as it were because it happened in order for me to discard it. I heard a priest speak to us, boys, in a youth organisation and what he said shocked me, revolted me so much that I decided to check whether what he had said could possibly be true. We were teenagers, preparing to re-conquer Russia sword in hand and here was a man who spoke of Christ and spoke of nothing but meekness, humility, forbearance, turning one cheek when one was hit on the other, giving us an image of what was not manly. I came home determined to make sure and to finish with the Gospel if that was the Gospel and that was Christ. I counted the chapters of the Gospels because as I expected no good from the reading. I thought that the shortest would be the best and so I was landed with St. Mark's Gospel, a Gospel written for young ruffians like me, the youth of pre-Christian Rome. And then something happened to me which you may interpret either as a hallucination or as a gift of God – between the beginning of the first and the end of the second chapter of his Gospel, of St. Mark's Gospel, I suddenly became aware with total, absolute certainty that on the other side of the desk the Lord Jesus Christ was standing alive.

This kind of experience is the only source of a totipotent kerygma. The "final and fundamental substance" of the kerygma can be found only in participating in the real experience of Jesus. How this will happen and what results it will have we do not know, any more than the first Christians in Jerusalem could have envisaged the Christian Churches as they exist today. Of this, however, we can be sure. If there is to be a world Church in the future, it will definitely be very different from the ones we have today.

PART TWO

SHARING WITH THE WORLD

11

Roadmaps to the Adjacent Possible: Evolution's Ebb and Flow

Felipe-Andrés Piedra, PhD.
Department of Molecular Virology & Microbiology, Baylor College of Medicine, Houston, TX, USA

Donald R. Frohlich, PhD.
Professor, Department of Biology, Nesti Center for Faith and Culture, University of St. Thomas Houston, TX, USA

Abstract: *Can Earth's life history inform our present and future? We summarize paleo-history to discover where we might go. Life as evolution is the consequence of a creative, non-equilibrium universe. Modern science has developed from the ideas that nature is governed by fixed laws and that natural phenomena are fully knowable, and thus, predictable and controllable. Our dominion appeared limitless. But, scientists and philosophers have come to realize that our creative universe exceeds our predictive abilities. In light of our limitations and current global conditions, we discuss the general steps that humanity could, and those we should, take into the unprestatable adjacent possible.*

Keywords: *adjacent possible, creative universe, evolution, history of life, extinction, emergence, hierarchic transitions*

"One of the greatest potential scientific dangers arises from the ruthless application of partial knowledge on a vast scale."[1]

1 Øjvind Lidegaard and Ian Milsom. 1997. *The Lancet*, Volume 349, Issue 9065, 31 May, pp 1622-1623

Life in a Creative Universe: Potential and Possibility

Life on Earth dawned some 4 billion years ago, and while its origins are obscure, its history is less so: biological evolution has been and is tumult and churning of flourishing ecosystems, the emergence of fundamentally new types of living things and relationships, and cascades of extinctions. Life on Earth has always been and will always be in flux.

The unfolding of life is only possible away from thermodynamic equilibrium – i.e., there is no life absent net flows of matter/energy. A dynamic universe, one that since birth has been expanding and whose decreasing mass-energy density has led to all manner of creations – elementary particles, the elements, stars, planets, galaxies, us –, is the only kind that can support life's emergence and evolution. Our universe, a creative one, is necessarily non-equilibrium.

We can define *potential* as what can happen and has, and *possibility* as what could happen and has not. Potential creates possibilities that become new potential when realized, leading to new possibilities. Stuart Kauffman defines the *adjacent possible* as the space of possible events, relationships, processes, and objects that could be (Kauffman 2000). After two centuries of attempts to realize the Newtonian dream of a universe that can be fully harnessed and controlled (so long as we know all positions and momenta), Kauffman grasped and asserted that the universe, though partly knowable and partly predictable, is fundamentally creative, and unpredictably so. For Kauffman and many of us – physicists, biologists, philosophers – inspired by his work, the adjacent possible is *unprestatable*; thus, the particularities of the future of humanity cannot be known, *only aimed for*.

Herein we will attempt what is perhaps logically impossible: to consider our future as if we have no hand in making it, looking to life's past in order to understand what might be in store for us. Drawing on knowledge gained from the life sciences (biology, evolution, etc.), we will inevitably engage in prophecy. What is best in humanity seems to be our potential for encounter, providence, empathy, sympathy, and a desire to live meaningful lives at peace in greatest possible harmony with each other. That harmony will be fleeting at best unless we begin to cherish Our Common Home that birthed and nurses us.

Doppelgangers: Extinction and Adaptive Radiation, Time as Generational

To speculate on a large-scale and non-myopically short-term future of humanity, it is instructive to look to the past, and consider major trends on a time-scale close to 5 billion years. By some 4.6 billion years before the present (bybp), the planet formed from an accretion disc composed of large numbers of inorganic and organic particles orbiting the sun. Robust evidence tells us that liquid water condensed onto the planet at approximately 4.4 bypb, and many scientists agree that the earliest *possibility* of life as we know it would have been around 4.3 bybp. Most workers agree that the *evidence* puts the earliest appearance of life at 3.8 bybp and the date gets pushed back as the resolution of our technology increases, and new discoveries are made. Indeed, it appears that life 'happened' almost as quickly as possible.

Three processes or concepts that drive global biotic patterns are extinction, adaptive radiation, and generation time. We tend to focus on processes of extinction because we see the vivid remnants in the fossil record.[2] Outside of the Great Oxygenation event some 2.8 bybp, resulting from the evolution of photosynthesis among the ancestors of the cyanobacteria (most microbial anaerobes were poisoned by oxygen), paleobiologists largely agree that Earth has undergone at least five major planet-wide extinction events, interspersed among other smaller extinctions:

1. **440 million years ago, 86% of all species lost**; global cooling, sea-level drop
2. **375 million years ago, 75% of species lost**; magmatism, volcanism
3. **251 million years ago, 96% of species lost**; aka The Great Dying, meteor impact, volcanism
4. **200 million years ago, 80% of species lost**; causes contested
5. **66 million years ago, 76% of species lost**; massive comet, prolonged winter, non-avian dinosaurs lost

Currently, we are in the midst of the Holocene or Anthropocene extinction, which is largely a result of human activity, consequent habitat fragmentation, and unrestrained use of the water, land, and air as dumping grounds for unwanted agro-industrial byproducts.

The fact of extinction is mirrored closely by ensuing adaptive radiations. Here, whole new groups of organisms evolve, and diversify, into niche[3] 'spaces' left by now-extinct occupants as well as unique niches created by new

---

2 The fossil record is both highly random and incomplete; skewed as it were. It is simply the nature of fossils that only those forms or characters that are capable of making impressions, being replaced by mineral deposits, or becoming trapped in rare tars and plant resins, will actually become fossilized. Biochemical pathways, soft tissues, behaviors, colors, and most genomes do not leave records. The chance of any organism dying or being trapped under conditions that promote fossilization is also extremely low. The vast majority of expired life forms are decomposed by microbiota; thus our estimates of diversity are surely on the low side. Add to these conditions, the likelihood of availability for discovery (2/3 of the planet is under water) and the chance that experts are in the right place, at the right time, make it amazing that we have been able to reconstruct as much of the past as we have.

3 We use term *niche* in the sense of G. E. Hutchinson (1957); the n-dimensional hyper-volume defined by the resource axes along which a species exists. No two species may occupy exactly the same hyper-volume space in any given habitat, although significant

conditions. For example, the Cambrian Explosion wherein all of the modern animal phyla body plans (among others now extinct), except one, evolved, was preceded by receding glaciers and warming oceans. Evidence also suggests that there may have been a sudden oxygenation of marine waters that would have promoted the evolution of complex animals capable of high metabolism and fast movement. Regardless, the very presence of newly evolved organisms creates new habitats and niches, as well as legion possibilities for Exo- and Endosymbioses; in other words, opportunities for new relationships and inter-dependencies. The salient point is not what was here, so much as *what relationships emerged?* The hard-fact history may be geological, but the ontological framework is significantly more relational than substantive.

A pattern seldom discussed outside of the natural sciences is the concept of 'time' in evolutionary biology. Like most people we find it almost unfathomable to think about the sheer number of years chronicled in geologic time. However, the underlying complexities of that scale with respect to evolution become magnified when we begin to consider how variation in populations is passed from generation to generation, and how or why, new characters and features arise. By definition, **evolution** is the change in character frequency in a *population* that occurs *between* generations. Individuals do not evolve. Individuals develop and age; only populations can evolve. Central to evolution is the process of getting genetic information from one generation to the next, altered or otherwise. As each generation produces gametes, genetic information is copied (replicated), and parents reproduce. Replication cannot be of one-hundred percent fidelity, thus occasional mistakes are made. Variability is also introduced during gamete production when chromosomal sections are mixed and recombined. Depending upon the environment, some of that variability may or may not stay in the next generation. If particularly well adapted to current local environmental conditions, the number of copies of that suite of adaptations will increase over time. If particularly disadvantageous, that variability may become extinct in the extreme case. Thus, the rate at which we see new variability arise is highly dependent not only on local conditions, and ensuing changes in the environment, but importantly also on the time between which generations occur.

Let's compare two short-lived and well-known laboratory models to humans. *Escherichia coli* is a common bacterium whose populations double in size every 40 to 65 minutes depending on temperature and nutrients (Plank and Harvey 1979). *Drosophila melanogaster*, better known as the fruit fly, is an intensely studied model organism in genetics that produces a new generation every 10 to 12 days (Peters and Berg 2017). Humans, relatively long-lived, have

overlap is seen in nature. (Hutchinson, G.E. (1957) Concluding remarks. *Cold Spring Harbor Symposia on Quantitative Biology. 22 (2): 415–427*) generational times between 20 and 33 years on the average, depending upon culture and historical time-frame (Coale 1972). Thus, for every *single* human generation, on average, 175,200 generations of *E. coli* are produced, and 720 generations of fruit flies flourish and die. If we were to multiply generation time over geologic time, and account for population sizes, we could easily see the astonishing number of possibilities for the introduction of variation as well as the enormous probabilities that *some* variation will randomly become lost (extinction). Yet, we know that conditions on earth have changed repeatedly, and evolution *per se*, seems to trend toward accumulating complexity.

Charles Darwin was a gradualist. That is, the good naturalist believed that populations of breeding plants and animals accumulated small changes over time to slowly become quite different from their ancestors. Modern data have uncovered a somewhat richer story. Indeed, some species and groups change slowly, but many others rapidly emerge and/or rapidly undergo extinction. Sometimes, as in the case of the five major earth extinctions, both novelty and demise have emerged hand-in-hand on a noticeably rapid and vast scale. Yet, some very successful approaches to life have remained remarkably stable over time. Sharks (450 million years old) have survived all five major extinctions to become both diverse and specialized; from predation to plankton feeding (Bird and Veríssimo et al. 2018). Conversely, some life forms that appeared within the 40-million-year period of the Cambrian explosion lasted only a scant few million years. The entire process is a rich tapestry of timelines upon timelines, interwoven threads around interwoven threads.

The evolution of life on Earth also embodies phenomena of emergence. Among these are the primary symmetry breaks from chemical to life-like systems of mutually constraining and promoting self-organizing systems[4]

---

4 Terrence Deacon (2012) recently proposed a conceptually simple and novel model of elementary life, a system he has termed *autogenesis*. An *autogen* is capable of minimally differentiated self-maintenance, self-repair, and reproduction. Autogenesis results from two co-dependent and complementary self-organizing processes; drawing on Stuart Kauffman's (2000) groundbreaking work on autocatalytic sets, Deacon proposed that an autocatalytic set where one member of the set not only catalyzes the formation of another but of a polymerizing species that self-assembles, at sufficient concentration, into a container that can capture and partition members of the autocatalytic set away from bulk media, can persist as an inert but poised (virus-like) structure before rupturing and making itself anew. Autogens, like autocatalytic sets, are simple and pre-biotically feasible; unlike autocatalytic sets, autogens are not merely 'self-organizing' but potentially self-sustaining. The logic of the autogen is, more than that of any solely 'self-organizing' system, consistent with the logic of life in that it is a system of matter that can maintain and reproduce itself. (Deacon, T. (2012). *Incomplete Nature: How Mind Emerged from Matter,* W.W. Norton & Co., ISBN 978-0-393-34390-8; Kauffman, S. (2000). *Investigations,* Oxford University Press, ISBN 0-19-512105-8)

and early cells. The list goes on to include emergence of the Eukarya[5], multicellularity, sexual reproduction, sociality, consciousness, and mind. Of these, our models are most robust for the endosymbiotic origin of Eukarya. All approaches to living are highly interdependent, complex, and relational in nature.

The Art of Being Human: Mixed Media

Life is a mosaic of mosaics. All living organisms are simultaneously a web of symbioses and individuals. Now thought of as *holobionts*, individuals are actually enclosed ecosystems that function as entities with relationships among themselves and the many other organisms that occur in unique environs. Human holobionts are both host to, and an assemblage of, a diversity of microbiomes, spread over numerous tissues and organs, that we have only now recognized as important contributors to health. For example, strong evidence has been recently reported that microbial flora in human guts has significant effects on brains and social behaviour (Katerina et al. 2018).

We would be mistaken to view our complete history without reference to our reticulated composition as a one-time flourishing group of human species. Our genus *Homo*, is only some 1.5 to 2.5 million years old, and *Homo sapiens* arose barely 200 ka (thousand years ago). Modern humanity (*Homo sapiens*) is a hybrid of both Neanderthal and Denisovan humans with clear and unique signatures in our genome. 'European' Neanderthal exhibit two major admixtures of *Homo sapiens* expanding from Africa; one 47-65 ka, and another 50-60ka in modern-day Siberia (Ackerman et al. 2016). By 30 ka Neanderthal themselves are believed to have gone extinct. A fourth human species, popularly referred to as Hobbit Man because of their small stature (*Homo floresiensis*), flourished on a few small islands in the Indonesian archipelago until 12 ka; many of those islands supported several species that today exhibit island dwarfism or gigantism. Modern Aboriginal Australian culture is well known to be at least 60 ka. The actual overlap of species distributions and chronologies is certainly underestimated, and more reticulate than we imagine.

Human extinction is hardly unthinkable. Our prejudice, centred in western history, makes well known numerous civilizations lost and replaced by successors around the Mediterranean and on the Near and Far Asian continent. Rarely, however, do we stop to think about whole 'High' civilizations now gone, and never replaced. Within the past year, LiDAR (Light Detection and Ranging – pulsed laser) remote sensing, and partial preliminary physical examination has uncovered close to 62,000 structures under dense lowland jungle cover in Guatemala that are the remnants of a Maya civilization that

5 Cells with membrane bound nuclei and organelles as opposed to Prokarya, represented by modern Eubacteria and Archea.

dates from 600-900 CE. Now vanished, the population is extrapolated to have been some 7 to 11 million inhabitants across 95,000 km^2. That population density works out to approximately 80-120 persons per km^2 and does not account for agricultural or other activities that would have left behind non-detectable structures or signatures (Canuto et al. 2018).

Homo sapiens now find itself in an unprecedented Anthropocene extinction. We are enamoured of our own power and individuality, yet we are blithely unaware of our mosaic constitution and remain stuck in intellectual dualisms and near-fictional hierarchic modes of thinking and behaviour.

Gathering to Meet the Challenge: Potential for a New We

The sixth mass extinction is of our own making. We have rapidly grown, are more and more rapidly growing, and radically restructure the Earth to meet our immediate needs (both real and less real) as we go. The last two millennia of our existence dramatically illustrate that, to paraphrase Nietzsche (1883-91), there is *chaos in us, and we can still give birth to a dancing star...* Concomitant with our capacity to radically reshape our world and gravely upset its balances is an ability to abstract and imagine the less visible but deeply important consequences of our actions, to test the hypotheses that result, and to change course where necessary –of life on Earth, we are alone in our potential for making both chaos and harmony.

We have emphasised the gravity of our present situation by pointing to life's history: mass extinctions can be cascades resulting from the disappearance of only a few highly important (hub-like) relationships among species leading to a chain of loss that propagates rapidly. We are in the midst of another and have only partial knowledge of the relationships that sustain us. It is therefore urgent that we act now to bandage the wounds of progress and become true global citizens – one population of Earth's most powerful and therefore most liable and obligately responsible stewards.

What remains to be seen is whether we can transition sufficiently rapidly from a patchwork of autonomous cultures, polities, concentrated wealth, and far too narrowly interested corporations, to a global society; one that highly values cultural diversity while acting consistently with the urgent idea of humanity's unity within itself and with the world. We well know the nature of power: those who hold it do not relinquish it willingly, and violence begets violence. What can give us hope? What makes possible a collective transition of the kind needed? The history of Life on Earth hints at answers.

From its origins to the present day, the evolution of life on Earth has been highly hysteretic. Although extinction and creation are two mutually dependent realities of biological evolution that perhaps imply reversibility, organismic change over large time-scales is highly irreversible (i.e., path-dependent). Heraclitus was correct in observing that "nothing endures but change." Although the bulk of the Earth's biomass consists of organisms obeying ancient modes of structure and process (bacteria, archaea, and viruses), life's 4 billion-year-old history has witnessed the emergence of organisms and relationships of ever-increasing complexity. Some of life's most world-changing events involve the emergence and stabilisation of new dependencies among previously autonomous agents. Only decades ago, Lynn Margulis (1970) succeeded in convincing the world of our own endosymbiotic origins. We, and every single-celled protist, plant, and animal come from an ancient and intimate symbiosis between non-eukaryotic microbes. The multiple independent emergences of multicellularity and extreme dependence among organisms of the same species (eusociality) are also examples of evolution's irreversibility and the increasing complexity of life.

Biologist Terrence Deacon (2018) has described a logic governing some of life's leaps in complexity as "hierarchic transitions." Hierarchic transitions are the emergence of new living wholes. The occurrence of a chance synergy among separate organisms, where each organism directly supports the persistence of at least another, can lead to a mutual dependence of increasing intensity as each living part is free to degrade in a complementary way. The mutual dependence can become so extreme that formerly free-living organisms lose their autonomy to each other and form higher-ordered beings. Our cultural transition from so many competing neighbours to one-world could be a hierarchic transition in the making. Its emergence is not guaranteed, but our future, one worth hoping for, requires it.

A Human Future: Reading the Tea Leaves

Based on economic and spiritual modes of living we see two possible scenarios that we would explore: economies of scarcity and economies of abundance. Thomas Malthus (1798) described an apocalyptic future world where war, plague, famine, poor health, and economic conditions act in concert to limit the growth of human populations. Post- and Neo- Malthusians more-or-less agree, but argue over the relative contribution of each kind of population check to a 'Malthusian catastrophe' where population growth exceeds available resources. Granted, Malthus (1798) himself, did not believe in population growth overshooting resources but rather wrote that population checks (mentioned above) would prevent human populations from outstripping agricultural growth. Biologists, like ourselves, know the commonness of environments and habitats whose resources restrain population size, and act through natural selection to reduce the reproductive fitness of those individuals unable to utilize them, and accommodate those variants that do. Be it food, nesting sites, breeding grounds, and so on, populations of living organisms cannot and do not surpass (outside of agricultural monocultures) the carrying capacities of environments (Hui 2006). This is neither the place nor time to argue climate change, declining natural resource availability, or pollution and human poverty. These are obvious, and we simply assume them.

Given that Pope Francis is correct in *Laudato Si'* (Pope Francis 2015), our global culture is quickly losing a so-called middle class where scant resources have become increasingly concentrated in the hands of a few and where large numbers of humanity (often displaced as refugees) exist at margins of health and economic parity. The model responsible for said scenario is an economy of scarcity wherein *enough* is quite simply, *never enough*.

One oft-discussed and attractive avenue of escape from conditions of an unpredictable future is found in the current darling of technologists and academics (pro and con), broadly known as transhumanism (TH). Here, technology is combined with living aspects of human organisms to vastly enhance both physical well-being and intellect. TH is based on a grave misunderstanding of life and mind: that both are mere mechanism, not merely analogous to, but of the same kind as our most popularly bewildering and abundant technology – computers and all their varied manifestations. As computer scientist Pedro Domingos has remarked, "People worry that computers will get too smart and take over the world, but the real problem is that they're too stupid and they've already taken over the world." Computers are our tools, and they can assist or hamper us. One would not suggest crutches as 'assistive walking devices' to an able-bodied person. In addition to its faulty intellectual foundations, TH will only ever be available to the wealthy and can only exacerbate the growing divide between have and have-not. TH serves only the material interests of the powerful, and with a collective lust for accumulation and consumption, presently has us in a chokehold that continues to tighten. TH would also very potentially leave a poisoned planet in its wake. For example, Tim Maughan (2015), for the BBC, writes of a toxic waste dump in a dystopian artificial lake in Inner Mongolia known as the Baogang Steel and Rare Earth complex. The facility, and associated city of Baotou has ballooned from a complex of 97, 000 workers in 1950 to over 2.5 million in 2015 and chiefly mines and refines neodymium and cerium; both used in the manufacture of smart electrical products (phones, tablets) and green technology – transhumanist byproducts? The lake itself is formed from a once-river-bed and productive crop land, and with a size of 10 km^2 is easily visible with its multitude of fill-pipes on Google Earth. A preferential option for the poor and vulnerable? (Pope Francis 2015). The irony is painful to escape.

Our brief comments, and this volume honour the life work of Fr. Kurien Kunnumpuram S.J. The good anthropologist penned in 2006, "Christian spirituality is a spirituality of hope … Now to hope is to look forward to the new, to what is not yet there, and strive to bring it about. Hence hope is forward-looking and forward moving. That is why a spirituality of hope is a spirituality of change … Those who refuse to change regard the past or the present as the final state of humankind. We are not yet in the new heavens and the new earth. We are on our way to them. And so our spirituality is a spirituality of hope and change."

We too advocate hope. Kunnumpuram has spent his life engaging the many layers of Indian culture in all of its current and ancient expressions from the kind forest peoples, to adherents of mainstream Hinduism and Christianity. Even among the mainstream, and most certainly among the indigenous, there are mosaics within mosaics; a droplet of the ocean, and an ocean within a droplet. Finally, and hardly clairvoyant, we can only point to a richly woven planetary past and quote Alfred North Whitehead (1964): "The misconception which has haunted philosophic literature throughout the centuries is the notion of 'independent existence.' There is no such mode of existence; every entity is to be understood in terms of the way it is interwoven with the rest of the universe."

In actuality, we live in an economy of abundance. This planet and its vast unexplored wealth grace humanity with the tools and the spiritual call to recognize, and embrace, the transcendent within the immanent; the I in the thou. Indeed, we reach for the stars – only to find that the stars are within us.

References

A Q&A with Pedro Domingos: Author of 'The Master Algorithm.' Langston, J. (2015) *University of Washington News,* https://www.washington.edu/news/2015/09/17/a-q-a-with-pedro-domingos-author-of-the-master-algorithm (accessed 29 September 2018).

Ackermann, R.R., et al. (2016) The hybrid origin of "modern" humans. *Evolutionary* Biology, 43 (1): 1-11.

Bird, C.S., and Veríssimo, A., et al. (2018) A global perspective on the trophic geography of sharks. *Nature Ecology & Evolution, 2 (2): 299–305.*

Canuto, M.A., et al. (2018) Ancient lowland Maya complexity as revealed by airborne laser scanning of northern Guatemala. *Science 361 (6409): 1355.*

Coale, A.J. (1972). *The Growth and Structure of Human Populations*. Princeton University Press, pp. 18–19.

Deacon, T. (2018) The Process Underlying Hierarchic Transitions in Evolution. *Manuscript in preparation.*

Encyclical Letter Laudato Si' of The Holy Father Francis On Care For Our Common Home (official English-language text of encyclical). 18 June 2015.

Hui, C. (2006) Carrying Capacity, Population Equilibrium, and Environment's Maximal Load. *Ecological Modelling, 192 (1-2): 317–320.*

Katerina, V., and Johnson, A., et al. (2018) Why Does the Microbiome Affect Behaviour? *Nature Reviews Microbiology 16 (10): 647-655.*

Kauffman, S. (2000). *Investigations,* Oxford University Press, ISBN 0-19-512105-8

Kunnumpuram, K. (ed) (2006). *Life in Abundance: Indian Christian Reflections on Spirituality.* Mumbai: St. Paul's.

Malthus, T.R. (1798/1999). *An Essay on the Principle of Population,* Bristol: Routledge/ Thoemmes Press.

Margulis, L. (1970). *Origin of Eukaryotic Cells,* Yale University Press, ISBN 0-300-013531

Maughan, T. (2015) The dystopian lake filled by the world's tech lust. *BBC,* http://www.bbc.com/future/story/20150402-the-worst-place-on-earth? (accessed 28 September 2018).

Nietzsche, F. (1883-91/*2010.. Thus Spoke Zarathustra.* Edinburgh: Edinburgh University Press.

Peters, N.C., and Berg, C.A. (2017) In Vitro Culturing and Live Imaging of Drosophila Egg Chambers: A History and Adaptable Method. *Oogenesis: Methods and Protocols, Methods in Molecular Biology 1457: 35-68.*

Plank, L.D., and Harvey, J.D. (1979) Generation time statistics of Escherichia coli B measured by synchronous culture techniques. *J Gen Microbiol. 115 (1): 69-77.*

Whitehead, A.N. (1964). *Science and Philosophy,* Adams & Co.

Wikipedia contributors, "Homo," *Wikipedia, The Free Encyclopedia,* https://en.wikipedia.org/wiki/Homo (accessed 25 September 2018).

12

Inter mirifica heute: Eine Relecture im digitalen Zeitalter

Christian Bauer
Professor, Practical Theology, University of Innsbruck, Austria

Abstract: *In the context of the modern social media, the author wishes to understand the Vatican II document, Inter mirifica, which deals with the Church's teaching on social communication. Basing himself on Gaudium et spes, the authors seeks a "reinforcement of our presence in the world". This does not necessarily demand a conversion motive, but solidarity and openness to our "fellow pilgrims," since "We share the same life-journey." This article is dedicated to the author"s friend Professor Kurien Kunnumpuram, the Indian pioneer of Second Vatican Council .*

Keywords: *Inter mirifica, Gaudium et spes, social communication, social media, fellow pilgrims.*

Nicht selten kommt das Neue weniger aus dem Zentrum eines Diskurses, als vielmehr von dessen Peripherie. Ähnliches könnte mit Blick auf eine neue Phase der Konzilsrezeption auch mit dem Zweiten Vatikanum und seinem wohl marginalsten Dokument[1] *Inter mirifica* geschehen. Ausgerechnet dieses kleine, teilweise auch zu Recht vergessene Randdokument des Konzils bietet die Chance für ein kraftvolles *Aggiornamento* von dessen heutiger weltkirchlicher Gesamtrezeption. Denn es ist, bei allen Schwächen des Textes,

1 Diese marginale Position zeigt sich bereits in dem Umstand, dass sich das IM zugrundeliegende vorkonziliare Schema im Band der ersten gedruckten Textentwürfe, die im August 1962 an die Konzilsväter erschickt wurden, an vorletzter Stelle befand.

eine passagenweise sogar erstaunlich aktuelle kirchliche Ressource für den Umgang mit dem, was in den 1960er Jahren noch nicht am Horizont stand und die Welt von heute dennoch massiv bestimmt: dem Internet. Vielleicht kann *Inter mirifica* sogar erst im digitalen Zeitalter sein volles pastorales Potenzial entfalten. Dazu braucht es allerdings eine Hermeneutik des Neuen[2], welche die Lehren des Konzils als komplexe Textkonstellationen betrachtet, deren pastoral orientierte dogmatische Gesamtaussagen vom jeweils Diskontinuierlichen her zu interpretieren sind. Dabei ist nicht das Neue auf das Alte hin auszulegen, sondern vielmehr das Alte auf das Neue hin: weitergehende Aussagen bilden den Interpretationsrahmen für weniger weitgehende. Das gilt auch für *Inter mirifica*. Daher nun:

1. Ansatzpunkt einer gegenwartsbezogenen Textauslegung im Horizont der Pastoralkonstitution *Gaudium et spes*

Das Internet macht nicht nur gegenwärtige Zeitsignaturen sichtbar und zugänglich, seine allgegenwärtige Präsenz ist auch selbst eines der machtvollsten Zeichen unserer Zeit. Das Konzilsdekret über die sozialen Kommunikationsmittel ist heute mit Blick auf dieses global wirksame ‚Megazeichen' auszulegen. *Inter mirifica* ist in diesem Zusammenhang von *Gaudium et spes* her und darauf hin zu lesen. Dabei ist zu beachten, dass die jeweiligen Zeichen einer Zeit niemals einfach nur einwertig positiv oder negativ erscheinen, sondern immer in ihrer ganzen mehrwertigen Ambivalenz. Wenn *Inter mirifica* in einer konzilstypischen Integration von Altem in Neues von der Alternative "Segen oder Fluch" (IM 11) spricht, dann ist es sich dieser konstitutiven Ambivalenz bewusst:

> "Die Kirche weiß sehr wohl [so IM 1], dass diese Instrumente bei rechtem Gebrauch den Menschen eine wirkliche Hilfe bieten, denn sie dienen zur Erholung und Ertüchtigung des Geistes und somit auch der Ausweitung und Stärkung des Reiches Gottes. Zugleich weiß sie aber auch, dass die Menschen diese technischen Erfindungen gegen Gottes Schöpfungsplan und zu ihrem eigenen Schaden missbrauchen können." (IM 1).

Diese ambivalenzfähige Gesamteinschätzung erhält im Vorwort von *Inter mirifica* ein positives Vorzeihen. Dabei fallen zunächst einmal die beiden programmatischen Titelworte ins Auge: "Inter mirifica technicae artis inventa…[unter den erstaunlichen bzw. bewundernswerten Erfindungen der Technik…]" (IM 1). Wie später *Gaudium et spes*, so setzt auch *Inter mirifica* sein Thema, die sozialen Kommunikationsmittel, zunächst einmal positiv an – und damit auf Höhe jener Pastoralkonstitution, die nicht defizitorientiert mit "Trauer und Angst" (GS 1) der eigenen Gegenwart beginnt, sondern

2 Vgl. Bauer, Christian: Optionen des Konzils. Umrisse einer konstellativen Hermeneutik des Zweiten Vatikanums, in: Zeitschrift für katholische Theologie 134 (2012), 141-162.

vielmehr ressourcenorientiert mit deren "Freude und Hoffnung" (GS 1)[3]. Dieses höchstlehramtliche Verbot des Kulturpessimismus verpflichtet auch jede heutige Interpretation von *Inter mirifica* auf einen positiven, gleichwohl nicht unkritischen Gegenwartsbezug. Dogmatisch eingebettet ist dieser wohlwollende Erstzugang in einen schöpfungstheologischen Gesamtrahmen, in dem von der Technik gesagt wird, die "menschliche Geisteskraft" (IM 1) habe ihre erstaunlichen Wunder "mit Gottes Hilfe aus der Schöpfung hervorgebracht" (IM 1). *Inter mirifica* bewegt sich hier auf einer schöpfungstheologischen Diskursspur, die bereits M.-Dominique Chenu mit seiner Theologie der Arbeit gelegt hatte, die den Menschen als *co-creator bzw. co-creatrix* Gottes begreift. Dieser thomasgeprägte Grundansatz wird im Vorwort von *Inter mirifica* in weltpastoraler Entgrenzung universal heilsfinalisiert, wenn es heißt, das gesamte Dokument solle "nicht nur auf das Heil der Gläubigen, sondern dem Fortschritt der ganzen menschlichen Gesellschaft dienen" (IM 1).[4] Denn, so *Inter mirifica* später: "Die Wirksamkeit der sozialen Kommunikationsmittel [...] macht die Einzelnen zu Bürgern der ganzen Menschheit [...]." (IM 22). Damit komme ich zu meinem zweiten Punkt:

2. Digitalisierung als markantes Zeichen unserer Zeit, das *Inter mirifica* eine überraschende Aktualität verleiht

Angesichts der "normativen Kraft des Kontrafaktischen"[5], die in der Welt von heute zu einer zunehmenden Tribalisierung von Kirche und Gesellschaft in Filterblasen und Echokammern führt, kann *Inter mirifica* in diesem Zusammenhang vielleicht eine ganz neue, prophetisch-kritische Rolle zuwachsen. Denn es gilt, die heutige digitale Kultur mit "echt humanem und christlichem Geist zu beseelen, um so den großen Erwartungen der Menschheit und dem Plane Gottes voll zu entsprechen" (IM 3). Nicht nur mit Blick auf Kinder und Jugendliche ist dabei unter anderem mit der "Eindruckskraft" (IM 4) auch des Internets zu rechnen, die "so groß sein kann, dass es den Menschen, insbesondere den unerfahrenen, schwerfällt, sie [...] geistig zu verarbeiten und

3 Diese ersten Worte der Pastoralkonstitution waren in einen früheren Textentwurf zunächst überkreuz gestanden: Freude und Trauer, Hoffnung und Angst. In einem bewussten lehrmäßigen Akt entschied man sich, die beiden positiv besetzten Gefühlslagen („Freude und Hoffnung") an den Anfang zu stellen – ohne die beiden negativ besetzen („Trauer und Angst") zu verschweigen. Man setzt also ‚ressourcenorientiert' bei den Stärken der eigenen Zeitgenossen an und nicht ‚defizitorientiert' bei deren Schwächen (vgl. Sander: Die pastorale Grammatik der Lehre, 197ff).

4 Diese ersten Passagen von *Inter mirifica* entsprechen dem im universalen Heilswillen Gottes verwurzelten pastoralen Grundansatz des Konzils, wie er auch im *Geistlichen Testament* von Papst Johannes XXIII. zum Ausdruck kam: „Mehr denn je [...] sind wir heute darauf ausgerichtet, dem Menschen als solchem zu dienen, nicht mehr bloß den Katholiken." (zit. nach Kaufmann/Klein: Johannes XXIII, 24).

5 Vgl. Hölzl: Die normative Kraft des Kontrafaktischen.

sich ihrer gegebenenfalls zu erwehren" (IM 4). In Zeiten von *fake news* und *hate speech* gilt es zudem darauf zu achten, dass die jeweilige "Mitteilung inhaltlich stets der Wahrheit entspricht" (IM 5) und "ethische Grundsätze sowie die Rechte und Würde des Menschen beachtet werden" (IM 5). Denn auch das Internet kann "leicht niedrige Instinkte wecken" (IM 7). Gerade angesichts des weltweiten Aufstiegs autoritärer Populismen ist auch heute die Freiheit der Medien "zu verteidigen und zu schützen" (IM 12) und "Rücksicht auf das Gemeinwohl" (IM 12) einzufordern.

Hier wirkt sich eine häufig und mit Recht kritisierte Schwäche des Textes, sein zeitkritischer Kulturpessimismus, gegenwartstheologisch positiv aus. Die prophetische Kraft dieser Negativaussagen von *Inter mirifica* wäre heute allerdings durch andere kirchlichen Lehraussagen zu balancieren, die den sozialen Medien auf der Höhe von *Gaudium et spes* in positiver Weise begegnen: "Say yes before no"[6] – auf diesen Nenner brachte das der irische Kurienbischof Paul Tighe, der als zuständiger Sekretär des Päpstlichen Rates für die sozialen Kommunikationsmittel eine entsprechende kirchliche Netzpolitik konzipierte und dabei auch eine bemerkenswerte Öffnung des Vatikans zu den neuen sozialen Medien vorantrieb.

Zurück zur Digitalisierung als einem markanten Zeichen der Zeit. Mit Blick auf die heute allgegenwärtige Herrschaft der Algorithmen hat Adam Greenfield vor kurzem in seinem vielbeachteten Buch *Radical technologies* (Untertitel: *The Design of Everyday Life*) von einer "Kolonisierung des alltäglichen Lebens"[7] gesprochen – und somit die Habermasche These von der "Kolonialisierung der Lebenswelt"[8] durch "systemische Mechanismen"[9] für den gegenwärtigen Strukturwandel der globalen Öffentlichkeit aktualisiert. Auch deren Mechanismen lassen sich zweiwertig nutzten: einerseits zur Kolonisierung der Lebenswelt, andererseits aber auch zum "Widerstand"[10] dagegen. Das Internet erscheint heute vielen wie eine kolonisatorische Macht – und doch ist es auch zugleich der Ort einer subversiven Umkehrung der herrschenden Verhältnisse: "Wo Macht ist, findet sich auch Widerstand."[11] Michel de Certeau stellte den gesellschaftlichen "Machtdispositiven"[12] entsprechende lebensweltliche Mikropraktiken des Widerstands gegenüber,

6 Paul Tighe am 14. September 2017 auf einem pastoraltheologischen Kongress in Augsburg-Leitershofen.

7 The Guardian, zit. nach Greenfield: Radical technologies, Klappentext.

8 Habermas: Theorie des kommunikativen Handelns [Band 1], 522.

9 Habermas: Theorie des kommunikativen Handelns [Band 1], 293.

10 Vgl. Habermas: Theorie des kommunikativen Handelns [Bd. 1], 579.

11 Vgl. Foucault: Dispositive der Macht, 211.

12 Foucault: Dispositive der Macht.

die systemische Mechanismen in den Freiheitspraktiken einer alternativen "Mikrophysik der Macht"[13] selbstbestimmt unterlaufen und umwenden:

> "Die wirkliche Ordnung der Dinge besteht in [...] 'populären' Taktiken, die diese Ordnung zu ihren eigenen Zwecken umwenden, ohne sich der Illusionen hinzugeben, dass sich in Kürze etwas ändern wird. [...] Folgen wir der Zunahme jener Handlungsweisen, die sich [...] in wuchernder Gesetzeswidrigkeit [...] entwickelt haben und in die Netze der Überwachung eingesickert sind. [...] Ich möchte einige dieser multiformen, widerborstigen, listenreichen und hartnäckigen Praktiken folgen, die der Disziplin entkommen ohne ihren Einflussbereich zu verlassen [...]."[14]

3. 'Komplizenschaft' mit Akteurinnen und Akteuren digitaler Widerstandspraktiken als pastorale Mission der Kirche

Bereits in seinem 1983 publizierten Essay über den "Alltag der Kommunikation"[15] sprach Michel de Certeau von "Netzen, in denen man sich um eine miteinander geteilte Leidenschaft oder Überzeugung versammelt"[16] und die zugleich einer entsprechenden "Zirkulation von Waren, Personen, Informationen, Bildern und Tönen"[17] dienen. Damit dieser "magische Enzyklopädismus, der ohne Zugangsprobleme jederzeit verfügbar ist"[18] auch wirklich allen offen steht, braucht es eine umfassende "Demokratisierung der Technik,"[19] die auch subalternen Personen jene *prise de parole* ermöglicht, von der Certeau mit Blick auf die "Ergreifung des Wortes"[20] im Jahr 1968 sprach. Gerade mit Blick auf das Internet wird dabei Certeaus mikropolitische Unterscheidung von Strategien und Taktiken neu relevant – angesichts der Strategien von Internetkonzernen wie Google, Facebook oder Amazon und der Taktiken, mit denen abertausende Nutzerinnen und Nutzer deren Macht unterlaufen:

---

13 Certeau: Arts de faire, XXXIX.

14 Certeau: Arts de faire, 46; 145f.

15 Vgl. Certeau: L'ordinaire de la communication.

16 Certeau: L'ordinaire de la communication, 5. Das Internet lässt sich in diesem Zusammenhang analog zu der Weise verstehen, in der Certeau damals das "Abenteuer der freien Radios" (ebd., 7) deutete: als ein zumindest potenziell "für alle" (ebd.) offenes mediales "Werkzeug für den Ausdruck des lokalen sozialen Lebens" (ebd.). Und wie das Fernsehen zur Zeit Certeaus eröffnet es heute im eigenen Mobiltelefon die ganze Welt eine "Landschaft im Innenraum der eigenen Wohnung" (ebd. 14).

17 Certeau: L'ordinaire de la communication, 5.

18 Certeau: L'ordinaire de la communication, 14.

19 Certeau: L'ordinaire de la communication, 22

20 Certeau: La prise de parole, 27.

> "Als Strategie bezeichne ich ein Kalkül von Beziehungen der Kräfte untereinander […], das einen Ort voraussetzt, der […] als Basis für die Organisation seiner Beziehungen zu einer bestimmten Außenwelt […] dient. […] Von einer Taktik spreche ich hingegen, wenn ein Kalkül vorliegt, das nicht mit etwas Eigenem rechnen kann […]. Sie hat nur den Ort des Anderen. Sie dringt teilweise in ihn ein, ohne ihn jedoch voll erfassen zu können […]."[21]

Dass in diesem Zusammenhang auch die immer noch gängige Unterscheidung von Digitalem und Analogem aufgehoben wird, zeigt Judith Butler in ihren vor kurzem publizierten *Anmerkungen zu einer performativen Theorie der Versammlung*. Darin betont sie, dass eine entsprechende "Politik der Straße"[22] auf der Performativität von "verkörperten Handlungen"[23] beruhe, da nicht nur sprachliche, sondern auch "körperliche Handlungen"[24] performativ sein können: "Körper versammeln sich […] und […] erheben Anspruch auf einen bestimmten Raum als öffentlichen Raum."[25] Diese "Körperallianzen"[26] verbinden das, was der Internettheoretiker Manuel Castells[27] den *space of places* und den *space of flows* nennt und weisen dank ihrer medialen Vermittlung über den jeweiligen Ort des Geschehens hinaus.

> "Wird die Szene übertragen, ist sie sowohl dort als auch hier […]. Ihre Lokalität wird dadurch, dass sie über sich selbst hinaus kommuniziert […], nicht in Abrede gestellt; sie hängt vielmehr von dieser Vermittlung ab, um als das Ereignis stattfinden zu können, das sie ist. […] Etwas Ortsgebundenes bleibt […], das nicht auf diese Weise verbreitet werden kann […]; […] die Szene wäre nicht dieselbe, wenn wir nicht verstehen würden, dass hier Menschen in Gefahr sind und dass es genau die Körper auf der Straße sind, die das Risiko tragen […], Auge in Auge mit denen, denen sie entgegentreten, ungeschützt, verwundbar […], beharrlich, wenn nicht aufständisch."[28]

Menschliche Körper und technische Dinge werden dabei im Sinne Bruno Latours zu gleichberechtigten "Akteuren"[29] eines einzigen großen Netzwerks:

---

21 Certeau: Arts de faire, XLVI.

22 Butler: Anmerkungen zu einer performativen Theorie der Versammlung, 91. Siehe auch Castells: Networks of Outrage and Hope.

23 Butler: Anmerkungen zu einer performativen Theorie der Versammlung, 15.

24 Butler: Anmerkungen zu einer performativen Theorie der Versammlung, 43.

25 Butler: Anmerkungen zu einer performativen Theorie der Versammlung, 15f; 96.

26 Butler: Anmerkungen zu einer performativen Theorie der Versammlung, 91.

27 Vgl. Castells: The Rise of the Network Society, 453-459. Dazu später auch Ders.: Grassrooting the space of flows.

28 Butler: Anmerkungen zu einer performativen Theorie der Versammlung, 124f.

29 Vgl. Latour: Eine neue Soziologie für eine neue Gesellschaft.

> "Es ist von Bedeutung, dass diese Körper Handys dabei haben, mit denen sie Nachrichten und Bilder versenden. [...] Lässt sich das Handeln des Körpers von der Technologie trennen […]? […] Was Körper tun, wenn sie demonstrieren, hängt fundamental damit zusammen, was Kommunikationsgeräte […] tun […]. […] Die Medien brauchen die Körper auf der Straße, […] ebenso wie die Körper die Medien brauchen […]."[30]

Technik und Körper, Digitales und Analoges, *space of flows* und *space of places* bilden komplexe Erfahrungseinheiten, die in unseren heutigen Gesellschaften entsprechende "Mikroresistenzen"[31] bedingen und ermöglichen. Dem Medienwissenschaftler Felix Stalder zufolge stellen diese vor die Entscheidung, ob wir in einer "postdemokratischen Welt der Überwachung und der Wissensmonopole" [32] oder in einer "Kultur der Commons und der Partizipation"[33] leben wollen:

> "Die Kultur der Digitalität hat […] zwei […] politische Entwicklungsrichtungen hervorgebracht. Diejenige hin zur ‚Postdemokratie' schafft eine im Kern autoritäre Gesellschaft, in der […] Menschen […] kaum mehr Einfluss auf die [...] Strukturen […] ausüben können. […] Dem gegenüber führt die Entwicklungsrichtung hin zu den Commons zu einer Erneuerung der Demokratie [...]. Im Zentrum steht eine neue Verbindung ökonomischer, sozialer und […] ökologischer Dimensionen des Alltags auf der Basis datenintensiver Beteiligungsverfahren."[34]

Es entspräche der pastoralen Mission der Kirche nach *Gaudium et spes*, diese mikropolitischen Alternativen zum realexistierenden Kapitalismus in solidarischer "Komplizenschaft"[35] mit allen Mitteln zu unterstützen. Das Schlusswort soll darum der bereits genannte Kurienbischof Teigh haben. Als dieser 2017 auf dem WebSummit in Lissabon sprach, erntete er hinterher

---

30 Butler: Anmerkungen zu einer performativen Theorie der Versammlung, 125ff.

31 Giard: Histoire d'une recherche, I-XX, XIII.

32 Stalder: Kultur der Digitalität, Klappentext. Stalder bezieht sich auf Jacques Rancières Begriff der Postdemokratie „Rancière argumentierte, dass die unmittelbare Präsenz des Volkes (Demos) abgeschafft und an dessen Stelle Prozesse der Simulation und Modellierung getreten seien, etwa Meinungsumfragen, Fokusgruppen und Szenario-Planung, angeleitet von Technokraten. Der Charakter der politischen Prozesse hätte sich verändert: vom Streit darüber, wie man einer prinzipiell offenen Zukunft begegnen wolle, hin zur Verwaltung vordefinierter Notwendigkeiten und alternativloser Konstellationen. […] Aus Demokratie […] wird Governence." (Stalder: Kultur der Digitalität, 206; 208).

33 Stalder: Kultur der Digitalität, Klappentext.

34 Stalder: Kultur der Digitalität, 279f.

35 Vgl. Ziemer: Komplizenschaft.

wohlmeinende Kommentare wie: “Gut, dass Du an die Peripherien gehst”[36]. Seine Antwort: “Nein, ich gehe ins Zentrum” – nur eben nicht der Kirche, sondern der digitalen Welt. Genau darum geht es auch bei einer Aktualisierung von *Inter mirifica* im Horizont von *Gaudium et spes*: um ein “reinforcement of our presence in the world”[37], oder besser noch um “presence, not new evangelization”[38]. Dabei darf es keine missionarischen Hintergedanken geben, vielmehr braucht es die solidarische Offenheit von “fellow pilgrims:”[39] “We share the same life-journey.”[40]

Literaturnachweise

Bauer, Christian: Optionen des Konzils. Umrisse einer konstellativen Hermeneutik des Zweiten Vatikanums, in: Zeitschrift für katholische Theologie 134 (2012), 141-162.

Butler, Judith: Anmerkungen zu einer performativen Theorie der Versammlung, Berlin 2017.

Castells, Manuel: Grassrooting the space of flows, in: Urban Geography 20 (1999), 294-302.

Castells, Manuel: The Rise of the Network Society. The Information Age: Economy, Society, and Culture (Vol. 1), Oxford ²2009 [Erstausgabe 1996].

Castells, Manuel: Networks of Outrage and Hope. Social Movements in the Internet Age, Cambridge 2012.

Certeau, Michel de: Arts de faire. L’invention du quotidien (Bd. 1), Paris 1980.

Certeau, Michel de: La prise de parole. Pour une nouvelle culture, Paris 1968.

Certeau, Michel de: L’ordinaire de la communication, Paris 1983.

Foucault, Michel: Dispositive der Macht. Über Sexualität, Wissen und Wahrheit, Berlin 1978.

Giard, Luce: Histoire d’une recherche, in: Certeau, Michel de: Arts de faire. L’invention du quotidien I, Paris 1990, I-XX, XIII.

Greenfield, Adam: Radical technologies. The Design of Everyday Life, New York 2017.

Habermas, Jürgen: Theorie des kommunikativen Handelns. Handlungsrationalität und gesellschaftliche Rationalisierung [Band 1], Frankfurt/M. 1995.

Hölzl, Michael: Die normative Kraft des Kontrafaktischen. Populistische Positionen zwischen Ideal und Lüge, in: Lesch, Walter (Hg.): Christentum und Populismus: Klare Fronten?, Freiburg 2017, 187-198.

Kaufmann, Ludwig/Klein, Nikolaus: Johannes XXIII. Prophetie im Vermächtnis, Fribourg 1990.

Latour, Bruno: Eine neue Soziologie für eine neue Gesellschaft, Berlin 2010.

Sander, Hans-Joachim: Die pastorale Grammatik der Lehre – ein Wille zur Macht von Gottes Heil im Zeichen der Zeit, in: Wassilowsky, Günter (Hg.): Zweites Vatikanum – vergessene Anstöße, gegenwärtige Fortschreibungen. QD 207, Freiburg/Br. 2004, 185-206.

Stalder, Felix: Kultur der Digitalität, Berlin ³2017.

Ziemer, Gesa: Komplizenschaft. Neue Perspektiven auf Kollektivität, Bielefeld 2013.

---

36 Paul Tighe, 14. September 2017 in Augsburg-Leitershofen.

37 Paul Tighe, 14. September 2017 in Augsburg-Leitershofen.

38 Paul Tighe, 14. September 2017 in Augsburg-Leitershofen.

39 Paul Tighe, 14. September 2017 in Augsburg-Leitershofen.

40 Paul Tighe, 14. September 2017 in Augsburg-Leitershofen.

13

Das zweite Vatikanum und die Kirche in Indien: Blitzlichter auf den Dialog mit Hindus und Buddhisten im Lichte von Nostra Aetate

Andreas Vonach
University of Innsbruck / Austria

Abstract: *Undoubtedly, Prof Kurien Kunnumpuram SJ has been the pioneer of the message and vision of Vatican II in India. This article looks at the Church in India and dialogue with Hinduism and Buddhism, especially in the light of Nostra Aetate. The author hopes that the spirit of dialogue of the Council will be carried forward in the Indian Church, inspite of resistance and opposition. Encountering religions and traditions and learning from them has been the key point of Vatican Council. The World Church has a lot to learn from the Indian Church in this regard.*

Keywords: *Buddhism, Hinduism, Encounter with religions, Nostra Aetate, Second Vatican Council.*

In Europa, aber auch in weiten anderen Teilen der Welt, ruht das Hauptaugenmerk bezüglich der Erklärung *Nostra Aetate* (in der Folge: NA) des zweiten vatikanischen Konzils ganz eindeutig auf deren vierten Artikel, der das Verhältnis der Kirche zum Judentum thematisiert. Diese Fokussierung erfolgt durchaus mit einem gewissen Recht, war es doch das Anliegen Papst Johannes XXIII. im Rahmen des von ihm einberufenen Konzils eine eigene "Judenerklärung" zu veröffentlichen, in der er eine Neubesinnung auf die besondere Beziehung legen wollte, die die Kirche mit dem ersterwählten Volk

Gottes verbindet.[1] Dass es zu einem solchen Dokument letztendlich nicht gekommen ist, hat vielfältige kircheninterne wie in der Außen- und Weltpolitik begründete Ursachen.[2] Stattdessen ist der Artikel 4 von NA übriggeblieben. Diese Verankerung in der Erklärung der Kirche zu den "nichtchristlichen Religionen" trägt nicht einmal der Tatsache Rechnung, dass der Papst die "Judenfrage" bereits im Jahr 1960 aus tiefen theologischen Erwägungen dem Ökumenereferat einverleibt hat. Nichtsdestotrotz hat der mit Abstand umfangreichste und auch strukturell den Höhepunkt markierende Artikel 4 im Endeffekt dem gesamten Dokument zu weltweiter Beachtung und zu herausragender Bekanntheit verholfen.

Der Aufbau der Erklärung folgt gleichsam dem Schema "vom Allgemeinen zum Besonderen", selbstverständlich aus dem damaligen innerkirchlichen Blickwinkel, wobei die Artikel 1 und 5 eine Art globalen Rahmen bilden.

Der erste Artikel setzt mit der Feststellung ein, dass die Welt globaler wird und damit interkulturelle, interethnische und interreligiöse Begegnungen vermehrt einhergehen. Daraus wird die Notwendigkeit und der Wille der Kirche abgeleitet, ihr Verhältnis zu den nichtchristlichen Religionen neu zu bestimmen und soweit möglich auch in Dialog mit ihnen zu treten. Dabei bekennt sich das Konzil dazu, das Verbindende vor das Trennende stellen zu wollen und formuliert die folgenden alle Religionen (und Menschen) einenden existentiellen Grundfragen: "Was ist der Mensch? Was ist Sinn und Ziel unseres Lebens? Was ist das Gute, was die Sünde? Woher kommt das Leid, und welchen Sinn hat es? Was ist der Weg zum wahren Glück? Was ist der Tod, das Gericht und die Vergeltung nach dem Tode? Und schließlich: Was ist das letzte und unsagbare Geheimnis unserer Existenz, aus dem wir kommen und wohin wir gehen?"[3]

Artikel 2 fokussiert sodann auf die religiösen Gefühle oder Urinstinkte, die die Menschheit seit dem Beginn ihrer Existenz auszeichnet und geht von verschiedenen Wegen aus, die zur Anerkennung einer verborgenen Macht führen. Hinduismus und Buddhismus werden in diesem Zusammenhang als einzige Vertreter solcher nicht der abrahamitischen Tradition verpflichteten Religionen dezidiert angesprochen und vorsichtig gewürdigt. Gleichzeitig wird kein Hehl daraus gemacht, dass man sich grundsätzlich mit derartigen Ansätzen eher schwer tut. Darauf wird in der Folge noch ausführlicher einzugehen sein.

---

1 Siehe dazu Oesterreicher, *Kommentierende Einleitung*, 406-414.

2 Vgl. ebd., 414-470.

3 Als Textgrundlage dient die lateinische Fassung, die in den *Acta Apostolicae Sedis* 58 von 1966 publiziert wurde, deren deutsche Übersetzung im selben Jahr in *Verlautbarungen des Apostolischen Stuhls*; in diesem Beitrag jeweils zitiert nach LThK. ZweitesVatikanum II. Freiburg [2]1967, 488-495.

Im dritten Artikel werden die Muslime “mit Hochachtung betrachtet”[4], deren Glaube an den einzigen Gott hervorgehoben und andere inhaltliche Anknüpfungspunkte aufgezeigt. Gleichzeitig ermahnt das Konzil die Christen gerade in diesem Zusammenhang insbesondere dazu, das Gemeinsame mit den Muslimen zu sehen und zu fördern sowie Zwistigkeiten und Feindschaften, die im Laufe der Geschichte entstanden sind, hintanzustellen und nach Möglichkeit zu überwinden suchen.

Damit steuert das Dokument auch gleichsam seinem Höhepunkt, nämlich Artikel 4, zu. Dieser ist wie gesagt der mit Abstand umfangreichste Teil der Erklärung und behandelt die Beziehungen der Kirche mit dem jüdischen Volk. Dabei gedenkt man zunächst “des Bandes, wodurch das Volk des Neuen Bundes mit dem Stamme Abrahams geistlich verbunden ist”[5], um sodann von den Ursprüngen bis in die Gegenwart die gemeinsamen Wurzeln und das gemeinsame geistliche Erbe sowie die Verbundenheit in der Heilsgeschichte herauszustellen. Ein Plädoyer gegen jegliche Formen des Antijudaismus rundet diesen Abschnitt ab, ohne jedoch das eigene diesbezügliche Versagen in der Vergangenheit direkt einzugestehen.

Nostra Aetate mündet mit dem 5. Artikel schließlich in einem neuerlichen Bekenntnis zur Gottebenbildlichkeit und damit gleichen Würde aller Menschen und ruft die Christgläubigen dazu auf, sich um ein friedvolles Zusammenleben aller zu bemühen.

Fr. Kurien Kunnumpuram sj, dessen Andenken ich diesen Beitrag gerne widme, hat sich Zeit seines Lebens für eine lebendige und sichtbare Umsetzung des Zweiten Vatikanischen Konzils im Allgemeinen und der Erklärung Nostra Aetate im Besonderen eingesetzt und engagiert. Sein Augenmerk galt dabei besonders der Rolle der Kirche in Indien sowie einer organischen Entfaltung derselben innerhalb einer Minderheitensituation angesichts einer zunehmend fundamentalistischer und nationalistischer werdenden hinduistischen Mehrheit. Wie sich das zweite Vaticanum dem Hinduismus gegenüber positioniert, soll im Folgenden anhand einer näheren Auseinandersetzung mit dem Artikel 2 von NA in den Fokus der Überlegungen gerückt werden. Dabei muss zunächst nochmals in Erinnerung gerufen werden, dass dieser Artikel sich grundsätzlich mit den nicht ausdrücklich monotheistischen Religionen beschäftigt und in diesem Zusammenhang Hinduismus und Buddhismus als einzige solcher Bewegungen explizit beim Namen nennt. Damit gelangt der indische Subkontinent automatisch in ein gewisses Zentrum, wenngleich natürlich der Buddhismus zwar aus dem Hinduismus heraus entstanden, in der Folge dann aber selbst zum Opfer hinduistischer Unterdrückung und Vertreibung aus dem indischen Kerngebiet geworden ist.

4 LThK, 2. Vat. II, 491.

5 Ebd.

Die Einleitung von Artikel 2 im Wortlaut: *Von den ältesten Zeiten bis zu unseren Tagen findet sich bei den verschiedenen Völkern eine gewisse Wahrnehmung jener verborgenen Macht, die dem Lauf der Welt und den Ereignissen des menschlichen Lebens gegenwärtig ist, und nicht selten findet sich auch die Anerkenntnis einer höchsten Gottheit oder sogar eines Vaters.*[6]

Die Kirche erkennt hier mit bis dahin völlig unbekannter Klarheit in "eindeutigen Worten die religiöse Erfahrung der verschiedenen Völker [...] als authentisch an"[7]. Freilich tut man dies im Endeffekt nicht wirklich ganz unterschiedslos, wenn doch jene "Wahrnehmungen einer verborgenen Macht" extra hervorgehoben werden, die "eine höchste Gottheit oder sogar einen Vater" kennen. Dass man sich mit diesen im konkreten Dialog aufgrund des Vorhandenseins eines klaren und zentralen gemeinsamen Anknüpfungspunktes natürlich wesentlich leichter tut, liegt jedoch auch auf der Hand.

Der Konzilstext nimmt sodann nochmals auf alle Völker Bezug und führt weiter aus: *Diese Wahrnehmung und Anerkenntnis durchtränkt ihr Leben mit einem tiefen religiösen Sinn. Im Zusammenhang mit dem Fortschreiten der Kultur suchen die Religionen mit genaueren Begriffen und in einer mehr durchgebildeten Sprache Antwort auf die gleichen Fragen.*[8]

Jegliche Artikulationen der Wahrnehmung dieser verborgenen, die Welt und das Leben durchdringenden Macht, werden also vom Konzil dezidiert als "Religion" anerkannt[9] und grundsätzlich wertgeschätzt. Die "genaueren Begriffe" und die "mehr durchgebildete Sprache", mittels derer verschiedene Religionen "Antwort auf die gleichen Fragen" zu geben versuchen, erlauben, ermöglichen und erleichtern den Dialog dieser unterschiedlichen Religionen miteinander und untereinander. Nichtsdestotrotz muss an dieser Stelle wohl kritisch angemerkt werden, dass sich das genannte "Fortschreiten der Kultur" an verschiedenen Orten auf unterschiedliche Weise und mit stark differierender Geschwindigkeit ereignet. Dies bedingt zwangsläufig, dass der Dialog mit den einzelnen Religionen auf jeweils unterschiedliche Art geführt werden muss. Die Anerkennung als nach Wahrheit strebenden Religionen seitens der Kirche ermöglicht zunächst das Gespräch, über Umstände und Qualität desselben entscheiden freilich die dem jeweiligen Einzelfall zugrunde liegenden konkreten Umstände. Hier ist und bleibt Sensibilität auf Seiten aller Gesprächspartner gefragt.

Bezüglich des Hinduismus nun – mit dem sich das Konzil aufgrund des oben Dargelegten zwangsläufig leichter tun muss als mit dem Buddhismus – wird konkret ausgeführt: *So erforschen im Hinduismus die Menschen das*

---

6 Ebd., 489.

7 Rahner / Vorgrimler, *Konzilskompendium, 350.*

8 LThK, 2. Vat. II, 489.

9 Vgl. Rahner / Vorgrimler, *Konzilskompendium*, 350.

göttliche Geheimnis und bringen es in einem unerschöpflichen Reichtum von Mythen und in tiefdringenden philosophischen Versuchen zum Ausdruck und suchen durch aszetische Lebensformen oder tiefe Meditation oder liebend-vertrauende Zuflucht zu Gott Befreiung von der Enge und Beschränktheit unserer Lage.[10]

Cyril Papali ordnet diese Würdigung des Hinduismus durch NA mit Recht wie folgt ein: "Diese Worte des Konzils sind nicht als Beschreibung des Hinduismus gedacht, sondern als Hinweis auf einige seiner hervorstechenden geistigen Werte, die als Ausgangspunkt für den Dialog mit ihm dienen können."[11] Allerdings sind diese "geistigen Werte als Ausgangspunkt für den Dialog" weitaus weniger konkret dargestellt, als es jene bezüglich Judentum und Islam sind. Dies ist klarerweise der Tatsache geschuldet, dass letztere monotheistische Gemeinschaften sind und mit dem Judentum sowieso eine ganz spezifische Verbindung und Verzahnung besteht. Insofern scheint der grundsätzliche theologische Dialog mit diesen auch vordringlicher und notwendiger für das eigene christliche Selbstverständnis zu sein. Zur Bewältigung essentieller gesellschaftlicher Fragen für eine friedliche und angstfreie Koexistenz indischer Christen mit der Mehrheitsbevölkerung des Subkontinents ist allerdings eine ernsthafte und tiefgreifende Beschäftigung mit dem Hinduismus unumgänglich; eine solche führt ja zudem an die Wurzeln indischer Identität und Lebensweise auch der dortigen christlichen Bevölkerung. Beide Bezeichnungen, "Hindu" und "Inder", leiten sich bekanntlich vom Fluss "Indus" ab und beschrieben ursprünglich die arische Bevölkerung des gesamten Subkontinents. Auf diese historische Zuschreibung rekurrierend, erheben heute vor allem nationalistisch-fundamentalistische Kreise die politische Forderung, dass letztlich alle "Inder" auch per definitionem "Hindus" zu sein haben, und sehen in ihren nicht hinduistischen Mitbürgern meist eine Art Verräter am eigenen Volk. Allein das zeigt schon die Dringlichkeit – aber auch die Schwierigkeiten und Grenzen – eines Dialoges gerade der indischen Christen mit dem Hinduismus möglichst auf Augenhöhe auf. Dabei ist es allerdings alles andere als einfach, die Komplexitäten und Divergenzen des hinduistischen Glaubens- und Lebenssystems auch nur annähernd begreifen und ansatzweise verstehen zu können. Cyril Papali fasst die Hauptmerkmale des Hinduismus wie folgt zusammen: "Anerkennung der *Veden* (der heiligen Bücher der Hindus) als unfehlbare Wahrheit, Glaube an das *Karma-samsāra* oder die Seelenwanderung gemäß dem Gesetz der Vergeltung und die Praxis des *Varṇa-ācrama-dharma*, das heißt des Gesetzes, daß jedes Individuum seiner Kaste und seinem Stand gemäß lebt."[12] Dies verlangt nun einem nicht

---

10 LThK, 2. Vat. II, 489.

11 Papali, *Hinduismus*, 478.

12 Ebd.

hinduistischen Dialogpartner einiges an Voraussetzungen ab. Zu allererst sollte sich ein solcher mit den zentralen Inhalten der – sehr umfangreichen – Veden einigermaßen vertraut machen. Sodann ist er gut beraten, das philosophisch-theologische System der Seelenwanderungslehre zu studieren; und schließlich muss er die Bereitschaft mitbringen, das Kastenwesen von seinen Ursprüngen und Entwicklungen her zumindest nachzuvollziehen. Gerade Letzteres ist für christliche Gegenüber alles andere als einfach, sind es doch gerade die Christen in Indien, die aufgrund des Glaubensprinzips der Gottebenbildlichkeit und daher gleichen Würde aller Menschen stets für zumindest eine Relativierung und Nivellierung der Kastenzuschreibung im öffentlichen Leben in Indien plädiert haben. Dabei ging es zumindest darum, dass im Schul- und Bildungssystem sowie bei Jobvergaben echte Chancengleichheit für alle garantiert wird, indem auf eine Berücksichtigung der Kastenzugehörigkeit zumindest für diese und ähnliche Lebensbereiche verzichtet wird. Gerade an diesem Thema wird sich die Qualität und praktische Relevanz eines christlich-hinduistischen Dialoges erweisen und auch messen lassen müssen. Fingerspitzengefühl seitens beider Dialogpartner ist speziell in dieser Frage jedenfalls gefordert. Auf der anderen Seite bieten die Veden – und hier vor allem die eher jüngeren Entwicklungen innerhalb der Upanishaden – überraschend viele Anknüpfungspunkte an die jüdisch-christliche Tradition, von schöpfungstheologischen Prinzipien über lebensweisheitliche Lehren bis hin zu vorsichtig monotheistischen Ansätzen.

Wie komplex und vielschichtig *die* hinduistische Lehre als Resultat einer mehrfachen Synthese verschiedener Richtungen im Endeffekt aber dennoch geblieben ist, bringt Papali prägnant auf den Punkt: "Sie ist erklärtermaßen monotheistisch, ohne sich jedoch von der Last des metaphysischen Pantheismus und der des mythologischen Polytheismus frei machen zu können."[13]

Aller Komplexität zum Trotz sind es einerseits zahlreiche Impulse aus den Veden und andererseits die hinter der Seelenwanderungslehre stehenden existentiellen menschlichen Fragen, die einen theologischen christlich-hinduistischen Dialog nachhaltig fruchtbar erscheinen lassen. So ist die Vorstellung der Seelenwanderung geprägt von den Fragen nach dem Woher, Wozu und Wohin der Schöpfung im Allgemeinen und des menschlichen Daseins im Besonderen. Und am Ende einer schier endlos langen Abfolge von Geburten, Toden und Wiedergeburten steht im Normalfall die zutiefst ersehnte endgültige Erlösung – so wie sie letztlich auch das Christentum am Ende der Zeiten glaubend erhofft.

Wie nahe in diesem Zusammenhang schöpfungstheologische Erwägungen gerade in späteren Teilen der Upanishaden jenen der jüdisch-christlichen Bibel sein können, zeigt der folgende Text:

13 Ebd., 480.

Da war nicht Nichtsein, und da war auch Sein nicht.
Nicht war das Luftreich, noch der Himmel drüber.
Was regte dort sich? In wessen Obhut?
Gab es das Wasser und den tiefen Abgrund?
Nicht Tod und nicht Unsterblichkeit war damals,
nicht gab's der Tage noch Nächte Anblick.
Von keinem Wind bewegt das Eine atmet' aus eigener Kraft.
Nichts Anderes war als dies nur.

Von Finsternis verborgne Finsternis,
Ein lichtlos Wogen war dies All im Anfang.
Von Öde zugedeckt das Leere.
Eine: Durch innrer Gluten Kraft ward es geboren.

Daraus erhob zuvörderst sich die Liebe.
Sie, die des Geistes erste Samenkraft war.
Des Seins Verwandtschaft fanden in dem Nichtsein
die Weisen, einsichtsvoll im Herzen suchend.

Quer haben ihre Meßspur sie eingezogen,
gab es ein Unten dort? Gab es ein Oben?
Da waren Samenspender, waren Mächte,
drunten selbsteignes Dasein, Spannkraft droben.

Wer weiß in Wahrheit, wer mag zu künden,
woher sie ward, woher sie kam, die Schöpfung?
Die Götter reichen nicht in jene Ferne –
Wer ist's, der weiß, von wo sie ist gekommen?

Von wannen diese Schöpfung ist gekommen,
ob sie geschaffen, ob sie ungeschaffen:
Das weiß nur er, der Allbeschauer droben
am höchsten Himmel – oder weiß er's auch nicht?[14]

Solche und ähnliche altindische Überlieferungen bieten zumindest auf theologischer Ebene gute Ansatzpunkte für einen Dialog mit dem Hinduismus. Diesen dann auf sozialethisch und politisch relevante Fragestellungen auszuweiten, bedarf wie gesagt einigem Feingespür und gutem Willen auf beiden Seiten. Kurien Kunnumpuram war Zeit seines Lebens einer, der über diese Sensibilität verfügt hat. Ihm war die Umsetzung des Zweiten Vatikanums nicht nur in innerkirchlichen Fragen ein Anliegen, sondern auch hinsichtlich der Hinwendung zur Welt und zu Andersgläubigen.

---

14 Aus: Upanishaden, 1958, 123.

Der Dialog mit dem Buddhismus spielt zwar für die Kirchen in Indien insgesamt eine weniger große Rolle als jener mit dem Hinduismus, sollte aber dennoch nicht unterschätzt werden. Einerseits ist die buddhistische Tradition in einigen Regionen Nord- und Nordostindiens nach wie vor vorherrschend, andererseits sind es gerade Elemente buddhistischer Spiritualität, die in christlichen Kreisen zunehmend auf Interesse stoßen und nicht selten inkulturiert werden. Mehr Wissen und Verständnis für deren Herkunft und Wurzeln sowie ein offener Austausch mit deren eigentlichen Trägern ist so gesehen jedenfalls hilfreich und wertvoll.

NÄ bleibt bezüglich des Buddhismus noch vager und unverbindlicher als hinsichtlich des Hinduismus: *In den verschiedenen Formen des Buddhismus wird das radikale Ungenügen der veränderlichen Welt anerkannt und ein Weg gelehrt, auf dem die Menschen mit frommem und vertrauendem Sinn entweder den Zustand vollkommener Befreiung zu erreichen oder – sei es durch die eigene Bemühung, sei es vermittels höherer Hilfe – zur höchsten Erleuchtung zu gelangen vermögen.*[15]

Das Konzil nimmt demnach als Spezifikum des Buddhismus genau jene spezifisch spirituelle Ausrichtung wahr, die eben grundsätzlich von etlichen christlichen Gruppierungen immer mehr entdeckt zu werden scheint. Grundsätzlich fordert es von den Christinnen und Christen, dass sie durch Gespräch und Zusammenarbeit mit den Angehörigen der nicht abrahamitischen Religionen die "geistlichen und sittlichen Güter und auch die sozial-kulturellen Werte, die sich bei ihnen finden anerkennen, wahren und fördern".[16]

Worin aber bestehen nun diese Güter und Werte konkret beim Buddhismus? Grundsätzlich gilt auch für den Buddhismus, ähnlich wie für den Hinduismus, dass er sich in verschiedenen Ausformungen präsentiert. Allen gemeinsam sind in der Tat die Wahrnehmung eines radikalen Ungenügens dieser veränderlichen Welt als Grundlage sowie die Erlangung höchster Erleuchtung als Ziel. "Eigene Bemühung" und "höhere Hilfe" als Mittel zur Erlangung dieses letzten Zieles müssen sich nicht unbedingt gegenseitig ausschließen, skizzieren aber die Spezifika der beiden großen buddhistischen Hauptströmungen Mahâyâna und Theravâda.[17]

Wenn auch die höchste Erleuchtung das letzte Ziel und Meditation der Hauptweg zur Erreichung desselben darstellen, so hat der Buddhismus durch seine philosophisch-weltanschaulichen Elemente doch wesentlich das Sozialleben, die Kunst und die Kultur der durch ihn geprägten Regionen nachhaltig beeinflusst. Diese Elemente sind es wohl, bei denen ein Dialog mit dem Buddhismus sinnvoll und gewinnbringend einsetzen kann und muss.

---

15 LThK, II. Vat. 2, 489f.

16 Vgl. ebd., 491.

17 Siehe dazu Dumoulin, *Buddhismus*, 482.

Das vom Konzil angesprochene am Anfang stehende Wahrnehmen eines "radikalen Ungenügens der veränderlichen Welt" wird von Dumoulin in die vier Grunderfahrungen "ungenügend, leidvoll, begrenzt und vorläufig"[18] expliziert, wobei weder eines der vier Elemente absolut gesetzt, noch eines weggelassen werden darf. So gesehen eignen sich diese vier menschlichen Grunderfahrungen in der Tat als Ansatzpunkt für einen Dialog praktisch jeder anderen Seinsphilosophie oder Religion mit dem Buddhismus. Gerade Christen müssten in Regionen, in denen der Buddhismus weit verbreitet ist, über diese gemeinsamen existentiellen Grunderfahrungen mit diesem relativ ungezwungen in Gespräch kommen können. Auch die im Dokument verwendete Wegmetapher ist dem jüdisch-christlichen Denken alles andere als fremd. Fingerspitzengefühl in einem derartigen Dialogprozess ist freilich bezüglich der Qualität der Erfahrung übernatürlicher Wirklichkeiten geboten. Hier sind die Unterschiede, gerade im Blick auf atheistisch geprägte Anhänger und Schulen des Buddhismus, doch sehr erheblich. Dumoulin ist wohl recht zu geben, dass gerade in der Praxis richtig verstandener, tiefdringender Meditation eine Chance für gemeinsame Erfahrungen und gemeinsame Erkenntnisse liegen kann.[19] Bezüglich der Transformierung buddhistischer Meditationsformen in die westliche christliche Welt hinein und vor allem was die damit verbundene Qualitätskontrolle betrifft, kommt den Kirchen in Indien, Indonesien, China oder auch Japan eine ganz besondere Rolle und Bedeutung zu. Das grundsätzliche Interesse gerade der westlichen Kirchen an östlicher Spiritualität birgt jedenfalls eine große Chance für bewusstes Gespräch und tiefer gehenden Austausch miteinander. Kurien Kunnumpuram war einer, der dieses Gespräch immer gesucht und den Austausch mit Buddhismus, Hinduismus und anderen indischen Religionen stets gepflegt hat. Ich bin stolz darauf, ihn gekannt, geschätzt und von ihm gelernt haben zu dürfen.

Gerade in seinem Sinne ist zu hoffen, dass dieser dialogische Geist des Konzils weiter lebendig und stark bleibt und sich nicht durch anderweitige Kräfte übertünchen und unterdrücken lässt. In Indien, Israel, aber auch europäischen und anderen Regionen sind es derzeit vor allem radikal nationalistische Kräfte, die den offenen und dialogorientierten Kurs des Zweiten Vatikanischen Konzils zurückzudrängen und zu nivellieren drohen. Im Sinne eines Miteinanders der Religionen und Völker gilt es dem entschieden entgegen zu treten. Gerade von den indischen Kirchen lässt sich in diesem Bereich viel lernen.

18 Ebd., 483.

19 Vgl. ebd., 484.

Literaturverweise

Dumoulin, Heinrich: *Exkurs zum Konzilstext über den Buddhismus*. In: Lexikon für Theologie und Kirche. Das Zweite Vatikanische Konzil II. Freiburg ^{2}1967, 482-485.

Oesterreicher, Johannes: *Kommentierende Einleitung* zu "Erklärung über das Verhältnis der Kirche zu den nichtchristlichen Religionen". In: Lexikon für Theologie und Kirche. Das Zweite Vatikanische Konzil II. Freiburg ^{2}1967, 405-495, hier 406-478.

Papali, Cyril B.: *Exkurs zum Konzilstext über den Hinduismus*. In: Lexikon für Theologie und Kirche. Das Zweite Vatikanische Konzil II. Freiburg ^{2}1967, 478-482.

Rahner, Karl/Vorgrimler, Herbert: *Kleines Konzilskompendium*. Sämtliche Texte des Zweiten Vatikanums mit Einführungen und ausführlichem Sachregister. Freiburg ^{23}1991.

Upanishaden: *Altindische Weisheit aus Brahmanas u.a.* Düsseldorf 1958.

14

Eucharistic Liturgy: An Ecological Perspective

Isaac Parackal OIC

Faculty of Philosophy, Jnana-Deepa Vidyapeeth, Pune

Abstract: *The Eucharistic liturgy of St. James presents before us a God who is the continuing Creator. The creation is not a past event that took place once and for all, but it is a dynamic event in which God manifests himself. Creation is not a noun but a verb which takes place every moment. God lives, unfolds himself, creates and loves. God is the mystery of love and creation is love's contagious existence. It is the overflowing love of the Loving Existence - God. Each day, creation is new. God's continuous presence is manifested in the world processes and everything in nature in one way or other proclaims the presence and glory of God. God is not only the God of humans but also the God of the universe. The cosmos is the primal expression of the Divine. Creation is the manifestation of God's gratuitous love and every being is a Theophany - the manifestation of the Divine. Therefore, our attitude to nature should be of respect, awe and gratitude.*

Keywords: *Eucharistic liturgy, Creation, Continuing Creator, Cosmotheandric Order, Eco-theology, Priest of creation, Symbiont.*

Introduction

Here is a story related to the environment, in which a boy who was a very good painter made a big painting of scenery. There were big mountains covered with trees, except a few in the far background which looked snow-covered. From one of the mountains flowed a beautiful river. Down in the valley could be seen a few cosy cottages surrounded by gardens, a few butterflies, some birds soaring high in the air and little children are playing happily in the open fields. Indeed, it was a beautiful painting.

The boy had a little brother. He also wanted to try his hand at painting. As soon as he got the chance, he picked up the brush and painted the mountain all black. The sparkling blue-white water of the river became brown, and with just one stroke of his brush, the flowers and trees and butterflies disappeared. His older brother was heartbroken. The only consolation was that the child who destroyed the painting was so small that he had done it in ignorance. Though it would require a lot of time and effort, the painter could paint another picture.

Something very similar is happening in our lives. How many of us have looked at nature's beauty, a thousand times more beautiful than any painting can ever be, and realized how fragile it is? Just like the child's stroke of the brush, one action of ours can destroy this beauty – be it the mountains with their forest cover or the sparkling streams and rivers of life-giving water, be it the immense sand deserts or our oceans which are teeming with life; be it our lush green rain forests or the stark beauty of our cold deserts. But, and this is an important but, there is a major difference. While the painting was spoiled by an ignorant child, our earth and its environment are being spoiled by adult humans. Even more significant is the possibility that if nature's system or what we call the environment is destroyed, the effect may be fatal for many species. Reckless borrowing against earth's exhausted bounty is driving the planet toward an ecological "credit crunch". Growing demand on natural capital-such as soil, air and biodiversity – already outstrip the world's capacity to renew these resources by a third. If our demand on the planet continue to increase at the same rate, by the mid 2030s we would need the equivalent of two planets to maintain our lifestyles. A European Union study calculates that the world is losing between two and five trillion dollars in natural capital every year due to the degradation of the ecosystems. The world is currently struggling with the consequences of over-valuing assets. But a more fundamental crisis looms, an ecological credit crunch caused by undervaluing the environmental assets that are the basis of all life and prosperity.[1]

In this paper, we shall analyze the inherent and inevitable relation between God, human beings and nature and how it is depicted in the Eucharistic liturgy of the oriental tradition (Liturgy of St. James) which is the unfolding saga of this intimate relationship. Eucharistic Liturgy invites us to be the priest and celebrant of creation which is the divine sacrament.

1 *Times of India*, Pune Edition, October 31, 2008, 13.

Creation as Dynamic and Continuing

The Eucharistic liturgy of St. James pictures before us a God who is the continuing Creator of the world. The creative process is dynamic and in this process, God *lives*, *unfolds* himself, *creates* and *loves*. God is the mystery of love and creation is love's contagious existence. Each day, the creation is new. The creation is not a past and 'once and for all' act but is new in each moment of the evolving process. In the preparatory service the priest prays: "The floods have risen up, O Lord, the floods have lifted up their voice; the floods have risen up with purity. The Lord is mightier than the noise of many waters, yes, than the mighty breakers of the sea; the Lord on high is glorified."[2] God's continuous presence is manifested in the world processes and everything in nature in one way or other proclaims the presence and glory of God. God is not only the God of humans but also the God of the universe.[3] The cosmos is the primal expression of the Divine. Creation is the manifestation of God's gratuitous love and all creatures are products of the divine love and recipients of that ongoing love.[4] In that way, every being is a *Theophany* - the manifestation of the Divine. Here, we arrive at the Hebrew understanding of a "living God" who is continuously revealing Himself and cares for His creatures. The Eucharistic liturgy of St. James brings to light the unfailing presence of God in the cosmos as "Immanuel." Our experience also reveals that we experience God not in vacuum but in and through the created cosmos. That is why the holy Eucharist is an act of continuous praising, glorifying and worshipping the Creator God who continues to sustain the world through his all-pervading Spirit. Just before the Sanctus, the priest and the whole congregation acknowledge that it is meet, right and fitting to praise and glorify God who is the Creator of the whole universe.[5] The whole creation together with the angels glorifies God as their Creator and sustainer. In almost all the prayers of St. James' Liturgy the Holy Spirit is depicted as the "life giver" of all things. We encounter the Creator God in and through the all-pervading and life giving Spirit. This life giving power is permeating the whole creation and without it not even a blade of grass can move. Without this life there is no beauty. A thing is beautiful because there is life in it. This life is the gift of the Divine Spirit. It is in this Spirit that we live, move and have our being.[6] The entire creation, the trees, the birds, animals, stones and rivers are full of life. Life is not just biological life. Life includes the consciousness that oozes into everything. This shows

2 *Malankara Qurbono English Taksa*, trans. Dr. C. A.Abraham, 1986, 8

3 Cf. R. Panikkar, *Cosmotheandric Experience*: *Emerging Religious Consciousness*, ed., Scott Eastham, Maryknoll, Orbis Books, 1983., 74.

4 Cf. Psalms 136: 1-9.

5 Cf. *Malankara Qurbono English Taksa*, 28.

6 Cf. Acts 10:28.

the intense relationship between the whole creation and the Trinitarian God who gives continuing sustenance and life to the world. The Spirit continues to penetrate the core of every being, and brings in a transformation from chaos to unity, thus ensuring the continuous process of creation. Interestingly, the Bible begins and ends with the symbolism of water which depicts the incessant presence of the divine Spirit. In the first chapter of Genesis, we read, "In the beginning when God created the heaven and the earth, the earth had no form and was void; darkness covered the deep, while the spirit of God hovered over the waters." In the last chapter of Revelation (Ch. 22:1), we see again the symbolism of water through the image of river of life which is gushing from the throne of God. In both these expressions there is one common element- the dynamic and continuing presence of the divine power in the cosmos who gives life to it through its continuous and unfailing action.[7]

The World as Sacrament

God is present in the world in and through the creative processes of the world. In the holy Eucharist the creative process, through which God recreates and saves the world is unfolding. In the silent prayer before the consecration words, priest addresses God as the "King of the world and giver of holiness" which implies royal relation between God and the cosmos.[8] A king is supposed to protect and maintain his kingdom without failure. Like that the unfailing presence of God is throughout the world and God protects and maintains it without falling apart.[9] If God is the giver of holiness and the one who sanctifies, then the world could be seen as the sacrament of God. We can see this sacramental notion in two dimensions-symbolic function and instrumental function. In the first dimension, the world is a symbol for "it is a mode of God's revelation, an expression of His truth and beauty which are 'spiritual' aspects of its reality."[10] Secondly, the world is instrumental because "God is effecting instrumentally through it (world), what He does for men in and through it."[11] The whole world could be seen as an instrument and ground of life. "The Earth, however, not only grounds reality, she yields reality. The Earth is fertile, she is the womb of beings. She receives the seed of the Divine and transforms it into abundant life. The Earth is where – and how – the Divine manifests its bounty and its power to man."[12] In Genesis, the Priestly author explains us that God Himself

7 Here, I appeal to the Hindu symbol of *Nataraja,* the dancing Siva, by whose continuous dance the cosmos is maintained and preserved in existence.

8 Cf. *Malankara Qurbono English Taksa*, 28.

9 Cf. *Malankara Qurbono English Taksa*. 8.

10 A.R. Peacocke, *Creation and the World of Science*, Oxford, Clarendon Press, 1979, 290.

11 A.R. Peacocke, *Creation and the World of Science*, 290. Brackets are mine.

12 R. Panikkar, *The Cosmotheandric Experience*, 132.

has declared that every aspect of creation is ordered and good.[13] The Oriental Theologian Alexander Schmemann writes: "God blessed the world, blessed man, blessed the seventh day(that is time) and this means that He filled all that exists with His love and goodness, made all this 'very good'."[14] Corroborated by the Genesis understanding we can maintain that all things can be a revelation of the divine wisdom and goodness.[15] When we say that we are God's creation we are affirming indirectly that God' voice is constantly speaking within us and saying to us, 'God saw everything that he had made, and behold, it was very good.'[16] In the words of Teilhard De Chardin, "Everything that is active, that moves and breathes, every physical, astral or animate energy, every fragment of force, every sparkle of life is equally sacred: for in the humble atom and the most brilliant star, in the lowest insect and the finest intelligence , there are radiant smiles and thrills of the same Absolute."[17] In the words of A. R. Peacocke, "the whole world of creation, then will be good and the revelation of the Divine and therefore, human had to do with one supreme Creator God "whose will was steadfast - and so the created order should in principle be a regular manifestation of the supreme 'mind' of the Creator."[18] All the worldly processes are sacramental and the world is a sacrament of God's continuous actions. In sacraments, especially in the Eucharistic celebration, we are using the natural things as the medium of God's grace and we believe that the invisible grace is coming to us through these visible natural objects. In the same manner the whole nature should be seen as the divine sacrament through which we receive the grace and blessings of God.The world is viewed as the *instrument* whereby God is effecting some cosmic purpose by acting on it. The world is our family where God's continuous presence is felt.

Human Being as Celebrant and Priest of Creation

Humans' role in creation can be seen as that of a celebrant of the sacrament of creation. The complex of proper responses of humans to nature suggests that his or her role may be perceived as that of priest of creation, as a result of whose activity the sacrament of creation is reverenced and dignified.[19] Human being has a privileged role in creation as he or she is the only creature in the

---

13 Cf. A.R. Peacocke, *Creation and the World of Science*, 279.

14 Alexander Schmemann, *Sacraments and Orthodoxy*, *Sacraments and Orthodoxy*, New York, Herder and Herder, 1965, 15.

15 Cf. A.R. Peacocke, *Creation and the World of Science*, 279.

16 Cf. Alexander Schmemann, "Liturgy and Eschatology", *Sobornost*, 7/1, 1985, 13.

17 Ursula King, *Pierre Teilahrd De Chardin,: Selected writings*, Maryknoll, Orbis Books, 1999, 46.

18 A.R. Peacocke, *Creation and the World of Science*, 280.

19 Cf. A.R. Peacocke, *God and the New Biology*, Gloucester, Peter Smith, 1994, 104.

world capable of relating with the Creator.[20] Since God is immanently present in the world, the world is to be seen as the manifestation of God's action. God is everywhere and at all times in the processes and events of the natural world, which could be seen as the vehicle and instrument of God's action and as capable of expressing His intentions and purposes –as our bodies are agents of ourselves. Human being should have the respect for the nature in the same way he or she has respect for his or her own body or those of other persons. We do not consider the body of the other as mere aggregates of flesh, but as a person. In the case of the natural world, if it is God who is the agent who is expressed therein, human attitude to nature should show a respect which is transmuted into reverence at the presence of God in and through the whole of created order, a derived sacredness or holiness as the vehicle and instrument of God's own creative action. In other words, humans have the sacred duty to revere the nature as he or she does to other persons. To be a priest means to be a *mediator*. So a priest has the sacred duty to gather together the offering of creation and present it back to God. "The priest is first and foremost the sacrificer. He or she is the one who can say "thank you" to God."[21] The basic definition of human being is that he or she is priest. Human being stands at the centre of the world and unifies it in his or her act of blessing of God, of both receiving the world from God and offering it to God –and by filling the world with this Eucharist, he or she transforms his or her life, the one that receives from the world, into life in God, into communion. This meeting of encounter between God and humans is the centre from where one moves to God and to the world. The Eucharist where humans meet God is the sacrifice of the whole world to God, the intercession for the whole world before God. "May the just and righteous, the prophets, apostles and martyrs and confessors, and the holy mother of God and all the saints who in all generations were pleasing to you, O God, be intercessors and suppliants to you. By their prayers and supplications wrath may be removed from your people and may peace and tranquility dwell in the four quarters of the world."[22] These prayers show the solidarity and great concern for the whole cosmos. In fact, the ideal world is the one where humans and all the created beings co-exist in peace and tranquility. The Eucharist is directed towards the "whole"- to the entire creation and the whole world. In this sense, the human being is an intermediary between God and world. He is cooperating with God in the creative activity and fulfils God's purposes within it.

---

20 Cf. A.R. Peacocke, *God and the New Biology*, 103.

21 Alexander Schmemann, " Sacrifice and Worship" *Theological Reflections of Alexander Schmemann*, 129-135.

22 *Malankara Qurbono English Taksa*,13.

Human Being as Steward, Manager and Symbiont of Creation

The modern cosmology has been developed based on Newtonian physics and of the Cartesian Scientific method which considered the world in terms of dualistic terms-matter and spirit. In the modern anthropocentric cosmos, human beings are seen as beings above other beings and masters over everything. Human beings try to have "mastery" even over the "mysteries" of the world. In their efforts to dominate the world, the world is even reduced to mere natural resources which are completely devoid of their autonomy. Again, human beings reduced the world to an object of an *experiment* rather than that of *experience*. Humans exploited the earth for their selfish motives and *agriculture* became *agribusiness* where *maximum* has become the motto instead of *optimum*. Further, humans valued *quantity* moreover *quality*. In the creation story of Genesis, human being is presented as having 'dominion' over the creation. Though the terms like steward, trustee or manager could be appropriate it is observed that these terms "introduce a nuance of 'domination' into the Biblical concept of 'dominion' and, in modern English, they do not adequately convey the 'caring' component inherent in the Biblical understanding. The stewardship is accompanied with a high sense of responsibility. The charge of "till and keep" the earth is literally to 'serve and preserve'. The human beings are the *oikonomo* (trustee) of the *Oikos* (house). The term 'dominion' has got a kingly reference. However, caring and preserving are part of kingly qualities. A king is supposed to look after his Kingdom and the subjects. He is not expected to exploit his people for his own purposes.[23] Humans would fail in his or her royal office of dominion over the earth were he or she to exploit the earth's resources to the detriment of the land, plant life, animals, rivers seas etc. What is decisive is the responsibility of humans for the conservation of what has been entrusted to them. He or she can show this responsibility by exercising his or her royal office of mediator of prosperity and well-being, like the kings in the ancient world.[24] Even though 'dominion' has the kingly reference, it is a caring 'dominion' exercised under the authority of the Creator, and so it is a more accurate reflection of the meaning of the Genesis myth to say that it describes humans as steward, or manager, or trustee (as of property, or a charity) as well as exercising the leadership of the king of creation. Therefore, humans must be responsible and are thereby accountable to God for the faithful preservation and maintenance of it. T.N. Khoshoo writes, quoting Gandhiji in *Mahatma Gandhi: An Apostle of Applied Human Ecology*, that "it is an arrogant assumption to say that human beings are lords and masters of the lower creatures. On the contrary, being endowed with greater things in life, they are the trustees of

23 Cf. *Psalm* 72, for virtues of a King.

24 Cf. C. Westermann, *Creation*, SPCK, London, 1974, 61.

the lower animal kingdom".[25] The delicate and holistic balance that exists in nature has to be respected and maintained. Human life "cannot henceforth dissociate itself from this earth-the proper *Oikos* of any ecumenism, the habitat of the human family - and every effort toward salvation now calls for a genuine integration with the entire universe."[26] From the smallest cells of our bodies to finest creations of our minds we are very much part of the cosmos. We are not isolated or independent beings rather we exist symbiotically. The creation, being a symbol of God's meaning and a vehicle and instrument of His purposes, can properly be seen as sacramental – as a 'sanctuary' even- and is worthy of human beings' reverence. Such a reverential attitude to all creation was, indeed, also a consequence of biological appraisals of humans as *symbiont* in relation to other living organisms.[27] The harmony between human beings and the mother earth is lost. Without this harmony, humans cannot save themselves. The earth is a victim of the voraciousness of human beings, who have abused her more than all the other living beings put together. "Humans have not simply taken their sustenance from the earth. They have further exploited and violated her, trying to climb to heaven - although this tower of Babel begins to crumble even as it is built."[28] The mother Earth is returning to life and recovering the soul, which she has lost due to the mistreatment of human beings.[29] The human being as symbiont must bring everything in nature to concord and symbiosis.

Human Being as Co-Creator

The universe was created in a state of journeying towards perfection, and the ultimate perfection is yet to be attained, to which God has destined it. In the words of Teilhard De Chardin, we are 'evolution conscious of itself'. Through this process, we, human beings have realised our immense possibilities and responsibilities. We are partners with God in a covenantal relationship. "The salvation of man and the transformation of nature are one since in the thought of the Greek fathers man is a "microcosm" whose destiny

25 Cf.T.N. Khoshoo, , *Mahatma Gandhi: An Apostle of Applied Human Ecology*. New Delhi: Tata Applied Research Institute. 1995.

26 R. Panikkar, "Towards an Ecumenical Ecumenism", *Journal of Ecumenical Studies*, XIX, no.4 (Fall 1982), 784.

27 Cf. A.R. Peacocke, *Creation and the World of Science*, pp. 314-315; also see 298.

28 R. Panikkar, *Blessed Simplicity The Monk as Universal Archetype*. New York, Seasbury Press, 1982, 52.

29 Cf. R. Panikkar, *Blessed Simplicity*, 52. To work for the Earth does not mean to exploit her for one's own gain. It means to cultivate her as one would a friendship or garden, not as one would plunder a mine…Mother Earth is returning to life and recovering the soul which from ancient times she has always been believed to possess: *anima mundi*.

is inseparably connected with that of creation."[30] The whole creation,, which is the macrocosm,, is intimately and inseparably connected with humans –the microcosm. The destiny of the universe is in the hands of humans who co-work with God to lead it to fulfilment. In the Eucharistic Liturgy, we pray to God to bless the whole creation: " Bless O Lord, the air, the dews, the rains, the seasons of the year and fill all things living with good will."[31] The prayers in the Eucharist demand a radical response from the humankind to cooperate with God in the continuing process of co-creating. When we pray in the Eucharist, "Lord, bless the seasons with your grace and enhance the fruits of nature,"[32] this enhancement of nature is not solely expected from the part of the Creator, but it extends an invitation to humans to cooperate with God in the creative enhancing process. Receiving the Holy Communion the priest says silently: "In my hand, I take you, Lord, who sustain the universe in your palms, and on my tongue, I receive you who rule the depths of the universe."[33] This shows the intimate relationship between the Creator and creation. As we receive the body and blood of God we become one with the cosmotheandric web of life and partners of the mystery of creation.

Holy Eucharist: A Call to Cosmotheandric Order (Rta)

In the Indian religious tradition, harmony among the Divine, human and the cosmic is well expressed in the notion of *rta*. *Rta* is the upholding of the cosmic order where God the Creator, the cosmos and the humans are in perfect harmony. *Rta* in its deepest sense means dharma-the right action and behavior as opposed to a-dharma- the wrong and unnatural action. Dharma implies a fundamental concern and respect for the whole creation and includes a moral and social order and symmetry. The whole creation itself could be seen as a passage from chaos to order. Human beings are called to uphold this harmony in which all forces of nature from electromagnetic to the divine, from angelic to human are intertwined and interrelated.

The holy Eucharist is the sacrifice by which the *rta*-order of the universe is maintained. Sacrifice by nature is a *theandric act*, an act in which God and humans have to work together in order that the world be conserved; it is a cosmic act because the sustenance of the world depends on it. The sacrifice, the sacrifice, and the sacrificed meet together in the holy Eucharist. The goodness and order in creation are celebrated in the Eucharist. It is well expressed in Eucharistic *anaphora* by raising the offerings to God. "The divine liturgy-

30 Zizioulas, "Ortodossia", in *Enciclopedia del Novecento*, Vol. 5, Roma, Istituto della Enciclopedia Italiana, 1980, 17.

31 *Malankara Qurbono English Taksa*, 31

32 *Malankara Qurbono Malayalam Taksa*, 2001, 300.

33 *Malankara Qurbono Malayalam Taksa* , 2001, 66. Translation is mine.

the continual ascent, the lifting up of the church to *heaven* , to the throne of glory, to the unfading light and joy of the kingdom of God-is the focus of this experience, simultaneously its source and presence, gift and fulfillment."[34]

In the Eucharistic celebration the bread and wine placed upon the altar symbolize the whole creation. They act as vehicles of the whole world in its entirety.[35] The word "Eucharist" comes from the Greek word, '*eucharistein*' which means thanksgiving. It is because of the predominance of the themes of praise and thanksgiving that the whole *anaphora* prayer is called "Eucharistic prayer." In this sense, holy Eucharist is in fact the "offering back" of the whole world to God in thanksgiving. The whole world is a God-given gift to humans whose task is to protect and conserve it. In the holy Eucharist we see this great symbolism of cosmotheandric unity which proclaims the interdependent, interrelated and harmonious structure of creation which is entrusted to human beings. In other words, Eucharist calls us to maintain *rta* – the cosmic order through dharma, the right action. In the present ecological crisis this symbolism has got great relevance. Human beings who are supposed to maintain the ecological well-being and order go against will of the Creator which results very much in the climatic changes and disorders in the atmospheric conditions such as global warming, tsunami, acid rains, ozone depletion, tornados, earth quakes etc. Any laxity in maintaining this cosmic order or *rta* has an effect on every web of life and it adversely affects the mutual and intimate relation among God, cosmos and humans.

Concluding Reflections: Towards an Eco-Theology

The experience shows that the development in the physical realm makes humans more and more unhappy. We cannot claim that we are better or happier than our ancestors, though we have made all types of advancements in science and technology. Modern facilities and technological devices make humans a foe to nature rather than a friend. Most of the modern technologies are provocative than evocative. They do not evoke in humans any respect for nature but alienate us further from both God and nature. The distance between human beings, God and the world becomes wider and wider with every new scientific discovery. For instance, the splitting up of atom in the name of scientific progress seems to be the cosmic abortion, which jeopardises the natural balance. For the sake of scientific achievements we experiment and explode atom bombs and launch missiles with high explosive chemicals which affect the rhythm and balance of the cosmic system. Now a days, even the deserts are not deserted but they have become the place of destructive experiments.

34 Alexander Schmemann, *The Eucharist: Sacrament of the Kingdom*, trans. Paul Kachur, NewYork, St.Vladimir's Seminary Press, 1988, 164.

35 Cf. Alexander Schmemann, "The World as Sacrament" , *Church, World, Mission*, ed. Alexander Schmemann, New York, St. Vladimir's Seminary Press, 1979, 217-227.

The modern human being is always on the go and he or she thinks that the quicker the better in order to gain time. Acceleration is the great discovery of modernity. The most important characteristic of techno-centric civilization lies in having introduced acceleration, less in the mathematical-physical than in the global sense: acceleration of rhythms, of times, of all happenings on this earth.[36] Humans want to speed up everything including the natural processes. Nature has a spontaneous rhythm and we cannot accelerate it without making harm to fulfil itself. This natural rhythm serves to the equilibrium of the cosmos. If this equilibrium is lost the cosmos cannot tolerate it, rather it will respond aggressively: this violent reaction of nature is manifested as tsunami, acid rains, earthquakes, drought, flood etc. The polluted atmosphere, the contaminated rivers, the stained seas, the extinct species, the exhausted natural resources and the denuded forests stand as evidence to this ecological disaster.

In this scenario of ecological crisis, holy Eucharist invites us to respect nature and cherish the fellowship*(koinonia)*. It reminds us of the great truth that *nature is not a slave to be raped but a partner to be cherished.* The Eucharist challenges us to cultivate a sense of responsibility(response-ability) and duty, which inspire us to work for the welfare of the whole world. The offering of bread and wine in the Eucharist reminds us of the offering of the whole world back to God in thanksgiving and thereby demands our sincere effort to make it a perfect offer pleasing to God. Any offering which is not flawless and perfect cannot fulfil the aspect of thanksgiving. However, an offering of thanksgiving is to be offered with an unblemished heart which seeks the welfare of every creature in this cosmos. This depends on a radical *metanoia*, a complete turning of mind, heart and spirit. The holy Eucharist challenges us to take a radical turn back (*metanoia*) that would enhance us to regain the lost harmony and confluence in the whole cosmos. The Holy Eucharist reminds us of our awareness and connectedness with the Divine, manifested in the whole creation which participates in the mystery of the Eucharist in and through the natural symbols used.[37] A mystic like Teilhard reminds us of this great cosmotheandric vision as he writes in, *Mass at the Altar of the Universe*, "Since once again, Lord...I have neither bread, nor wine, nor altar, I will raise myself beyond these symbols, up to the real majesty of the real itself; I, your priest, will make the whole earth my altar and on it will offer you all labours

---

36 Cf. R. Panikkar, *A Dwelling Place for Wisdom*, trans. Annemarie S. Kidder, Delhi, Motilal Banarsidass Publishers, 1993. 26: "Nowadays one thinks that the natural rhythms, the changes of day and night, of walking and sitting, of winter and summer-as in farming, for example-are no longer sufficient. One wants to progress faster. And the kind of acceleration resulting from this shatters the rhythms of the whole environment and of being in general."

37 Cf. Siji Noorokariyil SJ, *Children of the Rainbow*, Delhi, Media House, 2007, 124

and sufferings of the world."[38] A meaningful celebration of the Eucharist should awaken in us a sense of the divine presence in the cosmos, enabling us to cultivate a Cosmotheandric spirituality that revitalizes us to work for the well-being and integration (*lokasamgraha*) of the whole cosmos.

38 Ursula King, *Pierre Teilhard De Chardin: Selected Writings*, Maryknoll, Orbis Books, 1999, 80.

15

Theological Understanding of Ecoanthropology in *Laudato Si'*

A. L. Christopher Roach
Good Shepherd Seminary, Coimbatore, Tamil Nadu

Abstract: *This article is a theological reading of Pope Francis' Encyclical Laudato Si' in order to unearth the ecoanthropological dimensions found in it. The goal of this article is to make the human life holistic by maintaining the constant relationship with God and other creatures and to overcome by all means an excessive anthropocentric approach towards other creatures. The real understanding of the very being, dignity and responsibility of human beings will enlighten them to understand better the value and role of other creatures and will also indicate the damage caused by humans to the harmony of the nature. Ecology and anthropology are closely related because both are formed out of the earth (though, on the other side, humans are distinct from other creatures by the fact of being created in the image and likeness of God) and both contribute to their mutual and peaceful coexistence. Human responsibility over creatures is nothing but to work for the survival of the creatures and thus to serve the Creator, God. When and wherever the nature is threatened and destroyed the adverse effects are borne by the poor people. Hence it is necessary to work simultaneously for the liberation of the nature and the poor in our society. Further, human environment and the natural environment are closely knit together. Therefore, it is necessary to protect the cultural riches of the people. Laudato Si' invites humans to become aware of their dignity and responsibility, to learn from the wisdom of the creation and* *to work for the harmonious coexistence of humans with other creatures for the greater glory of God. This interrelated life will lead to the emergence of universal praise to God by both humans and other creatures.*

Keywords: *Ecoanthropology, Triad: God-humans-other creatures, interrelated, uniqueness, harmony, responsibility, poor, ecocare, cultural ecology and ecoanthropocentric life.*

Introduction

The encyclical of Pope Francis titled "*Laudato Si'*" apparently gives the picture that it is about ecology or environment but a closer reading brings to light that it is dealing with humans in relation to the environment. The Pope, by way of highlighting this idea, asserts that "there can be no ecology without an adequate anthropology".[1] In the present context of ecological degradation and threats it is necessary to have a proper understanding about humans, their dignity and their vocation. The true biblical and theological understandings of human beings never promote anthropocentrism rather they bring to the forefront the interrelationship that exists between the triad namely God, humans and other creatures. If humans are seen as special creation of God, and are also closely related to other creatures, then the human approach towards creatures and environment will result in care, concern and a holistic growth. This holistic attitude is necessary today to make a healthy life on the earth, our common home.

Who Are Human Beings?

Among the existential questions that humans raise about themselves the question "who am I?" occupies a central place. The following section will try to present answer to this question from the point of view of ecoanthropology.

a. Humans are Created by God

God created the universe, earth, water, light, animals, birds etc and found them good. According to Genesis 2:7, God created humans out of the earth (LS 18 subtly indicates this fact by using the term biological evolution). This is an indication that humans bear a material element in their very constitution; they are part of nature.[2] Leonardo Boff asserts that humans are sons and daughters of the earth and goes further on to state that they are earth itself.[3] So we can say

1 Francis, Enc. *Laudato Si'* (24 May 2015), Trivandrum: Carmel International Publishing House, 2015, no. 118 (hereafter *Laudato Si'* will be noted as LS).

2 Ross Langmead, "Ecomissiology," *Missiology vol 30, no. 4 (October 2002), 506.*

3 Leonardo Boff, "Earth as Gaia: An Ethical and Spiritual Challenge," *Concilium no.3 (June 2009),* 25.

that "humans are Earth-creatures".[4] Pope John Paul opines that in the creation of Adam and Eve, God established a fixed relationship between humans and the rest of creation.[5] Humans who remained good in the eyes of the Creator will continue to be good if they remain faithful to the Creator God and to other creatures.

b. Uniqueness of Humans

God created human beings in his likeness and image and they are 'person' with immense dignity. Therefore, they are "not just something, but someone". The divine image and likeness in human beings makes them distinct from the rest of creation. Cardinal Turkson puts it more sharply that the humans are distinct from other creatures because of bearing within themselves the breath of God.[6]Humans are gifted with self-knowledge, self-possession, freedom and ability to enter into communion with other human persons.[7]Even, if humans, who are created by God, are seen as an outcome of an evolutionary process, Pope Francis affirms that they possess unique features namely "capacity to reason, to develop arguments, to be inventive, to interpret reality and to create art, along with other not yet discovered capacities."[8] These abilities are considered unique because they transcend the spheres of biology and physics. Besides, the creation of humans as personal beings presupposes the direct intervention of God and humans are also enabled by God to enter into dialogue with him, the eternal Thou.[9] So humans, on the one side, belong to nature and on the other side, they are not mere objects but gifted to be personal partners of God in dialogue. Both the naive and lofty character of humans are well balanced in *Laudato Si'*.

c. Harmonious Relationship between Humans and Creatures

God who created both humans and other creatures placed them together in a harmonious situation. The Garden of Eden portrays a flawless ecosystem with peace and harmony between humans and other creatures.[10] Gen 2:19-20

---

4 Robert W. Lannan, "Catholic Tradition, the New Catholic Theology and Social Teaching on the Environment," *The Catholic Lawyer* vol 30 no. 4 (November 2017), 366.

5 John Paul, "Message for the World Day of Peace on 1 January," 1990 (8 Dec., 1989), no. 2, http://w2.vatican.va/content/john-paul-ii/en/messages/peace/documents/hf_jp-ii_mes_19891208_xxiii-world-day-for-peace.html (accessed on 30.06.2018).

6 Cardinal Turkson, "Human Ecology Fraternity and Communion," *L'Osservatore Romano* 51, no. 30 (27 July 2018), 4.

7 LS 65.

8 LS 81.

9 LS 81.

10 T. John Chakkuvarackal, "Biblical Perspectives on Creation, Ecology and Human Responsibility," *Mission Today vol 6, no. 4 (October-December 2004), 344.*

mentions that Adam gave names to all living creatures and they were with him without causing any danger for his existence. It is in this harmonious situation that God entrusted to humans the responsibility to take care of all creatures. God's intention was mutual coexistence, mutual sharing and mutual assistance. Human concern for other creatures and fellow humans is not an act of generosity but an expression of the acceptance of their interdependent existence. Each creature is valuable in the eyes of God and each possesses a particular goodness and perfection of its own. Hence, human beings who are endowed with intelligence, are expected to respect each creature, the laws of nature and to maintain the delicate equilibrium that exists between the creatures.[11] Human responsibility over creatures is nothing but maintaining the harmony established by God. The life of harmony is a life to be lived in a common home with mother (earth) and with brothers and sisters (creatures).[12]

Since there exists a harmonious relationship between human beings and other creatures the Bible urges humans to invite creatures like the sun, the earth, the moon, the waters above the heavens, the waters on the earth etc to praise God (Ps 136:6; 148:3-5, Dan 3: 60-81).[13] The biblical authors looked forward to the moment that a universal praise to God unanimously be given by both human beings and other creatures.

What Do Humans Continue to Do?

Humans in the present scenario are much worried about the ecological degradation and environmental threats caused by capitalist and technological domination. But the real crisis lies not in the environment but in the human heart. It is the human sin that causes ecological problems. Therefore, it is necessary to look into the inner world rather than the external world.

a. Excessive Anthropocentrism

Humans place themselves at the centre and they decide everything according to their convenience. They begin to consider other living beings as mere objects and subject them to their domination. This is a grave mistake on the part of humans. That is why Pope decries the modern tendency of humans to see them as the ultimate measure of what is right and good.[14]Judeo-Christian traditions are accused of promoting ecological crisis by exalting human dominion over

---

11 LS 68-70.

12 LS 1; Chakkuvarackal, "Biblical Perspectives on Creation, Ecology and Human Responsibility," 353-354.

13 LS 72.

14 Nagle, John Copeland, "Pope Francis, Environmental Anthropologist" vol 28, 7 (2015). *Journal Articles.* Paper227.http://scholarship.law.nd.edu/law_faculty_scholarship/1227 accessed on 09.07.2018, p. 18; LS 82, 116, 122-123.

the world and other creatures. This general accusation may not be fair but this indicates how Christian tradition has ignored the creation and environment in their theological treatment and catechesis. The Church was also not prompt in responding to ecological threats.[15]Further, modern anthropocentrism motivated by a technological mind sees nature and its resources as mere objects to be used.[16] Pope John Paul II in *Centesimus Annus says, "at the root of the senseless destruction of natural environment lies an anthropological error which unfortunately is widespread in our day".*[17] By excessive, arbitrary and disordered use of natural resources humans lose sight of their real picture and become cause for destruction of both humans and nature.[18]

b. Eco-care Not at the Cost of Human Care

It is true that creatures have a sacred character due to the close link that they have with God. Hence, creatures must be respected and protected. The eco-care or protecting the species should not become an obsession to the extent of denying any pre-eminence to the human person. Environmental activists should not lack tenderness, compassion and concern for the fellow human beings especially the poor. Since everything is interrelated the protection of nature and the protection of vulnerable human embryo (so abortion is not justified) are to be given equal importance otherwise ecoactivists will be accused of doing injustice to the humanity. In other words, Pope Francis says, the "sense of fraternity excludes nothing and no one".[19]

c. The Poor as the Scapegoat for Ecological Carelessness

Ecological carelessness which leads to ecological degradation always causes adverse effects in the life of the poor. As a result of ecological problems, the livelihood of the poor is affected; and they experience the loss of residence, displacement, uncertainty regarding their livelihood, lack of good drinking water, lack of fresh air, suffering caused by diseases like cholera, dysentery etc, premature deaths and denial of basic rights.[20] Pope Francis explains the indescribable sufferings and dangers to the poor as follows: "The extreme poverty experienced in areas lacking harmony, open spaces or potential for integration, can lead to incidents of brutality and to exploitation by criminal organizations. In the unstable neighbourhoods of mega-cities, the daily

15 Sebastian Athappilly, *Mystery and Destiny of the Human Person: A Theological Anthropology*, Bangalore: Dharmaram Publications, 2007, 70-71.

16 LS 115.

17 John Paul II, Enc. *Centesimus Annus, (1 May 1991), Trivandrum: Carmel International Publishing House, 2005, 37.*

18 John Paul II, Enc. *Centesimus Annus, 37.*

19 LS 90-92, 120.

20 LS 26, 28-30.

experience of overcrowding and social anonymity can create a sense of uprootedness which spawns antisocial behaviour and violence".[21] It is because they are poor they are not able to fulfil their basic requirements and they are also deprived of ways to fulfil economic needs. "The gravest effects of all attacks on the environment are suffered by the poorest".[22] Therefore, ecological dangers degrade and affect the life and future of the poor.

d. Ecological Sins

Laudato Si' mentions clearly humanity's sins against other creatures. Natural environment suffers grave damage due to human domination and irresponsible behaviour. It is due to human attitude of seeing themselves as 'masters', creatures are misused, abused and overused. Humans commit sin by destroying biological diversity, by causing climate changes that lead to degradation of earth's integrity, by destroying forests and wetlands, by poisoning the rivers and water bodies, by destroying grazing lands of cattle, by polluting the breathing air and by draining the earth resources for selfish motive at the cost of future generation etc. *Laudato Si'* declares, "The earth, our home is beginning to look more and more like an immense pile of filth".[23] Hence, each human being is responsible at a smaller or bigger level for the disfigurement or destruction of creation. Therefore, each one is urged to acknowledge his or her sins against creation and ask pardon from the Creator, and to make reparation for the sins committed through various possible ways.[24]

What Do Humans Need to Do?

"What kind of world do we want to leave to those who come after us, to children who are now growing up?" is the question raised by *Laudato Si'*.[25] By way of answering this question, humans need to work for the betterment of the earth along with its natural resources. A few aspects which humans can concentrate and thus contribute for the betterment of the earth, our common home are discussed below.

a. Promotion of Proper Ecoanthropology

One thing that Pope Francis wants of human beings is to have a proper understanding of ecoanthropology and to pass on the same understanding to their fellow humans. The proper or correct anthropology sees God, humans and other creatures not as three closed compartments but as three interrelated

21 LS 149.

22 LS 48.

23 LS 21.

24 LS 6, 8.

25 LS 160.

partners in the sustenance of life in the world. Human beings possess "a particular dignity above other creatures; it thus inculcates esteem for each person and respect for others".[26] Pope St. John Paul II in this regard says that not only nature is entrusted with humans as God's gift, but human beings are also given as God's gift to human beings. Therefore it is demanded from humans that they should respect the natural and moral structure of humanity.[27] Pope Francis for his part mentions that a genuine human ecology involves accepting one's human body, taking care of it and respecting its fullest meaning. At the same time human beings are also part of other creatures. Therefore they can neither keep aloof from other creatures nor degrade or use them for human selfish motive.[28] LS declares that humans "are part of nature, included in it and thus in constant interaction with it".[29] If we look at the human body from an ecoanthropological point of view, we cannot limit to biological body because the world outside or the nature is also seen as extension of human body. One must begin to think about nature as not only world around us but also a world within us.[30]"Our relationship with the environment can never be isolated from our relationship with others and with God"[31] and vice versa. "Everything is connected"[32] is the proclamation of Pope Francis to the whole world. Hence, a correct ecoanthropology needs to do justice to both vertical relationship and horizontal relationship of human beings.[33]

b. Dignity to Be Expressed in the Responsible Care of Creatures

It is true that humans are created in the image and likeness of God therefore they enjoy an irrevocable and undeniable dignity. However, the dignity that flows from the fact of being created in the divine image is to be expressed significantly by human care and service towards the creatures. The human dignity which is understood in terms of service involves in bringing back the original harmony that was existing between human beings and nature.[34] The

---

26 LS 119.

27 John Paul II, Enc. *Centesimus Annus, 38.*

28 LS 155.

29 LS 139.

30 Athappilly, *Mystery and Destiny of the Human Person: A Theological Anthropology*, 72; Human beings form part of the whole of creation so both are interdependent. It becomes evident in God's covenant with Noah where he made covenant not only with humans but also with all animals and birds (Gen 9: 9-10).

31 LS 119.

32 LS 91.

33 Copeland, "Pope Francis, Environmental Anthropologist" 19-20: Ecotheology gives equal importance to God, humans and creatures therefore it does not promote either theocentrism or anthropocentrism or biocentrism.

34 LS 66.

term dominion mentioned in the first account of creation is clarified in the second account by using two terms namely 'tilling and keeping'. 'Tilling' refers to make the land productive by cultivating and 'keeping' refers to taking care of everything so that the earth continues to be the home of all.[35] So human 'dominion' is to be understood as a responsibility to see the survival of the other living creatures. As a consequence, humans are to act on behalf of God in the ongoing process of creation and redemption.[36]Pope Francis regarding human responsibility puts succinctly as follows: "Living our vocation to be protectors of God's handiwork is essential to a life of virtue; it is not an optional or a secondary aspect of our Christian experience".[37] Hence, humans are to keep the creation as God keeps it (Ps 145:15-16).

c. Protecting the Poor

The poor are those who lack necessary resources to make a decent life. Pope Francis calls for setting up priorities to eliminate extreme poverty in the poor countries and for promotion of their social development. This call involves combating corruption, ensuring protecting laws for the poor and the minorities, encouraging less polluting forms of energy production, tapping solar energy, curtailing industrial pollution, waste management, encouraging diversified agriculture and rotation of crops, protecting the poor farmers' lands, encouraging local and poor farmers and industrialists.[38] The developed countries must first of all abstain from draining energy and raw materials of poor countries, must help the poor countries to overcome their debt and must assist the "poor countries to support policies and programmes of sustainable development".[39] As a result the life of the people in the poor countries will make a considerable improvement.

According to ecotheology the term poor refers not only to economically poor people but also the earth and creatures that lack protection from damage. In this sense the liberation theologians linked concern for environment with the liberation of the poor. The protection of the poor ultimately protects the environment and vice versa.

35 LS 67; Turkson, "Human Ecology Fraternity and Communion," 4-5.

36 LS 67; Lannan, "Catholic Tradition, the New Catholic Theology and Social Teaching on the Environment," 366,371.

37 LS 217.

38 LS 172, 180.

39 LS 52, 90, 152.

d. Promotion of Cultural Ecology

The human environment and the natural environment are closely knit together. Therefore, they both either live (develop) together or deteriorate together. Human beings are cultural beings. So genuine ecology involves itself in protecting the cultural treasures of humanity. The word 'culture' refers to all that refines and develops man's diverse mental and physical endowments. "Culture is a system of values" that "expresses the essential authenticity of the needs, the natural inclinations and the aspirations of the human person".[40]Culture is not something that we have inherited from the past but it is a present lived reality of humans. Therefore, efforts should be made to protect the cultural riches and their variety from the levelling effects of global culture. Efforts are to be made to protect cultural identity of human communities because disappearance of culture is more serious than disappearance of a species of a plant or animal.[41] It is necessary, therefore, to ensure the cultural environment for the betterment of humans and also other creatures.

e. Practical Guidelines of *Laudato Si'* for Ecoanthropocentric Life

Becoming conscious of the network of relationship between the triad, i.e. God, humans and other creatures will push forward humans to lead a life of harmony. Besides, only "a culture of care" will be able to stop the environmental degradation.[42] Hence *Laudato Si'* proposes the following practical ways to lead an ecoanthropocentric life: providing ecoconsciousness through education programmes, providing waste management, turning off unnecessary lights, tapping solar energy, encouraging use of common transport system, providing protection for the poor affected by ecological degradation, protecting lands of indigenous communities, initiating projects to help poverty stricken countries and communities, use of alternative fuel, planting trees and establishing green zones, praying with nature and for nature, and leading nature-related life. Living an ecoanthropocentric life means learning the wisdom of creation and living together in harmony with it and within the *oikos*.[43]

Conclusion

Pope Francis in *Laudato Si'* declares boldly that there can be no renewal of humans' relationship with nature without a renewal of humanity itself and that there can be no healing of relationship between humans and nature without

40 Adriano Bausola, "The Authentic Progress of Culture," *Laity Today, 39 (1996): 147.*

41 LS 143-145.

42 LS 231.

43 Alicio Caceres Aguirre, "Eco-theology: Epistemological Approaches," *Concilium no.3 (June 2009), 63.*

healing of all human relationships.[44] This article is a moderate attempt to understand well the being and doing of humans so that the threats posed by humans to ecology can be gradually eliminated in the world. Ps 133:1 says "How very good and pleasant it is when kindred live together in unity". The ecoanthropology of *Laudato Si'* encourages and looks for this unity and peaceful coexistence of humans with other creatures, and, this is the real need of the hour.

44 LS 118-119.

16

Catholicism and Modern Science: Vatican II on Science and Technology

Job Kozhamthadam SJ
Professor (Emeritus), Systematic Philosophy and Former President, Jnana-Deepa Vidyapeeth, Pune

Abstract: *Although the Second Vatican Council touched extensively and profoundly practically all the important aspects of the Church, in this paper, the author focusses on its groundbreaking spirit and statements on the relationship of the Catholic Church with modern science and technology. The aggiornamento inaugurated by Vat II is a long and challenging process that needs to continue. Both the Church and modern science need to collaborate in this noble task. Science, with its amazing findings of the secrets of nature and its well-proven powerful methods, can be a great boon in this process. The perennial truths and the rich tradition of the Church too should serve as facilitators rather than obstacles in this venture. The truths and insights of religion can ensure that the ongoing process does not deviate from the right path of holistic progress of humanity and the cosmos. The Christian tradition can make available centuries of rich experience as a source of inspiration and guidance. Vat II has opened the door for such a constructive and collaborative mission to respond responsibly to the challenges of our contemporary world.*

Keywords: *Vatican II, aggiornamento, Science-Religion Dialogue, Technology, Science.*

Introduction

Althoughh the Catholic Church is expected to be a Spirit-initiated, Spirit-filled and Spirit-governed institution, certain events in its 2000 odd history lead a critical mind to question this expectation or claim, particularly in our own time. However three events in recent times assure me that the Spirit is very much present and active in the Church: First the gift of Pope John XXII, second the Second Vatican Council and third the gift of Pope Francis.[1] To me, arguably, these three unexpected, out of the blue, happenings come across as a special Epiphany of the Spirit leading, guiding and protecting the Church of Christ. The central player and connecting link of these three, is, of course, Vatican II, undoubtedly the most important event in the history of the Catholic Church in the 20th century. Pope John is intimately linked to it as the inspirer and convener of Vatican II and Pope Francis as the one who has been making a heroic effort to put the path-breaking spirit and ideals of the Council into the practice, particularly since they went through a "lukewarm period" for several decades, mainly due to certain conservative and vested interests within the Church. As the Apostolic Brief *In Spirito Sancto* rightly points out, "The Second Vatican Council... must be remembered without a doubt among the greatest events of the Church."[2] Several details about this Council unmistakably reveal the hand of the Holy Spirit in initiating and carrying through this special event. As Pope John XXIII said in his opening speech, "It (the first announcement of the Council on January 25, 1959, within merely three months of his Pontificate) was completely unexpected, like a flash of heavenly light, shedding sweetness in eyes and hearts."

Furthermore, historically in the past, an ecumenical council was convened when there was a crisis, particularly a doctrinal one, and the Church was seriously threatened. This was not the situation when Vat II was convened. According to the "Opening Speech" of Pope John XXIII, "The salient point of this Council is not, therefore, a discussion of one article or another of the fundamental doctrine of the Church which has repeatedly been taught by the Fathers and by ancient and modern theologians, and which is presumed to be well known and familiar to all. *For this no Council was necessary.*"[3] But there was a pressing and potent reason: "Today the Church is witnessing a crisis underway within society. While humanity is on the edge of a new era, tasks

---

1 It is interesting to note the tremendous similarity between Pope John XXIII and Pope Francis, particularly in their lifestyle, general attitude and the special circumstances they were elected to be the Successors of St. Peter. See "The unlikely election of John XXIII," https://www.catholicireland.net/the-unlikely-election-of-john-xxiii/, accessed on 11/12/2018.

2 "Papal Brief Declaring the Council Completed," Walter M. Abbott, SJ, General Editor, *The Documents of Vatican II (London: Geoffrey Chapman, 1967), p.738. Henceforth Abt.*

3 Abt, p.715. Emphasis added.

of immense gravity and amplitude await the Church, as in the most tragic periods of its history. It is a question in fact of bringing the modern world into contact with the vivifying and perennial energies of the gospel, a world which exalts itself with its conquest in the technical and scientific fields, but which also brings the consequences of a temporal order which some have wished to recognise excluding God. This is why society is earmarked by great material progress to which there is not a corresponding advance in the moral field."[4] Thus the Council was intended to remedy the serious mismatch between the advances in the world of science and technology and in that of religion and morality. The Pontiff was quick to add that the Church has not been caught unaware of this situation: "If we turn our attention to the Church, we see that it has not remained a lifeless spectator in the face of these events, but has followed step by step the evolution of peoples, scientific progress, and social revolution."[5] The convening of the Council gives clear evidence to this ever vigilant and solicitous attitude of the Church. These statements of Pope John XXIII clearly indicate the importance he and the Church attach to scientific and technological developments and the well-recognized impact they have on society, particularly the Church.

Although the Council touched extensively and profoundly practically all the important aspects of the Church, in this paper, my principal focus will be its groundbreaking spirit and statements on the relationship of the Catholic Church with modern science and technology. Vat II commenced on October 11, 1962, under the Pontificate of Pope John XXIII and closed on December 8, 1965, under the Pontificate of Pope Paul VI. Not only was this Council unprecedented in its goal, but several other firsts also distinguished it. It had the largest number of participants – the attendance at the Council peaked up to 2540. Furthermore, it was considered the richest experience of its kind because of the careful, profound and open-minded way the questions were discussed all through its four long sessions. Another factor that made it special was its timing: it came at the opportune time, when the world needed it most, "bearing in mind the necessities of the present day, above all it sought to meet the pastoral need."[6] Its universal and open spirit also made it a special event. It was conspicuous by the presence of non-Catholics who were invited as observers, particularly from the Eastern Orthodox Churches. "Nourishing the flame of charity, it has made a great effort to reach not only the Christians still separated from communion with the Holy See, but also the whole human family."[7]

4 "Pope John Convenes the Council," Abt, p.704.

5 Ibid., ABT, p.704.

6 "Papal Brief," Abt, p. 738.

7 Ibid., p. 738. See also Second Vatican Council Ii Closing Speech - Papal Encyclicals, http://www.papalencyclicals.net/Paul06/p6closin.htm (accessed July 14, 2019).

The Goal of the Second Vatican Council

Since the circumstances that led to the convening of Vat II and hence its stated goals were intimately interlinked with developments in science and technology, a brief discussion of these goals is quite appropriate. *Lumen Gentium*, "Dogmatic Constitution of the Church," often considered by the topmost scholars in the field as "the most imposing achievement of Vatican II,"[8] describes this point in detail.[9] Today humans are "buffeted between hope and anxiety and pressing one another with questions about the present course of events, and they are burdened down with uneasiness."[10] According to the Council, this spiritual agitation and the changing conditions of life are part of a broader and deeper revolution. Giving a careful and precise analysis of the situation, it continues: "Intellectual formation is ever increasingly based on the mathematical and natural sciences and on those dealing with man himself, while in the practical order the technology which stems from these sciences takes on mounting precedence."[11] Furthermore, "Technology is transforming the face of the earth, and is already trying to master outer space."[12] The advances in the biological and social sciences too are equally powerful and effective: "Advances in biology, psychology, and the social sciences not only bring men hope of improved self-knowledge. In conjunction with technical methods, they are also helping men to exert direct influence on the life of social groups."[13] In short, in our contemporary world, intellectual formation is very much coloured and controlled by science and technology. The impact is not confined to the intellectual field only; it reaches out to the cultural field and plays a major role in shaping our mode of thought and value system. Indeed, a new age has ushered in, thanks to developments in science and technology.[14] As mentioned earlier, Pope John correctly diagnosed that there was no proportionate growth in the moral field to ensure balanced and harmonious growth of contemporary humans. The Council was intended as a timely move to remedy this serious imbalance.

Aggiornamento, the Catchword of Vatican II

"Aggiornamento," making up-to-date, which became the catchword for the Council, expressed its set goal better than any other word or concept. The Church must be brought up-to-date, must adapt itself to meet the challenges

8 Avery Dulles, SJ, "Introduction ," Abt, p. 13.

9 See "Gaudium et Spes," nos. 4 and 5, Abt, pp. 203-204.

10 Ibid., p. 203.

11 Ibid., p. 203.

12 Ibid., p. 203.

13 Ibid., p. 203.

14 See "Gaudium et Spes," no. 54, Abt, p.260.

of modern times, mainly due to the astounding developments in science and technology. Pope John called for a renewed, serene and tranquil study and reflection on all the teaching of the Church in its entirety and preciseness, in the light of these developments. He wanted the Church to make use of modern means and methods, well-proven for their efficaciousness and accuracy, to expound and explicate the ever-alive Christian teaching and rich heritage. Thus the Council would be "a step forward toward a doctrinal penetration and a formation of consciousness in faithful and perfect conformity."[15] Far from being intimidated by modern developments and techniques and then taking the negative and defensive attitude of debunking them, he wants to welcome them as practical tools from the ever-solicitous God to render the Church more relevant and meaningful to contemporary men and women.

Aggiornamento in the theological context should not be reduced to an exercise of rephrasing conventional theological teaching in contemporary terminology. The Council clearly states that such "old wine in new skins" simply defeats the purpose "for recent studies and findings of science, history, and philosophy raise new questions which influence life and demand new theological investigations."[16] Pope John Paul II in his letter to Fr. George Coyne, SJ, Director of Vatican Observatory, on June 1, 1988, was even more emphatic: "Contemporary developments in science challenge theology far more deeply than did the introduction of Aristotle into Western Europe in the thirteenth century."[17]

At the same time, it must be emphasized that this aggiornamento in no way meant any break with the fundamental teachings of the Church. To dispel any doubt on this matter, Pope John clarified: "The substance of the ancient doctrine of the deposit of faith is one thing, and how it is presented is another. And it is the latter that must be taken into great consideration with patience if necessary, everything being measured in the forms and proportions of a magisterium which is predominantly pastoral in character."[18]

The scientific developments had a pivotal role to play in motivating the Pope to convene the Council, and the predominant atmosphere was one of optimism and appreciation for scientific advances. But this allowed no compromise with spiritual values the Church has always stood for. Nor has the

15 "Pope John's Opening Speech to the Council," Abt, p. 715.

16 "Gaudium et Spes," no. 62, Abt, p.268.

17 Letter of Pope John Paul II to Reverend George V. Coyne, SJ, Director of the Vatican Observatory, I June, 1988, in Robert Russell, William Stoeger, SJ, and George Coyne, SJ, eds., *Physics, Philosophy and Theology: A Common Quest for Understanding (Vatican City State: Vatican Observatory Publications, 1988), p. M12. Henceforth Ppt. See also* Father Tomislav Vlasic's Letter To Pope John Paul II, http://www.medjugorje.org/vlasic1.htm (accessed July 14, 2019).

18 "Pope John's Opening Speech," Abt, p. 715.

Church failed to admonish humans against the wrongs that often accompany an excessive emphasis on the material and the scientific. In Pope John's own words: "The Church has not watched inertly themarvellouss progress of the discoveries of human genius, and has not been backward in evaluating them rightly. But, while following these developments, she does not neglect to admonish men so that, over and above sense – perceived things – they may raise their eyes to God, the Source of all wisdom and all beauty."[19] In fact, this aggiornamento, far from diminishing the importance and relevance of the spiritual dimension, should enhance and strengthen it. "Illumined by the light of this Council, the Church ... we confidently trust they will become greater in spiritual riches and, gaining the strength of new energies she will look to the future without fear. In fact, by bringing herself up to date where required, and by the wise organization of mutual cooperation, the Church will make men, families and peoples really turn their minds to heavenly things."[20] Clearly, one of the goals of this Council was to help contemporary humans living in a world dominated by science and technology to achieve a delicate balance between the scientific and the religious, between the material and the spiritual – an extremely challenging but crucially vital task.[21]

Some Special Features of Second Vatican Council

In order to understand and appreciate adequately Vat II's attitude towards science and technology, we need to look at the overall spirit that animated the Council. Some of the special features of the Council had a major role to play in determining the attitude it took towards modern developments, particularly towards those in the field of science and technology.

It could be said that Vat II ushered in a new age in the life and attitude of the Catholic Church. Gone was the age of unhelpful comparison and unhealthy competition. Instead the spirit of humility and fraternity was ushered in. Gone was the spirit of confrontation and condemnation, in its place the spirit of understanding and compassion was ushered in. As Pope John announced, "The Spouse of Christ prefers to make use of the medicine of mercy rather than of severity.[22] Taking a positive approach, "she considers that she meets the needs

19 Ibid., p. 714.

20 Ibid., p. 712.

21 It may be noted that several eminent scholars around this time also sounded alarm bells about the serious mismatch between the wealth of the material, scientific developments, on the one hand, and the poverty of the spiritual in humans, on the other, together with the consequent *monstrous growth the world was experiencing. In this context the writings of the humanist Marin Luther King Jr. and the scientist Louis de Broglie, both Nobel winners, are particularly remarkable.*

22 Ibid., p. 716.

of the present day by demonstrating the validity of her teaching rather than by condemnation."[23]

All these developments brought in newness and a positive spirit, thereby justifying the new appellations conferred on the post-conciliar Church. Pope John XXIII referred to it as a "New Pentecost," Pope Paul VI called it an "Epiphany," and Pope John Paul II spoke of a "New Advent." Pope John Paul II went further to say that it has brought about a substantially new relationship: "The Second Vatican Council laid the foundation for a substantially new relationship between the Church and the world, between the Church and modern culture."[24] I discuss some of the most salient elements at the foundation of this new relationship.

a. Emphasis on the Pastoral Rather Than on the Doctrinal Dimension

Vat II can best be characterized as a "people-friendly" council,in a sense here the focus of attention was meeting the pastoral needs of the faithful rather than affirming or clarifying some doctrinal details. Time and again in his opening speech, Pope John challenged the Fathers of the Council to a positive and pastoral attitude. The documents of the Council, particularly "Gaudium et Spes" and "Lumen Gentium," took special pains to understand the present predicament of contemporary men and women, and explored the best ways to meet their needs.

b. Spirit of Magnanimity, Universality, Optimism and Openness

The newness of the Council became most manifest in the spirit that animated it all through the many deliberations and, in some ways, afterwards: a universal outlook that cut across geographical, racial and cultural boundaries; a spirit of magnanimity that expressed itself in respectful acknowledgement and warm acceptance of non-Catholics and non-Christians; a spirit of optimism and positiveness that readily appreciated the good in other religions and systems; and a spirit of openness to new possibilities even when they looked challenging and demanding. In the words of Pope Paul VI, "From the start the Council has propagated a wave of serenity and of optimism, a Christianity that is exciting and positive, loving life, mankind and earthly values ... an orientation of making Christianity acceptable and lovable, indulgent and open, free of medieval rigorous and pessimistic understanding of man and his customs."[25] Unity in some ways became the central theme: unity within the Church, unity with our non-Catholic brothers and sisters (the Separated Brethren), unity with

23 Ibid., p.716.

24 Pope John Paul II, College, December 22, 1980. Quoted in http://www.wandea.org.pl/second-vatican-council.htm

25 Pope Paul VI, Doc. Cath. No. 1538, in http://www.wandea.org.pl/second-vatican-council.htm

the whole humankind, irrespective of creed, race, caste, colour, nationality, etc. According to Pope Paul VI, "The Council is a solemn act of love for mankind, love for men of today, whoever and wherever they may be, love for all."[26] The Council gave official and solemn testimony to this spirit of unity and universality when "The Constitution of the Church," considered by many the most important document of Vat II, called the Church "the sacrament of union with God, the sacrament of the unity of the whole of the human race."[27]

This spirit of unity and universal outlook contrasts conspicuously with the ideas of certain past theologians and other scholars. For instance, in the past theologians and other teachers used to describe the Church as "a perfect, independent society, often in competition with other social systems."[28] Also in the past at times, a narrow legalism and a consequent self-referential and self-righteous mentality used to dominate certain sections of the ecclesiastical milieu. Debunking and belittling of other traditions, cultures and religions was another trademark of this attitude. The successful expansion of colonialism and Church's association, in some ways, with it added to this spirit of triumphalism and elitism which placed other religions at loggerheads with Christianity, particularly in the East, isolated it from other cultures, thereby undermining the universality of Christ and his mission. Vat II was a heroic and much-needed initiative to undo the harm done by such uncalled for superiority feeling and triumphalism.

A spirit of humility and brotherly attitude was also very visible in Vat II. As Abbott points out in his footnote, there were several speakers in the Council calling for a reconsideration of the Galileo episode and for taking appropriate steps to forestall any recurrence of such embarrassing events.[29] In fact, Pope John Paul soon after taking over as the Supreme Pontiff in 1979 appointed a Pontifical Commission to reexamine the Galileo case to set the record straight. This Commission completed its work in 1992 and presented the Pope a report of its findings which found that mistakes had been committed by the Church officials involved in handling Galileo's case. The Commission's recommendation that "these mistakes must be frankly recognized" was endorsed by the official Church. A more dramatic demonstration of humility and brotherliness was witnessed on December 7, 1965, when the Roman Pontiff Pope Paul VI and the Patriarch of Constantinople, Athenagoras I, formally and publicly expressed their regret for the mutual excommunications pronounced

26 Pope Paul VI, Bodart, La Biologie et l'avenire de l'home, in http://www.wandea.org.pl/second-vatican-council.htm

27 This idea is found in many passages of "Gaudium et Spes," although the exact phrase occurs in the "Constitution on the Sacred Liturgy," no. 26, Abt 147.

28 "Second Vatican Council," http:///www.christurex.org/www1/CDHN/v1.html

29 Abt, p. 234, note 99.

by their respective predecessors Pope Leo IX and Patriarch Cerularius in 1054.[30]

A genuine openness by the Church to new ideas without losing its rootedness in tradition was another hallmark of Vat II, particularly from the world of modern physical and social sciences. Pope John emphasized this point already in his opening speech: "The Church should never depart from the sacred patrimony of the truth received from the Fathers. But at the same time,, she must ever look to the present, to the new conditions and new forms of life introduced into the modern world, which have opened new avenues to the Catholic apostolate."[31] Lawrence Cardinal Shehan of Baltimore, one of the prominent members of the Council, summarized his view of the Council: "Taken as a whole, the documents are especially noteworthy for their concern with the poor, for their insistence on the unity of the human family and therefore on the wrongness of discrimination."[32]

c. Willingness to Embrace a Dynamic Worldview

The Aristotelian world was very much a static one and gave rise to a static worldview. One could say that in this ancient Greek system also there was room for change and growth, but it certainly was very limited, being confined to the limits set by the intrinsic nature of each species. The species themselves were immutable, and the world as a whole could not change and evolve. Christianity, through its process of Hellenization, subscribed to this static worldview, with far-reaching theological and moral implications. According to this perspective, in the beginning, God created humans and the universe in the perfect stage. Through Adam's fall, this original pristine perfection was lost. The whole redemptive mission aimed at restoring lost purity and perfection. Progress in this context is achieved by going back to the good old days and state, not in going forward to a better and glorious future.

The scientific worldview, although it remained somewhat static in the initial stages of its development, gradually became dynamic and progressive, particularly with the advent of the theory of evolution. Today, thanks to further developments in science and the philosophy of science, it is claimed that everything is subject to change – everything in the universe changes and evolves, and everything in science is subject to change and evolution.

The scientific worldview and its consequent idea of evolution and progress are alien to the traditional Christian worldview. Vat II, in some ways, announced a departure from this static view and initiated a move towards a dynamic one. "Gaudium et Spes starts with a long tale of changes affecting

30 See Abt, p.xiii.

31 "Pope John's Opening Speech," Abt., p. 714.

32 Lawrence Cardinal Shehan, "Introduction," Abt, p. xvii.

humankind, the perpetual justification for innovation. Everything changes – the world, time, but especially man who is described as participating in a perpetual 'progression.' John XIII believed there had been a 'real progress of humankind's collective moral awareness through always deeper discovery of its dignity... and that divine providence was leading us to a new order of human relations.... Vatican II proceeded to make this principle magisterial."[33] Vat II gave evidence of this view when it said: "The human race has passed from a rather static concept of reality to a more dynamic, evolutionary one."[34] The consequences of this paradigm shift are enormous and the Council, well aware of this fact, observes: "In consequence, there has arisen a new series of problems, a series as important as can be, calling for new efforts of analysis and synthesis."[35] Pope Paul VI echoed some of these consequences when he said: "If the world changes religion should also change.... the order to which Christianity tends is not static, but an order in continual evolution towards a higher form."[36] This sensitivity to the dynamic worldview of modern science and this openness to its consequences are crucial for defining the Council's attitude to science and technology. They can play a pivotal role in fostering a constructive and creative dialogue between Christianity and modern science.

d. Concern for a Balance between the Divine and the Human

Some scholars point out a sharp contrast between Christ and Socrates when confronted with death. The Gospels tell us that in the Garden of Gethsemane Christ was extremely disturbed and frightened at the thought of his impending death. "My soul is sorrowful to the point of death," he told his apostles. (Mark 14:34). On the other hand, Socrates laughed and cracked jokes at the moment of his death. Whatever interpretation scholars may give to this remarkable contrast, it brings out the marked difference between Christ's way of looking at human life and the Hellenistic way. The Socratic school of philosophy, particularly Plato and Aristotle, made a sharp distinction between the celestial and the terrestrial, assigning the former a far superior status and value. Life on earth was neither desirable nor significant compared to the life after death in the celestial world. On the other hand, Christ had a balanced view towards human life on earth. He certainly was not attached to the world and to life in this world, but he did find true meaning and value for human life on earth.

As Christian theology developed, particularly in the Middle Ages, the Socratic view became dominant and the life of the world-to-come was given

33 http://www.wandea.org.pl/second-vatican-council.htm

34 Gaudium et Spes," no. 5, Abt, p. 204.

35 Ibid., p. 204.

36 Pope Paul VI, "Dialogues, Reflections on God and Man," quoted in http://www.wandea.org.pl/second-vatican-council.htm

all the attention at the expense of life in the present world. Connected to this was the over-glorification of the spiritual at the expense of the material, of the supernatural at the expense of the natural, of the divine at the expense of the human. Critics point out that this lopsided and unchristian view was exploited by the powerful and influential, both in the religious and in the secular world, to their selfish advantage – they could indulge in their selfish exploitation of the underprivileged and console the oppressed with the thought of the great reward to come in the next world. This exploitation was used by atheistic-minded critics of the Church to unleash their vehement attack on religion and God. For instance, Karl Marx called religion "the opium of the people," Frederick Nietzsche accused the Church of transferring all the good things to the world to come.

Although there have been several attempts by the official Catholic Church to rectify this one-sided view, many still felt that enough was not done to give a balanced Christian perspective. It seems to me that Vat II took special pains to remedy this imbalance. In this context the following words of Pope Paul VI are very pertinent: "We must never forget that the fundamental attitude of Catholics who wish to convert the world must be, first of all, to love the world, to love our times, to love our civilizations, our technical achievements, and above all, to love the world.... The Council puts before us, a panoramic vision of the world; how can the Church, how can we, do other than behold this world and love it?"[37] No doubt, this is not the usual traditional expression and language of Pontiffs. But it seems to me that the Pope has captured the sentiments of the Council quite aptly and accurately. A very positive attitude towards the world that was created by God who "found it good" can never be alien to the Church of God.

From this positive attitude towards and appreciation for the world of God's creation follows an equally positive appreciation for human activity, particularly in the positive sciences. The Council clearly states that there is a close bond between human activities like the sciences and religion. In fact, "Such is not merely required by modern man but harmonizes also with the will of the Creator. For by the very circumstances of their having been created, all things are endowed with their own stability, truth, goodness, proper laws, and order."[38] An important footnote to this text clarifies the matter even better: "The Council shuns any fundamentalism in dealing with the findings of science, whether ecclesiastical or natural."

In conclusion the Council states: "Therefore if methodical investigation within every branch of learning is carried out in a genuinely scientific manner

---

37 Pope Paul VI, Bodart, La Biologie et l'avenire de l'homme, in http://www.wandea.org.pl/second-vatican-council.htm

38 "Gaudium et Spes," no. 36, Abt, p.233.

and in accordance with moral norms, it never truly conflicts with faith. For earthly matters and the concerns of faith derive from the same God."[39]

At the same time, it must be emphasized that the Council's was no blind endorsement of everything scientific. It has taken pains to distinguish between "excesses associated with a spirit of scientism and the permanently valid achievements of the positive sciences over the past few centuries. In doing so, it remains faithful to the spirit of Leo XIII, Pius XII and John XXIII, Pontiffs who made notable efforts to establish fruitful contact and collaboration with the sphere of modern science and culture."[40]

The Main Ideas of the Council on Science and Technology

a. Warm and Positive Attitude

It is quite clear that a very warm and appreciative attitude prevailed towards science and scientists before, during and after the Council. As we have seen, one of the prime motivations for convening this historic Council came from the recognition of the importance of scientific developments and the urgent need to update the Church in the light of them. During the long course of it also the same spirit persisted, as was evident from the deliberations of the Council and the repeated reference of several council fathers to set aright the Galileo controversy. As we will see, after the Council, there was an even more appreciative and collaborative attitude. Perhaps the words of the "Closing Messages" give us the best testimony to this spirit. The importance the Council gave to science can be seen from the fact that it had a specific closing message "To Men of Thought and Science" read out by Paul Emile Cardinal Leger of Montreal, assisted by Antonio Cardinal Caggiano of Buenos Aires and Norman Cardinal Gilroy of Sydney, Australia.[41] It is remarkable to note that the special message begins with a special salutation: "A very special greeting to you."[42] Although there were closing messages addressed to many other groups, to none was extended such a special and warm greeting. For instance, immediately after greeting the scientists, the Council addressed the artists. But it began with the cold words "We now address you, artists."[43] It seems to me that this small detail should not be overlooked: this indeed was an indicator of the importance the Council attached to the world of science and scientists. That this special greeting was not perfunctory but was really intentional became clear from the very first sentence of the message: "Why a *special greeting* to

39 Ibid., p. 234.

40 See "Gaudium et Spes," no. 57, footnote 190.

41 "Closing Messages of the Council," Abt, p. 730.

42 Ibid., p. 730.

43 Ibid., p. 732.

you?"[44] The Council itself answers this question in terms of the common quest the Church shares with science: "Because all of us, bishops, and Fathers of the Council, are on the lookout for truth."[45] That this warmth and cordiality was not a passing formality, but was a foundation for a lasting relationship and a plea for close collaboration was evident in the memorable letter of Pope John Paul II to Fr. George Coyne, SJ, Director of Vatican Observatory: "We (science and Catholicism) need each other to be what we must be, what we are called to be."[46] He specified the point further in the letter: "For the truth of the matter is that the Church and the scientific community will inevitably interact; their options do not include isolation."[47]

b. Scientists as Friends and Fellow-seekers of Truth

The common bond linking scientists and the Fathers of the Church is the truth and the untiring quest for it. The scientific community and the Christian community share a common goal and a common quest. "Hence, our paths could not fail to cross. Your paths are never foreign to ours."[48] The Fathers of the Council reassured the scientists of their support and collaboration in the different aspects of their challenging search for truth: "We are friends of your vocation as searchers, companions in your fatigues, admirers of your successes and, if necessary, consolers in your discouragement and your failures."[49] These are deeply personal and intimate words of encouragement. I wonder whether even the secular world has ever expressed their support to the scientific community in such touching words.

The Council has a very specific message for the scientific community: "Continue your search without tiring and without ever despairing of the truth."[50] The spirit that should animate this untiring quest is the same as that of St. Augustine who said: "Let us seek with the desire to find, and find with the desire to seek still more."[51]

The specifically Christian contribution to this common quest for truth is "the light of our mysterious lamp, which is faith."[52] Only when genuine scientific efforts are coupled with deep faith in the one who said "I am the light of the world, I am the way, and the truth and the life," can we hope to

44 Ibid., p. 730. Emphasis added.

45 Ibid., p. 730.

46 Ppt, p. M14.

47 Ppt, p. M13.

48 "Closing Message," Abt, p. 731.

49 Ibid., p. 731.

50 Ibid., p. 731.

51 Ibid., p. 731.

52 Ibid., p. 731.

apprehend real truth, the whole truth. Today the time is ripe for such a meet between science and faith: "Never perhaps, thank God, has there been so clear a possibility as today of a deep understanding between real science and real faith, mutual servants of one another in the one truth."[53] Finally, the "Closing Message" exhorts scientists "not to stand in the way of this important meeting [between science and faith]. Have confidence in faith, this great friend of intelligence."[54]

c. Appreciation for the Achievements of Science

Gone is the stormy, confrontational attitude that clouded the sky of the relationship between science and religion in the past. Instead, a healthy attitude of dialogue and collaboration is moving in, thanks to a positive approach towards science and its achievements. According to Vatican II, far from being the devious devices of the devil, they are a boon to humanity, ordained by divine dispensation. "By divine favour, especially in modern times, human genius has produced from natural material astonishing inventions in the field of technology."[55] In her solicitude for the wellbeing of humanity, the Church is happy about these developments and gladly welcomes them. "As a Mother, the Church welcomes and watches such inventions with special concern... Mother Church, to be sure, recognizes that if these instruments are rightly used, they bring solid nourishment to the human race."[56]

In a way, science is a powerful affirmation of human dignity and greatness and provides humans with a most effective means to collaborate with the Creator in the ongoing plan of creation.[57]

> For when, by the work of his hands, or with the aid of technology, man develops the earth so that it can bear fruit and become a dwelling worthy of the whole human family, and when he consciously takes part in the life of social groups, he carries out the design of God. Manifested, at the beginning of time, the divine plan is that man should subdue the earth, bring creation to perfection and develop himself. When a man so acts, he simultaneously obeys the great Christian commandment that he places himself at the service of his brother men.[58]

---

53 Ibid., p. 731.

54 Ibid., p. 731.

55 "Decree on the Instruments of Social Communications," no. 1, Abt, p. 319.

56 .Ibid., p. 319.

57 See "Gaudium et Spes," no. 57, Abt, p. 262.

58 Ibid.., p. 262. See also The Professions And Society - Aromagosa.easycgi.com, http://aromagosa.easycgi.com/christianhumanism/professionsworkshop/professionsan (accessed July 14, 2019).

A prudential, judicious engagement in science can elevate humans to a higher and more sublime level of moral and intellectual life. "Furthermore, when a man applies himself to the various disciplines of philosophy, of history, and of mathematical and natural science, and when he cultivates the arts, he can do very much to elevate the human family to a more sublime understanding of truth, goodness, and beauty, and to the formation of judgments which embody universal values."[59]

d. Science as a Means to Meet the Challenges

Continuing its positive attitude, the Council further says that science and technology provide us with the best means to respond to the challenges and exigencies of our contemporary world. After a penetrating and perceptive analysis of the various ferments in the air today and the accompanying restlessness and aimlessness, it rightly points out that "today's spiritual agitation and the changing conditions of life are part of a broader and deeper revolution."[60] In its attempt to spell out the far-reaching consequences of this revolution, it admits that the conditions of the world are changing profoundly. For one thing, the traditional base of intellectual formation is getting changed. Today science and technology constitute a powerful foundation for the intellectual formation of humans all over the world. The technological revolution afoot in our society is transforming the face of the earth. The sweeping wave of the new scientific spirit is reshaping both our cultural sphere and mode of thought. I have quoted earlier the words of the Council on this point. In more recent times Pope John Paul has reiterated the same sentiment in his letter to Fr. George Coyne, SJ: "The scientific disciplines too, as is obvious, are endowing us with an understanding and appreciation of our universe as a whole and of the incredibly rich variety of intricately related processes and structures which constitute its animate and inanimate components. This knowledge has given us a more thorough understanding of ourselves and of our humble yet unique role within creation."[61] Not only the physical sciences, the social sciences and still more the life sciences also are affecting our world profoundly, especially in the wake of the genetic revolution with its astounding strides in genetic engineering, cloning, etc.

Another salutary outcome of this revolution principally triggered by developments in science & technology is the shift from an individual or person-centred worldview to a community-centred one. "The destiny of the human community has become all of a piece, where once the various groups

59 Ibid. , p. 263.

60 Ibid., no. 5, p. 203.

61 Ppt. P.M5.

of men had a kind of private history of their own."[62] The overall outcome of these revolutionary changes is that the old static worldview has given way to a dynamic one, with drastic consequences.[63]

> Indeed, because of all these developments, the living conditions of modern man have been so profoundly changed in their social and cultural dimensions, that we can speak of a new age in human history. Fresh avenues are open, therefore, for the refinement of the wider diffusion of culture. These avenues have been paved by the enormous growth of natural, human and social sciences, by progress in technology, and by advances in the development and organization of how men communicate with each other.[64]

In this new world naturally a new series of problems has arisen," a series as important as can be, calling for new efforts of analysis and synthesis."[65] The Council believes that for tackling these problems, a new approach using new techniques is needed, and here the findings of science & technology should play an active role. Here too Pope John Paul II presents a more contemporary view when he talks of the great contribution technology has made in the field of transportation, communication, etc., and concludes: "Such knowledge and power, as we have discovered, can be used greatly to enhance and improve our lives or they can be exploited to diminish and destroy human life and the environment even on a global scale."[66]

e. The Autonomy of the Sciences Upheld

The Council takes special pains to acknowledge and uphold the rightful autonomy of the sciences.

> The sacred Synod, therefore, recalling the teaching of the First Vatican Council, declares that there are 'two orders of knowledge' which are distinct, namely, faith and reason. It declares that the Church does not indeed forbid that 'when the human arts and sciences are practised they use their own principles and their proper method, each in its own domain.' Hence, 'acknowledging this just liberty,' the sacred Synod affirms the legitimate autonomy of human culture and especially of the sciences."[67]

Nor is it ashamed to admit its past lapses. It accepts that this principle of independence was not always preserved in the past and deplores the mistakes committed. "Consequently, we cannot but deplore certain habits of mind,

62 "Gaudium et Spes," no. 5, Abt, pp. 203-204.

63 Ibid. , no. 54, p. 260.

64 Ibid. , p. 260.

65 Ibid. , no. 6, p. 204.

66 Ppt. P. M5.

67 "Gaudium et Spes," no. 59, Abt, p. 265.

sometimes found too among Christians, which do not sufficiently attend to the rightful independence of science. The arguments and controversies which they spark lead many minds to conclude that faith and science are mutually opposed."[68]

Pope John Paul II took up this point more explicitly when he addressed the Pontifical Academy of Sciences in 1979 and said: "Certain attitudes (not unknown among Christians) deriving from a short-sighted view of the rightful autonomy of science: they have occasioned conflict and controversy and have misled many into thinking that faith and science are opposed."[69] The Pope emphasized that he was following up on the declaration of the Council and he took up the Galileo episode as a concrete instance: "To go beyond this stand taken by the Council, I hope that theologians, scholars and historians, animated by a spirit of collaboration, will study the Galileo case more deeply and, in loyal recognition of wrongs from whatever side they come, will dispel the mistrust that still opposes, in many minds, a fruitful concord between science and faith, between the Church and the world."[70] He echoed once again the same theme of respectful autonomy and mutually enriching collaboration between science and faith in his letter of 1988: "Both religion and science must preserve their autonomy and their distinctiveness. Religion is not founded on science, nor is science an extension of religion. Each should possess its own principles, its pattern of procedures, its diversities of interpretation and its own conclusions."[71] "Science and faith are called "to live in a collaborative interaction in which we are called continually to be more."[72]

At the same time, the Council is quick to point out that it does not endorse the false sense of independence, which "is taken to mean that created things do not depend on God, and that man can use them without any reference to their Creator."[73]

Some of the excesses and consequent dangers the scientific spirit can lead to also have not escaped the Council.

> No doubt today's progress in science and technology can foster a certain exclusive emphasis on observable data, and an agnosticism about everything else. For the methods of investigation which these sciences use

---

68 Ibid., no. 36, p. 234.

69 Pope John Paul II, "Proceedings of the Pontifical Academy of Sciences," November 10, 1979, PDF files, p.1. For more details see Mathew Chandrankunnel, CMI, *Science and Religion: From Warpath to Wholeness (Bangalore: Dharmaram Publications, 2004),m p. 213.*

70 Ibid., p. 213.

71 Ppt, p. M8.

72 Ppt, p. M14.

73 "Gaudium et Spes," no. 36, Abt, p. 234.

> can be wrongly considered as the supreme rule for discovering the whole truth. By virtue of their methods, however, these sciences cannot penetrate to the intimate meaning of things. Yet the danger exists that man, confiding too much in modern discoveries, may even think that he is sufficient unto himself and no longer seek any higher realities.[74]

For instance, at times a belittling of religious beliefs, an agnosticism towards matters of religious life, etc., are looked upon as "requirements of scientific progress or of a certain new humanism."[75] But these areas of concern and possibilities of deviation should not be exaggerated and used as an excuse to close the door of science and technology. The document goes on to say that "these unfortunate results, however, do not necessarily follow from the culture of today, nor should they lead us into the temptation of not acknowledging its positive values."[76]

f. The Pastoral Dimension of Science

The Council readily acknowledges and appreciates the positive values accruing from the scientific spirit. They are:

> Scientific study and strict fidelity toward truth in scientific research, the necessity of working together with others in technical groups, a sense of international solidarity, an ever clearer awareness of the responsibility of experts to aid men and even to protect them, the desire to make the conditions of life more favourable for all, especially for those who are deprived of the opportunity to exercise responsibility or who are culturally poor.[77]

From these considerations flows the apostolic dimension of science & technology because the values mentioned above can prepare the ground for sowing the seeds of the gospel. "All these values can provide some preparation for the acceptance of the message of the gospel – a preparation which can be animated with divine love by Him who came to save the world."[78]

In pastoral care too science and its findings can be beneficial. "In pastoral care, appropriate care must be made not only of theological principles, but also of the findings of the secular sciences, especially of psychology and sociology. Thus the faithful can be brought to live the faith in a more thorough and mature way."[79]

---

74 Ibid., no. 57, p. 263.

75 Ibid. , no. 7, p. 205.

76 Ibid., no. 57, p. 263.

77 Ibid., pp. 263-264.

78 Ibid. , p. 264.

79 Ibid. , no. 62, p. 269. See also"The Errors Of Vatican Ii - Sspxasia.com." Insert Name of Site in Italics. N.p., n.d. Web. 20 Jul. 2019 https://www.sspxasia.com/Documents/

g. The Importance of Science Education

Having appreciated the tremendous power science wields in our world by influencing not only how we live, but also how we think, the Council emphasizes the teaching of scientific ideas and methods in educational institutions. In its "Declaration on Christian Education," it takes special care to remind all that, although primary education is important and must be continued, "considerable importance is to be attached to those schools which are demanded in a particular way by modern conditions, such as so-called professional and technical schools,...."[80] It goes on to say that in institutions of higher learning, the Church wants "in a systematic way to have individual branches of knowledge studied according to their own proper principles and methods, and with due freedom of scientific investigation. She intends thereby to promote an ever-deeper understanding of these fields, and as a result of the extremely precise evaluation of modern problems and inquiries, to have it seen more profoundly how faith and reason give harmonious witness to the unity of all truth."[81] The Council is even more direct and emphatic when it says: "Since the sciences progress chiefly through special investigations of advanced scientific significance, Catholic colleges and universities and their faculties should give the maximum support to institutes which primarily serve the progress of scientific research."[82]

h. Science and Priestly Formation

From what has been said already, the conclusion follows naturally that the Council wants the imparting of the scientific spirit to be made an integral part of the priestly formation. This point is made explicit in the "Decree on Priestly Formation," particularly when it talks about the teaching of philosophy. "Philosophy should be taught in such a way that students will be led to acquire a solid and coherent understanding of man, of the world, and of God. Basing themselves on a philosophic heritage which is perennially valid, students should also be conversant with contemporary philosophical investigations, especially those exercising special influence in their own country, and with recent scientific progress."[83]

Speaking of theological study and research Pope John Paul urges all engaged in theological reflection to incorporate the findings of contemporary science to complement and enrich their service to the Church and the world. "As these findings [of science] become part of the intellectual culture of

---

SiSiNoNo/2004_January/errors_of_vatican_II.ht.

80 "Declaration on Christian Education," no. 9, Abt, p. 648.

81 Ibid., p. 648.

82 Ibid., no. 10, p. 649.

83 "Priestly Formation," no.15, Abt, p. 450.

the time, however, theologians must understand them and test their value in bringing out from Christian belief some of the possibilities which have not yet been realized."[84] At the same time, he is quick to caution that "theology is not to incorporate indifferently each new philosophical or scientific theory."[85]

i. The Impact of Science on Theology

The Council is of the opinion that theology is an important beneficiary of these scientific developments because they can "stimulate the mind to a more accurate and penetrating grasp of the faith. For recent studies and findings of science, history, and philosophy raise new questions which influence life and demand new theological investigations."[86] Hence the Council urges theology to be in constant touch with developments in the sciences. "Through a sharing of resources and points of view, let those who teach in seminaries, colleges, and universities try to collaborate with men well versed in the other sciences. The theological inquiry should seek a profound understanding of revealed truth without neglecting close contact with its own times."[87]

More recent proclamations of the Church are even more emphatic on this point: "Theology has been defined as an effort of faith to achieve understanding, as *fides quaerens intellectum.* As such, it must be in vital interchange today with science just as it always has been with philosophy and other forms of learning. Theology will have to call on the findings of science to one degree or another as it pursues is a primary concern for the human person, the reaches of freedom, the possibilities of the Christian community, the nature of belief and the intelligibility of nature and history."[88] Nor is the Pope content with a purely speculative theorization, he wants it to be implemented in the practical realm. "It would entail that some theologians, at least, should be sufficiently well versed in the sciences to make authentic and creative use of the resources that the best-established theories may offer them."[89]

These developments in science and technology have significant bearings on morality as well since they put us in close association with the contemporary life situation. Hence the Council urges all Christians: "May the faithful, therefore, ... blend modern science and its theories with Christian morality and doctrine. Thus their religious practice and morality can keep pace with their scientific knowledge and with ever-advancing technology."[90]

84 Ppt, p. M10.

85 Ibid., p. M10.

86 "Gaudium et Spes," no. 62, Abt, p. 268.

87 Ibid., p. 270.

88 Ppt, p. M10.

89 Ibid., p. M11.

90 "Gaudium et Spes," no. 62, Abt, p. 269.

Conclusion

Our brief study reveals that Vat II was not just another council convened to tackle a particular doctrinal problem vexing the Church. It was far more than that. It really aimed at an aggiornamento, a genuine, comprehensive effort to make the Church be at home in our contemporary world dominated by science and technology. It was a revolution-making event that brought about a paradigm shift not only in the Church's view of the world but also in its attitude towards science and technology. Far from being intimidated by the impressive strides of science, the Council gladly welcomes them as God's special gift to the universe to be used for its betterment. Far from looking at it as a formidable rival, Vat II looks at it as a respectful partner with a common mission. We have seen that recent developments in science and technology not only gave impetus to convene the Council, they also in some ways helped to redefine Church's new role in the world and suggested some ways of using the findings of science to play that role expeditiously and effectively.

The aggiornamento inaugurated by Vat II is a long and challenging process that needs to continue. Both the Church and modern science need to collaborate in this noble task. Science with its amazing findings of the secrets of nature and its well-proven powerful methods can be a great boon in this process. The perennial truths and the rich tradition of the Church too should serve as facilitators rather than obstacles in this venture. The truths and insights of religion can ensure that the ongoing process does not deviate from the right path of holistic progress of humanity and the cosmos. The Christian tradition can make available centuries of rich experience as a source of inspiration and guidance. Vat II has opened the door for such a constructive and collaborative mission to respond responsibly to the challenges of our contemporary world.

PART THREE

DIALOGUING WITH OTHER RELIGIONS

17

Encounter between Religions

Joseph Mattam SJ
Professor (Emeritus) Systematic Theology, Founder, Gujarat Jesuit Regional Theologate (RTC) and Gujarat Vidya Deep (GVD), Baroda

Abstract: *This article wants to look at Jesus' attitude to other religions, with a view to promote encounter between religions, which is demanded in our time. While continuing to affirm the centrality of Jesus in our life, as Christians, we affirm his unique role in the plan of God, as we have known it. We believe that he is meant for all, or as Pope Francis says, he has answers to all our problems in the world. We proclaim him to all and invite all to become his disciples. Jesus is the concrete human manifestation of what God wants to tell all people through the ages concerning our attitude towards God and the society in which we live.*

However, we do not say that he is the only way for all; we cannot say that God works through him only; for God has many ways unknown to us; what is known to us is limited in the plan of God; just because we know one way, we do not hold that is the only way; we do not know all the ways of God; we are not justified in imposing our terminology on all; even the language of logos, spirit is Christian and should not be imposed on others.

Keywords: *Encounter, Dialogue, Other religions, Jesus' centrality, Fulfilment theory.*

Since we follow Jesus, it is proper that we first look at Jesus' attitude to people of other religions. Jesus was a Jew. Jesus has not spoken explicitly about any other religions; hence, obviously, he does not condemn any religion, either. He also does not condemn anyone due to his/her religious affiliation. He seems to have accepted people for who they are; he saw their goodness, not based on their religion. His Jewish society had a rather negative attitude towards the Samaritans, yet as examples of good behaviour he brings in the Samaritans. The story of the Good Samaritan (Lk 10.30-37), the person who comes back to thank him after he had been cured was also a Samaritan (Lk 17.11-19). His dialogue with the Samaritan woman (Jn 4.5-42) shows his positive attitude. She thinks of what divides the Jews and others, for example, the Temple/mountain; Jesus thinks of what unites them: worship in spirit and truth, not on any mountain or in a temple. A Samaritan village did not welcome Jesus and his disciples (Lk 9.51-55); the disciples wanted to destroy that village, Jesus understands them, and without condemning them goes to another village. When a Roman Centurion asks for help, Jesus willingly offers to go and heal his servant, though the Centurion does not feel himself worthy to receive Jesus in his house (Matt 8. 5ff). He heals the sick of Gennesarath (Mk 6.53ff; Matt 14.34ff) without any precondition. Similarly, at Geresa, a gentile territory, he heals the daughter of a Canaanite woman (Mk 7.24ff), and he heals a deaf-mute (Mk 7.31ff).

The Encounter of Jesus

All through his public life, he is open to people of all faiths; he dialogues with them and emphasised the commonality; his formulation of religion was non-sectarian; it was universal and genuinely humanist, going against the ritualism of the traditionalists. This, of course, led him to incur their displeasure, and they would want him killed. We need to follow the lead given by Jesus and promote true humanism, appreciating the genuine life of faith wherever it is found. We will respect human dignity irrespective of faiths and religions, culture and traditions.

Jesus, we notice, was very open to all religions and he did not deal with people based on religious affiliations. But when we come to the era of the Church, things would change. To understand the Church's attitude to other religions, we need to look at its recent history.

The Relation between the European Church and Other Religions

It is necessary, however, to place the theme we study in its proper historical perspective. Only in the context of the general East-West encounter and in the light of the attitude of the universal Church to other religions in the 19th and early 20th centuries can the attitude of the Church in India be understood. We may point out three major attitudes which characterized the relation of the Church and of Europe to non-Christian religions and eastern cultures.

The first is what Dr. Cuttat calls a *Wertblindheit,* blindness to the values of religions and cultures other than one's own. It resulted in an attitude of polemics and exclusivism, based on a one-sided appreciation of one's own religion and culture and the ignorance of those of others. Missionaries, with some exceptions, followed a theology, which, owing to a very narrow and exclusivist interpretation of the axiom, *extra ecclesiam nulla salus*, believed that the eternal salvation of 'infidels' depended on conversion to Christianity. This attitude was found, for example, even at the beginning of the last century in *Maximum Illud* of Benedict XV who expressed the aim of missionary activity as "to bring light to those dwelling in the shadow of death and to open the way to heaven to those hurrying to destruction" (*Acta Apostolicae Sedis* 1919:446). Given the conviction that the followers of non-Christian religions were "hurrying to destruction", it is quite understandable that missionaries did not attempt to learn the spiritual wealth of the people to whom they had to preach the Word of God, but tried rather to refute and destroy them. Besides, there was a deplorable confusion between culture and Christianity, or more precisely, between Western culture and Christianity. Christianity had become so much identified with its expression in the West that another expression of it could not be conceived. But whatever may have been the shortcomings of the missionaries; they succeeded in 'planting' the Church in many parts of Asia and Africa, and their handing on of Christ's teaching has borne fruit.

Another attitude that gained currency in the nineteenth and early twentieth centuries among pioneers of Orientalism may be called descriptive, pragmatic or scientist. Thanks to the linguistic developments one was able to 'understand' Asia, but the Europe that Asia encountered was a Europe on the way to de-Christianization. Orientalists like Max Muller and Sylvain Levi were humanists with an open mind on the 'horizontal' plane, but closed to the 'vertical', owing to a positivist philosophy which dispensed with the supernatural. Scientism may thus be considered part of the beginning of secularism. Understandably the 'spiritual' East refused to yield to those who approached it with an a priori denial of everything beyond the observable and the measurable. The error of scientism was not in making abstraction of the transcendent order while it analysed the order of immanence – that would have been legitimate – but in denying transcendence in the name of science. Orientalism, however, so long as it remains within the field of description can render excellent service to an East-West encounter of religions.

If at one extreme we have polemics and opposition, at the other we find syncretism. Syncretism in a religious sense means "a mixing of inharmonious, conflicting religious elements" (Kraemer 1954: 258). It holds an "essential unity" of all religions at a "higher metaphysical plane", at the level of an Absolute beyond all gods, and sees all conflicting "truths" of religions as merely different expressions of the same Reality. Its exponents like Frithjof Schuon and Rene Guenon try to 'iron out' all differences between religions, maintaining that they are only apparent and valuable only on a lower level. Religious truths which are in fact essentially different, they try to present as really equivalent and interchangeable; and in Hinduism, they find a welcome partner. The syncretic tendency is not scientifically serious because it ignores the real existing differences and the opposing claims of different religions, and sees only the similarities. From a Christian point of view, it is unacceptable because of the Church's certain and absolute claims like the uniqueness of Christ, but it has a value in its desire for universalism.

At the beginning of the twentieth century, there emerged a tendency different from opposition and syncretism and even from a merely scientific approach, a new positive religious attitude which regards other religions not only as something to be tolerated but as containing positive values for Christ and His Church. The pioneers of this new attitude were faced with serious challenges. When the triumphalist, exclusivist and conquering spirit still prevailed in the thought of many, to speak of positive values, say, in Hinduism, was to court trouble. The words of Brahmabandhav Upadhyay aptly describe the prevalent attitude in India at the beginning of the last century. Though not referring specifically to Catholic missionaries, what he wrote about Christian missionaries is enlightening. "Sectarian missionaries for nearly half a century have been labouring under the delusion that the more it can be shown that the Hindu Scriptures are so many lies, the more rapid will be the propagation of Christianity in India. Hence the uncharitable attempt on all sides to trample and crush everything Hindu .... Educated India has been thoroughly estranged, and she looks upon Christianity as a destroyer, not as a fulfiller and perfector of what is true and good in the country" (Mattam 1975: 12). But the danger of syncretism was also real. Given such a background, we can appreciate the courage and dedication of men like Brahmabandhav and Johanns.

Brahmabandhav and Johanns

A Bengali convert, Brahmabandhav Upadhyay claimed that Christ had come to fulfil not only the religions of Israel but also the religions of India. He considered Christianity as the fulfilment of Hinduism – a thought that became popular with the book of J.N. Farquhar, *The Crown of Hinduism*. Among the catholic missionaries Fathers W. Wallace, P. Johanns and Dandoy were among the first to develop the fulfilment theory and work out its consequences.

The statement by the representatives of Bishops from all over the world gathered in the Synod in 1974 is the latest in a series of official and semi-official expressions of the change of attitude of the Catholic Church towards other religions. The Bishops declared: "Confident in the Holy Spirit's action which overflows the bounds of the Christian community, we wish to further dialogue with other religions which are not Christian, thus to achieve a deeper understanding of the Gospel's newness and of the fullness of Revelation" (Mattam 1975: 9). In India the changed attitude of the Church was briefly expressed by the All India Seminar of the Church in India, in one of its Resolutions: "The age of polemics is past; today we cultivate courtesy, kindness and confidence because of what God has given us and our neighbour in Christ". This resolution made by the representatives of the Laity, Clergy, Religious and Bishops of the Catholic Church in India clearly marks the passing from one era of her history to another. The spirit of this era has been carried on and further developed at the International Theological Conference at Nagpur in 1971 and the All India Consultation held at Patna in 1973. In various seminars and meetings held during the past few years, the Church has become more and more aware that she is called to be a partner in dialogue with other believers and non-believers in search of "an ever-fuller realisation of the Ultimate Mystery." She manifests an increased openness and is ready to enter into communion and collaboration with people of other faiths or no faith. The CBCI Commission for dialogue is organizing meetings all over the country to prepare the local Churches for dialogue with other religions. Theologians in India are becoming increasingly aware of the need for creative theological thinking and of hastening the process of Indianization. The Church in India, then, following the pattern of the universal Church, is definitely entering into a new era of her history.

It was the careful and daring attempts by many people in the country that has led to this new thinking. We thank all those pioneers like Fathers Dandoy and Johanns in Calcutta; Jules Monchanin and Abhishktananda in the South and many others.

Along with the changes in the attitude towards other religions, owing to decolonisation and a growing sense of nationalism, there is also an increasing awareness of the identity of the local ecclesial communities. They begin to appreciate better their right place in the universal Church and their responsibility for other local Churches. Even though there is some opposition in some areas to foreign missionaries, their presence in the missions is seen as an expression of the universality of the Church and of the concern each Church has for every local Church.

The New Approach

Our approach to other religions depends on our mission theology. Hence, we must also look at the changes in that area. Mission in the past was understood almost exclusively as proclaiming the Good News to bring about a conversion in people. Now mission is interpreted very differently. Many factors have led to this change. One obvious factor is the changed approach to other religions, some of which are older than Christianity itself, with claims similar to our own.

We have to understand Mission from the point of view of God, the source of mission. God's interest is the well-being of all humans in society, as is revealed by Jesus. Jesus subordinates everything, all laws, even the most sacred

Sabbath, to the well-being of the human. For Jesus, the human comes first, and all laws are to be at the service of the human; the Jews had reversed this in their legalism. Similarly, he subordinates sacrifices and all temple practices to the more critical concerns of justice, brotherhood as Yahweh had done (cf. Is 58, Matt 5. 23ff; 25 .31ff). We need to keep this background clearly in mind in order to understand what our mission today is; we cannot claim that in the past the Church had kept this in mind when it went out triumphantly to conquer all for the Lord.

One of the basic principles behind the new approach is the unity of all things, the unity of the plan of God: the unity of source and goal. The dichotomy between the natural and the supernatural has to be transcended and reality ought to be looked at as one which Jesus had realized and lived accordingly. Most of the mission theology of the past suffered from the separation of grace/nature, religious/secular, spiritual/material and salvation of the soul/needs of the body. The Church chose the first of these pairs as its proper domain of mission, with the consequent opposition between evangelisation and development, culture, etc. The social and temporal dimension of Jesus' ministry was obscured and hence a new approach to mission takes these two not as separate but merely as dimensions of the one reality, the one world God so loved and sent his Son to save.

One has moved away from a geographical concept of mission to a new understanding where the emphasis is on people, relationship, outlook and value system. Mission is a matter of human relationship; the areas of relationships, which are not yet redeemed, which enslave and are against the total well-being of people, and where people are suffering, are under some form or other of enslavement that is a mission field. The socio-cultural, economic aspects of human life are as much areas of mission as the geographical "mission field". Every area of human life that is still not sufficiently transformed by the values of the Kingdom, our politics, social relations, trade relations, economic structures which leave the majority in poverty and misery; the mass communications and culture, in general, are all mission fields. The Churches and their pattern of relationships, their structures are also mission territory. The mission land is the world, humankind, and every area of life and relationship, structures, processes, value systems at work in the world which are not divinely ordained, "foreign" to the Gospel of Jesus, not wholly formed by love, not totally fraternal.

The enemy is no more other religions, but evil in every form. Therefore, we must look around and study the structures and the value systems in the present pattern of national life, group life, Church life and international relationship - economic, political, and military. "God is calling out to us and bidding us to…. get to action for liberation, for the struggle against the great lords, the great powers that keep God's people in chains and oppressed. This becomes a major concern from the days of Moses… to the days of Jesus, to our day" (Mattam

1997: 55-75). Today globalization and its effects on the poor, the culture of death that reigns in the world are equally mission territory.

In light of the above-changed attitudes, Evangelisation is seen as transforming cultures and ideas affecting every strata of society. Some talk of the aim of mission as "creating a counter-culture"; it looks to a cultural transformation, "a change of peoples' world views and systems of values. The roots of such a cultural transformation will be a spirituality that motivates, inspires, and enables people to search for a fuller life for all.... To be counter-cultural is to be prophetic. It is to challenge people in the name of a vision of what they ought to become, by embodying that vision. In this sense, it will always be critical of the present" (Amaladoss 1996: 235-241).

With these changes affecting mission, now the mission is seen as dialogue. Because the context affects the mission, our mission will mean a threefold dialogue with Asia's poor, cultures and its many religions. A Christian understanding of Dialogue has passed through various stages, like seeing it as a preparation, means for evangelization, to now seeing it as mission, as meaningful in itself. Dialogue cannot continue with just sharing religious themes or experiences; it has to move also to the socio-political levels. In our present world, there are various types of inter-religious conflicts with economic, political and social causes, religious fundamentalism, religions justifying violence, and becoming tools of political parties and ideologies, and finally secularism. In such situations, the inter-religious dialogue would mean that different religious groups come together in view of promoting the common good of all.

Our mission is a call "to share the riches of our Christ-experience with our countrymen and women, by respectful dialogue with them" (T.K. John 1992: 109-134) and by collaboration with them for better human communities of freedom, love and justice. We do not hesitate to continue to share the good news of Jesus with everyone, while we accept the salvific value of other religions. We recognize that we have moved from rigid and exclusivist existence "to enter into a *dialogical relationship with the religions* of the country," (T.K. John 2005: 713-730) precisely because we have begun to discover rich treasures in these religions which were ignored for centuries. We will need to walk with other co-pilgrims. Eventually dialogue should become a way of life, not just sharing and talking. Dialogue is a celebration of diversity. Dialogue is a coming together to enrich each other through sharing and through allowing the other to enter into one's own horizon or world view.

Obstacles to Dialogue

What are the obstacles to dialogue – what led to the opposition and intolerance? We may just mention a few of the elements without going to details. Learning about others in order to put them down, like cutting the others' leg to make oneself look taller; the Church's claims that the Church is the one and only true religion; it possesses the fullness of revelation and salvation; Christ is the fullness of revelation; Jesus is the only saviour of the world; All salvation is in and through Jesus only; No salvation outside the church/Christ; misinterpretation of scripture texts; narrow view of salvation; near-total ignorance of other religions; the European view of things which was taken as final; Exclusivism; Mono culturalism and its position as final; Inclusivism; Pluralism and Syncretism. Added to the above, there is the history of the Church with its active opposition to Hinduism and all other religions; triumphalism; dishonesty in our approach. We had in the past ignored religions other than Hinduism, like for example, the tribal religions, Sikhism, Jainism, Islam, and Popular religions.

My own experience with dialogue: when I was in Delhi, at Vidyajyoti, the Archbishop of Delhi appointed me in charge of dialogue in the Archdiocese. When I contacted various Hindu, Muslim, Sikh and Buddhist leaders and began our dialogue meetings, they said openly: Since you Christians have not succeeded in converting us through your direct confrontational ways, now you are attempting to do that by dialogue; we do not trust that you are really genuine about your desire to dialogue; you want to convert us to your religion. It was really difficult to make them see that we were not looking for their conversion, but wanted to get to know them and work with them for some common good.

In the present time, there is a formidable difficulty by the rise of the Hindutva ideology, which is not Hinduism, but religion-based nationalism.

Why do we look for dialogue with other religions? We believe in one God, who is the God of all but known under various names. There is a basic unity of all human beings; we are humans first and foremost; only then we are different in terms of religious affiliations. All humans have a common destiny; here too we use different names for that ultimate destiny: salvation, *nirvana*, *mukti*, etc. Humans are interconnected and interdependent; hence opposition to one another is not the ideal we look for but collaboration, cooperation, co-working for common goals. For which dialogue between religions can be very helpful. God has a plan for the salvation of each one. We do not know what God's plan is; all we can do is to respect the diversity; listen to each other with respect.

In dialogue we do not look to convince the other anything; we look merely to understand the other. God had God's own ways from the beginning of humanity; Christianity came into the world only 2000 years ago; we may add another 1000 years to Judaism; beyond these two religions, God has been at work for thousands of years with God's people in God's own ways, unknown to us. Hence claims like salvation is possible only in Christianity, or only in Jesus are claims that cannot be sustained.

What we can say, and we need to say, is that we have experienced God's saving plan and action in the life, death, resurrection of Jesus; we believe that Jesus' teaching is meaningful and valid for all; hence we continue to proclaim the good news of God's love revealed in Jesus, but we do not make any claims that God works only in ways known to us. We affirm God's ways as revealed in Jesus. Jesus is meaningful for all.

Concluding Remarks

In conclusion, we may say that we continue to affirm the centrality of Jesus in our life. We affirm his unique role in the plan of God, as we have known it. We believe that he is meant for all, or as Pope Francis says, he has answers to all our problems in the world. We proclaim him to all and invite all to become his disciples. Jesus is the concrete human manifestation of what God wants to tell all people through the ages concerning our attitude towards God and the society in which we live.

However, we do not say that he is the only way for all; we cannot say that God works through him only; for God has many ways unknown to us; what is known to us is limited in the plan of God; just because we know one way, we do not hold that is the only way; we do not know all the ways of God; we are not justified in imposing our terminology on all; even the language of logos, spirit is Christian and should not be imposed on others.

References

Amaladoss, M. "Mission in a Post-Modern World: A Call to be Counter-Cultural", in *Sedos Documentation* 1996, p.235-241.

H. Kraemer "Syncretism as a Religious and Missionary Problem", in *The International Review of Missions*, 43, 1954, 253-273.

Mattam, Joseph, "Mission as Social Concern in Official Church Documents and Recent Missiological Literature", in J. Mattam & S. Kim (Eds.): *Mission Trends Today: Historical and Theological Perspectives*, Mumbai, St Paul's, 1997, pp: 55-75.

Mattam, Joseph: *Land of the Trinity: Modern Christian Approaches to Hinduism*, TPI, Bangalore, 1975.

T. K. John, "Formation in Context" in D'Sa, Thomas (Ed.): The *Church in India in the Emerging Third Millennium,* NBCLC, Bangalore, 2005, pp.713-730.

T.K. John, "Formation for Mission", in *Formation in Mission*, JCSA, New Delhi, 1992, pp.109-134.

18

The Salvific Significance of Other Faiths in the Teachings of Post-Conciliar Documents

Anoopa Anto MSMI
Research Scholar, Systematic Theology, JDV, Pune

Abstract: *the Second Vatican Council articulated a paradigm shift in the church's self-understanding and her relationship with the people of other faiths. The Council opened a new vision of the Church and her mission in the world. Against this background this article dialogue with the post-conciliar understanding of the Church's mission and the vision of late Kurien Kunnumpuram concerning the Church's relationship with the adherents of other faiths. In a world where intellectual arguments and scientific proofs versus the divine truths, genuine Christian witness based on faith experience play a vital role to convey the gospel message. For Kunnumpuram, the Church is the home for all people and religions. As he acknowledges the salvific meaning of other religions, he encourages Christians to appreciate the positive values in those religions. Therefore, this article attempt to respond to the views of Kunnumpuram Kurien, in the light of Evangelii Nuntiandi, Redemptoris Missio and Ecclesia in Asia.*

Keywords: *Salvation, mission, Kingdom of God, other faiths, evangelization, proclamation, witness, dialogue.*

Introduction

In the contemporary world, there is a growing awareness that the Church need to be attentive to the temporal affairs of humankind. The post-conciliar documents have shown the need for a more holistic understanding of the Church's mission. Hence we ask: how do we account for the salvation of adherents of other faiths in the light of post-conciliar documents? According to Kunnumpuram, the Church's positive approach to other religions calls for a radical rethinking of the missions. For him, missionary activity is "the manifestation of God's will and the fulfilment of that will in the world and world history."[1] He finds a paradigm shift in the Church's self-understanding and her relationship with the world. The post-conciliar documents find in other religious traditions immeasurable 'seeds of the Word' and consider them as a true 'preparation for the Gospel'. John Paul II exhorts: Though we appreciate the spiritual and moral goods God has bestowed on every people, we do not separate those gifts from Jesus Christ, who is at the centre of God's plan of salvation. *Ecclesia in Asia* affirms: Jesus is the universal Mediator between God and people for their salvation. The documents add that even for those who do not explicitly profess faith in him as the Saviour. Salvation comes as a grace from Jesus Christ through the communication of the Holy Spirit.

Mission of the Church in the Post-Conciliar Documents

In *Evangelii Nuntiandi* Paul VI gives a synthesis of the Church's religious and secular mission as he states "the Church is certainly not willing to restrict her mission only to the religious field and dissociate herself from humans' temporal problems"[2]. In his encyclical, *Redemptoris Missio* John Paul II, explores the theme of the kingdom of God and highlights it as the purpose of Jesus' mission, precisely, the proclamation and establishment of God's kingdom.[3] Hence, the Church is called to partake with God's liberative activity. The post-Synodal Apostolic Exhortation by John Paul II, *Ecclesia in Asia* deals with the new evangelisation in Asia. The document emphasises that "The Church's first purpose then is to be the sacrament of the inner union of the human person with God."[4] In this light, we proceed to explore the significance of evangelization and missionary activities in a multi-religious context.

1 Kurien Kunnumpuram, *Ways of Salvation: The Salvific Meaning of Non-Christian Religions According to the Teaching of Vatican II* (Pune: Pontifical Athenaem, 1971), 93-94.

2 Paul VI, *Evangelii Nuntiandi,* 4 December, *Acta Apostolicae Sedis* 53 (1943),§13.

§14. Kunnumpuram, *Towards a New Humanity: Reflections on the Church's Mission in India Today*, 14.

3 John Paul II, *Redemptoris Missio,* 4 December, *Acta Apostolicae Sedis* 53 (1943), §26.

4 John Paul II, *Ecclesia in Asia,*6 November, *Acta Apostolicae Sedis* 92 (1999),§24. Kunnumpuram, *The Indian Church of the Future*, 47.

a. *Evangelii Nuntiandi*

The background of the formulation of the Apostolic exhortation *Evangelii Nuntiandi* by Paul VI was 10th anniversary of the closing of the Second Vatican Council. The main objective of this Apostolic exhortation is stated as to make the Church of the 20th century ever better fitted for proclaiming the gospel to the people of this century.[5] On 22 June 1973 Paul VI reminded the Sacred College of Cardinals to search for means to convey Christian message to the modern world. He further added, "it is absolutely necessary for us to take into account a heritage of faith that the Church has the duty of preserving in its untouchable purity, and of presenting it to the people of our time, in a way what is as understandable and persuasive as possible." [6] In the following, we analyze major themes which Paul VI discusses in the document about the mission of the Church in the present context.

i. Proclamation of the Kingdom of God

The core of the Christian mission is the transformation of the present. This involves a conversion of the human heart, which in turn calls for a conversion of the society. Thus, the Christian community has become the salt, light and leaven in society (cf. Mt 5:13-14), all of which are minority images. Paul VI repeated this call in *Evangelii Nuntiandi,* "For the Church evangelizing means bringing the Good news into all the dimensions of human life and society and through its influence transforming humanity from within and making it new."[7] It combines splendidly a wide spectrum of views expressed in the Synod of Bishops in 1974 and thus arrives at a global concept of evangelization. *Evangelii Nuntiandi* asserts the need for the proclamation of the kingdom of God. He explains that it would lead more human persons to understand and to sincerely accept the good news. Through the power of this acceptance and of shared faith, they may gather together in Jesus' name in order to seek together the kingdom, to build it and to live it. He affirms that the proclamation of the Christ-event and proclamation of the kingdom of God are complementary.[8] The mission is centred on the resurrection of Jesus from the dead, which gives

---

5 Paul VI, *Evangelii Nuntiandi,*§2.

6 Paul VI, *Evangelii Nuntiandi,*§3.

7 Paul VI, *Evangelii Nuntiandi,*§8. Antony, D'Cruz, *The Church and the Kingdom of God: Towards a Contextual Ecclesiology for India,* 107. Kurien Kunnumpuram, "Towards a Theology of Ministries," in *Creative and Affirmative Action in Today's India,* ed. Alwyn D'Silva (Pune: National Vocation Service Center, 1984), 28-29.

8 Paul VI, *Evangelii Nuntiandi,* §13. Vadakkumpadan, Paul. *Evangelization Today: Understanding the Integral Concept of Evangelization in the Light of Contemporary Trends in the Theology of Mission* (Shillong: Vendrame Missiological Institute, 1989), 135. Kunnumpuram, *Towards a New Humanity: Reflections on the Church's Mission in India Today,* 16.

universal scope to his message.[9] Hence, the proclamation of the good news by the Church should be the proclamation of the values of the kingdom.

ii. Commitment to Evangelization

A decade after Vatican II, Paul VI underlined the essential nature of the kingdom of God in Church's Evangelization. Jesus himself, the good news of God, and he preached the message of the kingdom of God. The core of his proclamation is salvation i.e., liberation from sin and oppressive evils. Jesus had accomplished it through his death and resurrection. However, it must be carried out in order to be realised fully on the day of the final coming of Christ.[10] *Evangelii Nuntiandi* highlights that Christ is not only an external model of evangeliser but is the effective intimate cause of the evangelisation. The Church is an evangeliser. However, she begins by being evangelised herself. She is the community of believers therefore, "she has a constant need of being evangelised, if she wishes to retain freshness, vigour and strength in order to proclaim the Gospel." This constant conversion and renewal are necessary in order to evangelise the world with credibility. The purpose of evangelisation is interior change through the divine power of message she proclaims.[11] Evangelisation is not identical with the cultures, but the hearers of the gospel message are linked to a culture, and the building up of the kingdom cannot avoid borrowing the elements of human culture or cultures. Therefore "every effort must be made to ensure a full evangelisation of culture or more correctly of cultures. They have to be regenerated by an encounter with the gospel. But this encounter will not take place if the gospel is not proclaimed."[12] Hence, *Evangelii Nuntiandi* clarifies further that even in the face of the highest forms of natural religions, the Church believes that she has a unique mission on earth: to be the sacrament of salvation, which, in the words of Kunnumpuram as the sacrament of unity.[13] Nevertheless, the good news of the kingdom of God is meant for all people of all place and times.

9 Joseph Puthenpurakal, *Evangelizing Mission* (Shillong: DBCIC,2008), 95.

10 Paul VI, *Evangelii Nuntiandi*,§9.

11 Paul VI, *Evangelii Nuntiandi*, §14.

12 Paul VI, *Evangelii Nuntiandi*,§20. H. Staffner opines that the Church being aware of her mission that the instrument of God's self-communication to people regards the other faiths are not so much as rivals but rather as cultures which have to be purified and perfected by the Spirit. H. Staffner, "Mission Method According to Vatican II,"*Indian Missiological Review* 8 (October-1986): 230.

13 M. M James H. Kroeger, "Recent Popes and Interreligious Dialogue," in *Interreligious Dialogue: Catholic Perspective*, ed. M. M James H. Kroeger (Davao City: Mission Studies Institute, 1990), 44-45. John Paul II, cautions Christians that the members of other religions are indeed not lacking the treasures of human spirituality but can make Christians ashamed being themselves so disposed to doubt concerning the truths revealed by God and

iii. Witnessing Life and Explicit Proclamation

Christians are called to lead a witnessing life by which they transmit gospel values and become true evangelizers. However, witnessing life remains insufficient, which points to the necessity of due explanations of it. In other words, proclamation and witness life are as essential as two sides of a coin. For the Church, the first means of evangelization is the witness of an authentic Christian life, based on the love of God in communion with one's own neighbour.[14] The exhortation points out that the good news proclaimed by the witness of life has to be substantiated by the word of God. There is "no true evangelization unless the name, the teaching, the life, the promises, the kingdom and the mystery of Jesus of Nazareth, the Son of God are proclaimed."[15] In this respect, *Evangelii Nuntiandi* assigns a prominent place for kerygma and catechesis have given an important role in evangelization. The proclamation attains full development when it is listened, accepted and assimilated, and when it arouses a genuine adherence in its hearers.[16] Therefore, evangelization has to begin with the witnessing life of Christians. Christians are called to be like leaven to transform the society in which they live.

b. *Redemptoris Missio*

The missionary thinking of the Church is often articulated in certain remarkable mission documents. John Paul II's Encyclical *Redemptoris Missio* is one of them which has assigned due importance for both theological and practical dimensions of mission. One can find this document as positive and optimistic teaching to lead, guide, encourage and challenge the whole Church to a renewed commitment of mission, to re-evangelization and new-evangelization. John Paul II highlights that "it is the Spirit that impels the Church to proclaim Christ and also guides it to discover its gifts to other people, to foster them and receive in dialogue."[17] The kingdom of God brought about by Christ and in

---

proclaimed by the Church. John Paul II, *Redemptor Hominis,* 4 March, *Acta Apostolicae Sedis* 71 (1979), §6.

14 Paul VI, *Evangelii Nuntiandi*, §41.

15 Paul VI, *Evangelii Nuntiandi*,§22.Chethimattam states that it is the task of theologians to provide the common people a sense of moral and religious values and of meaning in their life emphasized by the life and teaching of Jesus Christ. John B. Chethimattam, "Problems of an Indian Christian Theology: A Critique of Indian Theologizing" in *Theologizing in India*, ed. T. K. John, Gispert-Sauch and M. Amaladoss (Bangalore: TPI, 1978), 205.

16 Paul VI, *Evangelii Nuntiandi*,§§22&23. Staffner, "Mission Method According to Vatican II," 236.

17 John Paul II, *Redemptoris Missio*,§29. Michael Amaladoss, "Interreligious Dialogue 50 Years After Vatican II: Challenges and Opportunities," *VidyaJyoti* 79 (February-2015): 88. Pope Francis affirms that the same Spirit everywhere brings forth various forms of practical wisdom which help people to bear suffering and to live in greater peace and

Christ. The Church continues his mission by works and prayer for its perfect and definitive realization.

i. Kingdom of God in the Person of Jesus

God manifested his plan of salvation for all in the person of Jesus of Christ. After receiving the Holy Spirit at his Baptism, he declared "The time is fulfilled, and the kingdom of God is at hand; repent and believe in the Gospel" (Mk 1:14-15; cf. Mt 4:17; Lk 4:43). The proclamation and establishment of God's kingdom are the purposes of his mission. However, the novelty and vitality of his message and identity as a messenger is that Jesus himself is the "Good News." He declares at the very beginning of his mission in the synagogue at Nazareth when he applies to himself the words of Isaiah about the anointed One sent by the Spirit of the Lord (cf. Lk 4;14-21). Hence, John Paul II highlights that since the "Good News is Christ, there is an identity between the message and the messenger, between saying, doing and being. His power, the secret of the effectiveness of his actions, lies in his total identification with the message he announces; he proclaims the Good News not just by what he says or does, but by what he is."[18] We continue our discussion by portraying Church's mission as the servant of kingdom.

ii. The Church as the Servant of the Kingdom

There are different ways of looking at the mission of the Church. John Paul II affirms that the Church is effectively and concretely at the service of the kingdom. The Church serves the kingdom by spreading the gospel values and guiding people to mature in their faith. Kunnumpuram substantiates that the mission of the Church is to establish the kingdom of God; in other words, it is to bring about the liberation of humanity. Consequently, the Church is at the service of humanity, and she has a ministerial role in the world. However, it is not only purely spiritual or other worldly undertaking; rather, it is also concerned with the welfare of human beings here on earth. He cautions, we must not reduce the mission of the Church into mere a humanitarian service but need to emphasize the religious dimension of the mission of humankind. Because it is concerned with the ultimate meaning and purpose of human life.[19] While carrying other activities such as dialogue, promotion of human

---

harmony." Francis, *Evangelii Gaudium*, 24 November (Trivandrum: Carmel International Publishing House, 2013), §254. Amaladoss, "Interreligious Dialogue," 97.

18 John Paul II, *Redemptoris Missio*, §13.Kurien Kunnumpuram, "Priests as Prophets of the Lord," in *The Dharma of Jesus: Interdisciplinary Essays in Memory of George Soares-Prahbhu*, ed. Francis X. D'Sa (Gujarath: Gujarath Sahitya Prakash, 1997), 248.

19 Kunnumpuram, *Towards a New Humanity: Reflections on the Church's Mission in India Today*, 29.

dignity, commitment to justice and peace, education and the care for the sick and abandoned, Church serves the kingdom by her intercession.

iii. Commitment to Evangelization and Dialogue

Inter-religious dialogue is one of the most widely discussed and debated topics in the socio-religious circle today. *Redemptoris Missio* understands inter-religious dialogue as a method and means of mutual knowledge and enrichment. It is not in opposition to the mission; indeed, it has special links with the mission and is one of its expressions.[20] In light of the economy of salvation, the Church sees no conflict between proclaiming Christ and engaging in inter-religious dialogue. Decree on Ecumenism *Unitatis Redintegratio* warns that dialogue should be conducted and implemented with the conviction that "the Church is the ordinary means of salvation and that she alone possesses the fullness of the means of salvation".[21] In dialogue, conviction and openness are held in balance, and the partners speak as religiously committed persons on subjects of common interest. The Christian missionary, while listening and sharing the religious experience with others, does not compromise with his or her Christian identity but continues to witness and proclaim the Gospel message in all circumstances. The dynamics of dialogue should lead Christians to listen and to understand that which other believers communicate to in order to profit from the gifts which God bestows so generously.[22] Kunnumpuram suggests that renouncing all sense of superiority, one can consider dialogue as a "sign of respect, as an act of love, as an expression of the search for the fullness of truth or as a means of fostering mutual understanding-in the concrete situation of India."[23] The Church in India takes up seriously the task of inter-religious dialogue and collaboration with people of other faiths.

c. *Ecclesia in Asia*

In the post-Synodal Apostolic Exhortation, *Ecclesia in Asia,* John Paul II reiterates the teachings of *Redemptoris Missio.* While he stresses the necessity of proclaiming Jesus Christ as the Saviour of the world, he strongly emphasises

---

20 John Paul II, *Redemptoris Missio*,§52.

21 "*Unitatis Redintegratio*," §3. Sebastian Painadath, "Dialectics between Spirituality and Religion,"*Jeevadhara* 42 (2012): 351. Kurien Kunnumpuram, "The Church and Peace," in *World and Peace*, ed. Kurien Kunnumpuram (Mumbai: Better Yourself Books, 2007), 226.

22 Secretariat for Non-Christians, "The Attitude of the Church Towards the Followers of Other Religions: Reflections and Orientations on Dialogue and Mission," in *Interreligious Dialogue: Catholic Perspectives*, ed. M. M James H. Kroeger (Davao: Mission Studies Institute, 1990):5.

23 Kunnumpuram, *Towards a New Humanity: Reflections on the Church's Mission in India Today* , 25.

the urgency of inter-religious dialogue and the service of human promotion.[24] According to Kunnumpuram concerning the theological understanding of the Church's mission, *Ecclesia in Asia* does not go beyond *Redemptoris Missio.*[25] However, this exhortation highlights practical ways to fulfil the mission in the concrete situation of Asia today. In the following, we narrow down our focus to three important concepts discussed in *Ecclesia in Asia,* namely, the centrality of the Holy Spirit, Word of God, and the gospel witness.

i. Centrality of the Holy Spirit

In *Ecclesia in Asia,* Pope John Paul II presents his vision for doing Christian mission in Asia. He gives strong affirmation to the need for a new drive for evangelizing in Asia and expressed a fervent hope that Asia will turn to Christ in the third millennium. He also emphasizes the centrality of the Holy Spirit and Word of God in presenting the mystery of Christ through the active participation in the liturgy. The Holy Spirit is the first manifestation of the love of the Triune God and is present in the world as its life-giving force. John Paul II explains, "Universal presence of the Holy Spirit, therefore, cannot serve as an excuse for failure to proclaim Jesus Christ explicitly as the one and only Saviour. On the contrary, the universal presence of the Holy Spirit is inseparable from universal salvation in Jesus."[26] It is the function of the Spirit to preserve the bond of communion between Christ and his Church, empower and shape the Church to continue and to accomplish his mission as the seed of the kingdom of God as she looks eagerly for its final coming.[27] Her identity and mission are inseparable from the kingdom of God, which Jesus announced and inaugurated in all that he said and did, above all in his death and resurrection. The Spirit completes Jesus' mission with creative newness and diversity of charismas in fellowship and communion of communities.

ii. Centrality of the Word of God

The Word of God, and a community's faith response to it are essentials for the effective mission of the Church. God makes Godself known to his children as a mystery of infinite love in which the Father eternally utters His Word in the Holy Spirit. Christian communities have to be rooted in the experience of God

24 John Paul II, *Ecclesia in Asia*, §§31&32. Kunnumpuram, *Towards a New Humanity: Reflections on the Church's Mission in India Today*, 17.

25 Kunnumpuram, *Towards a New Humanity: Reflections on the Church's Mission in India Today*, 17.

26 John Paul II, *Ecclesia in Asia,* §17. Pope Francis points out that the Holy Spirit enriches the entire evangelizing Church with different charisms. These gifts are meant to build up the Church. Francis, *Evangelii Gaudium*, §130.

27 Jonathan Tan Yun-Ka, "Approaches to Christian Mission is in India," *Vidyajyoti* 67 (November-2003): 215.

which flows from a living faith and this will mould them as more authentic witnesses which will enable them to proclaim the fulfillment of God's kingdom in Jesus to others. In order to fulfill this task one needs to have attentive and faithful reading and contemplation of the Word of God.[28] *Dei Verbum* affirms that throughout the history of the Church people of God have always found strength in the Word of God, and in present time also the ecclesial community grows by hearing, celebrating and studying the Word of God.[29] Benedict XVI writes, "The Word, who from the beginning is with God and is God, reveals himself in the dialogue between the divine persons, and invites us to share in that love."[30] Therefore, created in the image and likeness of God who is love, humankind can understand the identity as children of God and members of His kingdom only in accepting the word of God and in docility to the work of the Holy Spirit.

iii. Centrality of the Gospel Witness

In every case it is clear that there can be no true proclamation of the Gospel unless Christians offer the witness of lives in harmony with the message they preach. The Apostolic exhortation reminds: "The Church is called to bear witness to Christ by taking courageous and prophetic stands in the face of the corruption of political or economic power; by not seeking her own glory and material wealth; by using her resources to serve the poorest of the poor and by imitating Christ's own simplicity of life."[31] . The first form of witness is the very life of the missionary which is taking place in the Christian family, and in the ecclesial community. The Christian family and community of believers reveal a new way of living by striving to imitate Jesus of gospel. This way of life is the best possible way of being a missionary.[32] The people of today "put more trust in witnesses than in teachers, in experience than in teaching, and in life and action than in theories"[33] Missionary activities are not limited to the preaching but extend to the involvement of humanitarian movements of the society such as in the schools and hospitals, among the migrants, and tribals, and in the pursuit of justice and human rights.[34] Church in Asia has blessed with many missionaries who bore heroic witness to God's love among the peoples of the continent in the past. Their missionary spirit and zeal have

---

28 John Paul II, *Ecclesia in Asia*,§23.

29 "*Dei verbum,*" §2.

30 Benedict XVI, *Verbum Domini*, 30 December (Trivandrum: Carmel International Publishing House, 2010), §6.

31 John Paul II, *Ecclesia in Asia*, §43.

32 John Paul II, *Ecclesia in Asia*, §42.

33 John Paul II, *Ecclesia in Asia*, §42.

34 John Paul II, *Ecclesia in Asia*, §42.

become an inspiration for Christians in Asia to witness Jesus Christ and his Gospel.[35] We continue our discussion of the concept of salvation in the post-conciliar documents.

Salvation in the Post-Conciliar Documents

Acts of the Apostles more concretely affirms: "there is salvation in no one else, for there is no other name under heaven given among mortals by which we must be saved" (Acts 4:10:12). The incarnation of the Son of God united himself with every human being. Therefore, believers are obliged to hold the truth that the Holy Spirit offers everyone the possibility of sharing the merits of the paschal mystery of Jesus.[36] With this in mind, in the following paragraphs we briefly analyze the concept of salvation and the salvific significance of other religious traditions in the light of *Evangelii Nuntiandi, Redemptoris Missio* and in *Ecclesia in Asia.*

a. *Evangelii Nuntiandi* on Salvation

Basing on the Scripture and tradition the Church is deeply aware of her duty to preach the good news of salvation to all including people of other religious traditions. In *Evangelii Nuntiandi* Paul VI highlights: neither respect and esteem for other religions nor the questions raised by people of other faiths prevent Church from the proclamation of Jesus Christ. On the contrary, the Church acknowledges that entire humanity has the right to know the mystery of Christ and his message. The Church respects and recognizes other religious traditions because they are the living expression of the soul of vast groups of people. They are in search of God and have a quest which is "incomplete but often made with great sincerity and righteousness of heart."[37] They inherited an impressive patrimony of deeply religious texts, rituals and customs by which they relate to ultimate reality. Therefore, *Evangelii Nuntiandi* affirms: other religions traditions are all impregnated with immeasurable 'seeds of the Word' and can represent a true 'preparation for the Gospel'.[38] Acknowledging that the gospel message is not reserved to a small group but is destined for everyone, Church continues her mission to proclaim the good news of salvation to people of all time and all places.

b. *Redemptoris Missio* on Salvation

The universal salvific will of God and salvation in Christ is asserted throughout the New Testament. Jesus Christ is the one mediator between God and people:

35 John Paul II, *Ecclesia in Asia*, §42.

36 John Paul II, *Redemptoris Missio*, §6.

37 Paul VI, *Evangelii Nuntiandi*,§ 53.

38 Paul VI, *Evangelii Nuntiandi*,§ 53. "*Gaudium et spes*,"§6, "*Ad gentes*," §11, "*Lumen Gentium*," §16,17.

"For there is one God, and there is also one mediator between God and humankind, Christ Jesus, himself human who gave himself as a ransom for all", (1Tm 2:5-7; Heb 4:14-16). Therefore, no one can enter into communion with God except through Christ, by the working of the Holy Spirit. John Paul II points out that participated forms of mediation "acquire meaning and value *only* from Christ's own mediation".[39]And they cannot be understood as parallel or complementary to him. The universality of salvation refers that it is granted not only to those who explicitly believe in Christ and have entered the Church rather salvation is offered to all, and it must be made concretely available to entire humanity.[40] However, as in the past, many people do not have opportunity to come to know Jesus Christ or accept his gospel. For such people salvation in Christ is accessible by "virtue of a grace which, while having a mysterious relationship to the Church, does not make them formally part of the Church but enlightens them in a way which is accommodated to their spiritual and material situation."[41] This grace comes from the merit of Christ's death and resurrection; and is communicated by the Holy Spirit. In order to attain salvation each person need to cooperate with this offer of salvation in Christ which is gratuitous gift from God the creator all creation.

c. *Ecclesia in Asia* on Salvation

Christians believe that Jesus Christ, true God and true man, is the one Saviour who accomplished the Father's universal plan of salvation. As the definitive revelation of the mystery of the Father's love for all, Jesus is indeed unique, and "it is precisely this uniqueness of Christ which gives him an absolute and universal significance, whereby, while belonging to history, he remains history's centre and goal."[42] Risen from the dead, Jesus Christ is present to all and to the whole of creation in a new way. In him, values of all religious and cultural traditions, namely mercy and submission to the will of God, compassion and righteousness, non-violence and morality, filial piety and harmony with creation find their fullness and realization.[43] *Ecclesia in Asia* asserts*:* "Jesus is the one universal Mediator for the salvation of the world. Even for those who do not explicitly profess faith in him as the Saviour,

39 John Paul II, *Redemptoris Missio*,§5.

40 John Paul II, *Redemptoris Missio*,§5.

41 John Paul II, *Redemptoris Missio*,§5. In the perspective of Felix Wilfred, experience is the gateway to truth therefore the Church in India, cannot close itself on its own experience alone. Hence she has to be open to the new possibilities of "listening to the truth of God's Word and to move on to the ever new experience of the salvific action of God." Felix Wilfred, "The Problem of a Valid Starting-Point For Theologizing in India" in *Theologizing in India*, ed. T. K. John, Gispert-Sauch and M. Amaladoss (Bangalore: TPI, 1978), 142.

42 John Paul II, *Ecclesia in Asia*,§ 14. John Paul II, *Redemptoris Missio*,§255.

43 John Paul II, *Ecclesia in Asia*,§ 14.

salvation comes as a grace from Jesus Christ through the communication of the Holy Spirit."[44]Jesus is the Good News for the men and women of every time and place in their search for the meaning of existence, purpose of life and for the truth of their own humanity.

In my readings of Kunnumpuram's work entitled as *Ways of Salvation: The Salvific Meaning of Non-Christian Religions According to the Teaching of Vatican II,* and his other claims mentioned above his concerns for the people of other faith in terms of Jesus as the unique and universal saviour. His scholarly presentation of the theme in the light of the Second Vatican Council manifests his critical engagement with the teachings of pre-Vatican II and the writings of the fathers of the Church. He addresses the issues concerning the salvation outside the Church and necessity of the Church for salvation. Kunnumpuram understands the Church as the sacrament of unity.[45] For Kunnumpuram, genuine faith accepts Jesus Christ wherever it encounters him.

The theological vision of Kunnumpuram becomes very clear concerning the significance of the Church as a 'sacrament of salvation' amidst of religious pluralism. He is in this sense a visionary who has foreseen the post-conciliar teachings on the theme while developing his theology. He calls for a decentralization of the Church, where the uniqueness of Christ and his good news of salvation are highlighted than the power of the Church and her heritage as an organized institution. Kunnumpuram speaks about people's model Church that "The Gospel is proclaimed and the people responded to it positively. The Holy Spirit is present in each of the believers, the local community and the whole Church. Led by the Spirit, the local community shapes its ecclesial life in accordance with the socio-cultural situation of the people."[46] In his writings, we see a blending of teachings of the second Vatican council and post-conciliar documents. When he speaks about the Church as people of God, he invites readers to look at the world and people of other faiths in a wide spectrum.

Conclusion

We deduce certain concluding remarks from our discussion on the mission of the Church and other faiths in the light of post-conciliar documents and reflection on Kunnumpuram's writings. Paul VI and John Paul II exhort people

44 John Paul II, *Ecclesia in Asia*,§ 14.

45 Kurien Kunnumpuram, "The Church as the Sacrament of Unity," in *The World as Sacrament: Interdisciplinary Bridge-Building of the Sacred and the Secular, Essays in Honour of Joseph Neuner on the Occasion of his 90th Birthday*, ed. Issac Padinjarekuttu, Jacob Parappally and Francis X. D'Sa (Pune: JDV, 1998), 149.

46 Kurien Kunnumpuram, "Inculturation and Ecclesiology," *Indian Missiological Review* 19 (March 1997): 53. Kurien Kunnumpuram, "Thinking with the Church in the Context of the Second Vatican Council," *Ignis Studies* 1(June-1983):11.

of Asia in general and of India, in particular, to proclaim the kingdom of God and engage with the world's spiritual and temporal affairs. The *Evangelii Nuntiandi* reminds the importance of proclamation and witnessing life in the multi-religious context of Asia. John Paul II encourages people of India to dialogue with other faiths without compromising one's own faith and tradition. The post-Synodal Apostolic Exhortation, *Ecclesia in Asia,* emphasizes the work of the Holy Spirit, the centrality of the Word of God and its inevitability of witnessing life for the authentic missionary activity of the Church. In a similar vein, Kunnumpuram's theology reveals the fact that his concerns are post-conciliar. While upholding the teachings of the council that the Church as the universal sacrament of salvation Kunnumpuram, calls for a decentralization of the Church, centring her vision not on herself but altogether on Christ. However, it is essential to understand the particular context of the other when we engage in dialogue with world religions. Any Holy approach in this context would not be acceptable. The claims mentioned above centring the presence of Christ and the salvation of people of other faiths may appear as mere arbitrary claims unless they are clarified to them. Therefore, it is the task of theologians to elaborate a rich and satisfactory theology remaining faithful to one's own faith and *magisterium* of the Church.

19

Christayan: PhiloYoga for an East-West Complementarity Consciousness Continuum

Mathew Chandrankunnel CMI
Director, Ecumenical Christian Centre, Whitefield, Bangalore

Abstract: *India and Greece were two of the very ancient civilizations which had so much in common. Philosophy, love for wisdom was generated in Greece while yoga, spirituality became the symbol of India bridging body, mind and soul. The philosophical traditions, namely the six systems in Hinduism and the three main turnings of Buddhism, namely, Hinayana, Mahayana and Vajrayana consisting of innumerable philosophical positions by different schools and the logical argumentations in Jainism really exhibit the grandiose ethos and heritage of India. Thus, the philosophy evolved in Greece has a counterpart, namely a Darsan in India. Greek philosophy became the bulwark of the Western development of philosophy, theology and later science and ultimately the renaissance spirit that gave rise to the integrated effect of the Western Culture while the East brought mindfulness, yoga, spirituality in connecting the body, mind soul continuum. Thus the author pleads for a spirituality that integrates, drawing insights from both East and West. Integrating the yoga awareness, Buddhist meditative techniques and the hesychasm of the Jesus-Prayer can help us to transform ourselves into the consciousness of Christ as St. Paul had shown us. In his epistles, especially that of Philippians, Paul's consciousness has totally transformed, fused and merged into the consciousness of Christ. He was able to say that for me to live is Christ.*

Keywords: *Christian prayer, Buddhist meditation, Yoga awareness, East-West synthesis, Gita.*

India and Greece were two of the very ancient civilizations which had so much in common. Philosophy, love for wisdom was generated in Greece while yoga-spirituality became the symbol of India. The philosophical traditions, namely the six systems in Hinduism and the three main turnings of Buddhism, namely, Hinayana, Mahayana and Vajrayana composed of innumerable philosophical positions by different schools and the logical argumentations in Jainism exhibit the ethos and heritage of India. Thus, the philosophy evolved in Greece has a counterpart in India. Greek philosophy became the bulwark of the Western development of philosophy, theology and later science and ultimately the renaissance spirit that gave rise to the integrated effect of the Western Culture. The Indian philosophical systems and religions also traversed in time and transcended geography and became the foundation for the Eastern Culture. So the integration of the West and the East would be beneficial for the progress of humanity in a globalized world driven by science, technology and market forces. These driving forces are mostly from the West, and gradually, a recent phenomenon that is being woven into the globalized context is that of spirituality. Fr. Kurien Kunnumpuram SJ is someone who always dreamt of such integration, and I knew him through his articles and lectures. An important factor was that his niece was my teacher and came to know about him through her when I was a schoolboy. The theological oeuvre of Kurien Kunnumpuram is vast, and I thought of picking up the complementary approach for a globalized theology and spirituality where the possibility for an East-West fusion could be thought of would be a fitting tribute to Fr. Kunnumpuram. This spirituality could definitely generate a deeper theology that will be more holistic and leading to wellness and holiness. It will also be capable of achieving the stillness and awareness which the ancient Indian sages where practising through yoga while the Greek saints from Mount Athos practised through hesychasm and spilled over to the Slavic region such as Russia, Ukraine, Poland, Belarus and at present gripping all over the world. Today yoga and hesychasm is spread like wildfire in all over the globe, leading the practitioners to awareness and de-stressing themselves and to find meaning in life. So I am trying to integrate these two foundational traditions, through the love of yoga or Philo-yoga, fusing the best contributions from the West and the West. This is only a primal attempt and much has to go for better integration and fusion. So I request the critiques to be sympathetic to my intention and also the following attempt in integrating them.

Today Yoga is trendy and spread all over the world, because of its ability to transform a human person. The Medical Profession is promoting Yoga because of its power to calm the human mind, eliminate stress, keep the body agile with a vibrant brain. With enthusiasm, the corporate world embraced Yoga because of its ability to refresh the worn-out mind and body. The

Spiritual world from time immemorial experienced the Yogic power to bind the body, mind and soul into a continuum of consciousness and its ability to transcend from the natural to supernatural, from the mundane to the ethereal. It is a powerful tool to raise the body to a higher dimension of experience, to a level of transcendence, towards a higher state of consciousness. Yoga is holistic, binding the body, mind and soul into a continuum of consciousness; physical matter, the plant life, animal life, human life and the Divine fused into an inextricable intertwining. Yoga is one of the most significant contributions of India towards humanity, just like Ayurveda, number zero and the Indo-Arabic Numerals etc. One may find a young woman squatting on a mat as an advertisement, placed at the Time Square in New York conspicuously so that everybody can see it, as if trumpeting the importance of Yoga and a call to everyone, all over the world to practice yoga and become an adept of yoga. Yoga is spreading like wildfire across the globe, as a spiritual practice, relaxing technique and for heightened consciousness, eliminating stress, toxicities from body and mind. It has the unique quality to integrate the body, mind and soul into a holistic whole and transcend from the natural to the supernatural. Thus, both science and religion, now promote Yoga because of its healing power, as a transformation technique and as a unique means of transcendence towards an integral whole, the mundane, human and the divine, matter, life and mind into an inextricable intertwining singularity.

Mount Athos became the spiritual centre of the Orthodox Christianity. I had the opportunity to visit Mount Athos and breath into the Jesus Prayer and the spirit of hesychasm, by staying in the Holy Lavra Vatopedi during the Pentecost festival and Xenaphontos and a few other significant monasteries in this abode of spirituality. From the 5th century onwards, people moved to the mountain ranges of the island and evolved into a spiritual sanctuary. Twenty monasteries are at present filled up with spiritual seekers, and they pray the Jesus Prayer – "Lord Jesus, have mercy on us, sinners" – and long for stillness, awareness and happiness. In the 1950s, Elder Joseph, a spiritually acclaimed master who was endowed with supernatural gifts, brought a flow of seekers from all over the world. People who are actors, advocates, doctors who were all well accomplished in life but felt the lack of meaning, flowed to Mount Athos and became monks. During my stay there, I could find many such spiritual seekers who renounced the world and took refuge in the depth of spirituality. Jesus Prayer and hesychasm is now spread into the nook and corner of the world, inspiring young minds in search of meaning, wellness, wholeness and holiness. The practice of hesychasm and yoga has many things in common. First, I shall narrate the yoga, and then hesychasm and then, the integrated, holistic account of ***Philoyoga***.

Yoga

In the religious landscape of India, Yoga has an important role to play and is indeed deeply rooted in the cultural matrix. From time immemorial, even from the proto-history of India, that is, from the Indus Valley civilisation onwards, the influence of Yoga is visible. In *Mohenjodaro* and *Harappa*, the prominent cities of the Indus civilisation, archaeological excavations unearthed sculptures imitating animal forms. Figures of men, with wide-open mouth and bulging eyes, that looks almost like a roaring lion, an imposing meditating person, sitting cross-legged and austere which is popularly known as Pasupati which became popular in the later cultural periods of India and found in many temples, amulets depicting women who came to be called yogins all show how the yogic tradition became a template for the cultural heritage of India, transcending the time and space linking the past, present and the future. This fact has been acknowledged by many thinkers like the prominent philosopher of religion, Mircea Eliade.

The Rigveda depicts ascetics undergoing self-discipline through practices of austerities such as standing in the hot sun or holding the hand over the head for a prolonged time known as *tapas* to transform the consciousness. During the time of the Upanishads, different forms of Yoga are described. Achieving stillness of the *Atman*, often interpreted as the inner self or soul, through the control of the breath is mentioned in the *Chandogya* and *Bruhadaranyaka* Upanishads. The later Upanishads, such as Svetasvatara and Maitri, describe how it is possible to be a person of balance by controlling the breath. *Bhagavadgita*, the exhortation of Krishna to a depressed Arjuna, within the context of a battle, especially the sixth chapter, known as the science of self-realization, describes how a person can become a yogi, through practising desireless actions by which an individual consciousness can ascend to the supreme consciousness. Gita elaborates, how the *Dharma* (righteousness), *Svadharma* (self-righteousness), *Moksha* (liberation) can be attained through three different modes of Yoga, namely, *Karma* (action), *Bhakthi* (devotion) and *Jnana* Yoga. Different authors have given numerous interpretations basing on emphasizing these verses giving importance to any of these types of Yogas. Some interpreters give superiority to one among these three modes, and some claim these modes as leading from one to the other and climaxing in the *Jnana*. Gita integrates the six philosophical schools and shades of many different religious traditions and hence promotes the synthesis of the cultural heritage of India. The first verse in the sixth chapter itself describes the method of becoming a yogi, a renunciate by practising *Nishkamakarma,* which is elaborated through the other 47 verses. The Indian independence movement was inspired by Mahatma Gandhi, who interpreted Gita with a Karma Yoga vision. To the preface of the English translation of his Gujarati

Gita commentary, Gandhi wrote how the book gave him solace and courage in the face of tragedies and misfortunes in order to become a Karma Yogi.[1]

> I find solace in the *Bhagavadgītā* that I miss even in the Sermon on the Mount (Gospel of St. Mathew, chapter 5). When disappointment stares me in the face and all alone I see not one ray of light, I go back to the *Bhagavadgītā*. I find a verse here and a verse there and I immediately begin to smile in the midst of overwhelming tragedies – and my life has been full of external tragedies – and if they have left no visible, no indelible scar on me, I owe it all to the teaching of *Bhagavadgītā*.

Yoga Vasistha is another exhortation on Yoga. Here the context is the depressed prince Rama who went for a tour in the kingdom and found the depressing situation of the people. He fell into a mood of disinterestedness. Seeing the situation as fertile to get enlightenment, father of Rama arranged *Maharshi Vasistha* to admonish Rama so that his frustrations could be eliminated and bring him to enlightenment. Explaining consciousness, the book exhorts how to get liberation by becoming a yogi. The seeker or the *sadhaka* or the yogi is called into enlightenment by *Yoga Vasistha* by distinguishing between the eternal and the worldly, permanent and the impermanent and by cultivating a dislike for worldly pleasures and acquiring mastery over the physical, the psychological and the mental and thus transcending the world, *Samsara*, through a path of discipline encompassing knowing, desireless action into a stage of perpetual bliss known as *Turiya*. Such a person is known as *Brhmavidvarishta*, the one who is permanently wedded to absolute reality. The exhortation is from the perspective of the monistic or *Advaitic* though the book is a syncretic work comprising *Vedanta*, Jainism, *Saiva Siddhanta*, and Mahayana Buddhism. It integrates the various religious, philosophical traditions into an integral whole exhorting the seeker to follow the path of discipline and attain the true consciousness of the absolute reality by interpreting everything else as unreal, imagination and momentary. Vir Savarkar, one of the founders of RSS was so impressed by the work that it became a foundational vision for his whole enterprise. Hence, the book received prominence even today and is promoted by the right-wing thinkers of India.[2]

> All of a sudden I fell upon the *Yoga Vashistha*, and I found it of such absorbing interest that I have come to regard it ever since as the best work on the Vedanta Philosophy. The propositions were so logical, the verse is so beautiful, and the exposition is so thorough and penetrating that the soul loses itself in raptures over it. Such a fine combination of philosophy and poetry is a gift reserved only for Sanskrit poets.

1 S. Radhakrishnan, *Bhagavadgita*, Harper and Collins, 1993, quoted Gandhi, *Young India*, p.1078-1079.

2 Damodar Vinayak Savarkar, *My Transportation for Life*, p.151.

Around second century AD, Patanjali Maharshi compiled the *Yoga Sutras*, from the oral tradition synthesizing the theoretical text and the practical advice into an integral, holistic account with a philosophical vision derived from the *Samkhya Darsana* that is one among the six philosophical traditions. *Yoga Sutras* is hence considered to be the most essential textual account, and authoritative source on yoga for its philosophical vision and the eightfold exponential purposive processes that lead towards a transformative ideality of happiness and bliss termed as *Samadhi*, ecstasy, absorption, or mindfulness. Patanjali integrated the different religious, philosophical traditions and schools to such a beautiful synthesis that it would not be possible to refer it or name it belonging to a particular religion or philosophical heritage. He transformed the entire heritage into an integral whole, helping the one who practices, irrespective of his or her caste, religion, creed, race or times to achieve the goal. So one can fearlessly say that Patanjali transcended the divisions and placed Yoga, as an eternal contribution to humanity with a universal vision. So nobody can claim that Yoga belongs to Hinduism or of Vedic Period since yoga, though it borrowed concepts from all the Indian religions, has definitely transcended them all. Therefore any adept belonging to any place, any beliefs irrespective of land, creed, sex and race can follow yoga and achieve the purpose envisaged in the yoga sutra. The beauty and power of Patanjali's synthesis is that yoga became a tool of transformation not particularly being reserved to any school of philosophy or religious tradition and even atheists or agnostics could practice it without any internal conflict or mental struggle. However, there are tendencies claiming that yoga belongs to the Vedic or Hindu tradition, and it is against the Christian or Islamic religions. In fact, one can definitely observe that yoga transcends space and time and all types of fragmentations and divisions.

The eight-fold path of yoga is indeed successive eight steps starting with an attitudinal form, internal and external cleansing, a moderate life vision endowed with ethical and spiritual principles, deeply founded on a spiritual template with physical exercises leading to a concentration on the breath. This path gradually shifts its focus on the ethical, spiritual dimensions and exponentially progresses and ascends towards the apex of happiness or ecstasy synthesizing the body, mind and soul into an integral whole unified with the absolute or the ultimate which is kept as undefined in order to escape from the narrow divisions that may emerge from the mundane hair-splitting rational explanations of the society. The individual has the right to interpret the ultimate in his own terms, and thus, any religious follower can practise yoga without any mental conflict or guilt, and it is not against his or her religious tradition. Jain, Buddhist and Hindu religious philosophies can easily be visible in the spiritual foundation of yoga. It can also be seen that Jina, Buddha and other leading religious exponents were the practitioners of yoga and have contributed to the propagation of yoga. Therefore, it is important to elucidate the eightfold limb of yoga. They are, *Yama* (code of ethics), *Niyama,* (code of discipline) *Asana* (set of physical exercises), *Pranayama* (breathing techniques), *Pratyahara* (sense of withdrawal or control of the senses), *Dharana* (concentration or awareness), *Dhyana* (meditation) and *Samadhi* (bliss or ecstasy experienced because of the union with the divine).

Yama corresponds to the universal morality or the fundamental spiritual principle on which the whole life is to be constructed. *Yama* is further divided into five, namely, *Ahimsa* (non-violence-compassion), *Satya* (commitment towards truthfulness), *Asteya* (non-stealing), *Brahmacharya* (celibacy, sense control or continence), *Aparigraha* (non-possessiveness). These five principles are five attitudes to be cultivated through practice and powerful enough to control the need of the senses and the desire of the mind. So it is a holistic breaking system for both the body and mind to have a refined personality, with balance and equanimity. *Ahimsa* binds anyone to keep non-violence as a method in his relation with the life world, considering with compassion and controlling one's own passion for violence and vengeance. So holistically it promotes the negative and positive attitudes so that one may be careful in dealing with creatures with respect and mindfulness. It is both a duty and a responsibility. For any genuine relationship, honest and truthful communication is necessary and thus *Satya* governs the life of an adherent. As the edict goes, truth should be thought, said and acted upon and unpalatable truths should be withheld rather than said publically. So this principle of truthfulness makes one's life honest and trustworthy in the relationship with an individual, in the society or in governance. Mahatma Gandhi promoted these two principles as the bedrock for his freedom struggle as *Satyagraha* and *Ahimsa*. It could be seen that with these tools, Martin Luther King in the United States of America and Nelson Mandela of South Africa attained freedom for their people without an armed struggle **or** spilling blood following the example of Gandhiji. This shows that these values are meaningful even today and hence to be promoted as life principles applicable in every culture. These two principles are said to be derived from the Jain religion and philosophy and integrated into the yoga system. *Asteya* and *Aparigraha* are again two sides of the same coin, promoting non-stealing and non-possessiveness.

The desires of the mind and the needs of the body are to be curtailed with these principles. What is given is only acceptable and by limiting desire to the minimum is indeed an antidote for today's consumerist and hedonist attitudes of greed and avarice. Here the personality is refined through the limitation of the needs of the body and the desires of the mind and thus promote and define a balanced (one as a person) way of being rather than that of having with unlimited possessions and ambitions. *Brahmacharya* defines the seeker to be always following the path of the Divine, with undivided attention towards it. It curtails the bodily aspirations of pleasures and concentrates one on the mind towards the ultimate or the absolute. However, for a householder, it is by limiting his passions towards the partner and for the unmarried focussing their attention towards the Divine in their own different contexts but enabling both as seekers of the Divine in two orientations with equal levels of perfection. It is the control and emancipation of the sexual energy to regenerate the spiritual self continuously and uniquely. These five traits are individual attitudes that form a seeker to concentrate on their own contexts and perform their thought, speech and action in alignment with the Divine.

Niyama also has five subdivisions. These form a more intimate and personal code of conduct that cleanses the body, mind and soul. *Sauca* (purity), *Santosha* (contentment-tranquillity), *Tapas* (austerity), *Svadhyaya* (self-study), and *Iswarapranidhana* (surrender to the Divine) are the five physical, mental and spiritual templates on which the life has to be built upon. *Sauca* means both the external and internal cleanliness. As the body is cleansed from the physical pollutions, the mind is also to be freed from the mental pollutions such as passion, anger, lust, hatred, vengeance, greed, delusion, pride etc. This physical and mental cleanliness and purity lead one towards holiness and holism and help to tread the path with undivided attention and convert and focus the extra energy towards a divine dimension. *Santosha* helps one to be content with what one has and happy with it rather than crave unnecessarily and be deluged with unattainable aspirations. It is a mental attitude of feeling fine with what one already possesses irrespective of either physical or mental context of lacking.(Happiness is the soul mode relying on what you already have and encompass.?? =happiness is the soul's acceptance of what you have and what surrounds you??) It is a frame of mind and curtails both greed and desire. *Tapas* literally means to heat the body. It is disciplining both the body and mind and channelling the creative energy towards a definite goal. It is austerity. It is again burning the desires and pruning the needs so that the goal of life is always focused. It is a kind of catharsis, purging the body and mind with the discipline to clean, crystallize and to transform it towards further perfection. *Svadhyaya* is self-study, meaning ever watchful of oneself through examinations and cultivating a self-reflective consciousness. It is intentionally finding self-awareness and refining the personality every day. *Iswarapranidhana* is the acceptance of a transcending superiority and surrendering towards it wholeheartedly and gleefully. Every action of one is submitted to this supreme transcendence, often termed as God. This is the purposiveness, the driving force that guides the whole yoga process; one is seeking from the beginning to the end of the process. Patanjali never mentions with the usage or name of a particular religious term and hence perfectly places this method for every human being irrespective of caste, creed and race. This is the beauty of this technique, and anyone can, therefore, place their own concept and name of God in this process and thus realize the ultimate goal of being with the Divine. It is a realization process. Even atheists could easily follow the path by placing here their own humanistic values towards which they would like to strive. Unfortunately, there is a tendency prevalent today to define it, promote it and reserve it with definite religious colouring. However, it must be said that those who do such promotions are doing a disservice to the intentions of the Patanjali Maharshi who was not at all sectarian and wanted to promote the technique universally. Also though there are a few religiously driven detractors such as Christian fundamentalists who consider and condemn Yoga as it belongs to a particular religious tradition, mainly Hinduism and thus deny the benefits of this wonderful technique of binding the body, mind and soul into an integral whole with the absolute, Divine or God to their adherents. In short, Yoga is a universal technique, a spiritual practice that transcends narrow religious bias. By practising it, nobody is going to be becoming an adherent to a particular religion and it is not reserved for any particular religion.

Asanas are physical exercises to control and tame the body. It has therapeutic significance, and by controlling the body, the mind can also be controlled. The body-mind mechanism is a two-way process; by having a healthy body a sound mind can also be generated. The mind controls the bodily emotions and aspirations and by strengthening the body, in a reciprocal way mind is also streamlined. There are more than 200 physical postures of which most of them are derived from the postures and behaviour of the animals. In the second chapter, Patanjali describes the purpose of performing the postures as physical exercises repeatedly in order to gain "steadiness and ease, resulting in relaxation of effort and endless unity". Not much attention is given by Patanjali to this section and later exponents have given adequate representation to it which further developed as *Hatha Yoga*. Many of the postures carry the names of birds and animals such as *Mayurasana* (Peacock posture), *Kukudasana* (Rooster Posture), *Garudasana* (Eagle Pose), *Slabhasana* (butterfly pose), *Nagasana* (Snake pose), *Bhujangasana* (Cobra pose), *Gomukhasana* (Cowhead pose), *Kurmasana* (Tortoise pose) Vrishikasana (Scorpion pose) Simhasana (Lion pose). etc. These postures would also instil the grace and power of these birds, animals and creatures in the practitioner and thus inculcate a feeling of oneness with the totality of the life-world in which we live. Thus, these postures incorporate an ecological dimension to the human being as part of the biological continuum instead of being a dominant user and abuser but a custodian of them. A series of postures are combined together to increase the flexibility of the body such as *Suryanamaskara* which is invoking the sun with twelve continuous and flowing postures to strengthen both the body and mind while deriving the energy from the sun. A feeling of interentwinedness, focus, sense of pride, the refreshing and energizing experience is achieved through the practice of these yoga postures. If these exercises are practised for a prescribed time slot, it would indeed prepare the adherent to encounter the world with greater agility, balance and confidence with a renewed and redefined sense of body and mind. The contemporary neurophysiology describes the evolutionary development of the human brain containing the crawling lizard type, animal type and the human type brain sections. The fight or flight mode is lizard brain; the emotional mode is the animal monkey brain and the rational mode as the advanced human brain that are significantly active as different evolutionary sections in the integral development of the human brain. These different sections would definitely connect the human being into these various evolutionary stages of human life sharing with the biological continuum which links towards an integral whole. Thus the asanas guide and heighten the natural and biological dimension of our existential relationship with an inextricable interconnectedness with our intertwining biological continuum.

Pranayama is the control of the breath, and through it, the whole energy and metabolism are measured and focused. When one is depressed, the breathing is slow, while anxious, the breathing becomes irregular and fast. Thus the bodily emotions often control the metabolism. Hence when the breath is controlled, consequently a psychic effect is evolved, leading to the control of the emotional imbalances. This refining and modification of the breath generate inner heat or cooling of the body leading to a shift in the predominant metabolism of the body, establishing self-purification and discipline of the body and mind. Calmness, mindfulness and equipoise are established through the *Pranayama* by soothing the respiratory system, nervous system and the entire limbs of the physical body. So control of breath, *Pranayama* is an essential part of the Yoga system.

Pratyahara, the next stage of the Yoga process means withdrawing from whatever that nourishes the senses. Hence it is a withdrawal from the external and internal things and environment that feed the needs and desires of the body and mind with a decision to accept life with the bare minimum. When the stimulants are restrained the senses become more controllable and follow a definitive purpose. The senses are thus restricted and focused towards an attainable goal leading to emancipation and creativity. Thus unhappiness and uneasiness are all eliminated due to the restraint of the flood gates of the stimuli that aggravate the senses. The withdrawal, hence promotes concentration, meditation and mindfulness leading to the next stage of yogic life.

Dharana is the unrestricted and immovable concentration of the mind. It is the focused cultivation of inner perceptual awareness. When the seeker or the *Sadhaka* is withdrawing the sensuality and increasing the sensibility by tempering the body and mind through *asanas* and controlled by *pratyahara* and being driven and fired by the inner heat of *pranayama*, the body and mind is integrated into a holistic continuum being engrossed with a single-minded attention and devotion towards a purposiveness that which is simultaneously immanent and transcendent. Reflection and contemplation are the right conditions for both the body and mind for further heightened consciousness. The oscillations of the body and mind are restricted, purified, focused and guided towards a transcendent reality. No more is the body or the mind fluctuating in the presence of stimulus because through the elimination of the ego and its root causes of sensuality, sensibility and driving away from the totality of *Ahamkara*; the human person is purified and filled in with selflessness and service. The body and mind are attuned towards the Lord, and gradually, the descent of the snow of saintliness begins as the soul is reaching towards the heightened, peak level of consciousness.

Dhyana is the next stage of development of the yoga process. The body is cleansed, the veils are eliminated, and the mind is focused, and thus, the visualization is clearer. The reality is seen as the one, beautiful and the good, *Unum*, *Verum* and *Bonum* in the Western concepts while in the Indian tradition it is envisaged as *Satyam*, *Shivam*, *Sundaram*. Unhappiness and fear are eliminated without any trace. The reality is perceived as the One, Absolute and all others are considered as mere illusions and unreal leading to the merging with the reality. The individual consciousness existing as body, mind and soul are collapsing into the Supreme Consciousness without each one having distinct existence. It is the attainment of *Samadhi*, being merging into the One, the Good and the Beautiful that are inextricably interwoven. It is the end of this purposive movement that passes through the seven stages and falling into the supreme Bliss or *Ananda*. It is an identity without differentiation. It is the logical end of this eightfold path, being fused into the totality of the infinity, the Divine Consciousness. Initiated through the different conditions as stages step by step, by an exponential integral affirmative process, the body, mind and soul transcend and merge with the Supreme reality or indwell in it. The body is aware, the mind is mindful, and the soul merges with the Supreme one without a second. The finite Atman is merging into the infinity of the Brahman, a *Rencontre* between the particular and the universal, the individual and the Supreme. Samadhi is indeed the merging into the Divine totality. So yoga is a spiritual inquiry, an integration process, an openness towards the natural order, refining the human to ascend towards the Divine and merge or collapse into this infinite bliss of unlimited happiness. The natural, the human and the Divine are synchronized into an inextricable intertwining holistic continuum.

Samadhi is of two types, namely, *Samprajnata Samadhi* (Conscious Aloneness or Oneness) and *Asamprajnata Samadhi* (Super conscious Oneness). In the Samprajnata, the object of meditation is still remaining as an object of oneness while in the Asamprajnata, the object, the process and the Consciousness all merge into interwoven fusion without any differentiation. Here all mental modifications are ceased while for the *Samprajnata* the consciousness still concentrated on the object of meditation.

Patanjali's *Yoga Sutra* has four sections, namely, the *Samadhi Pada* (Union with the Absolute), *Sadhana Pada* (Practice or Discipline), Vibhudi Pada (Supernatural Powers) and Kaivalya Pada (Liberation). The *Samadhi Pada* defines what is meant by Yoga; it is the cessation of all mental fluctuations; *Citta Vrutti Nirodha*. This section describes the unity of the individual consciousness merging with the Supreme Consciousness and the ways and means of attaining this integration. In the *Sadhana Pada*, the eightfold path of Yoga is illustrated as well the *Kriya Yoga* or *Karma Yoga*, two perspectives on attaining this integration. Karma Yoga is further illustrated in the third chapter of the *Bhagavadgita*. In the *Vibhuti Pada*, the supranormal powers or manifestations are described. It is also warned that the *Sadhaka* or the seeker should never be seeking such powers because it is never the aim of Yoga. These manifestations are indeed distractions for the mind, and they may deviate the mind from the purposive goal it was seeking and might be lost if the manifesting power is sought after. The *Kaivalya Pada* illustrated how the seeker is achieving the liberation.

The *Yoga Sutra* of Patanjali is based on the Philosophy of *Samkhya* where the phenomena are divided into twenty five *tattvas* or principles. *Purusha*, the Self Consciousness and *Prakriti* (Primal Nature or phenomenal world), *Buddhi* (intellect), *Ahamkara* (ego), *Manas* (mind), five *buddhindriyas* (sensory capabilities), five *karmendriyas* (action capabilities) and ten elements. *Yoga Sutra* also incorporated the three *gunas* or qualities, namely *Sattva* (illumination, lightness), *Rajas* (passion, dynamism) and *Tamas* (inertia, darkness, heaviness). *Prakriti* is unmanifested and it is in, and through the presence of *Purusha*, *Prakriti* evolves into the twenty-four principles. Kapila, the proponent of *Samkhya* philosophy, does not incorporate God, and it is therefore considered an atheist tradition. However, Yoga integrates *Isvara* defined as a distinct consciousness without afflictions. For *Samkhya,* liberation is attained in and through acquiring knowledge while Yoga accepts *Bhakti*, devotion and *Karma* action as different means of attaining liberation.

Many have given commentaries on *Yoga Sutra*. Prominent thinkers like *Sankaracharya* and *Swami Vivekananda* of Hinduism and Haribhadra of Jainism have all made commentaries on the *Yoga Sutra*. Haribhadra of the eight century almost followed the epistemology of Patanjali and formulated the eightfold path integrating it with the fourteenfold path of Jainism towards liberation; but he assigned titles in the feminine gender and identified *Isvara* with *Jina*. Thus there are many commentaries on *Yoga Sutra* written from the perspective of different religious traditions in attaining the final goal. Thus, Patanjali's *Yoga Sutra* incorporated all these religious traditions and hence without much doubt, one can say that his brilliant vision transcended the divisions and fragmentation of the narrow and parochial subdivisions with a universal message of attaining a single goal. Therefore this universal vision and mission of Patanjali is to be appreciated very much definitely because the twenty-first century is becoming more and more fragmented through various influences, traditions and religious polarisations.

Patanjali Maharshi is, therefore, a great synthesizer; a poet and a scientist. He dissects and analyses human reality like a logician and mathematician in order to put them together to an integral whole. He purifies the body and the mind to reach out to the highest level, a consciousness without any object, a seedless consciousness. He transcends the ego that is termed as *ahankar* and *asmita,* which is analysed as the root cause of needs and desires leading to violence. The goal of Patanjali is to arrive at the seedless consciousness and it is like, experiencing the rose with thorns and then, rose with the flower, then even the flower disappears without any impressions, an effortlessness, pure awareness, a thoughtless thought. Patanjali distinguishes three different types of seekers; when a person makes a casual inquiry, it is curiosity; like a scientist, a person who makes an intense inquiry is a *jignasu*; the *mumukshu* does the inquiry to liberate himself or herself; the inquiry is due to the desire to be desireless; they are the balanced, equipoised beings without irritation, anger etc. They are soft, *mrudu*, according to Patanjali, a desert-like being who is a second-degree seeker; the third-degree seeker is the one who does all efforts with sincerity and intensity to transform oneself into bliss; it is into them the snow of holiness and bliss would descend. In Samadhi, every blur disappears, and the reality is God, the only existing thing, everything disappears; the atman dissolves into the Brahman, the merging of the individuality into the totality, into the infinity. It is the path of surrender to God, aloneness with God, merging into the One, the good and the beautiful, potentiality and actuality are fused into the one and the same. Untouched by the afflictions of life, the individual dissolves into the Divine Consciousness.

In order to dissolve into the Divine Consciousness, Patanjali exhorts that an individual needs a master; someone who has already experienced the Divine. The individual places the trust in him or her, having a rapport. Just like a river flowing into the ocean, the master helps the initiate flow into the ocean, the ultimate flowering of the individual consciousness. A master makes you be discontinuous so that you can make the leap; to a higher state of consciousness, from the routine everyday life, to be reborn as a new consciousness, as in terms of the Hegelian dialectics, from thesis to antithesis to synthesis, to jump the gaps to make quantum leaps to remain in the flowering of the consciousness, to be there forever. That is why there is no time in the flowering consciousness, in the *Samadhi*. Yoga is the method to become one's, own master. As said in the quantum mechanics 'the observer is observed', the object of one's meditation gradually transforms oneself into it, becoming ultimately the object itself. That is the reason why Patanjali says that the object of your meditation should be on someone who has gone beyond the desires, the desireless, he or she will flood you with happiness and will crystallize you into a discontinuous quantum leap towards a new existence of desirelessness where the body, mind and the soul fused into a transcendental continuum. In the translation of *Patanjali Yoga Sutra*, (III, 3.) Swami Vivekananda narrated the outcome of yoga as illumination. "When the field of observation and the observing intelligence merge as if their own form is abolished and the total intelligence shines as the sole substance or reality, there is pure choiceless awareness without the divided identity of the observer and the observed – that is the illumination."

Tibetan Buddhist Meditation

Meditation has become now popular in the West, and to some extent, it was due to the spread of Tibetan Buddhism through His Holiness Dalai Lama. Earlier the Japanese Zen Buddhism was a special interest to many in the West, and now because of the influence of Dalai Lama and the spread of the Tibetan Meditation practices, it is also spreading widely in the West. As a Professor of Physics at the Sera Je Monastery in Bylekuppa, I had the opportunity to interact with many monks who are studying for their doctorate known as Geshe and who practice the Tibetan meditation. Moreover, my interactions with His Holiness Dalai Lama also gave me some of the deeper aspects of the Tibetan meditation practices. These monks taught me the Tibetan styles of meditation, and I found how it is useful in my meditation as well. I have incorporated into my meditation process and compiled a method that can enhance the awareness and spirituality evolved from the yoga tradition.

Tilopa, Naropa, Marpa and Milarepa said to be the Guru-Shishya Parampara who were the prominent monks known for their meditative styles. Naropa was the Vice-Chancellor or Rector of the Nalanda University and a highly intellectual monk. One day when he was reading a book, an angel appeared to him and asked him whether he understood the meaning and logic of the book! When Naropa said he understood the meaning, the angel laughed, and therefore he said, he would also know the logic. Surprisingly, the angel cried, and hence, Naropa asked for the reason, and it was revealed to him that he was lying and did not know the logic. Therefore, he prayed how he would know the logic and he was asked to find Tilopa and learn from him. For twelve years, Naropa searched for Tilopa and could not find him but undergone temptations. Desperate, he was about to commit suicide, Tilopa appeared and invited him to be his disciple. For another twelve years, he had undergone training, and he became an accomplished meditator. Naropa moved from knowledge towards wisdom. His was a transformation from Pundita towards a Siddha. The case of Milarepa was also extraordinary. He moved from vengeance to compassion. They meditated for more than 30 years at a stretch, and even now there are meditators who are in the Himalayas meditate for many years continuously.

Tibetan meditation is based on visualization. The present neuro-biology speaks about the firing of neurons even when we are simply visualizing things. As we are lifting the hand, certain neurons will be fired in our brain and the same neurons will be firing even when are merely imagining to raise our hands even though we are not really raising the hand. So visualization is a very powerful meditative technique, and this has now evolved into psychological treatment such as Mindfulness for correcting illnesses and behavioural phobia and neurosis etc. Buddhist meditations like Tummo is practised in generating inner heat and even conducted like a meditation. During cold winter in the Himalayas, Buddhist monks are asked to get wet themselves and dry as many wet clothes as possible through their body heat. There are many who could dry more than five and the one who dry the highest number of clothes are given awards. So all these meditative styles are now spreading all over the west, and people are now turning towards meditation. These meditative practices could help someone who is meditating to transform oneself. There are books like that of Shantideva's Boddhisattuvacharyavatara, which helps one to transform oneself by subduing one's own anger and other repressive forces. This classic work of the 8th century illustrious monks will be taught for a year for all doctoral students of Tibetan Buddhism in the Sera Je Monastery.

Philokalia

The prominent hesychasm method is that of Jesus Prayer and it is given through the illustrious spiritual classic known as *Philokalia*.[3] It's a love of beauty. Philokalia is the collection of spiritual exhortation from the monks from the fifth century to the 15th century who were deep into the search for awareness, steadfastness in prayer, wellness and happiness in life. It is strange to find that in the first volume, there is a section written by St. John of Karpathos for the Indian monks. Perhaps, it is observed that these Indian monks mentioned here might be from Ethiopia rather than real Indians. However, the connections

3 Philokalia, translated by Dr. Cherian Eapen, Carmel Publishers, Thiruvanathapuram, 2006. It is Dr. Cherian Epen or Dr. Roy Cherian who was instrumental in translating and publishing the full text of Philokalia in English and Malayalam simultaneously. He had worked hard in bringing together the Church leaders and translators and meticulously gone through the translations as he is also an expert in Russian. He has also visited the Optima monasteries and Valamo monasteries and helped to revive them after the collapse of communism. In my sojourn in Russia, Dr. Cherian Epaen shared with me the spirit of Philokalia and Hesychasm and introduced me to the Saint Theophan the Recluse of whom I was enchanted and took him as one of my favourite saints. I also had the opportunity to visit many monasteries in Vladimir-Suzdal Diocese of Russian Orthodox Church where St. Theophan was bishop. Enchanting monasteries and Lavra's like that of St. Vladimir, who Christianized Russia are here in Suzdal city. I thank my friends, Dr. Natalia Markova and Dr. Ivan Vikulov professors at the University of Vladimir who gave a great vision of these centuries of spiritual revolutions that was and is underpinning in Russia.

between ancient Greece and India in terms of philosophy and spirituality seem to be deeply rooted.

The spiritual classic Philokalia was compiled by the monks of Mount Athos, namely, Nikodemos and Makarios and was used as a means for the spiritual transformation in the monasteries. This book later translated into Russian and it became a household name through the book, *The Way of the Pilgrim*, a pilgrim who makes the pilgrimage from one spiritual centre to another while he was reading the Philokalia. Several translations were made in Russian and later in English and many other foreign languages and became a bestseller. Those who want to follow the spiritual path it became a must-read book. It's fame spread into the West, and many renounced their jobs and went in search of meaning and spiritual wholeness to Mount Athos. I met even the younger generation who was indeed said to be Wizkids who renounced their possible excellence in computer science and other technological fields, and joining the orthodox Churches and practising the hesychasm involved with Philokalia. Now there are translations in English, the full five volumes, even translated into Malayalam by my friend Dr Roy Cherian who has a doctorate in Engineering from the Moscow University and propagated it all over India, in both the English and Malayalam translations. Thus I found how the Indians are also experiencing this Greek spiritual classic for the benefit of their spiritual growth.

In Orthodox Christianity, the prayer method of Jesus prayer incorporates the control of the breath. They use the Jesus prayer in a rhythmic way while inhaling and exhaling. The fifth book of the *Philokalia* describes how this prayer method is to be synchronized with the breath. Thus prayer could also be synchronized with the breathing and *Pranayama* could induce initial conditions for meditation. In Indian tradition, mantra yoga is another method just like the Jesus prayer that can integrate with the breathing to form a meditative practice. Thus East and West to a certain extent use breathing for orienting the human towards the Divine.

Christayan

Integrating the yoga awareness, Buddhist meditative techniques and the hesychasm of the Jesus-Prayer can help us to transform ourselves into the consciousness of Christ as St. Paul had shown us. In his epistles, especially that of Philippians, Paul's consciousness ahs totally transformed, fused and merged into the consciousness of Christ. He was able to say that for me to live is Christ. These diverse, spiritual techniques can enable a seeker to transform oneself into the consciousness of Christ who could be encountered through the Gospels and the epistles as an embodiment of compassionate love. For Christians, Lord, Christ Jesus is the embodiment of the divine in whose footsteps every Christian should follow. Christayan is the turning of one's own self into the mindfulness or consciousness of Christ, in terms of the yoga and meditation as illustrated by St. Paul in his letter to the Philippians. (Phil 2). It is a process or a Sadhana by integrating the spiritual elements of both, the West and the East. Yoga, one of the greatest contributions of India, through its eight-way path, leads one to concentrate and fall oneself into the union with God. Creating attitudes of physical and mental cleanliness, being truthful, non-possessiveness and surrendering totally to God, one journeys towards and attains the highest union with God. The Buddhist meditation techniques employ the art of mindfulness in raising oneself to the highest form of consciousness. Both Yoga and Hesichasm (Jesus Prayer of the Orthodox Christianity – *Philokalia*) employ control of the breath and synchronizing the breath with chanting the name of God in attaining stillness or Samadhi. In the Gospel of John, Jesus is the eternal master, Sanatana Sat Guru, the embodiment of new life and eternal life. Visualizing him and his qualities, one can transform one's own self creatively into the compassionate love of Christ, the Sacred Heart of Jesus, Dharmaram (garden of righteousness – Sacred Heart of Jesus). So Christayan or Philoyoga is a process of attaining new Life, awareness, transformation through meditative mindfulness, combining the best contributions of the East and the West, to transform oneself into Dharmaram, to achieve the compassionate love of Christ, turning oneself into a process of transformation into Christ, a Christayan.[4] The yogic practices with its eight limbs, Buddhist meditative mindfulness and the Christian meditative practices of hesychasm of transforming oneself into the consciousness of Christ, the Sanatana Sat Guru, embodied with compassionate love is a means of integrating the best heritage of the East and the West and the body, psyche and the pneuma into a consciousness continuum.

4 Christayan retreats are already conducted by the author in India and Europe many times and the author practices himself.

20

God in the Religious Other and the Experience of the Divine in Shared Religious Spaces

James Ponniah
Dept of Christian Studies, University of Madras

Abstract: *This paper seeks to examine the meaning of 'the other' encountered in situations of shared religious spaces and to understand them as potential venues of divine encounter. Focusing upon such instances in the multi-cultural, multi-ethnic and multi-religious nations of South Asia, the essay draws the reader's attention not only to the kinds and contexts of shared religious spaces but also to the characteristics of divine encounter in the shared religious spaces. In our world wherein fundamentalism, religious bigotry and communal violence are steadily on the increase, the other is seen as a threat. Thus the hope for a peaceful and harmonious human life in our world seems very bleak. To restore humanity's hope, we need to identify and acknowledge existing sites of optimism in contemporary times. This article on shared religious spaces has drawn our attention to one such site wherein the others' religious spaces are accepted, and their divinities are worshipped, venerated and celebrated.*

Keywords: *Shared experience, shared religious space, institutional space, the other, sacredness of space.*

Introduction

Most of the philosophical or theological works have deliberated upon the question of 'the other' with the help of sources such as scriptural, philosophical or theological traditions. Departing from such approaches, this paper seeks to examine the meaning of 'the other' encountered in situations of shared religious spaces and to understand them as potential venues of divine encounter. Focusing upon such instances in the multi-cultural, multi-ethnic and multi-religious nations of South Asia, the essay draws the reader's attention not only to the kinds and contexts of shared religious spaces but also to the characteristics of divine encounter in the shared religious spaces.

What is a Shared Religious Space?

More than ever before, our contemporary era is marked by the co-existence of a multiplicity of cultures, faiths and ethnicities. While western scholars call this multiculturalism in the context of the globalized world, scholars of South Asia and Asia contend that diversity, plurality and heterogeneity have always been the constituent characteristics of South Asian ethos and culture. A fund of beliefs, customs and practices have been held in common by the people of different faith traditions living in a given geographical location. These religious overlaps which transcend religious boundaries set by the organized and institutionalized religions have given rise to the emergence of shared religious spaces. These shared religious spaces include not only the sites and locales, but also the occasions and situations that make it possible for the people of one faith to participate in the religious events and experiences of another faith tradition. What makes some sacred places different from others is that people, irrespective of gender, caste and religious affiliation, can gain access to the divine energies and sacred powers in these places through certain customs, events and religious practices.

Kinds and Contexts of Shared Religious Spaces

One witnesses different kinds of shared religious spaces in multi-cultural, multi-ethnic and multi-religious nations of South Asia. These spaces can be either public or domestic; permanent or transient; institutional or popular. While public shared spaces refer to famous shrines and pilgrimage sites, domestic shared spaces are those homes that accommodate divinities from different faith traditions. While both these spaces are more or less permanent in nature, transient or temporary shared spaces refer to public roads and streets that are temporarily turned into a sacred space when religious events like processions take place and make available a particular deity's power to the people of other faiths. Institutional sacred spaces refer to the interfaith sacred spaces produced in Indian Christian ashrams by the religious elites, namely, the clerical class, while the popular sacred spaces refer to those produced by the lay people in shrines and homes. That said, the following pages will describe each of these categories at length.

Shrines as Shared Spaces

To the category of public shared spaces belong numerous shrines or holy sites in South Asia like temples, churches and Dargahs, either well-renowned or locally known to the people in a given area, which attract people of different faith traditions. The works of Selva J. Raj (2002, 2004, 2006, 2017), Vasudha Narayanan (2004, 2006), Paul Younger (1999), Joanne Punzo Waghorne (2002), Margaret Meibohm (2002), Brigitte Luchesi (2008), Damaris Luthi (2008), to name a few, have discussed how the rituals performed by the people of different religions in a given shrine render it as a shared religious space which is open to common public. People of other faiths visit these shared spaces to access the supernatural divine power to overcome their limit situations.

What makes a shrine a shared religious space are its seven-fold characteristics. 1. It is not static but dynamic. What transforms this space into a shared religious space is that it is a site of dynamism and activity wherein religious subjects from multiple religious backgrounds come to worship the deity and perform rituals in search of supernatural power for varying purposes. 2. Shared religious space is an open, inclusive and democratic space. Its frontiers are open to all as everyone can gain access to the divine energies and sacred powers through certain customs, events and religious practices. It is inclusive as it remains accessible to people of different faiths, castes and classes. It is also democratic in a sense it is produced by ordinary people's investment of religious sensibilities. This investment process does not discriminate people based on gender, caste or class. Nor does it privilege one set of people over others. It is also more democratic as it is least controlled by the religious elites, the clergy 3. It is fluid and less structured. In contrast to the rigid structures either of the official liturgy in Churches or of prescribed *agamic poojas* in temples, shared religious spaces are characterized by religious and ritual activities that are fluid and less structured. People enjoy more freedom here to chart the course of their ritual activities and follow their own sequence. It is not that there are no customs and traditions specific to a particular site. But they are less rigid and remain open for improvisation by the practitioners. One of the important properties of fluidity is that it renders boundaries porous, admitting the influx of different traditions that intermingle and overlap with one another resulting in what some theologians would term as syncretism while scholars of religion call it hybridity. 4. It is a site of common ritual system. Various forms of ritual vows offered at shrines like Our Lady of Health at Vailankannie or Mount Mary Church at Bandra or Shaul Hamid Dargah at Nagore such as offering of facsimile (imitation of various bodily parts) or coconut saplings or shaving of head etc., show that Christians, Hindus and Muslims not only share a common ritual system. Selva Raj's works mentioned above draw our attention to the fact of not only the Hindus who come to Catholic shrines such as Vailankannie or Oriyur to perform rituals and fulfil their vows (in fact he notes that some of the Catholic shrines are frequented more by the Hindus than by Christians) but also the Christian devotees of St. John De Britto who visit famous Hindu deities like Karupasami in the neighboring village. Thus, just as the fulfilling of vows draws Hindus to Christian site and Christians to a Hindu place, such vow-related practices serve as important intersections "for the dialogue not only of rituals and devotees but of sites and deities as well" (Raj 2006: 62) 5. The shared space is fundamentally a liminal space to borrow Victor Turner's idea. In the context of a shared shrine or a religious procession that takes place on a public road, what happens is the temporary suspension of the regular identity of places and peoples. For instance, when the devotees in Vailankannie perform Hindu-like vow rituals of shaving the head and offering coconut saplings, the religious boundaries of what is Christian and what is Hindu is temporarily suspended, transcended or at times violated and as a result, the religious places in question or the people therein are neither this nor that. A Christian, rolling himself/herself on the ground in the fulfilment of a vow or a Hindu, joining the recitation of the Rosary and partaking in the central Catholic liturgy of the Eucharist is neither strictly Christian nor Hindu. Nor the Christian shrine which receives the offering of a basket of coconuts or/and flowers and gives it back to the devotees as *prasad* is strictly Christian. What prevails over such places and occasions is the loss of homogenous identity. 6. It represents the common heritage and cultural landscape of a given region. Shared religious spaces are characterized by local flavours that manifest themselves in beliefs, practices, performances, rituals, myths, arts and architecture. When we observe the way people discharge their religious beliefs, fulfil their vows, decorate their religious places, adorn their deities and carry out their religious processions, there is hardly any difference among Hindus, Muslims and Christians. Susan Bayly (1989) shows that the Hindu temples, Christian Churches and Muslim dargahs across South India imagine their deities as warriors who would protect them against any impending dangers. Accordingly, temples, churches and dargahs share a common form and structure of public religious processions that display a deity's protective power over a territory. David Mosse (2012), Susan Visvanathan (1993) and Rowena Robison (1998) have also confirmed the prevalence of such situations in Goa, Kerala and in other parts of Tamilnadu. Nathan Katz (2000), too, has shown how the synagogue in Cochin has drawn upon the customs and traditions of the temple for its architecture and ritual repertoire. More often than not, the local traditions and myths consider the local Hindu folk deities and the Christian divinities like Mother Mary as kinsmen and kinswomen as they fulfil a similar function. Hence the common folk among the Christians and Hindus visit each other's sacred sites and worship the deities of the religious other. Their appreciation and celebration of these deities are also recorded in folk songs prevalent among both Christians and Hindus. The instances mentioned above point to the existence of a common cultural universe in which religious traditions are embedded, and it is this cultural universe which provides the substratum for the emergence and continuation of shared religious spaces. 7. It is a site of the exigencies of human life. What drives the common people to these shared spaces is their existential predicaments of limit or crises. Faced with stalemates in personal lives like the loss of a job or a mysterious illness or financial crisis the common people are compelled to seek supernatural interventions and find a solution to their life-threatening issue. In such an impasse, contemporary religious subjects make all efforts to overcome their problems by transcending their traditional religious boundaries. Under such circumstances, as Selva Raj notes "the devotee deems cross-religious rituals and pilgrimages as necessary and salutary in the quest for a solution to a human or spiritual crisis or problem" (Raj 2006: 63).

Domestic Space as a Shared Religious Space

People's allegiance to such deities in the shrines is likely to continue when people install in their homes the statues or pictures of these deities which they have brought from the shrines and add them to the pantheon of domestic deities making a Christian deity become part of the Hindu household or vice versa. The deity that has come into this shared religious space is easily accessible to the veneration of the relatives and visitors to the Hindu household. Shared domestic religious spaces are brought about by default in the context of interfaith marriages. Homes of such marriages, in most cases, as my study has indicated (James Ponniah, forthcoming), often have interfaith altars invariably transforming their home into inter-religious spaces. Such homes are bound to accommodate beliefs and practices from two different traditions. Such developments become more pronounced and conspicuous at the time of the celebration of the life cycle and other rituals, such as birth, christening, puberty, marriage, death etc., Practice of two faith traditions within a home on such occasions is not always possible without conflicts. However, such conflictual situations in most cases, lead to conversations and consensus among the couples making inter-faith homes more democratic and less structured.

The procession as a Shared Religious Event

While the spaces mentioned above, be they public or domestic, enjoy the status of permanent shared religious space, there are other locales that are turned into shared religious spaces temporarily. The public roads during the time of religious procession of famous deities belong to this category. Religious processions are particular displays of religion that lay claim to public space. Just as processions move towards a sacred space of a temple or church or dargah, they make the public spaces en-route sacred as they progress.

Transportation of gods through the streets makes public road a sacred ground, though temporarily. When a deity is taken around in procession on a public road, people of different faith traditions not only display deference towards the gods and goddesses of another faith tradition but also go to worship the deity to get blessings. When this takes place, a public road, though temporally, is turned into a shared religious space which functions for a while as an epicentre of multi-faith religious experiences wherein a Hindu places himself or herself for the *darshan* of a Christian God and vice versa. Religious processions on public roads can invoke both positive and negative reactions from the religious other. In a positive reaction, the religious others place the significance of religious processions within their personal narratives of a deity's benevolence towards them and their family. In a negative reaction the religious others fail to share the rationale of the religious subjects in holding a religious procession. The latter takes place when the state is seen to act in favour of a tradition. For instance, when religious processions take place, the traffic on certain key roads get suspended and the vehicle-routes are diverted to facilitate processions. While such developments point to the state's policy of religious accommodation, they equally help unravel the soft power of religion to turn public places into liminal spaces in which the normal activities of the traffic and other behaviours are suspended in deference to a religious event. When this occurs, negative reactions can come from three camps: i) Internal religious other: opposition to the public religious events or process need not always come from the external religious other. i.e, (i.e., to a Hindu event from Christian groups or to a Muslim event from the Hindus) but from internal religious other, i.e,, to a Catholic Christian procession from protestants or to a Pentecostal event from Catholic/Protestant Christians, or to a Sunni Muslim event of Muharram from Shias or to a Saivite religious celebration from Vaishnavites. ii) From communists/atheists/ rationalists: Celebration of religious events in public places and State government's support for the events can also face opposition from such people as communists, atheists and some rationalists who reject God and the influence of religion on society iii) From religious fundamentalists: opposition to such events can also come from religious fanatics who deny the legitimacy of any religion other than their own to exist in this world. While the third group and their supporters tend to locate the narrative about the religious other within a larger political framework of pseudo-secularism, the second camp indicts the state for its failure to maintain neutrality. While the minorities tend to name this stance of the nation towards the majority as anti-secular, the majority would label the pro-minority stance of the state as pseudo-secular. Such attempts of politicisation of religion which are on the increase in recent years do impact the way the deity of the religious other is perceived and experienced as a source of divine experience.

Indian Christian Ashrams as Institutional Shared Spaces

In addition to the publicly shared spaces, India also has a relatively new phenomenon called institutional shared spaces, namely Indian Christian Ashrams, produced by the mainline churches when they wanted to inculturate or indigenise Christianity in India. The movement of Indian Christian ashrams talked about and experimented with by Indian Christian leaders like K.T. Paul and N.V. Tilak in the 1910s, acquired a more permanent stature with the founding of Christukula (Family of Christ) Ashram by two Protestant Christians, Dr S. Jesudason and Dr E. Forrester-Patón in Tirupattur, about 140 miles southwest of then Madras city 1921. The first Catholic ashram was founded by Brahmachari Rewachand Animananda, also known as Swami Animananda, in Ranchi around 1940. Richard W. Taylor (1977) in his analysis of Indian Christian Ashrams classifies Protestant and Catholic ashrams in India as *khadi* and *kavi* ashrams, respectively. In his view, Protestant ashrams are more oriented toward social service and social transformation, following the Hindu ideal of *karma marga,* whereas Catholic ashrams are dedicated to contemplative and devotional spirituality enjoined in the Hindu ideal of *jnana-bhakti* yoga. However, both ashrams developed "within the established churches, rather than in opposition to them," as Helen Ralston (1989: 114) noted. Be that as it may, the practices such as vegetarianism, celibacy, adoption of Hindu symbols, wearing of saffron saris by woman, dhotis, *kurtas* and shawls by men, squatting on the floor during Mass and the chanting of Sanskrit *slokas*, and the incorporation of Hindu rituals, symbols, images, architecture, customs, and other institutional practices into their religious life etc., make these Christian ashrams become visible signs of indigenized Christianity, resembling Hindu monasteries known as Mutts. A more detailed description of the Catholic ashrams will prove this point.

To begin with, the chapels in these ashrams are built in the style of a typical Indian Hindu temple. Statues of Jesus, Mary, and other saints like Benedict, Francis of Assisi, etc., would adorn the chapel *gopuram* (towers). The inner sanctum of the chapel would be darkened to resemble the *mula sthanan* (inner sanctum) of a Hindu temple. One of the popular Hindu symbols like an inverted lotus may serve as the altar on which Eucharist can be offered. The Eucharistic liturgy is consciously crafted to incorporate various Hindu symbols and gestures. The sanctuary walls or pillars in the chapels are often dotted with dark triangular niches for little oil lamps *(deepa).* The tabernacle in the sanctuary is likely to be built in the shape of a *linga* or of a miniature temple. In the chapel, there would be a prominent stone cross in an enclosed circle with the symbol "OM" inscribed in the middle. Sanskrit *slokas* from the Vedas and the Upanishads, as well as readings from other Hindu scriptures and the Bible, would be part of their morning, noon, and evening prayers.

These prayer services also include popular Hindu rituals such as prostrations or the *arati* (waving of the lamp in front of the tabernacle). In some places like Shantivanam at Thannirpalli near Trichy or Anjali Ashram in Mysore sandal paste is distributed in the morning as the symbol of grace and divinity, *kumkum* (auspicious red powder) at noon as the symbol of the third eye of wisdom, and ashes in the evening as the symbol of the impurities burnt away. *Bhajans* on Jesus – often sung in Sanskrit or Hindi – are a regular feature in the liturgical and para-liturgical celebrations. The above-mentioned description of an ashram clearly shows that these Catholic Christian Ashrams, while preserving their Catholic identity, have Hindu forms in their art, architecture, inmates' style of life, dietary practices, worship and rituals. Thus they have become both Hindu and Christians spaces with a goal to facilitate Indian Christians to have Christ or God experiences through Hindu forms and frames.

The Characteristics of Divine Encounter in Shared Religious Spaces

1. *Experience of the Divine Other through Darshan*: One of the important characteristics of the divine encounter in South Asia is the act of beholding and touching the deity's image. Known as *darshan*, this mode of encountering the divine power is not only central to South Asian religious life, but it also constitutes the shared religious spaces at the same time. *Darshan* is a reciprocal act, i.e., it involves not only seeing and touching the deity but also being seen and touched by the divine, which results in receiving a blessing from the deity. Thus ringing the bell in the temples or clapping the hands in front of the deity or approaching the deity's image as close as possible in religious processions or establishing contact with the deity's image through physical touch etc.. are all meant to ensure not only that the devotees get the maximum attention of the deity but also that the power of the deity imparted to a devotee is felt as powerfully as possible. It is the possibility of this aspect of the *darshan* that attracts the religious other towards a deity either in a religious site or in procession. The more powerful a deity is in the people's perception, the more diverse constituency of devotees it draws to itself, which in turn makes a religious site a better shared religious space. In a similar vein, religious processions are meant to take the deity out of the temple or a church into the neighbourhood territories so that the deity's blessings and benevolence are made available to people of all faiths through the act of *darshan*. Thus *darshan* becomes an effective means of encountering the deities of the religious others, deities who reach out to people of other faith traditions and present themselves as kind, benevolent and powerful.
2. *Experience of the Divine through the Material and the Tangible:* It is through the embodied cultural practices that people experience the divine of the religious other. It is true of religious sites both public and domestic,

permanent and temporary, the institutional and the popular. For instance, Paul Younger, Selva Raj, Vasudha Narayanan and others in their works on Catholic and other shrines detail how embodied practices and material objects in shared religious sites such as taking a cleansing bath in the sea or tank, rolling around the church, walking on the knees, tying pieces of cloth around tree branches or the flagpole as token of individual wishes, offering of hair at the shrine, offering of baskets with incense sticks, candles and coconuts and the presentation of flower garlands (which are touched to the feet of the image before being returned) etc., are found very commonly not only in Christian shrines as in a Hindu Temple but also in Muslims Dargahs. Many of these characteristic elements of the Christian veneration of Mary and other saints in Catholic churches and shrines play a central role also in Muslim Dargahs as in South Asian Hindu worship. In this regard, Selva Raj observes that "the Catholic system retains the basic principles, idioms, vocabulary, content, and the rubric of the Hindu system" (Raj 2006: 60). These common South Asian or Tamil cultural practices become very powerful means through which the Tamil Hindus and Christians experience the divine power. It is through the world of material objects and the tangible ritual-based bodily expressions that a Hindu, an otherwise a disinterested outsider to the Christian world of the ordered liturgy in the church, becomes an insider and a devotee of a Christian shrine. Luchesi (2008) and others have also discussed how the Catholic churches in Germany, Norway and Switzerland first allowed, then encouraged and facilitated the practice of vernacular Catholicism for the Sri Lankan Tamil Diaspora. By bringing in Tamil priests and creating Tamil chaplaincy in different places, they not only made the Christian Tamil diaspora feel welcome and took care of their religious needs, but also provided world of hope to the Tamil Hindus as well who regained their access to the divine power through the mediation of Mary and other saints who were part and parcel of their religious life back in their home country. Luchesi (2008) in her work has shown how practices such as going to have a glimpse of the miraculous picture, touching it, lighting candles inside and outside the churches in Kevelaer, are the same both for the Hindus and the Christians as these practices were followed back in their homeland. These religious possibilities provide a new sign of hope for the Tamil Christians and Hindus who were in a state of anxiety, uncertainty and fear in a foreign land as refugees.

3. *Experience of the Divine Other through Ritual Hospitality:* One of the common practices in shared religious space, be it shrine or home or ashram, is providing a communal meal to the religious visitors and guests. The practice of the age-old Indian saying 'Atithi Devo Bhava' ('The guest is equivalent to God') is very evident in shared religious

space. In the context of shrines, the climax of the fulfillment of a vow often culminates in a communal meal served first to the poor, the beggars and the destitute who are believed to take the place of the deity to whom the cooked food is offered. This ritual hospitality assumes a special significance in the case of *asanam. Asanam* tradition requires that the vow-taker himself/ herself serves the food on banana leaves to a group of thirteen honoured "ritual guests," who are basically beggars. The climax of this *asanam* is the act of reverse begging. Having served the meal to the "ritual guests" on banana leaves, the principal vow-taker goes on his/her knees in front of each of the thirteen invited beggar guests and begs for a handful of food from each. With the food collected through reverse begging, s/he sits beside the thirteen beggars and eats the ritual meal. Only after the "ritual guests" have been fed to their satisfaction, can family members partake of the "ritual meal." What interests us in this tradition is that this ritual hospitality not only enables us to treat and encounter the divine in the vulnerable other, but also makes the host to totally identify himself/herself with the poor and the marginal people.

4. *Experience of God as a Consoler of the Afflicted*: One of the important reasons why hundreds and thousands of people go to the shared religious space of the shrines is to get rid of their sorrows and distress. This shared sacred space of shrines provides the afflicted devotees with comfort, motherly care, healing and hope. The experience of the divine power as solace in these sites is equally shared by Christians, Hindus and Muslims. As South Asian scholars have noted, these shrine-based interreligious experiences point to how the common people see in the image of the divine other the reflection of their own deity's divine attributes. For instance, they argue that just as Christians consider Blessed Mary as the Mother of God, Hindus understand her as the Divine Mother, which for the common people is unproblematic. 'The Mother of God' in Catholicism becomes 'The Divine Mother' in Hinduism. According to Annette Wilke (2013), this difference is expressed in two different Tamil words Christians and Hindus use to address Mary. Christians use *mata* (Mother), whereas Hindus prefer *taye*, a Tamil word meaning 'divine mother' which is reserved for goddesses. It is this perception of Mary as *taye* (divine mother) that drives them to the shrines of Mother Mary whom they approach without any hesitation as she cares for those who suffer various forms of ills in life.

5. *Experience of the Divine in the Ordinariness of Life:* Another important characteristic of shared religious space, especially the one produced by religious processions is that it makes it possible to experience God on the streets. It is this availability of the divine presence on the road and in the hustle and bustle of the streets and markets that automatically

elicits veneration and deference on the part of the religious others. What is significant about this sacred space is that it produces the experience of the divine other outside the deity's regular abode (church or temple), namely, in the sacredness of the secular and the ordinary. Religious minded as they are, South Asians spontaneously tend to worship the divine figure who has come out of his/her regular abode on to the streets to visit them in their localities. As the deity on procession is believed to possess enormous power, it enlists the veneration of the onlookers and bystanders who, irrespective of religious traditions, welcome the deity into their area to obtain the blessings.

6. *Encountering the Divine in the 'Sacredness of the Other'*: Shared religious spaces provide new possibilities to believers to encounter God by inviting them to partake in other's ideas of the sacred. They make the believers respect and honour the religious sensibilities of the religious others, thereby enabling them to participate in the metaphysics of the religious other's transcendence. Sharing other's way of seeing involves sharing other's way of knowing. In doing so, shared religious spaces make people accept the differences in religious others. In other words, such developments are capable of mapping out new terrains of interfaith epistemologies and metaphysics.
7. *The Divine in the Intersectional Space:* In the globalised and digitalized world of today, no religious tradition can claim to be totally a sanitized religious space and to remain completely disconnected from the religious world of the other. Whether or not desired or intended, religions are faced with the situations of interactions, exchanges and at times of conversations between them. Religious sensibilities in today's world inform us that there are no religious 'heterotopias,' to borrow from Foucault's views, an autonomous religious space of a tradition that exists totally outside all other religious spaces. It means that today's world is an intersectional space between various religious traditions which are inter-related if not inter-dependent. Religions will do well by realizing their inter-relatedness to serve humanity by synergizing their resources and energies to tackle the issues of poverty, ecology and lack of human dignity in the world. That said, shared religious spaces illustrate an optimism that is predicative of intersectional space in that they embody appreciation, respect and positive outlook the people have towards the religious others and their scared locales. Tapping the opportunities provided by shared religious spaces, religion can take the optimism of the intersectional space to the next level by addressing the issues and concerns of the people who frequent the shared religious spaces to enhance their well-being.

Conclusion

In a world like ours wherein fundamentalism, religious bigotry and communal violence are steadily on the increase, the other is seen as a threat. Thus the hope for a peaceful and harmonious human life in our world seems very bleak. To restore humanity's hope we need to identify and acknowledge existing sites of optimism in contemporary times. This article on shared religious spaces has drawn our attention to one such site wherein the others' religious spaces are accepted and their divinities are worshipped, venerated and celebrated. This essay written in honour of Prof. Kurien Kunnumpuram whose life and works had profound respect and appreciation for others, their views and ethos is also my humble tribute to an intellectual who stood strongly for peace and harmony among diverse religious traditions of India.

References

Bayly, S.B. (1989) *Saints, Goddesses and Kings: Muslims and Christians in South Indian Society, 1700-1900.* Cambridge: Cambridge University Press.

Katz, Nathan (2000). *Who Are the Jews of India*, Berekely, Los Angeles and London, University of California Press.

Luchesi Brigitte (2008) "Seeking the Blessing of the Consolatrix Afflictorum: The Annual Pilgrimage of Sri Lankan Tamils to the Madonna in Kevelaer (Germany)" In Knut A. Jacobson and Selva J. Raj (eds.) *South Asian Christian Diaspora: Invisible Diaspora in Europe and North America*, Surrey, Burlington: Ashgate, 75-96.

Luthi Damaris (2008), "Perpetuating Religious and Social Concepts in the Extended Motherland: Tamil Christians in Berne (Switzerland)" In Knut A. Jacobson and Selva J. Raj (eds.) *South Asian Christian Diaspora: Invisible Diaspora in Europe and North America*, Surrey, Burlington: Ashgate, 97-116.

Meibohn, Margaret. (2002). "Past Selves and Present others: The Ritual Construction of Identity at a Catholic Festival in India" in Selva J.Raj and Corinne G.Dempsey (eds.) *Popular Christianity in India: Riting Between the Lines*, Albany: State University of New York, 61-84.

Mosse, David. (2012) *The Saint in the Banyan Tree: Christianity and Caste Society in India.* Berkeley, Los Angeles and London: University of California Press.

Narayanan, Vasudha. (2004) "Sacred Land, Common Ground, Contested Territory: the Healing Mother of Velankanni Basilica and the Infant Jesus Shrine in Bangalore," *Journal Hindu Christian Studies,* 17, pp. 20-32.

Ponniah, James (forthcoming) "Women Make It Work: The Story of Inter-religious Marriages in Urban India" in Ponniah, J. (ed.) *Culture, Religion and Home-Making in and beyond South Asia.* Fortress Press.

Raj, Selva.J. (2002) "Transcending Boundaries, Transcending Turner: The Pilgrimage Tradition at the Shrine of St.John de Britto" in Raj, S.J. and Dempsey, C. G. (eds.) *Popular Christianity in India: Riting Between the Lines*. Albany: State University of New York, pp. 85- 114.

__________ (2004) "Dialogue 'On the Ground': The Complicated Identities and the Complex Negotiations of Catholics and Hindus in South India." *Journal Hindu-Christian Studies*, 17, pp. 33-44.

_________ (2006) "Shared Vows, Shared Space, and Shared Deities: Vow Rituals among Tamil Catholics in South India" in Raj, S.J. and Harman, W.P. (eds.), *Dealing with Deities*. Albany: State University of New York, pp. 43-64.

_________ (2017) "Being Catholic the Tamil Way," in Locklin, R.B. (ed.). *Vernacular Catholicism, Vernacular Saints: Selva J. Raj on "Being Catholic the Tamil Way*. Albany: State University of New York Press, pp. 1-16.

Ralston, Helen (1989) *Christian Ashrams: A New Religious Movement in Contemporary India, Studies in Religion and Society 20 [Lewiston, NY, and Queenston, ON Edwin Mellen Press, 1989).*

Richard W. Taylor, "From Khadi to Kavi: Toward a Typology of Christian Ashrams," Religion and Society 24 (December 1977): 19-37.

Robinson, R. (2009) "Negotiating Traditions: Popular Christianity in India," *Asian Journal of Social Science,* 37 (1), pp. 29-54.

_________ (1998). *Conversion, Continuity and Change: Lived Christianity in Southern Goa*, New Delhi: Oxford University Press.

Visvanathan, Susan (1993). *The Christians of Kerala, History, Belief and Ritual Among the Yakoba.* Madras: Oxford University Press.

Waghorne, Joanne Punzo (2002) "Chariots of the God/s: Riding the Line Between Hindu and Christian, " in Selva J. Raj and Corinne G.Dempsey (eds.) *Popular Christianity in India: Riting Between the Lines*, Albany: State University of New York, 11-38.

Wilke, Annette (2013) "Tamil Temple Festival Culture in Germany: A New Hindu Pilgrimage Place" In U. Hüsken and A. Michaels (eds.) *South Asian Festivals on the Move*, Wiesbaden: Harrassowitz, 369-395.

Younger, Paul (1992) "Vailankanni Calling: Hindu Patterns of Pilgrimage at a Christian Shrine" in Alan Morinis (ed.), *Sacred Journeys: The Anthroplogy of Pilgrimage*, Westport, Conn.: Greenwood Press. 89-99.

21

Advaita and *Theosis* The Spiritual Encounter between the Spirituality of the Upanishads and the Experience of Being *in Christ*

Sebastian Painadath SJ
Sameeksha, Centre for Indian Spirituality, Kalady, Kerala

Abstract: *This article explores the mystical convergence between advaita and theosis. Five elements of the Upanishadic advaitic tradition are located first: the Divine as mystery, and as the ultimate subject, the divinisation of the human, the immanence of the Divine in cosmos, and the resultant freedom. Then the three-fold dimension of the divine consciousness of Jesus is articulated: being sent by the Father, being in the Father and being one with the Father. John's Gospel shows that Jesus wanted to communicate this threefold experience to us. This is what Church Fathers called theosis, the divinisation of the human; this is a birthing process. Having explained the terms advaita and theosis, the convergence and divergence between the two are explored. The article concludes with the proposal that Hindus and Christians could move on as spiritual co-pilgrims, who share their deep mystical experiences with one another and get enlightened and enriched by each other.*

Keywords: *Aadvaita, Theosis, Divinisation, Mystical experience, Dialogue, Upanishads.*

The Upanishads, composed in the light of the mystical experiences of the great sages between 800 and 400 BCE, contain an *advaitic* experience: deep oneness with the all in the Divine. The great Church Fathers (100-600 CE) described the core of Christian faith in terms of *theosis*, the divinisation of the human. In this paper I would like to explore the scope of a theological encounter between these two perceptions: *advaita* and *theosis*.

The Dynamics of Spirituality

Spirituality is the universal experience of being gripped by the divine Spirit, the experience of being awakened to the dimension of Transcendence: it is the sense of the Holy, the orientation to the Absolute, the ultimate concern. In spirituality, one experiences the Divine as Spirit: as breath, as movement, as vibration. In spirituality, one resonates with the expansion of the Divine into infinite horizons. The Spirit explores the *depth* of the Divine (I Cor. 2:11).

Often one gets access to spirituality through faith. Spirituality is universal; faith is particular. Spirituality is the unfolding of the Divine in consciousness; faith is related to a concrete revelatory event. Faith finds expression through symbols, which are taken from particular cultures: symbol is the language of faith. Through the mediation of symbols, spirituality evolves as religion.

Religious symbols evolve in four areas: creed, cult, code and community. In each area the believing community appoints authoritative persons: theologians, priests, teachers and leaders. In all these areas there are ambiguities rendered by social, political, economic and psychological factors. There is a constant struggle of the divine Spirit with these factors. This critique of the Spirit finds expression through mystics and prophets. Often mystics are silenced and prophets are killed by the authorities; every religion has a criminal history. Religious symbols in their function are ambivalent: they can open the way to the Divine, they may also block the way.

In this article we focus attention on the encounter of two mystical traditions of the East and that of the West: concretely on the interfacing of *advaita* and *theosis*.

The Spirituality of the Upanishads

The Upanishads offer an authentic source of the Indian mystical heritage. They have been composed at different times between 800 and 400 BCE. Though the Upanishads are not given the same revelatory value (*sruti*) associated with the Vedas, they are held in high esteem in the scriptural corpus of Hinduism for, these contain the recollections (*smriti*) of the sages who went into the depth of the unity of reality in the Divine. Upanishads uphold the absolute transcendence of the Divine (*Brahman*) as well as the deep immanence of God (*Atman*) in the world. The transcendent mystery of the Divine is revealed through its immanence in the world: Atman is Brahman – *ayam ātma Brahma* – this is a basic insight of the Upanishads.

Five elements can be located in the mystical worldview of the Upanishads:

a. The Divine is Absolute, Incomprehensible, Ineffable Mystery

An abiding sense of the all-pervading, and all-transcending mystery of the Brahman vibrates in all the Upanishads. When speaking of the Divine the sage says:

> "There the eye does not reach, nor speech, nor mind: we do not know it nor do we know how to teach it. Indeed it is other than the known, and also beyond the unknown. Thus have we heard from the ancient sages who have spoken about it." (Kena Up. 1.3-4)

This being the case, the only way to reach out to the divine mystery is the way of negation: *neti...neti...*(not this, not this) (Birth. Up.4.5.15). "That from which words return along with the mind not attaining it - that is the blissful Brahman." (Tait. Up. 2.9.)

The Divine is "ungraspable, unperceivable, indescribable", (Mund. Up. 1.1.6), "formless eternal silence" (Chand. Up. 3.15), "subtler than the subtlest" (Swet Up. 4.14). If asked what its form is, one should answer: "Its form is formlessness" (Swet. 4.19).

b. The Divine is the Ultimate Subject Of Consciousness

The human mind can grasp something only in so far the latter is objectified. The mind wants to put everything into a definite form. But the Divine is formless, and hence, it is not an object for the mind to grasp. Hence the only way to grasp the Divine is to dive into a deeper level of consciousness. Upanishads invite the seeker to dive from the mind (*manah*) to the introspective intellect (*buddhi*), from the mental level to the intuitive level, from analysis to awareness, from the objectified mode of perception to the experience of the true subject (Kath. Up. 3:10). This process is a matter of human effort that involves asceticism and renunciation, concentration and meditation. But the attainment of the experience of the Divine as the ultimate Self is a matter of grace.

> "The Self cannot be attained by instruction, nor by mental exercises, nor through much hearing. He can be attained only by the one whom the Self chooses. To such a one the Self reveals his true nature" (Kath Up.1.2.23).

> "That which is not thought by the mind, but by which the mind thinks, that is Brahman; not what people worship here. That which is not expressed through speech, but by which speech is expressed, that is Brahman; not what people worship here" (Kena Up. 1.5-6)

The Upanishadic sages demand that a true spiritual seeker should not get stuck at any particular image of God. Any categorical experience may be affirmed, but it should constantly transcend towards the Brahman that is ever-beyond. The seeker should constantly ask himself/herself: how can I know the Knower? *Vijnātāram kena vijaneeyāt.*

c. The One Who Knows the Divine Becomes One with the Divine

The true awakening to mystery of the divine subjectivity takes place not in the framework of the dualistic mind but through the unfolding of the intuitive buddhi. Only by becoming one with the Divine does one really know the Divine, for the Divine is not so much object of our knowledge, but subject of our consciousness:

> "Only in oneness is it to be seen, the stable *atman,* immeasurable, free from blemish is it, beyond space, unborn, great, unwavering" (Brh. Up, 4,4,20 cfr. Kath.Up.9,13; Swet.Up. 6,13: Mait Up. 6,17).

In the depth of consciousness, one enters into an experience of mystical union with the Divine. "The one who knows the Brahman, verily becomes Brahman!" (*brahmavid brahmaiva bhavati*, Mund.Up.3.2.9) "By knowing the Brahman one merges into the Brahman" (Swet.Up.2.7). One has thus transcended the phenomenal level of consciousness (Tait.Up.2.2.1) and entered into the mystical awareness of the divine Self within. In deep oneness with the Self one may exclaim "I am Brahman!" (*Aham brahmāsmi,* Brih Up. 1.4.9) Here one touches upon a level of experience that is far deeper than the mental level. This experience of mystical union cannot be evaluated in terms of the conceptual framework or philosophical theories of the mind. Hence any attempt to label this experience as monism or self-annihilation, or to judge it as denying the reality of the individual and the world would be off the mark. What is essential is to see how such an inner pilgrimage and the unitive experience improve the quality of a person's life.

d. The Entire Universe Is Permeated by the Divine Self (Atman)

With the intuitive experience of the Self inside one looks at the world outside. And one perceives "the same Self in all and all in the Self" (Isa. Up.6) It is an ecstatic experience of the universal theophany. The divine light shines through everything (Mund. Up. 2.2.1), the divine life permeates everything (Swet.Up. 1.6), the divine vibration - OM - resonates in everything (Chand.Up.2.23.3). The universe is the divine abode, the body of the Lord (Chand.Up.5.18.2). The entire universe is permeated by the divine Lord (Isa Up.1).

> "Verily this whole world is Brahman. Everything takes birth from it, moves in it and finally merges with it. Tranquil one should meditate on it" (Chand. Up.3.14.1). "That from which these beings are born, that through which

> they live and that into which they finally enter - that is Brahman"(Tait. Up.3.1.1). "He who dwells within the earth (and everything), yet distinct from the earth, whom the earth does not know, whose body the earth is, who controls the earth from within, he is the Self, the inner controller (*antaryāmin*) the immortal One" (Brih. Up. 3.7.3). "This verily is the Lord of all beings. As the spokes are held together in the hub and felly of a wheel, just so in this Self, are all beings, all gods all worlds, all living beings, all these selves, held together" (Brih.Up-2.5.15).

The Upanishadic sages use a highly poetic language to describe the experience of the universal immanence of the divine Self. They do not identify the finite world with the infinite Brahman; they taste and see the power and presence of the Brahman in every atom and every living cell. They realise that the whole universe is soaked in the divine energy sphere. The divine presence is felt as permeating and enlivening everything like butter in milk (Swet.Up.4.16), like salt in sea-water (Brih.Up.1.4.7), like oil in the seed (Swet.Up.1.15), like the vital sap in the tree (Chand. Up.6.11.1). This is a highly mystical worldview. This cannot be judged with logical categories or evaluated with the dogmatic framework of another religion. Any attempt to label this as pantheism or idolatry would miss the point. What is important is to see how this world view communicates a sense of ecological harmony. When the cosmos is experienced as the dance of the Divine, human persons would live with great respect for everything, animate and inanimate.

e. Inner Freedom Is the Character of the Enlightened Person

The experience of the divine presence within oneself and in everything makes one sensitive to the grace and demands of divine presence in the world. The basic characteristic of one's relation to realities outside would then be inner freedom. "The one who sees all beings in the Atman, and the Atman in all beings, is free from fear" (Isa Up. 6). If the Lord permeates everything, one cannot possessively cling on to anything. Hence the sage exclaims: "renounce and enjoy!" (Isa Up.1). The Upanishadic masters describe greed (*kama*) as the root cause of all suffering and alienation in life. (Mund. Up. 3.2.1) Through greed one gets fixated on one's ego (*ahamkāra*) and thereby the way to inner spiritual freedom is blocked (Swet.Up. 4.7). Besides, through greed, one destroys the resources of God-given nature and manipulates other human beings for one's ego-gratification. The way to overcome greed is to develop the attitude of non-possessiveness (*aparigraha*).

> "Two motivations bind a person: that which leads to the auspicious (*srēyah*) and that which brings about the pleasurable (*prēyah*). Each has a distinct purpose to attain. The wise man pondering over them prefers the auspicious to the pleasurable. But the ignorant man chooses the

> pleasurable for worldly benefits, and thus fails of the true aim of life" (Kath.Up.1.2.1-2).

A man of inner freedom is above the duality of good and evil. The integral mystical vision of life gives rise to a holistic view of nature and society.

> "On knowing the Self one becomes a liberated person. His whole life is oriented to the Divine. He has risen above the desire for wealth and worldly benefits. He has risen above the feeling of having done something good or evil. What he does, does not bind him to this world at all" (Brih. Up. 4.4.22).

The one who perceives the Divine in all, becomes concerned about the integral welfare of the others. Compassion would be the hallmark of such an ethical attitude. When the Creator Lord was asked, about the basic virtues of life, he answered: be self-controlled, (*dama*) be generous (*datta*), be compassionate (*daya*) (Brih.Up.5.2.1-3). The last instruction given by the master to the student as the latter enters upon his family life offers a summary of the ethical teaching of the Upanishads.

> "Always speak the truth, incessantly pursue the dharma, continue the self-study. Never swerve away from truth and dharma. Let there be no neglect of your welfare and the prosperity of all beings. Let there be no neglect of the duties to the ancestors and the responsibilities to the life-forces of nature. May your mother and father, your teacher and guest be God for you. May the good dealings you found in me inspire you further. What you give to others, give in faith and humility, with sympathy and generosity. (Tait. Up.1.11.1-4)

Being *in Christ*

What happens when the Gospel of Jesus encounters the spiritual world of the Upanishads? What happens when faith in Christ meets the mystical experience of the Upanishadic sages? How would an encounter with the spiritual world of the Upanishads deepen the faith experience of a Christian?

The Foundational Experience of Christian Faith

The Logos became flesh in Jesus Christ. God so loved the world that he sent his only begotten Son to the world. In Christ God has reconciled the world to himself. The old is gone, everything has become new. We live in Christ – these are some of the key expressions (*mahavākyas*) of Christian faith. When a Christian says these words to a Hindu shaped by the Upanishadic heritage, he will be confronted with the question: have you experienced the power of these words? Has the Gospel really deepened your consciousness, and transformed your life? Experience is the primary source of authenticity in the mainstream

Hindu heritage. Hence the insistence on asceticism, meditation, discipline and simplicity of life.

Experience of the Divine is basically the experience of oneness with the Divine. There is a constant insistence in the Upanishads that every form of duality conceived at the mental level has to be transcended by the consciousness of the unity of reality in the Divine. This is an invitation to a deep mystical consciousness. This is a challenge to Christians to awaken the mystical dimension of Christian faith. There is a tendency in us Christians to overemphasise the I-thou relationship with God. God is conceived primarily as Father, Lord, Saviour, King. This personification of the Divine with male symbols is evident in our prayers and liturgy, in our theology and Church structures. The mystical sages of the Upanishads bring our attention to the mystery dimension of the Divine, to the experience of God as the Subject of our being, to the consciousness of being one with the Divine. We are here helped to look deeper into the God-experience of Jesus: Jesus experienced the Divine as the inner source of his being, as that-out-of-which he came forth. (The following references are from the Gospel according to John)

a. 'The Father Sent Me' (3:16, 4:34, 5:36-38, 7:28-29, 10:36, 17:3)

Jesus had an abiding consciousness of being *sent* by the Father. Here the Father is the one who sends the Son with the redemptive mission. The Son understands his mission as 'doing the will of the Father' (4:34, 5:30, 6:38), as 'completing the work of the Father' (4:34; 6:29; 9:3). What is perceived here is a certain distinction between the one who sends and the one who is sent. The relation between the Father and the Son is an *inter*-personal relation.

b. 'I Am in the Father and the Father Is in Me' (5:26, 8:28, 14:10; 17:21,23).

Jesus knew that the Father who sent him is with him, in him (8:16,29, 16:32, 14:10). Here the Father is the one who gives life to the Son from within. The Son constantly takes birth from the Father (5:26; 6:57; 8:24; 16:28). The Father is the source and *generator* of the Son. Between them there is total mutual immanence, intense compenetration (*perichoresis*). The Son is the expression and unfolding of the Father (14:10; 12:49). There is no Father without the Son, no Son without the Father. The relation between the Father and the Son is an *intra*-personal relation.

c. 'The Father and I are One' (10:30: 17:11,21,22.)

This is the articulation of the deepest experience of Jesus in relation to the Divine. He had the consciousness that his being and life and work have been totally transparent to the divine source, which he called the Father. Father and Son are essentially one. The being of the Father unfolds itself through the being of the Son. The Son is the self-communication of the Father. There is absolute unity between them. The relation between the Father and the Son is a *trans*-personal relation, in the sense that it goes far beyond the personalist structures of the human mind. The oneness in the depth of the Divine cannot be expressed in personalist categories. These three aspects of Jesus' consciousness may not to be taken as three phases or spheres, but as the three integral dimensions of his God consciousness.

And Jesus wanted to communicate to us this inner experience:

Just as the Father sent me into the world, so do I send you into the world (17:18).

Just as the Father knows me, and I know my own (10:14)

Just as the Father has loved me, so have I loved you (15:9;17:26).

Just as I remain in the love of the Father, so will you remain in my love (15:10).

Just as I draw life from the Father, so will you draw life from me (6:57).

Just as I am in the Father, and the Father is in me, so am I in you and you are in me (17:21;14:20).

Just as the Father and I are one, so may you all be one in us (17-21-22).

The Greek preposition *kathos* (just as) has a great significance here. Jesus wanted all those who believe in him make the same inner journey that he made, and participate in the same inner experience that shaped his consciousness. Our life evolves not so much before Christ as in Christ, not before God as within the inner-trinitarian process of life. We are called to participate in the filial experience of Christ: we are daughters/sons of God.

Theosis: The Divinisation of the Human

The early Fathers of the Church found in the process of the divinisation of the human (*theosis*) the core of Christian faith experience:
"God became man so that man may become God!" (*Deus homo factus est, ut homo fieret Deus*, Augustine, PL.38,1997).

"Through his immense love the Word of God became what we are, so that we may become perfectly what he is" (Iraeneus PG. 7,1120).

"When our consciousness is completely purified and through contemplation elevated above the material realm, it will be divinised by God."(Origen, *Comm. on John 32,27*).

"With Jesus human and divine nature begin to be woven together so that by fellowship with divinity human nature might become divine, not only in Jesus, but also in all those who believe and go on to undertake the life which Jesus taught."(Origen, *Contra Celsum, 3,28*).

"We have not only become Christians, but Christ himself. Stand firm in awe and rejoice: we have become Christ." (Augustine, *Commentary on John's Gospel, 21,8*)

"The Word became man, so that we humans may become Divine..Theosis means the re-forming of the Image of God according to which we have been created by the Word." (Athanasius, *De Incarnatione 3,101*).

"In the Spirit the Word divinises us." (Athanasius, PG.25, 192; 26,589). "Christ takes shape in us through the Holy Spirit who reinstates the divinity in us." (Cyril of Alexandria, PG.75,1088).

"Theosis is participation through grace in the nature of God." (John of Damascus, *Expositio Fidei, 88,18*).

"Through theosis we are brought into the energy-field of God." (Gregorios Palamas, *Holy Hesychasts*).

Divinisation means the reinstatement of the image of God fully in us. What humanity had lost through the *Fall* has been reinstated through the salvific event of Jesus Christ. What hides our true nature is being removed by the light of the risen Christ in us. In the power and presence of the Spirit we recognize who we truly are.

The Spirit makes us realize that we are no more slaves but daughters and sons of God, participating in the divine nature through Christ. The Fathers of the Church do not equate human soul with the preexistent divine Son, but they emphasis that through the Incarnation of the divine Word the Divine that is dormant in us is awakened in Jesus; through Christ we have been graced with the realisation that we participate in the new humanity that is one with the divinity of Christ. We are grafted onto the tree of Christ (Rom. 11:17). So we put on the new Man (Col. 3:10), and become a new creation (II.Cor. 5:17). We live *in Christ*.

Faith in Christ means, therefore, participation in the divinisation process that takes place in and through the Spirit of Christ. The Spirit continuously transforms our life and makes us participate in the divine life. Everyone who is united with the Lord is "one Spirit with him" (1 Cor.6:17). We are called to "be partakers of the divine nature" (1.Pet.1:4), "to be transformed into the image (of God in Christ) that we reflect in brighter and brighter glory" (II Cor.3:18). In faith we find ourselves in a process in which "we get fully mature with the fullness of Christ himself" (Eph. 4:13), a process through which "we are filled with the fullness of God" (Eph.3:19). And this process in the Spirit leads to the final state in which "God will be all in all" (1 Cor.15:28). For the early Fathers and the mystics of the Church the experience of divinisation (*theosis*) has been a foundational element of Christian spirituality. We do not participate in the divine essence, but in the divine nature.

This is a *birthing* process: God gave birth to us; we give birth to God. Origen, Gregory of Nyssa and Augustine use the imagery of the *birth of God in the soul*. We are all called to become not only children of God but also mothers of God. "What once happened in a bodily way in the virgin, Mary continues to happen in every human soul that is totally open to God: to become mother of God."(Gregory of Nyssa, *Comm. on Mathew, 12,50*) "When God works in the soul, the soul receives the Word and becomes pregnant in the Spirit. Thus the soul becomes like a mother giving birth to God."(Origen, *Comm. on Song of Songs*). Reflecting on what happened in Bethlehem Augustine preached: "Christ is born; may he be born in our hearts. Mary bore him in her womb; may we bear him in our hearts. The virgin became pregnant through the Spirit; may our souls be pregnant through faith in Christ. Our souls must bring forth God into the world." (Quoted in Kurt Ruh, *Meister Eckehart*, Munich 1985, 142).

For Meister Eckhart we are all called to be virgins (fully open to the divine Spirit) and mothers (bringing forth God into this world). "I give birth to the one who gave birth to me." (Sermon, *Ave gratia plena*). This perspective of the Fathers and mystics of the Church helps us to perceive what is happening deep within us: the divinisation of the human. Creation is experiencing the birth pangs of the divine Spirit, and this birthing takes place through human persons. Our consciousness is being transformed by the Spirit and elevated to a divine consciousness *just as* it came to a full blossoming in the consciousness of Jesus. We are being reborn in Christ, and we give birth to Christ in all the spheres of the Christification process. It is in this process of *christophany* that we discover our true identity.

What would be the concrete effect of theosis in human life? The person being reborn in God will be highly sensitive to the sufferings and agonies of people as well as of creation. The dealings of that person will be characterised by mercy. One who lives from a divine centre of life will be a merciful person. The face of God manifest in Jesus has been the merciful face of God. By being inserted to the birthing of the Spirit one experiences the birth pangs of the new creation. In the lives of the poor and on the faces of the broken humans one discovers the healing presence of the God who creates everything new. In their wounds, and in the woundedness of the mother earth, one discovers the *wounded God*. At the same time one experiences the regenerative power of resurrection too in this broken world. This world of ours is God´s world, the body of the divine Spirit.

Christians Encountering the Upanishadic Vedanta

The inner experience of Jesus, and the Christian heritage of the mystical experience that evolved out of it, help us to look deeper into ourselves and discover our true identity within the inner-divine process. The 'Spirit that searches the depth of God' (I Cor. 2:11) enables us to realise that we are being reborn in the Spirit and that we give birth to the Word in the world. Those who drink from the divine fountain unfolded in Jesus will be impregnated by the Divine Spirit and hence will give birth to the new creation. (Jn.7:37-39). God gives birth to himself in and through us. Our true self-identify consists of total transparency to the divine power and presence.

At the level of this mystical experience Christians meet the sages and seekers of the Upanishadic heritage. The Upanishads give witness to the experience of the sages who discovered their true identity within the inner-divine dynamics of *sat-chit-ānanda* (Being-consciousness-bliss). They felt that they were being constantly transformed by the self-outpouring stream of divine life, and enlightened by the self-manifesting beam of divine light. They were led from the objectifying activity of the mind to the contemplative pursuits of the buddhi. Their consciousness was deepened and enlightened by the divine light. They could perceive the entire reality with its diversity in its ultimate depth of divine unity. *Prajnānam Brahma*, consciousness is divinised (Ait. Up. 3.1.3) - they could exclaim. Here the subject-object polarity is transcended. Here one discovers and realizes one´s true nature as one with the divine nature. *"Brahmavid brahmaiva bhavati"* (the one who experiences the Divine *becomes* Divine) - this is the ultimate mystical experience in the spiritual heritage of the Upanishads. "Everyone united with the Lord *becomes* one Spirit with him" (1 Cor. 6:17). This is the deepest mystical experience in the spiritual heritage of the Church. There is a certain convergence in these two streams of mystical introspection: one deepens the other, one enlightens the other.

Without unnecessarily polarising them or unduly ignoring the specific differences, the question may be asked from each side: what does the other evoke in me? With this question, the Christian believer reads the Upanishads from within her own spiritual depth, and the Hindu seeker reads the New Testament from within the inner cave. The Christian feels the movements of the Spirit that awakens the mystic in him/her and the Hindu experiences the movements of the same Spirit that alerts the prophet within him/her. The Christian is moved to the perception that no integral spirituality can be genuine without contemplative pursuits and the ascetical elements demanded by them. The Hindu is led to the realisation that no liberative spirituality is possible without a genuine concern for human welfare and the resulting commitment to justice. The Christian is then helped to see the power and presence of the

Divine in nature and thus draw the ecological consequences of the life of faith. The Hindu is helped to discern the liberative presence of God in the events of history and thus become sensitive to the challenges of social life. The Christian thus learns to look at nature as the body of the divine Spirit and to deal with it with greater respect and concern. The Hindu is motivated to look at a human person as the temple of the Spirit and meet them with the concerns of equality and justice.

Spiritual Co-Pilgrims

Here it is not a question of one teaching the other on the path of spiritual progress, nor is it a matter one interpreting the Scripture of the other in the light of one´s revelatory experience. Rather, the Hindu and the Christian understand him/herself as a co-pilgrim with the other. On the way of this common pilgrimage, they read the Scriptures of the other, open themselves to be challenged, criticised, enriched and guided by the other. It is, in fact, a process rediscovering one's spiritual identity in an encounter with the other. It is through the *thou* that I become *I*. The mystical and prophetic streams are the dialectical elements of spiritual integration. In every religion, both are at work manifestly or implicitly. There are, for instance, mystical streams in Christian Scriptures and traditions; but to a great extent, these are not fertilising Christian theology or the day-to-day life of Christians. In the highly structured patterns of community organisation and the dogmatic framework of theological thinking in the Church, the mystical elements have often been marginalised, if not suppressed. In today's world, there is a global quest for mystical experiences. Many Christians unable to find mystical wellsprings within their community and heritage seek them at the feet of Eastern masters or in the New Age Movements. This is a phenomenon which Christianity has to take seriously and listen to what *the Spirit is telling the Church* today. Church has to discern the unseen work of grace in the hearts of all human persons. The Upanishads open to Christians infinite horizons of searching the mystery of the Divine. If one's mind is attuned to the relentless quest of the Upanishads, one cannot be fixated on the particular forms of God's revelation, nor can one be dogmatic about the concrete formulations in theology. Such openness of the mind does not mean relativising faith in Christ but seeing it in relation to the universal process of the divine self-manifestation. Church will then be understood not primarily in terms of the visible structures and closed traditions but as the Spirit-determined community, the pilgrim-community that is ever on the move "to grasp the breadth and the length, the height and the depth of the love of God revealed in Christ" (Eph.3:19).

At a depth of the Upanishads and the New Testament, there is a mystical experience of oneness with the Divine. The Christian experience of union with the Divine has been later interpreted in terms of *theosis*; the Upanishadic experience of merging with the Divine has been taken up in *advaita*. They are ways of understanding at the mind-level the deep mystical oneness-experience that one has at the heart-level. The Church Fathers who advocated theosis made a consistent distinction between the divine essence and divine nature; humans participate not in the divine essence but are raised to divine nature. "...that you should share the divine nature..." (II. Pet. 1:4). Gregory Palamas makes the distinction between the non-participable divine essence and the participable stream of divine energies. In some advaita schools of thought; however, there is a tendency to speak of humans merging into the divine essence (*sat*), for ultimately reality is non-dual (*a-dvaita*). Reflecting on theosis Thomas Aquinas said: "the one who knows God, becomes God-like" (*quisque Deum intelligit, deiformis fit, ST. 1.12.5.ad 3*); the Upanishadic sage would say: "the one who knows God becomes God" (*brahmavid brahmaiva bhavati*, Mund. Up. 3.2.9). These are attempts to interpret the deep mystical experience that in fact eludes every mental perception and verbal articulation. "There the mind does not reach, nor the words" (Kena Up. 1.3) "If you know God, it is not God" (Augustine, PL.8.663). It is important that one goes beyond the mind and reach out to the intuitive faculty of the buddhi / *nous* to enter the cave of the heart, wherein the merging / union / oneness of the human with the Divine takes place. This is an unending spiritual pursuit. One could find here converging lines between Christian spirituality and Upanishadic experience, between *theosis* and *advaita*. At the heart level, East and West meet. This is what Abhishiktananda through his deep entry to the Upanishadic wisdom discovered.

In this spiritual pursuit, the Christian theologian meets the Hindu Vedantin as a spiritual co-pilgrim; the interpretation of the spiritual dynamics of the New Testament is deepened by the mystical insights of the Upanishads. The anthropocentric world-view of Christianity is balanced by the cosmic world-view of the Upanishadic sages, and the social initiatives are integrated with ecological concerns. The prayer of Jesus was that *all may be one*: that all human persons irrespective of the differences in religious affiliations and cultural patterns may experience their deep oneness in the triune divine reality. On the way to grasp the mystical meaning of the divinisation that takes place deep within us, the Upanishads throw a lot of light. There is, therefore, tremendous scope for Christian theology to be spiritually fertilised by the Upanishads.

22

Encountering God: A Liberative and Societal Experience

VM Jose SJ

Moral and Pastoral Theology, Jnana-Deepa Vidyapeeth, Pune

Abstract: *Everything in our life, today just as in Jesus' time, begins with an encounter. An encounter with this Man, the carpenter of Nazareth, a man like all men and yet different. There is an encounter between people, an encounter between people who were in the street". And this, he commented, is "something unusual". In fact, "when we go into the street, every man thinks of himself: he sees, but does not look; he hears, but does not listen"; in short, everyone goes their own way. And consequently "people pass each other, but they do not encounter each other". Because, Pope Francis clarified, "an encounter is something else" entirely, and this is "what the Gospel proclaims to us in our context: an encounter between a man and a woman, between an only son who is alive and an only son who is dead; between a happy group of people — happy because they have encountered Jesus and followed him — and a group of people who weep as they accompany the woman", who is a widow and is on her way to bury her only son. The Church should create spaces for critical reflection, spaces where poor people can meet and reflect about God's presence in their concrete situations. Also these spaces should be places of communion among equals, where real participation is lived out. These spaces should be witness of God's presence among the people, a presence of communion, equality and "new creation".*

Keywords: *Liberative, Passover lamb, Incarnation, Liberation Theology, Clericalization, Trinitarian model, Culture of encounter.*

> *"Everything in our life, today just as in Jesus' time, begins with an encounter. An encounter with this Man, the carpenter of Nazareth, a man like all men and yet different. The first ones, John, Andrew, and Simon, felt themselves to be looked at into their very depths, read in their innermost being, and in them sprang forth a surprise, a wonder that instantly made them feel bound to Him, made them feel different."* –Pope Francis

Introduction

What is encountering God, what is liberative and societal experience? Without some clarity on these terms we cannot have a meaningful understanding of the subject. Encounter in this context is meeting God face to face. In my younger days, it was confined to having daily family prayer, going for mass and receiving communion once in a while. Sometimes we helped the poor, basically giving alms to the poor. If we did all these, I thought we had fulfilled the obligation and encountered God. In other words, it was encountering the Living God. Liberative and societal experience leads us to a wider realm, which is related to the wider society. Pope Francis explains this term very explicitly. It is an invitation to work for "the culture of encounter", in a simple way, "as Jesus did": not just seeing, but looking; not just hearing, but listening; not just passing people by, but stopping with them; not just saying "what a shame, poor people!", but allowing yourself to be moved with compassion; "and then to draw near, to touch and to say: 'Do not weep' and to give at least a drop of life". Pope Francis used these words in one of his homilies. Pope Francis on a regular basis has spoken of a Culture of Encounter as a goal for human society. A society that espouses a Culture of Encounter facilitates the right relationship among humans and involves a spirituality that emphasizes a personal friendship with God who first encounters us in love. I believe that the term, *culture of encounter*, Pope Francis uses, is a loaded term. To make an encounter, part of our culture means that every one of us is expected to practice it in our day to day life. The Culture of Encounter may be explained as, the structuring of a society in which persons encounter each other, and thus they are able to encounter the Living God.

Encountering God

In the First Book of Samuel, the young boy ministered to the Lord under the direction of Eli. We read that in those days, the Word of the Lord was rare; there were not many visions. We know that Samuel's sleep is interrupted because he hears someone calling his name. He gets up and goes naturally into Eli's bedroom to see what he wants, only to find out that the preacher has not called him. Only after three disruptions of sleep that Eli-the-priest, realized what was going on. “Samuel,” he said, “Go and lie down, and if you hear that voice calling you again you say, “Speak, Lord; for your servant hears you’” (1 Samuel 3:9). So Samuel went and did just as the prophet asked, and God spoke to Samuel that night in a special way.

The above-mentioned experience of Samuel is a classic example of encountering God personally. If this experience remains within the personal self, it has no substantial effect. On the other hand, if we understand the meaning of, *speak Lord, your servant hears*, we will understand that the Lord will tell us to reach out to others. Lord tells his ministers to carry on with their services to society. Psalm 24: 3-4 clarifies the perspective. Who may ascend the mountain of the Lord? Who may stand in his holy place? The one who has clean hands and a pure heart, who does not trust in an idol or swear by a false god.

Obstacles to Encountering God

"If a man cannot get through to God, it is because there is a secret thing he does not intend to give up." We are so preoccupied with the secret thing that we refuse to give up such things, and we enjoy ourselves being in such situations. But unless we give up such a stubborn nature, there is no way of coming close to God through prayer. To experience Him and His power personally, we have to be real with God and search for Him in our selves daily. When we sin against others, our relationship with them is affected, so naturally, our relationship with God is breached. We have the example of Adam and Eve hiding from God behind the fig leaves; we too are ashamed and likewise hide. We have many ways of hiding from God; we hide behind our daily routines, work, family responsibilities, recreation, or even spiritual ministry. We have to understand, therefore, how sin affects our relationship with God and so constant prayer is very important.

Another obstacle that prevents us encountering God is brooding over painful past events: “Stop dwelling on past events and brooding over times gone by; I am doing something new; it's springing up - can't you see it? I am making a road in the desert, rivers in the wasteland” (Is 43: 18-19). Many of us go through traumatic experiences in our life, and quite naturally, we find it difficult to experience God. We want to experience happiness and fulfilment in life. Unfortunately, we feel we are caught up in our past. How can we find a way out of this situation? At least on some occasions, we can find some helpful method by meeting a close friend, a loving Christian or a right counsellor. We have to open our heart to receive the grace of God through their kind words of encouragement and hope. God does intervene in our life through many people and events. Through such ways, we can deal with the painful past and overcome it. In other words, God's love and healing are available to us always provided we rely on His love to heal our wounded heart.

Holding grudges against others: "Make every effort to live in peace with everyone and to be holy; without holiness, no one will see the Lord" (Heb 12: 14). An easy way of keeping God away is to keep grudges against others and keep the bitter feelings against them. Since it is our own choice to keep grudges, the power of the spirit will not enter into us, and we will not encounter God. We will not be prompted to think of God or to pray. There will be no personal desire in us to be reconciled or to forgive others whom we have wronged or others who have wronged us. We should realize that our faith is mainly about forgiveness, as Jesus has mentioned. Jesus has given us as a free gift, and we, in turn, are expected to share this gift with others. As believers in Christ, we are obliged to follow the way of Christ. "Let all bitterness and wrath and anger and clamour and slander be put away from you, along with all malice. Be kind to one another, tender-hearted, forgiving one another, as God in Christ forgave you" (Eph 4: 31-32).

Stubbornness in unbelief: "Yet they did not listen to me or incline their ear, but stiffened their neck; they did more evil than their fathers" (Jer 7: 26). One of the main barriers which block us from coming close to God is unbelief. Unless and until we keep unbelief apart and believe in Jesus, we cannot find God. If we persist in unbelief, we cannot understand what it means to have a relationship with Jesus Christ. We need to understand what is said in the NT. He cried out to Jesus, "I believe; help my unbelief" (Mark 9:24).

With a little effort, we can become believers. Though it is a simple thing, many people don't care about it and thus do not believe. They harden their heart and choose unbelief over belief. They choose to reject God and ignore Him. Unless we break this barrier of unbelief, we cannot have contact with God. By accepting Jesus as saviour, we are forgiven, and we can encounter God.

Community Encounter of God

We read in the Old Testament when the Hebrews were held in slavery by the Egyptians; God chose Moses to be His instrument to rescue them, because He had seen their trouble, had heard their cry for help and had decided to come down and set them free. The Lord said, "I have indeed seen the misery of my people in Egypt. I have heard them crying out because of their slave drivers, and I am concerned about their suffering. So I have come down to rescue them from the hand of the Egyptians and to bring them up out of that land into a good and spacious land" (Exo 3). Such a God is someone who is very close to the people, and people can easily encounter Him as their redeemer, father and saviour.

Further, we understand that God acted to save His chosen people as a community special to him. After many difficult and troubling situations, God designed to persuade Pharaoh to let the people go free. Finally, God sent the angel of death to take the first-born of every family so that the chosen people are set free. God wanted to assure His people that He cared for them as a community. Then Moses summoned all the elders of Israel and said to them, "Go at once and select the animals for your families and slaughter the Passover lamb. Take a bunch of hyssops, dip it into the blood in the basin and put some of the blood on the top and on both sides of the door frame. None of you shall go out of the door of your house until morning. When the Lord goes through the land to strike down the Egyptians, he will see the blood on the top and sides of the door frame and will pass over that doorway, and he will not permit the destroyer to enter your houses and strike you down" (Exo. 12).

What we can conclude here is, death was not going to affect God's people if they obeyed His word and trusted in the blood of the lamb. They had to paint their doorposts. As a community, they obeyed the instructions and found themselves safe although death had visited every Egyptian house. Thus the Hebrews encountered the saving power of God in their life because they listened to their God.

As committed Christians, we know that the same power of God can work in our life. All that we need to do is to trust in the power of God and be washed in the blood of the lamb. We have to remind ourselves often of the awesome power of God that redeems us and leads us through great trials and tribulations. Since we are part of the church we don't have to face these struggles by ourselves; the encouraging support of the church is always available. Thus we can also help one another to encounter God!

Ways to Encounter God

There are many and different ways to encounter God, for instance, through the beauty of nature, through prayer and meditation; there are also sudden and tremendous encounter such as St. Paul's experience on the way to Damascus. Each encounter depends on the situation in which we live and when God who wants to reveal himself to us. The Peruvian liberation theologian, Gustavo Gutierrez had another way of encountering God. His option for the poor enabled him to see the Lord in the faces of the poor in Latin America. He acknowledges that "Christ hides himself behind the faces of those whom we tend to avoid because they have little importance in the eyes of the society." According to him, to be followers of Jesus requires us to walk with and commit ourselves to the poor. In doing so, we encounter the Lord who is simultaneously revealed and hidden in the face of the Poor.

Encountering God: Old Testament

Based on the understanding that the Biblical God is close to human beings, first of all, Gutierrez reflects on the first covenant that speaks about God dwelling in the midst of his people. God said, "I shall dwell in the midst of the Israelites, I shall become their God, and by my dwelling among them, they will know that I am the Lord their God who brought them out of Egypt. I am Lord their God" (Exod.29: 45; 26: 11-12). The presence and the dwelling of God among his people emphasized the relationship between God and human beings. To despise one's neighbour (Prov.14: 21), to exploit the humble and poor worker, and to delay the payment of wages, is to offend God: "You shall not keep back the wages of a man who is poor and needy" (Deut.24: 14-15; Exod.22: 21-23). Therefore, to love God and to love our neighbour means to do justice to the poor and the oppressed.

Encountering God: New Testament

In the New Testament God becomes present in the Incarnation of the Word. Through the Incarnation, the Word made Flesh, every person is the presence of God. Gutierrez notes: "Since the incarnation, humanity, every human being in history, is the living temple of God."

This is the key element for speaking about an encounter with God. Gutierrez puts it this way: "If humanity, each person, is the living temple of God, we meet God in our encounter with others; we encounter God in the commitment to the historical process of humankind." The Trinitarian understanding of God has been taken very seriously by Liberation Theology. Such seriousness was also recognised by the Pope's (John Paul II) visit to Puebla on the occasion of the Latin American Bishops assembled there, when he stated that, "Our God, in his most intimate mystery, is not a solitude, but a family. For he intrinsically contains paternity, filiation, and the essence of the family that is love: this love in the divine family is the Holy Spirit". However, the belief in the Triune God for the faithful throughout the world is a real struggle. According to Liberation Theology, it is possible to emphasise a political and a religious reason for such a struggle. In the political arena we are used to political authoritarianism which is expressed in a heavy concentration of power. It is sad that the family is is fashioned around an old patriarchal figure that does not allow equality for male and female. Unfortunately, the political and social situation has suggested that, just as there is one God, so there must be one ruler and one rule. In the religious sphere, according to liberation theologians, we find a similar phenomenon, that is, the centralization of power in the hands of a single person, though in theory, it is said to be different. Similarly, the clericalization of the Church has led to the accumulation of power in the hands of priests who often exploit this power.

Trinitarian Dimension: Praxis Oriented Approach

The model of Trinity as communion can be seen as the ground where the struggle of impoverished people is rooted. Moreover, the communion model can uphold and sustain the utopia of a new form of society. Today there is an emphasis on the communion model as it can challenge the Church and her praxis in the world. We need to ask why the Church should be involved in the struggle of marginalised people. The preferential option for the poor helps people in the church and the world. Pope Francis says very explicitly, "I prefer a church which is bruised, hurting and dirty because it has been out on the streets, rather than a church which is unhealthy from being confined and from clinging to its own security."

We know that Jesus revealed God. He is the central person, in order to understand the Trinity. Jesus revealed a God full of compassion for poor, marginalized and oppressed. Jesus revealed a God who made a clear option for the outcasts and marginalized of society. If we understand liberation theology, we know that the Trinity is not impartial and universal. Through the incarnation, the Trinity opted for the poor. Therefore, the Church, in order to remain faithful to the God revealed by the Son, is called to renew her option for the poor. A society inspirited by Trinity is a society that cannot tolerate class differentiation, domination and marginalisation. On the contrary, a society rooted in the Trinitarian model is an inclusive society where equal opportunities are granted to all people.

Conclusion

Without contemplation, prayer, thanksgiving to God, there is no Christian life, and the fulfilment of the Christian life is in commitment, solidarity and love of neighbour. These two ways are not separated, and they need each other. The integration of these two approaches is the best way to link justice and spirituality. Since we cannot approach God without carrying the longing of our brothers and sisters with us.

Pope Francis expressed, "the Word of God speaks of an encounter. There is an encounter between people, an encounter between people who were in the street". And this, he commented, is "something unusual". In fact, "when we go into the street, every man thinks of himself: he sees, but does not look; he hears, but does not listen"; in short, everyone goes their own way. And consequently "people pass each other, but they do not encounter each other". Because, Pope Francis clarified, "an encounter is something else" entirely, and this is "what the Gospel proclaims to us in our context: an encounter between a man and a woman, between an only son who is alive and an only son who is dead; between a happy group of people — happy because they have encountered Jesus and followed him — and a group of people who weep as they accompany the woman", who is a widow and is on her way to bury her only son. The Church should create spaces for critical reflection, spaces where poor people can meet and reflect on God's presence in their concrete situations. Also, these spaces should be places of communion among equals, where real participation is lived out. These spaces should be witnesses of God's presence among the people, a presence of communion, equality and "new creation".

References

Ricky Jones, "Pope Francis on the Mystery of the Encounter with God" https://sfvacts.org/pope-francis-on-the-mystery-of-the-encounter-with-god/. Accessed on November 2, 2018.

Pope Francis, "Morning Meditation in the Chapel of the Domus Sanctae Marthae, For a culture of Encounter," *L'Osservatore Romano*, Weekly ed. in English, n. 38, 23 September 2016.

Dan Delzell, "Barriers to Getting Through to God," *Christian Post Contributor*, July 1, 20144.

Gustavo Gutiérrez, *We Drink from Our Own Wells: The Spiritual Journey of a People*, Orbis Books, Maryknoll, 2002.

Gustavo Gutierrez, *The God of Life* (trans. Matthew J. Connell), Orbis Books, Maryknoll, 1991.

Pope Francis, *Amoris Laetitia: The Joy of Love*, Exhortation Published on March 19, 2016.

PART FOUR

SEARCHING FOR TRUTH AND DIGNITY

23

Theological Language: What Has Been and What Could Be

Johnson J. Puthenpurackal OFM Cap
Vijnananilayam, Janampet -534475, Eluru, Andhra Pradesh

Abstract: *This article a reflective look-back and a look-ahead: a look back into what theological language has been, and a look ahead into what theological language could be. In this context the author asks: Can we still continue to confine God and theology in a suffocating language of conceptual precision with a presumption of truth and objectivity? Should not we let the Divine 'speak to' us, rather than our 'speaking about' the Divine, reducing theology to be an epistemology of God? Should not our theological language be more humble, without any presumption of having 'captured' (comprehended) the Divine with absolute certainty? We need, hence, a radical shift in our religious discourse and theological language. It is high time that we begin theologizing and conveying theological approaches to God-Human-Cosmos in the form of street-plays, musical dramas, inspiring quotes, traditional dance-forms, stories, parables and anecdotes, etc.; these forms transcend the either/or structure of truth and falsity. Every event is a story of the Divine insofar as it communicates the Divine, not in informative statements, but in the form of a constantly disturbing call to be appropriated by a response of fundamental option or radical commitment. It is our conviction that the purpose of theological language is not for giving dispassionate information about God, but for passionately waking us up from our religious slumber!*

Keywords: *Theological language, God concept, Logical precision, Poetic openness.*

Introduction

Without any claim of competence in theology or theological language, an attempt is made in this study to make a reflective look-back and a look-ahead: a look back into what theological language has been, and a look ahead into what theological language could be. Since it is not a strictly theological question, we think that reflecting on this question of practical relevance can be done by any serious thinker and genuine believer, and not necessarily by the so-called official theologians.[1] Hence, with presumed reflective freedom, we begin by a preliminary clarification of the central phrase of this study, namely, 'theological language,' with Christian theology as its background.[2]

Although 'theological language' is closely related to 'religious language,' there is a difference between them. "Religious language, arising out of personal experiences of God, accepts divine existence as a given and seeks existential appropriation of the transcendental world available to devotees of a tradition."[3] Since it is born of one's religious experience, it is more primordial than theological language.[4] Both have God as their referent. But as the language used in theology, which is an apologetic and systematic science, theological language tends to be more scientific, logical and systematic. For our purpose in this study, we take 'theological language' as the human discourse about the divine in itself and in its mutual relation to humans and to the cosmos. Theological language is not a divine language, but the human language used in their discourse about the divine. Since theological language is devised by humans, there remains the possibility of humans' perceptive weakness showing itself in their language as well. As we proceed with our reflective journey, we shall see how and why our theological language has taken a deviated growth.

Theological Language: What Has Been

We find that there is a parallel and close relation between God being reduced to a human concept, religion being organised as an institution, and theological

---

1 It is generally considered that those have made formal academic studies in theology and are engaged in theological research and discussions are the official 'theologians.'

2 In fact, the expressions, theological language and religious language, can be taken as referring to any religion; but we limit our use of these terms only to Christian—more precisely to Catholic—religion and theologizing.

3 James M. Reese, OSFS, "Language, Religious," in *The New Dictionary of Theology*, ed., Joseph Komonchak et al, first Indian edition (Bangalore: Indian Theological Publications, 1993), 564.

4 Some religious thinkers have rightly referred to theological language as 'Secondary Religious Language' as different from the 'Primary Religious Language,' which is same as what is ordinarily known under the name, 'Religious Language.' Ibid., 564-65.

language becoming a logical language of conceptual precision.[5] Before we consider the nature of the hitherto theological language, we shall take a cursory look at the conceptualised God and the structuralised religion (Christianity).

a. God as a Concept, Religion as a Structure

It was nothing but a logical consequence of philosophy becoming a rational structure that the notion of God has been reduced to a concept. Heidegger's philosophy has brought it out explicitly through his insightful analysis. According to him, as a result of Christianity adopting the western metaphysical philosophy of conceptual precision, the Biblical notion of God gradually gave way to a metaphysically precise concept of God. The doctrine of the two-tier world of Plato got baptized as the theory of the natural and the supernatural realms. God was confined to the supernatural realm and was superimposed with metaphysical attributes of superlative degrees, such as eternal, infinite, omniscient, omnipresent, all-perfect, etc. God is thus made *an object of human estimation*.[6]

The characterization of God in high-precision concepts is indicative of the humans' presumptuous monopoly over the truth of God in human concepts. According to Heidegger, it is a degradation to reduce God to an object of human estimation. The metaphysical theologians have been busy with formulating an epistemology of God in the innumerable theological books. Aligning himself with the Nietzschean proclamation of the death of God, Heidegger shows thus the caricature of the metaphysical God. Metaphysics thus nurtures a pseudo-God, a product of human representation. God is made a dead concept to be subjected to rational analysis and manipulation by humans.

The rational philosophy of precision not only mummifies God to a human concept but also solidifies religions to mere institutions. Baked in conceptual philosophy, the western mind has been trying clearly to demarcate the precise boundary for the religions, as a result of which the ontological religiosity of the humans gradually got epistemologised – got shaped into organised structures.[7] This process of giving conceptual clarity and structural boundary to God and

---

5 The basis for such transformation of God, religion and language into precise conceptual structures is the change in the understanding of philosophy as a result of the pre-Socratic poetic insights and artistic intuitions transformed into logically precise metaphysical concepts—a shift from *mythos* to *logos*, from *art* to *philosophy*. Western philosophy gradually became epistemology with the subject becoming the arbiter of truth, enframing reality in conceptual clarity.

6 Heidegger, The *Question Concerning Technology and Other Essays,* trans., W. Lovitt (New York: Harper Torchbooks, 1977), 105.

7 'Defining' refers to 'specifying the boundary' of something. It is possible only when the boundaries are clear; the more organized something is, the more definable it becomes.

religion has been going on for the last two millennia, and it is most evidently seen in Christianity. Hence, in order to see the process of the structural growth of religion, it is best to look at the growth of Christianity.

Christ was a movement, a charismatic figure, whose life and message shows that he did not care so much for the structure as for the persons. Christianity was the fruit of an upheaval, a revolution against the Judaic structures. The movement-aspect of Christ was faithfully lived and was vividly manifest during the early periods of the Church. With the conversion of Constantine to Christianity, life and charism gradually gave way to structure—a powerful institution, with well-defined moral-codes, precise dogmas, ecclesiastical structures, bureaucratic centralisation, positions and titles, etc. To support this power-structure, there developed a theology.[8] Although the ecclesiastical power was referred to as of Divine origin, it follows the logic of human power structure—a secular structure with religious garb.[9] Thus we find the gradual transition of Christianity from being a dynamic and revolutionary *movement* to a well-structured *institution*. Under the heavy blanketing of organizational stagnation, the attention was directed to giving clarity and precision to the language used for the discourse on God and religion. In his *Phenomenology of Religious Life*[10] Heidegger discusses, among other issues, the question of "a return to the original [religious] experience"[11] from a 'dogmatic' interpretation of religious experience.[12] This takes us to the kind of theological language that has been hitherto used.

b. Theological Language to Be Logically Precise

Insofar as God is reduced to a *dead* concept and Christianity is organized as a *dead* structure with as much conceptual and logical precision as possible, it is a natural consequence that the language employed for theological discourse be a language of logical precision.

---

8 Leonardo Boff, *Church: Charism and Power*, trans. John W. Dierckmeier (New York: Crossroad Publishing Co., 1988), 51. Christ is presented as the emperor, the cosmic Lord. Lk. 10:16 "whoever hears you, hears me, ..." was interpreted not in the missionary context of church-world, but in the context of hierarchy-community.

9 Although the picture of the church drawn by Leonardo Boff is rather bleak, it is very much founded on historical basis. It is to be specially noted that Boff acknowledges the respectability and moral authority that the Church has gained during the last few decades. Ibid., 47.

10 Transl., Matthias Fritsch and Jennifer Anna Gosseti-Ferencei (Bloomington: Indiana University Press, 2004).

11 Heidegger, *The Phenomenology of Religious Life*, 50. Dear to him are the expressions like "original religious phenomena," the "primordial Christian religiosity," etc.

12 Ibid., 50.

Humans are essentially *linguistic* beings insofar as they are gifted with language. In the popular understanding, language has been looked at as an 'expression' (*Ausdrücken*) and an 'activity' (*Tätigkeit*) of the humans.[13] It is the means by which we, the humans, give expression to what is within us—our understanding and knowledge, our dream and vision of reality. With the help of language, we try to describe or *picture* the already existing reality, and hence Wittgenstein holds that "language is the picture of reality."[14] In picturing or expressing reality, language is expected to be a perfect picture of reality, resembling it in every aspect.[15] In expressing the reality, we try to be as precise as possible. In the western metaphysical tradition, the preoccupation has been to make a precise language with logico-scientific exactitude.[16] When reality is *expressed* in language, it is placed within so precise a boundary that there is a one-to-one correspondence between reality and its expression. Language as picture or expression comes about as a result of the human activity; the picture is drawn by the humans; and as per this understanding, language is a human creation.[17] Insofar as language is a human activity, there exists the danger of using it as a means of human manipulation and domination, in which case the subject dictates and controls the object by means of language; it is very evidently seen in the language of *propaganda* and *advertisement*. Truth is manipulated and presented by the subject as 'objectively' true. Thus language as a 'precise expression' and a 'human activity' reiterates that it is a subject-controlled language since it is the same subject that 'creates' and 'pictures' the truth. Hence by making the picture of language perfectly corresponding to the truth of reality, we cannot claim any 'objectivity,' since the truth of reality is itself a subjective creation!

The above-clarified subject-controlled language is referred to as 'logical language' with a presumption of 'objectivity' under the ploy of 'precision.' The

13 Heidegger, *Unterwegs zur Sprache*, 6. Auflage (Pfullingen: Neske, 1979), 11; *Poetry, Language, Thought,* trans., Albert Hofstadter (New York: Harper & Row, 1975), 192.

14 This is a pervading theme in Wittgenstein's *Tractatus Logico-Philosophicus*, written in 1922.

15 Wittgenstein came to this conviction when he saw in a magazine the vivid account of a motor-car accident both by picture and language. When the narration of that accident was read, the 'picture' of that accident became visible to him. If the narration is very precise, the 'picture' that emerges too will be clear and precise. Just as there is a perfect correspondence between the parts of the picture and those of the reality pictured, so also is the case with language and reality.

16 The emergence of logico-scientific language can be understood better in the light of Heidegger's critique of Western metaphysics as a conceptual enterprise.

17 Such a conception of language as a human activity has been perpetuated in the history of western thought; it is evident from the terms used in the different languages to refer to 'language': language, *langue*, *lingua*, *glossa*, (meaning 'tongue', the main organ of speech); *Sprache*, *taal*, (referring to the activity of speech).

logically precise language (language as *logos*) represents or pictures reality as faithfully as possible. It has the logico-scientific precision and conceptual exactitude. As the meaning is 'enframed' in logical language, it can exhaust the meaning. Scientific language merely 'pictures' the one and only meaning placed within the precise boundary of definition, giving us the conclusive and definitive information. The boundary of definition is fixed by some subject; and the one meaning is so precisely specified that one can easily assign the label of truth or falsity on any fact based on its conformity to the definition of human construct.

The hitherto theological language has been using a language of precision. It was necessitated by what took place as a result of Christianity having adopted the western metaphysical philosophy for its theologizing. As we have summarily shown above, God is reduced to a concept of human making, and the God-human-world relation is specified with structural clarity and epistemological certainty. The conceptual clarity and epistemological certainty are such that there is hardly any room for doubt. The numerous books on God and on Christian life, especially those written before the Vatican II, are ample proofs for it. The formulation of theological language had to be done with extreme care and conceptual precision, as though the use of linguistic expressions can change the 'reality' of God! The first division in Christianity took place regarding the use of one word, '*filioque*'![18] In order to formulate the various Christian dogmas, human experts in language are used; what is humanly formulated is presumed to be divine in content and expression. After having conceived the concept about God and God-human-cosmos relation, and formulated the same in language, the humans forge the signature of God; the human-made truth and language is fakely given a divine authority!

By using the high-precision linguistic expressions in theological language, it has been presumed that what is conveyed through it is absolutely 'true' beyond any human doubt. Clarity and veracity are mistakenly taken as mutually implying. Christian theology and theological language have been making a triumphant march for almost two thousand years, conveniently forgetting the human presumption that they have the total monopoly over all matters divine. The absolute certainty and arrogance with which the humans have been analysing and laying God bare in theological jargons are incomprehensible for the thinking humans!

Thus the hitherto theological discourse has been employing a conceptually and logically precise language, in which all theological issues and questions lay buried and they are made to remain dead since all issues are conclusively defined with universal and perennial validity. In the rigid confines of logical

18 The theological question was whether the Holy Spirit proceeded from the Father, or from the Father and the Son; the Church got divided on this issue!

language, any re-visiting of the theological issues is hardly possible. The stagnated theological 'truths' are made to be more 'dead' within the secure confines of a rigidly conceptual language of precision.

Theological Language: What Could Be

When God was reduced to a human concept, and religion was organized as an institution, the theological language was necessitated to be a logical language of conceptual precision. But when the Divine is considered as dynamic presencing and theology as live thinking, theological language cannot be the same.

a. God and Theology as Dynamic

Traditional thought pattern has been considering reality as static and mute presence; being is anything that is *present*, and thus it got entified – Being (*Sein*) was identified with entity (*Seiendes*), anything that is mutely present. Such an understanding of reality facilitates a conceptual thought that encapsulates reality within a precise conceptual boundary. This static understanding has been in vogue till the twentieth century, until Heidegger brought about a revolution in his understanding of reality or thing, not as something that *is*, but as something that *things*,[19] not as something that is *present*, but as something that is *presencing*.

In the contemporary period, western thinkers are not, nor do they want to be, mere analysts of dead reality; they are mostly poetic thinkers and aesthetic mystics. Persons with such an open disposition are philosophers, theologians, thinkers, mystics, poets,…; they 'see'[20] reality as dynamic presencing—reality as speaking, moving and alive. They do not 'see' reality as statically present to be analyzed, to be defined and to be placed within conceptual precision. This shift towards a dynamic way of understanding reality has influenced Christian theology as well; God is no more to be taken as a static presence, but dynamic presencing, and theology consists, not of dead definitions and statements, but of active thinking by the existing humans in their relation to God who is dynamically involved in the spatio-temporal world of humans. God as dynamic presencing to the humans cannot be encapsulated in a logical language of precision. We need, hence, to look for another type of language for theological discourse.

---

19 Heidegger, *Vorträge und Aufsätze*, 4. Auflage (Pfullingen: Neske, 1978), 170; *Poetry, Language, Thought,* trans., A. Hofstadter (New York: Harper & Row, 1975), 177-78.

20 The term 'see' has a deeper meaning than its empirical meaning, namely, 'seeing with our external eyes'; we take 'seeing' in the phenomenological sense of 'perceiving with the consciousness,' or as taken in Indian thought: 'seeing with one's inner self.' Philosophers, according to Indian thought, are referred to as 'seers' (*d#r^anika*).

b. Theological Language to Be Poetically Open

The changed approach to theological language takes us to a phenomenological understanding of language that considers it neither as an *expression* of reality nor as a human *activity*—language created by the human subject in order to express reality as seen by the subject. Instead of considering language as a creation of the human, Heidegger in his phenomenological look reflects on the 'essencing' (*wesen*),[21] 'coming-to-be' or the '*languaging*'of language. "How does language as language come to be [*west*]? We answer: language speaks [language languages]."[22]

The 'essencing' (*Wesen*)[23] or the coming-to-be takes place in the primordial 'speaking' (*Sprechen*) by reality and the corresponding speaking (*Ent-sprechen*) by the humans.[24] In the silent speaking by reality there is present a call to the humans to 'speak'—to speak in response to the reality speaking. It is the humans who give voice to the silent speaking of language in reality. Heidegger sums up his central thesis of language in a sentence: "Language speaks. Man speaks only insofar as he corresponds [*ent-spricht*] to language."[25] The humans, by attuning themselves to the tune of the silent speaking of language in reality, give sound to it. Thus the human is neither the creator of language, nor even the speaker of it, but only the 'responder' to the primordial speaking of language.[26]

The humans respond primarily, not in any logical language, but in forms such as poetic sparks, mythical stories and parables, spontaneously expressed works of art, etc. A poet gives out poetic sparks in response to his/her *being gripped* by reality; s/he gives 'sound' to what s/he is *touched* with; and this 'giving sound' is human speaking. When I say 'this flower is beautiful!,' I am

21 Heidegger takes '*Wesen'* both in its verbal and nominal sense. 'Essencing' is used to refer to the verbal sense of '*wesen.*'

22 "Wie west die Sprache als Sprache? Wir antworten: *Die Sprache spricht.*" Heidegger, *Unterwegs zur Sprache*, 12; *Poetry, Language, thought*, 190.

23 The term '*Wesen*' ordinarily means 'essence.' But Heidegger takes it in the verbal sense of 'essencing' (coming-to-be), which is primordial to 'presencing' (*An-Wesen*) and 'absencing' (*Ab-Wesen*). Since 'essencing' does not sound well in English, many prefer to use the expression 'presencing' to mean 'essencing' in the Heideggerian sense.

24 Just as the world worlds (*Weltweltet*), thing things (*Ding dingt*), time times (*Zeit zeitigt*), so also language languages—language speaks—(*Sprache spricht*). In German the expression '*Sprache spricht*' shows the close relation between the noun and its verbal form. In English it is normally rendered as 'language speaks.' To make it more Heideggerian in meaning and style, we prefer to use the expression: 'language languages.'

25 "Die Sprache spricht. Der Mensch spricht nur, indem er der Sprache entspricht." *Phänomenologie und Theologie* (Frankfurt am Main: Vittorio Klostermann, 1970), 41.

26 Johnson Puthenpurackal, *Heidegger, Through Authentic Totality to Total Authenticity: A Unitary Approach to His Thought in Its Two Phases* (Louvain: Leuven University Press, 1987), 219.

not giving out my subjective opinion, but rather I am giving expression to what I am spoken to—the flower speaks to me by being present to me as beautiful.[27] When a professor values the answer-papers and gives a particular grade for a student, s/he is in fact listening and responding to what the answer-papers speak to him/her. When one is really conscientious in making a valuation, one experiences struggle within oneself, not knowing whether one has rightly 'heard' what the answer-papers have truly spoken! When the subject takes the upper hand by 'creating' a language of one's choice and precision, it tends to be a conceptually clear, but subjectively manipulated language. In advertisements, we find the manipulative language, controlled and constructed by the subject! Thus the primordially responded language has an independence and autonomy from the human 'speaker' or 'writer.' It is not the humans that speak through the language, but rather language 'speaks'—the way it speaks[28]—to the humans to 'cor-respond' to it by their primordial response. Such a profound language we find, not so much in scientific treatises of the literate (logico-conceptual language), but more in the 'spontaneous' expressions of the so-called illiterate (mythico-poetic language)!

The '*mythico*-poetic' language[29] is more primordial a response than '*logico*-conceptual' language. This primordial or 'aboriginal language' consists of the spontaneity of the 'mother-tongue' (*Muttersprache*). Such a language may lack scientific precision and conceptual exactitude, but it has greater profundity as it does not 'enframe' reality by giving the exhaustive meaning; rather it is creative of meaning by breaking the 'boundary' of scientific precision. Mythico-poetical language, thus, functions as evocative *pointers* rather than informative *concluders*. The spontaneous response of the humans to reality is given a precise 'shape' by the manipulative human intervention

27 When the judges make a judgment on a person—as guilty or innocent—they are giving a united 'sound' to the way that person shows oneself with regard to a particular case. When the beauty-queens from the various countries walk on the stage in front of the judges, they are 'speaking' silently, yet loudly. The judges are asked to 'gather' their speaking, and make it 'audible' to others in the form of a statement; namely, so-and-so is the 'Miss-World' of this year. Every human expression, linguistic or non-linguistic, is a giving sound to what is silently spoken, giving visibility to what is invisibly shown.

28 The 'speaking' of language is not dictated by the humans; it is the 'play' of being. In Heidegger, the notion of 'play' is very important. There is no '*why*' it plays; but only '*that*' it plays. For more on the notion of 'play' in relation to Heideggerian thinking of Being, cf., Puthenpurackal, *Heidegger: Through Authentic Totality to Total Authenticity*, 192-95.

29 In the contemporary thought-pattern the notion of '*mythos*' has gained added importance. It can no more be taken merely as a 'myth' in the sense of some imaginary and untrue stories. The profundity of the notion of mythos is evident from the lengthy consideration, given in *Historisches Wörterbuch der Philosophie*, vol. 6, 281-318.

in logico-scientific language, which can either be true or false; whereas in mythico-poetic language we cannot speak of truth and falsity.[30]

In light of the above-clarified understanding of language, we can now propose the thesis of ours. It is our humble contention: theological language today is in need of a radical shift from being a conceptually precise language of the human construct to a mythico-poetic language of openness. Christianity took pride in its dogmatic language of precision, not knowing that it was a language of domination confining God and theological truths within conceptual boundaries. Theology was reduced to an epistemological science that clearly specifies and distinguishes between what is theologically true and false,[31] determined by the humans. Humans decide what the Divine is! In their presumptuous arrogance, the humans claim to have a monopoly even over the truth of the Divine!

One of the important characteristics of the postmodern thought is that it does not make any absolute claims on the truth of our knowledge, even with regard to the physical world. Our knowledge is merely 'from one perspective,' and hence 'under erasure'—all these expressions[32] point to the same direction: our knowledge is radically finite. As humans are spatio-temporally limited, so is their knowledge. If we cannot have definitive and conclusive knowledge about spatio-temporal reality, how can we claim to have absolute knowledge about matters divine, and express it in a logically precise language?

Today we have a better understanding of language as the human response to the speaking of reality; this understanding is better suited for theological language, since it should not be the human speaking about God, rather God speaking to the humans. Humans can only 'give sound' to what is being spoken by the Divine. Hence, subjective manipulation has no role in any language, much less in theological language. A genuine theologian has to be a thinker, a poet, a mystic, who is receptively open to the Divine speaking; and from out of such a non-manipulative openness will flow genuine theological discourse.

From what has been said above, it is clear that theological language has primarily an evocative function, rather than a 'picturing' function. When the language is taken as the picture of reality, it is presumed to picture the reality as perfectly as possible, that is to say, the whole reality is captured in the picture. Can any person of common sense imagine that the reality of God can be

30 It is in line with this thought that we cannot speak of truth or falsity with regard to aesthetic expressions; hence the meaninglessness of such questions: "Has the artist or poet *correctly* expressed this notion?"

31 It was the presumption that what we held was true, with the necessary conclusion that the other with another approach was false, that led the Church to many an anathema and condemnation!

32 These expressions are used mainly by Jacques Derrida, one of the prominent postmodern thinkers.

captured and contained in theological language of human construct? Hence it can function only as an *evocative pointer*, which is best carried out in mythico-poetic language, such as meaningful stories and parables, poetic sparks and relevant anecdotes, mythical narratives and proverbial sayings, symbolic expressions[33] and spontaneous works of art (dancing, drawing, singing, etc.). The Bible has used an evocative language; it instils into us perennial values, such as love, forgiveness, simplicity, etc., and not *dead truths*. The Biblical narration of the parable of the Good Samaritan and the act of Jesus multiplying the loaves, is not meant to give us a detailed picture and *information* about what was done by the Samaritan on the way to Jericho, and by Jesus in the context of the hungry multitudes in Galilee, but to evoke and challenge us as to what we should do on our 'way' of life, and in our 'situations' of life and work.[34] We do not think that theology is a 'science' that defines and deposits 'dead' truths. It is our conviction that religion and religious language are not meant to lullaby the people to slumber, but to disturb and wake them up from their religious slumber. This what Jesus did, and this is what we are expected to do.

Concluding Remarks

In the light of the above-given reflections, can we still continue to confine God and theology in a suffocating language of conceptual precision with a presumption of truth and objectivity? Should not we let the Divine '*speak to*' us, rather than our '*speaking about*' the Divine, reducing theology to be an *epistemology* of God? Should not our theological language be more humble, without any presumption of having 'captured' (comprehended) the Divine with absolute certainty? We need, hence, a radical shift in our religious discourse and theological language. It is high time that we begin theologizing and conveying theological approaches to God-Human-Cosmos in the form of street-plays, musical dramas, inspiring quotes, traditional dance-forms, stories, parables and anecdotes, etc.; these forms transcend the *either/or* structure of truth and falsity. Every event is a story of the Divine insofar as it communicates the Divine, not in informative statements, but in the form of a constantly disturbing *call* to be appropriated by a response of fundamental option or radical commitment. It is our conviction that the purpose of theological language is not for giving dispassionate information about God, but for passionately waking us up from our religious slumber!

---

33 There is a close relation and difference between the symbolic and the aesthetic. Cf.,

34 The poets through their poetries, novelists through their novels, story-tellers through their parables and fables, people of wisdom through their wise sayings, have been making people reflect on their lives, challenging and disturbing them from their peaceful slumber of comfort. If this is what mythico-poetic language can do in our 'human' life, it must be much more so in the religious sphere.

24

A Philosophical Reading of the Theology of Praxis

Nishant A. Irudayadason
Professor of Philosophy, Jnana Deepa Vidyapeeth, Pune

"The Spirit aids me: now I see the light!
'In the Beginning was the Act,' I write."
–Johann Wolfgang von Goethe

Abstract: *This paper explores the theology of praxis from a philosophical point of view. Taking inspiration from the works of Paul Ricoeur and Jurgen Habermas, this paper highlights the richness in the understanding of praxis while drawing attention to its complexity. It affirms the importance of language, communication symbols and power structures that are inherent to the theology of praxis. Caution is made not to idealize certain notions like respect and benevolence—however noble they may be—without taking actual cognisance of the actual asymmetrical structure of power relation. An analysis of collective praxis both in terms of conflict and co-operation is done so as to invite the readers to the constant need to be open to new possibilities of appropriating the praxis of Jesus in changing times and contexts.*

Keywords: *Action, communication, language, practice, pragmatic semantics, symbolic.*

In my opinion, all theology must have a practical nature. When we talk about the practical nature of theology, we usually refer to the importance of the narrative of salvation for human experience. However, in recent years, some theologians prefer to focus on human action than on human experience. For example, a French theologian Claude Geffré holds that theology should not only begin from praxis or human action but must also allow itself to be challenged by it.[1] Another French theologian Camil Ménard, inspired by the writings of a Brazilian theologian Clodovis Boff, states that the theological methodology moves an initial praxis to a praxis transformed by the indispensable mediation of one or more theories.[2]

Focusing on praxis or action has some benefits. First, the modes of action are more precise than those of experience. Secondly, action is more susceptible to analysis and based on the analysis, action can be improved. Thirdly, focusing on practices involves both personal and collective dimensions, whereas experience usually involves a personal dimension. Fourthly, action can be thought of only in relation to a context; it is woven into a specific historical milieu with its history, tradition, symbols and agents of action. Fifthly, action is dynamic and it is a locus of relationships, conflicts, judgments, and personal and collective transformations. Finally, action is often critical of acquired knowledge, including knowledge acquired through experience; the study of a particular action makes it possible to understand the gap between professed and enacted theories,[3] an analysis that calls for and offers new knowledge and capabilities.

The theology of praxis makes at least two vital demands on us. First it invites us to improve both our awareness of the situation and our commitment to engage in action. Secondly, it invites us to develop a more rigorous theological method to better understand the significance of our actions for our faith. Although the theology of praxis is primarily about action, there is hardly any reflection on the very concept of action. There is more literature on the relationship between theory and practice. But a clear understanding of the concept of action seems to be essential for research in the theology of praxis. This seems all the more important for the Church as ecclesial practices are said to be the result of divine inspiration or of a mission granted from above. A Christian cannot deny that the Spirit plays an important role in ecclesial practices, but these are nonetheless related to the complexity of human actions.

We need to recognize that the theology of praxis cannot be limited to human actions alone; it must be interested in the divine action as well. The divine action, however, is already the subject matter of systematic theology

1 Claude Geffré , *Le christianisme au risque de l'interprétation* (Paris: Cerf, 1983), 343.

2 Camil Ménard, "L'urgence d'une théologie pratique nord-américaine comme théorie critique de l'agir chrétien au service de la société," in Petit and Breton (eds.), *Seuls ou avec les autres? Le salut chrétien à l'épreuve de la solidarité* (Montréal: Fides, 1992), 300.

3 See Chris Argyris and Donald Schön, *Theory in Practice: Increasing Professional Effectiveness* (San Francisco: Jossey-Bass, 1974).

which thematises it, for example, in terms of revelation, creation and salvation. Theology of Praxis focuses specifically on the divine action manifested through human actions as is the case in the New Testament: the Gospels present to us the actions of the historical Jesus and the Acts of the Apostles (*praxeis apostolon*), speaks to us about the actions of the members of the early Christian community. Thus, theology of praxis is a theological discipline determined by an empirical-hermeneutical relation to actions, particularly but not exclusively to the actions of believers. Its challenge is to bring to light the connection between the divine action and human actions for salvation. Theology of praxis focuses on the interaction between divine and human actions for the transformation of the world; it is theology rooted in reality and therefore relevant and sometimes normative.

Elements of the Philosophical Tradition

A quick glance at the development of the term praxis in the philosophical tradition can help us to understand its meaning. In Greek, the verb *prasso* means I act, I do an activity, I do it, and "our doing, our conduct, our praxis result from our own deliberation and choice under the guidance of the practical wisdom that Aristotle named *phronesis* and Aquinas named *prudentia*."[4] Activities involving physical labour reserved for slaves were excluded from praxis and were designated by the term *poiesis*. Aristotle, for example contrasts praxis which refers specifically to ethical-political action with *poiesis* which involves productive action; "For production [poiesis] has its end beyond it, but action [praxis] does not, since its end is doing well itself." (NE 1140b) It is within this framework that Aristotle made praxis one of the three fundamental human activities that he considered three modes of knowledge: *theoria*, *praxis* and *poiesis*.

The Marxist tradition distinguished the term practice from praxis, giving the latter a reflexive character which it denied to the former. In this context, practice seems closer to the ancient *poiesis*.[5] Althusser defines *poiesis* as "any process of transformation of a determinate given raw material into a determined product, a transformation effected by a determined human labour, using a determinate means (of production)."[6] Practice, thus understood, is rooted in particular contexts far from ideal. Praxis incorporates the characteristics of practice, but it is distinguished by its reflexive dimension. David Tracy, who intends to distinguish praxis from practice identified with the application of

4 Bernard Lonergan, "Theology and Praxis," CTSA Proceedings, 32 (1977): 1.

5 In philosophy, *poiesis* (from Ancient Greek: ποίησις) is the activity in which a person brings something into being that did not exist before. *Poiesis* is etymologically derived from the ancient Greek term ποιεῖν, which means to make.

6 Louis Althusser, *For Marx*, trans. Ben Brewster (London: Verso, 2005), 166.

a theory, defines it as "the critical relationship between theory and practice whereby each is dialectically influenced and transformed by the other."[7] The theory-practice relationship is important in theology of praxis marked by its desire to uncover, criticize and improve the dialectical influence between theory and practice in contemporary situation. The Marxist distinction between practice and praxis has become less important today, so we can focus on the concept of action rather than practice (though these terms are used interchangeably) and recall with Paulo Freire that praxis is "the action and reflection of men and women upon their world in order to transform it."[8]

Heidegger took up the Aristotelian triptych[9] by making each of its activities fundamental dispositions for the unveiling of the Being. Praxis proves to be the most basic mode of Dasein, mode in which *theoria* and *poiesis* are determined respectively in contemplative and productive disposition. As in Marx, praxis in Heidegger determines and reveals the subject as well as his or her world. MacIntyre identifies praxis with "any coherent and complex form of socially established cooperative human activity through which goods internal to that form of activity are realized in the course of trying to achieve those standards of excellence which are appropriate to, and partially definitive of, that form of activity, with the result that human powers to achieve excellence, and human conceptions of the ends and goods involved, are systematically extended."[10] By interpreting Bourdieu's notion of *habitus*[11] in his book *The Logic of Practice*, Graham specifies that "practices are not merely 'rule-governed behaviour,' but symbolic, purposeful strategies with many layers of meaning.[12]

---

7 David Tracy, *Blessed Rage for Order: The New Pluralism in Theology* (Chicago: The University of Chicago Press, 1996) 243. See also his book *The Analogical Imagination* (New York: Crossroad, 1981), 69.

8 Paul Freire, *Pedagogy of the Oppressed* (London: Penguin Books, 1996), 60.

9 Aristotelean triptych is the artful repetition employed in rhetoric. It comprises of three activities: 1. Tell them what you are going to tell them, 2. tell them, 3. then tell them what you told them.

10 Alasdair MacIntyre, *After Virtue: A Study in Moral Theory* (Notre Dame: University of Notre Dame Press, 2007), 187.

11 The French sociologist Pierre Bourdieu developed the notion of 'habitus' to capture the permanent internalisation of the social order in the human body whilst recognising the agent's practice, his or her capacity for invention and improvisation. In Bourdieu's theory of practice, the world's structural constraints form permanent dispositions. These are schemes of perception and thought, extremely general in their application, such as those which divide up the world in accordance with the oppositions between the male and the female, east and west, future and past, top and bottom, right and left, etc., and also, at a deeper level, if the form of bodily postures and stances, ways of standing, sitting, looking, speaking, or walking.

12 Elaine L. Graham, *Transforming Practice: Pastoral Theology in an Age of Uncertainty*, 101

a. Praxis in the Philosophy of Paul Ricoeur

Ricoeur makes a distinction between praxis and practice. He refers to practices as "complex actions ruled by precepts of all kinds whether technical, aesthetical, ethical or political."[13] For him, practices consist of chains of actions endowed with structures that are primarily logical, then teleological or historical, prescriptive, and ethical. They are logical because they present relations of coordination and subordination, teleological because they are enshrined in plans of life and in the unity of a life that unfolds from birth to death, prescriptive because they are governed by rules or precepts, ethical because they are marked by an asymmetrical dynamic inviting or respect for others (ethics). It is in practices that subjects express themselves, their goals, the choice of means to achieve their goals, the results of their choices, and their relations to other subjects and the given circumstance in which they act.

Praxis is the plan of life in which practices are expressed, the narrative unity of life, which captures and integrates praxis into a story, the wish for a good or accomplished life in the Aristotelean sense. From the conceptual point of view, it is only a limited idea: the good life is a goal, towards which are directed all our individual actions. The content of good life is, "for each of us, the nebula of ideals and dreams of achievements with regard to which a life is for more or less fulfilled or unfulfilled"[14] The good life is the horizon towards which all our actions tend.

However, such finality goes beyond individual action, of which it nevertheless constitutes the internal dynamic. This proves that the individual life is not a set of closed practices. "This opening, which fractures practices otherwise held to be closed in upon themselves when doubts rise about the direction of our life maintains a tension, most often a discrete and tacit one, between the closed and the open within the global structure of praxis".[15] It concerns above all the text of the action, but also the moral agent who interprets himself or herself in his or her action. Thus, if we accept that understanding the action is for the agent to understand himself or herself, we can say that self-esteem at the ethical level is what the self-interpretation is at the reflexive level. This is the meaning of the good life, the first moment of the ethical goal. But ethics is also concerned with the other whom it institutes as my fellow being who also requires me reciprocally.

13 Paul Ricoeur, "The Teleological and Deontological Structures of Action: Aristotle and/or Kant?" in A. Phillips Griffiths (ed.) *Contemporary French Philosophy* (Cambridge: Cambridge University Press, 1987), 99.

14 Paul Ricoeur, *Oneself as Another*, trans. Kathleen Blamey (Chicago: University of Chicago Press, 1992), 179.

15 Ibid., 179.

b. Dimensions of Action in Habermas

In the wake of Weber, Jürgen Habermas developed a typology of action, which is useful for analysing actions. Habermas distinguishes four types of action: teleological, normative, dramaturgical and communicative.[16] The concept of teleological action (directed to one end) is fundamental to the other types of actions because the teleological structure is present in all four types of action. In fact, what differentiate these four types of action from one another are the conditions according to which we pursue our goals and the manner in which we relate our actions to those of others.

Teleological action is characterized by its focus on the relationship between the means and the end. The success of the action implies the choice and the coordination of the means to arrive at the desired end. The criteria for this action are the knowledge of the external world (means) and the effectiveness of the intervention in this world (end); it is the right coordination between the means and the end of the action. Depending on how the knowledge and interests of the agent of the action meet, this type of action can be a source of cooperation or conflict. But when we are over preoccupied with the right coordination between the means and the end, we risk turning our action into instrumental or technical.

Normative action refers to the common values of a group by which members of the group orient their actions. The criteria for this action are legitimacy of norms and conformity of actions to the norms of a social group. Admittedly, norms are found in every action, as Ricoeur points out while referring to the rules of action, but there are actions that are entirely defined by its relation to norms and therefore characterized as normative.

Dramaturgical action is that in which participants mutually constitute an audience for one another. Habermas holds that this action is often parasitic of the preceding ones and that it rarely exists in the pure state. The criteria for this action are truthfulness and the authenticity of communication to the internal subjective world, involving the risk of communication becoming manipulation and transforming the dramaturgical action into instrumental.

Communicative action opposes a purely performative or utilitarian objectifying attitude of partners in action and therefore implies a moral dimension. It aims at the interaction of acting subjects in search of agreement or consensus that allows them to coordinate their action plans. Interpretation is its principal task: "the task of mutual interpretation is to achieve a new definition of the situation which all participants can share. If their attempt

16 Jürgen Habermas, *The Theory of Communicative Action Vol. 1: Reason and Rationalization of Society*, trans Thomas McCarthy (Boston: Beacon Press, 1984), 75ff.

fails, communicative action cannot be continued"[17] In communicative action, before arriving at a mutual understanding on coordinating mechanism of the action, subjects agree to relativize their expressions when their validity is disputed by the other participants of the action. Hence the triple criteria of this action: the first related to truth (the statement is true in relation to the objective world), the second to justice (the linguistic action is just in relation to the normative context in force) and the third to truthfulness or authenticity (the intention expressed by the speaker is his or her thought as he or she expresses it). Peukert expresses very eloquently the meaning and the mechanism of this action:

To speak implies the creative projection of an interpretation of the subjective, social and objective reality on to my conversation partner in a way that both opens up to an understanding to that person and invites my partner to share her or his own creative interpretation with me."[18]

The Richness and Complexity of Praxis

Literature often uses the terms action or social action to refer to praxis. We shall therefore do the same, while stating however that praxis involves repetition of action for a certain duration and commitment to it over a period of time. We must also acknowledge that praxis has a social dimension though society consists of cooperating and conflicting individuals with their knowledge and interests. Recent literature on praxis revolves around two poles. One emphasizes the systemic aspect, objectifies praxis and considers individual agents of action as one of elements in praxis. The other is pragmatic and places the agent of the action at the heart of praxis. Although there is tension between the two camps, it seems to us that they are not irreconcilable. We cannot understand the agent of action outside the system of action and the reverse is also true. This tension nevertheless remains fruitful, making it possible to escape reductionism on both sides, and it invites us to understand these apparently conflicting poles as complementarity.

By borrowing largely from Paul Ricoeur, we shall define praxis as a complex system of actions and interaction of agents of action, oriented towards one or many ends, including relations of coordination and subordination, regulated by rules of different types, marked by a dissymmetry among the agents of action living in a context—whether institutional, sociocultural or religious that influences the action and gives it meaning, but also allows to be influenced by the action. To understand praxis, we need to study the system

17 Jürgen Habermas, *Communication and the Evolution of Society* (Boston: Beacon Press, 1979), 3.

18 Peukert, "Enlightenment and Theology as Unifinished Products," in Don S. Browning and Francis Schussler Fiorenza (eds.), *Habermas, Modernity and Public Theology* (Crossword Publishing Co., 1959), 59.

of action through its semantics and structural poles by investigating "who does what, where, when, how and why". For Ricoeur, "it is in terms of the entire network crisscrossing the semantics of action that we understand the expression 'agent'."[19] He further adds:

Actions have goals, goals which are anticipated and which have results. But actions towards goals imply motives, the reasons for engaging in the actions that allow one event to be connected to another. These motives are held together by agents who are capable for the consequences of their actions, and consequently a network of interactions is constructed, each item complementing the other. These elements, and more besides, allow narrators and listeners to answer questions like 'what,' 'why,' 'who,' 'how,' 'with whom' or 'against whom' with regard to any action.[20]

If praxis is a complex system of voluntary and goal oriented actions, it involves the goal of individual subjects. These individual subjects interact with others in action, thus praxis is inevitably related to the meaning of human existence.[21] Through the system of action, the human subject makes meaning of human existence.[22] Action therefore involves physical, emotional and spiritual subjects with needs and desires, capable of judgment and choice, capable of coordinating actions and goals according to ideologies of self-representation and representations of the world in diverse and overlapping contexts (personal, social, ecclesial), which influence them and largely determine their representations, goals and actions.

There is no action without a subject and there is no subject without an action. Action is thus the locus both of understanding and of transformation of self and the world. Action influences the subject's being and understanding. In this sense, action is the un-concealment and transformation of the self and the world. Heidegger considers praxis as a mode of Dasein's existence and relates it to the notion of care. Action is the unfolding of the human subject and his or her relation to the world.

a. Praxis as a Hermeneutical Act

We orient our actions according to their perceived or constructed meaning. Thus, hermeneutics is an important aspect of action related to the public dimension of an action, to a meaning that is publically available, as Jervolino points out: "It is a structured symbolic system, a public one, which furnishes

19 Ricoeur, *Oneself as Another*, 95.

20 Paul Ricoeur, Time and Narrative, Vol 1 (Chicago: University of Chicago Press, 1984), 55.

21 Thomas W. Ogletree, "Dimensions of Practical Theology : Meaning, Action, Self," in Don S. Browning (ed.), *Practical Theology* (San Francisco: Harper and Row, 1983), 85

22 Ricoeur criticizes the semantics of action as the occultation of the subject. See Ricoeur, *Oneself as Another*, 56 ff.

single actions with a context and makes them, in a certain sense, readable."[23] The subject as part of the world makes his or her interpretation of the self, others and the world, an interpretation that is susceptible to change and transformation by his or her action. The complex interaction between theory and practice is thus woven, which has relevance for a theology of praxis. Led by the meaning making project in which reality is confronted with interpretation, practice is intrinsically related to theory, as is ethics to hermeneutics.

Interpretations are in process and in conflict. As there are many agents of action, Actions allow for multiplicity of interpretations leading to conflict as there are many agents of action. Both conflict and cooperation are part of an action. This makes complex not only an action but also its analysis, interpretation and evaluation. Which interpretation should be privileged and on what basis? Hence the need for Ricoeur's hermeneutical process or Habermas' communicative action to determine which vision, narrative and metaphor are best suited to the givenness of the world, the interests of the "narrators," and the significance of the action that is likely to transform both the "narrators" and the "listeners." Interpretation, however, has a dramatic dimension for those who are refused the right of a narrative.

The human subject is an indispensable element in the system of action. The subject wishes to inscribe something of his or her self in the system in which he or she evolves. When the subject makes a manifestation of his or her self in the world through the system of action, he or she may have a kenotic experience: in action the subject is divested at least a part of his or her self. Thus, a tragic dimension of praxis is added to its dramatic dimension. The hermeneutical act must be attentive to the dramatic and tragic dimensions of praxis.

The entanglement between the laws of the system and the desire of the subject is problematic.[24] It is because of this entanglement, every action represents the power of the subject, his or her ability to perform certain actions. Von Wright calls this interference, which according to Ricoeur, "consists in joining together the ability to act, of which an agent has an immediate understanding with the internal relations that condition a system."[25] According to Ludwig von Mises, an economist and one of the pioneers in praxeology, human beings determine their course of action based on three conditions:

23 Domenico Jervolino, *The Cogito and Hermeneutics: The Question of the Subject in Ricoeur* (Dordrecht: Kluwer Academic Publishers, 1990), 128.

24 See Ricoeur, *Oneself as Another*, 88-112.

25 Paul Ricoeur, *From Text to Action: Essays in Hermeneutics*, II, trans., Kathleen Blamey and John B. Thompson (London: Continuum, 2008), 212. Cf. Paul Ricoeur, *Time and Narrative, Vol. 1*, trans. Kathleen McLaughlin and David Pellauer (Chicago: University of Chicago Press, 1984), 135; Paul Ricoeur, *Time and Narrative, Vol. 3*, trans. Kathleen Blamey and David Pellauer (Chicago: University of Chicago Press, 1990), 231.

uneasiness over an existing situation, possibility of a greater satisfaction when the existing situation changes, and representation of the power to act: "to make a man act, uneasiness and the image of a more satisfactory state alone are not sufficient. A third condition is required: the expectation that purposeful behaviour has the power to remove or at least to alleviate the felt uneasiness."[26]

Consciousness of the power to act is a necessary prerequisite for action. We may have good reasons to engage in transformative action but not doing it only because we know that we do not have the power. This is the reason why we feel helpless in the face of a unjust economic system, polarizing national political climate, the inhuman form of globalization, oppressive social structures and mass genocides. According to Ricoeur, When we say "I can" we affirm implicitly of our consciousness of the power to act: "It is only in this phenomenology of the 'I can' and in the related ontology of the body as one's own that the status of primitive datum accorded to the power to act would be established definitely.[27] No ethics is possible without this consciousness. This dynamics of the power to act has not been given enough attention in various theologies of liberation including Feminist, Dalit and Tribal theologies.

Praxis is founded in the will to transform reality; it works through the dynamics of power and makes the human subject commit to action. It is therefore the locus of competition, struggle, domination, submission, exchange and cooperation. Recent studies on construction of power structures inform us that power is not equally shared. Every action is therefore marked by a structural inequality. Whatever be our convictions about kindness and cooperation, to act is to make an intervention often though persistent persuasion. Ricoeur remarks that the other "is potentially the victim of my action as much as its adversary."[28] Following the Weberian and the Marxist traditions, Habermas has pointed out the effects of instrumental action on the subject who may be reduced merely to a means in the Kantian sense. In our enthusiasm to idealize action, we tend to forget that power is at work in every action and it can create conflict. Praxis is constantly accompanied both by cooperation and conflict resulting from the dynamics of power. To deny this is to turn a blind eye to the ethical call at the heart of the theology of praxis. The asymmetric relation of power is often a problem in ecclesial practices as elsewhere and I wonder if we give pay enough attention to this. We pretend to have an idealized concept of praxis, especially because of our ideology of respect, benevolence and love

26 Ludwig von Mises, *Human Action: A Treatise on Economics* (San Francisco: Fox and Wilkes, 1996), 14

27 Ricoeur, *Oneself as Another*, 111. See also page 112 and 181.

28 Ricoeur, "Ethical and Theological Considerations on the Golden Rule," in *Figuring the Sacred: Religion, Narrative and Imagination* (Minneapolis: Fortress Press, 1995), 294.

of others, whilst the actual practice in the Church is to hold an asymmetrical relation which we cannot afford to ignore.

b. Praxis as Communication

The fact that a subject enters in relation with other subjects in action whether through cooperation or conflict suggests that praxis is a locus of communication. The effectiveness of an action depends on the communication among its agents and with the context. To act is to make oneself heard of one's vision of the world and to listen to the vision of others. Thus human action becomes communication. "Human action concerns intended activity. As such it includes communication acts as well as bodily movements."[29]

Austin and Searle highlighted the practical dimension of communication: "to say is to do." However, it also seems to me that "to do is to say," or again "to act is to say." We can confuse "to do" with "to act" as Hannah Arendt has pointed out in her *The Condition of Modern Man*. However, the level of a pragmatics of communication, "to do" can be taken as synonymous to "to act." This equation may have other implication but it does have a meaning even if it is the complicity of political silence. To the idea speech is action, the school of Palo Alto adds the idea 'action is speech,' thus suggesting that human behaviour is a form of communication,[30] a position which Habermas refutes.[31] We shall be prudent and be content in affirming that action says something.

The pragmatics of language considers discourse as an act and a performance. However, this act and its meaning depend on the context of interlocution that is, on its location, the dynamics of relations between the interlocutors, their positions, culture, beliefs and intention. We know from Heidegger and Wittgenstein that language serves not only to represent the world but also to complete an action by directing oneself to build the world. To speak is to act, or to commit to act on self, others and the world. It is to establish meaning rendering speech into action. When a speaker says something to someone, he does it with an intention to make an impact on the person whom he or she is addressing. The speaker may intend to frighten, to impress, to coax, to seduce or to comfort his or her addressee. The illocutionary force of speech, what one does in speaking, is action.

---

29 Donald Polkinghorne, *Methodology for the Human Sciences: Systems of Inquiry* (Albany, New York State University Press, 1983), 172.

30 See Paul Watzlawick, J. Helmut Beavin and D. Jackson, *Pragmatics of Human Communications* (New York: Norton, 1967).

31 See Habermas, *Communication and the Evolution of Society*, 44-50.

What we have discussed here is not strange to the hermeneutical theology of action. Paul Ricoeur has invited us to read action as a text.[32] On the one hand, action offers the structure of a locutionary act because it has a certain propositional content and internal features that bring it closer to the act of speech. On the other hand, it also has an illocutionary force insofar as it aims to influence not only the external world but also the human environment within it. We can thus think of a typology of action and ecclesial action, modelled after the illocutionary acts of Austin and Searle. This is not surprising if we remember that pragmatics (of *pragmata*, actions) is precisely based on actions intended and carried out by the speech act. Since the illocutionary force of discourse is primarily about action, we find these features in praxis. Praxis therefore communicates something.

The first feature of Searle's typology, the assertive trait (by which something is said to be true), seems less obvious. Yet, praxis communicates to us a perception of reality as a truth claim. To lock up mad people in an asylum, for example, is to say that they have no place in our neighbourhood. Praxis, as we have stated earlier, is also an act of interpretation.

The guiding trait of praxis is more evident than the previous one as it is directly oriented to action. It aims not only to change the external world but also to influence human persons, who inhabit it, to engage in action. In fact, it is from an understanding of discourse as performative, and therefore as action, that pragmatics has thematised this trait.

The commitment trait is also obvious: if someone shows commitment in word, he can also do it in action. To give one's presence, time and energy is to commit oneself to the other. Admittedly, there may be tenderness, trickery and other hazards of action, but these also mark the acts of speech.

The expressive feature of praxis is related to the dramaturgical action of Habermas and to the pragmatics of Watzlawick mentioned above. Practice is where the human person expresses what he or she is with his or her possibilities and limits, and through which he or she says what really matters to him or her, what he or she wants to be, and what he or she wants the world to become.

The act of declarative language accomplishes what it says, a realization that is directly related to action. Declarations of different sorts—declaring a session open, declaring someone as married, elected or dismissed—are already encoded in action in specific contexts, without which these declarations would be false.

32 Paul Ricoeur, *From Text to Action: Essays in Hermeneutics*, II, trans., Kathleen Blamey and John B. Thompson (London: Continuum, 2008), 140-163. See also Charles Taylor, "Interpretation and the Science of Man," in *Review of Metaphysics*, 25 (1971): 3-51. Clifford Geertz had already proposed to do ethnography as one reads a manuscript: "Thick Description: Toward an Interpretive Theory of Culture", in *The Interpretation of Cultures* (New York: Basic Books, 1973).

Let us add one last element to these communicative features of praxis. It is also the locus of mutual recognition, which in my opinion, constitutes its radical aspect of communication attested by the pragmatics of Palo Alto. The human person's ability to be with (*Mitsein*) others is unique. In the words of Martin Buber, "the basis of man's life with man is twofold, and yet one: the wish of every man to be confirmed as what he is, even as what he can become, by men; and the innate capacity in man to confirm his fellow men in this way."[33]

Communication has "the function of constantly rebuilding the self concept, of offering this self concept to others for ratification, and of accepting or rejecting the self-conceptual offering of others."[34] It is through praxis that the ongoing construction of the concept of the self and identity exchanges are done. In this sense, praxis as communication has a broader meaning than that of Habermas' "communicative action."

Conclusion

The meaning of action emerges partly from its agents and partly from the system of action, which is situated in a larger context. It is detached from the event itself and from the agents of action. Just like the meaning of the text is distanced from the event of writing and its author, the meaning of an action surpasses the intention of its agents not only because of its public nature, but also because of its entanglement with the system of action and of multiple agencies. We can agree with Ricoeur that an action is detached from its agent in the same way that a text stands out from its author and develops its own meaning. Similarly, the meaning of the action no longer coincides with the intentions of its agents, but resides in the action itself. Like a text, it is open to anyone who knows how to read it. It can therefore receive different interpretations from those made by its agents.

The importance and significance of an action goes beyond its original relevance and meaning. In this, an action opens a world of possibilities. Paraphrasing what Ricoeur says about the comprehension of a text, we can say that what is to be understood in an action is neither the agents' presumed intention, nor the inherent structures of the action, but the outcome of the action.[35] We are at the heart of the hermeneutical work of the theology of praxis articulated in its empirical work. Praxis opens many possible meanings that can be realized in new contexts. Thus, a Christian theology of praxis is always

33 Martin Buber, "Distance and Religion," in Asher D. Biemann (ed.), *The Martin Buber Reader: Essential Writings* (New York: Palgrave Macmillan, 2002), 210.

34 John Cumming as cited by Watzlawick and others, *Pragmatics of Human Communications*, 84.

35 Paul Ricoeur, "Toward a Hermeneutic of the Idea of Revelation," *Harvard Theological Review* 70, no. 1-2 (April 1977): 1-37.

open to new possibilities of actualizing the praxis of Jesus in new ways, thus enabling us to live the Christ event in our own context.

It is on the open-ended aspect of praxis that we conclude our reflections, a choice that is obviously not fortuitous. If Faust replaced the aphorism "In the beginning was the Word" with "In the beginning was the Act," it is because action Praxis and logos, or action and proclamation, are woven together and the theology of praxis must take this into account.

25

"All Truth is God's Truth:" Towards a New Christian Philosophy from the Perspective of Edith Stein

M.D. Joseph

Research Scholar, Science and Religion,

Jnana-Deepa Vidyapeeth, Pune 411014

Abstract: *Edith Stein (1891-1942), who took the religious name Teresa Benedicta à Cruce (Teresa Benedicta of the Cross), was beautified in 1987 and canonized eleven years later on October 11, 1998, by Pope John Paul II. When the beatification process began in 1962, the advocates focused on her life and good works, arguing for her case based on heroic virtue; however, in 1983, Joseph Cardinal Hoffner proposed a different route to beautification and sent a letter to Rome requesting that she be considered a martyr because of her clear theology of suffering, her willingness to follow the path of the Cross and offer her life as a sacrifice, and the circumstances under which she, her sister Rosa, and approximately 300 other baptized Christians of Jewish descent were sent to Auschwitz. In 1987 Stein was confirmed by the Congregation for the Causes of Saints both as a martyr and as someone of heroic virtue, the first person confirmed as both in the 400-year history of the Congregation.*

In this article the author wants to study her approach to Christian philosophy, as a perennial search for Truth, as Prof Kurien Kunnumpuram through his words and works have shown. Like Kurien, her starting point is the phenomenological (thrown existence) where she embraces everything to reach the final and eternal truths and truth.

Keywords: *Edith Stein, Truth, Philosophy, Phenomenology.*

Introduction

As Sarah Borden points out in her work titled, *Edith Stein that* Edith Stein (1891-1942), who took the religious name Teresa Benedicta à Cruce (Teresa Benedicta of the Cross), was beautified in 1987 and canonized eleven years later on October 11, 1998, by Pope John Paul II. When the beatification process began in 1962, the advocates focused on her life and good works, arguing for her case based on heroic virtue; however, in 1983, Joseph Cardinal Hoffner proposed a different route to beautification and sent a letter to Rome requesting that she be considered a martyr because of her clear theology of suffering, her willingness to follow the path of the Cross and offer her life as a sacrifice, and the circumstances under which she, her sister Rosa, and approximately 300 other baptized Christians of Jewish descent were sent to Auschwitz. In 1987 Stein was confirmed by the Congregation for the Causes of Saints both as a martyr and as someone of heroic virtue, the first person confirmed as both in the 400-year history of the Congregation.[1]

In this article I want to study her approach to Christian philosophy, as a perennial search for Truth, as Prof Kurien Kunnumpuram through his words and works have shown. Like Kurien, her starting point is the phenomenological (thrown existence) where she embraces everything to reach the final and eternal truths and truth.

Her Life and Works

Her life and works have influenced such a great person like St. Pope John Paul II. Thus he writes in his *Rise, Let us be on Our Way* that his personal philosophical outlook moves, so to speak, between two poles: Aristotelian Thomism and phenomenology. He says that he was particularly interested in Edith Stein, an extraordinary figure for her life story as well as her philosophy; born into a Jewish family in Wroclaw, she discovered Christ, was baptized and entered the Carmelite convent, spent some time in the Netherlands, but who was deported from there to Auschwitz by the Nazis, died in a gas chamber and her mortal remains were burned in a crematorium. She had studied with Husserl and had been a colleague of the Polish Philosopher Ingarden.

The Pope says that he had the joy of beatifying her in Cologne and then canonizing her in Rome. The Pope also proclaimed Edith Stein, Sister Benedicta of the Cross, as a copatron of Europe, together with Saint Bridget of Sweden and Saint Catherine of Siena: three women alongside the three male patrons: Cyril, Methodius, and Benedict. He further says that he was interested in her philosophy, as he read her writings, especially *Endliches und Ewiges Sein* (*Finite and Eternal Being),* but what fascinated him most was

---

1 M.D. Joseph, *Thrown into The World: An Existentialist's Approach to Life* (India, Guwahati: EBH, 2016), 157-158.

her extraordinary life and her tragic destiny, intertwined with that of millions of other defenseless victims of our era, a disciple of Edmund Husserl, an impassioned seeker after truth, an enclosed nun, a victim of Hitler's regime: hers is a truly unique human story.[2] The purpose of this article is to see her development of a new Christian philosophy as this the title of this article indicates, "All Truth is God's Truth:" Towards a New Christian Philosophy in the Perspective of Edith Stein.

A New Christian Philosophy

It is seen that during the 1920s and early 1930s, Stein gave lectures for the Catholic circuit and translated Christian texts, and her philosophical writings of the following years reflect these activities, which reveal her interest and capability as a person in formulating the theoretical position concerning the traditional Christian dogma, and her sympathetic concerns regarding the medieval scholastic tradition.[3] As regards to Stein's view of Christian philosophy Borden points out that though Stein's primary intellectual formation, however, was as a phenomenologist, one can see throughout her work of this period a clear project of creating a dialogue between more contemporary philosophy and the great medieval Christian tradition.[4]

In her efforts to the contribution towards Christian philosophy, Stein acknowledges the influence of Fr. Erich Przywara in her preface to her work *Finite and Eternal Being,* especially his formidable text *Analogia entis.*[5] Fr. Przywara was little known now. But in European Catholic circles of the day, who was a powerful force, editing the journal *Stimmen der Zeit* [Voices of the Time] and in regular exchange with the major theologians, including Karl Barth [1886-1968], Paul Tillich [1886-1965], Hans Urs von Balthasar [1905-1988], and Karl Rahner [1904-1984]. Although not agreeing on all details, Przywara and Stein shared a vision of integrating phenomenology, and scholastic philosophy. And both were concerned with the Church's response to the 'Modernist Crisis.'[6]

As Borden points out that during the turn of the century among the Catholics in Germany, there was something of a ghetto mentality; during the late nineteenth century, with Bismark's *Kulturkampf* (cultural wars), Catholics were ostracized and understandably, came to see much of mainstream culture as hostile also between the years of 1890-1914, the Catholic Church in Europe was caught up in the Modernist Crisis, battling theologians and intellectuals,

2 John Paul II, *Rise, Let us be on Our Way* (London: Jonathan Cape, 2004), 90-91.

3 Sarah Borden, *Edith Stein, Edith Stein* (London: Continuum , 2003), 90.

4 *Ibid.*

5 *Ibid.*

6 *Ibid.*

who embraced and those who appeared to embrace German Idealism with its historicist understanding of religion and religious belief.[7] As Borden points out there were certainly dangerous intellectual waters to be negotiated, – the response to the philosophical challenges was reactionary at best. And both in this situation Stein and Fr. Pryzywara, however, saw in the contemporary phenomenological movement resources for responding to German Idealism and an opportunity for Catholic thought to converse with contemporary thought and culture.[8]

Borden points out that all the works of Stein between 1929 and 1939 present such a dialogue.[9] The year 1929 marks the publication of Stein's contribution to the *Festschrift* volume in honor of Husserl's seventieth birthday ('Husserl's Phenomenology and the Philosophy of St Thomas Aquinas' [HT] and 1936, the completion of *Finite and Eternal Being*.[10] Thus, Stein, in her *Festscherift* article compares Husserl and Aquinas on several philosophical points including the nature of the philosophical project and a discussion of what can be known and how it is known, pointing out their philosophical compatibilities, although Aquinas where their paths diverge.[11] Thus, as Borden points out that the article was intended as a first, brief comparison of the two thinkers.[12] And when six years later, when Stein wrote *Finite and Eternal Being*, she was no longer interested in a strict comparison, but, rather, presents her own metaphysical positions, which reveal the influence of both phenomenology and medieval scholasticism, which are reducible to neither.[13] During this time, Stein attempted once again to obtain a university position and wrote a *Habilitationsschrift, Potency and Act*, working through many of the questions which would be more fully developed in *Finite and Eternal Being.*[14]

In her work a *Habilitationsschrift, Potency and Act*, develops a vision of philosophy as not only foundational to other intellectual disciplines but also as comprehensive, grasping all of being and increasingly central to her writing is her conception of Christian philosophy.[15] Thus, Borden points out that in this work, Stein develops a vision of philosophy as not only foundational to other intellectual disciplines but also a comprehensive, grasping all of being. Borden says that increasingly central to her writing is

7 M.D. Joseph, *Thrown into The World: An Existentialist's Approach to Life*, 194-195.

8 *Ibid.*, 195.

9 Sarah Borden, *Edith Stein*, 91.

10 *Ibid.*

11 *Ibid.*

12 M.D. Joseph, *Thrown into The World: An Existentialist's Approach to Life*, 195..

13 Sarah Borden, *Edith Stein*, 91.

14 *Ibid.*

15 *Ibid.*

her conception of Christian philosophy. According to Borden in all of her work following her conversion, Stain is a Christian thinker, but also an explicitly Christian philosopher. She offers critiques of the more agnostic (Husserlian phenomenology that clearly favour the Christian philosophy of St Thomas (while also noting points of real compatibility between the two), and in *Finite and Eternal Being*, she articulates her understanding of Christian philosophy and develops arguments for the existence of God. Borden points out that prior to turning to her more metaphysical claims regarding being, essence, and personhood, which are central to her mature synthesis of medieval and contemporary thought, (which Borden discusses in her *Edith Stein*: Chapter 6; Metaphysics and Epistemology of the Later Work, p. 103), Stein's critical examination of Husserl's phenomenology and claims regarding the nature of Christian philosophy, arguments for the existence of God, and the mark of the Trinitarian God on nature should be considered.[16]

Questions Regarding Phenomenology

The spirit of the Scholastics, certainly imprinted phenomenology. Thus, Husserl was reported as saying that phenomenology 'converges towards Thomism and prolongs Thomism.'[17] But after the publication of Husserl's publication of his *Logical Investigations,* his thought was hailed as the 'new scholasticism.'[18] And as Borden points out that while these were initial receptions of Husserlian phenomenology, the two schools have not, since then, always been thought to be good bed-fellows.[19] However, according to Stein a primary similarity between St Thomas Aquinas and Husserl is their general conception of – optimism regarding – the philosophical task as both Saint Thomas Aquinas and Husserl search for the logos and intelligible structure of all that is.[20] There is a prevailing conviction guiding their philosophical work that 'it is possible for our knowledge to uncover, step by step, more and more about this logos, if it takes the lead in conformity with the strictest intellectual honesty,' [(*Husserl's Phenomenology and the Philosophy of St Thomas Aquinas,* pp. 130-131/9) (Borden follows Baseheart's translation but will provide the page numbers from both English versions)].[21]

But it is seen that beyond this general conviction, however, the starting points of the two thinkers differ. Thus, Stein in her *Festschrift* article, and again in her comments at Juvisy and in *Potency and Act*, Stein questions

16 M.D. Joseph, *Thrown into The World: An Existentialist's Approach to Life*, 196.

17 Sarah Borden, *Edith Stein*, 92.

18 *Ibid.*

19 *Ibid.*

20 *Ibid.*

21 *Ibid.*

Husserl's general project.[22] Thus, Borden points out how Stein presents her critiques as *questions* that Husserl needs to answer, not as direct criticism and it is possible that he could respond to at least some of her critiques.[23] Husserl's phenomenology is method that begins with consciousness, analyzing how experience presents itself to us and moving to a greater understanding of essences, that is, the basic ways in which our experiences are structured.[24] Stein suggests, however, that once transcendental phenomenology as for example, Husserl's post-*Logical Investigations* variety, makes the subject or consciousness the philosophical starting point, there is little way to move beyond the subject.[25] Thus, Stein writes in *Husserl's Phenomenology and the Philosophy of St Thomas Aquinas*, p. 136/32;

> [t]he world which is constructed in the acts of the subject always remains a world for the subject. It could not succeed in this way – as was objected again and again to the founder of phenomenology by his circle of pupils – in winning back from the sphere of immanence, that objectivity from which he had proceeded and which it was his aim to safeguard: a truth and reality free from all subject-relativity. With the new interpretation, which was the result of the transcendental inquiry, existence, equated with manifesting itself to a consciousness, will never satisfy the truth seeking intellect.[26]

The Husserlian orientation of phenomenology, which is directed to consciousness, prevents it as she suggests that from achieving the objectivity that Husserl claims it is after. Thus, Borden says that putting the critique perhaps too simply: Stein fears that Husserl will not get the real world but merely the world as it appears to the individual.[27] As Borden points out that while Husserl was clearly not a relativist, Steins thinks that his method may end up in the very idealism that Husserl set out to fight.[28]

While in contrast to Husserl, in Thomas's writings, the realist thesis is never suspended. Thus, she writes in, *Husserl's Phenomenology and the Philosophy of St Thomas,* that St Thomas never advocates bracketing the existence of the world as he is not interested in analyzing possible worlds; rather, his philosophy searches for ' the most complete image of this world.'[29] Thus, as Borden points out that while both Thomas and Husserl search for

22 *Ibid.*

23 *Ibid.*

24 *Ibid.*

25 *Ibid.*

26 *Ibid.*, 92-93.

27 *Ibid.*, 93.

28 M.D. Joseph, *Thrown into The World: An Existentialist's Approach to Life*, 198.

29 Sarah Borden, *Edith Stein*, 93.

the essences and essential structures, Thomas does not look for them as the condition for possible worlds but rather as a way to investigate this world.[30]

In a similar fashion, phenomenology can only be oriented toward objective truth as a regulative ideal. Thus, Husserl cannot posit the existence of objective truth, or the whole truth, without compromising the transcendental method.[31] While for Thomas, the whole truth exists and is not merely an ideal regulating his search.[32] For this the whole truth is the world as divinely known and that because there is a divine knower, revelation is possible.[33] Therefore, Thomas argues that while natural reason can get us to truth, it is not the only path.[34] Thus, both Thomas and Husserl agree that the whole truth is that toward which natural reason leads.[35] But Thomas's claim that the whole truth is real rather than a regulative ideal broadens the possible sources by which we acquire truth.[36]

Further Borden points out;

> For Husserl, objective truth functions as the goal toward which reason leads. Thomas agrees that *ratio* or reason aims at truth: however, he separates *ratio* into natural and supernatural reason, a distinction Husserl does not make. In making this distinction, Thomas insists that there is a limit to our natural reason. We can and must use our faculties, and we can no more free ourselves from our intellectual faculties than we can escape our shadows. But our reason is not supernatural reason, and any attempt (such as Kant's for example) to find the limits of reason from within and by means of human reason itself are problematic. They lack, so it appears, an Archimedean point, outside ourselves from which to ask the question about our own limit. Because he begins in consciousness and limits himself to that one field, Husserl cannot provide a critique of the limits of reason. There is no point from which to conduct such a critique, whereas for Aquinas, such a principle exists in the thesis of God. (Aquinas does not place God first in the 'order of knowing'; however, God is first in the 'order of being.' Stein implies that this might offer a point from which to critique human reason, understanding the limits of reason through study of revelation).[37]

30 M.D. Joseph, *Thrown into The World: An Existentialist's Approach to Life*, 198-199.

31 Sarah Borden, *Edith Stein*, 93.

32 *Ibid.*

33 *Ibid.*

34 *Ibid.*

35 *Ibid.*

36 *Ibid.*

37 *Ibid.*, 93-94.

As one goes through the critique of Stein, one finds that Stein is more towards St Thomas than Husserl directly. Thus, the bulk of Stein's critique which as written for the 1929 *Festschrift*, and it does not appear again in *Finite and Eternal Being*. In Finite and Eternal Being her concern turns away from the evaluation of these two thinkers to the positive task of articulating her own metaphysical claim.[38] Thus, Borden says that some scholars have suggested that in presenting her own views, she abandoned phenomenology and turned instead to Thomism, motivated perhaps by 'docility to the magisterium.'[39] But her study of scholastic thought and adoption of Thomistic categories cannot be taken as a simple replacement of phenomenology with the more explicitly Christian philosophy of St Thomas.[40] And as Borden claims that while Stein found phenomenology lacking as she attempted to articulate the theoretical bases for Christian doctrine, she also frequently chose phenomenological approaches over scholastic ones.[41] Thus, rather reading her as phenomenologist turned Thomist, it is more accurate to see her as a thinker trained in phenomenological method who began seriously studying and integrating scholastic thought into her work, using it to supplement the shortcoming she found in phenomenology.[42] Thus, Borden points out "nonetheless, her vision of philosophical project differs significantly from her earlier view, and she argues in her later writings for a distinctively Christian philosophy."[43]

The Nature of Christian Philosophy

Stein devotes the final section of the opening chapter of her opus *Finite and Eternal Being* to a discussion of the nature of Christian philosophy.[44] As Borden says that for many, the idea of 'Christian philosophy' is contradictory.[45] For if it is Christian, it depends upon revealed truth, and if it is philosophy, it cannot appeal to any special revelation but only to what is accessible through natural experience and reason.[46] In like manner, even St Thomas Aquinas holds that when one moves from natural reason to belief, one also moves from philosophy

38 *Ibid.*, 94.

39 M.D. Joseph, *Thrown into The World: An Existentialist's Approach to Life*, 200.

40 Sarah Borden, *Edith Stein*, 94.

41 *Ibid.*

42 *Ibid.*

43 M.D. Joseph, *Thrown into The World: An Existentialist's Approach to Life*, 200.

44 Sarah Borden, *Edith Stein* 94.

45 *Ibid.*

46 *Ibid.*

to theology.[47] However, Stein says that there is a way to understand 'Christian philosophy,' which is both Christian and philosophy.[48]

In order to bring out the nature of Christian philosophy, Stein employs Jacques Maritain's[49] distinction between the nature and condition of philosophy.[50] The first, the nature refers to nature of philosophy *per se,* that is, as a discipline using only natural reason and experience.[51] Thus, according to their natures, philosophy and theology differ.[52] But philosophy is also a historical science, developing within time and under various historical conditions.[53] Thus, as Borden affirms that given a Christian context of development, one may have a Christian *condition* of philosophy.[54] Christianity would then offer categories and concepts which may be scrutinized philosophically.[55] Example for such Christian condition for philosophy would be medieval Europe, which developed under the undeniable influence of Christianity.[56] Thus, many of the philosophical tasks and questions arose in relation to and conjunction with theological concerns, and terms arising originally from revelation came to have philosophical significance.[57] For Stein the best examples for such are the notions of *creature and Creator.*[58] For example, one can compare for an understanding of this world as created with the interpretation that sees this world as simply here or, as Aristotle did, as eternal.[59] Thus, the doctrine of creation, coming from faith, may have been the occasion for looking at our experience anew; one can, however, look away from revelation as such and analyze the claims purely philosophically.[60]

47 *Ibid.*, 94-95.

48 *Ibid.*, 95.

49 *Ibid.*, 102,The French philosopher Jacques Maritain (1882-1973) is best known for his work on Thomas Aquinas and is considered a leader in the Thomistic revival. When Stein was in Juvisy, near Paris, for a conference in 1931, she met Maritain and his wife. The three of them became friends, and a number of letters between them have been published. See *Letters d'Edith Stein. Textes de Raïssa Maritain* (Papers of Jacques Maritain, 25, December 1992) and 'Vier Briefe Edith Steins and Jacques Maritain' in *Katholicsche Bildung*, 94 (1993): 581-4.

50 *Ibid.,* 95.

51 *Ibid.*

52 *Ibid.*

53 *Ibid.*

54 M.D. Joseph, *Thrown into The World: An Existentialist's Approach to Life*, 201.

55 Sarah Borden, *Edith Stein*, 95.

56 *Ibid.*

57 Sarah Borden, *Edith Stein*, 95.

58 *Ibid.*

59 *Ibid.*

60 *Ibid.*

Thus, Borden points out;

> Likewise, theological claims put before philosophy questions it otherwise may have been unlikely to consider, including the problem of two natures in one person and one nature and three persons. From these questions, philosophical concepts such as *person* versus *nature* were developed. Thus, revealed truths such as God's creation, *ex nihilo*, the Incarnation, and the Trinity provide ways to understand natural experience and can be a motive for making distinctions that might not otherwise have been made. In this, however, the philosopher must articulate and defend these concepts not only as a believer but also as a philosopher, and the conclusions of these analyses then become the philosophical 'goods' of all later philosophy.[61]

However, from the Middle Ages philosophy has changed significantly. For Thomas philosophy was a discipline covering much that a twentieth- or twenty-first-century person would consider part of another field.[62] In this regard, we now make more divisions among the tasks allotted to natural reason, distinguishing biology, physics, political science, psychology, and sociology.[63] Thus, Stein writes in her *Endliches und ewiges Sein,* pp. 19-20 that it is not the performance of any one of these sciences but, rather '[t]he clarification of the foundations of all the sciences.'[64] And as such, it aims to articulate the nature of *being* itself (regardless of whether it is the being of an ant or a cantaloupe), the construction of beings as such, and the essential division of beings according to species and genera.[65]

In order to clarify the foundations of all the sciences and articulating the nature of being itself, Stein has a further way to understand the relationship of philosophy and revealed truths.[66] Thus, she says that the philosopher wishes to remain faithful to one's goal of understanding being in itself and the fundamental structure of all being *and* the philosopher is convinced of the truths of faith, believing that there are certain truths accessible only through revelation, then such a thinker cannot limit his (her) work simply to what accessible through natural means, (*Endliches und ewiges Sein*, p. 23).[67]

As Borden points out further that if something is made visible to the thinker through a higher Light, then it is unreasonable to attempt to understand the ultimate structure of reality depending only on what is known through one's own light, particularly when convinced that it is indeed a meager light

61 *Ibid.*

62 *Ibid.*

63 *Ibid.*, 95-96.

64 *Ibid.*, 96.

65 *Ibid.*

66 *Ibid.*

67 Sarah Borden, *Edith Stein*, 96.

as what has been revealed is not simply incomprehensible.[68] It is intelligible in itself and intelligible to us in the measure to which we have been given light to see.[69] Thus, Stein claims that if a philosopher wishes to understand being in all its fullness and depth, then, he (she) cannot remain simply within more natural reason but, rather, must enrich one's philosophy with theology, without it, however, becoming theology.[70] Thus, Stein distinguishes the two tasks, claiming that:

> [i]f it is the task of theology to establish the facts of revelation as such and to work out their proper meaning and connection, then it is the task of philosophy to bring into harmony what it has worked out by its own means with that which it has borrowed from belief and theology," (*Endliches und ewiges Sein*, p. 24).[71]

According to Stein if philosophy stops before a question that it cannot answer with its own resources for example, the origin of the human soul, and uses belief as a source of knowledge, then it is no longer a pure and autonomous philosophy.[72] At the same time she does not, however, think that it is right to call it *theology.*[73] For this, she uses an analogy as she says that one can write a historical work about physics without writing a book that would be classified as 'natural science,' likewise, one can write a philosophical book including theology without thereby doing theology.[74] And as Borden points out that she adds, however, one qualification that there is clearly a disanalogy here insofar as the historian does not ask about the genuineness of the physicists' claims.[75] While the philosopher takes the claims of faith *as true.*[76] However, in both cases the researcher in the one field expands his (her) work by including the claims from another field and may only proceed in his (her) own work with those claims.[77] Thus, Stein holds that the philosopher must acknowledge the loan from faith and cannot claim that they are one's own, independent conclusions, but one may, nonetheless, think philosophically with claims from faith as she quotes Przywara, saying, 'philosophy is completed "*through* theology, not as theology," (*Endliches und ewiges Sein,* p. 26).[78] Here one can find the unity of

68 M.D. Joseph, *Thrown into The World: An Existentialist's Approach to Life, 202.*

69 Sarah Borden, *Edith Stein,* 96.

70 *Ibid.*

71 *Ibid.*

72 *Ibid.*

73 *Ibid.*

74 *Ibid.*, 96-97.

75 M.D. Joseph, *Thrown into The World: An Existentialist's Approach to Life*, 203.

76 Sarah Borden, *Edith Stein*, 97.

77 *Ibid.*

78 *Ibid.*

the Eastern and the Western thinking as the greater schools of Indian thought cannot be discussed separately from theology.

For Stein, Christian philosophy, thus understood, aims at a comprehensive understanding of being as a unity 'which natural reason *and* revelation make accessible to us,' (*Endliches und ewiges Sein*, p. 97).[79] Developing the stream of Stein's thought of the nature of Christian philosophy, Borden points out that the *summa* of the medieval thinkers have such a goal, and, for Stein, all human knowing by nature aims at such completion, to know all that can be known.[80] For example an unbeliever will take the truths of faith included in philosophy as 'hypotheses' rather 'theses,' as the believer will understand them.[81] However, she believes that if one proceeds honestly, acknowledging what is borrowed from faith, one may continue to do philosophy while also incorporating truths of faith.[82] Thus, if both the author and the reader are as free of prejudices as, in their philosophical conviction they should be, then neither will shrink from such an attempt.[83]

Defending the Existence of God

There is a philosophical honesty in Stein's argument as regards to the existence of God. However, it is not a *proof per se* for God's existence, but an argument pointing to one place where we can come to the concept of God and then arguing that it is reasonable to believe in existence of God[84] (divine). At the same time, she also acknowledges quite firmly that her 'argument' requires a leap of faith (like that of Kierkegaardian leap of faith) as she writes that a believer will easily jump the chasm, whereas the unbeliever will stop before it, (*Endliches und ewiges Sein*, p. 10).[85]

In the final section of Chapter 2 of *Finite and Eternal Being,* Stein begins by limiting herself to the phenomenological sphere namely the real of consciousness, where she says that we have an unreflexive self-awareness.[86] She holds that even if we are deceived about all else, we cannot be deceived about our own being though our being is temporal and always in the tension between being and non-being.[87] Thus, Stein affirms that our ego has a longing, however, 'not only for the endless continuation of its being, but also for the

79 *Ibid.*

80 *Ibid.*

81 *Ibid.*

82 *Ibid.*

83 *Ibid.*

84 *Ibid.*

85 *Ibid.*

86 *Ibid.*

87 *Ibid.*

full possession of being,' (*Endliches und ewiges Sein*, p. 54).[88] Thus," Borden points out;

> We come to the idea of the fullness of being. We ourselves do not have that being, but we taste it in our temporal existence and long for the full possession of being. In this idea of a *pure being*, that is, one that neither gains nor loses its being but always has the fullness of being, we have the idea of God. Thus, we can get the idea of an eternal being from the temporal passage of experiences, leading us to the idea of something without such becoming and passing away, but which *is* fully.[89]

In a similar manner, Stein approaches the same argument from a slightly different angle, as she says that we live in a 'now' suspended between what is already and what is not-yet, yet we *are* in each moment.[90] And in any moment, we have something of the fullness of being, albeit only momentarily.[91] Thus, in this momentary fullness, we find an image of the eternal, albeit a very weak and distant image, and the conscious I is, therefore, (very distantly) analogous to the Eternal.[92]

It has been often remarked by many of contemporary philosophers that belief in God is not only incapable of proof but also unreasonable.[93] Stein addresses this point in a number of places, clearly concerned about this criticism of faith.[94] Thus, she challenges this claim by drawing an analogy between our trust in a support for our being and a child's trust in her mother.[95] On the other hand, Martin Heidegger in his *Being and Time,* describes *angst* as the basic human emotion. According to him angst, a fear of nothingness, of death, of ceasing to be, and the avoidance of angst is an avoidance of an authentic mode of being (existence).[96]

In contrast, Stein writes in *Endliches und ewiges Sein,* p. 56, '[a]angst is certainly not ordinary the ruling life feeling.'[97] According to Stein it is only in cases of illness is angst such a foundational feeling.[98] Whereas our ordinary experience is one of confidence and a great security about our own being even when we can hide our own finitude from ourselves, our security in being is

88 *Ibid.*, 97-98.

89 *Ibid.,* 98.

90 *Ibid.*

91 *Ibid.*

92 *Ibid.*

93 M.D. Joseph, *Thrown into The World: An Existentialist's Approach to Life*, 205.

94 Sarah Borden, *Edith Stein*, 102.

95 *Ibid.,*98.

96 *Ibid.*

97 *Ibid.*

98 *Ibid.*

not merely the result of self-deception just as a child is not *unreasonable* in trusting that her mother will not drop her.[99] So too our confidence in our own being is not an unreasonable assumption.[100] For Stein, it is truth that death will come, but our lives to be authentic we need not be ordered by an angst in the face of our own inability to maintain ourselves in being.[101]

Stein continues saying that this appropriate confidence, however, is analogues to the child's confidence in its mother in a further respect that the child is secure is that she (he) has a strong arm upholding her; so too do we have a support and ground for our being as we are not the source of our being (existence), but the overwhelming fact of our confidence suggests that there is such a support.[102] In order to bring forward the ground of our being, Stein puts forward two paths by which people understand that support and ground to be the Eternal Being viz., the way of faith and the way of reason, using proofs for God's existence.[103]

As Borden points out that in the previous arguments, Stein simply argued that there are sources within consciousness and our immediate experience from, which to gain the *idea* of God.[104] In the final section Chapter 2, Stein develops a stronger argument for God's existence using Aquinas' 'third way,' (as he states in his *Summa theologica* 1, q. 2, art. 3).[105] Thus, she argues that we – and all finite things (beings) are contingent.[106] And therefore must receive our being and existence from where else, and making this argument she points both to our (existential) need to be placed in existence and to be maintained in existence.[107] Clearly, the I is not identical with the Eternal Being as there are holes in our knowledge, mysteries regarding where we come from and where we are going as we are finite beings.[108] As Borden points out that Stein quotes Heidegger, claiming that we find ourselves thrown into being,[109] which is basically the common human experience as humans.

Thus, Stein writes in *Endliches und ewiges Sein,* p. 53 that we are not the origin of our own being and thus must receive it (as thrown into the world from somewhere at some time). But such a 'reception of being independent of

99 *Ibid.*

100 *Ibid.*

101 *Ibid.*

102 *Ibid.*

103 *Ibid.*, 98-99.

104 *Ibid.*, 98.

105 *Ibid.,* 99&102.

106 *Ibid.,* 99.

107 *Ibid.*

108 *Ibid.*

109 *Ibid.*

an eternal being is unthinkable' because there is nothing outside of an eternal being that possesses its own being.[110] Stein says that it could be that my flowing being has a ground in something finite - the finite, however, cannot be the final support and ground.[111] But we are more confident about our continuance in being than such a limited support suggests that the security of being, that felt in my flowing being points to an *immediate* anchoring in the final support and ground of my being (notwithstanding the possible mediating supports), (*Endliches und ewiges Sein*, p. 58).[112] As Borden points out that though this feeling is a dark feeling and hardly counts as *knowledge*.[113] But it does suggest strongly that there is something, which is the ground of our being as humans more than finite supports.[114]

Thus, as Borden affirms that as regards to Stein's argument for the existence of God is given with a much more tentative note than most traditional arguments.[115] Nonetheless, it has been a central theme in all her philosophical works, as a believing philosopher should use all sources of truth, not only imply accessible to natural reason, in attempting to understand being – given that she makes clear when she is using truths of revelation.[116] It is in this sense that Stein uses truths of revelation. Thus, it could be pointed out that Steins' philosophy of God is an approach rather than a proof for a conclusion as her phenomenology, which leads to a self realization of the finite as that of an Eternal Being.[117]

Trinitarian Aspects of Being

One of the significant Christian elements that Stein has developed in *Finite and Eternal Being,* is the doctrine of the Trinity, which is one of the central themes of Christian belief and faith.[118] Thus, she asks;

> [i]f the Creator is the archetype of creation, should we then not find in creation a reflection (even if still a distant one) of the three-in-oneness of Original Being? And should not a deeper understanding of finite being be gained from that? (*Endliches und ewiges Sein*, p. 328).[119]

110 *Ibid.*

111 *Ibid.*

112 *Ibid.*

113 M.D. Joseph, *Thrown into The World: An Existentialist's Approach to Life*, 207..

114 Sarah Borden, *Edith Stein*, 99.

115 M.D. Joseph, *Thrown into The World: An Existentialist's Approach to Life*, 207.

116 Sarah Borden, Edith Stein, 99.

117 M.D. Joseph, *Thrown into The World: An Existentialist's Approach to Life*, 207.

118 Sarah Borden, *Edith Stein,* 99.

119 *Ibid.*

In order to bring out the Trinitarian nature being, Stein dedicates Chapter 7 of her *Finite and Eternal Being* as she dedicates to the image of the Trinity in creation and she claims that all of creation has the mark of the Trinitarian God. [120] Thus, for example, according to her human beings as unities of body, soul, and spirit; while angels as unities of spiritual matter, essence, a carrier; and being itself as divided into three types.[121] Likewise, according to Stein the notion of spirit as a going-out-of-itself, where we can see a reflection of the Trinity.[122] Thus, Stein writes; "God as the 'I am' is also an 'I give myself wholly to a You,' am one with a You,' and therefore a 'We are' (*Endliches und ewiges Sein,* p. 324)."[123] As Borden points out that the interior life of the Trinity is love and self-surrender, and Stein similarly claims that at the root of all creation is communion and community.[124]

Further, Borden claims;

> Stein's vision of being is thus deeply Trinitarian and deeply communal, and the final Chapter of *Finite and Eternal Being* culminates with a discussion of our unity in the Body of Christ. (The chapter is titled, 'The Meaning and Foundation of Being Individual,' yet her discussion of being individual ends in a description of the ways in which we are fundamentally communal). Being a member of the human race is the foundation for being a member of the Mystical Body of Christ, although recognizing that membership requires maturity and growth. We begin by understanding ourselves as members of our families, of small communities, and of a state, seeing other communities as foreign and even dangerous. Only by recognizing our membership in humanity as a whole do we come to see no other person as foreign; this insight, further, 'binds us to human beings of all times and heavenly realms, despite all differences,' and enriches us through contact with differently formed humanity (*Endliches und ewiges Sein,* p. 446).[125]

According to her such claim regarding our fundamental unity is foundational for making sense of the Christian doctrines of the Fall, the Incarnation, and Grace as (the Christian) salvation history is the history of humanity, and our participation in humanity is what enables it to become our personal story.[126] Thus, in summarizing Stein's view regards to the Trinitarian

---

120 *Ibid.,* 100.

121 *Ibid.*

122 *Ibid.*

123 *Ibid.*

124 M.D. Joseph, *Thrown into The World: An Existentialist's Approach to Life*, 2008.

125 *Ibid.*

126 Sarah Borden, *Edith Stein*, 100.

aspects of being, Regina van den Berg points out as she writes in her *Community in the Thought of Edith Stein,* p. 272;[127]

> [w]ere it not for the presupposition that all humanity is one, and that man (humans) belongs by nature to the community of humanity, then original sin, whereby in one man, all have sinned, would be entirely unintelligible. Adam acted *as* a member of humanity; therefore, his act affects all the members.[128]

In similar fashion Borden points out;

> Likewise, if all were not one, it would make no sense for *one* man's act to save humanity. Christ participated in humanity and, only thus, could save humanity. Further, His grace 'radiates out to the members because they are united already *from nature* with the Head and are capable – as spiritual beings and in virtue of their free self-opening – to take within themselves His divine life' (*Endliches und ewiges Sein*, p. 47). All human beings are united from nature, Stein claims, and we may be further united, through grace, in the Mystical Body of Christ. This Body what makes possible the Christian story as a series of historical events that are relevant for all human beings, regardless of how remote their lives may seem to be from the original parents or the Jewish carpenter.[129]

Conclusion

From the above passages it can be said that Stein explicitly defends a notion of Christian philosophy in incorporating both natural reason and revelation, although critical of Husserl's transcendental philosophy, she develops her own arguments for (the defense of) the existence of God even though a non-traditional understanding of such an argument beginning with the phenomenological starting point, viz., the immediate experience of our own consciousness.[130] Thus, Borden points out that Stein's project is, as she somewhat sheepishly admits in the Foreword to her opus, an unabashedly comprehensive one, attempting to understand all of being with the help of whatever truth is available. Thus, she draws from phenomenology and contemporary philosophy, the medieval tradition, revelation, and, as her discussions of matter in Chapter 4 of *Finite and Eternal Being* reveal, even from the latest science. Stein does not quote Justin Martyr's famous saying, but her work reveals a resounding affirmation that 'all truth is God's truth,' something Prof Kurien Kunnumpuam whole-heartedly agree![131]

---

127 *Ibid.*, 102.

128 *Ibid.*, 100.

129 *Ibid.*, 99-101.

130 M.D. Joseph, *Thrown into The World: An Existentialist's Approach to Life*, 209.

131 *Ibid.*

Bibliography

Baba, Dan, S. J. "Edith Stein." *In Christo30, no.1* (January 1992): 46-48. Borden, Sarah. *Edith Stein.* Continuum, London: British Library Cataloguing-in-Publication Data, 2003.

Joseph, M.D. *Thrown into The World: An Existentialist's Approach to Life.* India, Guwahati: EBH, 2016.

Paul, John II. *Rise, Let us Be On Our Way.* London: Jonathan Cape, 2004.

Puthenpurackal, Johnson J. "The Irreconcilability of Thomism and Phenomenology: A Thinking beyond Edith Stein." *Living Word93, no. 5* (October 1987): 325-338.

"Teresa Benedict of the Cross Edith Stein," available from http://www.vatican.va/news_services/liturgy/saints/ns_lit_doc_19981011_edith_stein_en.html (accessed February 5, 2015.

26

Fostering Values and Dignity in a Globalizing World

Thomas Menamparampil SDB, DD
Archbishop (Emeritus) of Guwahati, Assam

Abstract: *How do we face the globalised world? How can we trace values in this complex world? Can we move away from the market-driven world? What is the role of an enlightened person in today's context? How can intellectuals foster a sense of dialogue? How do we promote hope in our conflicting world? What can we do to foster peace and prosperity among us? These are some of the issues the author takes up in this article, written in honour of Prof Kurien Kunnumpuram, who has been a person embracing everyone and everything. In troubled times like ours, we need new motivators to urge society on. It is for us to develop motivation for carrying a hope-filled message to the whole world. "Let your aims be common, and your hearts be of one accord, and all of you of one mind, so you may live well together" Then we can consider the family of humankind as one.*

Keywords: *Freedom, Responsibility, Respect, One Family.*

How do we face the globalised world? How can we trace values in this complex world? Can we move away from the market-driven world? What is the role of an enlightened person in today's context? How can intellectuals foster a sense of dialogue? How do we promote hope in our conflicting world? What can we do to foster peace and prosperity among us? These are some of the issues that I take up in this article, written in honour of Prof Kurien Kunnumpuram, who has been a person who embraces everyone and everything. Like him, we need to foster an inclusive culture of freedom, responsibility and respect.

Pressed hard by the raw realities of a globalizing society, people in the Developing World, especially those who belong to humbler and weaker communities, are beginning ask questions. Some become apologetic about their cultures and hesitant about the cultural assumptions of their own community, particularly when they do not seem to help them in coping with the problems in a fast-changing world. To them, their own traditional values appear outdated. They stand for outright rejection of the old in an eager desire to profit by what is new.

Others, in response, emerge as proud asserters of their cultural identity and inherited traditions. They are determined to offer fierce resistance to anything unfamiliar and alien. Some among them do not hesitate to go to exaggerations and enjoy making a display of their attachment to their traditions, even to what has become irrelevant, obsolete and unhelpful.

While the former forget the importance of historical and cultural continuity, the latter show no confidence in the dynamic element at the heart of their own culture that knows how to adapt to changing situations without compromising the core values of their collective identity and inner genius.

The Role of Enlightened Persons

These are contexts which invite enlightened persons to study changing trends and new ideas with an open mind and self-confidence in order to draw profit from whatever is good. They should, at the same time, deepen their understanding of their own heritage and cultural values in order to re-interpret them to the other members of their community and make them respond to contemporary needs.

It is when diverse streams of thought converge, they fertilise each other, and a 'new world of ideas' comes into existence, holding out hope for the coming generations. The convergence of thought and the complementary nature of human aspirations invite us to affirm our belongingness together.

Reflection on the Values of One's Own Culture is in View of Dialogue and Mutual Sharing

A reflection on the values of one's own culture in the Developing World is not meant to be chauvinistic self-assertion of emerging nations, nor a claim to superiority. It is merely a humble search for a community's core identity and an expression of an intense desire to re-interpret its cultural assets to respond to the needs of the times and share the resulting insights within the community and among others who are interested. Some of these insights may prove to be a lamp on humanity's path to the future.

Similarly, the affirmation of Asian or African values is not intended to be a defence of various forms of cultural nationalism or national fundamentalism that are arising in some places on these continents. Nor is it an underestimation of modern concepts like human rights, the rule of law, accountability, democracy, participation, political-economic-gender equality, the dignity of the individual. What these modern concepts stand for were present in diverse formulations in diverse cultures in different periods of history. After all, all human values have their roots in identical human nature.

What we would like to emphasize is that today, the various incarnations of these values must be brought to dialogue with each other with mutual respect so that our common destinies can be shaped purposefully. I wish that this International Conference helps toward that end.

The Danger that Values Decline and Fall in a Market-driven Society

Of course, in a market-driven society, the values that are esteemed most are efficiency, productivity, speed, marketability, management and such others. The traditional Indian emphasis on self-search, the Chinese on self-cultivation, or the African on community solidarity, is not a denial of the importance of practical values in a world where Economy has assumed immense importance. Asian or African values do not stand on the way to the rationalization of the Economy, but they insist that the Economy be also human and humane.

Christopher Dawson said decades ago that society is seriously impoverished if it is "emptied of all the values that are not explicable in economic terms" (Dawson 26). It is good for us to be aware of what disasters await human society when a value-free market is allowed to dominate human lives.

When people are evaluated only in market terms, i.e., when human beings are classified merely as 'labour' or evaluated solely in reference to the 'market', their status sinks. In other words, when their worth is calculated only in terms of their use to the economy, they become less than human beings and bearers of dignity. And yet, the tragedy today is that entire nations are opting for this form of self-abasement by making economic growth their sole goal.

Dangers When Profit-making Becomes the Sole Goal of a Society

When mighty enterprises like Big Corporations or Government Departments make profit-making as their sole ethical norm, they become less and less accountable to anybody. Today's top managers have the power to set their own remuneration, with no upper limit (Piketty 24). They can amass enormous sums by bringing business and political power to join hands together towards that end. They manipulate mass media, impose uniform ways of thinking and acting on society, monopolise knowledge, subject people to consumeristic habits, imprison them in artificial environments and even isolate them from natural settings. They flaunt their wealth, humiliating the poor whom they see as getting poorer and poorer. Those who fall victims to their mesmerising and psychologically numbing influence, lose their concern for society, attitude compassion, and commitment to solidarity; they lose sight of ecological responsibilities and grow in their greed for wealth (Hathaway xvii), often acquired unethically.

Adam Smith had argued that the economic dynamism stimulated in society by the self-interest of individuals can benefit the entire society, even when not intended. However, Nobel Laureate Liu Xiabao points out that to make the self-interest of the majority purposeful, we need a minority of moral giants who can make 'selfless sacrifice'. "The appearance of a single martyr can fundamentally turn the spirit of a nation and strengthen its moral fibre." Liu was referring to Mahatma Gandhi. "Gandhi was such a figure," he said (Guha 39).

Corrupt Practices Have Risen to the World Stage

The tragedy in our times is that corrupt practices have risen to the world stage. No one can plead to be totally innocent. That is why all must join hands together to wipe out this plague from society. Corruption is not only about the wrong use of money, but also about the wrong use of power. It is not only about taking bribe in government offices, but also about various forms of manipulation and blackmailing, political arm-twisting, pushing a particular party's or ethnic group's interests through underhand ways, unfairness of dominant classes and castes to weaker sections, the imperceptible manner of bulldozing or marginalizing legitimate claims, silencing the voices of the weaker communities, physical elimination of political opponents or commercial competitors, interfering with election processes, using 'strong men' for vacating land or realizing bills, fixing matches, selling drugs. Corruption also has reference to hidden transactions, unpaid salaries, underpaid employees, unfair pressure.

The globalized world has become a hiding place for corrupt business. The global market provides distances, creates anonymity, gives opportunities for dishonest deals, enables one to take advantage of the weak, evade laws, and make an unfair proportion of profit. Let us make a distinction: 1. if greater profits are made through harder work, greater efficiency, more effective customer service or through path-breaking innovation, it is undoubtedly legitimate. 2. But if it is made by underpaying the worker, evading taxes, ignoring safety laws, producing counterfeits, ruining the environment, abusing customer confidence, falsifying accounts or labour figures, double book-keeping, deceptive advertisements, industrial espionage, it is undoubtedly criminal.

Investigative journalism has often highlighted specific cases of dishonesty and unfairness. But media men also can bend to mammon, and sell their services for money: cooking up stories to defame or defend a party leader, distorting facts to press an argument, presenting allegations as proven truth for minor favours. Plagiarizing, pirating cassettes, and violating intellectual property rights are very common in our days. Engineers in government service get opportunities to embezzle huge amounts. Doctors are accused of patronizing particular pharmaceutical companies or diagnostic centres, and even dealing in human organs. When citizens are not alert, the mechanisms of accountability and sanction are not activated, and structures of enforcement lie idle. Society remains silent. You and I give tacit approval.

Do Our Ancestors Have a Message in Such Contexts?

Allow me to cite certain Asian sources that can inspire us in such a situation, e.g., a message from Buddha's teachings. The economy had grown brisk in his part of India in those days: credit, debt, interest and market—everything was in full function. There were rich people going bankrupt and poor people gathering a fortune, honestly and in other ways. A warning against corruption was timely. A passage from early Buddhist poetry says, "Let no one deceive anyone else, nor despise anyone anywhere. May no one wish harm to another in anger or ill-will" (Samyutta Nikaya 146-8).

Similarly, a Chinese Taoist teaching says, "When rulers live in splendour and speculators prosper, while farmers lose their land and the granaries are emptied; when governments spend money on ostentation and weapons; when the upper class is extravagant and irresponsible, indulging themselves and possessing more than they can use, while the poor have nowhere to turn. All this is robbery and chaos. It is not in keeping with the *Tao*" (Tao TeChing 53). Are we in such an age? At another place, the Tao Te Ching says, "The sage does not accumulate. The more he does for the people, the more he saves. The more he gives to people, the more he has" (Tao TeChing 81).

In the Chinese Confucian tradition, a gentleman is concerned with what is right; the inferior man with profit, with material welfare. Mencius too looked down on the profit motive. Science, technology, and efficient economy have given us good things, but they must be regulated by the norms of wisdom contained in our cultural traditions. Truly, "A gentleman takes as much trouble to discover what is right as lesser men take to discover what will pay" (Tao TeChing 81).

In the West, the first generations of capitalists were models of self-regulation. Their aim was to earn, build up capital, invest, and not to overspend. In fact, Weber and Keynes refer to high accumulation and low consumption (Sachs 150). Today's capitalists, on the contrary, tend to profligacy, an eagerness to display: they believe in lavish parties, weddings, anniversaries, election victories, particularly in India. Concentration on fortune-hunting has thrown up a class of super-rich and dumped the weak in dire poverty (Sachs 152).

Imbalance in Economy

An economy organized on a vast scale, whether controlled by the Government or by Corporations, tend not to respect persons, human concerns, families, communities, values, natural environment. Gigantism always has its victims. No wonder Henri Bergson thought that man was designed for very small societies. We are not, of course, opposed to the bigness of things, but are anxious that its weaknesses should be recognized. Correctives should be sought. There is evidently some imbalance when "Companies are competing against countries--not just other companies"(Charan 7).

The manner in which some companies do that looks more like an expression of the aggressive and destructive streak in human nature than of its constructive instincts. They ignore the inner worth of human beings; underestimate persons, communities, cultures, nature's gifts to humanity, ethical and aesthetic traditions. After having invaded and damaged millions of human lives and ruined the environment, when things go wrong, the only solution that profit-makers can propose are drugs, tranquillizers, sedatives, stimulants, and antidepressants (Fleischcker 16); not silence, reflection, self-criticism or self-improvement, as our Asian sages would have suggested.

When Giants Fail, Poor People are Asked to Help

Meantime consumer goods are in abundance, and most people are happy. They do not know what they are missing, how they are losing values that have taken shape over centuries, and what their fate ultimately will be. Gradually speculators and self-interested fortune-hunters take over the economy. And then, of course, there comes the collapse. If a collapse had not taken place, one would not believe that it was possible. But it has taken place: in Europe (1990s), Asia (1997-98), Brazil (1998-99), Argentina (2001), even in the US (2008-09) (Fukuyama 6). The reasons for these economic collapses are not hard to find: narrow self-interest and irresponsibility.

And when, during periods of recession, corporations and banks collapse and are gasping for breath, it is the taxpayer's (the average man's) money that is being used to bail them out. It is as though the poor are rushing to the rescue of the rich. This may sound paradoxical, but this is what is actually happening.

It is similar to the paradox about International aid that has not reduced inequality or brought the needed assistance to the poor. International aid so often turned out to be the poor in rich countries coming to the aid of the rich in poor countries, and then the poor in poor countries being compelled to pay back the debt to the rich in rich countries. Thus, even plans formulated with good intentions go wrong in unforeseen ways.

Postcolonial Anxieties

There was a time when the main Afro-Asian anxiety was about winning freedom. Once freedom was won, other problems began to manifest themselves. Newly independent nations had to deal with outdated economic systems and fiscal policies, shortage of capital, land reforms, and codification of law. Many of them had to build up for the first time political institutions like parliaments, electoral commissions and parties; judiciary; national consciousness in the face of strong ethnic, linguistic and regional loyalties. They had to make primary education and health care access; maintain roads and railways; equip the army, bureaucracy; handle chronic hunger, illiteracy, unemployment, red tape, corruption and religious fanaticism. The task was not easy for newly born nations nor their leaders inexperienced in administration. It is no use finding fault with the leaders of that era. They were trying to achieve what more advanced countries had done over the centuries.

They had other worries as well. The right sort of political climate had to be created that would favour democratic participation and healthy collaboration. The concept of nation-state developed at the Treaty of Westphalia in 1648, with the more or less homogenised citizenry, did not suit many of the multi-ethnic, multi-cultural, multi-religious nations of Asia or Africa. Ethnic minorities thought their interests would be neglected by the dominant majority. It is no surprise that discontented ethnic groups went in for secessionist wars wanting to set up independent nations. Diverse communities began fighting among themselves, going at times to the point of violence. Neighbouring countries claimed portions of each others' territories which they felt belonged to them in some earlier period history. And again, during the Cold War period, most nations were dragged into ideological polarisations, and ideology-led groups clashed within nations.

After the '80s, injustice was no more perceived along class-lines alone; it was more understood in terms of the neglect of weaker groups: women, lower castes, regional minorities, ethnic or linguistic minorities, migrants, poor indebted nations, victims of globalization and of new forms of poverty, of human rights violations, damaged environment, wounded cultures, cultural rootlessness, and communal violence. Many uncertainties also remained as to how to deal with social problems like alcoholism, drug abuse, out of wedlock pregnancies, and sexually transmitted diseases. Speaking of values, new questions came up like cell research, euthanasia, death penalty. Traditional value-systems failed to adapt to new problems and to respond to the new needs. We have then a long way to go. But we can do it together.

Erosion of Cultures and Family Values

The mobility of job-seekers as a result of rapid commercial and industrial growth has led to the enfeebling of social bonds which used to be nourished by the extended family, tribal loyalties, and neighbourhood communities. At the production centres, workers can be reduced to status of production-machines: culture-less, personality-less, individuality-less, humanity-less, soulless. This evidently stands for a disaster.

In rural areas, whence majority of the workers come, social life has been so transformed as to cause the erosion of cultures where values are generated. This in turn leads to the breakup of families, especially when members live apart for reasons of work, and weakening of communities within which ethical convictions are handed down. This has reduced the effectiveness of the traditional patterns of social formation and the handing on of cultural traditions, social norms, and religious convictions from one generation to the next. This leads further to the weakening of the codes of moral behaviour, and even more of the handing on of ancestral values and spiritual motivations.

Difficulties in Introducing Democracy

When younger nations seek to introduce modern type of democracy, they are likely to meet with some difficulties, particularly if similar institutions were not part of their older heritage. We may look at a few examples. When Australia gave independence to the Solomon Islandsin the 1970s, Westminster style of government was triumphantly introduced. But the entire system was so new to the cultural world of the local communities that it was difficult to get it functioning meaningfully. A political system that had developed in the western world through the efforts of centuries was being thrust upon the Pacific islands where the leaders were chosen for their ability to grant favours, not for the quality of their ideology or value of their political programmes. Nor was it easy to rouse national feeling or enthusiasm for political parties where social relations were largely confined to their own kinsfolk, clans and related ethnic groups. The chaos that followed was understandable.

Even Eastern Europe struggled hard with the processes of the democratization of their nations after the fall of the Berlin Wall. Total success is still far ahead. In Latin America, democracy gained considerable ground after the 1970s, but even on that continent, there is a reversion of late. Cases of non-functioning democracies or faulty democracies are in large number. Thus, countries like Russia, Venezuela, and Iran reportedly manipulate elections, close down independent press, control opposition activities, thus weakening checks and balances that are typical of modern democracy, and causing the erosion of the rule of law. Some of the successor states to USSR in Asia have developed an uncertain position: neither authoritarian nor meaningfully democratic. They belong to a grey zone (Fukuyama 2011:4).

There are again other nations that are democratic but are not able to deliver the basic services people expect. We may look at some interesting cases. In Ukraine, the ruler ousted in the Orange Revolution was called back and re-elected when his democratic opponent was found incompetent. Thus, governance-failure plagues many of the so-called democratic countries, perpetuating gross inequality. In Latin America again, there are countries like Venezuela, where minority ethnic communities feel excluded and where class hierarchy represent racial and ethnic divides. Inability to deal with social and economic problems undermines the legitimacy of democracy (Fukuyama 2011:5). Fukuyama alleges that Indian democracy is weakened by criminal politicians, fractious groups, extreme inequality, corruption and chaos. It is true, China is efficient and gets its plans executed without delay and with amazing efficiency, but the government is undemocratic.

Thus the ailments of functioning democracies are many: authoritarianism (Russia), corruption (India), failed-states status (many countries in the developing world); entrenched interest groups (United States) (Fukuyama 2011:10). No one is totally free. Then, there is no use to finding fault with only Afghanistan, Iraq, Syria or other countries in the developing world. All need to be understood, encouraged and helped. If the path to democracy had been hard for those countries that have long been on the road, it would mean the same for others. Nation-building is laborious and costly, and much effort has to be put into political institution-building. There are many things that can help: expanded access to education, intelligent use of information technology, the spread of ideas, especially on the benefits of democratic values and their relationship with the modern economy. Unfortunately, for all these efforts, there are places where extreme poverty has led to the formation of gangs, narcotrafficking, sense of insecurity, and organized criminality...and where violence prevails.

Unfortunately, Violence has Become the General Way of Protest

When values fail to exert moral authority in society, the force comes to play a greater role in obtaining social compliance, whether imposed by the Administration or inflicted on each other by fellow-citizens. Force used in excess takes the form of violence. Violence, once unsheathed, cuts in all directions. For example, if it was used for the struggle for freedom, it remains on for a long time in various shapes to harass societies even after independence.

Similarly, there is the danger that communities that feel marginalized along class, caste, ethnic, cultural, regional or religious lines, grow convinced that their voice would have persuasive power only if it is accompanied by a show of strength, not excluding violence. With this sort of conviction, fear of imposed unreasonableness can catch up with society at various levels and influence various sections.

A response to it is likely to be equally unreasonable. After all, all radical ideologies in Africa or Asia in recent history were a response to intense pressure under which a people/nation laboured. The more radical the pressure, the more radical the response. One exaggeration invites another. In such an atmosphere, even traditionally peaceful societies lose confidence in the peaceful styles taught by their wise ancestors. If a sense of balance and moderation is ignored and values are forgotten, and if strong self-assertion becomes the norm across all emerging nations, tensions are bound to arise, with many uncertainties for our common future.

There is also an eagerness in all emerging nations to catch up with the developed world. Impatience for quick achievement runs the risk of surrendering to persons who over-claim power, which in turn can lead to power-struggle and initiate a cycle of violence. Similarly, in the economic field, growing anger against mounting inequality can threaten the future of our societies.

Meantime natural resources are being over-tapped, the environment is in peril, and stiff competition rises to merciless heights.

Reflection on Values Has Become Absolutely Necessary Lest We Perish

Sayyid Qutb said years ago in *Milestones* “Humanity is standing today at the brink of an abyss...because humanity is bankrupt in the realm of ‘values’, those values which foster true human progress and development” (Mishra 270). Already in 1916, Yan Fu had called for a return to Asian values in the face of gross injustices he witnessed, “How different are the principles of Confucius and Mencius, as broad and deep as Heaven and Earth, designed to benefit all men everywhere” (Creel 237). Sun Yat-sen wrote in 1924; the oriental civilization is one of Right not Might (Mishra 214).

These are lessons that many Africans and Asians forget today. Ultimately we may have to learn some of our own teachings from others. In 1896, Liang Qichao pointed out, Mencius had taught that the rulers must be close to the people; now, he said, it is from the democratic West that we have to learn this lesson today so that we may be truly ourselves (Mishra 144). One thing is certain: we all have to learn from each other.

Ancient Values Will Have to be Reinterpreted for Our Times in Our Own Cultural Contexts and Given a Dynamic and Relevant Meaning

Society keeps changing. New situations call for new responses. In one period of Jewish history, they realized that they should express their relationship with the divine not merely by offering sacrifices of rams, goats, and oils, but acting justly, mercifully and remaining humble (Micah 6:7-8). There was a radical change of perception, new importance being given to justice, which grows even stronger in the other Israelite prophets.

Mahatma Gandhi reinterpreted the ancient concept of *Ahimsa* (non-violence) to suit a new need when he courageously brought it to the political field. He gave the word new connotations never perceived before. Non-violence was, for him, not mere passivity or weakness, or a sign of helplessness. On the contrary, it had a transformative quality, with immense power to change a situation, for example, by confronting an unjust law with active civil disobedience. By reinterpreting the concept of *Ahimsa* in this way, Gandhi universalized the message, making it meaningful to everyone in a similar situation anywhere in the world. Martin Luther King, Mandela, others felt inspired by Gandhi while pressing for their rights.

Similarly, Gandhi gave to the Indian concept of renunciation a dynamic content, linking it with intense political and socially beneficial activity and making it sturdy, and giving it a spiritual purpose. It was not arbitrary instrumentalization of an idea but in keeping with the Indian inclination of making concepts and norms context-sensitive.

And again, Gandhi introduced the concept of "strong persuasion" by appealing to the conscience of the opponent in respectful protest, in a non-violent and courteous manner of expressing non-acceptance. Similarly, his understanding of God as Truth made him inclusive, tolerant, and open. He was open to new ideas from anywhere in the world. However, he insisted on the 'language of continuity' between his society's past and future (*Guha 123*).

Self-Search, Self-discipline and Self-Enhancement Are for Social Good

The Muslim jurist-mystic Ayn al-Qudat al-Hamadhani (d. 1131) defined ethics as the 'opinion of the heart'. Mahatma Gandhi had a similar expression, the 'inner voice'. Cultivating this inner voice is calculated to remove the influence of all negativities like avarice, anger, resentment, self-seeking, in order to be able to create a serene atmosphere with the rest of the world. It generates a new set of attitudes and spiritual values like self-control, benevolence, patience, peace, non-injury, truth, endurance and tranquillity. Nearly all Asian traditions give importance to the development of the inner self through inner striving and discipline for creating an ethical climate in society.

Interestingly, Paul Ricoeur's understanding of ethics is something similar: he sees ethics springing from our desires, needs and strivings towards self-actualization (Schweiker 548). All these efforts are then calculated to self-actualization. But this attention to the personal self is for social benefit. Patanjali says a person who has become master of his/her self, hears "the cries of all creatures", offers friendship, compassion, joy, impartiality, and sensitivity to others.

Historically, values evolved in different cultures in different ways to suit the needs of individual societies. The difference often is in the emphasis. Personal effort can never be neglected. "Be yourself your own lamp and your own refuge," says Mahaparinibbana Suttanta (Chandra 170). For, you can set yourself right with sincere effort. Even accumulated evil in one's heart can be transformed and set right by a moment's action of the mind. According to the Upanishads, *Moksha*, unfettered condition, comes from withdrawal and reflection on the deeper nature of things. "Sitting in forgetfulness" (meditation) is considered most helpful for attaining the highest perfection and purity of oneself, *Nirvana* (Chandra 153). The Christian concept of 'contemplation' is not very different.

The Indian practice of cultivating Mindfulness can help one to reinterpret values in each context; for example, to decide how to combine justice with mercy, and wisdom with compassion. Asian sages always urged a holistic approach to ethical problems basing on the wisdom of doctrinal texts, philosophical principles, and also lived experiences. Hardened conceptual tools may not always help. In Buddhism, there are the Four noble truths to guide one in living a balanced and moderate life.Secular scholars would like to seek assistance from practical reason and the findings of human sciences as well.

Traditional values must be brought to social contexts, e.g. corruption in offices, adulteration of goods in commerce, student indiscipline in universities, abuse of women in homes, exploitation of the weak in slums, provocation of an opponent in the political scenario. This is what makes Gurucharan Das emphasise the need for education in citizenship and 'public *Dharma*' (Das 148), which would mean the ethic of uprightness in the public sphere.

Collective Self-Awareness, Healing of Collective Memories

As there are things to be set right in the inner consciousness of a person, there are wounds to be healed in the collective self-consciousness of a community, an ethnic group, a language group, a religious group, a society, a nation, a civilization. It is in this mighty undertaking that we keep failing at the global level and in individual contexts right round the world. Generally, we study the immediate causes of tensions and conflicts and suggest remedies. Our social analyses have remained at a superficial level and often ideologically conditioned. We should not be satisfied with the obvious but should dig further down and search into the collective psyche of communities.

Could there be a profound sense of hurt kept alive by the memories of humiliations one's community has suffered (e.g. during the colonial or post-colonial period) or of by the guilt feelings for injuries one's community/nation has inflicted on others? Psychic wounds remain, whether they be personal or collective until they are healed. Anger and resentment of a community/nation/civilization remain submerged, and even if ineffective today, tomorrow they find self-expression in hate-speech or outright violence. We need to attend to the ongoing sense of victimhood and bring healing to the ire that remains buried deep within the consciousness of communities and nations.

Until we succeed to handle collective grievances with the delicate skill of a physician, and help each other and get over our postcolonial complexes, we do not become truly free; we have not yet become independent.

Similarly, lingering wounds may be in the collective unconscious of an ethnic minority, a language group, a religious community, or a nation, prompting a belated response in one manner or the other. These wounds need to be healed. The task I am proposing certainly is not easy. But that is the mission of responsible intellectuals in the world today. In this endeavour, they need to have a non-sectarian, non-partisan attitude, guided solely by the values one cherishes for the common good. It is a world-transforming undertaking.

Wounds Inflicted by One's Own Success is Hardest to Heal

While hurts inflicted by an opponent is hard of healing, those inflicted by oneself is harder. The complacency and over-confidence that come upon oneself from unqualified success are the hardest to heal. Christopher Dawson argues that many successful civilizations/nations fell victims to these very weaknesses precisely in periods of their eminent success, weaknesses to which they grew blind. When they began marginalizing the values by whose strength they had grown and attained success, they were placing themselves on the way to decline.

For example, he says, the Hellenic civilization collapsed on its own with the "disappearance of those vital characteristic types in which the spirit of the culture had embodied itself". Once they cut off their roots with their past, true Greek values and institutions disappeared, and their society became an impersonal exploitative hierarchy. There was clearly "the degradation of the Greek type". Thus, "Hellenism withered from within" (Dawson 62-63).

Dawson makes similar comments on the decline of Roman society with the weakening or Roman values. "Rome became more and more a predatory state that lived by war and plunder and exhausted her own strength with that of her victims" (Dawson 67). Cities became parasitic.

These are weaknesses to which any culture or community can descend. But if a community cultivates collective self-consciousness and social sensibility, it paves the way to social healing. Responsible members of the community, therefore, should reflect on the vexed questions that harass the community, e.g. growing economic inequality, gender prejudice, ecological degeneration, memories of collective humiliation, communal tensions.

Similarly, in a politically competitive world, there can be lingering fear in countries and communities that have gone through negative experiences, if they see a show of strength in neighbouring peoples and excessive eagerness to outsmart others, before which they feel inadequate. On the contrary, they are edified when they see self-restraint and mutual assistance. And they rejoice at the success of an achieving neighbour.

We All Have to Learn from Each Other

In this globalized world, we all have to learn from each other. "The great civilizations of the past have often been focused on their own cultures. In the future, they will increasingly study the greatness of other civilizations" (Martin 388). Even the most developed nations are beginning to recognise their own incompleteness without others. There is general recognition of human interdependence, a conviction that we belong together, that our needs are identical, and that we need each other. Despite growing distances between self-centred communities, there is visible convergence of thought, fusion of longings, and a desire for togetherness.

For example, there is a sudden revival of interest among environmentalists to study the traditions of tribal communities in remote areas when exploring ways to control pollution, ecological destruction, species' extinction, over-tapping of non-renewable energy; ecological balance, appropriate use of land, harmony between humans and other species. They have sought inspiration from personalities like Tagore or Gandhi who manifested great esteem for life in the villages, the simplicity of the people and the beauty of uncontaminated nature.

While we do not claim that such models have the final word on these matters, they seem to propose a corrective to industrial recklessness, an impersonal economy, and over-confidence individual civilisations. Wisdom consists of drawing profit from each others' experiences.

Communities, Cultures, Ideologies and Religions Must Dialogue

Gradually people are awakening to the fact that Economy is dependent not only on capital and labour, but also on values like traditions of trust, skills developed in cultures, and habits of the mind, which we call the social capital of a society. They are sustained by ethical convictions deeply embedded in cultures. These values can be brought meaningfully to day-to-day social processes only if cultures, communities, ideologies, disciplines, and religions, dialogue. Life together becomes possible only by searching for consensus among these various traditions.

As we have already seen, ancient values have to be made relevant by bringing them to concrete situations and face to face with issues that society considers important today, e.g. democracy, economics, technology, natural sciences; ecology, feminism, and postmodern perceptions. They have to be put in relationship to responsibilities in the activities of real life, like, accounting, management, finance, marketing, communication technology, treatment of workers, and others. Only in this way will the global civilisation emerge as truly human and meaningful.

A Search for Global Ethics

Let us take another example. The best way to confront the so-called 'terrorist' force is not the use of greater force. Human ingenuity must suggest other solutions as well. We have referred to some of them in earlier sections. Gandhi believed that mind-power is stronger than muscle-power and gun-power in the long run.

When we fail to agree on moral values among ourselves, various types of inter-community tensions and social fragmentation are bound to occur. Common codes of conduct must be evolved. Increasing cybercrimes, for example, call for a global ethical code. In 1993 Hans Kung suggested a Global Ethic in the Parliament of World Religions in an effort to broaden areas of agreement (Schweiker 488).

The values of various cultures are complementary, and not one exclusive of the other. Diverse needs compelled communities to emphasize diverse values as required in specific circumstances. However, the Golden Rule of 'doing unto others as one would like others to do to you' seems to have the widest acceptance. In the same way, the sense of responsibility and benevolence for the poorest and the most neglected may be considered universal. Some societies emphasize justice, others compassion; Africa may give importance to 'communal ties and social cohesiveness', the western society to individual rights, Asians to family values. These are complementary.

Religious Believers and Ardent Secularists Must Dialogue

Those with secular convictions accuse religious believers of being partisan, forgetting that they too often show themselves partisan when they apply 'rationality' only to some areas and not to others. That is why religious and secular voices must engage one another; national and civilizational leaders must talk.

Values that are more widely acceptable must emerge from their conversation. That is the only way to solve problems like social tensions, civil wars, cultural oppression, political autocracy, economic stagnation, forced migration, and increase in the volume of refugees.

Humanity Has Become Interconnected and Interdependent

It is not that no progress has been made in matters of common interest. Kishore Mahbubani lists a number of areas where common understanding has been deepening at the global level: there is growing acceptance that rulers are accountable to the people (*Mahbubani 40*); that a win-win approach is better than cutthroat competition; that the work ethic of discipline, competence, teamwork is required to make a breakthrough in economy; that the health of the masses is the best asset of the nation; that healthy food and clean water are a must to ensure high production; that the future of a society depends on fair access to education for all people.

It is usually believed that ideals converge while practical interests divide peoples. Mahbubani argues that in the present day,, the opposite is true. In our times, it is evident that economic interests are bringing peoples and nations together. In this area all speak the same language (e.g., the language of science and technology, economic growth and development). The strategic interests of the developed and underdeveloped world have become interdependent. Global trade keeps growing in volume. There is visible upward mobility everywhere; many more millions have risen to the levels of the Middle Class. Global interests in the areas of ideas, ideals, information, compassion, assistance keep widening. International travel is expected to touch 1.6 billion by 2020. So, Mahbubani argues that in today's situation, material interests of people converge; but it is their minds that have not found the way to move forward together (Mahbubani 81-82).

A new human consciousness must emerge, one that encourages togetherness (Mahbubani 74). But if each nation seeks only its own interests, the common good comes to be clean forgotten. What actually happens is that national leaders are caught in strategies of populism and are eager to advance their own personal interests, or those of the dominant group, or the nation's own short term interests. There are few statesmen who are able to transcend these limitations.

But we know that the future belongs to those who ensure a fair deal across different income classes, ethnic groups, regions, and nations, and put their collective interests in relationship to the global good.

The Role of Intellectuals

You have become a disciple in order to benefit the world (Silabhadra, the Buddhist professor of Nalanda University, to Hiuen Tsang from China)

Jesus said to his disciples, teach them all that I have taught you (Mt 28:20)

Intellectuals must develop a sense of responsibility. "The ideas of economists and political philosophers, both when they are right and when they are wrong, are more powerful than is commonly understood. Indeed, the world is ruled by little else", said John Maynard Keynes. Practical men (actual rulers) are often slaves to outdated ideas; he argued (*Stiglitz 151*). Hence even the most anti-intellectual society today has need for people who have ideas towards togetherness if they wish to make headway.

The recent book of Thomas Piketty, *Capital in the Twenty-first Century*, refers to the "rising human capital hypothesis," which argues that 'human capital' is far more important than financial capital and real estate (*Piketty 21-22*).

However, 'human capital' is not only knowledge and skills, but also values like motivation, a sense of purpose, a sense of belonging, mutual trust, energies for resilience, and absolute determination. While knowledge and skills will decide the direction of the economy, values alone will ensure cohesion to a community and a future to society. Here is where intellectuals with vision can help. They are more powerful than actual power-wielders (Mahbubani 64). I call them "Philosopher-Friends," not the philosopher-kings of Plato.

Confucius taught, "Persons of humanity are like this: wanting to develop themselves, they also develop others; wanting to achieve things themselves, they also allow others to achieve what they want (*Analects 6.28.2-3*). And again, "But if even a simple peasant comes in all sincerity and asks me a question, I am ready to thrash the matter out, with all its pros and cons, to the very end" *(Analects IX,7)*.

The ancient Indian classic Rigveda had said, "One ignorant of the land asks of the one who knows it; he travels forward, instructed by the knowing-one. This, indeed is the blessing of instruction, one finds the path that leads straight forward" (*Rigveda X, 32.7*).

In times of troubles, we need new motivators to urge society to go on, just like Kurien Kunnumpuram did in his own modest ways. It is for us to develop motivation for carrying a hope-filled message to Africa, Asia and the rest of the world. " Let your aims be common, and your hearts be of one accord, and all of you of one mind, so you may live well together" (*Rig Veda 10.191.2-4*). "Consider the family of humankind one" (Jainism, Jinasena, Adipurana).

References

Chandra, Ramesh & Mittra, Sangh, *Buddha: A Revolutionary and Reformer*, Commonwealth Pub. New Delhi, 2003

Charan, Ram, *Global Tilt,* Random House Books, London, 2013.

Creel, Herlee G., *Chinese Thought: From Confucius to Mao Tse Tung,* Chicago, 1971).

Das, Gurucharan, *India Grows at Night*, Allen Lane (Penguin), London, 2012.

Dawson, Christopher, *Dynamics of World History,* ISI Books, Wilmington (Delaware), 2002.

Ferguson, Niall, *Civilization*, Allen Lane (Penguin), London, 2011.

Fernandez-Armesto, *Civilizations*, Pan Books, London, 2001.

Fleischacker, Samuel, *The Ethics of Culture*, Cornell University Press, New York, 1994.

Friedman, George, *The Next Decade*, Anchor Books (Random House), New York, 2012.

Fukuyama, Francis, *The Origins of Political Order*, Ferrar, Straus and Giroux, New York, 2011.

Guha, Ed. Ramachandra, *Makers of Modern Asia*, Belknap Press Harvard, Cambridge, 2014.

Hathaway, Mark & Boff, Leonardo, *The Tao of Liberation*, Orbis Books, New York, 2009.

Hobsbawm, *Fractured Times*, Eric Little, Brown New Delhi (Noida), 2013.
Mahbubani, Kishore, *The Great Convergence*, PublicAffairs, New York, 2013.
Martin, James, *The Meaning of the 21st Century*, Eden Project Books, London, 2006.
Mishra, Pankaj, *From the Ruins of Empire*, Allen Lane (Penguin), London, 2012.
Picketty, Thomas, *Capital in the 21st Century*, The Belknap Press, Harvard, 2014.
Sachs, Jeffrey, *The Price of Civilization*, The Bodley Head, London, 2011.
Schweiker, William, Ed., *Religious Ethics*, Blackwell Publishing, Oxford, 2008.
Sharma, Ruchir, *Breakout Nations*, Allen Lane (Penguin), London, 2012.
Stiglitz, Joseph, *The Price of Inequality*, Allen Lane (Penguin), London, 2012.

27

Dual Faces of Human Dignity: Secured Worth and Required Recognition

J. Charles Davis
Humboldt Research Fellow
Albert Ludwig University of Freiburg, Germany

Abstract: *History informs us the varying use of the term human dignity from a status of rank, inherent value to a dignified way of living. Human dignity has intrinsic, attributed and inflorescent variants, inheres in human individuals as well as collectively in human species, plays positive and negative roles of empowerment and constraint, functions as a principle as well as a rule and is self-respect, self-esteem and social recognition in acknowledgement of the secured, inviolable, intrinsic worth. It prohibits self-degradation and social degradation of individuals and humanity as a whole. It inheres not only in rational-moral capacities but includes all basic human needs. Humanity is dignity, and every human individual is a concrete, experiential face of the existential dignity. Human dignity is neither vague nor useless, but the supreme moral-legal watchdog principle of complementarity for bioethics, biolaw and biopolitics to protect humans against misuses under the mask of freedom of research in biosciences and biotechnologies.*

Keywords: *Human dignity, Worth, Recognition. Philosophical Basis, Socio-Political Expressions*

Professor Kurien Kunnumpuram SJ is an appreciable, admirable and inspiring personality. He is a reputed, renowned professor of theology and an expert of the second Vatican documents. As a man of clarity in his interactions, he was most of the time chosen to be a moderator of dialogues, meetings and conferences. He is gentle and a man of friendships across all walks of life. He respects every man and woman with dignity and equality. His contributions to the academia of ecclesiology, the formation of religious leaders, development of Indian church and promotion of human rights are enormous and praiseworthy. The eminent Indian ecclesiologist, Professor Kunnumpuram used to quote frequently the opening statement of the *Gaudium et Spes*: "The joys and the hopes, the griefs and the anxieties of the men of this age, especially those who are poor or in any way afflicted, these are the joys and hopes, the griefs and anxieties of the followers of Christ" (1965, no. 1). The Church is not an abstract concept but consists of people for the people. The term dignity is mentioned 51 times in this Pastoral Constitution on the Church in the Modern World *Gaudium et Spes* by His Holiness Pope Paul VI. This document of the Second Vatican council talks all about human dignity, human community and human activity. Human dignity is the hallmark of his living and teaching. As his student, secretary and friend, I am privileged to write a *festschrift* in honour of Kurien on his 85th birthday on human dignity here.

What is Human Dignity?

Leszek Kolakowski says, "It is difficult to define what human dignity is. It is not an organ to be discovered in our body, it is an empirical notion, but without it, we would be unable to answer the simple question: what is wrong with slavery?"[1] History informs us the varying use of the term human dignity from a status of rank, inherent value to a dignified way of living. Today, however, "there is a taken-for-granted assumption that dignity is good for the human condition and that it is part of our moral DNA. It has been acknowledged that violations of human dignity can be identified and recognized (torture and slavery are obvious examples) even if the abstract term cannot be defined with precision."[2] The concept of human dignity, even without a clear definition, is increasingly used in the international and national declarations of human rights after World War II and commonly accepted that human dignity is inviolable.

Mass killings with biotechnological weapons that have potentials to annihilate humanity prompted the framers of human rights constitutions, declarations and conventions to protect humans intuitively and more urgently and immediately than to look for philosophical, legal and socio-political

---

1 Leszek Kolakowski, "What Is Left of Socialism," *First Things* 126 (October 2002) 42-46, 46. Cited in Leon R. Kass, "Defending Human Dignity," in: E. D. Pellegrino (ed.), *Human Dignity and Bioethics* (Washington, DC: The President's Council on Bioethics, 2008) 297-331, 297.

2 Judy McGregor and Edward Sieh (eds.), *Human Dignity: Establishing Worth and Seeking Solutions* (London: Palgrave Macmillian – Springer Nature, 2017) "Preface" viii.

justifications. They presumed, however, that the superstructure human rights have their foundation on human dignity, and violation of human rights meant the violation of human dignity which is sacrosanct or uninfringeable. National constitutions and intergovernmental declarations explicitly or implicitly accept a hypothesis that humans have certain rights such as the right to life on account of inviolable dignity. Violations of human rights are vehemently opposed in these documents not only to preserve political peace in the society but primarily because they are acts of indignity and desecrations of inviolable human dignity.

In this article, I aim to fathom the idea of the dignity inherent in every human individual who (must) enjoy the value by virtue of being human prior to the state, society or social contract. I shall first analyze the meanings of human dignity and then discuss the relationship between human dignity and human rights. The article is an attempt to show intrinsic dignity to be a principle that protects humans and prevent them from adversary uses in biosciences and biotechnologies.

The Three Senses of Human Dignity

Daniel P. Sulmasy categorizes the one and the same human dignity into three senses, namely, intrinsic, attributed and inflorescent dignity.[3] *Intrinsic* dignity means "worth, stature, or value that human beings have simply because they are human, not by virtue of any set of biological, psychological, social, economic, or political conditions, nor of the views of other persons, nor of any particular set of talents, skills, or powers."[4] Intrinsic dignity is present in each and every human being, thus in whole human species, simply by virtue of the fact that they are human. This sense of human dignity reveals and designates a pre-existing value which is not conferred or created by human choices. It is prior to any human attribution and all that humans must do is to recognize and respect the intrinsic dignity in others. Discriminations against humans are vehemently opposed not because they would violate or destroy or remove the intrinsic dignity but because the discriminated humans who have dignity get insulted. Insult is incompatible with human dignity. The affected entity is not the abstract concept of dignity, but individual humans who have dignity.

The second sense is an *attributed* human dignity, which is a value conferred upon others by acts of attribution. It is always a choice. It is attributed

3 See Daniel P. Sulmasy, "The Varieties of Human Dignity: A Logical and Conceptual Analysis," *Medical Health Care and Philosophy* 16 (2013) 937-944, 938; Daniel P. Sulmasy, "Dignity and Bioethics: History, Theory, and Selected Applications," in: E. D. Pellegrino (ed.), *Human Dignity and Bioethics* (Washington, DC: The President's Council on Bioethics, 2008) 469-501; See Daniel P. Sulmasy, "Death, Dignity and the Theory of Value," *Ethical Perspectives* 9 (2002) 103-118,

4 Sulmasy, "The Varieties of Human Dignity," 938.

to dignitaries in acknowledgement of their talents and skills. The attributed human dignity is not intrinsic but a conventional social value that can be gained or lost depending on social rank or political power. Some speak of the need of attribution since attribution is the duty of recognizing the dignity in others as one claims in oneself. There is a nuanced distinction between intrinsic and attributed human dignity. Attributed dignity need not be understood only as a social value conferred on humans on account of their public offices, but it could also be interpreted to be a mere recognition through attribution of intrinsic dignity. In any case, attribution seems to important, since humans cannot live alone but in society. Therefore, attribution can be thought to be a mere acknowledgement of the intrinsic worth of humans. This aspect demands respect for intrinsic dignity.

The third sense is called *inflorescent* dignity, which describes the worth or value of a process that is conducive to human excellence. Inflorescence refers to flourishing or flowering or blossoming as human beings in consistent with and expressive of intrinsic dignity. This sense of human dignity can be compared to the understanding of dignity as a virtue – "a state of affairs by which a human being habitually acts in ways that express the intrinsic value of the human."[5] It expresses an idea of dignified or undignified behaviour, which is different from that of the intrinsic dignity of humans. Alan Gewirth elaborates:

> The sense of 'dignity' in which all humans are said to have equal dignity is not the same as that in which it may be said of some person that he lacks dignity or that he behaves without dignity, where what is meant is that he is lacking in decorum, is too raucous or obsequious or is not 'dignified'. This kind of dignity is one that humans may occurrently exhibit, lack, or lose, whereas the dignity in which all humans are said to be equal is a characteristic that belongs permanently and inherently to every human as such.[6]

While we may admire a dignified conduct, we know that this does not add anything to the intrinsic dignity of those whose conduct is admirable. The three senses of human dignity are not mutually exclusive. It is the same intrinsic dignity that is simultaneously at play and present in all human beings requiring an "attribution" creating blossoming conditions for "inflorescence." Intrinsic dignity is essentially prior to the attributed and inflorescent dignity. Thus, Sulmasy concludes that "the attributed and inflorescent uses are logically and linguistically dependent upon the intrinsic sense of the word."[7] Sulmasy uses the debate about euthanasia to explain how proponents and

5 Sulmasy, "The Varieties of Human Dignity," 938.

6 Alan Gewirth, *Human Rights* (Chicago: University of Chicago Press, 1982) 27-8.

7 Sulmasy, "The Varieties of Human Dignity," 941.

opponents use the same notion of dignity differently conveniently in favour of their arguments.[8] Realists like American Physician Leon Kass (1939- CE) who was also Chairman of the President's Council of Bioethics (2001-2005) argue that euthanasia ought to be illegal because it is undignified for humans to flee from realities of life and avoid confrontation with human limits or finitude.[9] Proponents want to legalize euthanasia arguing that human beings should not be forced to prolong life and accept the indignities caused by terminal illnesses. Proponents seem to equate dignity with the autonomy to have control over the circumstances of their own situations including death.[10]

Harris, Macklin and Cochrane contested the usefulness of human dignity in bioethics because it is too general or vague,[11] while others find the generality or vagueness of the concept of human dignity to be a blessing to allow many interpretations in the interests of the human society in order to be used in a variety of ways in a variety of settings.[12] The problem does not really seem to be about existence, the ambiguity of definition, moral content or normativeness of the concept of human dignity, but the application of the various senses of dignity differently in practical issues make the concept appear ambiguous.

8 See Daniel P. Sulmasy, "Death, Dignity and the Theory of Value," *Ethical Perspectives* 9 (2002) 103-118.

9 Leon Kass "A Commentary on Paul Ramsey: Averting One's Eyes, or Facing the Music? One Dignity in Death," *Hastings Center Studies* 2/2 (1974) 67-80.

10 Sulmasy, "The Varieties of Human Dignity," 938; T. Quill, "Death and Dignity: A Case of Individualized Decision Making," *New England Journal of Medicine* 324 (1991) 691-694.

11 Their argument, as summed by Sulmasy (937), is that "If dignity can mean one thing to one person and another thing to another person than (sic) [then] it cannot serve to resolve any ethical disputes." Ruth Macklin, "Dignity is a Useless Concept," *British Medical Journal* 327 (2003) 1419-1420; J. Harris, "Cloning and Human Dignity," *Cambridge Quarterly of Healthcare Ethics* 7 (1998) 163-167; A. Cochrane, "Undignified Bioethics," *Bioethics* 24 (2010) 234-241. Roberto Andorno, "The Dual Role of Human Dignity in Bioethics," *Medical Health Care and Philosophy* 16 (2013) 967-973, 968: "Lack of definition does not by itself prove that dignity is an empty concept or a purely rhetorical notion. As a matter of fact, defining dignity in clear-cut terms would be as difficult as defining 'freedom,' 'justice,' 'solidarity', or whatever other key social value (which by the way are never defined by law). It is not because the idea of human dignity is too poor, but because it is too rich that it cannot be encapsulated into a straightforward definition with which everybody agrees. In reality, its core meaning is quite clear and simple and embodies a very basic requirement of *justice* towards every individual."

12 P. R. Johnson, "An Analysis of Dignity," *Theoretical Medicine and Bioethics* 19 (1998) 337-352; A. Gewirth, *Self-fulfillment* (Princeton, NJ: Princeton University Press, 1998) 159-174; L. Nordenfelt, "The Varieties of Dignity," Health Care Analysis 12/2 (2004) 69-81; D. P. Sulmasy, "Human Dignity and Human Worth," in: N. Lickiss and J. Malpas (eds.), *Perspectives of Human Dignity: A Conversation* (Dordrecht, Netherlands: Springer, 2007); D. Schroeder, "Dignity: One, Two, Three, Four, Five, Still Counting," *Cambridge Quarterly of Healthcare Ethics* 19/1 (2010)118-125; M. C. Jordan, "Bioethics and Human Dignity," *Journal of Medicine and Philosophy* 35 (2010) 180-196.

However, the concept itself is not unambiguous and it is not useless either. The loaded term dignity is rich with boundless but at least three meanings mentioned here that people interpret it the way they want, but that actually that need not compromise but complement the intrinsic value of humans.

Dual Philosophical Faces of Human Dignity

The legal and state philosopher Paolo Becchi speaks about the two faces of human dignity that continues to exist down the history from the Roman antiquity to the 21st century.[13] It was used in twofold meaning and continued to develop in history without losing its core substantially: human dignity designates a special status of humans in the universe as well as a self-achieved social status. The former is ontological and the latter is relational and evaluative. The expression of dignity thus refers both to the reality that human differentiates himself from the rest of the nature because the human is the only animal rationale as well as to the active role of a human in the public life that distinguishes him/her from other individuals and confers a special value. In the sense of the first variant of the meaning, the human as such has dignity because the human stands at the top of the hierarchy of nature; in the sense of the second variant, dignity is graduated depending on the status in the social hierarchy. For Cicero, who was the first to emphasize these two meanings, a human who relinquished the enjoyment of the senses, violated the dignity of his/her rational nature; whereas a personal dignity grew out of the deeds which he had brought to the common good.[14] The first refers to the very being and the second refers to the aspect of becoming human(e). The rational nature and behaving rationally is the key point for Cicero.

The first meaning of dignity is universal, which the human species possesses the universal dignity essentially as a natural gift or endowment. The second meaning is particularistic and dependent on performance or accomplishments that some individuals generate and others not.[15] Dignity in the first meaning is absolute that a human can neither increase nor diminish it, but in the second is a social dignity that a human can acquire or lose it. Social dignity was first equated to public office as such and not to the human who held the appointment. Subsequently, social dignity was associated with the title that s/he had as member of a specific standing and not on account of own achievements. Finally, social dignity was also attached to any occupation or

13 Paolo Becchi, *Das Prinzip der Menschenwürde – Eine Einführung* (Berlin: Duncker & Humboldt GmbH, 2016) 11-19.

14 See Becchi, *Das Prinzip der Menschenwürde*, 11; M. Tullius Cicero, *De Officiis*, ed. and trans. W. Miller (Cambridge, MA: Harvard University Press, 1913) I.30: 105-6.

15 See Becchi, *Das Prinzip der Menschenwürde*, 11; For the twofold meaning, see H. Hofmann, "Die versprochenen Menschenwürde," *Archiv des öffentlichen Rechts* 118 (1993) 353-377.

function with which a human contributes to the material and spiritual progress of the society.[16] The two faces of the same intrinsic and social dignity continued to survive in history similar to the two side sides of the same coin.

During the Renaissance, the ontological understanding of dignity took a back seat behind the thought that dignity must be earned that it becomes a special value only when it is attained by humans gifted with reason. The Italian Renaissance philosopher Giovanni Pico della Mirandola (1463-1494 CE) expressed the idea of the human as the master of own destiny and for the English philosopher Francis Bacon (1561-1626 CE), scientists and researchers stood first in the grade of dignity for their contribution through new knowledge to the society.[17] In this sense, there is a possibility for the *homo faber* to obtain more dignity. While the Dutch jurist Hugo Grotius (1583-1645 CE) considered that a respectful handling of the dead would confer dignity, for the English philosopher Thomas Hobbes (1588-1679 CE), humans, according to their (cap)abilities, had a market price, which could be fixed and changed by the needs of the judgement of the buyers.[18]

The German jurist and political philosopher Samuel Putendorf (1632-1694 CE) seems to be the first to speak of human dignity based on moral abilities of humans going beyond the rational ability and social status of humans to the fundamental freedom which is prerequisite for the existence of moral order. He makes a clear distinction between *entia physica* and *entia moralia* of the natural order. It is not simply the nature but the moral freedom of humans that alone confers them dignity.[19] Putendorf believes that human species in the natural world is the only being that can set limits to own acts and subject to laws that are naturally given. Therefore, human dignity belongs to humans not because of any special place in the nature but because s/he is a morally acting subject. To appreciate the whole meaning and originality of this new approach, it could be contrasted with two other concepts for nuances: a contemporary thought of Blaise Pascal (1623-1662 CE)) from whom Putendorf sharply differs and later with the view of Kant (1724-1804 CE) whose view is already anticipated by Putendorf. For Pascal, the whole dignity of humans lies

---

16 See Becchi, Das Prinzip der Menschenwürde, 12.

17 See G. Pico della Mirandola, *De hominis dignitate* (Bologna, 1496), German translation: A. Buck (ed.), Über die Würde des Menschen, trans. N. Baumgarten (Hamburg: 1990); F. Bacon, *Novum Organum* (London: 1620) 1: CXXIX; Francis Bacon, *De dignitate et augmentis scientiarum,* London: 1605.

18 See Becchi, *Das Prinzip der Menschenwürde*, 15, T. Hobbes, *Leviathan*, J. Schlösser (trans.) and H. Klenner (ed.) (Hamburg, 1996) 72.

19 See Becchi, Das Prinzip der Menschenwürde, 15, S. Putendorf, De jure naturae et gentium, 2. Buch. 1. Kapitel, §5). See H. Welzel, Die Naturrechtslehre Samuel Putendorfs (Berlin: 1958).

in thinking faculty.[20] Naturally, Putendorf does not deny that the human stands out in the order of nature through thinking capacity. However, this capacity does not confer dignity but in that moral capability which alone reveals the true human nature. Without doubt, Putendorf anticipated the unmatched, well-known, decisive, effective potential concept that we find at the culmination of the 18th century Enlightenment Age of Reason in the works of Kant.[21]

The distinction between *entia physica* and *entia moralia* by Putendorf is parallel with the kingdom of nature and the kingdom of ends (*Reich der Natur und Reich der Zwecke*): dignity belongs to humans not on account of their primacy in the nature, but because of their affiliation to the kingdom of ends. For both Kant and Putendorf dignity of humans meant that they are certain beings that morally act and follow the rules of the universally commanding reason. The real difference between Putendorf and Kant is: while Putendorf considered God as the guarantor for obtaining the highest good, Kant remained within the bounds of reason that can at best be a motivation for moral conversion.[22] Kant signifies the clearest break with hierarchical notion of dignity that seems to be the best-known articulation of the idea of intrinsic human dignity that anchors for human rights and duties.[23] According to Putendorf and Kant, the foundation of human dignity does not lie in mere biological existence but in a moral practical reason that prescribes us to treat the humanity (dignity) in one`s own person as well as in the person of the other always as an end and never as a means.[24] Human dignity is violated through the instrumental use of reducing a person to a thing, as the Italian legal philosopher Cesare Beccaria[25]

20 See Becchi, Das Prinzip der Menschenwürde, 15. B. Pascal, Pansées (1670) in: *Œuvres* completes (Paris: 1963).

21 See Becchi, Das Prinzip der Menschenwürde, 15-16.

22 See Becchi, Das Prinzip der Menschenwürde, 16.

23 See Deryck Beyleveld and Roger Brownsword, *Human Dignity in Bioethics and Biolaw* (New York: Oxford University Press, 2001) 52.

24 "Handle so, dass du die Menschheit sowohl in deiner Person, als in der Person eines jeden anderen jederzeit zugleich als Zweck, niemals bloß als Mittel brauchst" (Immauel Kant: *Grundlegung zur Metaphysik der Sitten* (1785) in: in: W. Weischedel (ed.), *Werke*, Vol. IV (Wiesbaden: 1956) No. 429. Only in the later work on *Metaphysics of Morals* (1797), Kant speaks of human digntiy explicitly: "Die Menschheit selbst ist eine Würde; denn der Mensch kann von keinem Menschen (weder von anderen noch sogar von sich selbst) bloß als Mittel, sondern muß jederzeit zugleich als Zweck gebraucht werden, und darin besteht eben seine Würde (die Persönlichkeit)" Immanuel Kant, *Metaphysik der Sitten*, No. 462. For the English editions, see: Immanuel Kant, *Groundwork of the Metaphysics of Morals* (1975) in: H. J. Paton (trans. with introd.) *The Moral Law* (London: Hutchinson, 1948); *The Metaphysics of Morals* (1797), trans. and ed. Mary Gregor (Cambridge: Cambridge University Press, 1991).

25 Cited in Becchi, *Das Prinzip der Menschenwürde*, 17. See C. Beccaria, *Dei delitta e delle pene* (1764), ed. F. Venturi (Torino: 1965): "Non vi è libertà ogni qual volta le leggi

seems to have incidentally remarked about 20 years before Kant. Unlike the Hobbesian a market value of Humans, the Kantian human has a priceless, non-exchangeable intrinsic value.[26] In critique of the Kantian source of dignity, we might say that humanity (dignity) should not be reduced to a single aspect of moral reason. Humans are more than mere rational autonomy and moral capability.

The Scottish moral philosopher and behavioural political economist Adam Smith (1723-1790 CE) emphasized the intrinsic principle of sympathy that helps us experience the passion of others. This accounted for the dignity and equality of self-regarding and other-regarding.[27] The empiricist philosopher David Hume (1711-1776 CE), a friend of Smith, however, considered that human dignity occurs only through social action.[28] The dignity must be awarded to the human by others when his/her conduct with others evokes impressions. With Kant, the recognition of others grounds on the moral value of the human as the end (with)in himself, even if the behaviours of someone do not make any good impact on others. Indeed, the formulation and propagation of this idea of human dignity had a quite effective contribution to the abolition of torture and conquest of humiliating and cruel punishments. Despite excessive criminal rigorism, Kant entangled himself at times in self-contradictions, when he pleaded for castration and capital punishment.[29]

Despite strong philosophical roots of human dignity in history and occasional references in the early legal text, a full legal legitimacy, juridification or legalization of the moral principle of human dignity happened only after the World War II. Only thereafter it became legally obligatory as an ethical

---

permettono che in alcuni eventi l'uomo cessi di essere persona e diventi cosa" (50), in: T. Vormbaum (trans.), *Von den Verbrechen und von den Strafen* (Berlin: 2004): "Wo die Gesetze erlauben, dass der Mensch unter gewissen Voraussetzungen aufhört, Person zu sein, und zur Sache wird, dort gibt es keine Freiheit" (77).

26 See M. A. Cattaneo, "Menschenwürde bei Kant," in: K. Seelmann (ed.) *Menschenwürde als Rechtsbegriff*, SVRSP, Beiheft 101 (Stuttgart, 2004) 24-32.

27 Adam Smith, *The Theory of Moral Sentiments* (1759), trans. Walther Eckstein (Hamburg: 2004). Remy Debes, "Adam Smith on dignity and equality," *British Journal for the History of Philosophy* 20/1 (2012) 109–40.

28 David Hume, *An Enquiry Concerning the Principles of Morals* 1751, Appendix IV: On Some Verbal Disputes (London: A. Miller, 1777) 314: 4.3.: "But on the whole, it seems to me that although everyone agrees that there are virtues of many different kinds, what we chiefly have in mind when we call a man 'virtuous' or 'a man of virtue' are his social qualities, which are indeed the most valuable. All the same, an honest good-natured man wouldn't get that honourable label if he were notably lacking in ·any of the non-social virtues· such as courage, temperance, economy, industry, understanding, dignity of mind."

29 See Becchi, *Das Prinzip der Menschenwürde*, 18.

imperative to treat humans as humans as such.[30] Following disasters after the world wars, the *UNO Charta* invoked the faith in fundamental human rights, in dignity and value of human person and the *Universal Declaration of Human Rights* began with the statement: "recognition of the inherent dignity and of the equal and inalienable rights of all members of the human family is the foundation of freedom, justice and peace in the world." While addressing the origins of Totalitarianism, Hannah Arendt wrote: "We became aware of the existence of a right to have rights [...] only when millions of people emerged who had lost and could not regain these rights because of the new global political situation."[31] Arendt believed that dignity is the "right to have rights," which "needs a new guarantee which can be found only in a new political principle, in a new law on earth, whose validity this time must comprehend the whole of humanity."[32] Thus, the new international order witnesses the attempt to make a new beginning through recognition of human dignity as the universal and absolute value.

To be treated as humans and to guarantee the right to treat every other human independent of gender, race, language, religion, political affiliation, economic and social position means to restore *humanity,* that has fought against the national socialist (Nazi) ideology with the introduction of the category of *Untermenschen* (subhuman) and the myth of Aryan race.[33] A comparison of the German (Bonn) Grundgesetz 1949 and the Constitution of the Italian Republic (CIR) 1948 may be useful. According to the Grundgesetz, the constitution of fundamental rights derivates from human dignity. Precisely because humans possess a dignity differentiating them from other living beings, humans possess basic rights. Since the Grundgesetz grounds its foundation indissolubly on human dignity[34] and the inadmissibility of any change is explicitly prescribed in Article 79 (3),[35] universality, unavailability and unchangeability (so-called *Ewigkeitsgarantie* = eternal guarantee) of that principle is confirmed.

30 For example, many juridical documents, that refer to the concept of human dignity, were written down according to the *Charter of United Nations* (1945), the *Universal Declarations of Human Rights* (1948) and *Grundgesetz (Constitution or Basic Law) of Federal Republic of Germany* (1949) See P. Tiedemann, *Menschenwürde als Rechtsbegriff: Eine philosophische Klärung* (Berlin: 2007).

31 Quoted in: Becchi, *Das Prinzip der Menschenwürde*, 19. See Hannah Arendt, *The Origin of Totalitarianism* (Cleveland/New York: 1951) 296.

32 Arendt, The Origin of Totalitarianism, IX.

33 See Becchi, Das Prinzip der Menschenwürde, 22.

34 Art. 1 (1) GG: Die Würde des Menschen ist unantastbar. Sie zu achten und zu schützen ist Verpflichtung aller staatlichen Gewalt.

35 Art. 79 (3) GG: Eine Änderung dieses Grundgesetzes, durch welche die Gliederung des Bundes in Länder, die grundsätzliche Mitwirkung der Länder bei der Gesetzgebung oder die in den Artikeln 1 und 20 niedergelegten Grundsätze berührt werden, ist unzulässig.

Naturally, due to the Nazi context that led to the World War II, philosophers, jurists, sociologists and theologians of the Land of Ideas, Germany, more than those of other countries, reflected upon human dignity extensively, since inhuman treatments representing a profound violation of human dignity took place at the concentration camps.[36] The psychologist Victor Frankl (1905-1997), who suffered in the KZ at Auschwitz himself, shares his experiences in *Man's Search for Meaning: An Introduction to Logotherapy* on inner freedom and will to meaning. Any amount of humiliation and suffering may not take away the intrinsic worth of humans, which is never lost though affected and disfigured. He says, "an incurably psychotic individual may lose his usefulness but yet retain the dignity of a human being."[37] This is a sort of Stoic understanding of dignity. All that one needed was to have a hope to live.[38]

The Marxist philosopher Ernst Bloch (1885-1977 CE), the legal philosopher Werner Maihofer (1918-1978 CE) and the sociologist Niklas Luhmann (1927-1998 CE) dealt with the theme of human dignity intensively in the 20th century. The emphasis shifted from the maxim "to respect" to "to protect," that should be achieved through a politics of *welfare*. The protection of human dignity contains the realization of the basic needs of humans through the social state. The earlier understanding of protection is thus not abandoned but much more extended in order to include the basic needs of humans in the practical world.[39] Luhmann did the initial analysis of the breakthrough concept of the Tübingen state law professor Günter Dürig (1920-1996 CE) who considered that human dignity is the highest constitutional principle of all objective rights and human dignity cannot undergo subjective considerations or be limited through other basic rights,[40] but spoke in favour of a "dynamic" against a "static" understanding of human dignity. Against the understanding of natural gift of dignity by virtue of being human, Luhmann advocated the dignity as a socio-cultural variable that must be established in the first place.

36 See Deryck Beyleveld and Roger Brownsword, *Human Dignity in Bioethics and Biolaw* (New York: Oxford University Press, 2001) 16-17.

37 Victor E. Frankl, *Man's Search for Meaning: An Introduction to Logotherapy*, trans. Ilse Lasch (Allahabad: St. Paul Press, 6th Print 2000) 119.

38 The original title of the book was "*trotzdem Ja zum Leben sagen: Ein psychologe erlebt das Konzentrationslager*" (1946), Victor Frankl, *Man's Search for Meaning* 1959 (USA: Beacon Press, 2006). He says that "even in the most absurd, painful, and dehumanized situation, life has potential meaning and that, therefore, even suffering is meaningful."

39 See Becchi, *Das Prinzip der Menschenwürde*, 30; Ernst Bloch, *Naturrecht und menschliche Würde* (Frankfurt a. M.: 1961); Hans Wagner, *Die Würde des Menschen* (Würzburg: 1992); Werner Maihofer, *Rechtstaat und menschliche Würde* (Darmstadt, 1962) 40-41.

40 See Günter Dürig, "Der Grundgesetz von der Menschenwürde: Entwurf eines praktikablen Wertsystems der Grundrechte aus Art. 1. Abs. 1 in Verbindung mit Art. 19 Abs. 2 des Grundgesetzes," *Archiv des öffentlichen Rechts* 81 (1956) 117-175 and "Kommentar zu Art. 1 Grundgesetz," in: *Grundgesetz: Kommentar* (1958).

The human can attain or lose in his self-representation as partner of social interaction. Dignity is the result of hard performance of representations that are subjected to constant risk of loss of dignity.[41] Luhmann thus revived the the social role of individuals signifying the dynamic character of human dignity. It is in social interaction that an individual realizes one's being of human and self-awareness. However, his original and unconventional interpretation did not get due attention in his time.[42]

Taking Stock

The two faces of intrinsic as well as social human dignity continue to be unwithering in history while shining forth as ever and unfolding in every branch of science and resist to lose their relevance even today. We can infer from history that the two aspects of human dignity can inclusively play a complementary role rather than exclusively one against the other. It seems to be two sides of the same coin. It requires only an acknowledgement that social dignity is the external recognition of intrinsic dignity.

The Socio-Political Expressions of Human Dignity

The approach of human dignity shifted in a new direction since the beginning of the 1970s. The philosophical, legal and political debate was dominated by the significant work of *A Theory of Justice* by the US-American political philosopher John Rawls (1921-2002 CE) who postulated the construction of a *fair* and in the sense of *well-ordered* society against the prevailing Utilitarianism that allowed harm against individuals in the interest of the greater common good of the society. The priority of the right over the good became the central and the basic principle of Rawls.[43] The new attention focused on more practical principles of liberty, equality, social contract and justice as fairness that a theoretical foundation of human rights was not of greater importance. However, the theme of human dignity gained the centre of discussion increasingly since the early 90s especially in Germany, where two prominent legal philosophers Hasso Hofmann (b.1934) and Ulfrid Neumann (b.1947) brought the concept dignity back. Neumann warned against a tyranny of dignity that could become a burden and block the discussion on ethically

41 Seee Niklas Luhmann, *Grundrechte als Institution: Ein Beitrag zur politischen Soziologie* (Berlin: 1965) 53-83. See See Becchi, Das Prinzip der Menschenwürde, 31.

42 See Becchi, *Das Prinzip der Menschenwürde*, 31; R. Stoecker, "Die Würde des Embryos," in: D. Gross (ed.) *Ethik in der Medizin in Lehre, Klinik und Forschung* (Würzburg, 2002) 53-71; K. Seelmann, "Repräsentation als Element von Menschenwürde," *Studia Philosophica* 63 (2004) 141-158.

43 John Rawls, *A Theory of Justice* (1971), Revised Edition (New York: Belknap Press, 1999); Otfried Höffe, *John Rawls. Eine Theorie der Gerechtigkeit,* Klassiker Auslegen. 2. Auflage (Berlin: Akademie Verlag, 2006).

sensible themes. On the contrary, Hofmann goes beyond the understanding of dignity as gift (*Mitgift*) and achievement (*Leistungstheorie*) to a social recognition (*soziale Anerkennung*).[44]

The legal, philosophical debate on human dignity found an interim endpoint in the new commentary of Mathias Herdegen (b. 1957) on Article 1 of the Basic Law, which introduces a classic of the constitutional commentaries.[45] Herdegen attempted to make a difference of core and marginal areas in human dignity and suggested that one of the core areas is not available for consideration (*Abwägung*). Ernst-Wolfgang Böckenförde accused him of having made an "Epochenbruch" over the previous interpretation of Günter Dürig known as object formula (*Objektformel*). According to Dürig, human dignity is moral value (*sittlicher Wert*), prepositive foundation (*vorpositives Fundament*) and natural law anchor (*naturrechtlicher Antiker*) of the Basic Law (*Grundgesetz*) and its human image. Herdegen degrades it to a constitutional norm on an equal level. Not only jurists, but also philosophers and moral theologians involve themselves in the extensive discussion about the normative content of human dignity.[46] Nevertheless, it should be noted that human digntiy appears as the new key concept ("*neues Schlüsselkonzept*") in a widely spread legal philosophical textbook.[47]

The debate on human dignity, after the considerable decrease in the discussion on Rawl's theory of justice, emerged with much more vigour in the ethical as well as legal philosophical areas in the Anglo-American contexts. The

---

44 H. Hofmann, "Die versprochenen Menschenwürde," *Archiv des öffentlichen Rechts* 118 (1993) 353-377 and "Methodische Probleme der juristischen Menschenwürdeinterpretation," in: I. Appel, G. Hermes (eds.), *Mensch-Staat-Umwelt* (Berlin: 2008) 47-79; Ulfrid Neumann, "Die Tyrannei der Würde: Argumentationstheoretische Erwägungen zum Menschenwürdeprinzip," *Archiv für Rechts- und Sozialphilosophie* 84 (1988) 153-166 and "Menschenwürde als Menschenbürde – oder wie man ein Recht gegen den Berechtigten wendet," in: U. Neumann (ed.) *Recht als Struktur und Argumentation.* Beiträge zur Theorie des Rechts und zur Wissenschaftstheorie der Rechtswissenschaft (Baden-Baden: 2008) 35-55.

45 Mathias Herdegen, "Kommentar zu Art. 1 Abs. GG," in: T. Maunz and G. Dürig (eds.), *Grundgesetz: Kommentar* (München: Beck, 1996).

46 Ernst-Wolfgang Böckenförde, "Die Menschenwürde war unantastbar. Abschied von den Verfassungsvätern: Die Neukommentierung von Artikel 1 des Grundgesetzes markiert einen Epochenbruch," *Frankfurter Allgemeine Zeitung FAZ* (3. September 2003) 33, 35, also in: *Recht, Staat, Freiheit.* erweitere Ausgabe (Frankfurt a. M.: 2006) 379-388.

47 K. Seelmann, "Menschenwürde: ein neuer Schlüsselbegriff," in: K. Seelmann, D. Demko (eds.), *Rechtphilosophie,* 6th ed. (München: 2014) 241-260, (2004) 3rd ed. 212-228; See Becchi, *Das Prinzip der Menschenwürde*, 32.

American philosophers Martha Nussbaum[48] (b.1947-) and Ronald Dworkin[49] (1931-2013 CE) are the two most prominent and important personalities in this discussion. Nussbaum seems to take up the idea of Bloch and Maihofer that dignity does not only belong to the abstract person as legal subject but to the concrete individual in his dependency on socio-economic conditions that at times do not even gurantee the minimum subsistence required for a dignified life. When a human is forced to live below the level of minimum subsistence and falls into an extreme poverty line, it indicates a violation of human dignity. Thus, the correlation between human dignity and material needs became decisive.[50]

For Nussbaum, the human, in the first place, is neither an *animal rationale* nor is s/he an *animal morale*, but basically, phenomenologically and existentially a "*being with needs*." The dependency on Karl Marx by Bloch, Maihofer and Nussbaum is evident. The more a state and the society is able to fulfil these needs, the more is the dignity realized though them. Dignity is deprived not only when/where basic sustenance is lacking but also where the realization of *capabilities* is hindered by the exploitative social conditions. Dignity is due to all humans, but special efforts are required to create such conditions under which it can effectively unfold itself. The state must enable every citizen to make *capabilities* into flourishing. This is somewhat similar to Sulmasy's third sense of inflorescent dignity. Nussbaum's discussion on dignity is enhanced by strong emancipation: The addressees of dignity are no longer only the rational, self-conscious and autonomous individuals, but children, women, old, persons living under degrading conditions and at the same time are not able to realise own capabilities. An abstract Stoic understanding of intrinsic dignity is insufficient and problematic in many ways and "respect for human dignity is not just lip service, it means creating conditions favourable for development and choice,"[51] and thus her main emphasis is on social

48 Martha Nussbaum, *Women and Human Development: The Capability Approach (*New York: 2000), Hiding from Humanity: Disgust, Shame and the Law (Princeton: 2004), "Human Dignity and Political Entitlements," in: *Human Dignity and Bioethics: Essays Commissioned by the President's Council on Bioethics* (Washington, DC: 2008), and *Creating Capabilities: The Human Development Approach* (Cambridge, MA: 2011).

49 Ronald Dworkin, *Is Democracy Possible Here? Principles for A New Political Debate* (Princeton: 2008) and *Justice for Hedgehogs* (Cambridge, Mass.: 2011). In this book, Dworkin develops the principles of "self-respect" and "authenticity," pp. 203-204.

50 See Becchi, Das Prinzip der Menschenwürde, 33.

51 Martha Nussbaum, "Human Dignity and Political Entitlements," in: *Human Dignity and Bioethics: Essays Commissioned by the President's Council on Bioethics* (Washington, D.C.: 2008) 351-359. Nussbaum preferred "an Aristotelian-Marxian account of dignity, which sees the dignity of the human being as squarely a part of the world of nature and does not posit a sharp split between rationality and other human capacities. I shall show how such an account might ground basic political entitlements (in a non-metaphysical way

dimension of dignity that ensures the conditions for the realization of basic needs and capabilities.

Granting equal rights would mean, in the sense of capability approach of Nussbaum, a single political goal but people "are actually able to do and to be" with their capabilities for basic needs to live a life with dignity. In other words, respecting equal rights would mean to enable a human to obtain basic needs without deprivation. Nussbaum explains that "there is dignity not only in rationality but in human need itself and in the varied forms of striving that emerge from human need."[52] Political entitlements must, therefore, be equal and the same for all citizens including people with disabilities who must be respected as fully equal citizens. What happens if some individuals cannot attain the capabilities because of a disability? Nussbaum clarifies that "they still have these capabilities, for example, the right to vote and the right to own property, but that these capabilities in some cases will have to be exercised in a relationship with a guardian.

Moreover, even with guardianship, it is always better if the guardian can act as a facilitator rather than a substitute."[53] A human with disabilities will have all the same political entitlements equal to a normal human. An individual who has an intrinsic dignity lives in and represents the self through the society. Therefore, basic needs, social recognitions and political entitlements are significant. In this sense, Nussbaum has made a good contribution to take capabilities seriously. It could be interpreted that Nussbaum's understanding is referring to inflorescent conditions for a dignified life and she does not see the human uniqueness, without which, I believe, the very aspect of morality within humans and the claims of animal rights become baseless. Despite similarities in basic needs, there is definitely a clear distinction between humans and non-human animals. Otherwise, the old norm of survival of the fittest will return to rule. It is precisely the uniqueness and moral sense of humans that plead for respect for humans as well as non-human animals. While we should not exalt the gift of reason, it is precisely the same gift of reason that would be

suited to a pluralistic society)" 352. She critiques that "Stoics not only split humans off from other animals more sharply than the evidence supports, refusing to grant animals any share in intelligence, they also denied without argument that there is any dignity or end-like worth inherent in those human capacities in which animals also partake, such as sentience, everyday (non-moral) practical reasoning, emotion, and the capacity for love and care. Thus, the split not only slights the other animals, it also slights elements in human life that would appear to have worth, urging us to respect only a small sliver of ourselves" (354-355). She says that Stoics would still hold that a woman would not lose her dignity despite rape, Nussbaum says that rapes violates the bodily, mental, and emotional life of woman, affecting all her opportunities for development and functioning (358).

52 Nussbaum, "Human Dignity and Political Entitlements," 363.

53 Nussbaum, "Human Dignity and Political Entitlements," 364.

able to ensure the political entitlements. Her theory of political justice does not substantiate the source of human dignity, it only ensures what could contribute to respecting human dignity or making life worthy of dignity.

Dworkin highlighted primarily the individual dimension of dignity, which contains two basic principles of self-respect and authenticity. The first suggests that "each human life has a special kind of objective value," that belongs as "intrinsic value" to every human in the form of a "potentiality". That is why society has to facilitate basic conditions for realization of dignity from the beginning of life. The second principle, on the other hand, supports that "each person has special responsibility for realizing the success of its own life." This means that it is rightly a predominant duty of every individual to actualise the "intrinsic value." According to Dworkin, "these two principles together [...] the basis and conditions of human dignity."[54]

In the ongoing debate on human dignity, the publication of *The Decent Society* by the Israeli philosopher Avishai Margalit gained a great significance in the German-speaking regions. Margalit aimed at a "decent society" that always remained in the background of Rawls' "well-ordered society." Decent is a society whose institutions do not humiliate humans, rather protect the self-esteem of every individual. Humiliations violate a human in self-esteem because dignity, according to Margalit is nothing other than "a representation of self-respect."[55] The connection between human dignity and self-respect is far from self-evident.[56] To begin with, a human may not be in a position to determine whether dignity is humiliated or not; namely, someone can be seen from outside as humiliated through certain acts, without feeling the humiliation in oneself. A human may still uphold self-respect when s/he is actually humiliated, and vice versa a human can forfeit self-respect without being subjected to degradations. The dignity of a raped woman is certainly violated but she has not lost her self-respect due to the rape. On the other hand, a man who becomes drunk every evening loses his self-respect, even though

54 See Becchi, *Das Prinzip der Menschenwürde*, 34. Becchi also makes a comparison of Dworkin's position with the european tradition: "Diese zwei Würdedefinitionen stehen den Bedeutungsvarianten nahe, die wir in der europäischen Tradition ausgemacht haben: Würde als Mitgift oder aber als Leistung." Dworkin, *Is Democracy Possible Here?* 9-10.

55 Avishai Margalit, *The Decent Society* (Cambridge, Mass.: 1996), trans. Politik der Würde (Frankfurt a. M.: 1999) 53; P. Schaber, "Menschenwürde und Selbstachtung: Ein Vorschlag zum Verständnis des Menschenwürde," in: *Menschenwürde/La dignité de l'être humain*, in: *Studia Philosophica* 63 (2004) 93-106, 101: "Jemanden zu erniedrigen heisst demanch, ihm die Möglichkeit zu nehmen, sich selbst zu achten." Cited in Becchi, *Das Prinzip der Menschenwürde*, 34.

56 Becchi, Das Prinzip der Menschenwürde, 34. See R. Stoecker, Menschenwürde und das Paradox der Entwürdigung," in: Menschenwürde: Annäherung an einen Begriff (Wien: 2003) 133-151 and "Selbstachtung und Menschenwürde," in: Studia Philosophica 63 (2004) 107-119.

no one has violated his dignity. It is not, however disputed that humiliation plays a role in the violation of dignity. Humiliation violates dignity. Strictly speaking, the moral evaluation of the matter does not depend on self-respect but on violation of the due respect by mutual partners.[57]

Dignity thus has to do with social interaction.[58] Whoever cannot bear the gaze of the others, loses the social face and loses social dignity. Understood this way, humiliation effects a disturbance in self-representation of the image that one wanted to give about oneself. Dignity is violated due to the infringement of private domain of self-representation. Every person has the right to positive protection of what s/he owes to the public as well as to the negative protection of what s/he reserves to oneself in privacy. Right to self-representation can be limited only in exceptional circumstances. The more we become transparent to the public, the greater is the need for the protection of core privacy. Here, respect for private life finds a philosophical justification. Becchi enlists the following acts intrusion into privacy: tapping of telephonic conversations, unauthorized disclosure of protocols, personal documents or pictures, also through the procedural use of lie detector, are therefore problematic since they come in conflict with the exclusive right of self-representation that is due to every human.[59]

The application of human dignity is extended to a whole range of other offences as well. The dignity of a human can be not only violated through torture or degrading treatment, but also a public insult, publication of sensitive private affairs in text or picture or through disclosure of statements that are inconsistent with a public position. In all these instances, the affected person is harmed in his image that s/he wants to present to the public. Humiliation is worse when it has affected the self-image, self-respect and self-esteem. If s/he does not get an opportunity to present the actual image, then the reputation of the person is permanently damaged. This understanding of dignity, too, has to accept an objection: not every abatement is condemnable; sometimes it is justifiably revealed, what is really behind some facades since the right to respect for private and family life cannot be stretched indefinitely. Hence, the difficult task remains to define precisely, which contemptuous behaviours violate the human dignity. Legally seen, it is certainly easier to implement the protection of dignity against discrimination and misuse than condescension.[60]

---

57 Becchi, *Das Prinzip der Menschenwürde*, 34-35.

58 Considered from a social point of view, see R. Sennet, *Respect in a World of Inequality* (New York/London: 2003). Paolo Becchi suggests a literature on social recognition: see H. Honneth, *Kampf um Anerkennung und Missachtung* (Frankfurt a. M.: 1994). Becchi, *Das Prinzip der Menschenwürde*, 35, f. 15.

59 Becchi, Das Prinzip der Menschenwürde, 35.

60 Becchi, Das Prinzip der Menschenwürde, 36.

The journey through the new understandings of dignity makes it clear that the old idea of dignity is still valid. The ethnic cleansing in Ex-Yugoslavia, the genocide in Ruanda as well as in Sri Lanka, the tortures and humiliations of Iraqi prisoners through US soldiers in Abu Ghraib as well as the inhuman conditions of detentions of suspected terrorists in Guantanamo, the ongoing killings through infiltrations in Kashmir are a few examples to mention in recent times that testify the importance of protection of human dignity against violation of human rights in armed conflicts. More concerned than a mere fact is a justification of using torture even today as a weapon against terrorism.[61] Should torture belong to the catalogue of police investigation methods on grounds of internal state security, it would be a dangerous regression that must necessarily be avoided at all costs if we do not want to fall back to the barbarianism. However, if we invoke the principle of human dignity as the protective shield of every person, including those who have committed the heinous crimes, then there would be a greater justice in the light of the basic and unconditional character of this principle.

Taking Stock

The concept of human dignity has assumed new meanings in the light of human rights traditions. Humans rights are natural rights corresponding to inherent human dignity and they are not conferred by the society, rather they are to be recognized, asserted and protected, while interpretations and applications of human rights may vary especially when they are weighed against in conflict situations by the society and the state, namely, by the constitutions and jurists. Natural law may undergo changes in the sense that interpretations are subject to contexts. Among all philosophical and legal traditions, the modern Kantian understanding of human dignity has greatly gained a universal significance that prohibits to degrade a human to a thing.

Dual Roles of Dignity: Empowerment and Constraint

The historical-philological enquiries, philosophical-religious traditions or empirical-legal examinations discuss the question: *who has the dignity*? Many of them indicate that dignity does not only belong to individual humans but to the whole of humanity as a whole.[62] Some of them defend that it is the

61 See Linus Sonderegger, *Die Rückkehr der Folter? Anwendung von Zwang bei der Vernehmung im Deutschen und US-amerikanischen Recht*, Schriftreihe des Max-Planck-Instituts (Berlin: Duncker & Humboldt, 2012). Sonderegger says that there is a distinction between the use of coercion during interrogation for criminal procedural purposes and those that serve to avert an imminent danger or to combat terrorism.

62 For example, Micha Werner, "Individual and Collective Dignity," in: M. Düwell, J. Braarvig, R. Brownsword, D. Mieth (eds.) *The Cambridge Handbook of Human Dignity* (Cambridge: Cambridge University Press, 2014) 345-352; Deryck Beyleveld and Roger

special value of humanity as a species that demand the same value to be shared among its members. It is obvious that every human being is (and grows as) a member of the species *homo sapiens* and nothing else. Particularly in the contexts of modern biotechnological threats through cloning and germline interventions to the identity and integrity of the human species, it is important "not only to promote respect for the intrinsic worthiness of every individual but also of *humankind as a whole*."[63] There is a challenging question: which takes precedence in conflicting situations: is it the individual human dignity or the dignity of the society, namely, the public order?[64] For example, can the state justify the death penalty to a terrorist? Can we permit homosexuality which may be contrary to certain religious or cultural beliefs? A conservative communitarian approach may treat "human dignity as the ground not only for permitting individuals to make their own choices but also for setting limits to the sphere of free choice."[65] Feldman explains that

> we must not assume that the idea of dignity is inextricably linked to a liberal-individualist view of human beings as people whose life-choices deserve respect. If the state takes a particular view on what is required for people to live dignified lives, it may introduce regulations to restrict the freedom which people have to make choices which, in the state's view, interfere with the dignity of the individual, a social group or the human race as a whole… The quest for human dignity may subvert rather than enhance choice… Once it becomes a tool in the hands of the lawmakers and judges, the concept of human dignity is a two-edged sword.[66]

It may not be correct to put the whole weight of human dignity on respect for autonomy and self-determination. Dignity, whether individual or

---

Brownsword, *Human Dignity in Bioethics and Biolaw* (New York: Oxford University Press, 2001) 25-28; Marcus Düwell, "On the Border of Life and Death: Human Dignity and Bioethics," and "Human Dignity and Future Generation," in: M. Düwell, J. Braarvig, R. Brownsword, D. Mieth (eds.) *The Cambridge Handbook of Human Dignity* (Cambridge: Cambridge University Press, 2014) 526-534 and 551-558;

63 Andorno, "The Dual Role of Human Dignity in Bioethics," 970.

64 Brownsword says that, "there is a fault line in international jurisprudence of human dignity. Whereas, one the one side, we find a liberal ethic that treats human dignity as the underpinning of human rights, on the other, we have a conservative ethic holding that the fundamental duty is not to compromise human dignity." Quoted from R. Brownsword, "Human Dignity from A Legal Perspective," in: M. Düwell, J. Braarvig, R. Brownsword, D. Mieth (eds.) *The Cambridge Handbook of Human Dignity* (Cambridge: Cambridge University Press, 2014) 1-22, 7. See also R. Brownsword, "Bioethics Today, Bioethics Tomorrow: Stem Cell Research and the Dignitarian Alliance," *University of Notre Dame Journal of Law, Ethics and Public Policy* 17 (2003) 15-51.

65 Brownsword, "Human Dignity from a Legal Perspective," 8.

66 David Feldmann, "Human Dignity as a Legal Value: Part I," *Public Law* (1999) 682-702; 685. See also "Human Dignity as a Legal Value: Part I," *Public Law* (2000) 61-76.

collective, is larger than self-respect. Robert E. Goodin is right in saying that the "entitlements arising out of [respect for dignity] may vary somewhat with time and place... [For] what [others] mean by their actions is crucial, and performance intended to humiliate in once culture might be intended to honour in another."[67] Therefore, there is always room for careful considerations to see what promotes human dignity at best and what violates human dignity at worst. There is no ready-made, clear-cut answer to the problem of indignities either. One area where we can easily understand that dignity is at risk is when the right to life is violated, since (i) it is only in and through a body that a human life can exist at all, (ii) bodily-life is the most fundamental good of human life and (iii) the right to life is the most fundamental right. In such cases, there is no weighing of human dignity against any principle. Dignity is neither available for compromise, nor can it be subjected to autonomy.

A tension between human dignity as the empowerment of autonomy and human dignity as constraint existed in the German legal decision on the well-known Peep-Show case:[68] The Federal Administrative Tribunal denied a licence for the peep-show on the ground that the performance would violate Article 1(1) of the Basic Law. Affirming that "respect for and protection of human dignity are constituent principles of the Basic Law," and that in the peep show, "the woman is placed in a degrading position" and "treated like an object,"[69] the Tribunal said:

> The consent of the women concerned can only exclude a violation of human dignity if such a violation is based only on the lack of consent to the relevant actions or omissions of the women concerned. However, this is not the situation here because in the case at issue... the human dignity of the women concerned is violated by the exposition typical of these performances. Here, human dignity, because its significance reaches beyond the individual, must be protected even against the wishes of the woman concerned whose own subjective ideas deviate from the objective value of human dignity.[70]

The objective value of human dignity is present in the whole species of humanity going beyond the individual. If an act violates the objective value in anyone, then human dignity is said to be violated irrespective of whether

---

67 Robert E. Goodin, "The Political Theories of Choice and Dignity," *American Philosophical Quarterly* 18 (1981) 91-100, 99.

68 BVerwGE 64 (1981) 274. Cited in Beyleveld and Brownsword, *Human Dignity in Bioethics and Biolaw,* Ch. 2: "Human Dignity and the New Bioethics: Human Dignity as Constraint," 29- 47, 34.

69 Beyleveld and Brownsword, Human Dignity in Bioethics and Biolaw, 34.

70 BVerwGE 64 (1981) 277-279. Quoted in Beyleveld/Brownsword, *Human Dignity in Bioethics and Biolaw,* 34.

the concerned party freely agrees to perform such act or not. Free choice is irrelevant when human dignity is at stake. The individual as well as collective recognition of human dignity as an objective value, namely, in particular, human being and in humanity as a whole, can be used in two specific ways: human dignity as a moral principle or norm for the empowerment of human life and as a rule of constraint to restrict undignified individual and collective human acts. At the legal level, human dignity can be used as a constitutive norm to guide the public as well as private human life. Brownsword says, "human dignity is deployed not only to give protection to human life from the point of conception (including human embryos) but also to constrain actions which, although *prima facie* merely self-regarding, are judged to compromise human dignity (whether located in the actor's own person or humanity or, so to speak, in the community's collective conscience)."[71]

Seen from a liberal-individualist and conservative-collective approaches, human dignity can pose a challenge that one can stand against each other. While the former stresses upon respect for individual choices, the latter will set limits to individual freedom. While the former focuses on the rights of individuals, the latter speaks of duties of the state and the society. While the former speaks of empowerment of human choices, the latter constrains actions contrary to the individual and collective human dignity. Unlike many might see these two perspectives in a conflictual manner, there is a possibility of seeing them in complementarity. That is possible in a shared common understanding of human dignity that it is foundational and prior to human features and activities, the state and the society. Clearly, human dignity precedes human autonomy. It is not autonomy that renders human dignity; rather autonomy is only an indicative factor to authenticate human specialness for protection-worthiness. In this sense, neither the individual nor the society can impose something against each other. As Feldman cautions that, "once it becomes a tool in the hands of lawmakers and judges, the concept of human dignity is a two-edged sword."[72] This double-edged sword needs to be carefully used.

Taking Stock

We have seen the two natures of human dignity: (i) as an inherent property of individual humans and (ii) as a collective conscience. Further, the inherent human dignity operates as an empowerment of individual human life and as a constraint on free choice. While the former plays a background role and the latter plays a foreground role. As a background justification for the recognition of human rights and as the source of the fundamental freedoms, the idea of

71 Brownsword, "Human Dignity from A Legal Perspective," 6.

72 David Feldman, "Human Dignity as a Legal Virtue: Part I," *Public Law* 14 (1999) 682-702, 685; Quoted in: Brownsword, "Human Dignity from A Legal Perspective," 8.

intrinsic human dignity as empowerment comes with the right to respect for one's dignity as a human as well as the right to the conditions in which human dignity can flourish. Thus, human dignity as empowerment plays a double role: (a) as a negative right will oppose unwilled interventions by others and through the freedom of researches in biosciences and biotechnologies,[73] (b) and as a positive right will render support and assistance to secure circumstances and conditions essential to flourish as a human. Thus, any hurdle to the dignity as empowerment is therefore a double offence: (i) a denial of rights and dignity as well as (ii) a denial of responsibility.[74] In the background court of human dignity as empowerment, autonomy is prioritized and the informed consent rules empowerment bioethics.

Human dignity as constraint does exactly the other way. Dignity in the foreground puts a constraint on free choice. In its rule, either paternalism or social defence prevails and autonomous consent (no matter how free or informed) is no more decisive. Human dignity as a rule of constraint can restrict autonomy in favour of the collective good of society's vision and rules that it is wrong to compromise one's own dignity as it is to compromise the dignity of others.[75] Yet, it is the one and the same intrinsic human dignity that is at play with roles of empowerment and constraint. In the constraint mode, we refer to the dignity of the human being to prevent indignities, and in the empowerment mode, we promote the dignity of being human. And we can be friends of both concepts. They are complementary and not opposites. The principle of respect for human dignity thus as a *negative* requirement forbids certain practices without any balance with other principles, and a *positive* requirement promotes the improvement of quality of life.[76]

---

73 Leon Kass explains: "In [...] domains of clinical medicine and research involving human subjects, appeals to human dignity, while tacitly employing an ideal of proper treatment and respect, function explicitly as bulwarks against abuse: patients should not be reduced to "thing-hood" or treated as mere bodies; research subjects should not be utilized as mere means or treated only as experimental animals. This "negative" function of the concept of human dignity in these domains makes perfect sense, inasmuch as it is intended – and needed – to restrain the strong in their dealings against the weak." Kass, "Defending Human Dignity," 301.

74 Beyleveld and Brownsword, *Human Dignity in Bioethics and Biolaw*, 11-16.

75 Beyleveld and Brownsword, *Human Dignity in Bioethics and Biolaw,* 11, 29-47.

76 This can be also connected to the concepts of sanctity of life and quality of life. The former is the mirror of human image; the latter is facilities for human life for instance, better schools, hospitals, transport system, etc. see Roberto Andorno, "The Dual Role of Human Dignity in Bioethics," *Medical Health Care and Philosophy* 16 (2013) 967-973, 969.

Human Dignity: Foundation of Human Rights

Habermas says that morality is a unified code and dignity is the moral source from which all of the basic rights derive their meaning.[77] The equal human dignity of everybody demands the membership of everyone in a constitutional political community, which in turn must protect human dignity by granting equal rights and preventing violation of these rights.[78] Habermas states that human rights that arose against despotism and oppression have always been associated with dignity in its appeal for justice to remedy suffering and humiliation. In fact, the moral content of human rights lies in the normative character of human dignity. In the line of thinking of Habermas, Misztal says that "the centrality of human dignity in all historical struggles against various forms of domination and humiliation explains why, in order to prevent mass crimes and to construct just political order, there has always been the need to fufil `the moral promise to respect the human dignity of every human person equally`."[79]

The first and the most fundamental right of humans is the right to life, whose moral credence springs forth from human dignity. Life is the most fundamental good of any living entity. Taking away a life is the violation of the right to life. Taking away any life does not pose the same weight of a moral problem, but in humans, the right to life becomes absolute in the sense of practical moral reason, and in the natural world, no life is absolute. Every physical entity dies one day. As Kant equates humanity with dignity, we could say that dignity is inseparably intertwined with the right to life. There is no more any possibility for the talk of human dignity, when the life is interrupted as in the case of abortion or suicide or euthanasia. We may still treat a dead body with certain respect, but death brings the end to life, all dignity-talks and moral considerations.

The concept of human dignity is nowhere clearer than in bioethics to defend humans against life-destroying choices or decisions. Human dignity makes no compromise when the right to life is at risk. In this sense, it functions not only a principle but becomes a norm or rule. The exception to this rule or norm can happen only when two lives are in conflict with each other. Therefore, it is "the most useful and the primary and supreme concept" as against all criticisms of dignity as a "useless concept" by Ruth Macklin who

77 Jürgen Habermas, The Concept of Human Dignity and the Realistic Utopia of Human Rights," *Metaphilosophy* 41/4 (2010) 464-480, 466.

78 Habermas, "The Concept of Human Dignity and the Realistic Utopia of Human Rights," 464.

79 Barbara A. Misztal, "The Idea of Dignity: Its Modern Significance," *European Journal of Social Theory* 16/1 (2012) 101-121, 113-4.

equated dignity with "respect for autonomy." Andorno speaks of a minimal threshold of the dignity of every human being in the legal systems:

> The meaning of dignity can indeed be better grasped by considering what is *contrary* to it rather than what is in conformity with it. Evil is easier to identify than goodness. It is when we are confronted with the worst things that can be done to a human being that we better understand, by contrast, what "dignity" means. Even the Kantian categorical imperative according to which on one is to be treated as a mere means to another's end can be regarded as an example of this *via negativa.* Therefore, it can be claimed that the first and primary task of the principle of human dignity is to set a minimal threshold of respect for a human being, i.e. to clearly indicate what practices are absolutely incompatible with a civilized society. Only after having established that minimum, the legal system can seek to promote people's well-being in positive terms.[80]

Human rights systems and declarations have an assumption that people have inherent dignity and therefore are entitled to fundamental rights to protection and non-humiliation. Andorno says it succinctly that "legal norms do not create from nothing; [...] people's rights are not the capricious invention of lawmakers, who could legitimately revoke them in a change of humour. Rather, individual states, as well as the international community, are morally *obliged* to recognize that all people have basic rights (i.e. that they have equally valid claims to basic goods) because this latter derive from the dignity which is inherent in every human being."[81] Article 6 of the Universal Declaration of Human Rights says that "everyone has the right to recognition everywhere as a person before the law." Recognition denotes the formal acknowledgement of what is already existing.[82] It is noteworthy that legal systems do not define human dignity as an arbitrary legal fiction or as a metaphysical hypothesis or as a religious symbol. The reason behind this is also to avoid any affiliation to a particular culture or religion or school of thought.[83] It creates a sense of plurality and universal validity.

Legal systems present human dignity as the "*indispensable basis for the fair functioning of human society.* All human beings qua humans are regarded as really deserving to be treated with unconditional respect and entitled with basic rights regardless of age, sex, physical or mental abilities, ethnic origin, religion, political ideas, socio-economic status, or any other particular condition

80 Andorno, "The Dual Role of Human Dignity in Bioethics," 969.

81 Andorno, "The Dual Role of Human Dignity in Bioethics," 968.

82 J. Nickel, *Making Sense of Human Rights: Philosophical Reflections on the Universal Declaration of Human Rights* (Berkeley: University of California Press, 1987); Andorno, "The Dual Role of Human Dignity in Bioethics," 968.

83 Andorno, "The Dual Role of Human Dignity in Bioethics," 968.

or circumstance. This is the core idea behind the concept of human dignity."[84] In this sense, humans have no rights apart from human dignity; rather human dignity is the only word that stands under carrying human rights on its head. Thus, human dignity is the overarching and shaping principle of international bioethics. Human rights require state recognition, but the ultimate validity of human rights is the acknowledgement of dignity that already exists. In other words, "basic rights are grounded on the inherent worth of every human being and not on a merely contingent decision of lawmakers or of the international community, [and] they cannot be taken away by any authority."[85] Andorno gives a fitting, precise explanation of the relationship between human dignity and human rights:

> Why do we need the notion of dignity if we already have that (much more concrete) of human rights? Is dignity not a mere collective term to refer to rights? The fact is that international law clearly distinguishes between dignity and rights: rights *derive* from human dignity; human dignity is not a kind of super-right, but rather the ultimate source of all rights. The idea of human dignity intends to respond to the question "why do human beings have rights?" And the answer is that they are entitled to rights precisely because they possess intrinsic worth.[86]

Far from being a 'vacuous figure of speech'[87], human dignity, as the 'primacy principle' (Principle I.5 in Helsinki 1964), reveals the fundamental idea that "the person does not have to reach any functional standard to be valuable as a person or to be treated with full respect."[88] Human rights belong to existing individuals yet are insufficient to cope with the new biotechnological challenges that affect humanity as a whole. Hence, human dignity plays the role of an overarching objective principle to protect human image and humanity as a species against biotechnological threats as well as of a concrete subject standard for self-respect and self-esteem. Both human dignity and human rights recognize the inherent value of humans. They are complementary and inhere in human being(s). Human rights derive from human dignity and should never violate their source. There are no human rights without human dignity.

---

84 Andorno, "The Dual Role of Human Dignity in Bioethics," 968.

85 Andorno, "The Dual Role of Human Dignity in Bioethics," 968.

86 Andorno, "The Dual Role of Human Dignity in Bioethics," 970.

87 G. Helgesson and S. Eriksson, "Against the Principle that the Individual Shall Have Priority over Science," *Journal of Medical Ethics* 34/1 (2008) 54-56.

88 Colin Parker, "The Moral Primacy of the Human Being," *Journal of Medical Ethics* 36/9 (2010) 563-566. Quoted in Andorno, "The Dual Role of Human Dignity in Bioethics," 969.

Conclusion

Human dignity has intrinsic, attributed and inflorescent variants, inheres in human individuals as well as collectively in human species, plays positive and negative roles of empowerment and constraint, functions as a principle as well as a rule and is a self-respect, self-esteem and social recognition in acknowledgement of the secured, inviolable, intrinsic worth. It prohibits self-degradation and social degradation of individuals and humanity as a whole. It inheres not only in rational-moral capacities but includes all basic human needs. Humanity is dignity, and every human individual is a concrete, experiential face of existential dignity. Human dignity is neither vague nor useless, but the supreme moral-legal watchdog principle of complementarity for bioethics, biolaw and biopolitics to protect humans against misuses under the mask of freedom of research in biosciences and biotechnologies.

28

The Spirituality of Fullness of Life: A Study of the Spirituality of Kurien Kunnumpuram Based on his Writings

Stephen Chundamthadam SJ
Samanvaya, Centre for Indian Studies, Kanjirapally, Kerala

Abstract: *People sincerely search for God experience through spiritual practises. Spirituality has to lead one to liberation and salvation. Liberation is from the oppressive and inhuman structures, and situations and salvation is a movement towards eternal life. One can experience God in nature, in the depth of one's own being, through the rites and doctrines of religion and in the socio-political involvements. In this sense, spirituality becomes an integrated one, integrating prayer and work and humanizing the person. Prayer improves the quality of a human person so that one may experience peace and joy in life. Christian Spirituality is meant to facilitate personal growth in the following of Christ for the service of our people. Spirituality is a lif-style and a way of life. It is an internal search for growth, meaning and holiness of life, which is revealed in the quality of one's life.*
Keywords: *inclusive spirituality, Abba experience, the spirituality of compassion, pilgrim of the Absolute, inhuman structures, people of God.*

Introduction

This is article is about the spirituality of Kurien Kunnumpuram based on his writings. He started his academic life in the context of Vatican II, which influenced his theological thinking and spirituality to a great extent.

Kunnumpuram developed an inclusive spirituality faithful to the teachings of Jesus Christ and Vatican II. This inclusive spirituality leading to the fullness of life for all was a deviation from the traditional understanding of Christian spirituality. The traditional Christian spirituality taught that salvation is possible only in and through the church. But spirituality in the wider sense is not restricted to any particular religion, tradition or culture. The common factor in all these is the belief in a transcendent divine power.[1] Christian spirituality is partaking in the Christ event (life, passion, death and resurrection of Jesus) through personalization of Christ mystery. Spirituality is a life of total detachment lived in the awareness of the indwelling and all-pervading spirit. "Christian Spirituality is, therefore, participation in the mystery of Christ through the interior life of grace, actuated by faith, charity and other Christian virtues. Vatican II opened up the understanding of salvation and spirituality. The life that the individual receives through participation in Christ is the same life that the Incarnate Word shares with the Father and the Holy Spirit."[2]

Inclusive Spirituality

Inspired by the vision of the Second Vatican Council, Kunnumpuram presented an inclusive spirituality, which envisages the salvation for all as the people of God. He makes a distinction between piety and genuine spirituality; the former is guided by the faithful performance of devotional practices and rituals whereas the latter is guided by the spirit of God which transforms the life and values of a person. There is an urgent need for true spirituality in the Church. Encouraged by the idea of Karl Rahner on spirituality, he makes it clear what we need today in the Church is not piety but true spirituality manifested in the life and values of a person. "The Church's public life even today (for all the goodwill which is not to be questioned) is dominated to a terrifying extent by ritualism, legalism, administration, and a boring and resigned spiritual mediocrity continuing along familiar lines."[3]

Though there are a number of religious congregations and pious and devotional practices, he wonders, how many of them have genuinely imbibed the spirit of Jesus' Abba experience which became the driving force behind

1 "In its widest sense, spirituality refers to any religious or ethical value that is concretized as an attitude or spirit from which one's actions proceed. This concept of spirituality is not restricted to any particular religion; it applies to any person who has a belief in the divine transcendent power and fashions a life-style according to one's religious conviction. In this context, one can speak of Zen Buddhist, Jewish and Muslim Spirituality as well as Christian Spirituality." Jordan Aumann, *Spiritual Theology*. London Sheed and Ward, 1979. P. 17.

2 Jordan Aumann, 1979.p. 18.

3 Quoted by Kunnumpuram, in his work, *Towards the Fullness of Life.* from K. Rahner, *The Shape of the Church to Come*, London: SPCK, 1972, p. 82.

his radical commitment to the kingdom of God. For him, religious life is not a monastic withdrawal from the world, but it is a prophetic commitment to the people to enable them to experience God in the midst of their struggles and sufferings.

Spirituality: A Way of Life

Spirituality, according to Kurien Kunnumpuram, is a life style and a way of life. It is an internal search for growth, meaning and holiness of life, which is revealed in the quality of life. In the final analysis, spirituality is the transformation by the touch of the spirit of God.[4] Kunnumpuram argues that this life style has to be simple and detached from the material riches; because, "attachment to riches can prevent us from being open to God and to other human beings."

For him:

> Spirituality is a way of life. It is our total inward quest for growth, meaning and authenticity. And it is manifested in the quality of one's life. In the last analysis, to be spiritual is to be touched and transformed by the Spirit of God. In a person who has been touched and transformed by god's Spirit the fruits of the spirit will be seen: "love, joy, peace, patience, kindness, generosity, faithfulness, gentleness and self-control." (Gal. 5:22-23).[5]

In this sense, spirituality aims at "personal growth in the following of Christ for the service of our people." Following Christ requires the reliving of his Abba experience of God as unconditional love.

> In moments of honest self-awareness, we can detect in ourselves a tendency to be greedy, demanding and fastidious, and to cling to whatever we have. We also tend to use our ministry and social position for the purpose of self-aggrandizement. It is here that the call to a simple lifestyle becomes relevant. It tells us to let go, to be simple, to be modest. It also asks us to share with others not only our possessions but also our time, talents, industry and creativity. It also demands from us a more responsible use of time and money.[6]

In short, spirituality is self-emptying and detachment from anything that is contrary to spiritual values. In this sense, spirituality is a call to unconditional love.

---

4 Kurien, *Puthiya Sabhakhum Puthiya Lokathinumvendi.* Ernakulam: St. Paul's, 2016 p. 102.

5 Kunnumpuram, *Towards the Fullness of Life.* Mumbai: St. Paul's, 2009 p. 35.

6 Kunnumpuram, "The Prophetic Dimension of the Religious Life." in *Shaping Tomorrow's Church.* Kurien Kunnumpuram, ed. Mumbai: St. Pauls, 2006. P. 398.

Spirituality is a Call to Selfless Love

Spirituality is a call to 'total and selfless love' and demands us "to deal with all beings-plants, animals, humans-tenderly and affectionately." He laments,

> In the world today there is a lot of pain and suffering inflicted not only on human beings but also on animals. Harm is also done to the inanimate creation. Humankind seems by and large to have lost true chastity, that is, the ability to touch persons and things without hurting and harming them. That is why there are so much cruelty and violence among us.[7]

Though the spirituality Kunnumpuram advocates demand compassion and care for the entire creation it gives an important role in the full development of the human person. He writes, "Mission of the Church is to collaborate with God in His Work for the Wholeness of the Human Person, the Human Community and the Cosmos according to the Pattern Revealed in Jesus Christ."[8]

The Spirituality of Compassion

The priests and the religious are called to live a spiritual life participating in the Abba experience of Christ. He is critical of the kind of spirituality practised today, which lacks compassion and forgiveness. "One is at times surprised that priests, religious and lay people who are obviously pious are manifestly unfair in their dealings with others. Some of them show so little compassion of Christ and are quite unwilling to forgive others."[9]

"All spirituality is meant to facilitate personal growth in the following of Christ for the service of our people."[10] Personal growth is for the service of the people of God. Following Christ involves recapturing Jesus' Abba experience, identifying oneself with the poor and the powerless, confronting the agents of oppression. Kunnumpuram thinks that the Church in India failed to be the agents of God experience to the faithful. As a result, the people search for God-experience elsewhere. It is true that the Charismatic movements in India, to a certain extent, hold back our faithful from joining Neo-Pentecostal Churches. Church in India is more concerned about the prestigious institutions and structures than leading people to God experience.

He laments:

> Our liturgy, too, has largely failed to mediate an authentic experience of God. There is an undue insistence on rites and rubrics, on law and structure, in our common worship. We cannot, of course, deny the need

7 Kunnumpuram, ibid p. 398.

8 Kunnumpuram, "The Church of My Dreams" 407; also in *Freedom and Liberation. Reflections on the Church's Vocation and Mission.* 131.

9 Kunnumpuram, *Towards the Fullness of Life.* p. 35.

10 Kunnumpuram, *ibid,* p. 36.

> for some general norms in this matter.... But sufficient room must be left for responsible experimentation. Since life is so rich and varied, meaningful liturgy, which is the celebration of life, will always be free and spontaneous, at least to some extent.[11]

Referring to the Asian Synod, Kunnumpuram argues that Christian spirituality in India has to resonate with the Asian spiritual traditions founded on experience. "The search for God... has always stirred the human heart and which is particularly visible in Asia's many forms of spirituality and asceticism." (*Ecclesia in Asia* 44). The Synod proposes faithful listening to the word of God and meaningful celebration of the sacraments, particularly the Eucharist as the means of God experience. (*EA* 22-23). Based on the teachings of Vatican II and some of the popes Kunnumpuram elucidates the main characteristics of spirituality for India.

Spirituality is Experiencing the Divine

Christian Spirituality is a spirituality of involvement in the world and not of monastic withdrawal from it. Involvement in the world brings in the different dimensions of the experience of the Divine. Some of the main characteristics of spirituality are experiencing God in nature, in the depth of one's own being, through the rites and doctrines of religion and in the socio-political involvements. In this sense, spirituality becomes an integrated one, integrating prayer and work and humanising the person. Prayer improves the quality of a human person so that one may experience peace and joy in life.

Prayer for him is the loving contact with God, which is possible only through loving contact with people. Love of God and love of people are the two dimensions of the most important commandment in Christianity. 'Compassion and kindness enabled the good Samaritan' to transcend the narrow restrictions imposed on him by the Jewish tradition and to reach out to his neighbour who was in need. Spirituality strengthens hope. "In the final analysis, Christian hope is not about what we can foresee, plan, control and manipulate. It is about our total surrender to the incomprehensible mystery of God, who cannot be controlled or manipulated, but who is perceived as the one who ultimately blesses, sanctifies and constitutes our salvation." [12]

The Spirituality of Suffering

In his work *Towards the Fullness of Life,* he writes:

> There is a tendency among many people to practice a spirituality which may not be quite Christian. They believe that the more they suffer, the

11 Kunnumpuram, "The Crisis of Values in the Catholic Church." in *Towards a New Humanity: Reflections on the Church's Mission in India Today*. Mumbai: St. Pauls, 2005.pp 240-251.

12 Kunnumpuram, *Towards the Fullness of Life*. p. 20.

> more pleasing to God they become. What kind of God is this who is happy to see us suffer? I firmly believe that God wants us to be happy here on earth. Besides, we Christians are committed to the removal of pain and suffering from the face of the earth.[13]

He continues, "It is not that God prevented me from experiencing pain, suffering or even failure... What I wish to say is this: In and through my mistakes and sins, and in and through the wise and foolish decisions of my superiors and others, God has guided my life according to his design."[14]

For Kunnumpuram, spirituality is a term with broader meaning; it doesn't limit itself to the socio-cultural and economic aspects of this worldly life; it goes beyond the empirical existence. Because, for him "The human person is not a soul living in a body, but an animated body, so perfectly integrated that the person in his totality can express himself/herself and be apprehended in any part."[15]

Spirituality of Salvation

As a soul animated body, a human person longs for liberation and salvation. Liberation is from the oppressive and inhuman structures and situations and salvation to eternal life. "The first and fundamental meaning of liberation, which thus manifests itself is the salvific one: man is freed from the radical bondage of evil and sin. In this experience of salvation, a man discovers the true meaning of his freedom, since liberation is the restoration of freedom. It is also education in freedom, that is to say, education in the right use of freedom. Thus to the salvific dimension of liberation is linked its ethical dimension."[16]

Salvation, according to Kunnumpuram, has a social dimension (*LG* 9), it is not attained through the individual, internal effort alone. "The universal plan of God for the salvation of mankind is not carried out solely in a secret manner" (*AG* 3). Nor it is limited to Christians alone; it is open to all people of goodwill.

> All this holds true not for Christians only but also for all men of good will in whose hearts grace is active and invisible. For, since Christ died for all, and since all men are in fact called to one and the same destiny, which is

13 Kunnumpuram, *ibid* p. 73.

14 Kunnumpuram, *ibid* p. 133.

15 Kunnumpuram, "Reflections of Christian Spirituality," 212. in *Life in Abundance: Indian Christian Reflections on Spirituality*, by Kurien Kunnumpuram, 211-220. Mumbai: St. Pauls, 2006.

16 Cited by Kunnumpuram from "Instruction on Certain Aspects of Theology of Liberation, 23 "Freedom and Liberation. Reflection on a New Document from Rome." p. 194.

> divine, we must hold that the Holy Spirit offers to all the possibility of being partners, in a way known to God, in the paschal mystery.[17]

Vatican Council teaches: "Seeds of the Word lie hidden in these cultural and religious traditions of people," these have to be respected. (*A G.*11), "they are precious elements of religion and humanity" (*G S.* 92). Whatever truth and grace are to be found among the nations is a sort of secret presence of God, because, "Doubtless, the Holy Spirit was already at work in the world before Christ was glorified." (*A G.*9.4). In *Perfecte Caritatis* we read, "The manner of living, praying, and working should be suitably adapted everywhere, but especially in mission territories, to the requirements of the culture and the social and economic circumstances." (*P. C.* no. 3). Culture, tradition and belief system play an important role in the formation of any spirituality. Three factors, i.e., God, world and human are inevitable for a better understanding of any spiritual tradition.

Love for Culture of Silence and Solitude

God speaks to us in the depths of our being. In order to listen to God, we need to cultivate the culture of silence and solitude. He proposed two kinds of prayers, i.e., the prayer of the mind, which includes vocal prayer, meditation and contemplation; and prayer of the heart where the mind is inactive. "We need to try ever new methods of prayer in order to find out those methods which help us to pray at this stage of our life. Methods that we found helpful at an earlier stage of our life may not be so right now... We learn to pray well by praying." [18]

The Need for Integral Spirituality in the Indian Context

Kunnumpuram feels that there is a strong longing for God experience in the minds of the ordinary people, which is revealed in various spiritual movements. The longing for God-experience is strong in the pluri-religious context in India.

Pope Paul VI during the Bombay Eucharistic Congress in 1964, addressing the non-Christian Religious Leaders said: "Yours is a land of ancient culture, the cradle of great religions, the home of a nation that has sought God with a relentless desire in deep meditation and silence and in hymns of fervent devotion."

On 2nd February 1986, Pope John Paul II in his address to the representatives of religions in Delhi said:

---

17 *GS* 22, cited by Kunnumpuram in *Ways of Salvation: The Salvific Meaning of Non-Christian Religions According to the Teachings of Vatican II.* Poona: Pontifical Athenaeum, 1971. p.89.

18 Kunnumpuram, *Towards the Fullness of Life.* Mumbai: St. Paul's, 2009 p. 33.

> Integral human development requires a spiritual vision of man- that man is a pilgrim of the Absolute, travelling toward a goal, seeking the face of God. From this spiritual vision of man comes the strength to preserve in the cause, as well as the clarity of thought needed to find concrete solutions to man's problems.

Pope John Paul 11, more than any other pope has been keenly encouraging a culture of inter-religious dialogue among the faithful. Through his worldwide travels, prayer meetings, meeting with heads of religious communities; his close acquaintance with other religious traditions, etc., created a better rapport with other traditions.

Conclusion

Inspired by the Second Vatican Council and encouraged by the pioneering theological efforts of Samuel Rayan and George Soares-Prabhu, Kunnumpuram argued for an inclusive spirituality. This inclusive spirituality leading to the fullness of life for all was a deviation from the traditional understanding of Christian spirituality. His understanding of spirituality included all irrespective of caste, religion, culture or tradition. He believed that the whole of creation has a role in the economy of salvation. Though Kunnumpuram advocated for compassion and care for the entire creation, he gave an important role in the full development of the human person. The distinction he made between piety and genuine spirituality is relevant in the Indian Church today, and he believed that there is an urgent need for true spirituality in the Church. For him, religious life is not a monastic withdrawal from the world, but it is a prophetic commitment to the people to enable them to experience God amid their struggles and sufferings. Spirituality, according to Kunnumpuram, is a lifestyle and a way of life. It is an internal search for growth, meaning and holiness of life, which is revealed in the quality of life. His thought-provoking insights that the Church in India failed to be the agents of God experience to the faithful, Indian Church has to resonate with the spiritual traditions of Asia based on experience, Christian Spirituality is the spirituality of involvement in the world and not of monastic withdrawal from it are challenges to the Church in India.

29

Carnal Hermeneutics and the Divine-Human Dynamism of Love

Victor Ferrao

Dean of Philosophy, Rachol Seminary, Goa

Abstract: *Following the carnal turn in hermeneutics, we wish to explore the divine human dynamics of love. We begin with an attempt to understand carnal hermeneutics; we then take up the flesh to flesh dynamism of humans as being-towards-the-world. Next, we attempt to theologise in the light of hermeneutics. While exploring the divine human dynamics of love, we realise that we relate to God, humans and creation primarily as embodied beings in-the-the-world. We live in flesh as 'Incarnate Cogito'. Therefore, one might say that carnal hermeneutics might produce a Copernican revolution in Theology as well as Philosophy. The immediacy of living in flesh can open us new dialogical way of relating God, humanity, and creation.*

Keywords: *Hermeneutics, carnality, dialogical way, locus theologicus, incarnation.*

Hermeneutics is a science that assists us to grasp how understanding takes place. With the rise of phenomenology, hermeneutics had a new lease of life. The work of Martin Heidegger, Hans George Gadamer, Paul Ricoceur, Jurgen Habermas and others open us to understanding and made it part of our everyday life.[1] Some thinkers assert that humans are hermeneutical

1 For a good introduction to hermeneutics read Hermeneutics by Richard Palmer's , Richard E. Palmer *Hermeneutics* (Evaston : Northwestern University Press, 1969), 7.

animals.[2] Although, these new developments have praise worthy applications, we have still not explored the profound depths and heights of what has been called as the hermeneutical turn in Philosophy. Unfortunately, the hermeneutical turn got trapped in the linguistic turn and remained largely locked into the intellectual and semantic dimensions of understanding. Phenomenology did its bit to rehabilitate our constitutive corporeal dimension, yet hermeneutics seem to remain trapped into the oculo-centric moorings of understanding.[3] Thanks to the work of Catholic philosopher Richard Kearney, we can trace a return to primordial aspects of hermeneutics that takes our bodily existence seriously.[4] These developments are profoundly vital as they bring new light that enables us to understand the Divine Human reaching out in Love. Love may not be fully understood outside our bodily existence. The essential bodily dimension of divine love is manifested in the mystery of divine incarnation and human quest for theopoesis.[5] There is a profound hermeneutical belonging together in the bond of love between Humans and God. The divine journey of love may be seen as reaching its climax in the word becoming flesh. In the incarnation God's love of humanity is revealed in flesh. If the divine journey is "Word becoming flesh", the human journey is "flesh becoming Word". Our study promises to open new horizons to understand the divine-human dynamism of love. This is why we turn to the carnal hermeneutics of Kearney in a Pastoral Year dedicated to the theme: "The love of Christ urges us on."

Following the carnal turn in hermeneutics, we wish to explore the divine-human dynamics of love. We begin with an attempt to understand carnal hermeneutics; we then take up the flesh to flesh dynamism of humans as being-towards-the-world. Next, we attempt to theologise in the light of hermeneutics. Finally, we try to explore the divine-human dynamics of love.

Understanding Carnal Hermeneutics

Hermeneutics is chiefly imprisoned into linguistic and intellectual chains. We seem to have surrendered to the dictum that teaches that we have no access to reality outside language.[6] May be this linguistic limit in the dynamic process of understanding forgets a primary aspect to it. Linguistic laden-ness of the dynamism of our understanding remains open to the oral and visual aspects of

---

2 See Cyril Desbruslais, *Interpretation of Transcendence* (Pune: Jnanadeepa Vidyapeeth, 1989).

3 See Richard Kearney , 'The wager of Carnal Hermeneutics' , in Richard Kearney, *Carnal Hermeneutics*, (New York: Fordham University Press, 2015), 16-17.

4 *Ibid.*, 15-56.

5 See Lancy Monteiro, "God's Divining Presence: an Adequate of Revelation for a Theology of Interreligious Dialogue" in *Vidyajoti Journal of Theological Reflection* (Delhi: Vidyajoti Welfare and Educational society, Nov 2017, No. 80), 53-54.

6 Jacques Derrida seems to takes this position when he says 'there is nothing outside the text'

opening ourselves to the world that continuously gives itself to us.[7] It seems to close itself to the other senses that enable us to sense the world even before we begin to speak. The carnal hermeneutics of Kearney opens us to this primordial sensing of the world.

Sensing the World

Humans sense the world and make sense of it even before they develop linguistic competence. Right from the moment of our birth and some may say that even during the developmental stages in the womb, humans access their world without linguistic abilities. This means that we have access to the world outside language. Our intense sense experience enables us to make sense of the world around us. The world is sensible and can be understood through our senses of touch and taste, maybe even before we begin to use linguistics categories of our intellect. We interpret the world with our bodily senses. This primordial sensing of the world is primary, while the intellectual apprehension of the world through the modes of language is secondary. Carnal hermeneutics of Richard Kearney dwells with this primary relation that we develop to make sense of the world. This primary sensing of the world gives us sense (meaning) of the world. The world before being intelligible is revealed as sensible and what we sense about the world makes us orient ourselves to the world. One might see intellection involved in the sensing of the sensible world. We may do well to bracket it to enter the hermeneutical horizons of flesh in the dynamism of understanding. We have to do this in order to free even our sense knowledge from the clutches of over intellection. Over intellection has enslaved us to binaries of sense/ nonsense, sensible/ intellectual and the like. In this context, we primarily follow the phenomenological attitude that remains open and passive and enable us to receive the revelation of the world through the primordial working of our senses.

Living in Flesh

We live in the flesh right from the moment of our birth. Some may say that this life in flesh begins at conception. Vitality at infancy is mainly a matter of taste and tact. The infant's main windows to the world are taste and touch. The touch and taste of mother's breast as the child opens its mouth for the first milk becomes the primary locus of sensing the world. This shows that humans are flesh before words and are striving to become words all our lives. Indeed, we can trace this human dynamism embedded in our quest for wisdom. The Latin word *sapientia* comes from the word *sapere* which means to taste.[8] We

7 Phenomenology teaches that it is world that primarily gives itself to us.

8 See Richard Kearney , 'The Wager of Carnal Hermeneutics' , in Richard Kearney, *Carnal Hermeneutics*, 16.

become open to wisdom through our dynamism of tasting. Breast being the first window to the world opens us to understand the world through taste. Melanie Klein, an English psychoanalyst, teaches that breast is the world to the child. The breast that gives milk is good, and the breast does not give is bad.[9] She teaches that we are primarily searching for substitutes for the milking giving breast in different ways all our adult life. These teachings seem to indicate that our deepest 'knowings' are tasting and touching. From the moment of birth, humans are condemned to sense the world through the tips of their tongue that enable us to discern between savoury and unsavoury. It is taste and touch that makes the world sensible and we become sensitive. This is why touch and taste are the primary locus of hermeneutics. There is a deep inextricable relation between sensing and interpretation.

Hermeneuticising Carnally

Carnal hermeneutics embraces a large spectrum of sense. It is our primary deciphering tool of life. Flesh mediates between us, world and God. We are incarnated and we keep incarnating into the world to understand and relate to it. Body enables us to begin living tactfully and sensitively. Body literally keeps us in touch with things.[10] It is our embodied existence that keeps us open to the world. The flesh is a medium of transition and transmission.[11] It keeps mediating and messaging between, inside and outside, self and other and more than human. This is primarily done through touch. Touch is something that we first do to the world. It is the touch that is something that the world does to us first too. There is a two-way mutual relation involved in relating to the world through touch. We touch the world and the world touches us. This does not happen in other ways of sensing the world. Sight requires us to see the world but the world does not see us as we see it. Same can be spoken of hearing and other senses too. In hermeneutical understanding, there is a kind of mutuality. We can notice a hermeneutical circle here. There is a sensing in the sense or receiving or making sense from someone or something other than myself. It is the flesh that mediates this otherness while it crosses back and forth between self and strangeness. This is where hermeneutics arises. This is the locus where what Martin Heidegger calls, 'the as structure' operates.[12] This mediation in the flesh is therefore interpretive even before we can use categories evolved though our linguistic competence. This means flesh mediates but remains

9 https://www.learning-theories.com/object-relations-theory-melanie-klein.html accessed on 5-04-2018.

10 *Ibid.*, 20

11 *Ibidem.*

12 *Ibidem.*

figural to us most of the time. It continuously pre-figure, con-figure and re-figure our experience.[13] We are figuring things out before we begin to speak.

Beings-Towards-the-World Through Flesh

Martin Heidegger taught us that humans are beings-in-the-world. This characterization of us as beings-in-the-world manifest humans as passively receiving the constant giving of the world. Although Heidegger tried to focus on the dynamic relation of being-in the world, his focus on humans as shepherds of being and language as the house of being seem to impose some kind of inertness in the dynamism of humans reaching out to word. The carnal hermeneutics stays open to the dynamism and views humans are beings-towards-the-world rather passive beings-in-the-world.

Hermeneutics of Ownness and Otherness

The flesh is the place where we exist in the world as suffering and acting in pathos and praxis. The flesh is both mine and most other. It is the paradigm of otherness. Paradoxically, it is close to me and furthest to me at the same time. It opens us to our embodied given-ness as well as the given-ness of the world. It becomes a ground of my own proper otherness while at the same time I am enabled to derive the strangeness of the other from my ownness. It is through the flesh that we have space of belonging to the self and its other.[14] It is the foundation of the I-THOU relation. It is the flesh that enables us to develop non-objectifying primordial relations. In order to make oneself part of the world, one does not just have to be oneself but has to be oneself as another-a self with others. This means that the otherness of the other as 'foreign' relates not only to the otherness of my flesh (that I am), but also exists before any reduction to my ownness.[15] Flesh can appear as a body among other bodies to the degree one is another among others, oneself as another as Ricoeur would teach us. It is a flesh that makes us self-with-its-other. This is why flesh is the foundation of one's intimacy to oneself as well as immanence to the other. Thus, flesh constitutes an intimate body (leib) for the self and physical body (korper) among other bodies.[16] This is the basis of carnal hermeneutics where I experience myself as someone in a shared world. The shared world exists for us from flesh to flesh. It is in this flesh to flesh relation that the other is given to me both as inscribed in embodied relation and as always already transcendent. Hence, the analogy becomes the ground of self and other relations.

---

13 *Ibidem.*

14 *Ibid.* 50-51.

15 *Ibidem.*

16 *Ibid.*, 53.

Carnal Difference of the Male and Female

Understanding the difference between male and female carnal experience will enrich humans. Several feminist are turning to the lived body as a better concept for analysis of subjectivity than the gender. Lived body brings the social-cultural experience alongside of the notion of a physically acting body. This brings body-in-situation to the centre of our attention. All persons face the martial facts of one's body and its relation to the environment. This dynamism sums up the carnal existence of humans. It involves our comportment, motility and spatiality. It constitutes our facticity but we have the freedom to construct ourselves in relation to this facticity.[17] The male and female have different facticity. Both respond differently to this facicity. A man exhibits more freedom while woman are governed by patriarchy. Hence, to large extent, women experience alienation. Often their bodily existence is eroticised, vouyerised and fetishised in a man's world.[18] Hence, time and again, women internalise the desire of man and silence their own female desire. Influenced by capitalism and materialist science, being is seen as being in solid objects, self-identical one and the same thing, to be observed measured, passed from hand to hand in a relation of commodity exchange. Unfortunately, in this scenario a woman's desire is organized to become an object of the male gaze and learn to find pleasure in the satisfaction of the male. Carnal hermeneutics opens us to the plight of women and opens them the possibilities of nurturing their own specific desire which is plural, fluid and interested more in touch than sight.

Heremeneutics of Biopower

Human bodies are involved in everything we do – in birth, in health, in work, in sport, in leisure and in death. All kinds of identities that we human form are embodied. Our living and moving bodies produce a physical culture that becomes a way of relating to our environment, ourselves, other humans and God. All liturgies are embodied rites. In the power of technology, we are now moving into techologized bodies. Bodies are biological as well are socially constructed. Body politics is irrupting from the bodies as they are radicalised, marked by caste, medically named as disabled/ diseased/ fit, theologically disembodied, consumerised by the market, digitalised by communication technology, regimented by military and so on and so forth. Besides, body mediates our cultural and ecological process. In several ways body expresses power relations. The body becomes an important space where power operates in our society. Therefore, a critical study of the body results in the critical study of power in our society. The body is site violence as well as a point of its

17 https://real-philosophy.livejournal.com/348094.html accessed on 30-1-2018.

18 genderbitch.wordpress.com/2009/11/23/attraction-and-objectification accessed on 30-1-2018.

resistance. The body is socially interpreted or hermeneutised to produce and sustain unequal power relations in our society. Political-religious ideologies inscribed into patriarchy produce and maintain dominant power relations. All these dominant power relations are naturalised and normalised and they influence everyday habits of thinking. It is only through counter-discourse of body that we can contest and deconstruct the reigning oppressing biopower in our society. Carnal hermeneutics is a very powerful tool to produce such an emancipative discourse.

Theologizing in the Light of Carnal Hermeneutics

Our primary access to the world being taste and touch can let us convert the gustatory and tactile sense as a site of theology. 'Taste and see that the Lord is good' (Psalm 34:8) already articulates a theology developed through carnal hermeneutics. Often eschaton is portrayed as a festive meal and not merely a beatific vision that satisfies the eyes. This shows that carnal hermeneutics has been very central to theologising to both the Christians and the people of the Old Testament. This leads to a humbling in theology and saves us from masking our point of view as God's eye point of view. This also saves us from reducing intelligibility to visibility.

Carnal Hermeneutics in the Old Testament

The inaugural act of Abrahamic discernment is a scene of tasting wherein Abraham and Sarah greet strangers (*Hostis)* from the desert of Mamre who in sharing food revealed themselves as divine and announced the birth of an impossible child Isaac.[19] Later, the revelation of the name of Israel occurs a mutual touching of limbs between Yahweh and Israel.[20] The covenant in the Old Testament is sealed by the Passover meal (Ex 24:1-11). Food was an essential part of covenant making in the ancient near East. We can already find it illustrated in the Bible when Laban and Jacob made peace by breaking bread (Gen. 31: 51-54). The Old Covenant is also pictured through tactile images as one between God and his unfaithful wife (Jer. 21:1-5, Hos. 1:2). The promise of the New Covenant is also given through a taste image of a meal (Isa 25: 6-8). God's faithfulness is seen through various taste images through the feeding of his people with Mana (Ex 6.31, Nub. 11: 7-8) and providing water from the rock (Ex 17.1-7). This manifests that the primal way of relating to the world through the sense of touch and taste became central to the covenantal relationship between God and the People of Israel and manifests that intelligibility is more than mere visibility. The other senses also are valid

19 Richard Kearney, 'The Wager of Carnal Hermeneutics', in Richard Kearney, *Carnal Hermeneutics*, 18 .

20 *Ibidem.*

modes of relating to Goa and his creation. It is based on the principle that our embodied nature leads our body to sense and simultaneously be sensed as sensing.

Carnal Hermeneutics in the New Testament

The fact of Incarnation and bodily Resurrection are the foundational events of the New Testament. The event hermeneutics of the Paschal Mystery is inexhaustible and based in a carnal hermeneutics. In several ways, the New Testament demonstrates that Jesus came to the earth to taste and touch. The wedding feast of Cana, the table fellowship meals, the last supper, the Emmaus meal, manifest the gustatory dimension of his ministry while several of his acts of healings show the touch aspect of his public ministry.[21] We can see how carnal hermeneutics reaches its climax in the last supper, suffering and death on the cross and the victory over the cross in the resurrection of our Lord Jesus Christ But we have admonition not to touch, taste and handle in the teachings of St. Paul. The Apostle teaches that the kingdom of God is not meat and drink but peace and joy in the Holy Spirit (Rom.15:17). He further teaches that 'food does not bring us near God; we are no worse if we do not eat and no better if we eat (1 Cor. 8:8). But his teachings remain ambivalent as he teaches in the later days the Spirit some shall depart from the faith; commanding to abstain from meats (1Tim 4: 1-3). These texts are said to be taught mimically and not dogmatically. St. Augustine held this view and taught St. Paul taught abstinence to present him as a model. We can find thick carnal hermeneutics in St. Paul when he taught that the link between Christ and the Church, calling the church the body of Christ (Col.1: 14-19, 1 Cor. 12:12). But it reaches its climax when he teaches that Christ is suffering in our suffering in the flesh.

Towards a Carnal Theology

Richard Kearney opens a space to do theology via carnal hermeneutics. He teaches that flesh is a medium just like the word. Both inter-animate each other. The "Word becomes flesh" so that "flesh becomes Word." Flesh as a medium precedes all distinctions like subject and object. The flesh is always in a process of immersion into life. It is in the process of mediation. It introduces us body and soul into the flesh of the world. It is the flesh that makes it possible for us to touch as well as be touched by the world. It is flesh that enables us to crossover and recognizes other flesh. It is in and through the flesh that we can relate to everyone including the divine. It is this process of mediation that God embraces through the mystery of the incarnation. It only through 'this is my

21 *Ibid.*, 18.

body'[22] that we can relate to the world and God. Life becomes Eucharist for us all. It is as if we are challenged to live 'this is my body', and through this life in the flesh we participate in the Paschal Mystery of Christ. It is 'this is my body' that breaks into an encounter with God, humans and creation enter into a bond of love in the flesh. This breaking of the 'I' is breaking into an encounter of love and care that loves in the flesh. The 'I' that speaks word becomes the 'I' that is spoken in word. It is the 'I in the flesh' that relates to the 'THOU who became flesh'. It is true that there is no salvation outside the flesh. There is no Paschal Mystery outside the flesh. It is the Word that became flesh that saves. The Eschaton being the Resurrection of the Body cannot be an experience outside the hermeneutics of flesh and cannot be view in limited oculo-centric manner as beatific vision alone. It is also seen as a heavenly banquet that enables us to touch, smell, taste and sees and maybe even provides us occasion to hear everyone in the fellowship of the Saints.

Understanding Divine Human Dynamism of Love

The Divine and Human dynamism of love has a distinct carnal dimension. The carnal dimension brings in the cosmic dimension and brings creation in this love embrace. The divine, human and creation stay entangled in an embrace of love. Here we try to understand this love embrace with the help of familiar symbols of heart, cross and breath we share resonance with faith and carnal hermeneutics

Heart at the Heart of the Bible

The word heart (*lebab*, Hebrew and *Kardia* Greek) plays a key role in the entire Bible. It features in hundreds of places and is used in hundreds of ways in a wide variety of context bearing several meanings that were unknown outside the Jewish community in the Old Testament and early Christians in the New Testament. What we can clearly find is that these several uses of the word heart does not reduce it to a physical organ but becomes the central place of our identity (*ipseity*).[23] Hearts stands for what we properly are. In most cultures, the heart stands for volition but is not thought to be irrational. It is a seat of will and reason. Blasé Paschal famously said that the heart has reasons which reason does not understand.[24] Heart in the bible is an undivided whole and does not signify a distinct organ. But rare exceptions to this general usage are in Jeremiah and St. Paul. Jeremiah invites the people of Israel to a

22 Emmanuel Falque, 'This is my Body: Contribution to the Philosophy of the Eucharist', in Richard Kearney, *Carnal Hermeneutics*, 279- 294.

23 See Jean-Luis Chretien, 'From the Limbs of Heart to the Souls of Organ' , in See Richard Kearney, *Carnal Hermeneutics*, 93.

24 https://en.wikiquote.org/wiki/Talk:Blaise_Pascal accessed 1-2-2018.

spiritual circumcision when he says "remove the foreskin of your heart'.[25] In the same way, St. Paul prays for the Ephesians for spiritual awakening when he says 'May He (God) open the eyes of your heart that hope his call opens up to you'.[26] 'The senses of the heart' that is evoked in the bible can be appropriated with the carnal hermeneutics that we are studying here. It stands for the whole person. The spiritual dimension of the person is appropriated with the corporeal in the biblical context. Unfortunately, it is the old anthropology borrowed from the Greeks that emphasises the soul would later become dominant and humans will be thought to be souls trapped into a body. Thanks to carnal hermeneutics, we can return to holistic anthropology. This holistic anthropology invites us to enter into a hermeneutics of heart to understand and live into the loving embrace of God our Father. Christian tradition that looks at God's love through the symbol of the sacred heart of Jesus can become the locus of dwelling in this loving embrace of God.

Hermeneutics of the Cross

The cross becomes an important symbol of God's love manifested in the passion and death of Jesus Christ, His only Son. The cross produces at once disruptive, interruptive and provocative hermeneutics of God's Love. It presents the entire life of Jesus as a sacrifice on the cross offered for the love of humanity and creation. It produces the resonance of simultaneity of God's involvement, our involvement and world-involvement. It draws us to find a link with the cry, suffering and pain of humanity and creation. The cross becomes the divine embrace of humanity and the entire creation. It is in and through the cross that God, humanity and creation cross each other. The way of the cross becomes the way of God, humanity and creation in which the sacrifice of the cross become enacted in the entire cosmos. This means that the sacrifice of the cross opens our minds and hearts and enables us to view the cosmic sacrifice in the way of the cross of Jesus. This is why whoever follows Jesus Christ has to pick up his /her cross (human and the cosmic side of our life) and follow the Lord (Lk. 9: 23-24). The hermeneutic of the cross along with the hermeneutics of resurrection sparks the light of hope amidst darkness, suffering, disease and sin. This hermeneutics of hope is marked by Christ's victory over the cross. It is a faith that irrupts only after the victory over the cross. It is only through what we call the hermeneutics of the cross that we come to recognise the one born of Mary (Mystery of incarnation) is the Son God and saviour of the world who died on the cross. It is this faith that enables us to live a life of love that strives to establish God's reign in our society.

25 See Jean-Luis Chretien, 'from the Limbs of Heart to the Souls of Organ' , in Richard Kearney, *Carnal Hermeneutics*, 94.

26 *Ibidem*.

Living by the Original Breath

The original breath that was lost by the original sin is restored by the passion, death and resurrection of Jesus. The spirit of God that was hovering over the mighty oceans (Gen 1: 2) is blown into the nostrils of Adam, giving the first human the breath of life (Gen 2:7). Christian faith views the Holy Spirit as the breath of life signifying the giving of the super-abundance of life of God. Hence, the original breath becomes a hermeneutics of Pentecost, which becomes the explosion of God's love for humanity symbolised by the tongues of fire. The hermeneutics of the Spirit is open without closure. The spirit of God refuses all human mastery and always remains in the realm of mystery. The Pentecost proclamation of St. Peter crossing linguistic barriers and all people understand the message of the Apostle in his/her language. This shows that the original breath restored in Jesus Christ is both life-giving and life-affirming. Hence, the hermeneutics of the Holy Spirit invites us to live in the power of the original breath of God restored through the gift of the Holy Spirit. The original breath keeps us into the economy of Trinitarian plan of salvation in communion with the Catholic Church. The sacramental economy, the proclamation of the Word of God and the mission of God's Kingdom of the Catholic Church keeps the original breath of God in circulation both within and outside the boundaries of the Church. This makes the Church a visible sacrament of the communion of God, humanity and creation.

Conclusion

Our study has opened to us that we relate to God, humans and creation primarily as embodied beings in-the-the-world. We live in the flesh as *'Incarnate Cogito'* (Paul Ricoeur). Therefore, one might say that carnal hermeneutics might produce a Copernican revolution in Theology as well as Philosophy. The immediacy of living in the flesh can open us the new dialogical way of relating God, humanity, and creation. The cosmotheandric[27] experience of Humanity is essentially a flesh to flesh experience. It will open up new vistas for ethics and morality as a carnal hermeneutics can draw us to flesh to face encounter emphasised by Emanuel Levinas. Besides, it can be therapeutic as wounds of trauma and pain can require carnal healing. It also promises social emancipation and can become an important resource to contest racialised, caste marked human bodies, medically invaded human bodies through innovation in science and technology, and attacked by capitalist-driven markets. This is why the body has to be the new *locus theologicus* of theology.

27 http://www.raimon-panikkar.org/english/XXXIII-2-cosmotheandric.html accessed on 1-2-2018.

30

"Formation of the Heart:" An Essential (But Ignored) Element in Priestly Formation

P. T. Mathew SJ

Professor of Theology (Emeritus), Vidyajoti College of Theology, New Delhi

***Abstract*:** *Formation of priests was a major theme in the writings of Kurien Kunnumpuram, and the book Called to Serve is particularly noteworthy. In it Fr Kurien discusses four aspects of the formation of priests, viz. human, spiritual, intellectual and pastoral. In this article, the author continues his reflection on aspects of priestly formation. It particularly focuses on a grossly neglected area, viz. formation of the heart. The first part takes a look at the emerging paradox in priestly formation in the present-day context, and the second part reflects more in detail on some key elements in the formation of the heart!*

"What do I still lack?" was a question coming from the heart of a young man, and it required an answer from the heart. Hearing Jesus' answer, the young man went away sorrowful, for he expected an answer from the head, not the heart. Apathetic theology cautions us about the limits of answers from the head, whether in written word or spoken word. There is the 'empty space' beyond words, and that is the space occupied by the heart. Formation of the heart enables a pastor to be 'large-heated' and 'broadminded' reaching beyond the realms of words and reason. It means conscious effort to create space for others and their concerns, expanding one's horizon of relationships to welcome even the excluded. We need pastors with transformed hearts and are capable of transforming the hearts of men and women today.

Keywords: *Formation, Heart, Pastors, Justice and Discernment.*

Introduction

Fr Kurien Kunnumpuram SJ spent most of his active life in the formation of priestly candidates and in teaching them systematic theology. Both demanded of him a creative mind and an emotive commitment. Any thought of him brings up to my mind images of priestly formation with its multiple dimensions and contemporary challenges. Formation of priests was a major theme in his writings, and the book *Called to Serve* is particularly noteworthy.[1] In it, Fr Kurien discusses four aspects of the formation of priests, viz. human, spiritual, intellectual and pastoral. In this short paper, I would like to continue his reflection on aspects of priestly formation. I would like to particularly focus on a grossly neglected area, viz. formation of the heart. In the first part, we shall take a look at the emerging paradox in priestly formation in the present-day context, and in the second part, we shall reflect more in detail on some key elements in the formation of the heart.

The Emerging Paradox

Seminary formation can never remain insulated from what happens in the wider society and the changing cultural scenario. Most of the young men entering the portals of seminaries today are products of the new-gen culture. How do we mould such men as authentic pastors, equipping them with the necessary knowledge, skills and attitudes for effective apostolic commitment is the critical question before us. The sudden explosion in the field of media and communication keep the new-gen people 'engaged' 24x7. Our society is becoming increasingly noisy (and colourful) with little space or time for silence and solitude. Religious worship and celebration do not lag behind! Young priests take pride in displaying their eloquence from pulpits and at conventions adding to the noisy world around. Such is the real context in which priestly formation takes place today. The discrepancy between what is taught in formation houses with the insistence on intellectual formation, on the one hand, and the complexity of challenges in actual pastoral settings leave many young priests confused or disheartened. It is in such a context of paradoxes that we need to speak about the formation of the heart.

Deus Caritas Est, the first encyclical letter of Pope Benedict XVI (2005), underscored the importance of professional formation in the practice of charity. At the same time, it states that professional competence is not of itself sufficient. "Practitioners of Love require not only professional training

---

1 Kurien Kunnumpuram, *Called to Serve: Indian Christian Reflections on the Priesthood and Priestly Ministry in India*, Mumbai: St Pauls, 2012. See also *Shaping Tomorrow's Church: Formation of Priests and Religious for India*, edited by Kurien Kunnumpuram (Mumbai: St Pauls,2006).

but also the *formation of the heart*", he wrote.[2] Modern secular professions rarely speak of the dimension of the heart and its training. There is a growing awareness that this aspect can no more be ignored in professions that deal with human issues. Priestly training also has to face the apparent incongruity between the language of the heart and the language of secular professions, between cool heads and warm hearts. An untrained heart can talk volumes with little content! After all, "the heart has its reason which reason knows nothing of.... We know the truth not only by the reason but by the heart" wrote Blaise Pascal, the 17th century French thinker.

Give us Pastors with a Heart!

What else can the message of Christianity be except the message of the heart! We live in a world where 'heart' gets sidelined in the rush for heartless technology and soulless development. The world is witnessing more and more bleeding hearts – in broken families, old-age homes, communal riots, political rivalries, and urban anonymity. Troubled hearts and fractured world! The need of the hour is more and more merciful hearts. It is most unfortunate if pastors too 'lose heart', which is not uncommon. The world is in need of pastors who are able to hear the heartbeat of the 'sheep', and transcend the frame of mere rational logic. Recently while addressing the participants in the plenary assembly of the pontifical academy for life, Pope Francis said:

> Science and technology are not enough: doing good requires wisdom of heart.... Virtue is the best that the human heart has to offer.... Therefore, I encourage universities to consider all this in their programmes of formation, so that the students can improve those dispositions of the heart and mind, which are indispensable to receive and take care of human life, according to the dignity that belongs to it in any circumstance.[3]

What the pope said applies equally or more to priestly formation today. A priest is called to live a life with an awakened heart when he can say "I know my sheep and they know me" (John 15).

Apophatic theology or '*via negativa*' was always part of the Christian tradition, and it underscored the limits of a purely rationalistic approach in matters divine. Pseudo-Dionysius the Areopagite, the anonymous Syrian monk of the 6th century is mostly associated with the development of apophatic theology. It reminds us of the provisional nature of all knowledge about God and matters of faith. He looks at *via negative* as a plunge into that darkness beyond intellect where we not only run short of words but also remain speechless. Conceptual thought is built on binary logic (either this or that) while *via*

2 *Deus Caritas Est,* No. 31

3 From "Address of his holiness pope Francis to participants in the plenary assembly of the pontifical academy for life", 3 March 2016.

negativa frees us from the burden of binaries (neither this nor that). This is true freedom of the heart. Wendy Farley argues that the practice of apophatic theology transcends the limitations of conceptual thought and operates at the heart level, thus contributing to a deeper knowledge of matters divine.4 A theology of negation is necessary for a proper theology of affirmation.

Probably this is the wisdom that we get from the Buddhist tradition which speaks of 'empty heart'; it is empty of evil but filled with wisdom! Whatever is done is done with this divine wisdom. That is why Buddhist masters emphasize training of the heart and suggest various ways of training it. Ajahn Mun, the renowned meditation master from Thailand, speaks of 'reading one's own heart' and 'listening to one's own heart'. He writes: "Listening to your own heart is really very interesting. This untrained heart races around following its own untrained habits. It jumps about excitedly, randomly, because it has never been trained. Therefore train your heart! Buddhist meditation is about the heart; to develop the heart or mind, to develop your own heart.... You must discipline it with meditation, with *samādhi*. This is called "Training the Heart". Buddhism is the religion of the heart."[5] Meditation and awareness are at the centre of this training; it is nothing but training in compassion. The message to priestly formation is self-evident: in a fractured world, with many people with troubled hearts, a pastor has to be a messenger of a healing heart. No wonder, the Jesuit tradition labels the third and final stage of formation before final vows (*tertianship*) as 'school of the heart'!

Some Dimensions of Formation of the Heart

a. Human Heart as an Organ and as a Symbol

Proper formation of the heart has been a focal point in the biblical tradition from the very beginning. The term heart occurs over one thousand times in the Bible. It is the anthropological term the bible uses to denote a person's centre (core) not only physiologically, but also emotionally and morally. In the OT view, the heart is meant to understand, to discern and to give insight, just as the eye is meant to see, and the ear to hear. Heart is the inner forum where discernment takes place, decisions are arrived at, and commitments are made. 'Man looks at the outward appearance, but the Lord looks at the heart', asserts Prophet Samuel (1Sam 16:7). Jeremiah and Ezekiel were proposing a new heart that the Lord would give human persons (Jer 31:33; Ezek 36:26). David prays for a pure heart to replace his defiled conscience (Ps 51:10). The metaphor of writing on the tablet of the heart is also inspiring (Prov 3:3; Jer

---

4 Wendy Farley, "And what is a merciful heart?- Apophatic theology and Christian Ethics", in *Theology Today*, Vol.67 (2011), 405-418.

5 Ajahn Chah, "The Training of the Heart". http://www.ajahnchah.org/book/Training_Heart1_2.php. Accessed 20.08.2018.

17:1). Heart needs to be educated by filling it with God's heart (Prov 22:17-18). Jesus is unambiguous: "Where your treasure is, there your heart will also be" (Mt 6:21). He sums up the law with the call "love the Lord your God with all your heart…" (Mt 22:37).

The Lord promises through Jeremiah, "I shall give you shepherds *after my own heart,* who will pasture you wisely and discreetly" (Jer 3:15). It is the right of the people of God to have shepherds after his own heart. It affirms that the ability to pasture the flock 'wisely and discreetly' as essential to this pasturing. Every formation programme must be geared to preparing pastors who are wise and discreet. That is why Pope John Paul II chose this text as the title of his post-synodal apostolic exhortation, *Pastores Dabo Vobis*.[6]

b. Restlessness/Discontent as Valuable Resource

All pastoral engagement assumes human situations that demand urgent human/divine intervention. Only a person who is disturbed by a situation can creatively intervene in it. We have an excellent example in Jesus himself. After going around towns and villages in Palestine at the beginning of his ministry, Jesus felt deeply disturbed, "because they were harassed and helpless, like sheep without a shepherd" (Matt.9:35-38). This discontent becomes the beginning of an expanded form of ministry involving selection of a group of disciples, as narrated by Matthew in the following chapter. Jesus' initial focus was on the proper formation of his disciples, thus indicating what it means to be 'pastors after His own heart'.

Restlessness or discontent is not necessarily a negative quality; the heart looks at it in positive terms as a valuable virtue and as goal-oriented. The human heart is inherently restless, as St. Augustine spoke of. "You have made us for yourself, and our hearts are restless until they rest in you", he wrote.[7]It can become a spiritual power behind committed action. Late Julius Nyerere, former president of Tanzania and a devout Catholic, understood its value when he named it *Divine Discontent*. The conviction that we are transforming human discontent into divine discontent is at the core of genuine pastoral engagement. Unless guided by this vision, discontent can quickly degenerate into selfish aggression or irrational reaction. Resistance and conflict are inevitable in any action, but the heart prompts us to see them not as disasters, but as opportunities for renewal and enrichment. A formed heart prompts a pastoral worker never to be disheartened, however alarming the situation be.

---

6 John Paul II, *Pastores Dabo Vobis*, 1992.

7 *Confessions, I.i.l.*

c. The Heart Promotes Human Solidarity

"We must learn to live together as brothers, or perish together as fools", said Martin Luther King Jr. years ago, indicating the importance of human solidarity. Solidarity is the contemporary term for the classical Christian virtue of 'mercy', later called 'charity', and then 'commitment'. Pope John Paul II defines solidarity as "a firm and persevering determination to commit oneself to the common good, that is to say, the good of all and each individual, because we are all responsible for all."[8] Solidarity consists of two essential components: *inter-dependence* (awareness that I am deeply dependent on others), and *mutual responsibility* (that I am responsible for my brothers and sisters). Solidarity is an attitude, a commitment to participate in the life of the community/society to promote the common good. Theologically it rests on our identity as living images of the Trinitarian God, and in professing the mystery of the incarnation that our God is present in human history in the person of Jesus Christ to give us dignity as his children, as brothers and sisters.

Any pastoral engagement devoid of a sense of solidarity can easily degenerate into mere administrative strategies or political manoeuvring. The result would be the misuse of authority and neglect of the weaker members of the Christian fellowship. Today we witness many pastoral situations facing group conflict and power struggle, often becoming a public scandal. The strength of a chain is determined by the strength of its weakest link; the health of a society is determined by the wellbeing of its weakest member. Only a properly trained heart can perceive the weakest link and attend to its concerns. Pastoral formation is to be oriented not only in cultivating this sensitivity in pastoral workers, but also in enabling them to be promoters of the spirit of solidarity in pastoral situations.

d. Restorative Justice that Goes Beyond Distributive Justice

The contemporary world is characterised by growing awareness about the cry for justice and is proactive in its response. At the same time, its preoccupation seems to be with *distributive justice*. No doubt, distributive justice is crucial in a world marked by uneven access to resources and a widening disparity between classes. But the heart says that we need to go beyond distributive justice. The heart impels us to shift our focus onto *restorative justice*. Archbishop Desmond Tutu gives us valuable insights based on his South African experience. As a strong advocate of restorative justice, he incorporates the love principle taking justice beyond punitive or retributive justice. He affirms the centrality of restorative justice drawing from the African religious tradition of *ubuntu*; the core concern here is "the healing of breaches, the redressing of imbalances, the restoration of broken relationships, a seeking to rehabilitate both the victim

---

8 *Sollicitudo Rei Socialis*, No. 38

and the perpetrator, who should be given the opportunity to be reintegrated into the community he has injured by his offence."[9] Here justice is not sacrificed, instead is affirmed in its fuller sense. It builds up the community, and avoids creating victors and losers. All are destined to become victors.

Pastoral workers cannot but be messengers of restorative justice in human situations marked by an urge for vengeance and retaliation. Paul wrote to the Corinthians that Christ has given us the 'ministry of reconciliation'... 'entrusting to us the message of reconciliation' (2 Cor 5:18-19). So a pastor is an 'ambassador' of reconciliation. The ministry of reconciliation can easily get reduced to the ritual of confession, as history tells us, unless pastors are formed in the school of the heart. Pastors are called to be ambassadors of reconciliation and restoration, and so are to be trained accordingly.

e. Faith in the Power of Resurrection

Resurrection is the affirmation of life in the midst of misery and death. That is the meaning of Easter. Moments of discouragement and frustration, helplessness and hopelessness, of allegations and betrayals, are inevitable companions of pastoral workers at all times. Pastors may recall the cry from the cross, "My God, why did you abandon me" (Mk.15:34), as reflecting the agony of the heart in moments of utter frustration. We are reminded of the scene in the Old Testament where Moses hits the hard rock to produce water for the belligerent people of Israel in the desert (Exod 17:6; Num 20:10-11). Pastoral engagement often would lead us to the hard rock of the wilderness, asking us to work miracles. Archbishop Tutu would tell us how to make possible what appears impossible; after the collapse of the regime of apartheid, reconciliation of the white minority and the black majority appeared impossible. But the conviction that there is *no future without forgiveness* made the impossible possible through the work of the *Commission for Truth and Reconciliation*, of which Tutu was the chairperson.[10]

It also throws light on the meaning of success and failure in pastoral engagement. The heart would tell us that it is only when a grain of wheat falls into the ground and dies...it bears much fruit, and that "he who loves his life loses it, and he who hates his life...will keep it" (Jn.12:24-25). Obviously, it goes contrary to the logic of the head and of a world that upholds rationality as of supreme value.

---

9 Desmond Tutu, *No Future Without Forgiveness, New York: Image Book, 1999, 54.*

10 *No Future without Forgiveness* was the title of the book he wrote after completing the work of the Commission (New York: Image Book, 1999).

f. The Heart Can Teach Us the Art of Discernment

The secular world currently presents before us two dominant systems of decision making: *autocratic* (decision by the one who has absolute power), and *democratic* (decision by the majority). The majoritarian principle has been sanctified by the ideology of parliamentary democracy and contemporary political systems. But the heart shows us a third alternative: the *discernment approach* (decision guided by the Divine Spirit).[11] The assumption is that the discerning faculty rests with the heart. This approach has deep roots in the Christian spiritual tradition. We have the prayer of King Solomon asking Yahweh for a discerning heart (1Kgs.3:9). We see the early church practising it in their everyday life and ministry, in the election of Mathias (Acts 1), in the appointment of the deacons (Acts 6), and in the council of Jerusalem while settling disputes (Acts 15). Unfortunately, we have lost this rich heritage of the discernment approach. The attraction of centralised authority and power is too tempting in today's world. The majoritarian principle is often prone to manipulation to serve vested interests. We need to recover the spirit of the discernment approach in pastoral engagement, and it has to begin with priestly formation. A pastor has to guide people to walk with the Spirit while dealing with complex problems or while taking difficult decisions. "Be wise as serpents and innocent as doves", we are told (Mt.10:16); both are essential requirements for a pastor.

We can look up to the Ignatian spiritual tradition to learn more about the effective use of discernment approach in pastoral ministry. The dynamics of the *Spiritual Exercises* manifest consistent emphases on formation of the heart in the one making a retreat. The first introductory explanation states the goal as "preparing and disposing our soul (heart) to rid itself of all its disordered affections, and then, after their removal, of seeking and finding God's will in the ordering of our life."[12] It further explains the reason in clear terms: "For what fills and satisfies the soul consists, not in knowing much, but in understanding the realities profoundly and in savouring them interiorly."[13] This emphasis is kept alive all through the Exercises, particularly the contemplation on *Call of the King*, the application of the senses and the colloquy. The Ignatian insistence on the heart is most evident in the exercises on 'discernment of the Spirits' paying attention to the inner movements of the heart.[14] Ignatius was convinced that true transformation of persons consisted of transformation of their heart.

---

11 *Pastores Dabo Vobis* speaks of 'Gospel Discernment'. See no. 10.

12 George E. Ganss (Tr), *The Spiritual Exercises of Saint Ignatius, Anand: Gujarat Sahitya Prakash, 1992, Introductory Explanation, no. 1, p.22.*

13 *The Spiritual Exercises of Saint Ignatius, Introductory Explanation, no. 2, p.*22.

14 For more details on this, see *The Spiritual Exercises of Saint Ignatius, nos. 313-336 [Rules for the Discernment of Spirits].*

g. Pay Attention to the Language of the Heart

"Where words fail, music speaks," wrote Hans Christian Andersen, the well-known Danish author of the 19th century (1805-1875). He is reminding us that music is one mode of the language of the heart. The same is true of silence and dreams. To experience the power of silence in a noisy world is becoming more and more difficult. But it is inevitable for an effective pastor. "When we dream alone, it is just a dream; but when all dream together, it is the beginning of Reality", said Archbishop Dom Helder Camara. To pay attention to the dreams of oneself, and of others, demands of our facility with the language of the heart. Do we, in our pastoral engagement, enable people to dream together? Do we share our dreams with them? Do we let ourselves share in their dreams? Lord Buddha soon after his enlightenment rushed to Sarnath, near the holy city of Varanasi, to share his dream (his first sermon) with a group of disciples. Jesus' work among the dispirited people of Israel lasted only a short time, yet he succeeded to share his dream of the Reign of God with the small band of companions, and it flourished and reached the ends of the earth. Pastors are sharers and promoters of that vision, and formation programmes must enable trainees to be committed to that vision in pastoral settings entrusted with them.

Conclusion

"What do I still lack?" was a question coming from the heart of a young man (Matt 19:20), and it required an answer from the heart. Hearing Jesus' answer, the young man went away sorrowful, for he expected an answer from the head, not the heart. Apophatic theology cautions us about the limits of answers from the head, whether in written word or spoken word. There is the 'empty space' beyond words, and that is the space occupied by the heart. Formation of the heart enables a pastor to be 'large-heated' and 'broadminded' reaching beyond the realms of words and reason. It means conscious effort to create space for others and their concerns, expanding one's horizon of relationships to welcome even the excluded. We need pastors with transformed hearts and are capable of transforming the hearts of men and women today. Let us hope that those responsible for priestly formation will take these to heart.

31

Spirituality that Humanizes according to Kurien Kunnumpuram

Surekha Lobo BS
Department of Systematic Theology, Jnana-Deepa Vidyapeeth, Pune

Abstract: *According to Kunnumpuram, the mission of the Church is to collaborate with God in His work for the wholeness of the human person, the human community and the cosmos according to the pattern revealed in Jesus Christ. Hence, to realize such a vision, a spirituality that humanizes is the need of the hour. In this context, Kurien Kunnumpuram holds: "For as long as one half of humanity is discriminated against and oppressed, humankind cannot blossom fully." Together, we as Christians as well as people of goodwill in India could search for a "spirituality that humanizes" a spiritualty of understanding what it means to be human in an age which is set on promoting dehumanization.*

Keywords: *Spirituality, dehumanization, love of God and human beings, serving the poor.*

First and foremost, this paper is my humble tribute to my mentor and spiritual guide, Prof. Dr. Kurien Kunnumpuram. I feel honoured and privileged to have given me an opportunity to gather my thoughts and reflections on Kurien Kunnumpuram's theology of spirituality. Besides being my professor at JDV, Pune he has been a mentor, spiritual guide and a friend whose theological reflections and his presence in JDV campus has been a source of inspiration and resource. The theological insights I gained from his writings and my personal encounters with him become a cherished resource for my life as a religious and in my scholarly research since 2011. As a scholar myself, I have felt a special pride in having recourse to his theological and ecclesiological views and make them my own.

Secondly, I am very proud and blessed to speak about a priest who loved the Church more than anything else and who also inspired thousands of his students to do the same, at this painful time when the church is being rocked by scandal after scandal, sadly by a few of us who are called to love and serve the Church as a Sacrament. According to Kunnumpuram, the mission of the Church is to collaborate with God in His work for the wholeness of the human person, the human community and the cosmos according to the pattern revealed in Jesus Christ. Hence, to realize such a vision, a spirituality that humanizes is the need of the hour. The present paper, therefore, focuses mainly an appraisal of Kunnumpuram's views on the Spirituality that humanizes. Remaining faithful to his theological horizon I shall try to understand and communicate his spiritual considerations in relation to their relevance and significance to today's Indian context with its own unique problems and issues as powerfully comprehended and articulated by Kunnumpuram in his writings.

With this background, let me come to the point or rather bring me to the contemporary Indian context. In a multi-religious country like India where Christians make up just 2.3% of the population how do we dialogue and collaborate with people of other faiths and no faith who share common human and spiritual values in the struggle for social justice and social transformation? Where does Spirituality that humanizes come into the picture of the contemporary scenario? Therefore, this essay begins with the spirituality that humanizes in Kunnumpuram's Perspective, his contribution in the area of Christian theology. I shall then propose some of the possible ways to promote a spirituality that humanizes for the 21st century Indian situation.

Kurien Kunnumpuram's Perspective

The scholarly work of Kunnumpuram exhibits a far-reaching influence in a number of areas. Kunnumpuram was and has been called as a Church man, ecclesiology expert, the pre-Vatican theologian and a champion of Vatican II and so on. As a theologian, he has left no stone unturned in his search for imparting the Spirit of the Second Vatican Council. The central characteristics of Christian faith according to him are faith in one God and in Jesus who is God-with-us who is the centre and goal of the Christian life. Christians today experience the tangible presence and grace of God through the means of sacraments, basically through the sacraments of Baptism and Eucharist. All human beings by their very nature are directed toward God in that they have the same origin and destiny and share the image and likeness of God.

In his writings, Kunnumpuram mentions that there are many ways of understanding "spirituality" since spirituality is all about human beings in relation to God and God in relation to human beings. The role and meaning of spirituality has been discussed in various worldwide publications. Many tried to encode the term but there is not a widely agreed definition of spirituality. The phenomenon is used and understood very differently in today's context in comparison to its original root.1 Christian Spirituality is essentially concerned about the totality of human existence or a way of life that is manifested in the quality of one's life. It overflows from the faith experience of individuals in their own way. Kunnumpuram believes that every human person has different experiences and different ways to encounter and "be touched by the Spirit of God."[2] Thus, he says that spirituality is a universal human concern that is significant for the human enterprise as a whole. The Christian vision is one of the possible ways of understanding humanity.[3]

Humanity for Kunnumpuram is the humankind. The word humanity is from the Latin *humanitas* for "human nature, kindness." Human beings are created out of love and they are created in God's own image and likeness. The Bible underscores the special creation by stating that the human being is created 'in the image and likeness of God (Gen l: 27ff). The metaphor 'image of God' states that the human person is relational by nature. Therefore, for us Christians, says Kunnumpuram, that "the human person is the privileged *locus* of God-experience – one encounters God first of all in Jesus of Nazareth and then in every man, woman and child."[4]

Spirituality that Humanizes

While it is true that human being has always been restless, always on the move, searching for greener pastures but never satisfied. Only with those who have a profound God-experience are able to say that only in God can a human person find complete rest. What is needed today is spirituality that humanizes a total inward quest for growth.

---

1 Kurien Kunnumpuram, "Reflections on Christian Spirituality," in *Life in Abundance: Indian Christian Reflections on Spirituality*, ed. Kurien Kunnumpuram (Mumbai: St Pauls, 2006), 213. The word 'Spirit' comes from the Latin words '*spirare*', to breathe and '*spiritus*', the breath. Russ Moxley, *Leadership and spirit: Breathing new vitality into individuals and organizations* (San Francisco 2000), 22.

2 Kunnumpuram, "Reflections on Christian Spirituality," 213.

3 Pedro Arrupe says, "We receive Christ hungering in the world. He comes to us not alone, but with the poor, the oppressed, the starving of the earth. Through him they are looking to us for help, for justice, for love expressed in action. Therefore we cannot properly receive the Bread of Life unless at the same time we give bread for life to those in need whenever and whoever they may be." Padro Arrupe, *Address delivered at the International Eucharistic Congress*, Philadelphia, August, 1976.

4 Kunnumpuram, "Reflections on Christian Spirituality," 216.

Two-Fold Growth

Kunnumpuram says that Christian Spirituality is concerned about the totality of human existence or a way of life. It is that which is manifested in the quality of one's life. Therefore, spirituality is meant to facilitate personal growth in the following of Christ for the service of our people.[5] Spirituality takes its place in the world of every-day experience of every person. Spirituality will be truly human and transformative when we as Christians together with people of other faiths strive not only to transform community 'out there' which is always a difficult enterprise but when each of us truthfully tries transforming ourselves, for that is perhaps the most difficult task ahead! Towards this end, we need to critically examine where do each one of us stand in relation to personal and institutional power, the accumulation of wealth, poverty, social discrimination and othering? In the light of Kunnumpuram's writings, the spirituality that humanizes can achieve through two-fold growth: "growth in the following of Christ for the service" of the other.[6]

a. Growth in the following of Christ

The Scripture teaches us that the God of the Bible is a living and life-giving God. Jesus came into this world in order that we may have life, and have it abundantly. (Jn 10:10). According to Kunnumpuram to follow Christ means the following:

One, to follow Jesus Christ is to **recapture his God-experience**.[7] The Christian tradition begins with Jesus' experience of God. Jesus was gripped by the vision of God's reign. The vision propelled him forward to do courageous things.[8] According to Kunnumpuram, the thrust of Jesus was to bring home to his followers that God offers His love unconditionally and that it can transform one's life totally.[9] Two, to follow Christ is to **identify oneself with the poor and the powerless**. The incarnation[10] "is the manifestation of God's intense

---

5 Kunnumpuram, "Reflections on Christian Spirituality," 212-213.

6 Kurien Kunnumpuram, *Towards the Fullness of Life: Reflections on the Daily Living of the Faith* (Mumbai: St Pauls, 2009), 35-36.

7 Kunnumpuram, "Reflections on Christian Spirituality," 214.

8 As George Soares-Prabhu states: "If it is God-experience of Jesus that empowers him to identify with the poor and confront the rich, it is an act of solidarity with the poor that is the occasion for his experience of God." Cf. George Soares- Prabhu, "The Spirituality of Jesus as a Spirituality of Solidarity and struggle," in *Liberative Struggles in a Violent Society*, (ed.) J. Vattamattam (Hyderabad: Forum publications, 1991): 152-153.

9 Kunnumpuram, "Reflections on Christian Spirituality," 214.

10 The incarnation is that event where the second person of the Trinity, the Word, became flesh and dwelt among us. John 1:1, "in the beginning was the word, the word was with God, and the word was God." John 1:14, "And the word became flesh and dwelt among us . . . "

yearning to be one with us [humans]."[11] It symbolises the identification of Jesus with the poor. "By his incarnation, the Son of God has united Himself in some fashion with every human being" (*GS* 22). Therefore, the incarnation is always a call to follow Jesus in his solidarity with humankind, expressed concretely through his consistent and progressive identification with the poor. Three, to follow Christ is to **follow in his confrontation with all those who oppress the poor**. The mystery of the Cross, an image that emphasises the self-giving death of Christ as the symbol of this confrontation. The Cross is the ultimate expression of Jesus' love for the poor and the marginalised. It is on the Cross that Identification and confrontation have reached their furthest possible limits.

b. Growth in the Service of Others

To be a Christian is to share in the God-experience of Jesus. Jesus' own life finds expression in his prophetic mission of proclaiming liberation to the captives (Lk 4:18). Jesus goes up the mountain, a symbol of the place of encountering God, and calls the disciples 'to be with him' before they are 'sent out' with authority (Mk 3:13). He showed men that they were more precious to God than the lilies of the field and the birds of the air (cf. Lk 6:22-33) and that to God they mattered more than religious legalities of the Jewish culture and tradition.

According to Kunnumpuram, the development of the Catholic doctrine on spirituality that humanizes is based on the mystery of Incarnation, the mystery of God-with-us humans and the necessity of the followers "to become increasingly more human."

With Second Vatican Council "the joys and the hopes, the griefs and the anxieties of the people of this age, especially those who are poor or in any way afflicted these are the joys and hopes, the griefs and anxieties" (*GS* 1) of the people of God. The Second Vatican Council has brought to humankind light kindled from the Gospel and puts at its disposal those saving resources which the Church herself, under the guidance of the Holy Spirit, receives from her founder – Jesus Christ. Drawing upon the scriptures, the Christian faith has provided a rationale for the claim of the human person as *imago Dei* (Gen 1:27). Therefore, humans are not allowed to despise their bodily life. Rather, they are obliged to regard their body as good and honourable since God has created it" (*GS* 14).

Therefore, spirituality is to be understood as a reflection on our faith-experience in the light of tears and hopes; in other words, it is a reflection on life in the light of God encounter.[12] Spirituality that humanizes is nothing but a

11 Kunnumpuram, *Towards the Fullness of Life*, 99.

12 In the context of theology what Samuel Rayan reflects this spirituality: "We bring two – life and faith – to face each other, to dialogue, questioning and critiquing, exploring each other's depths and enriching each other." Samuel Rayan, "Doing Theology in India,"

faith seeking the dignity and honour of every woman and man. Kunnumpuram is convinced that spirituality capable of humanizing humanity will ever be springing forth at the meeting point of God and the social reality of our country, India.

Conclusion: Vision Ahead

Finally, it must be stated that God is more to be experienced than to be intellectually known. God experience is meant to facilitate the personal growth of an individual; and this growth always has the human society as an integral part of it; thus spirituality is also always meant to ensure the growth of the human person in society. This calls for cognitive change-the development of a new vision of life; an attitudinal change – imbibing a new set of virtues, values; and an internal or behavioural change – the adoption of a new way of living. Thus personal experience and encounter, a holistic vision, and the corresponding commitment and action are the essential components of true spirituality.[13] What we urgently need in the Church today is a spirituality that humanises. The marginalisation needs to be countered through the intensification of spirituality at all levels. In other words, to be spiritual is to be touched and transformed by God's Spirit and the fruits of the Spirit are to be reflected in one's life (Gal 5:22-23). More specifically, today, we focus not only on ourselves as individuals, but also ourselves as social beings in our contemporary 'global village.' True spirituality, therefore, means social action. See that justice is done – help those who are oppressed, give orphans their rights and defend widows (Is 1:17).

Today spirituality that humanises implies the attempt to create a secure place to live in. it should be capable of serving the wholeness of life.

What are some of the possible ways to promote a spirituality that humanizes today?

- It is to look at the human person through the eyes and vision of Jesus.
- It is a spirituality that promotes justice, which starts from taking sides with the marginalised as Jesus did. It means a close friendship with the marginalized, which is realised only in one's availability to the margins of society in India today.
- It is a spirituality of tolerance. Not the tolerance of indifference but that which is born of Christian love – where one respects the right of the other to be different.

---

in *Theologizing in Context*, ed. Jacob Parappally (Dharmaram Publications, Bangalore, 2002), 11.

13 Kurien Kunnumpuram, "Towards a Theology of Education," *Jeevadhara*, Vol. 12/ 69 (May-June, 1982): 172.

- It is to foster unity and promote a countrywide conscious sense of being proudly Indian, committed to the country and open to the country and the world at large.
- It is the process whereby a society of people with diverse origins, histories, languages, cultures and religions come together within the boundaries of a sovereign state with a unified constitutional and legal dispensation, a national public education system, an integrated national economy, shared symbols and values, as equals, to work towards eradicating the divisions and atrocities and hate.

Therefore, It is not two commands but one love command: Love of God in the love of neighbour and the service to woman and man is to service to God. The golden rule of the Gospel enshrined in the various sacred scriptures, "Do to others as you would have them do to you" (Lk 6:13) serves as a critique as well as a solid edifice on which justice, reconciliation, peace and love to reign in our land-India. Hence, respect for otherness, equality, mutuality, partnership and collaboration are the essential components of this spirituality. Hence, it is a spirituality that includes everyone irrespective of caste, creed and gender, especially those on the margins.

I conclude with a quote from Kunnumpuram: "For as long as one half of humanity is discriminated against and oppressed, humankind cannot blossom fully."[14] Together, we as Christians as well as people of goodwill in India could search for a "spirituality that humanises" a spiritualty of understanding what it means to be human in an age which is set on promoting dehumanisation.

14 Kunnumpuram, *Towards the Fullness of Life*, 7.

32

Love of Neighbour as the Axis of Pauline Ethics: A Brief Study of Gal 5:13-14 and Rom 13:8-10

Paulraj Mariapusham

Abstract: *Fr. Kurien Kunnumpuram SJ kept drawing my attention to two texts in the Epistles of Paul, namely Gal 5:13-14 and Rom 13:8-10 which speak about agapē as the fulfilment of the law. As one who always insisted on authentic human existence following the axiom of St. Irenaeus "Gloria enim Dei vivens homo, vita autem hominis visio Dei ," proper understanding of these two texts was vital for Kurien.*

Terminologically Paul's idea of love is expressed not only through agapē and its cognates (c. 136 occurrences) but also through phileō, eleeō and epipotheo and their cognates and includes both God's love for human beings, human beings love for God and human beings love for one another. Gal 5:13-14 and Rom 13:8-10 focus on the love of the neighbour.

These two texts occur at crucial places in two of Paul's most systematic, dogmatic epistles in which he, following the indicative-imperative pattern, invites every follower of Christ to live the through Christ gained freedom by loving one another which amounts to a singular way of fulfilling all the commandments and the law.

Keywords: *Love commandment, Love in St Paul, Love of neighbour, Love of God.*

Introduction

The greatest of all the biblical commandments is the one to love one another (the Greek agapē) and the whole of Christian message can be summarized in this one word 'love.' This is what each one longs for and wishes to share with our fellow human beings though at times we end up doing just the opposite of love. 'Love is the beauty of the soul' said St. Augustine. It is appropriate that such a topic is studied as part of the seminar conducted in honour of Fr. Kurien Kunnumpuram, SJ who always insisted on authentic human existence following the axiom of St. Irenaeus "Gloria enim Dei vivens homo, vita autem hominis visio Dei."[1] During the last few years when I got a chance to live with him in the Papal Seminary, Pune, he kept drawing my attention to studying these two texts, namely Gal 5:13-14 and Rom 13:8-10 which speak about agapē as the fulfilment of the law. A proper understanding of these two texts was vital for him.

'Love of Neighbour' in the New Testament

The New Testament is replete with 'love' and the 'love commandment.' However, the moment we hear of 'love-commandment' in the New Testament, the texts that immediately occur to our minds are either Jn 15:12-13 which speaks of the love of neighbour or Mt 22:37-40 (Mk 12:28-31; cf. Lk 10:25-27) which speaks about the two greatest commandments of which the second concerns the love of neighbour) or 1 Jn 4:7-12 which sees the love of neighbour as a direct consequence of the love of God for us revealed through Jesus' death[2] or 1 Cor 13:1-13 which is a hymn of praise on love. However prominent and important 1 Cor 13 may be, yet there are two other texts in Paul, namely Gal 5:13-14 and Rom 13:8-10 which speak of the love of neighbour and which play a foundational role for Pauline ethical exhortations.

In fact, when we turn the pages of Paul's Epistles to the Galatians and the Romans, we find him speaking against the 'law' and the 'works of the law.'[3] In

---

1 This Latin quote must be correctly translated as "For/truly the glory of God is a living man; and the life of man consists in beholding God" and not simply as "the glory of God man fully alive" thereby promoting the cult of self-fulfilment. The quote actually speaks about the fulfilment of human beings in beatific vision of God, namely in Christ (cf. Eph 3:18-19).

2 For a detailed study particularly of Mt 22:34-40 and 1 Jn 4:7-12 read: George M. Soares-Prabhu, "The Love Commandment," in *Biblical Spirituality of Liberative Action, ed. Scaria Kuthirakkattel (Pune: Jnana-Deepa Vidyapeeth, 2003), 65-71.*

3 By these terms 'law' and 'works of the law' Paul appears to refer to the legalistic and retributive / salvific understanding of and attitude to fulfilling the works of the law (the so called 613 prescriptions) which he clearly rejects as a possible means of salvation. While admitting that the law is good and holy (cf. Rom 7:12) and explaining that it was given as a 'disciplinarian' (Gal 3:24) to those who were disobedient, Paul goes on to affirm that

its place, Paul brings in another commandment, namely, the commandment of love which is even more demanding than the laws and prescriptions which Paul has rendered superfluous. Particularly the two texts which we intend to study in this short essay and which occur at key positions of the respective Epistles, also treat the love of the neighbour as the singularly important commandment. Let us begin our brief study by first taking a look at the terminology, foundation and specifications of this love as we find in the epistles of Paul.

'Love' in Paul: Terminological Clarifications[4]

Terminologically Paul's idea of love is expressed not only through agapē, a word well-known among the Christian circles and which occurs around 136 times in Paul in its different forms but also through phileō (c. 25x),[5] eleeō (c. 22x) and epipotheo (c. 21x) and their cognates. Now the meaning of the term agapē is not easy to define, though it usually refers to relationships based on love and charity, but the meaning of other terms can easily be specified. The term phileō refers to attachment or affection, eleeō to compassion or mercy and epipotheo to longing or yearning. Among them, the usage of eleeō applies exclusively to God's mercy and compassion, while the other three are used to include God's love for human beings, human beings love for God, and human beings love for one another. Among the three first, namely God's love for human beings, is the foundation on which the other two are built. Gal 5:13-14 and Rom 13:8-10 which use the cognates of agapaō focus on the love of human beings for one another.

Pauline Foundation of Neighbourly Love

For Paul, love is the basis of the divine plan of salvation. As the creation and the call of Israel through covenant express the love of God in the Old Testament, Christ's death on the cross does it in the New Testament. Paul himself experiences the mercy and grace of God in and through the sacrifice of Christ on the cross in his personal life (cf. Gal 2:19-20; 1 Tim 1:13-16). He then also understands that the same has been done to the whole of humanity (Rom 5:6-8; Eph 2:4-5; 2 Thess 2:16). This becomes evident from how he speaks of the revelation of the 'wrath of God' in his Epistle to the Romans.

---

after grace has been revealed in and through Jesus Christ, the Old Testament law has been rendered superfluous (cf. Rom 7:1-6).

4 The terminological clarifications made here are based on Kurt Aland, *Vollständige Konkordanz zum griechischen Neuen Testament unter Zugrundelegung aller modernen textkritischen Textausgaben und des Textus Receptus*, vol. 2 (Berlin: Walter De Gruyter, 1983); R. Mohrlang, "Love," *Dictionary of Paul and His Epistles,* eds. Gerald F. Hawthorne, Ralph P. Martin, Daniel G. Reid (Illinois: Inter Varsity Press, 1993), 575.

5 The numbers here refer to the number of occurrences of the terms and their cognates in the Epistles of Paul.

Having established the fact that the whole of humanity is under sin and the wrath of God in Rom 1:8-3:20, Paul should have gone ahead with explaining the punishment which would have been a logical consequence of sin and wrath of God. Instead he goes on to describe how in the place of the wrath, God reveals his righteousness. This suggests that in the logic of God as explained in the Epistle to the Romans sin is not followed by punishment but by God's righteousness.

This righteousness of God is understood in the biblical context not as an attitude or a virtue, but as the way God relates to human beings. In the Letter to the Romans Paul claims that God relates to the human in that he justifies everyone under sin by revealing his grace as a gift through the redemption in Jesus Christ whom he put forward as an expiatory sacrifice (Rom 3:23-25). The important point to be noted here is that Christ who knew no sin (2 Cor 5:21) was obliged by God the Father to die for human beings while they were still weak, ungodly, sinners and enemies of God (Rom 5:6-8). Paul thus describes how salvation has been offered both to the Gentiles and to the Jews as a gratuitous gift which is appropriated by humans by faith in Christ (Gal 2:16; Rom 1:16). Such a free offering of salvation and justification is due to the love of God (Rom 5:8). When Paul speaks about the love of God, the focus is on God's love for human beings from which the love for the neighbour flows.

This love of God is further expressed in the calling given to all people (Eph 1:4-5) and not only to Israel (Rom 9:13.15.18.21-24). For Paul, this love of God[6] is also the basis for Christian theology and ethics, for a believer's sense of security (Rom 8:31-39) and it is also the chief driving force (2 Cor 5:14-15) in the life of the Christians. Though Rom 8:28; 1 Cor 2:9, 8:3; 16:22; Eph 6:24; and 2 Tim 3:4 mention human obligation to love God, Paul does not emphasize the first great commandment (cf. Mt 22:34-40) in his ethical sections as much as he does with regard to the love of neighbour.

The two texts we study in this essay, namely Gal 5:13-14 and Rom 13:8-10 which stake the claim that love of neighbour is the epitome and kernel of the entire Old Testament moral law, also demonstrate through their structural placement in the respective epistles, how this love of neighbour flows from the love of God revealed through the sacrifice of Christ. It must be noted here that these two texts occur in two of Paul's most systematic, dogmatic epistles.

Indicative-Imperative Pattern

In the epistles of Paul, we find two types of material, the first consists of the descriptive or the dogmatic section on the basis of which he then makes certain demands which form an ethical section. Since all the epistles of Paul

6 When Paul uses the expressions 'love of God' and 'love of Christ,' he might refer either to our love for God or for Christ (*objective genitive) or God's or Christ's love for us (subjective genitive). In some places it is very ambiguous (cf. Rom 5:5; 2 Cor 5:14; 2 Thess 3:5).*

are addressed to Christian communities the descriptive section delineates how Christians have been included in God's plan of salvation in and through Jesus Christ and the ethical section contains admonitions or exhortations which guide the Christians to live a life worthy of the call that has been given to them (Eph 4:1). This way of dividing the writings of Paul has been named the indicative-imperative pattern by J D G Dunn.[7] Such a pattern can be easily traced in 1 Thessalonians, Galatians and Romans which the first part is in the indicative and the second in the imperative. In all the other epistles this pattern is followed in each of the individual issues dealt with.

Gal 5:13-14

As said above this unit occurs in the ethical section of the Epistle to the Galatians. Following the above suggested pattern, the Epistle to the Galatians can be structured in the following way:

> The Indicative Section: 1:1-5:12: (contains the descriptive section on how the Galatian Christians had been saved from sin through grace without having to be circumcised): 1:1-5: Foreword; 1:6-10: Shock of Paul; 1:11-2:24: Autobiographical Narratives to prove the authenticity of the gospel proclaimed by him; 2:15-21: Justification through Faith; 3:1-4:7: Law, Spirit and Son-ship; 4:8-31: Warning against Falling into Slavery; 5:1-12: Appeal to the Galatians concerning Christian Freedom.
>
> The Imperative Section:[8] 5:13-6:20 (contains the ethical admonitions): 5:13-26: Exhortations not to allow the Christian Liberty become an occasion for Self-Indulgence; 6:1-10: Further Exhortations to give concrete expression to Christian Freedom and Love; 6:11-18: Postscript.

Having explained the independency and the reliability of the Gospel proclaimed by Paul in Gal 1:11-2:21, Paul continued to demonstrate in Gal 3-4 that the Gentile Christians are saved without having to follow the prescriptions of the law, particularly the prescription of circumcision as a precondition for entering into a relationship with God. Thus, he concludes that the Christians have been made free from sin through the Christ Event alone.

---

7 Cf. James D G Dunn, *The Theology of Paul the Apostle* (Edinburg: T & T Clark, 1998), 626-631. Such pattern is found in texts like Rom 6:4ab; 1 Cor 5:7ab; Gal 5:1ab; Gal 5:13ab, Phil 2:12-13. However, one must also be aware that the indicative-imperative pattern is strictly followed by Paul in all his epistles. Often, he mixes them up.

8 The exhortative or the hortatory character of this section is made evident by the three imperatives used in 5:13-14: "Do not use your freedom as an ..." and "... but through love become slaves ..." in v 13 and "you shall love your neighbour as yourself" in v 14. One also finds eleven other imperatives in the section 5:13-6:10. Cf. J. Louis Martyn, *Galatians: A New Translation with Introduction and Commentary (New Haven: Yale University Press, 1997), 481.*

Paul begins the next section 5:1-12 with the noun 'freedom' in the dative case[9] in 5:1, thereby showing that Christ set us free for the purpose of freedom.[10] The first implication of Christian freedom, according to him, is that the Christians do not submit themselves once again to the yoke of slavery. That is, the obtained Christian freedom should not be understood as a license for doing the things according to one's own desires. Then in the succeeding verses of this section, namely in 5:2-12 he describes the Christian freedom which is the consequence of the justification brought by Jesus and which must find its expression in authentic love (v 6). This section also reveals that the principle of Christian liberty (freedom) is very close to Paul's heart[11] (cf. Gal 5:1; Rom 8:2).

Both 5:1 and 5:13 imply that to live by grace is to live in freedom, in the freedom of Christ. It is both freedoms from inner conflicts and external enslavements, that is, the inhibitions one carries along within oneself and the external structures and systems which enslave the human beings and destroy human dignity. Paul seems to suggest elsewhere that the inner conflict is due to the tyranny of sin (Rom 6:7-8.18; 6:23; 7:13). Though Christ has made the Christians free from all enslaving elements, yet Paul is aware that slavery to flesh on the part of the human beings is not yet overcome. That is why he begins his exhortation section by first reminding them of Christian freedom and by inviting them not to yield to self-indulgence. He writes in 5:13-14:

> 13 For you were called to freedom, brothers and sisters; only do not use your freedom as an opportunity for self-indulgence, but through love become slaves to one another. 14 For the whole law is summed up in a single commandment, "You shall love your neighbour as yourself."

Here Paul is making three main statements. First is a warning against self-indulgent behaviour which is actually a misuse of freedom; the second is an invitation to give expression to this freedom by serving one another, and the third contains an assurance that by practising love of neighbour one fulfils all the requirements of the law. From what follows in 5:19-22, we understand that this love of neighbour amounts to fulfilling the fruits of the Spirit.

The first statement gives a warning against turning Christian freedom into a license, which would then lead to self-indulgent behaviour. The original

---

9 Cf. Ernest De Witt Burton, *A Critical and Exegetical Commentary on the Epistle to the Galatians* (ICC, Edinburg: T & T Clark, 1962), 270-71.

10 This is the so called 'dative of place whither.' Cf. Smyth H. W., *Greek Grammar (Cambridge: Harvard Univ. Press, 1956), 1531. The dative of place shows the direction or the purpose of some activity. Here when Paul places 'freedom' in the dative case and relates it to Christ, it means that Christ, through his act of justification, has taken those who participate in this justification 'into the realm of freedom.'*

11 Cf. James D G Dunn, *The Theology*, 658-661.

word used in the text for self-indulgence is 'flesh', and it should not be understood merely as bodily flesh distinguished from spirit but as a supra-human power which can destroy the Galatian Christian community.[12] A more detailed presentation of this flesh as a dangerous actor is made in vv 16-20. In the same verses, he also speaks of the Spirit as another supra-human power which is always in conflict with the flesh. Such a conflict is further intensified by the lists containing the works of the flesh and those of the Spirit in vv 19-22. The freedom is given by the Spirit (2 Cor 3:17) whose fruits are "love, joy, peace, patience, Kindness, goodness, faithfulness, gentleness, self-controle" (cf. Gal 5:22) and who is opposed to the works of the flesh: "fornication, impurity, licentiousness, 20 idolatry, sorcery, enmities, strife, jealousy, anger, quarrels, dissensions, factions, 21 envy, drunkenness, carousing, and things like these" (cf. Gal 5:19-21). The test of Christian freedom lies in the capacity of the Christians to overcome the fruits of the flesh and live the fruits of the Spirit.

The second statement calls for mutual service in love. Here freedom is understood as the right of the individual not to pursue one's own interests but to be conditioned by the rights of the others in a community. By implication, the individual should be prepared to give up one's rights for the sake of one's neighbour. It is for the same reason Paul also forbids the Corinthian Christians from participating in the meals offered to the idols (cf. 1 Cor 8-10). Such an understanding of freedom appears paradoxical and comes as a puzzle to those who believe that freedom is for oneself.

Contrary to that this text affirms that this freedom is not for oneself but freedom from oneself, that is, a freedom "to be unselfish, freedom, that is, to live in love."[13] Living this life of freedom in love implies giving up the desires of the flesh and living the fruits of the Spirit referred to in the previous paragraph. Inability to love is an expression of one's incapability to free oneself from one's selfishness which again proves that one is not yet free. Freedom that does not include responsibility is not freedom at all.

The third statement confirms that the love of neighbor fulfils the whole law. It is surprising to note here that after arguing against the law in the previous sections of the Epistle, now Paul is making a claim to get the whole of the law fulfilled. What is actually meant here is not getting the prescriptions of the law executed, but Paul claims here that by loving the neighbor one behaves according to the will of God which is actually the purpose of the whole law. Here the meaning of the word 'fulfil' has to be understood in the sense of 'bringing to completion' or 'making perfect,' thereby implying that the one

---

12 Cf. J. Louis Martyn, *Galatians, 483.*

13 C K Barrett, *Freedom and Obligation. A Study of the Epistle to the Galatians* (London: SPCK, 1985), 62.

who loves the neighbor, fulfils the essence of the law. Such an understanding is clarified later in 6:2 of the same Epistle where it is claimed that by bearing one another's burden, the Galatian Christians will fulfil the law of Christ. Therefore, Christian freedom is not to be enjoyed in selfish solitude but it is for making oneself a 'slave' to all (1 Cor 9:19-22). Here love is defined as the concern to serve one another and Christian freedom is joined to active and passionate concern for one another.

Rom 13:8-10

As in the case of Galatians, the Epistle to the Romans can also be divided into two major sections with their subdivisions:

> *Indicative Section:* 1:1-11:36 (Explains the human situation of sin and the righteousness of God expressed through justification by faith in Christ which results in a free life in the Spirit) 1:1-7: Foreword; 1:8-15: Introduction: thanksgiving prayers and Paul's wish to visit Rome; 1:16-17: Thesis Statement; 1:18-3:20: The general guilt of humankind; 3:21-8:39: Revelation of God's righteousness as an expression of his love and life in the Spirit which flows from it) and 9:1-11:36: Righteousness of God and the People of Israel: Here Paul makes the claim that the whole of Israel will be saved.
>
> *Imperative Section:* 12:1-15:13: (contains exhortations which contain demands of upright Life in Christ) 12:1-13:14: Spirit-guided Christian life must be the proper worship to God - 13:8-10: Love Commandment; 14:1-15:13: The strong owe the duty of love to the weak there; 16:1-27: Postscript.

After addressing the duty to civil authorities in 13:1-7, Paul moves to the duty of love of neighbour that sums up the Mosaic Law in 13:8-10. Till now Paul has spoken of God's love for human beings (5:5.8; 8:35.37.39; 9:13.25) and the love of human beings for God (8:28), but now he takes up the question of human love for other human beings (12:9; 13:8-10; 14:15). This little passage consisting only of three verses summarizes basically Gal 5 and reverts to the theme of 12:3-13. The only difference between 12:3-13 and this text is that in ch 12 it is about love towards members within the Christian community, and here it is love for the neighbour in a universal sense. Now let us read the text:

> Rom 13:8-10: 8 Owe no one anything, except to love one another; for the one who loves another has fulfilled the law. 9 The commandments, "You shall not commit adultery; You shall not murder; You shall not steal; You shall not covet"; and any other commandment, are summed up in this word, "Love your neighbor as yourself." 10 Love does no wrong to a neighbor; therefore, love is the fulfilling of the law.

This text begins with an opening statement on loving one another and on the relationship between the love for one another and the rest of the commandments in v 8 and continues to provide an explanation as to the relationship between love and the rest of the commandments in v 9 before finally somehow summarising the points of the previous two verses in v 10. By doing so Paul brings all social relationship demanded by the law particularly by the Decalogue under the one umbrella of love of neighbour (12:9).

As said above v 8 contains all the main points of this unit. After speaking about the 'dues' (tas opheilas) to be paid to the civil authorities in terms of taxes, revenues, respect and honour in 13:1-7, now he explains what a Christian 'owes' (opheilete – v 8) to all human beings, namely love. Actually love cannot be a debt in the sense of a quid pro quo (something for something), yet Paul calls it a debt "to stress its role in all Christian conduct"[14] and to provide an effective link to the just concluded section in v 7 where he speaks about paying to all what is due to them. Further he clarifies that this love is not limited only to the Christians but also to the outsiders as is implied by the Greek ton heteron meaning 'the other' in v 8 and ton plesion sou meaning 'your neighbour'[15] in v 9. It means that the danger of reducing this love to the 'like-minded' person[16] who is congenial to me should be avoided and must be extended to the one who differs from me. And then Paul makes the third point of this verse by asserting that this exhortation on love fulfils all the obligations of the Christian life.

Now Paul takes up the same idea of Gal 5:14 where he has already affirmed that the love of neighbour fulfils all the law. However, while in Gal 5 this idea is expressed only once through the Greek peplērōtai, here the same is expressed through three terms peplērōken in v 8, anakephalaioutai (summed up) in v 9 and plērōma in v 10. Now, this idea of fulfilling or summing up the law should be understood in the context of Romans. In 3:31 he has said "Do we then overthrow the law by this faith? By no means!

14 Joseph A. Fitzmyer, *Romans: A New Translation with Introduction and Commentary* (New Haven: Yale University Press, 1992), 678.

15 In the Hebrew context 'neighbour' referred to a fellow Israel. Cf. Cf. C. G. Montefiore, *Rabbinic Literature and Gospel Teaching* (London: Macmillan, 1930), 60-68. However, in the context of Paul it cannot be limited only to the fellow Christians. Already in Jesus' language the neighbour includes an enemy (cf. Mt 5:43-44; Lk 6:28) and the alien, for according to Luke, Jesus told the parable of the Good Samaritan in answer to the question "And who is my neighbour?" (cf. Lk 10:30-37). Further we find in Mt 25:31 -44 the neighbours are the hungry, the thirsty, the strangers, the ill-clad, and the prisoners.

16 C K Barrett, *A Commentary on the Epistle to the Romans* (London: Harper & Bros, 1957), 250.

On the contrary, we uphold the law." Thus the law that is not in a position to re-establish the lost relationship between human beings and God is not overthrown. Again in 10:4, Jesus is Christ is seen as the end of the law. Jesus is also the goal of the law because he is the one who mediates the right relationship with God for the believers and through him the law obtains its original function of promoting life (cf. 7:10). Now Jesus enables the believers to fulfil the demands of the law. This happens through the love of neighbour, which is actually a response to the love of God that has been revealed in Christ himself (cf. 5:8). Both the Greek verbs plēroō (v 8) and the noun plērōma (v 10) used here to refer to the praxis / doing of the law.

In v 9 Paul lists four / five of the Decalogue (6, 5, 7, and 9 or 10) of Deut 5:17-21. Contrary to the 9th and 10th commandments, Paul does not specify the objects of covetousness. It may be due to the fact that he has already mentioned it in 7:8. And the expression "any other commandment" may refer immediately to the rest of the commandments in the Decalogue, but remotely it would refer to the whole of Tora and even to the Greco-Roman legal system. V 10a reminds us of 1 Cor 13:4-6, which illustrates that authentic human love should be void of every selfish motive. One cannot both love and do wrong. In fact, evil is overcome through love (12:21: "... overcome evil with good"). Thus according to Paul the law remains. However, the highest of all the laws is love. Love of neighbour is also a law coming from the Lord and it acknowledges the unique dignity of the individual and demands to love the neighbour as oneself. The basis of such a demand lies in God's love for us. Authentic love of neighbour consists of transforming oneself and of concretizing the good things that we want to do.

The explicit reference to the law in this section re-emerges the discussion on the law in 1:18-11:36. Throughout the Epistle Paul has identified the law with the ethnic Israel and has established that the Christians are discharged from the law (7:6) though it is good and holy (7:12). However, now that Paul has defined the Christians in non-ethnic categories, he has to provide a new centre similar to that of the law for the people of Israel, around which the rest of the norms for personal and social ethics could be built. Thus the triple emphasis on love of neighbour (vv 8, 9, 10) and bracketing emphasis on fulfilling the law (vv 8, 10) effectively gathers together and sums up the earlier scattered references on these themes (love – 5:5; 8:28; 12:9; fulfilment – 8:4).[17]

As in the case of Galatians, Romans too makes it clear that this love is the result of freedom which has been acquired through Jesus Christ. Cf. Rom 8:2 For the law of the Spirit of life in Christ Jesus has set you free from the law of sin and of death. Rom 8:14-17 [14] For all who are led by the Spirit of God are children of God. 15 For you did not receive a spirit of slavery to fall back into

17 Cf. James D G Dunn, *Romans 9-16* (WBC 38B; Dallas: Word Books, 1988), 775.

fear, but you have received a spirit of adoption. When we cry, "Abba! Father!"
16 it is that very Spirit bearing witness with our spirit that we are children of
God, 17 and if children, then heirs, heirs of God and joint heirs with Christ

Synthesis of Gal 5:13-14 and Rom 13:8-10

In these two texts, Paul invites every follower of Christ to live the through Christ gained freedom by loving one another which amounts to a singular way of fulfilling all the commandments and the law. The affirmation 'love fulfils the law' is made once in Gal 5:14 and three times in Rom 13:8-10. The formulation of this love of neighbour as "You shall love your neighbour as yourself" (Rom 13:9; cf. Gal 5:14) is a quotation from Lev 19:18. In doing so Paul appears to echo the saying of Jesus in Mk 12:28-34 (cf. Mt 22:34-40; cf. Lk 10:25-27) where he makes the love of God (Deut 6:4-5) and the love of neighbour (Lev 19:18) as the two most important of all the commandments. Matthew (22:37-40) also makes the same claim and adds that both the law and the prophets hang on these two (Mt 22:37-40).

Paul also makes the love of neighbour commandment as the foundation of the life of every disciple of Christ. However, Paul goes one step further than Mark and Matthew in speaking of this 'love of neighbour' as the single commandment that fulfils the whole of the Mosaic law. From the contexts of the two Epistles, it is clear that here the 'law' refers to the Mosaic law. In Galatians Paul has been contrasting faith with the law of circumcision and in Rom 13:9 he makes a direct reference to the Mosaic law (Decalogue). By implication what the people of Israel living under the law of Moses required to do as their covenantal obligation is now being fulfilled by those practise the love of neighbour. Thus by fulfilling the law, love only upholds it.

Specifications of this Love of Neighbour

Now in the writings of Paul, love for one another is intimately related to faith in Christ and these two concepts form two sides of the same coin. They occur in the initial thanksgiving of his epistles (Eph 1:15; Col 1:4; 1 Thess 1:3; 2 Thess 1:3; Philm 4-5). Most prominently these two terms occur in Gal 5:6 where Paul's summary of the Christian life is expressed as: 'faith working through love.' In the context of Pauline theology, "love represents the ethical outworking of the imputed righteousness bestowed by grace through faith, the outward expression of new life in Christ."[18]

For Paul love is never a 'self-attained' virtue but is the result of the transformed life filled with the Spirit of God who pours God's love into human hearts (Rom 5.5; Gal 4:6-7; Phil 1:8: Eph 5:18) and therefore lack of love calls

18 R. Mohrlang, "Love," in *Dictionary of Paul and His Letters*, eds. Gerald F. Hawthorne, Ralph P. Martin, Daniel G. Reid (Leicester: Inter Varsity Press, 1993), 576.

into question one's relationship to God (Rom 8:1-14). This love of neighbour is a joyful and grateful response to the grace received (Rom 12:1-2; 2 Cor 8:1-9). Thus there is a necessary correlation between faith in Christ and loving others. Love is the fruit of righteousness (Phil 1:11) and the fruit of the Spirit (Gal 5:22). God pours his love into human heart (Rom 5:5; Gal 4:6-7; Phil 1:8; 2 Cor 8:16) and it is not a self-merited achievement.

Everything a Christian does is to be an expression of love (1 Cor 16:14) and it is the first virtue above all the others (Col 3:12-14) and the one charism believers are to seek above all others (1 Cor 12:31-14:1). In the context of 1 Cor 12-14, which insists on using the Spirit-given charisms for the 'common good' (cf. 1 Cor 12:7) and on every one's readiness to restrain one's own conviction of charism for the benefit of the whole (1 Cor 14:28.30), love of neighbour understood as love without any self-interest (cf. 1 Cor 13:1-13) is made the guiding principle. That is why 1 Cor 13 is inserted between chs. 12 and 14. 1 Cor 13:1-13 qualifies this love as self-less. Real love demands self-sacrifice (Eph 5:25-33; Col 3:19; Tit 2:4) and self-denial. The contrast is the love of self and money (2 Tim 3:2-4). The invitation made by Paul to refuse to eat meat also involves this self-denial when he requests the Corinthian Christians to give up their right to eat meat for the sake of those Christians who are of a weaker conscience (Rom 14:15.20-21; 1 Cor 8:9-13; 10:23-33).

This love is not expressed only through gentleness. Sometimes it calls for harsh language (Gal 1:8-9; 5:12; Phil 3:2) which arises out of genuine concern (1 Cor 4:14; 2 Cor 2:4; 7:8-11; 12:19; 13.2-4.10; Gal 2:11-14). It is the intention of the heart or the motivation of the action which qualifies love as authentic.

This love is first related to the Christian community[19] (Gal 6:10) whose members must remain united (Rom 12:10.16.18; 14:1.19; 15:5-6; 1 Cor 1:10; 2 Cor 13:11; Gal 3:27-28; 5:22-23; 6:2; Eph 4:1-6; Phil 1:27; 2:1-4; 4:2; Col 2:2.19; 3:12-14; 1 Thess 5:13-14), should care for one another (1 Cor 12:25-26) and should help in mutual up-building (Rom 14:19; 15:2; 1 Cor 8:1; 14:3-5.12.17.26; Eph 4:15-16; 1 Thess 5:11), though it includes all humans into the fellowship (Rom 12:14.17-21; Gal 6:10; 1 Thess 3:12; 5:15). Though Paul invites the Christians to love the ton heteron and the ton plesion as we have seen in Rom 13, yet it has not gone the full way of calling the Christians to love even their enemies.

19 Cf. Hugh Montefiore, "Thou Shalt Love Thy Neighbour as Thyself," in *Novum Testamentum VII* (July, 1962), 157-170. In this article the author notes that a close examination of Paul's use of neighbourly love in his extant epistles confirms the view that Paul did not regard it as a Christian duty to go out of his way to love a non- Christian. The author's contention in this article is that the love of outsiders and even of enemies comes actually from Jesus himself which then gets narrowed down to the members of the Christian community at the time of the Early Church.

In the Hebrew context 'neighbour' referred to a fellow Israel. In Jesus' language the neighbour includes an enemy (cf. Mt 5:43-44; Lk 6:28) and the alien, for according to Luke, Jesus told the parable of the Good Samaritan in answer to the question "And who is my neighbour?" (cf. Lk 10:30-37).

Further we find in Mt 25:31-44 that the neighbours are the hungry, the thirsty, the strangers, the ill-clad, and the prisoners. Paul's use of neighbourly love in his extant epistles confirms the view that Paul did not regard it as a Christian duty to go out of his way to love a non-Christian. The love of outsiders and even of enemies comes actually from Jesus himself which then gets narrowed down to the members of the Christian community at the time of the Early Church as reflected in Paul. This is understandable from a person who is concerned first to set the things right in his own communities before extending it to the larger society.

The other aspect of the love of neighbour commandment in Paul is that it does not go to the extent of questioning the dehumanising structures of the times. The possible reasons could be that Paul's main focus was to strengthen the insiders (the Christians) in the context of an insider-outsider (non-Christians) tension. This was to attract the outsiders through an exemplary life by the insiders. Since the Church was in its fledgeling stage, Paul and the others could not afford to question the oppressive structures of the society. In some places, Paul even instructs the Christians to follow the 'customs' (cf. 1 Cor 11:13) in order not to scandalize the outsiders. In fact, Paul in his epistles and Luke in the Acts of the Apostles, try to present the Church as friendly as possible to the Romans. Maybe they did it for the sake of first establishing the church in the midst of all opposition and rejection so that the church can gain wings to take off in a much stronger way.

Critical Reflection

Paul rightly identifies the importance of 'love' as the central proclamation of Jesus and makes it the foundation of the ethical behaviour of all the Christians. Theologically 'love of neighbour' is rightly understood by Paul as the central proclamation of Jesus Christ. He does it by showing that Justification is a gratuitous gift which is appropriated by everyone who believes in Christ. By virtue of this justification, every Christian is made free and this freedom is only for loving one's neighbour as oneself. Living this life of freedom in love means giving up selfishness by avoiding all the desires of the flesh and living out of the gifts of the Holy Spirit.

However, pastorally when Paul is giving exhortations to the communities on this love of neighbour his main focus remains the love of the insiders, that is, the Christian brothers and sisters before the outsiders. For whatever reason Paul may have done it, in any case, it is clear that Paul has, to a certain extent, narrowed down the perspective of love of neighbour from that of the earthly

Jesus. Such an approach to love may not provide wide wings so that she can take off with a full swing, but might turn the Church communities become more and more inward-looking.

Conclusion

Gal 5:13-14 and Rom 13:8-10 presuppose Paul's description of the human situation of sin and the failure of the Mosaic law to really free them. Both the texts present God's response of love, grace and mercy in and through the cross of Christ as a gratuitous gift (initiative is from God). All those who come to believe in Christ are justified through the same Christ event, and they are made free from the desires of the flesh whose root cause is sin. All those who are freed by the cross are then led by the Spirit, who functions as a guarantee and guide. The Christian Freedom and the consequent life in the Spirit needs to be expressed through love of neighbour which replaces law and fulfils it at the same time.

CONCLUDING ARTICLE: BEING AN INDIAN CHRISTIAN

33

Free and Joyous:
The Challenge of Being an Indian Christian Today

Kuruvilla Pandikattu SJ
Dean, Faculty of Philosophy, Jnana-Deepa Vidyapeeth, Pune

Abstract: *Based on Kurien's last book, the author traces the person and theology of Kurien as "Freedom and Joy." The author shows that Kurien was a man of freedom and a larger vision. His commitment to the people was based on a deep and liberating experience of God. Truly, he was a man of joy. A liberated person who could accept and affirm everyone! A human (human, only and fully) and humane person, indeed! He was truly committed to the Church he loved and India, which was his home!*

Keywords: *Kunnumpuram, joy, freedom, Indian Christian.*

Prof Kurien Kunnumpuram, SJ, one of the most creative Indian theologians, is quite convinced that freedom and joy are essential characteristics of our Christian existence. This article, meant to pay homage to a creative Indian theologian, founder of *Jnanadeepa: Pune Journal of Religious Studies* and author of more than 20 books explores the basic content of his final book, *Freedom and Joy*, which, I believe, characterises his own life!

We first familiarise ourselves with the person of Kunnumpuram. Then we focus on his understanding of freedom as essential to every Christian. This is followed by his appraisal of joy, the core experience of a Christian, in spite of all the suffering we experience. Then we briefly dwell on Kurien as a creative thinker and eminent theologian. Then we focus on freedom and joy as the essential features of being a Christian in today's world. We conclude by affirming the creative contribution of Kurien to the Indian Church in the light of Vatican II.

The Person: Indian Pioneer of Vatican II Reform

Prof Kurien Kunnumpuram, SJ (1931-2018) is no more physically present with us. He completed his PhD on Second Vatican Council from the University of Innsbruck, Austria, in 1968, just three years after Vatican II. The next year he joined Papal Seminary Community, teaching at Jnana-Deepa Vidyapeeth and remained here till 2013. This means he has spent half of his years (44 years out of 87) in Pune. On September 25, 2018, he was admitted in the hospital in a coma state, due to a blood clot in the brain. Sadly, after 29 days in a coma, he breathed his last on October 23, 2018.

He is an eminent thinker and creative theologian. He started the journal *Jnanadeepa: Pune Journal of Religious Studies* in 1998. He worked as editor of *Asian journal for Religious Studies* for more than ten years. Through both the journals, he has been attempting to promote an Indian Christian theology, which is rooted in the rich Indian tradition and the deep Christian heritage. He was the first editor of *Encyclopedia of Christianity*, published by Jnana-Deepa Vidyapeeth, Pune. Author of more than 20 books in areas of Church (Ecclesiology), Anthropology and Spirituality, he has contributed significantly to theologising in the Indian context. On 17-18, October 2018 a seminar was organised in Kozhikode, to honour his contribution to Indian theologising, where more than 40 participants studied 18 papers and explored the adventurous journey of a Christian.

One of the creative and significant Indian theologians, Kurien's last book, aptly titled "Freedom and Joy"[1] signifies his own life. As you know, Gandhi, dared to say, "my life is my message." Kurien would not really make that claim, but his life came very close to the message of this book. He is quite convinced that freedom and joy are essential characteristics of our Christian existence. As the pioneer who introduced the reforms of Vatican II to the Indian situation in general and Jnana-Deepa Vidyapeeth, in particular, he had a tremendous impact on the new understanding of the Indian Church.

He, along with Francis D'Sa and George Soares-Prabhu, belonged to the second generation of theology professors at JDV, who brought about the emphasis on freedom (liberation theology) and Indian orientation

1 Kunnumpuram, Kurien. *Freedom and Joy: Reflections on the Essential Characteristics of Christian Life Today*, Jnana-Deepa Vidyapeeth, Pune and Christian World Imprints, New Delhi, pp. 177+viii, ₹ 325/- ISBN: 977-93-5148-320-5. Most of the quotes are from this book. See also Fr Kurien Kunnumpuram Sj Passed Away | Papal Seminary, Pune, http://www.papalseminary.in/2018/10/25/1202-fr-kurien-kunnumpuram-sj-passed-away (accessed July 14, 2019).

(inculturation) in the campus.[2] Further, as you know, he followed the footsteps of great personalities like Scripture scholar Fr Francis Pereira SJ (1931-2014), liturgist Fr Lorenzo Fernando (1947-2017) and Indian philosopher Fr Noel Sheth SJ (1943-2017). They tried to promote an ambience of freedom, transparency and joy in the campus and theological thinking.

Freedom of the Children of God

After a careful investigation of the Kingdom of God which was central to the life and ministry of Jesus, the great Scripture scholar George Soares-Prabhu has concluded that Jesus was the supreme example of the freedom of the Kingdom of God. Soares-Prabhu states: "Jesus moves through the pages of the Gospel as the supremely free man. He is driven by no demons of greed or ambition – for the Son of Man "has nowhere to lay his head" (Lk 9:58) and has come "not to be served but to serve" (Mk1K 10:45). He is daunted neither by the pressures of heteronomous law (Jn 8:1-10) nor by the violence of established authority (Lk 13:31-33). With supreme freedom, he challenges the most sacred institutions of his people when his concern for his fellowmen urges him to do so. He breaks the Sabbath (Mk 7:1-15), touches lepers (Mk 1:42), dines with the socially outcast and with sinners (Mk 2:15-17)."[3]

Jesus' mission was to liberate people. He said that the Spirit of the Lord "has sent me to proclaim release to captives and recovery of sight to the blind, to let the oppressed go free" (Lk 4:18). Jesus frees human beings from sin and guilt (Mk 2:1-12). He frees us from the routine of ritualism (Mt 6:7) and the oppressive burden of the law (Mt 11:28-3 and 23:4). He liberates us from the terrible isolation to which we can be condemned by social ostracism (Lk 19:1-10), ritual uncleanness (Mk 1:40-45) or mental ill-health (Mk 5:1-21). He calls his followers to freedom from possessions (Mk1:16-18; 10:1) and unhealthy family ties (Lk 9:61). He invites them to put all their trust in God so that they need no other security in life (Mt 6:25-34).

As a result of his personal encounter with Jesus, Paul exclaims: "For freedom, Christ has set us free. Stand firm, therefore, and do not submit again to a yoke of slavery (Gal 5:1).

In 2013 Pope Francis, in his Apostolic Exhortation, *The Joy of the Gospel* affirms: "God's mercy has willed that we should be free". Kurien will agree with it fully. So Kunnumpuram reminds us of the powerful words of St Paul: "For you were called to freedom, brothers and sisters" (Gal 5:13). This call, issued many centuries ago, is most timely today.

---

2 The first generation being Fr Lionel Mascarenhas, Fr Carlos D'Mello SJ and Fr Joe Miranda SJ.

3 See Fr Kurien Kunnumpuram Sj Passed Away | Papal Seminary, Pune, http://www.papalseminary.in/2018/10/25/1202-fr-kurien-kunnumpuram-sj-passed-away (accessed July 14, 2019).

The Joy of Being a Christian

When Jesus was born in Bethlehem, an angel of the Lord told the shepherds: "I am bringing you good news of great joy for all the people" (Lk 2: 10). In the gospel of Mark, Jesus begins his public ministry by proclaiming the good news that the Kingdom of God has come (Mk 1:14-15). Now joy is one of the fruits of the Kingdom (Rom 14:17). Towards the end of his ministry, Jesus declared: "I have said these things to you so that my joy may be in you and that your joy may be complete" (Jn 15:11). After a careful examination of the life and ministry of Jesus, Kurien finds Albert's conclusion relevant: " Joy was, in fact, the most characteristic result of all Jesus' activity amongst the poor and the oppressed. The meals he had with them were festive celebrations, parties. Jesus, obviously, had a way of ensuring that people enjoyed themselves at the gatherings. This scandalised the Pharisees. Rejoicing and celebrating with sinners was incomprehensibly scandalous (Lk 15:1). They could only assume that he had become a pleasure-seeker, 'a drunkard and a glutton' (Lk 7:34)." Jesus tried to explain this joy and this celebration to the Pharisees by telling them three parables: The parables of the lost sheep, the lost coin and the lost son (Lk 15). It is highly significant that each of these parables ends with joy and celebration. When the shepherd finds his lost sheep, he calls together his friends and neighbours and celebrates with them. And Jesus adds: "Just so, I tell you, there will be more joy in heaven over one sinner who repents than over ninety-nine righteous persons who need no repentance" (Lk 15:6-7). Something similar happens when the woman finds her silver coin, which was lost (15:9-10).

The last parable is extremely significant. After listening to the parable, one wonders: Who is the lost son? The younger son who went away from the Father and lived riotously with his women? Or the elder son, who, as a true Pharisee, kept the law most faithfully? The younger son was able to receive God's forgiving love, rejoice in it and celebrate it. But the elder son was not able to do so. So, he is really the lost son! To quote Nolan once again: "There can be no doubt that Jesus was a remarkably cheerful person and that his joy like his faith and hope was infectious… The poor and the oppressed and anyone else who was not too hung up on 'respectability' found the company of Jesus a liberating experience of sheer joy".

Pope Francis points out that the whole Bible speaks of joy. Jesus himself "rejoiced in the Spirit" (Lk 10:21). He promises his disciples: "You will be sorrowful, but your sorrow will turn into joy" (Jn 16:20). Then he adds: "But I will see you again, and your hearts will rejoice, and no one will take your joy from you" (Jn 16:22). The disciples "rejoiced" at the sight of the risen Lord. In the Acts of the Apostles, we read that the first Christians "ate their food with glad and generous hearts" (Acts 2:46). Because of the preaching of Philip and the miracles he worked "there was great joy in that city" (Acts 8:8). The newly baptized eunuch "went on his way rejoicing" (8:39), while Paul's jailer and his household "rejoiced that he had become a believer in God" (Acts 16:34).

Similarly, Pope Francis points out that the whole Bible speaks of joy. Jesus himself "rejoiced in the Spirit" (Lk 10:21).

Creative Thinker and Critical Writer

He certainly was one of the best and most eminent theologians of India. He has written scores of books and many theological articles based on research. His thinking and writings were marked by originality and creativity. He was bold in his thinking. Certainly, he remained within the faith of the Catholic Church, which was shaped by his study of the documents of Vatican II. His own doctoral thesis on the document of Second Vatican Council. He certainly was one of the best-read persons on Second Vatican Council. He would profusely quote and refer to the documents of Second Vatican Council. It is he who helped the student body and staff members in Papal Seminary and Jnana-Deepa Vidyapeeth to get more and more acquitted with Second Vatican Council. He certainly was an epoch in the history of the Catholic Church. I would say, he has greatly shaped, fashioned and impacted by Second Vatican Council, which opened the doors of the Church to the world.

Gaudium et Spec guided him to take the realities of the world seriously, with its hopes and dreams. This is how Kurien pursued his theological thinking and writing. Courageously, boldly and in the light of Second Vatican Council.

Fr Kurien, apart from being our friend, was an eminent theologian, a skilled writer and a good formattor.

Through the two journals he has been editing and more than 20 books he has written, he has impacted the theological life of Indian Christianity. The six Volumes of the Collected Works of Samuel Rayan he has edited have been remarkably influential in fostering a climate of freedom, responsibility and dignity.

At a personal level: He and I lived in the Papal Seminary for many long years. I can assert that even when I was a student and later as a staff that Kurien became the rallying point for the seminarians. The seminarians will turn to him in moments of difficulty. Kurien was always welcome them and make himself available to them. They trusted him, felt supported and encouraged by him. I could see that they loved him, and they were very fond of him. So I would say Fr Kurien was a good formator in the seminary for the generations of priests in the modern world, after Second Vatican Council.

I thank God for the person, the theologian and the formator that Fr Kurien was. He was a creative thinker, an innovative guide and a courageous dreamer. He certainly was a gift to the church in India and in his way to the Universal Church.

Conclusion: Empowering Presence

These reflections based on Kurien's last book aptly entitled, "Freedom and Joy," published by Christian World Imprints, was released on 17th October 2018 in a gathering of about 45 Christian thinkers, at SRC, Kozhikode, Kerala. They came together to reflect on the creative contribution that Prof Kurien Kunnumpuram to the Indian Church. Prof Kunnumpuram was then in a coma after a stroke and fall at Kozhikode. A few days later, on October 23, 2018, he breathed his last. May his soul rest in peace! May his vision of a Christian who is both free and joyous! And of an Indian who is truly open to other cultures and religions.

This experience of the joy of the first Christians should inspire all of us to find great joy in our Christian life. Unfortunately, according to Pope Francis, "there are Christians whose lives seem like Lent without Easter". Some of them walk through life as though they are taking part in a perennial funeral procession. Kurien reminds us of Pope Francis who invites Christians everywhere "to a renewed encounter with Jesus Christ". For "with Christ, joy is constantly born a new."

The freedom and joy that Kurien experienced and radiated make him an enabling, encouraging and empowering presence among us. He could accept and affirm everyone with their differences and unique qualities. It is because of persons like him that at Papal Seminary and Jnana-Deepa Vidyapeeth, we can experience an atmosphere of freedom, joy and fellowship. Inspired by him, may we all become free and loving persons: enabling, encouraging and empowering each other, by accepting and affirming each one of us. In spite of our weakness, differences and inabilities!

In spite of his limitations, Kurien was a man of freedom and of a larger vision. His commitment to the people was based on a deep and liberating experience of God. Truly, he was a man of JOY. A liberated person, who could accept and affirm everyone! A human (human, only and fully) and humane person, indeed! He was truly committed to the Church he loved and India, which was his home!

Truly Kurien cared for others, especially the poor and the broken people. His heart reached out to them and embraced them! He also shared with them his vision, dream and values. He lived for and dreamt of a egalitarian society in the Church and in the nation. He wished for a free and joyous community that cares, shares and dreams together both as Indians and as Christians. In this process he embraced the others, both non-Christians and non-Indians reverentially and respectfully!

Appendices on Kurien Kunnumpuam SJ

1. Highlights on Prof Kurien Kunnumpuram SJ

Prof Kurien Kunnumpuram SJ (1931-2018) is no more physically present with us. We are at a loss to comprehend the loss to the Jesuits, the Indian Church and Papal Seminary, Pune, India.

Fr Kurien was an enthusiastic, creative and intelligent person. He completed his PhD on Vatican II from the University of in 1968, just three years after Vatican II. The next year he joined Papal Seminary Community, teaching at Jnana-Deepa Vidyapeeth and remained here till 2013. This means he has spent 44 years out of 87 years in Pune. On September 25, 2018, he was admitted to the hospital in a coma state, due to a blood clot in the brain. Sadly, after 29 days in a coma, he breathed his last on October 23, 2018.

The milestones of his eventful life are as follows:

8 July 1931	Birth at Teekoy, Kerala, India
11 July 1950	Entered the Society of Jesus
24 March 1963	Ordination to the priesthood
1968	Completed Doctorate in Systematic Theology from the University of Innsbruck, Austria, on "Ways of Salvation."
1969	Started teaching Theology at Jnana-Deepa Vidyapeeth (JDV), Pune, India
1974-77	Dean of the Faculty of Theology, JDV, Pune
1987–1993	Rector of Jnana-Deepa Vidyapeeth, Pune, India
January 1998	Founded *Jnanadeepa: Pune Journal of Religious Studies* (also editor and publisher)
January 2002	Started editing and publishing *AUC: Asian Journal for Religious Studies*

8 July 2011	Eighty memorable years: Celebrated at Papal Seminary, Pune, with a mass and felicitation by Rt. Rev. Thomas Dabre, Bishop of Pune, India
31 August 2013	Returned to the Jesuit Province, Calicut (Kozhikode), Kerala.
17 November 2017	Stroke, Calicut (Kozhikode), Kerala. Recuperated gradually.
25 September 2018	A blood clot in the brain; went into comma; Calicut (Kozhikode), Kerala.
17-18 October 2018	National Seminar on "Kurien's Contribution to Indian Theological Vision", Calicut (Kozhikode), Kerala.
23 October 2018	Rest in Peace, at Nirmala Hospital, Kozhikodu, Kerala.

He was an eminent thinker and creative theologian. He started the journal Jnanadeepa: Pune Journal of Religious Studies in 1998. He worked as editor of Asian journal for Religious Studies for more than ten years. He was the first editor of *Encyclopedia of Christianity*, published by Jnana-Deepa Vidyapeeth. Author of more than 20 books in areas of Church (Ecclesiology), Anthropology and Spirituality, he has contributed significantly to theologizing in the Indian context. On 17-18, October a seminar was organized in Kozhikode, to honour his contribution to Indian theologizing, where more than 40 participants studied 18 papers on themes dear to Kurien's heart.

One of the creative and significant Indian theologians, Kurien's last book, aptly titled "Freedom and Joy" signifies his own life. As you know, Gandhi, dared to say, "my life is my message." Kurien would not really make that claim, but his life came very close to the message of this book. He is quite convinced that freedom and joy are essential characteristics of our Christian existence.

He, along with Francis D'Sa, and George Soares-Prabhu, belonged to the second generation of theology professors at JDV, who brought about the emphasis on freedom and Indian orientation in the campus. [The first generation being Fr Lionel Mascarenhas, Fr Carlos D'Mello SJ and Fr Joe Miranda SJ]. Further, as you know, he followed the footsteps of great Scripture scholars like Fr Rui de Menezes and Fr Francis Pereira SJ (1931-2014), liturgist Fr Lorenzo Fernando (1947-2017) and Indian philosopher Fr Noel Sheth SJ (1943-2017).

2. Rector's Letter to Provincial

Bhausaheb Sansare SJ

To
The Provincial
Christ Hall
Malapramba
Kozhikode
Kerala

October 24, 2018

Dear Fr M.K. George

We are saddened to hear of the demise of Fr Kurien Kunnumpuram SJ on October 23, 2018.

As you know Fr Kunnumpuram came to Papal Seminary in 1969 and had been teaching here till 2013. He served Papal Seminary and Jnana-Deepa Vidyapeeth in various capacities like Dean, President, Animators of various academies and councils.

His presence among us was a calming and reassuring one. The students profited immensely through his interaction. He contributed much to the growth and development of the Papal Seminary community. He had been an inspiration both to the students and the younger staff members in our collective search for God. He was a remarkably motivating and inspiring leader, who could enable, encourage and empower the seminarians.

Kurien had a way of dealing with problems impartially and compassionately. He could take the whole community with him, especially in community meetings and interactions. He was a visionary who could see much ahead of times. He has brought tremendous good will among our community members. Truly, he has been very productive pastorally and intellectually while being a member of our community.

He was an excellent teacher, insightful writer, inspiring formator and a good priest.

We want to thank you and the Kerala Province for giving Kurien to us, that too half of his life, where he has been really productive and creative. We know that even when he was in the Province, Kurien was always interested and involved in our community. His heart was also with us.

Our heart-felt condolences and prayerful wishes to you and the whole Kerala Province. It will be painful for you to bid him farewell. We will surely miss his gentle words of comfort and consolation. May we be inspired by Kurien's commitment and vision.

Yours truly
Rev Fr Bhausaheb Sansare SJ
Fr Rector and Community,
Papal Seminary, Pune

3. A Man of Vision and Commitment

Thomas Karimundackal SJ

Fr. Kurien Kunnumpuram, SJ (1931-2018) is no more physically present in our midst. We are unable to comprehend the loss to the Church, particularly the Church in India, and I am sure that his physical absence will create a vacuum in the theological circles and discussions. Though my life with him was short, Fr. Kurien has left behind immortal memories in my heart with his unembellished life. It is the same feeling that most people share about the undecorated and exemplary scholarly life of Fr. Kurien.

Fr. Kurien was a simple and cheerful person who could hide a thousand feelings behind his innocent smile. He was a simple man who enjoyed the simple things that life offered. He enjoyed the spiritual enrichment of simplicity until the very end of his life. He could make life comfortable with very minimum needs, and he never bothered about a secure life. I never heard him speak ill of anybody. He was a virtuous man who never had any complaint in life.

Fr. Kurien showed great enthusiasm to visit his students and friends and to maintain a close relationship with them. He used to walk with a meditative rhythm, and never in a hurry. So also in his quiet manner Fr. Kurien slowly walked into the lives of his friends and inserted himself into their hearts. He was always approachable. He received everyone heartily, welcomed them cordially and treated them warmly. That was his personal trait of being hospitable. He remained an affable and friendly person to all, the lay staff, as well as the public. Many approached him for advice and counsel.

Fr. Kurien was very systematic, regular, hardworking and totally committed to the task entrusted to him. He kept himself always busy, either reading or writing or counselling. One would never see Fr. Kurien is sitting idle. He had a fire in him that kindled other fires. He was a man who relentlessly gave love, received love and longed to love more. His family ties testify to this. His friends remember this. Even his detractors agree that he was a loving and lovable man.

Fr. Kurien's life-time achievement has been, apart from other things, the engaging way of teaching the essentials of theological anthropology, ecclesiology, and Mariology in a very clear and concise manner. As a teacher, he was very much loved and appreciated by his students. He knew the pulse of every student and treated him/her very personally. He gave freedom to the students and allowed them to grow responsibly.

Indeed, he was known for his intellectual calibre and clarity of thought. He completed his PhD on Vatican II with a special reference to "ways of salvation" from the University of Innsbruck in 1968, just three years after Vatican II. He has studied the documents of Vatican II taking the concern of every Christian believer in India, such as how to understand the meaning of his or her salvation through Christ in the Church in the face of the multi-religious context of India which claims to have various "ways of salvation". As Jacob Parappally observes, "Kurien Kunnumpuram's contribution to the understanding of the theological significance of other religions in God's plan of salvation according to the teachings and insights of the Vatican II not only highlighted the importance of entering into dialogue with other religions as an imperative to the self-understanding of Church but also showed the need for a theology of Non-Christian religions and developing a theology of Christian Missions." Indeed, his scholarly and erudite expositions on various theological themes answer the question: How can the Church remain a home for all peoples and religions in the light of the teachings of Vatican II?

Author of more than 15 books in areas of Ecclesiology, Anthropology and Spirituality, he has contributed significantly to evolve a method to theologize in the Indian context. He has articulated his creative theological reflections in the journal *Jnanadeepa: Pune Journal of Religious Studies,* a journal which he founded in 1998. He has edited the *Asian journal for Religious Studies (AUC)* for more than ten years. He was the first editor of Encyclopedia of Christianity, published by Jnana-Deepa Vidyapeeth. He, along with Fr. Francis D'Sa and George Soares-Prabhu, Fr Francis Pereira SJ, Rui de Menezes, who belonged to the second generation of theology professors at JDV, brought about the emphasis on doing theology in the context. Thus, the scholarly contribution of Fr. Kurien exhibited a far-reaching influence in several areas.

Fr. Kurien was a man of determination and total self-reliance. His 44 years of meritorious service in various capacities at JDV and Papal Seminary (1969-2013) substantiate this. As the dean of the faculty of Theology (1974-77), and the Rector of Jnana-Deepa Vidyapeeth (1987-93) he has given an orientation to the theological and priestly formation in India. He has dreamt dreams for JDV and realized them raising JDV to the standard of a premier theological institution in India. According to him, theological formation is meant to form the clergy to liberate people from the bondages – social, cultural, religious, and economical – rather than forming clergy for the routine ritual celebrations. In his opinion, priestly and religious life is not a withdrawal from the world, but it is a prophetic commitment to the people to enable them to experience God amid their struggles and sufferings.

According to Fr. Kurien, the mission of the Church is to collaborate with God's salvific work for the fullness of the human person and the human community, according to the pattern revealed in Jesus Christ. He says: "To follow Christ is also to identify ourselves with the poor and powerless as he did. The Incarnation is the symbol of this identification. Through his incarnation, he inserted himself into the human family and became one with us". According to him "the members of the Church are called to be the disciples of Jesus Christ. And the disciples of Jesus are the children of God". Therefore, in his opinion, to realize the Church's mission, a radical commitment to the values of Jesus is indispensable and necessary; values like righteousness, love, trust, forgiveness, sharing, genuine worship, avoiding ostentation, non-judgmental attitude etc.

Fr. Kurien is convinced that the Church, the dream of Jesus, is a joyful community and its mission is to proclaim joy and freedom, which calls for sensitivity to the needs of others. He says: "joy was, in fact, the most characteristic result of all Jesus' activity amongst the poor and oppressed". Therefore, according to him the experience of Joy that Jesus communicated to his hearers should inspire all of us to find great joy in our Christian life, and it should be the abiding quality of Christian life. The basis of such a liberating and enabling joy and freedom should be our Christian experience of God.

By integrating the teachings of Jesus in the Gospels and the Vatican II Fr. Kurien, through his writings and teachings, communicated an inclusive spirituality, a spirituality that humanizes. According to him, spirituality is not restricted to any particular religion, tradition or culture; rather it breaks the social, cultural and religious barriers leading to 'fullness of life for all'. This inclusive spirituality which he emphasized was against the traditional understanding of Christian spirituality. He made a distinction between piety and genuine spirituality; while the former is guided by the faithful performance of devotional practices and rituals, the latter is guided by the spirit of God which transforms the life and values of a person. He says: "There is a lot of piety among us, but not enough spirituality. Piety consists of the performance of external devotional practices and is measured by one's fidelity to these practices. Whether or not the faithful performance of these exercises of piety improves the quality of one's Christian life is a question that is seldom asked. One is at times surprised that priests, sisters and lay people who are obviously pious are manifestly unfair in their dealings with other people. Some of them show so little of the compassion of Christ and are quite unwilling to forgive others." He further claims: "Spirituality is a way of life. It is our total inward quest for growth, meaning and authenticity. And it is manifested in the quality of one's life. .... to be spiritual is to be touched and transformed by the Spirit of God. In a person who has been touched and transformed by God's Spirit the fruits of the Spirit will be seen: "love, joy, peace, patience, kindness, generosity, faithfulness, gentleness and self-control" (Gal 5:22-23)". Accordingly, Christian Spirituality is essentially concerned about a way of life that is manifested in the quality of one's life, a quality that makes one more human, liberative and close to God and fellow-human beings.

The memory of Fr. Kurien brings us hope of what a simple, dedicated and learned man can do to better humanity. His memory will remain with so many of us, as a true friend, a mentor, a fellow seeker and most importantly a man who dreamt for a society of freedom, joy, peace and justice. Fr. Kurien continues to live in our memory and in our lives, as an inspiration, as a model, and most significantly as a loving presence. May his soul rest in peace, and may our souls become restless to live out the dreams of Fr. Kurien.

[This article was republished from The Smart Companion, November 2018]

4. Farewell to Fr Kurien Kunnumpuram SJ, an Eminent and Creative Theologian

Papal Seminary

Prof Kurien Kunnumpuram, SJ (1931-2018) died on October 23, 2018, at Kozhikode, Kerala. His funeral took place at 11:00 AM on Thursday, October 25, 2018. There was a special memorial Eucharist presided over by Rt Rev Thomas Dabre, Bishop of Pune, both a colleague and personal friend of Fr Kurien.

Rt Rev Bishop Thomas Dabre, the main celebrant of the special memorial Eucharist, said that "Fr Kurien, apart from being my personal friend, was an eminent theologian, a skilled writer and a good formattor." He recalled that he had lived with Kurien in in the Papal Seminary for many long years. "I can say even when I was a student and later as a staff that Kurien became a rallying point for the seminarians. The seminarians will turn to him in moments of difficulty. Kurien was always welcome them and make himself available to them. They trusted him, felt supported and encouraged by him. I could see that they loved him and they were very fond of him." Bishop Dabre acclaimed Fr Kurien as a "good formator in the seminary for the generations of priests in the modern world, after Second Vatican Council."

Bishop Dabre opined: "He certainly was an epoch in the history of the Indian Catholic church. I would say, he has greatly shaped, fashioned and impacted by Second Vatican Council, which opened the doors of the Church to the world."

In the homily, Fr Kuruvilla described Kurien's contribution to the Papal Seminary, Jnana-Deepa Vidyapeeth and to the Indian Church briefly. Fr Kurien completed his PhD on Vatican II from the University of in 1968, just three years after Vatican II. The next year he joined Papal Seminary Community, teaching at Jnana-Deepa Vidyapeeth and remained here till 2013. This means he has spent 44 years out of 87 years in Pune.

Fr Kuruvilla added: "He is an eminent thinker and creative theologian. He started the journal *Jnanadeepa: Pune Journal of Religious Studies* in 1998. He worked as editor of *Asian journal for Religious Studies* for more than ten years." He was the first editor of Encyclopedia of Christianity, published by Jnana-Deepa Vidyapeeth. Author of more than 20 books in areas of Church (Ecclesiology), Anthropology and Spirituality, he has contributed significantly to theologizing in the Indian context. He recalled that on 17-18, October 2018 a seminar was organized in Kozhikode, to honour his contribution to Indian theologizing, where more than 40 participants deliberated on 18 papers.

One of the creative and significant Indian theologians, Kurien's last book, aptly titled "Freedom and Joy" signifies his own life. Kurien would not really make that his life is his message, as Mahatma Gandhi did. But Fr Kuruvilla pointed out that Kurien's life came very close to the, of this book. He is quite convinced that freedom and joy are essential characteristics of our Christian existence.

He, along with Fr Francis D'Sa SJ and Fr George Soares-Prabhu SJ, belonged to the second generation of theology professors at JDV, who brought about the emphasis on freedom and Indian orientation in the campus. He recalled that the first generation being Fr Lionel Mascarenhas, Fr Carlos D'Mello SJ and Fr Joe Miranda SJ. Further, Fr Kurien followed the footsteps of great men like Scripture scholar Fr Francis Pereira SJ (1931-2014), liturgist Fr Lorenzo Fernando (1947-2017) and Indian philosopher Fr Noel Sheth SJ (1943-2017) in Papal Seminary in shaping the lives of seminarians and giving a liberative dimension to their spirituality.

Rev Fr Bhausaheb Sansare SJ, Rector, Papal Seminary said that Fr Kurien's "presence among us was a calming and reassuring one. The students profited immensely through his interaction. He has contributed much to the growth and development of the Papal Seminary community. He has been an inspiration both to the students and the younger staff members in our collective search for God. He was a remarkably motivating and inspiring leader, who can enable, encourage and empower the seminarians."

He added that Kurien had a way of dealing with problems impartially and compassionately. Fr Sansare added: "He is a visionary who can see much ahead of times. He has brought tremendous good will among our community members. Truly, he has been very productive pastorally and intellectually while being a member of our community."

The minister of Papal Seminary, Fr Vincent Crasta SJ, highlighted three aspects of Fr Kunnumpuram. Firstly, he was a progressive thinker concerning the Church, priesthood and religious life, taking into considering the changing times. Secondly. He was truly a man of genuine detachment and interior freedom. Thirdly, he is a person "deeply concerned of other people, enquiring about them, supporting them." In other words, Fr Kurien was a man "who had spiritual depth, because of which he could relate to different people holistically.

"Fr Joe Francis from the Diocese of Aizawl, Mizoram was a student of Kurien. He reminiscences: "Fr Kurien was a calm in the storm. Always composed, patient and compassionate, he could deal with any situation with equanimity."

The Eucharist was attended by 170 seminarians and 40 religious from around Papal Seminary. Four of Papal Seminary priests, Fr Biju Joseph, Fr. Thomas Karimundackal, Fr Nishant Irudayadason and Fr VM Jose, represented papal Seminary at Christ Hall, Kozhikode, where the Eucharist and funeral were presided by Rt Rev Varghese Chakkalackal, Bishop of Kozhikode.

5. A Man for Others

Jose Thayil SJ
Rector, Papal Seminary, Pune 411014

I have known Fr. Kurien for the last 30 years or so. I have been a silent admirer of him during all these years. While I was the director of studies in Patna Regional Theologate, I have invited him a few times to come and give classes in Patna. His classes were very well appreciated.

There are very many things that I appreciate in Fr. Kurien. I like to mention a few of them. He is known for his availability. He is always willing to help out the staff and the students in any way he can. I have seen him volunteering to help out. He is a man who encourages others, especially to do well in academic matters such as reading, writing and publishing. I have found him to be a crusader for freedom. Though giving more freedom to seminarians brings along its own problems, he feels that true formation can take place only in an atmosphere of freedom. He is an optimist by nature. He tries to see the positive side of people and situations and gives a positive interpretation of the things that he hears and sees. He is a good observer. He can notice what many of us fail to notice at all.

He is known for his clarity in thinking, speaking, teaching and conducting meetings. That is why his classes are very well appreciated, and his articles and books are easy to read and understand. We can get many insights and practical suggestions from his classes and writings. He is invited time and again to be the resource person in chapters of both men and women religious. He is also highly sought after as a retreat director. He challenges people to be more human and spiritual rather than being "pious and holy". I have found him very human in his approach towards me and others.

As he will moving out of Papal Seminary to Christ Hall in Calicut in his home province, I wish him good health, good friends and God's abundant blessings. Fr. Kurien, as Papal Seminary has been your home for the last 45 years or so, you are most welcome anytime to this home of love. As we promise to keep you in our prayers, we request to keep Papal Seminary in your prayers and thoughts. Once again wish you all the best and may God bless you.

[Farewell to Kurien from Papal Seminary, August 2013]

6. Short, Sweet and Focussed

VM Jose SJ

"When life gives you a hundred reasons to cry, show life that you have a thousand reasons to smile."

Kurien Kunnumpuram SJ is seen as the ever young man here. Even though he is 82 plus, he is still very energetic, active and vibrant. Though he is in the list of emeritus, he still takes classes, gives retreats, talks and travels far and wide. He is a tremendous inspiration to youngsters. It is a pity that he is leaving JDV campus and Papal Seminary in particular.

Though I was in JDV for my philosophy (residing in De Nobili College, Pune), I did not meet Kurien those days. I first started my contact with him when he came to Vidyajyoti, Delhi, to teach theology. He taught Ecclesiology, and I confidently say that all the students appreciated his classes. He is very systematic, organized and comprehensive and moreover interprets topics to the contemporary situation in order to make it relevant for us today.

What I appreciate in Kurien is his straightforwardness in his comments. He does not beat around the bush but says directly what he has to say. He is very positively critical and appreciates the goodness in others. He is available to students when they call him for a talk or anything similar. His critical stand and commitment to issues and problems of society are praiseworthy. His talks are focused and to the point; short and sweet when needed. I appreciate the way he is concerned about the community here in Papal Seminary.

I thank him for his great contribution to theology in India and the world. Personally, he has helped me to study and understand the situation of Papal Seminary. Every time I want to have an honest opinion, I can go to him, because he gives me his opinion from the bottom of his heart. I appreciate the valuable remarks and suggestions he has offered about the day to chores, including liturgy of Papal Seminary.

Kurien, I pray that God bless you abundantly and give you the strength to reach out to and inspire many more people wherever you are.

"It's true that we don't know what we've got until we lose it, but it's also true that we don't know what we've been missing until it arrives."

[Felicitation Speech, Papal Seminary, Pune, August 2013]

7. "No More Words"

Ben Bose
Papal Seminary, Ramwadi, Pune 411014

"No more words. We know them all, all the words that should not be said But you have made our world more perfect and beautiful."

To gild (make golden) a lily would not be necessary because it is sublime in itself. So is Fr Kurien. Well! It is, indeed, an honour and privilege for me to express the deepest sentiments of feelings and gratitude to Fr Kurien for his wonderful being to each one of us. He is a person of integrity, a happy priest, lives his life with commitment, self-contentment and love. As he has been engaged in learning and teaching theology for 50 years, his very life has become a message: a life-promoting and growth-enhancing person.

As I was asked to share my experience of working with Fr Kurien, I would say he has played a predominant role in my life to deepen my faith, understanding of theology and convictions of life realities. But as time limits me, I would like to highlight them in three points: as a person of faith, as a person of hope and as a person of love.

A Person of Faith: As Abraham was a blessing, Dear, Fr Kurien, you are a blessing to us as you have been one of the stalwarts of Papal Seminary. Faith in God is the foundation of his theology as it is permeated throughout his life. The intellectual calibre, depth in his knowledge and experience, clarity of thoughts and precision in his words are the characteristics of his lectures and talks as they are the reflections of his faith understanding, which are very much demanding till today. His total surrender before the Lord, as a faith expression is very inspiring. An example is that whenever he comes to the chapel for the mass, he kneels down and pray devoutly and genuinely. Perhaps it looks very simple, but it means to me a lot and gave me a lot of inspiration.

A Person of Hope: Fr Kurien is a peaceful person. His words are hope-filled as they give consolation in the lives of the people who are in touch with him. Maybe a tremendous openness, an incredible optimism, joy and enthusiasm are the hallmarks of his towering personality. Whenever there are some serious issues or discussions in the community, Fr Kurien comes with three points to give us hope and encouragement. It is very true when we go for our spiritual direction or personal-sharing, he is always able to understand from the students' perspective and pinpoints the goodness in us. At any time, I approached him with serious difficulties; he used to tell me: "Don't worry, see Ben, you, do one thing, etc." Likewise, the amount of trust that he has shown in me made me more committed to life. Similarly, his constant support and encouragement enabled me to grow in several ways, and one of them is to opt for B. Th. Comprehensive Defence Paper.

A Person of Love: According to Fr Kurien, our relationship to one another was important for Jesus. That is why he asked us to love one another as he had loved us (cf. Jn 14:12). In one of the writes up, Fr Kurien says: "I am particularly thankful to God for creating me something of the goodness and loving-kindness of God. They have also shaped me as a human person. I would not have such basic human characteristics as the ability to love or to speak a language unless I was first loved and spoken to by other human beings." This reflects his loving relationship with God and human beings. Since he cherishes many loving relationships in his heart; he becomes an apple of everyone's eye in the seminary, campus and elsewhere. Therefore, no wonder to say that he is a man of parts as he is very dynamic and young in his hearts and thoughts.

As we come together to bid farewell to Fr Kurien, now I feel a feeling that you all feel that is to say: We miss you father! The song is ended, but the melody lingers on. "No more words. We know them all, all the words that should not be said but you have made our world more perfect and beautiful."

Dear Fr Kurien, we thank you very much for all that you have been to each and everyone's life. We wish and pray that may God grant you good health of mind and body to serve many more so that they may have life in abundance. ***Thank you!***

[Farewell to Kurien from Papal Seminary, August 2013]

A True Image and Likeness of God

Who Will Cry When You Die? is the title of Robin Sharma's recent book, a guiding light that leads us to a brilliant new way of living. So is Fr Kurien Kunnumpuram SJ, a true light for a new way of living, which enabled many lives towards the fullness of life. Indeed, I bitterly cried when he had departed to his heavenly abode. Still, he is alive and active in me as a source of inspiration and wisdom to move on to live life day to day. In this article, I would like to impart few thoughts and experiences with Kurien, my role model, guru and friend. Overall my relationship with him enabled me to know Jesus so dearly, to follow Him so closely, to love Him so intimately in and through Fr Kurien, whose deep faith in God, commitment in service, optimistic and analytic approaches in life as a humble humanitarian and joyful human person.

He often succinctly stated quoting Mahatma Gandhi: "Be the change that you wish to see the most in your world." As a mentor, he taught me to be optimistic in life, exhorting that under God's providence, our destiny is in our hand. In the same way, whenever people asked him for an autograph, he used to write as follows: "May this world be a better and happy place because you are lived in it." Thus he was interested in the personal growth of people around him by giving a positive outlook in life.

At a point of life, when I was undergoing my own trials and tribulations, he came across to my life as a true friend. He listened to me patiently and understood me as I am and guided me to improve the quality of my life. He used to tell me that I should never allow anybody to ruin my life even in any relationships. For him, friendship is a choice that one makes in life to be dependent. He added that in any friendship, I have to learn to respect others and to make sure that nothing affects my ministries. The recalled that Vatican II holds that the ministry of a priest sanctifies his life. Besides, he said at a juncture of life that struggles are good for me as it is a new learning process in life. He reminded me that I could re-arrange my room, but not my friends since they have their own freedom.

Finally, he said: "the food that we cook will perish, the building that we built will be demolished, and the book that we write will be outdated, but ultimately what remains is the capacity to love." Emphatically he reminded me in the retreat before my priestly ordination that "Father loved me as I have loved you. Therefore you love one another (cf. Jn 15:9-17)," which is the summary of Christianity existence.

Fr Kurien was interested in my personal growth, so he loved me very much and guided me carefully. When I was in Papal Seminary, Pune, he corrected my B.Th. Comprehensive thesis even the previous night of his transfer to Christhall, Calicut and handed over to me early in the morning before he left for the airport at 4 AM. When I did my personal retreat with him for my ordination at Christ Hall he reminded me finally of three things: (1) Have an hour of serious reading or study which is quite inspiring or challenging; (2) Prepare your homilies well and write it down for at least 3 years; and (3) Save some money, since I am a diocesan. It may help me when I am seriously ill, or even I can help students for education. After all, he exhorted me to have a sense of mission in life.

After my ordination, when I told him that I was appointed a prefect of studies of the seminarians, he told me three points, firstly to be fair to everyone secondly to help boys to grow and lastly to correct them respectfully. Similarly, when I started to teach in an Arts' College, run by the Diocese of Neyyattinkara, he advised me to be careful of three things viz. have a plan and prepare the lesson very well, don't condemn the students but have conversations and to be impartial. He also mentioned that the success of a teacher is to love the students. Apparently, I used to discuss with him and seek advice from him for many things. His accompaniment throughout my life was an enormous source of energy and support. From all these, I realise how he was interested in my personal growth and success.

In 2013 August, Fr Kurien transferred to Christ Hall, Calicut, since then I visited him more than twenty times till 2018. Since we both are born in July, we celebrated our birthdays together at Malabar Palace, a restaurant at heart of the city in Calicut where Nelvin, his nephew, had been working. Likewise, whenever I paid a visit to him, he used to share with his glorious days in Germany, Pune and even his nostalgic reminiscences over a dinner. I cherish those beautiful memories with him, and I remember once he said to me about the secret of his health firstly that he never overeat, secondly regular exercise (childhood days of swimming and later on evening walk) and very interestingly he always enjoyed every moment of his life.

On another occasion, he shared with me that he loved Pune very much and he always stood for the students and for their freedom because he says that where there is freedom, there is growth. I saw him in 2007 when I went for philosophy and since 2010 onwards I had been working with him in association with AUC, but he never spoke to me a single word in Malayalam either over the phone or even in personal talks. I enjoyed certain honour and privileges in the name of Fr Kurien such as an opportunity to felicitate him on his jubilee, enjoyed a special dinner with his close friends and the members of his family and took me for lunch out on the previous day of his transfer.

We are close friends and even once he asked me the same: "Ben, have you ever noticed that I consider you as equal." He took me several times to his home and made me stay with him too. He also paid a visit to my home and stayed with me. For the last time, he visited and stayed with me was on October 30, 31 and March 1, 2017. Among those days, one day he spent at home another day at my parish, then he came along with me to the college, where I am teaching, bishop's house and Kovalam. Gloriously I remember those beautiful days, especially that we had at Kovalam. His memory is really amazing, even the previous day he was admitted for the stroke for the second time he gave a phone call asking me when would I be visiting him and about my dad's health, my brother's transfer to Kashmir, matters at parish and college. He would remind me of the seminar on himself and would say that he had to discuss with Fr Kuruvilla SJ. It was unusual to talk more than what we used to be, and I was surprised how come he is so sharp ever after the stroke.

The very next day I contacted Fr Kuru, who informed me that Fr Kurien was in the ICU and really I was shocked.

He was loved and respected by everyone at Pune and Calicut. He once said that he got an analytic mind. It is true as he was precise in words and able to summarise things in three points as he is known for it. Merlyn Kunnumpuram, his niece, witnessed it and says how she was taught case studies for her management studies. Towards my last visits, many a time he mentioned how his friendship circle was closely connected with Kuru, Merlyn and myself. I feel privileged to have such a great personality in my life.

After my ordination when I made my personal retreat with him he emphasised that his theology and understanding of life is based on unconditional love of God. He also believed in the compassionate face of God. It was an eye-opening for me when he said, “The stupidities that we do may make us cry. It may weigh you down. But not those people who love you.” He urged me not to be anxious about life but to be depended upon God, and our life should be witness to others. So he proposed to me to do an exercise that at the end of the day that I may ask myself whether I am satisfied or feeling happy? Likewise, whenever he rang up to me, he used to ask me, “Ben, where are you?” The question resonates in me as it has very many things to communicate to me, and our conversations also ended with a note of hope, ‘keep well’. I always phoned up to him, whenever I felt sad, distracted or disturbed, then he would suggest a way out from all the troubles. As a result, I would be relaxed and rejuvenated. I do remember at a point of crisis I contacted him over the phone thrice or four times a day, but he never got angry. Rather he listened to me patiently and tried to understand me, and meticulously he made me come out of my struggles. Another incident I remember is that when he was undergoing surgery for a hernia, his niece (Merlyn Kunnumpuram) and I went to visit him at Christ Hall on the previous day. We both were perplexed how to face the situation and to talk to him. WE found him happy and optimistic, and he made us laugh with his sense of humour. We both were energized after meeting him. I wonder at his positive outlook on life and matters.

As I conclude this short sharing of my experience with him, I feel, perhaps my words and letters are not enough for me to speak about Fr Kurien.

I realise that he is my hero, guru, friend, mentor and a role model who reshaped my faith in God, life perspectives and understandings. He has moulded me and made me what as I am today. He was a visionary for me. He lives in me to be a better priest. May he rest in peace!

(July 21, 2019)

8. A Personal Story

Merlin Joseph Thomas

I was born in a small town/ village in Kerala, Thrissur. My schooling was done in a state syllabus school, and that yields to me just about acceptable English.

My earliest memories of Fr Kurien SJ come in as a Mentor who was an effective coach also. He would provide me with audio cassettes (the year 1992) to listen to English passages and stories to improve my colloquial and pronunciation and come to speed with the fast-moving city "English" and much-needed armour of communication. He, in fact, put me in touch with his very good friend Fr. Sabino SJ to talk to me daily to track the progress.

He ensured that he directed me well and throughout during my MBA in Pune University and thus set the tone for me to take up successful IT corporate career/ Job. Always positive and encouraging. He helped me learn /solve case studies in a methodical manner; it looked to me that he was a subject matter expert.

An incident etched in my memory is of a day when I was late for a meeting with him at the papal seminary. (He had a busy schedule as he was a JDV Rector that point of time). He was extremely unhappy with my behaviour and pulled out an article from his bookshelf with the caption: "One man was late for his funeral" and made me read it along with the famous author, Peter Dunker's book on "Time Management". Never once after that was I late for a meeting EVER. Such was his discipline towards small things that matter so much in life for personal and professional purposes, another synonym for punctuality.

I have always admired the kindness and care he had for the people around him. He was always ready to help and enjoyed imparting his knowledge and loved listening to people around him. He was ready to resolve issues and conflicts, no matter how small or big as he thought each challenge was a learning opportunity.

Relation wise, he was my Father's younger brother, but I always considered him to be my father, and we fondly called him "Kuriacha". His direction helped me in building my own career, married life and in the upbringing of my three children.

God blessed him with remarkable intelligence and exceptional memory who was always a Leader in all situations. He encouraged people to be thankful for the life that God has given as a gift. He has reinforced the spirituality in me.

His courage to face life at any point in time was a quality I always admired for and carried forward to my life as well.

My journey with him was on April 2018, where we travelled together to papal seminary from Calicut was a memorable one as we have together reflected our close association of 26 years.

I like to thank Fr. Kuruvilla SJ for giving me this opportunity to write about Fr Kurien Kunnumpuram SJ.

[Merlin is the niece of Rev Kurien Kunnumpuam)]

9. A Friend and a Theologian

Sebastian Painadath SJ

I first met Kurien in 1962: I was a student of philosophy and he was studying theology, both at the Pontifical Athenaeum, Pune. I found him very approachable and genuinely interested in cultivating mature companionship. In 1970 before my theological studies in Innsbruck, I spent a few weeks at De Nobile College. The advice he gave me in view of my theological formation was to look at Christian faith from the perspective of religious pluralism. This was a valuable orientation for me. He himself did a doctorate at Innsbruck on the openness of Vatican II to other religions. Back in India in 1978, I used to come to JDV occasionally for classes on some optional subjects. I was put up at the Papal Seminary, and I used to meet Kurien often for personal sharing or theological reflections. I was impressed by his clarity of thought, commitment to theologising in the Indian context and warm friendship. When in 1987 the Kerala Jesuit Province asked me to initiate the RTC at Kalady, Kurien was extremely supportive. He used to come every year to take a course at the RTC. He was very impressed by the ashram character of the Jesuit presence at Sameeksha. During the annual Province Meets Kurien would make very pertinent interventions with clarity and precision, with good humour and in a non-threatening way. As the editor of *Jnanadeepa,* he often asked me to contribute studied articles on inculturation and the spirituality of the Bhagavad Gita. I always found in Kurien a confrere genuinely encouraging others to grow and express themselves creatively. Warm friendship with individuals was an integral element of his spirituality. That is why a lot of priests trained at the Papal Seminary came to the funeral at Calicut. Kurien will live in the hearts of hundreds of his friends: sisters, priests, bishops and laywomen/men. The theological formation of the laity was for Kurien a personal concern. When the JDV Certificate Course for the laity was started at Sameeksha, he was always available to take them through the post Vat. II vision of the Church. He has published quite a lot on Indian ecclesiology; these theological perspectives will bear good fruits on the Indian soil in the coming decades.

10. Care, Concern and Compassion: A Tribute to Fr Kurien Kunumpuram SJ

Santan Nago FS

Superior General, Congregation of the Sisters of Our Lady of Fatima

The news of Fr Kurien Kunumpuram's death has deeply saddened us. He was a well-known and much-loved person by all Fatima Sisters. He has been a part of us for the last three and a half decades. Almost all the Sisters know him personally.

- Fr Kurien had moderated our two General Chapters. He had conducted Retreats to several groups of our Sisters.
- He had lectured at our seminars and renewal programmes for all categories of Sisters – Juniors, Seniors, Superiors, Formators, Headmistresses, Nurses, Social workers, Fatima Sisters Associates and our Novices.
- Fr Kurien had assisted us in updating our Constitutions twice, once in 2000-2001 and more recently 2016-17.
- He has edited our Congregations' historical books and several articles.
- Fr Kurien Kunumpuram was a priest, a brother, a guide and a dear friend to us. He has been a great benefactor to us, spiritually and morally. He had encouraged, strengthened and empowered so many of us in living our lives more fully and meaningfully.
- He always had time whenever we approached him for discussions on matters of concern and difficult issues. His wise suggestions and solutions put us on the right track. His deep faith in God and his personal relationship with Christ and the Catholic Church, has inspired and invigorated us.

Very dear Fr Kurien, you will be remembered for many things you taught and communicated to us. The three most beautiful qualities that can be attributed to your personality were:

1. **Your care:** You truly cared about us individually and as a Congregation and took time to listen and made us feel better, every time we came to you.
2. **Your concern:** You were genuinely concerned about our all-round progress, sharing our joys, sorrows, successes and failures.
3. **Your compassion:** You always looked at the positive side of things and found goodness in every situation, that refreshed and boosted us.

Thank you, dear Fr Kurien! God blessed you with a wonderful life; now, God awaits to embrace you in His Kingdom.

Good-bye Fr Kurien, till we meet again in heaven!

Sr Santan Nago FS, Fatima Sisters Generalate, Pune.

11. A Caring Gentleman

Chacko PC (Mash)
Trivandrum

I am privileged to write few words on Fr Kurien Kunnumpuram, whom I admire very deeply as a genuinely humane person. I know him for seventy years when I had the opportunity to be together. Later destiny took us to different paths, and we could not keep in touch.

Still, after about 60 years, I was fortunate to know Kurien as a professor, administrator and writer. I had the rare privilege of translating some of his books into Malayalam. This allowed me to know him more closely. He was a man open to the whole world, caring for all. He was also willing to share everything with others!

He was an optimist, who would always find positive qualities in others, including me. He encouraged me and empowered me. He listed to me with interest and showed special concern for my daily activities. He was truly a caring gentleman.

Further, as a thinker and theologian, Fr Kurien was a man of deep faith, which he expressed in his hope, trust and charity. He was a man who cared for others. He showed compassion to others. He encouraged each one to take his or her path and move on.

A caring gentleman! A person of good humour. A thinker with a vision. A religious who was open to God and other fellow human beings!

I was truly fortunate to come to know him.

12. Remembering with Gratitude! A Tribute to Late Rev. Fr Kurien Kunnumpuram, SJ

Rekha Chennattu, RA
Superior General, Religious of the Assumption, Paris, France

We, the Assumption Sisters of the Indian Province, owe much to Father Kurien Kunnumpuram as someone truly interested in our well-being and growth, as someone who loved, guided and inspired us for the last forty years. We will always remember him with much affection and gratitude!

I consider myself blessed to have known Fr Kurien personally first as a professor of Theology and then as my colleague at Jnana-Deepa Vidyapeeth, Pontifical Athenaeum, Pune. He was a creative teacher and dynamic theologian who was passionately in love with the documents of the Second Vatican Council. Father Kurien always encouraged me to become a biblical scholar who would make a unique feminine contribution to the universal Church. When I was part of the editorial team of the Journal, *Jnanadeepa* in the 1990s, he always supported and appreciated my efforts. I also had the privilege of working with him to edit a book on an *Indian Reading of the Letters of Saint Paul*. He came across to me as an optimistic and committed theologian who was never tired of serving the Church.

Whenever I visited him seeking his wisdom and guidance, he had a special grace of making me feel affirmed and empowered. I am always touched by his gracious generosity to help anyone who is in need, people from all walks of life. Enhancing life, promoting growth and fostering communion were the characteristics of his spiritual accompaniment.

Dear Father Kurien, we will miss you and your words of wisdom.

May the legacy of Father Kurien be a source of inspiration and hope for the universal Church. May he rest in peace and live forever in our hearts!

13. National Seminar Organised to Honour Indian Theologian Prof Fr Kurien Kunnumpuram SJ

News Report

What is the relevance of Vatican II for the Indian Church? How does acts of piety related to depth in spirituality? How can spirituality humanise us and take us to our fellow human being and God? These were some of the questions that Fr Kurien Kunnumpuram SJ reflected on and wrote about.

Fr Kurien remains one of the pioneering theologians of Vatican II and has been internationally recognised as a thinker and writer of eminence. A National Seminar on "Fr Kurien Kunnumpuram, SJ: A Theological Inspiration," was conducted at Socio-Religious Centre, Christ Hall, Kozhikode, Kerala, on 17-18, October 2018.

Fr George Mutholil SJ, Provincial, Kerala Province, inaugurated the Seminar. He remembered Fr Kurien as a man "who challenged me to grow." He saw Fr Kurien's life and writings as a challenge "to priests to practice a spirituality of active involvement in the lives of people and to practice an integrated spirituality – integrating life, prayer and work, instead of 'scattering their energies in many directions'." As a scholar and mentor, he had a way of accepting everyone personally and encouraging them to grow.

About 45 scholars in the fields of Philosophy and Theology came together to deliberate on the theological significance of Prof Kurien Kunnumpuram. There were 18 papers presented, which urged the Church to be open to dialogue, to become a community of love and to humanise our spirituality. Some of the prominent figures who participated in the seminar are Fr Johnson Puthenpurackal OFM Cap (Elluru), Fr Job Kozhamthadam SJ (Delhi), Fr Keith D'Souza SJ (Mumbai) and Fr Mathew Chandrankunnel CMI (Bangalore).

Fr Paul Raj, Papal Seminary, Pune, spoke of the love commandment of St. Paul, which is related to and different from Jesus' love commandment. Fr Paul Thelakkatt, editor "Light of Truth," Ernakulam, elaborated on the distinction between madness and sanity, in relation to contemporary society. Fr V M Joseph, Jnana-Deepa Vidyapeeth, Pune, spoke of the liberative and societal dimension of encountering God. Fr James Ponniah, University of Madras, elaborated on the shared sacred spaces that different people and communities live in. Prof Job Kozhathadam SJ, Director, Indian Institute of Sciences and Religion, New Delhi, Fr Stephen Jayard, Jnana-Deepa Vidyapeeth, Pune, spoke of the collaboration of the Church and with the world of science and technology.

Sr Surekha Lobo, Centre for Women's Studies, Pune and a Bethany Sister, spoke of a spirituality that humanizes and enables us to be better human beings. Fr Jacob Parappally MSFS, Chief Editor, "Journal of Indian Theology," elaborated on "ways of salvation" and "the way of salvation" which Kurien explored in connection to Vatican II. Fr Mathew Chandrankunnel CMI, Director, Ecumenical Centre, Bangalore, spoke of the need to dialogue with Hinduism and bring about an East-West complementarity continuum.

Fr Victor Ferrao, Rachol Seminary, Goa, spoke of the bodily dimension of divine-human love. Fr Thomas Karimundackal SJ, Papal Seminary, Pune, spoke of the Church of the poor, children and marginalised from the perspective of Luke's Gospel. Fr Nishant Irudayadason, JDV, Pune, tried to link theory and praxis in theologising. Fr EP Mathew SJ, Dean, Satya Nilayam, Loyola College, Chennai spoke of the future of anthropology from a Christian vision. Fr PT Mathew SJ, Christ Hall, Kozhikode, pleaded with the theologians to bring the heart dimension into theologising. Fr Johnson Puthenpurackal OFM Cap, former President, Association of Christian Philosophers of India, reflected on the dynamic tension between "what has been and what could be (possible)" in theological language. Fr Stephen Chundamthadam SJ, Samanvaya, Institute of Advanced Indian Spirituality, Kanjirapally, studied the humanising and integrating spirituality of Fr Kunnumpuram, that fosters freedom, joy and intimate experience of God, leading to fellow human beings.

During the seminar, Fr Kurien's last book "Freedom and Joy" was released. In the book, Kurien perceived freedom and joy as essential characteristics of a Christian. Fr Kuruvilla Pandikattu SJ opined that the person of Kurien himself personified both this freedom and joy of the Gospels.

Fr Kurien was born in 1931 at Teekoy, Kerala. He was a good athlete in his younger days. Because of his extraordinary intellectual talents, he was sent to pursue his doctoral studies in Innsbruck, Austria. "His must have been the first doctorate on Vatican II," opines Fr Sebastian Painadath SJ, one of his colleagues. Fr Kunnumpuram finished his PhD on "Ways of Salvation in Vatican II" in 1968. Then he joined the staff of Jnana-Deepa Vidyapeeth, Pune and taught Theology. He also served as the Dean and Rector of Jnana-Deepa Vidyapeeth, Pune.

He was the founder of the influential theological journal "*Jnanadeepa: Pune Journal of Religious Studies*," from 1998 onwards. He also edited another journal "*AUC: Asian Journal for Religious Studies*," and was the first editor of the "Encyclopedia of Christianity in India," published by Jnana-Deepa Vidyapeeth, Pune. He wrote more than 20 books and have made significant contributions to Indian theology. Therefore, the participants came to honour him and pay due respect to him. He was a remarkable person, who dreamt of a Church that is open to Indian traditions and that empowers all sections of the people.

Unfortunately, they missed Fr Kurien's physical presence during the seminar, since he was in Nirmala Hospital, Hospital, Kozhikode. Due to a blood clot in the brain, he has been in a coma for more than 20 days. But they felt his empowering presence, urging them to be more human and to experience God, especially in our neighbours.

The coordinators of the seminar were Fr PT Mathew and Fr Kuruvilla Pandikattu. They are planning to publish the articles of this research seminary. The event was organised by Kerala Province of the Society of Jesus. Fr Jose Thachil, Coordinator, Socio-Religious Centre, Kozhikode accompanied the participants gracefully.

14. An Innovative Thinker and Good Formator

Bishop Thomas Dabre

The passing away of Fr Kurien Kunnumpuram SJ on 23rd October 2018 at 10:30 PM was a shocking and saddening news to me. He was 87 years old and most of his priestly ministry was done in the Papal Seminary and in Jnana-Deepa Vidyapeeth (JDV). I am immensely grateful to Fr Kurien, since he encouraged me, guided and has made an immense contribution to what I am today. I shall remain always immensely grateful to him for his bonds of friendship and generosity with me.

He certainly was one of the best and most eminent theologians of India. He has written scores of books and many theological articles based on research. His thinking and writings were marked by originality and creativity. He was bold in his thinking. Certainly, he remained within the faith of Catholic Church, which was shaped by his study of the documents of Vatican II. His own doctoral thesis on the document of Second Vatican Council. He certainty was one of the best read persons on Second Vatican Council. He would profusely quote and refer to the documents of Second Vatican Council. It is he who helped the student and members of staff here in Papal Seminary and Jnana-Deepa Vidyapeeth to get more and more acquitted with Second Vatican Council. He certainly was an epoch in the history of the Indian catholic church. I would say, he has greatly shaped, fashioned and impacted by Second Vatican Council, which opened the doors of the Church to the world.

Gaudium et Spec guided us to take the realities of the world seriously, with its hopes and dreams. This is how Kurien shaped his theology. Courageously, boldly and in the light of Second Vatican Council.

Fr Kurien, apart from being my friend, was an eminent theologian, a skilled writer and a good formator. He and I lived in the Papal Seminary for many long years. I can say even when I was a student and later as a staff that Kurien became a rallying point for the seminarians. The seminarians will turn to him in moments of difficulty. Kurien was always welcome them and make himself available to them. They trusted him, felt supported and encouraged by him. I could see that they loved him and they were very fond of him. So I would say Fr Kurien was a good formator in the seminary for the generations of priests in the modern world, after Second Vatican Council.

I thank and praise God for the person, the theologian and the formator that Fr Kurien was. He was a creative thinker, an innovative thinker and a courageous thinker. He certainly was a gift to the church in India and in his own way to the Universal Church.

May his soul rest in peace!

[Rt Rev Thomas Dabre is the Bishop of Pune as well as an alumnus and faculty of Papal Seminary and Jnana-Deepa Vidyapeeth. So he has been a colleague and companion of Fr Kurien. This article is adapted from his homily on Kurien's funeral.]

15. Quotes by Kurien

"There is a lot of piety among us, but not enough spirituality. Piety consists of the performance of external devotional practices and is measured by one's fidelity to these practices. Whether or not the faithful performance of these exercises of piety improves the quality of one's Christian life is a question that is seldom asked. One is at times surprised that priests, sisters and lay people who are obviously pious are manifestly unfair in their dealings with other people. Some of them show so little of the compassion of Christ and are quite unwilling to forgive others."

"Spirituality is a way of life. It is our total inward quest for growth, meaning and authenticity. And it is manifested in the quality of one's life. In the last analysis, to be spiritual is to be touched and transformed by the Spirit of God. In a person who has been touched and transformed by God's Spirit the fruits of the Spirit will be seen: "love, joy, peace, patience, kindness, generosity, faithfulness, gentleness and self-control" (Gal 5:22-23). Besides, "where the Spirit of Lord is, there is freedom" (2 Cor 3:17).

"To follow Christ is also to identify ourselves with the poor and powerless as he did. The Incarnation is the symbol of this identification. Through his incarnation he inserted himself into the human family and became one with us. As Soares-Prabhu observes, "Jesus 'declasses' himself and adopts the life of an itinerant preacher without a home or means of subsistence"."

"Any genuine experience of God will send us out to serve those whom God loves. And working with people will make us aware of how much we are in need of God, of God's help and guidance. This will gradually usher in a rhythm of prayer and work – prayer leading to work and work leading to prayer. So the integration of prayer and work takes place existentially."

"Christian spirituality is a spirituality of hope. St. Paul believes that Christians are those who have hope (1Thess 4:13). Now to hope is to look forward to the new, to what is not yet there, and strive to bring it about. Hence hope is forward-looking and forward moving. That is why a spirituality of hope is a spirituality of change. According to Karl Rahner it is a sin against hope to refuse to change. Those who refuse to change regard the past or the present as the final state of humankind. We are not yet in the new heavens and the new earth. We are on our way to them. And so our spirituality is a spirituality of hope and change."

"God did not create the world in order to get anything for himself. In fact, there is no need of God's that we can supply, no luxury of His that we can provide. Actually, God created the world in order to bestow his blessings on his creatures and to give them a share in his own goodness."

"Christian hope asks us to regard every stage in the growth of a person and every phase in the development of the Church as merely provisional. It has to be transcended. We are still on our way to the final Kingdom."

"Freedom is for love and service. Our ability to give ourselves away in love and service is the true measure of our freedom. After having declared: "For you were called to freedom", Paul adds: "Through love become slaves to one another"."

"In recent times, we are becoming increasingly more aware of the cosmic dimension of salvation. The destiny of humankind and that of the cosmos are inextricably intertwined. In the past, Christians often thought of their relationship to the world in terms of domination, possession, use and enjoyment. There was little awe and wonder before the mystery of the universe. This arrogant and irreverent attitude to creation is largely responsible for the serious ecological crisis was are facing today."

Our Contributors

Dr A. L. Christopher Roach is a priest of the diocese of Coimbatore. At present, he is a professor of Systematic Theology at Good Shepherd Seminary, Coimbatore, Tamilnadu. He holds a Doctorate in Systematic Theology from Jnana-Deepa Vidyapeeth, Pune; a Licentiate in Dogmatic Theology from Urbaniana University, Rome and a Diploma in Pastoral Counselling and Religious Formation from NVSC, Pune. He is a frequent writer in the *Divine Shepherd's Voice* and he has also authored a few theological articles. He can be contacted at: aleoroach@yahoo.co.in

Dr Andreas Vonach is Professor of Department of Biblical Studies and Historical Theology, University of Innsbruck. He has several scholarly publications and has been closely associated with Jnana-Deepa Vidyapeeth, Pune. Email: andreas.vonach@uibk.ac.at

Sr Anoop Anto MSMI (Karippaserry Annamma) is a research scholar in systematic theology at Jnana-Deepa Vidyapeeth, Pune. She received her B.Th from Sacred Heart Theological College, Shillong and M.Th in Systematic Theology from Catholic University, Leuven. Email: anoopaanto121@gmail.com

Dr Christian Bauer is Professor and Head of the Institute of Pastoral (Praktische) Theology, University of Innsbruck, Austria. Email: Christian.F.Bauer@uibk.ac.at

Mr Denis Rodrigues has a background in Philosophy, Theology, Political science and Science. At different times of his life, he has taught philosophy and worked in the Social Development field. At present, he is in 'Vanaprastha', trying to work out a synthesis of all that he has experienced, in keeping with Kierkegaard's dictum that 'life is lived forward but understood backwards'. Email: audden@gmail.com

Dr Donald R Frohlich is a biologist and has published widely in evolution, behavioural ecology, molecular population biology, and the science/spirituality interfacing. He holds visiting professor appointments in Philosophy at Universidad del Rosario Bogotá CO, and JDV Pune India, and in 2015 was appointed University Fellow in Faith and Science at the Center for Faith and Culture, University of St. Thomas, Houston TX. A product of a liberal arts education and life, DRF is grateful to pursue a deeper understanding of the wholeness inherent in the universe with his many students and colleagues. Email: frohlich@stthom.edu.

Dr (Sr) Evelyn Monteiro SCC was Professor of Systematic Theology in the Faculty of Theology and Associate Professor, Jnana-Deepa Vidyapeeth, Pune. She is visiting professor in several theologates in India and abroad. She has authored and edited several books and published many articles in national and international journals. She is the co-founder of Ecclesia of Women in Asia (EWA). Email: srevelynm@gmail.com

Dr Felipe-Andrés Piedra obtained his PhD studying the self-assembly and dynamics of microtubules. Since his youth, he has been moved to celebrate, explore, and reveal the manifold sources of life's beauty. FAP is currently a post-doctoral fellow at Baylor College of Medicine, Houston, TX where he studies the effects of self-assembly on viral gene expression. He has taught evolutionary biology at the University of St. Thomas where he befriended Donald R Frohlich. FAP is devoted to encountering nature on its own terms, gleaning what knowledge he can, and keeping in sight the grandeur of the universe and its immortal mysteries. Email: piedra@bcm.edu.

Dr Francis X. D'Sa SJ is Professor (Emeritus) of Theology and Philosophy, Jnana-Deepa Vidyapeeth, Pune. He is a specialist in Indian philosophy and Raimon Panikkar and author of numerous books in philosophy and dialogue between religions. Email: francis.x.dsa@gmail.com

Dr Isaac Padinjarekuttu is Professor of Church History and Dean at Oriens Theological College Shillong, Meghalaya. He has authored/edited nine books and published more than a hundred articles on various theological topics. Email: padinjarekuttu@gmail.com

Dr Isaac Parackal OIC is a professor in the Faculty of Philosophy at JDV, Pune holding a doctorate in Philosophy, specialized in Metaphysics and Anthropology from the University of St. Thomas Aquinas in Rome. He did his post-doctorate studies at Sacramento, USA in the University of California. He belongs to the Order of the Imitation of Christ (Bethany Ashram). He has been teaching Metaphysics, Ancient and Medieval Philosophy and Ecology at JDV. Email: isaacparackal13@gmail.com

Dr J. Charles Davis is a Priest of Jammu-Srinagar Diocese. He has specialized in Bioethics and had been a Professor of Jnana-Deepa Vidyapeeth. His book "The Ethics of Human Embryonic Stem Cell Research: Proposals for A Legal Framework for India" has become authoritative in the field. Currently, he is back in Germany doing his habilitation at Albert Ludwigs University of Freiburg with the prestigious Alexander von Humboldt Research Fellowship. Email: davischarlesj@gmail.com

Prof Jacob Parappally MSFS is Dean, Theology, Tejas Vidya Peetha, Bengaluru. He was Dean and Professor of Theology at Jnana-Deepa Vidyapeeth, Pune. Email: parappally@gmail.com

Prof James Ponniah was Dean, Faculty of Philosophy, Jnana-Deepa Vidyapeeth, Pune. Currently, he teaches at the Department of Christian Studies, University of Madras. In addition to many articles, he has authored a monograph *The Dynamics of Folk Religion in Society:Pericentralisation as Deconstruction of Sanskritisation* (2011) and other books. He was awarded Collaborative International Research Grant by American Academy of Religions in 2015. Email: jamesponniah@gmail.com

Prof Job Kozhamthadam SJ is Professor (Emeritus), Jnana-Deepa Vidyapeeth, Pune and was also the Dean, Faculty of Philosophy as well as President, Jnana-Deepa Vidyapeeth, Pune. Currently, he is Director at Indian Institute of Science and Religion, New Delhi. He has been the pioneer of science-religion dialouge in India. Email: jobksj@gmail.com

Dr Joseph Mattam SJ is Professor (Emeritus) of Systematic Theology, had been the founder and for many years, Dean of the Gujarat Jesuit Regional Theologate (RTC) and later, of the Gujarat Regional Seminary (GVD); he lectures in various theological and other formation centres in India and abroad. He has authored seven books and has edited 12 books. He was the President of FOIM (Fellowship of Indian Missiologists), an Ecumenical Association.

Dr Johnson J. Puthenpurackal OFMCap is a Capuchin priest of Marymatha Province and a Heidegger-specialist with a Ph.D. from KUL (Belgium); he is a resident professor of Philosophy in Vijnananilayam, where he has been teaching for more than a quarter of a century. He is presently the President of the 'Indian Capuchin Research Forum' (ICRF). He is one of the pioneers of the 'Association of Christian Philosophers of India' (ACPI), and was editorially responsible for the publication of the *ACPI Encyclopedia of Philosophy*. He has lectured in many Institutes, and presented papers in numerous seminars. To his credit, there are several studies published. Email: johnsonjp@rediffmail.com

Dr K. Arul Samy ALCP/OSS is a member of the Apostolic Life Community of Priests in the Opus Spiritus Sancti (ALCP/OSS). Currently, he is the Assistant Superior General of his Religious Society and is living at the Holy Spirit Novitiate House, Mysore. Arul has Doctorate in New Testament Studies from Philosophische-Theologische Hochschule St. Georgen, Frankfurt am Main, Germany, which he completed in the year 2004. He was the Provincial Superior of his Religious Society in India from 2008-2014. He teaches in various seminaries and houses of formation. Email: arulkaspar@gmail.com.

Dr Kochurani Abraham completed her PhD from the University of Madras in Feminist Theology. Currently, she is the national convener of the

Indian Christian Women's Movement, which is an autonomous movement of women with feminist sensibilities and commitment to building gender justice in the churches and in society. Email: kochuabraham@gmail.com

Prof Kuruvilla Pandikattu SJ is the Dean of Philosophy at Jnana-Deepa Vidyapeeth and has been actively involved in Science-Religion Dialogue. His areas of interest: the meaning of death, anthropology, science and spirituality for human enhancement and life management. Email: kuru@jdv.edu.in

Dr M K George SJ is the Provincial of the Jesuits of Kerala Province. His expertise is in Andragogy, Sociology and Social Work. He was Principal, Loyola College of Social Sciences, Trivandrum, Kerala. Email: gmutholil@gmail.com

M. D. Joseph (Jose Mannukulangara) is a priest belonging to the Archdiocese of Guwahati, Assam. He is an author, writer and research scholar (Science and Religion) at Jnana-Deepa Vidyapeeth, Pune. E-mail: josemannuorama@gmail.com

Dr Mathew Chandrankunnel CMI has completed his PhD on Quantum Physics and has been a Professor of Philosophy at Dharmaram Vidyakhetram, Bangalore. Currently, he is the Director of prestigious Ecumenical Christian Centre, Whitefield, Bangalore, 560066. Email: chandrankunnel@gmail.com

Prof Nishant Alphonse Irudayadason is a Professor of Philosophy and Ethics at Jnana-Deepa Vidyapeeth: Pontifical Institute of Philosophy and Religions (JDV), Pune, India. Having obtained two doctoral degrees in Ethics and Philosophy from Université Paris-Est and Institut catholique de Paris, France, he has been actively pursuing his academic life. He has authored two books, edited two books and published many articles in National and International Journals as well as in edited books. He is a regular contributor to contemporary political analysis in "Light of Truth." Email: nishant@jdv.edu.in

Dr Paul Thelakat, a priest, belonging to the Archdiocese of Ernakulam-Angamaly, is the Editor of the popular Christian magazine, English Sathayadeepam (Light of Truth) in Kerala and was the spokesperson of Syro-Malabar Church. He has his PhD in Theology and Master's Degree in Philosophy. Email: thelakatpaul@gmail.com

Dr M. Paul Raj is a Catholic priest of the diocese of Sivagangai, Tamil Nadu, India. He has a doctorate in Biblical Theology from the University of Innsbruck, Austria, with specialization in the Epistles of St Paul. He is at present a member of the Scripture Department at the Faculty of Theology, JDV, Pune and resides in the Papal Seminary and helps out in the formation of the seminarians. Email: maprmay22@gmail.com

Dr PT Mathew SJ is a Jesuit priest belonging to Kerala Province and was formerly a member of the Faculty at Vidyajyoti College of Theology, Delhi. He holds a PhD in Christian Studies from the University of Madras.

His publications include *We Dare the Waters – the World and the Worldview of Mukkuvar* (Chennai: University of Madras, 2001), and *Human Persons in the World – Explorations in Christian Anthropology* (Anand: Gujarat Sahitya Prakash, 2017. He continues teaching in different theological centres and is presently Socius to the Jesuit Provincial of Kerala. Email: matpampa@gmail.com

Dr Sebastian Painadath SJ is Jesuit from Kerala, Director of Sameeksha, Centre for Indian Spirituality, Kalady, Kerala, India. He holds a Doctorate in Theology from the Univ. of Tübingen, Germany. He is engaged in spiritual ministries and inter-religious dialogue in India, Europe and the East Asian countries. He is the author of 32 books and about 400 articles in English, German and Malayalam. Email: spainadath@gmail.com

Prof Shalini Mulackal is a Presentation Sister, teaching Systematic Theology at Vidyajyoti College of Theology, New Delhi. She has authored a few books and published many academic articles. She was the first woman President of the Indian Theological Association, Member of Indian Women Theologians Forum (IWTF), Indian Christian Women's Movement (ICWM), former Coordinator of Ecclesia of Women of Asia (EWA), and Chairperson of Centre for Dalit Studies (CDS) Delhi. Email: smulackal@gmail.com

Dr (Sr) Surekha Lobo is a member of the Congregation of Sisters of the Little Flower of Bethany (Bethany Sisters), Mangalore, for North-East Province. Currently she is a JDV Staff as well as the Moderator of the Centre for Women's Studies, at JDV Pune. She has a Doctorate in Systematic Theology from JDV. She has her experience in formation and education as well. Email: surekhabs@gmail.com

Dr Stephen Chundamthadam SJ (Emeritus Professor, Indian Philosophy, JDV Pune) is the Director, Samanvaya Centre for Indian Studies, Kanjirapally. He belongs to the Society of Jesus, Kerala province. Areas of research: Advaitavedanta, Indian Spirituality and Yoga. For several years taught courses on Indian Philosophy, Indian Spirituality, World Religion, Yoga and Karate in Jnana-DeepaVidyapeeth, Pune. Presented papers in national and international seminars and published several researched articles in edited works and journals. Email: sthadam@gmail.com

Dr Thomas Karimundackal SJ teaches Scripture at JDV, Pune, and he is on the staff of Papal Seminary for three years. He has authored many articles both in national and international journals on various biblical themes and presented papers on various biblical subjects in different national and international conferences. His book, *A Call to Commitment: An Exegetical and Theological Study of Deut 10,12-11,32,* is published in the well-known research series Forschung zur Bible and received wide reviews. Email: tomksj@gmail.com

Rt Rev. Thomas Menamparampil S.D.B., DD, Archbishop (Emeritus) of Guwahati, Assam, India, is a prolific writer, effective communicator, a veteran missionary and an educator of North-East India. He was made the Bishop of the Diocese of Dibrugarh, Assam, on November 29, 1981. On April 21, 1992 he was transferred as the first Bishop of the newly erected diocese of Guwahati, Assam and then made the Archbishop of Guwahati on August 1, 1995. After having served the Archdiocese as its first Bishop and Archbishop before becoming its emeritus on January18, 2014. He was then made the apostolic administrator of the Diocese of Jowai, Meghalaya by Pope Francis

Dr Vadappuram M. Jose SJ is a full-time professor and Head of Department of Pastoral and Moral Theology, Jnana-Deepa Vidyapeeth, Pune and a resident of Papal Seminary, Pune. He has authored numerous articles and books and attended various national and international seminars. His areas of specialization: Liturgy, Pastoral Theology, Social involvement. Email: vmjose@gmail.com

Dr Victor Ferrao is a priest of the Archdiocese of Goa and the Dean of Philosophy, Rachol Seminary. He is a prolific writer in political philosophy and on science-religion dialogue. He has published numerous books and has participated in many national and international conference. Email: victorferrao@yahoo.co.uk